PERSONAL Trainer MANUAL

The Resource for Fitness Professionals

Richard T. Cotton
Editor

Christine J. Ekeroth
Associate Editor

Ace
AMERICAN COUNCIL ON EXERCISE®
www.acefitness.org

American Council on Exercise®
San Diego, California
Publisher

Library of Congress Catalog Card Number: 96-85138

Second edition
ISBN 0-9618161-6-3

Printed in the United States of America.

I J K

Distributed by:
American Council on Exercise
P. O. Box 910449
San Diego, CA 92191-0449
(858) 535-8227
(858) 535-1778 (FAX)
www.acefitness.org

Assistant Editor: Holly Yancy
Design: Grace Graphics
Production: Suzan Peterson
Photographer: Rick Starkman
Anatomical Illustrations: James Staunton
Technical Consultants: Richard Seibert, Deborah Ellison, Karen Nelson
Glossary: Karen Nelson
Index: Theresa Schaffer
Transcription: Kathie Marihugh, Yvonne C. Spencer
Copy Editors: Christina Gandolfo, Ronale Tucker
Proofreaders: Christina Gandolfo, Ronale Tucker
Chapter Models: Bryan Cochran, Diane Duray-Stoner, Kristen Edwards, Scott Fischer, Melissa Garner, Nancy Heyne, Sandra Leichliter, Tony Ordas, Christopher Ranck-Buhr, Darlene Ravelo, Theresa Schoppe, Holli Spicer, Karen Kay Spicer, Dan Trone
Cover Model: Eric Sams

Acknowledgements:
Thanks to the entire American Council on Exercise staff for their support and guidance through the process of creating this manual. A special thanks to Paul Jackson of Busy Body for providing the exercise equipment.

REVIEWERS

Douglas Brooks, M.S., is an exercise physiologist and international lecturer on exercise physiology, kinesiology, strength training and personal training. He is the author of *Going Solo, The Art of Personal Training* and *Program Design for Personal Trainers.*

Diane Buchta, B.A., is an ACE-certified Personal Trainer, and the owner of Tri Fitness, a personal training and consulting company. She also is the former strength coach for the United States triathlon team, and a contributing editor for *220 Magazine.*

Karen J. Calfas, Ph.D., is a licensed clinical psychologist and the assistant clinical professor in the family and preventive medicine department at the University of California, San Diego. She also serves as the director of health promotion at San Diego State University and conducts research in exercise adherence.

J. E. Lindsay Carter, Ph.D., is professor emeritus of exercise and nutritional science at San Diego State University. She is an international consultant and workshop presenter as well as the author and editor of several books and chapters. She conducts research in physique and performance.

Deborah Ellison, R.P.T., is a physical therapist in San Diego, Calif., and is the owner of Movement That Matters, an exercise consulting company. She also is the program design consultant for Reebok.

Larry Gettman, Ph.D., is the vice president of research and development for National Health Enhancement Systems, Inc., and adjunct professor of exercise science and physical education at Arizona State University. He formerly served as chairman of the ACE Board of Directors.

Louis Horwitz, M.D., F.A.C.E.P., is the director of the University Hospital Health System at the Bedford Medical Center Emergency Department. He is board certified in Emergency Medicine.

Gwen Hyatt, M.S., is president and director of education for Desert Southwest Fitness, Inc., and served as the chairperson of the ACE Aerobic Instructor Certification Examination and Accreditation Committees.

W. Larry Kenney, Ph.D., F.A.C.S.M., is a professor of applied physiology at the Pennsylvania State University, and a member of the Board of Trustees of the American College of Sports Medicine. He also is an ACSM Certified Exercise Specialist and Program Director and the senior editor of ACSM's *Guidelines for Graded Exercise Testing and Prescription.*

Brian E. Koeberle, J.D., is a sports/entertainment attorney and the director of operations for the Major League Baseball Players Alumni Association. He is the author of *The Legal Aspects of Personal Fitness Training,* and lectures on various sports and fitness and the law.

Karen P. Nelson, M.A., is the the director of Active Lifestyles Plus in Tucson, Ariz. She was formerly the director of certification for the American Council on Exercise, and has worked as a personal trainer for four years and as a clinician in spine and joint rehabilitation.

George Salem, Ph.D., is the associate professor in the department of physical education at California State University, Long Beach, where he also is the co-director of the biomechanics laboratory. His current research projects include biomechanical examinations of resistance exercise among intercollegiate women athletes and elder populations.

Barbara Scott, MPH, RD, is an associate professor in the nutrition education and research program and the department of pediatrics at the University of Nevada School of Medicine in Reno, Nev.

Mitch Sudy is the vice president of programs and services for the American Council on Exercise and served as the assistant executive director for the Lockheed Employee Recreation Association. He is the editor of the first edition of the *ACE Personal Trainer Manual,* and is a 13-year fitness industry veteran.

Steven P. Van Camp, M.D., is a cardiologist at the Alvarado Medical Group in San Diego, Calif., and served as the president of the American College of Sports Medicine for 1995-1996.

Larry S. Verity, Ph.D., F.A.C.S.M., is a professor of exercise physiology for the department of exercise and nutritional sciences at San Diego State University, and is a preventive and rehabilitation exercise specialist certified by the American College of Sports Medicine.

Denise Wiksten, Ph.D., A.T.C., is the assistant professor of athletic training/pre-physical therapy in the department of exercise and nutritional sciences at San Diego State University. She is a member of the National Athletic Trainers' Association and serves on its board of certification.

CONTENTS

FOREWORD

Personal training has come a long way since we first introduced this revolutionary manual in 1991. Since then, our body of knowledge has expanded not only in the area of exercise and physical activity for fitness, but we now understand the value of exercise in optimizing health and quality of life. In fact, there has never been a better, or more exciting, time to be a part of the fitness industry. With the release of the Surgeon General's Report on Physical Activity, we now have the muscle of the United States government behind us to help further the cause of promoting safe and effective activity to the American public.

Even so, the challenge to mobilize a nation where a mere 25 percent or less of the population exercises regularly, despite the fact that most of them intuitively know they should, can seem daunting. It is clear that not everyone is motivated by health issues and requires an added incentive to become more physically active. This brings us back to the instructor.

Of all the variables that can affect exercise compliance, perhaps the most important is the quality of the exercise instructor. Research has verified that the number-one factor affecting exercise compliance is the influence of qualified, enthusiastic professionals. Lending credence to this belief are the many effective exercise practices incorporated by qualified instructors such as prescribing progressive exercise to minimize injury, ensuring variety and fun during the session, establishing realistic goals, providing periodic evaluations, keeping adequate records and recognizing accomplishments through rewards and recognition.

This is one of the reasons why we receive nearly 1,000 calls each month from clubs and fitness organizations looking for qualified instructors and trainers who are certified by the American Council on Exercise. As the demand for quality exercise increases, the exercising public and the fitness employer demand better qualified instructors. As a personal trainer, you will be expected to be conversant with the information presented in this manual, experienced in the techniques and skills required to implement programs and current on emerging technologies and programs.

The fitness industry continues to grow and, by the year 2005, the U.S. Department of Labor predicts a 14 percent to 24 percent increase in the number of employed fitness professionals. With this growth comes innumerable opportunities for you to become a part of a profession dedicated to the health and well-being of others. If you are ready to be a vital presence in this growing force of change, this publication is an excellent first step. And remember, while the task is formidable, the cause is great.

Sheryl Marks Brown
Executive Director

INTRODUCTION

When the *ACE Personal Trainer Manual* was first issued back in 1991, most people had little idea of what or who a personal trainer was. The industry grew rapidly, however, and it wasn't long before the term personal trainer became a household word. Today, the requisite knowledge of a personal trainer has expanded at an equally rapid rate.

This new manual represents the most current, complete picture of the knowledge, instructional techniques and professional responsibilities personal trainers need to provide safe and effective exercise instruction to their clients. In addition to providing background education and information to personal trainers, the *ACE Personal Trainer Manual* is designed to serve as a companion and self-study aid to the American Council on Exercise's Personal Trainer Certification Examination. Since its launch in May 1990, more than 23,000 people have successfully passed the ACE Personal Trainer Certification Examination, making ACE the largest certifying agency of personal trainers in the world.

In developing the *ACE Personal Trainer Manual*, we brought together 18 experts from the fields of exercise physiology, nutrition and law. Each chapter is a building block of knowledge, arranged logically to give you an understanding of the basic principles and skills inherent to personal training.

Because you will be responsible for designing and supervising exercise programs, it is essential that you have a basic understanding of the principles of human physiology and anatomy. Chapter 1 explains how the body functions at rest and how it responds and adapts to many different types of exercises, while Chapter 2 explores the structure of the body and the relationships of the body parts to one another. Chapter 3 provides you with a broad understanding of human movement and how applying the principles of biomechanics (mechanics applied to living things) and kinesiology will enable you to design exercise programs that are safe, effective and compatible with the body's function and design.

Chapter 4 covers the broad science of nutrition, highlighting the fundamental knowledge personal trainers need in order to best advise their clients. While it is beyond a personal trainer's scope of practice to give specific nutritional advice, it is necessary for you to have a basic understanding of the components that comprise food and their affects on both health and performance.

The hallmark of ACE-certified Personal Trainers is their ability to work safely and effectively in promoting better health through physical activity for a wide variety of individuals. However, not all clients who seek your services can or should be trained by you. The purpose of Chapter 5 is to assist in screening for potential contraindications to physical activity, while Chapter 6 provides the tools necessary to assess the ability or readiness of your clients to participate in physical activity.

Chapters 7 through 11 provide you with the nuts and bolts of developing comprehensive physical activity programs for your clients, including cardiorespiratory fitness, muscular strength and endurance and flexibility. With an understanding of these major components of fitness, Chapter 11 brings it all together in helping you develop specific programs that suit the individual needs of each of your clients.

When it comes to physical fitness, what works for one individual may not work (or be appropriate) for another. This is particularly important when dealing with clients who have special needs. Chapter 12 helps you sort through what is, and what is not, appropriate for you to do for clients who have special needs or conditions.

Getting started is one thing — sticking with it is another. Keeping clients motivated is a challenge most personal trainers will face, so Chapters 13 and 14 focus on the principles of adherence and the skills you need to effectively communicate with your clients.

Even when programs are designed properly, injuries can happen. However, a properly conditioned client can rehabilitate an injured area quickly and more completely. Chapter 15 addresses potential musculoskeletal injuries your clients may experience, as well as how such injuries might be prevented. Chapter 16 covers several procedures for preventing and coping with emergencies. Although this information is a good overview of first-aid procedures, it is not comprehensive, nor is it a substitute for formal training in first aid. As an ACE-certified Personal Trainer, you should take the American Red Cross Standard First Aid and Personal Safety Course, and you are required to become certified in cardiopulmonary resuscitation (CPR). Finally, Chapter 17 gives you an overview of the legal system and the operation of various laws and legal principles that may have an impact upon your ability to serve your clients.

As a personal trainer, you have an abundance of information at your fingertips. Your challenge is to learn how to apply this information in a way that is appealing, brings about results, and ensures the long-term success of your clients.

A career in fitness can be both long and rewarding. It offers an opportunity to creatively apply scientific information to help people not only achieve their personal fitness goals, but live healthier lives as well. If you are considering a career in fitness, we hope this book entices you to pursue one. If you are already dedicated to fitness, we hope this book will aid you in your ongoing exploration and work in the fitness industry.

Richard T. Cotton
Editor

PART I

Exercise
Science

CHAPTER 1

Exercise Physiology

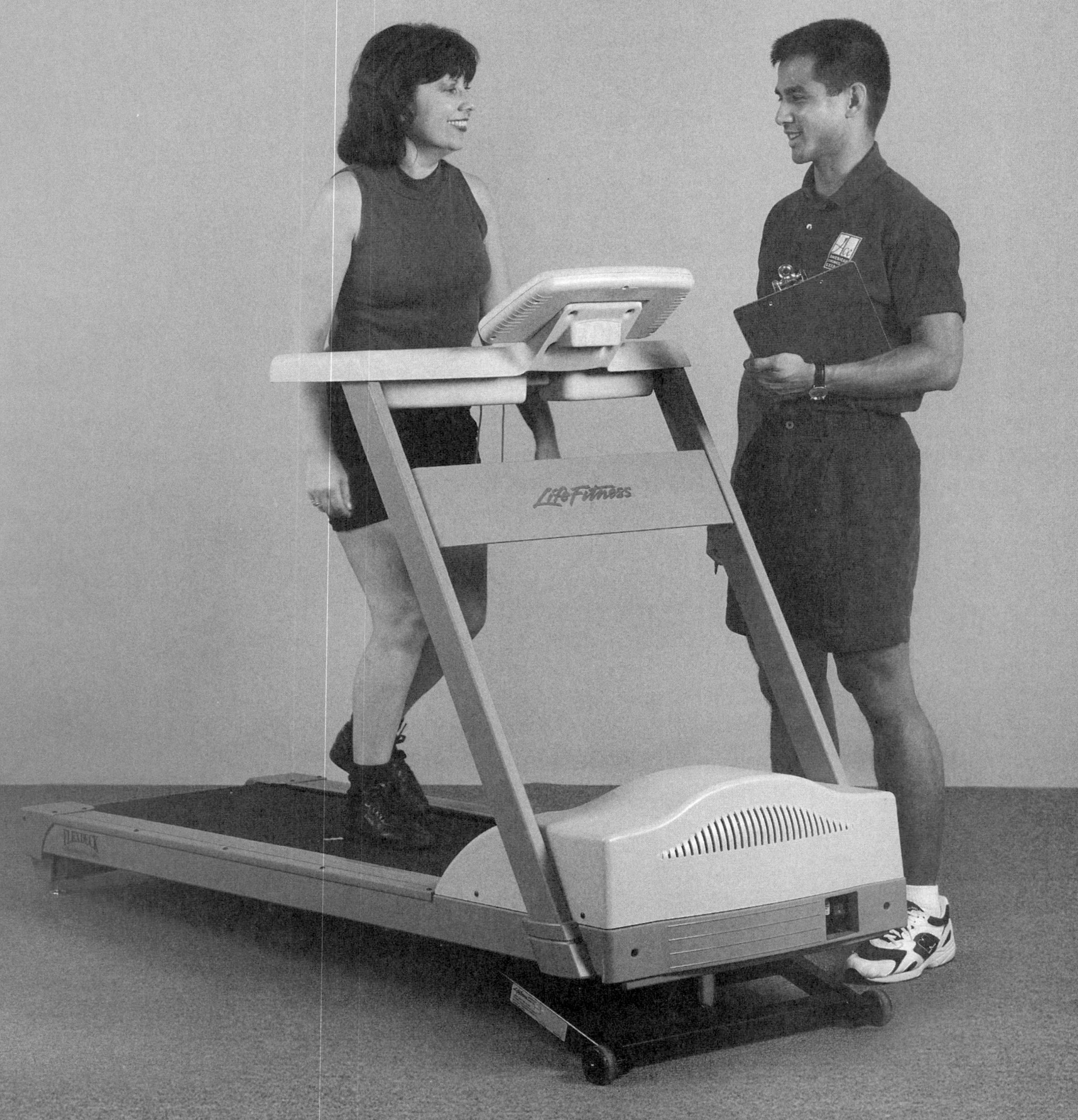

1

IN THIS CHAPTER:

Daniel Kosich

Daniel Kosich, Ph.D., is president of EXERFIT Consulting, senior consultant to IDEA, co-exercise science editor for Shape *magazine, contributing editor for* New Woman *magazine, and technical advisor to the Jane Fonda Workout. He is the author of* GET REAL: A Personal Guide to Real-Life Weight Management, *and has developed numerous fitness and nutrition education programs for fitness center personnel and*

Interest in physical fitness training for the general public has grown rapidly in the past decade. Those involved with designing or supervising exercise programs must have a basic understanding of the principles of human physiology and anatomy. Physiology is the study of the myriad functions in a living organism, and exercise physiology is the study of the ways cells and tissues of the body function during exercise. The study of exercise physiology challenges you, as a personal trainer, to first be familiar with how the body functions at rest, and to then understand how the body responds and adapts to many different types of exercises.

How does the body respond to a gradually increasing exercise pace? Does the body respond differently to a dramatic increase in pace, compared with a gradual increase? What are the differences between responses to lifting weights and running or cycling? Why is a slow, sustained stretch held with no pain much safer and generally more effective than rapid, bouncing stretches? These are all questions that you must be able to easily answer.

This chapter presents the fundamental concepts of exercise physiology that you must understand in order to design a safe and effective exercise program that will enable a healthy adult to achieve optimum fitness.

OPTIMUM FITNESS

There are many ways to define physical fitness. It may be helpful for you to think about physical fitness in relation to "specificity of training," which means that physiological adaptations to exercise are specific to the system worked during the stress of exercise. In other words, the type of exercise that develops **cardiovascular endurance** is not very effective for developing an optimum balance of muscular strength. **Flexibility** training usually increases the **range of motion** about a specific joint, such as the hip, but it is not effective for improving cardiovascular endurance or muscle strength. Resistance training, such as weight lifting, is the best way to increase strength, but it is not the most effective way to improve cardiovascular fitness.

Optimum physical fitness is often defined as the condition resulting from a lifestyle that leads to the development of an optimal level of cardiovascular endurance, muscular strength and flexibility, as well as the achievement and maintenance of ideal body weight. Because training is specific as described above, an individual must participate in cardiovascular (cardiorespiratory), strength and flexibility exercise to achieve optimum (balanced) physical fitness.

DEFINITIONS

Cardiovascular, or cardiorespiratory endurance, also referred to as aerobic fitness, describes the ability of the cardiovascular/cardiorespiratory system (heart, lungs, blood vessels) to deliver an adequate supply of oxygen to exercising muscles. (Some exercise physiologists prefer to use the term cardiorespiratory rather than cardiovascular, because cardiorespiratory includes the reference to the lungs [respiratory]. These terms will be used interchangeably in this chapter.) Blood must flow from the heart through blood vessels (vascular) to the lungs to pick up oxygen that can be delivered to exercising muscles.

Muscular strength is the maximum amount of force a muscle or muscle group can develop during a single contraction. Muscular endurance is the number of repeated contractions a muscle or muscle group can perform against a resistance without fatiguing, or the length of time a contraction can be held without fatigue.

Flexibility describes the amount of movement that can be accomplished at a joint (an articulation), such as the knee or shoulder, and is usually referred to as the "range of motion about a joint." Maintaining flexibility may help reduce the risk of injury, and can also help improve performance in many activities.

Healthy body weight represents a healthy **body composition**. An individual's weight on a scale is comprised of two dimensions: 1) body fat (adipose tissue); and 2) **fat-free weight** (muscle, bones, blood, organs, etc.). Body fat, which is the body's primary reserve of stored energy, is stored as **triglycerides** both in fat (adipose) cells located between the skin and muscles all over the body, as well as within skeletal muscles. While the energy available from fat is used throughout the body, exercising muscles can utilize a tremendous amount of fat to produce the energy necessary for muscle contraction. Percent body fat represents the percentage of total body weight that is carried as fat. In general, a healthy body-fat percentage falls in the range of 18 percent to 25 percent for women and 12 percent to 18 percent for men. Fat-free weight represents all the rest of the body's weight, excluding fat — muscles, bones, organs and nervous tissue. Achieving and maintaining a healthy body composition is an important part of health and fitness.

Fitness Testing

It is possible to measure one's level of fitness in each of the areas of optimum fitness using a variety of fitness tests. The most important value of fitness testing, which will be discussed in detail in Chapter 6 and referred to throughout this manual, is to establish a baseline against which improvements can be measured over time.

Fitness testing can be done in a controlled laboratory environment, which usually involves expensive, precision instruments. Gas analyzers for measuring true oxygen consumption, hydrostatic tanks with nitrogen or helium washout apparatus for measuring body composition, and calibrated static gauges on isokinetic machines for measuring strength are typical examples of laboratory testing devices.

Fitness testing also can be done with less sophisticated equipment using what are often referred to as "field tests." Field tests, which typically use prediction equations developed by comparing data with laboratory tests, give personal trainers the opportunity to perform accurate assessments without the need for expensive equipment. The 1.5-mile run/walk for estimating aerobic capacity, and the skinfold caliper and circumference measurements for estimating body composition are examples of field tests that are specific to your client's training (e.g., walking, running) and are often more accurate than submaximal lab tests such as stationary bike and stop tests.

PHYSIOLOGY OF THE CARDIOPULMONARY (CARDIOVASCULAR) SYSTEM

Physiology of the Cardiopulmonary (Cardiovascular) System

The cardiopulmonary system is primarily a transport network in the body. Blood serves as the vehicle to carry gases (such as oxygen) and nutrients (such as **fats**, **amino acids** and **glucose**) from where they are taken into the body to the cells where they are needed. Blood also picks up by-products (such as **lactic acid** and carbon dioxide) from the cells where they are made and carries them to where they can be expelled or metabolized.

Cardio (as well as cardiac, coronary and myocardial) refers to the heart. Pulmonary, as mentioned earlier, refers to the lungs. In the lungs, blood gives up carbon dioxide and picks up oxygen. Blood is transported in the body through an incredible network of blood vessels. Therefore, the cardiopulmonary system is composed of the heart, which pumps the blood; the lungs, where the blood picks up oxygen; and the blood vessels, which transport the blood throughout the body. Vascular refers to the blood vessels: arteries, veins and capillaries. The cardiovascular system, therefore, refers to the heart and all the vessels through which blood flows.

There are three kinds of blood vessels: arteries, capillaries and veins. Generally, **arteries** carry blood with a fresh oxygen (O_2) supply away from the heart to be delivered to the various cells and tissues. (An exception to this is the pulmonary arteries and veins. Pulmonary arteries have a low O_2 content and pulmonary veins have a high O_2 content.) **Capillaries** are very narrow, thin-walled vessels across which the exchange of gases, nutrients and cellular waste products occurs between the blood and the cells of the body. After passing through the capillaries, blood enters the veins. The systemic venous system provides the network of vessels through which the blood, now lower in oxygen content

Physiology of the Cardiopulmonary (Cardiovascular) System

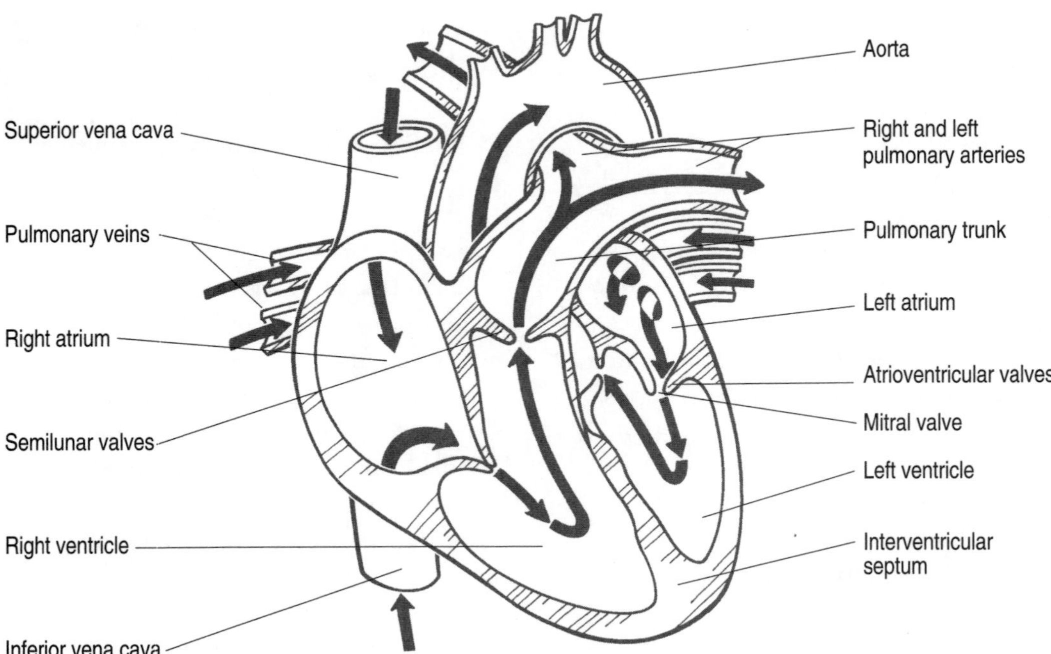

FIGURE 1.1
Anatomy of the heart and pattern of blood flow through it.

than arterial blood but with a much higher content of carbon dioxide, flows back to the heart to continue the cyclic blood flow.

The Heart

The heart muscle is divided into right and left sides, and each side is further divided into upper and lower chambers, making a total of four separate chambers. The upper chambers are called **atria**; the lower chambers are called **ventricles**. As depicted in Figure 1.1, the right side of the heart receives the venous blood (blood coming back to the heart through the veins), then pumps this blood to the lungs. All of the blood from the venous system enters the right atrium, then flows to the right ventricle. When the heart muscle contracts, the right ventricle squeezes against the volume of blood that has filled into the chamber and sends this blood to the lungs through the pulmonary arteries.

In the lungs, the blood picks up a fresh supply of oxygen and gives off carbon dioxide (CO_2) in the pulmonary capillaries. Oxygen and, to a limited extent, carbon dioxide are carried in red blood cells on a protein called hemoglobin. The freshly oxygenated blood returns to the left atrium through the pulmonary veins, then flows to the left ventricle. While the right ventricle contracts, the left ventricle also contracts and pumps the blood in its chamber through the largest artery in the body — the aorta — to be delivered to the rest of the body.

In essence, the cardiovascular system has two circulatory patterns: one is pulmonary circulation — from the heart to the lungs and back; the other, often referred to as systemic circulation, is the flow of blood from the left ventricle to the rest of the body and back. Remember, the right and left ventricles contract at the same time, and each side pumps the same amount of blood per contraction.

The two phases in the rhythmic pattern of cardiac contraction and relaxation are called the cardiac cycle: systole and diastole. **Systole** refers to the contraction phase of the cardiac cycle; **diastole** refers to the relaxation phase. During systole, the atria contract first, pumping blood to the ventricles. A fraction of a second later, the ventricles contract, pumping blood to the lungs and the body. Remember, the left

Physiology of the Cardiopulmonary (Cardiovascular) System

and right sides of the heart contract simultaneously, so at the same time blood from the right ventricle is pumped (ejected) to the lungs through the pulmonary arteries, blood from the left ventricle is ejected to the rest of the body through the aorta.

As the heart muscle relaxes during diastole, blood fills the left and right chambers of the heart in preparation for the next contraction. Note that during diastole, the heart muscle itself is supplied with its blood flow (therefore, its oxygen supply) through the coronary arteries. One of the many benefits of having a high level of cardiopulmonary fitness is that the heart spends more time resting (in diastole) at any submaximal exercise intensity, including rest, than when the system is poorly trained. We'll discuss the reasons for this later in the chapter.

Cardiac Output

Cardiac output (Q) is the amount of blood that flows from each ventricle in one minute. The cardiac output from the left and right ventricles is exactly the same. However, the blood in the left ventricle is ejected with significantly greater force than the blood in the right ventricle. This is because the blood from the right ventricle goes just to the lungs and back, whereas the blood from the left ventricle has to be pumped with enough force to send it throughout the rest of the body.

Cardiac output is a product of two factors. One is heart rate (HR), the number of times the heart beats per minute (bpm). The other is **stroke volume (SV)**, the amount of blood pumped from each ventricle each time the heart beats. Stroke volume is measured in milliliters (ml) per beat (1 ounce = 29.6 ml). If heart rate is multiplied by stroke volume, or the number of beats per minute is multiplied by the amount of blood pumped from each ventricle per beat, the resulting volume represents the cardiac output. Cardiac output can be expressed by the following equation:

$$Q = HR \times SV$$

For example, if the heart beats 60 times per minute (HR = 60), and 70 milliliters of blood are pumped each beat (SV = 70 ml), the cardiac output would be

$$60 \text{ bpm} \times 70 \text{ ml/beat} = 4200 \text{ ml/min}$$

This equals about one gallon of blood per minute, a fairly typical cardiac output at rest.

Ejection Fraction

The amount of blood that fills the ventricles during diastole is not always completely ejected (pumped out) during systole. The percentage of the total volume of blood in the ventricle at the end of diastole that is subsequently ejected during contraction is called the **ejection fraction**.

The ejection fraction at rest is only about 50 percent because there is minimal need for oxygen in the muscle cells at rest; the heart can supply adequate oxygen with minimal effort. But during work, when there is an increase in the need for oxygen in the muscles, the heart is able to completely empty the ventricles during contraction. During exercise, the ejection fraction can increase to 100 percent of the blood in the ventricles at the end of diastole. The importance of the increase in ejection fraction (which clearly increases cardiac output) as one goes from rest to increasingly higher exercise intensities will soon be clear.

Oxygen Extraction at the Muscles

As mentioned earlier, a primary purpose of the cardiovascular system during exercise is to deliver oxygen and other nutrients to the exercising muscle cells and to carry carbon dioxide and other waste products away from the muscles. Cardiac output represents the volume of blood (therefore, oxygen) flowing toward the muscles each minute. But another critically important factor, especially in exercise performance, is the amount of oxygen taken from the hemoglobin (remember, this occurs in the capillaries of the muscles) and subsequently used in the exercising muscle cells. This process is referred to as **oxygen extraction**.

Normally, all of the oxygen delivered to the cells via the arteries is not extracted in the capillaries. So, while the amount of oxygen in venous blood is certainly less than the amount of oxygen in arterial blood, there is some oxygen in the blood that returns back to the heart. In other words, we are able to load the blood with more oxygen in the lungs than our body is able to use at the cellular level. Therefore, in a healthy person, the inability to breathe fast enough is not the limiting factor in performance. A significant limitation to exercise performance is the capacity of the muscles to extract oxygen from the bloodstream to produce energy.

ENERGY PRODUCTION IN THE CELLS

Why is oxygen so important? An understanding of the functions of the cardiopulmonary system in oxygen delivery and extraction can help explain energy production in the cells, particularly in muscle cells.

ATP — The Energy Molecule

When a muscle fiber contracts and exerts force, the energy used to drive the contraction comes from a special substance in the cell known as **adenosine triphosphate**, or **ATP**. For our purposes, ATP is the body's energy source, just as gasoline is the energy source in an automobile engine. How quickly and efficiently a muscle cell produces ATP determines how much work the cell can do before it fatigues. While there is some ATP stored in a muscle cell, the supply is limited. Therefore, muscle cells must produce more ATP in order to continue working. Muscle cells replenish the ATP supply using three distinct biochemical pathways, or separate series of chemical reactions: the **aerobic system**, **anaerobic glycolysis** and the **creatine phosphate system**.

Aerobic and Anaerobic Energy Systems

The word "**aerobic**" means "with oxygen." The first system for producing ATP, the aerobic energy system, is dominant when adequate oxygen is delivered into the cell to meet energy production needs, such as when the muscle is at rest. Most cells, including muscle cells, contain structures called **mitochondria**. The mitochondria are the site of aerobic energy (ATP) production. The greater the number of mitochondria in a cell, the greater the aerobic energy production capability of that cell.

The other two energy systems, anaerobic glycolysis and the creatine phosphate system, are the primary sources of ATP when an inadequate supply of oxygen is available to the cell to meet its energy needs. In the absence of sufficient oxygen, as when a muscle needs to generate force quickly (e.g., to lift a heavy weight), the muscle relies primarily on the anaerobic systems, which provide a rapidly available source of ATP. "**Anaerobic**" means "without oxygen." The anaerobic production of ATP occurs inside the cell, but outside the mitochondria.

Most cells, such as those in the heart, brain and other organs, have little or no anaerobic capability. Therefore, these cells must be continuously supplied with oxygen, or they will die. For example, if a coronary artery (which supplies blood and oxygen to the heart muscle) becomes clogged with a build-up of cholesterol deposits, there will be a diminished flow of blood through that artery. This condition, in which blood supply does not meet the demand, is known as **ischemia**. The decreased blood flow can lead to an insufficient oxygen supply to the heart muscle, during rest or exercise, which often leads to a sensation of pain and/or pressure in the chest called **angina pectoris**.

Energy Production in the Cells

If the oxygen supply is cut off, such as when a blood clot forms where the coronary artery has become clogged, the area of the heart muscle (myocardium) beyond the blockage suffers a **myocardial infarction**, often called a heart attack. If enough of the myocardium is involved, the result is a fatal heart attack. In the brain, ischemia can lead to a **stroke**.

Unlike the heart and the brain, skeletal muscles such as the triceps and quadriceps, have a significant anaerobic capability. You must understand aerobic and anaerobic energy production in relation to what substances are used to produce ATP, as well as to exercise intensity, with rest and maximum effort representing the two extremes of possible intensity. The body uses an extremely complex chemical process to produce ATP. However, just a basic understanding of the process will assist you in designing effective exercise programs.

Fat (fatty acids) and carbohydrate (glucose) are the two substances the body's cells use to produce most of the ATP supply. Proteins, which are comprised of various combinations of amino acids, are not a preferred energy source. In an adequately nourished client, proteins play a minor role in energy production. However, when a diet does not supply sufficient calories, the body is capable of using amino acids, stored in tissues such as muscle, to produce the energy it needs. This is certainly not an ideal process.

When the body is at rest, and the cardiopulmonary system is easily able to supply adequate oxygen to the mitochondria of muscle cells, both fatty acids and glucose are used to produce ATP. In other words, at rest, most of the needed ATP is produced aerobically, using both fatty acids and glucose. In fact, the body produces about one calorie per minute at rest. (The actual number is related to lean body mass.) About 50 percent of this one calorie per minute comes from fatty acids, even in an untrained person. In a well-trained endurance athlete, fatty acids provide as much as 70 percent of the resting caloric expenditure.

With increasing exercise intensity, the cardiovascular system makes every attempt to increase its delivery of oxygen into the mitochondria of exercising muscles to aerobically produce enough ATP. At some point in increasing intensity, determined both by a client's level of aerobic fitness and by genetics, the cardiovascular system becomes unable to supply enough oxygen to the exercising muscles, so they call on the anaerobic systems to rapidly produce ATP. The intensity at which adequate oxygen is unavailable is referred to as the **anaerobic threshold**. (The terms respiratory and lactate threshold also are used.) As illustrated in Figure 1.2, the anaerobic threshold is reached before maximum effort, generally somewhere in the range of 50 percent to 85 percent of maximum effort.

The anaerobic systems cannot predominate for a prolonged period. The primary source of anaerobic ATP production is glucose, which is carried in the blood and also is stored in muscles and the liver as **glycogen** (a large molecule made up of chains of glucose). A second source of anaerobic ATP production is **creatine phosphate**, a molecule that can be quickly broken apart to help produce ATP. However, as with the muscles' store of ATP, there is an extremely limited supply of creatine phosphate. Research done nearly 20 years ago (J. Bergstrom et al., 1971) has shown that even in a well-trained athlete, the muscles store only enough creatine phosphate and ATP, together referred to as **phosphagens**, to last for about 10 seconds of maximal effort.

The unit of energy most often used in exercise science is the kilocalorie (kcal). One kcal is the amount of heat that will raise the temperature of one liter of water one degree centigrade.

To summarize, as long as a muscle cell is aerobic, it uses both fatty acids and glucose

Energy Production in the Cells

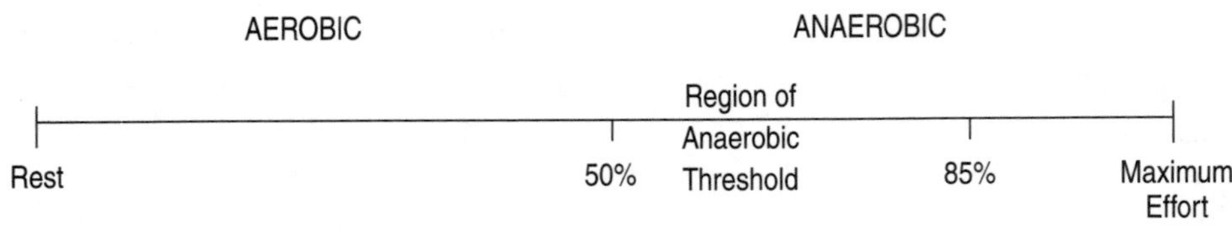

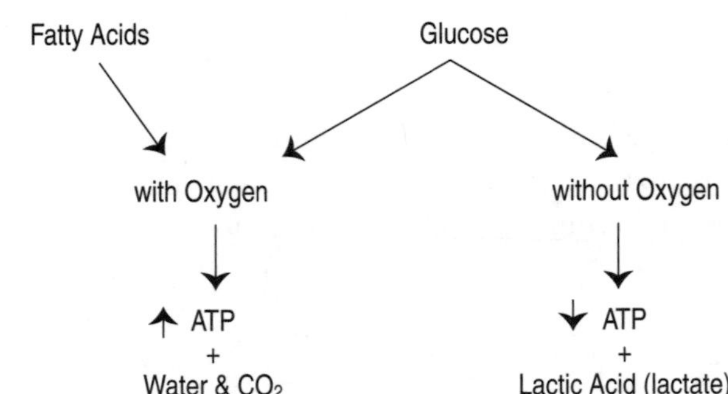

FIGURE 1.2
Energy production and relative intensity in an exercising muscle.

to produce ATP. The aerobic system produces much more ATP than the anaerobic systems, primarily because fat yields nine calories of energy per gram, while carbohydrate (glucose) and protein yield only four calories of energy per gram. Further, the end products of aerobic ATP production are water and carbon dioxide (CO_2). Both are relatively easy for the body to deal with, so that aerobic energy production does not lead to muscle fatigue.

When an exercising muscle becomes anaerobic, it relies on glucose (and to a limited extent the phosphagen system) to produce ATP. However, not only is much less ATP produced anaerobically than aerobically per molecule of substrate used, the by-products of anaerobic ATP production include **lactic acid**, heat and hydrogen ions. As the level of lactic acid and other by-products increases in a muscle, continued contraction of that muscle is soon inhibited. Lactic acid is thought to be the principal cause of the immediate soreness (the "burn") in an exercising muscle.

In addition to lactic acid build-up, muscles give other signals when they can no longer produce enough ATP aerobically. One is hyperventilation, defined as "breathing faster than is necessary at a given pace," an indication that anaerobic ATP production is predominating. When inadequate oxygen is available, the muscle signals the brain to increase the rate and depth of breathing. However, the limiting factor is not usually the ability to increase the rate and depth of breathing. It is primarily the ability to extract and use oxygen at the muscle. Therefore, hyperventilation is a futile process. Figure 1.3 summarizes the essential elements of the biochemistry muscles used to produce the ATP needed for contraction.

The chemistry that the body uses to produce ATP depends on proteins in the body called **enzymes**. Enzymes are needed to start and carry out the chemical reactions that produce ATP both aerobically and anaerobically. The fat-metabolizing enzymes are different from the carbohydrate-metabolizing enzymes. Further, separate enzymes are used to metabolize carbohydrate aerobically than are used to metabolize carbohydrate anaerobically. When we exercise at an intensity below the anaerobic threshold, the aerobic enzymes that metabolize fat and carbohydrate are dominating in the production of ATP. But when exercise is done above the anaerobic threshold, the anaerobic enzymes take over the dominant role in producing ATP.

Energy Production in the Cells

Energy System	Substance(s) Used	Limitation to Produce ATP	Primary Use ATP production
Anaerobic			
1. Phosphagen	Creatine Phosphate (CP) Stored ATP	Muscle stores very little CP and ATP	High intensity, short duration activities; less than 10 seconds to fatigue
2. Breakdown of Glucose	Glucose and Glycogen	Lactic acid buildup causes rapid fatigue	High intensity, short duration activities; from 1 to 3 minutes to fatigue
Aerobic	Fatty acids, Glucose and Glycogen	Depletion of muscle glycogen and sugar; insufficient oxygen delivery	Long duration, sub-anaerobic threshold activities; longer than 3 minutes to fatigue

FIGURE 1.3 Energy systems available to an exercising muscle.

Aerobic training will lead to an increased capacity in the aerobic system, but has little effect on anaerobic enzymes. Aerobic training significantly increases our ability to burn fat. Anaerobic training, on the other hand, will lead principally to an improved function in the anaerobic enzyme system — another application of the principle of specificity of training.

Aerobic Capacity (Maximal Oxygen Consumption)

The total capacity to consume oxygen at the cellular level is referred to as **maximal oxygen consumption or VO_2 max**. This phrase represents an individual's maximum aerobic capacity. VO_2 max depends on two factors: 1) the delivery of oxygen to the working muscle by the blood, or the cardiac output; and 2) the ability to extract the oxygen from the blood at the capillaries and use it in the mitochondria. Maximum oxygen consumption is represented by the following formula:

VO_2 max = (cardiac output max) x (oxygen extraction max)

VO_2 (the volume of oxygen consumed) is measured as either milliliters of oxygen consumed per kilogram of body weight per minute (ml O_2/kg/min), or as liters of oxygen consumed per minute (l O_2/min).

We can illustrate how much oxygen is actually used at rest when compared with a hypothetical* maximum aerobic capacity of a client who weighs 70 kilograms (154 pounds). If his resting heart rate is 60 beats per minute (bpm), stroke volume is 70 ml/beat (remember cardiac output = heart rate x stroke volume), and oxygen extraction is 6 ml O_2/100 ml of blood, then his resting VO_2 is:

* Personal trainers are unable to directly measure these values.

VO_2 = (60 bpm x 70 ml/beat) x (6 ml O_2/100 ml blood)

which equals 252 ml O_2/min. Divided by 70 kg, his resting VO_2 is about 3.6 ml/kg/min. During maximal exercise this man has a heart rate of 180 bpm, a stroke volume of 115 ml/beat, and an oxygen extraction of 15 ml O_2/100 ml blood. So his maximum VO_2 is:

VO_2 max = (180 bpm x 115 ml/beat) x (15 ml O_2/100 ml blood), which equals 3,105 ml O_2/min, or 44.4 ml/kg/min.

While the example represents a hypothetical client in moderate condition, it clearly illustrates that our bodies have a tremendous capacity to increase oxygen consumption, in this case by more than 12.5 times. While increases in both heart rate and stroke volume account for the increased cardiac output during exercise, the increase in **oxygen extraction** (referred to as arterio-venous oxygen difference, or O_2 diff.) results from different stimuli. During exercise, several changes occur that make it easier for oxygen to be taken off the hemoglobin molecule for use in aerobic energy production in the muscles. The changes include increases in temperature, acidity and level of carbon dioxide in muscles.

The resting VO_2 of 3.5 ml/kg/min is often referred to as one **Metabolic Equivalent**, or 1 **MET**. Activities are sometimes described in terms of METS; for example, volleyball has a range of about 3 to 6 METS, and high- or low-impact and step aerobics classes have a range of about 6 to 10 METS. To determine the VO_2 equivalent of any MET value, simply multiply the MET value by 3.5. Physicians often prescribe exercise by MET values for patients in cardiac rehabilitation programs and reevaluate the MET capacity of the patient as the rehabilitation progresses.

Not only does VO_2 max increase with aerobic training, the percentage of maximum effort at which the anaerobic threshold occurs also increases. Practically speaking, this means that a client is able to aerobically produce ATP at increasingly greater intensities in response to aerobic training. Further, the aerobically trained person generally can perform more intense activities than the untrained person, while still working aerobically.

CARDIOVASCULAR/CARDIOPULMONARY RESPONSES TO EXERCISE

Since maximal aerobic capacity is actually a function of cardiac output times oxygen extraction, you must understand how these factors change in response to aerobic training, as well as the guidelines for effective cardiovascular (aerobic) training.

Changes in Oxygen Delivery

As one begins an exercise session, heart rate and stroke volume (cardiac output) increase in order to increase the delivery of oxygen to working muscles. Blood flow is shunted from the abdominal area to the exercising muscles. This redistribution results from a **vasodilation**, or an increase in diameter, in the arterial vessels that supply blood to the exercising muscles, along with a **vasoconstriction**, decrease in diameter, of the vessels that supply blood to the abdominal area. The breathing rate also increases.

In addition, blood pressure changes. **Systolic blood pressure** generally refers to the amount of pressure generated by the contraction of the left ventricle (systole). Systolic pressure provides the force that propels blood through the system. **Diastolic blood pressure** represents the amount of pressure left in the system when the heart muscle relaxes between beats (diastole). Blood pressure of 120/80 means that the left ventricle generates 120 millimeters of pressure (mercury) during contraction and 80 millimeters of pressure remain in the vascular system when the heart is relaxing between beats. The driving force for blood flow is called pulse pressure, which is the difference between the systolic and diastolic pressures.

Blood pressure response is one of the important measures taken during a clinical stress test to evaluate cardiovascular fitness and health. During exercise, systolic pressure should increase as the cardiovascular system attempts to increase oxygen delivery to the muscles. Diastolic pressure, on the other hand, should stay the same or even decrease a little, because the dilation of blood vessels in the muscles (and in the skin to help get rid of heat as exercise continues) decreases the amount of peripheral resistance in the vascular system.

All of these changes occur in an attempt to deliver more oxygen to the exercising muscles. It is clear that when the muscles need to produce more ATP to meet the increased energy needs of exercise, oxygen consumption also increases. As long as enough oxygen can be delivered into the mitochondria to meet this increased energy need, ATP production will proceed primarily through the aerobic system.

Changes in Cardiac Output

In response to proper aerobic training, several adaptations occur in the cardiopulmonary system that lead to a significantly increased aerobic capacity. Resting heart rate decreases, in part because the interior dimensions of the ventricles increase; that is, the ventricles can hold more blood as the heart gets larger inside. Since the ventricles can fill with a greater volume of blood during diastole, stroke volume at rest also increases. The same cardiac output can be maintained at a lower heart rate. Because a given intensity of activity requires a given amount of oxygen, the cardiac output at a given intensity is essentially the same whether one is trained or untrained. Since more blood is pumped with each contraction, the heart beats fewer times per minute to achieve the necessary oxygen delivery. This increased efficiency is certainly a benefit to the heart.

In response to aerobic training, the stroke volume during exercise also becomes greater. Since a given intensity requires a given amount of oxygen, the heart rate at any given submaximal intensity will be lower, following as few as three months of regular aerobic exercise. If a given work effort (say, a 10-minute mile pace) raised the heart rate to 150 bpm before training, then the same work effort after training may raise the heart rate to only 125 bpm. In order to get to 150 bpm, the trained client will need to exercise at a greater intensity, perhaps an eight-minute mile.

Maximum cardiac output is significantly greater following training because of the increase in stroke volume. Maximum heart rate is determined by age, not by state of training, but a greater maximum stroke volume multiplied by the same maximum heart rate yields a greater maximal cardiac output.

Changes in Oxygen Extraction

In addition to increased stroke volume and maximum cardiac output, other changes occur that enable individuals to sustain exercise at a much greater intensity and still be "aerobic" following training (Figure 1.4). Recall that the other factor responsible for VO_2 is the extraction of oxygen from the blood and its subsequent use in the mitochondria of muscle cells. The exchange of gases and nutrients between blood and tissues occurs in the capillaries. One change in response to aerobic training is that new capillaries are produced in the active skeletal muscles, increasing the area for the exchange of oxygen. The other major change in response to aerobic training is a significant increase in the mitochondrial density, which means more of the muscle cell is occupied by mitochondria. This also leads to a significant increase in the amount of aerobic enzyme activity in the cell, since the mitochondria are the site of aerobic ATP production. The increased aerobic enzyme capacity allows a greater use of oxygen; thus, exercising at greater intensities can still be accomplished "aerobically." The increased ability to use O_2 also is part of the reason why resting and submaximal heart rates decrease with training.

The increased maximum cardiac output combined with the increased extraction capability yields not only a greater maximum aerobic capacity, but also an elevated anaerobic threshold. The greater the ability to aerobically make ATP at higher exercise intensities, the more "fit" a client becomes, and the greater their ability to "burn" fat.

Aerobic training also produces a number of other changes that influence

Guidelines for Cardiovascular Fitness

Cardiac Output Factors	Oxygen Extraction Factors
1. Decreased HR at any submaximal effort, including rest	1. Increased capillary density
2. Increased SV at rest, and at all intensities	2. Increased number of mitochondria
3. Increased maximum cardiac output	3. Increased activity of mitochondrial (aerobic) enzymes

↑ cardiac output + ↑oxygen extraction yields ↑ VO_2 max

FIGURE 1.4 Summary of adaptations to cardiovascular training.

performance during submaximal exercise. First, the body uses more fatty acids for ATP production at any submaximal intensity. Second, during submaximal exercise, the body stores more glycogen in trained muscles and produces less lactic acid, both of which lead to improved endurance. Aerobic training also increases the body's tolerance to the lactic acid that is produced during exercise. It is clear that aerobic exercise is beneficial. What follows are some specific guidelines for cardiovascular training.

GUIDELINES FOR CARDIOVASCULAR FITNESS

Any type of fitness training, whether it is aerobic training, strength training or flexibility training, is based on what exercise physiologists call the **overload principle**. Overload means that in order to train one of the body's systems, such as the cardiopulmonary system or the skeletal muscle system, that system must be made to work harder than it is accustomed to working. The overload to cause significant improvement in the cardiovascular system is an increased **venous return** sustained for a prolonged period. In simpler terms, the exercise(s) must cause a sustained increase in the amount of blood returning to the heart.

In order to maximize overload, aerobic training should follow four rules. The exercise should 1) be the correct type, 2) be done at the proper intensity, 3) be of sufficient duration and 4) occur with adequate frequency. Please refer to Chapter 7 for a detailed discussion of the variables to consider when developing a cardiovascular training program.

Type of Exercise

The type of exercise chosen is related to the **principle of specificity of training**. For maximum effectiveness, aerobic exercises need to be rhythmic and continuous and involve the large muscle groups. Generally, the hip flexors (iliopsoas, rectus femoris) and extensors (gluteus maximus, hamstrings), and the knee flexors (hamstrings) and extensors (quadriceps) should be involved. Walking, jogging, cycling, aerobic dance and stair climbing are examples of activities that use these muscle groups. Activities combining upper and lower extremity movements, such as cross-country skiing, rowing and swimming, can lead to high levels of aerobic capacity. However, for those with physical challenges, such as spinal cord problems that prohibit lower extremity movement, using large upper-body muscles — such as in upper-body ergometry — will clearly enhance aerobic fitness.

Rhythmic, large muscle movements are essential for an effective increase in blood flow back to the heart. The rhythmic squeezing action of the large muscles against the veins within them is called the "muscle pump." This muscle pump leads to a significant increase in venous return, which is required for effective aerobic conditioning.

Intensity of Exercise

The intensity rule is critical. The principles of aerobic and anaerobic energy production make it clear that exercise at too great an intensity for a client's level of fitness will rely on the anaerobic systems, not the aerobic systems. Research shows that optimum exercise intensity for fitness improvement is in the range of about 50 percent to 85 percent of maximum oxygen consumption. This corresponds to about 60 percent to 90 percent of maximum heart rate. The ranges are broad because of the effects of the level of fitness, as well as genetic factors. The higher a client's level of fitness, the higher the appropriate exercise intensity. Recent research also shows that untrained individuals will begin to improve aerobic fitness at intensities as low as 40 percent of VO_2 max (≅ 50 percent HR max).

Heart rate during exercise can provide an excellent monitor of intensity. Keep in mind that many factors will cause an increase in heart rate, and that an elevated heart rate is not necessarily an indication of an effective aerobic training pace. However, if the increased heart rate is accomplished by the correct type of activity, then the cardiovascular training potential is substantial.

Monitoring a **target heart rate (THR)** training zone provides an excellent indication of correct exercise intensity. Clients also monitor intensity by learning to recognize their anaerobic (lactate, respiratory) threshold. Exercising above this threshold leads to hyperventilation, lactic acid build-up and rapid fatigue. The **talk test** utilizes the hyperventilation response. The client should be able to carry on a comfortable conversation while exercising. If breathing is labored and difficult, the intensity is too great. Hyperventilation during exercise is normally accompanied by a burning, sometimes painful sensation in the active muscles because of lactic acid accumulation.

Another excellent way to monitor intensity is to use Borg's **Rating of Perceived Exertion (RPE)**. Clients can use this scale as a subjective way of measuring how hard they are exercising. For most people, exercising at a level of 12 to 15 (somewhat strong to hard) correlates well with an appropriate training heart rate. Please refer to Chapter 6 for a discussion of these and other heart-rate monitoring techniques.

Duration of Exercise

The third rule is that aerobic exercise must last for at least 15 to 20 minutes per session to lead to substantial fitness improvements over time. Once a client reaches the proper intensity, the activity must be sustained for the minimum time in order to cause adequate aerobic overload. Recent research suggests that two 10-minute sessions will lead to the same improvements as one 20-minute session if they are done at the same relative intensity.

Because aerobic training is related to the oxygen cost of activity, there is an inverse relationship between intensity and duration. If intensity is increased, the duration can be decreased and yet achieve a similar training effect. Conversely, if the intensity is decreased, the duration must be increased to achieve the same training effect. In general terms, when the cells of the body consume 1 liter (about one quart) of oxygen per minute, about five calories per minute have been expended (1 liter O_2/min ≅ 5 calories/min). If 2 liters per minute are consumed, the expenditure would rise to about 10 calories per minute. For example, walking costs approximately 5cal/min; jogging costs approximately 10cal/min. So jogging for 30 minutes would use about 300 calories (10 x 30 = 300), the same as 60 minutes of

Guidelines for Cardiovascular Fitness

walking (5 x 60 = 300). Therefore, walking for twice as long as jogging will result in approximately the same training effect. This is an especially important consideration for the untrained client.

A method of training that is increasingly being applied to the general public is interval exercise. There are two types of **interval training**: 1) performance interval training — a very high-intensity effort designed to enhance competitive performance in a specific sport, and 2) fitness interval training — a modest-to-vigorous intensity effort designed to improve general fitness.

Interval training has been used for many years by competitive athletes. In performance training, interval training often involves periods of maximal or near-maximal effort followed by short periods of rest. Such a method of training leads to significant performance benefits, largely because of an increased tolerance to the build-up of lactic acid. Performance intervals are generally recommended only for well-trained athletes. Because of the high intensity, an untrained person is at an increased risk for injury, not to mention quick fatigue, if performance intervals are attempted.

You can, however, encourage clients to perform fitness intervals. In fitness interval exercise, the client periodically increases intensity throughout a workout. The intervals are not rigidly defined as in performance interval training. Most importantly, the increase in intensity is capped when the anaerobic threshold is reached. At this point, the intensity is decreased. Figure 1.5 illustrates how interval exercise might look in a fitness training application.

Frequency of Exercise

The fourth rule for cardiovascular training is that the proper type of activity, done at the correct intensity and continued for a sufficient length of time, must be performed at least three days per week. While training three days per week may be sufficient, especially for those just beginning an exercise program, more frequent exercise, such as a brisk, daily walk, is certainly acceptable. It also will lead to more rapid improvements. Keep in mind that it is important to allow adequate rest and recovery to minimize the risks associated with over-training. Most experts encourage even competitive athletes to take at least one day per week for rest or a low-intensity recreational activity, like a round of golf.

Warm-up and Cool-down

Both a warm-up and cool-down period are an essential part of any exercise session (not just aerobic exercise). Warming up brings about important physiologic changes that reduce the risk of injury, as well as make the exercise session more comfortable. First, it causes an actual increase in the temperature of the muscle and connective tissue, thereby reducing the risk of soft tissue injury. Second, it allows the cardiovascular system to effectively adjust blood flow from the abdominal area to the active muscles where the need for oxygen is increasing in response to the exercise, while maintaining adequate venous return. This blood shunt is accomplished by constriction in arteries that supply blood to the gut, and dilation in arteries that deliver blood to the active muscles. Heart rate will quickly rise to near maximum in an attempt to supply adequate oxygen if the necessary three to five minutes of warm-up are not performed, especially if an intense pace is attempted too soon. Cool down to 18 to 20 beats per 10 seconds (108 to 120 bpm) to allow the system to reverse the blood shunt.

It may be difficult for you to impress the need for warm-up and cool-down to a client. The best activities for both are simply to work at a much lower pace in whatever activity the client is using for training. Examples include slow cycling for cycling, walking for jogging, and slow swimming

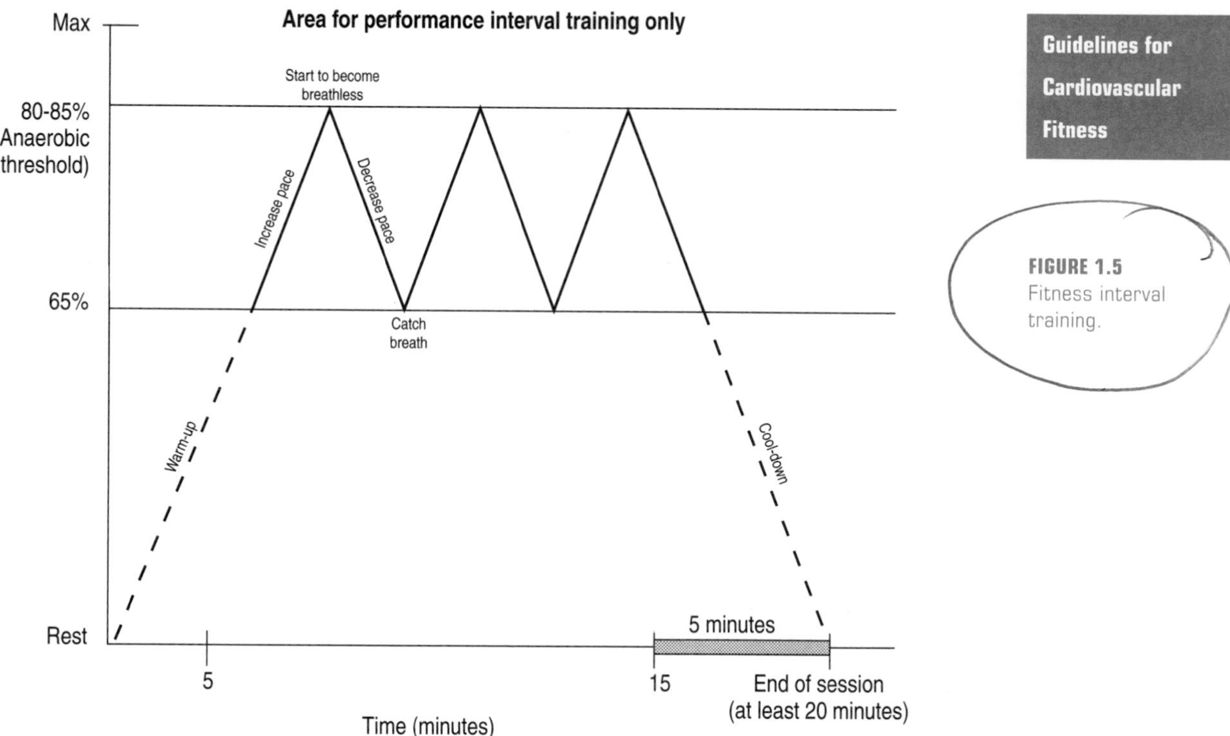

Guidelines for Cardiovascular Fitness

FIGURE 1.5 Fitness interval training.

for swimming. You should remind your clients that warm-up and cool-down not only reduce the potential for fatigue, but they reduce the risk of exercise-related injuries as well.

Benefits of Regular Aerobic Exercise

Research has shown that regular aerobic exercise has a number of significant health benefits, both for those who are apparently healthy and for those who suffer from various health problems. In addition to the positive body composition benefits, aerobic exercise has been reported to actually decrease appetite in many people. But even if it doesn't decrease appetite, the calorie-burning effects of regular aerobic exercise allow for a substantial daily calorie intake. In fact, competitive endurance athletes often consume 3,000 to 5,000 or more calories per day, and yet remain lean. Clearly, long-term aerobic training (combined with a sensible diet) is critical to achieving and maintaining a healthy body composition.

Weight-bearing exercises, such as jogging and brisk walking, have been shown to help strengthen the skeletal system. This not only helps reduce the risk for developing osteoporosis, but for those with physician approval to exercise, it may help stop further progress of the condition.

Since aerobic exercise training increases the sensitivity of the cells to insulin, aerobic exercise is often part of the treatment program for diabetics whose blood sugar is well controlled. Berger (1979) reported that less insulin is required to regulate blood sugar levels effectively in diabetics who exercised regularly. In several reported cases, type II diabetics who were medicated with drugs other than insulin were able to significantly reduce, or completely eliminate, medications by following a prudent course of exercise and healthy diet. The American Diabetes Association recommends that any diabetic considering beginning an exercise program consult with a physician to learn how to carefully monitor blood glucose levels before, during and after exercise. Eating a carefully designed diet is equally essential in the management of diabetes.

Aerobic exercise is often part of the

therapy for reducing the risk of **coronary artery disease** in high-risk individuals, as well as for those who have suffered a heart attack. Four primary risk factors for developing coronary artery disease are: 1) lack of adequate aerobic exercise, 2) high blood pressure (**hypertension**), 3) smoking and 4) high blood cholesterol levels (The American Heart Association). Aerobic exercise is effective in minimizing these **risk factors** for several reasons. First, many of those with high blood pressure also are overweight. Aerobic exercise definitely assists in reducing excess body fat and lowering blood pressure in those with hypertension. Second, many smokers find that regular aerobic exercise provides a great incentive to quit smoking. Third, regular, brisk aerobic exercise often leads to an increase in the level of **high density lipoprotein (HDL)**, or "good" cholesterol.

Aerobic exercise is frequently part of the therapy for those with arthritis. It certainly helps maintain aerobic fitness, as well as a healthy body weight, but most importantly, it increases joint range of motion.

It is essential to keep in mind that your role as a personal trainer in working with clients with significant health risk is to help implement the physician's recommendations. It is illegal, unethical and certainly not in the client's interest for you to attempt to diagnose a problem or suggest an exercise prescription for high-risk clients. See Chapter 12 for a discussion of considerations for working with clients' physicians to implement exercise programs for those with specific health problems.

Environmental Concerns

Altitude. Because there is less oxygen in the air at progressively higher altitudes, even well-trained athletes need to work at reduced intensity levels until they become acclimated to higher than their normal training altitude. While the length of the acclimatization process depends on a comparison of the new altitude, with the altitude the person is accustomed to, it takes about two weeks to acclimate significantly to altitudes up to about 8,000 feet, but can take up to four to five weeks to fully adapt to altitudes over 12,000 feet. However, noticeable improvements are generally observed within four to five days.

Since there is less oxygen in the air at higher altitudes, the heart will beat faster at any given sub-maximal intensity in order to deliver adequate oxygen to the muscles, even at rest. During exercise, the heart rate at any given intensity may be as much as 50 percent higher than normal, so pay particularly close attention to the onset of hyperventilation when beginning an exercise program at a high altitude. Decrease exercise pace to an intensity that allows the client to complete the session without becoming exhausted.

A number of potential problems are associated with high altitude, including headache, insomnia, irritability, weakness and dizziness. Be sure to report any such symptoms to a physician to reduce the risk of more severe complications. It might seem reasonable to assume that training at higher altitudes would enhance aerobic capacity upon return to a lower altitude. While it may be true in the short term, the changes the body makes to enhance oxygen carrying and delivery capacity to muscles due to the lower pressure at higher altitudes are lost within three to four weeks upon return to lower altitudes.

Heat. When exercising in an environment that is hotter than the body is accustomed to, blood vessels near the skin open to facilitate the transfer of body heat to the environment. This is so the body's internal temperature can be maintained. This causes a reduction in both venous return and stroke volume. At any given exercise pace, heart rate will be higher than usual as the cardiovascular system attempts to maintain cardiac output to meet oxygen needs in the muscles.

Because sweating is one of the most

effective means the body has of regulating internal temperature, exercising in hot, humid conditions is especially stressful to the unacclimated person. In order for sweat to dissipate heat, it must evaporate. When the humidity is high, sweat does not evaporate. So even though your client may be sweating profusely, there is a risk of severe heat problems. See Chapter 16 for a discussion of the signs and symptoms of heat-related problems.

The main concerns of exercising in the heat and humidity are replenishment of water and allowing the maximum amount of sweat to evaporate. To replenish water, drink at least 3 to 6 ounces every 10 to 15 minutes during exercise — the cooler the water the better, because cooler water empties more rapidly than warm water from the stomach into the intestines where it can be absorbed. Drink 8 ounces of water 20 to 30 minutes before exercise, and another 8 to 10 ounces of water in the 30 minutes following the exercise session. To allow evaporation of sweat, wear lightweight clothing. Light colors (white is best) reflect heat better than darker colors. Wear a light-colored hat to keep from absorbing heat through the top of the head. Never wear rubberized or waterproof garments that prevent the evaporation of sweat. Such a practice could lead to severe heat stress. Experts often recommend 100-percent cotton garments for exercising in the heat. In addition, there are now a number of specialized fabrics on the market that wick perspiration away from the body more effectively. Be sure to have your clients use sunscreen to reduce their risk of skin cancer.

Cold. It surprises some to learn that replenishment of body fluids is just as important when exercising in a cold environment as it is when exercising in the heat. Not only is water lost as vapor in exhaled air, but the kidneys increase urine production in the cold. Exercising in the cold generally produces enough body heat so that few problems occur during the exercise session. However, risks can become apparent when exercise is stopped, and the possibility of losing too much body heat increases.

The easiest way to be certain that the body doesn't overheat during exercise or lose too much heat during a rest period is to dress in layers. As the body temperature increases during high-intensity exercise, successive layers of clothing can be removed to allow the heat to dissipate. Layers can be replaced during rest or periods of low-intensity effort to help maintain body heat.

Be certain that the layers near the client's skin are made from fabrics that allow sweat to pass through, such as wool, polypropylene or any of the newer synthetic materials that wick moisture away from the skin. During a period of rest or low-intensity effort, a layer of wet clothing next to the skin will cause the body to lose heat. If the day is windy, the outer layer should provide wind protection to reduce chilling during a rest period. It is important to wear a hat when exercising in the cold, especially during periods of rest, since a significant amount of heat can be lost through the scalp.

BASIC SKELETAL MUSCLE ANATOMY AND PHYSIOLOGY

In addition to basic knowledge of function and training in the cardiopulmonary system, you must give similar attention to the skeletal muscle system. There are three primary types of muscle cells in the body:

1. Cardiac cells are muscle cells unique in structure and function and found only in the heart.

2. Smooth muscle cells are found in the walls of arteries, which allow for the blood shunt (the constriction and dilation in blood vessels) to redistribute blood flow, and in the walls of the intestines.

Basic Skeletal Muscle Anatomy and Physiology

3. Skeletal muscle cells are bound together to form the many skeletal muscles. Skeletal muscles attach to bones across one or more joints in the skeletal system. Coordinated contraction of the skeletal muscles causes movement at the joint(s), and, therefore, of the body.

Muscle Fiber Types

There are two primary types of skeletal muscle fibers (cells): **slow-twitch (Type I)** and **fast-twitch (Type II)** fibers. The determination of the different muscle fiber types is possible through a laboratory technique known as a muscle biopsy. In a muscle biopsy, a sample of muscle tissue is excised (taken out) using a needle that is inserted directly into the muscle. The section of tissue that is taken is mounted on a slide and stained for microscopic analysis. Based on the results of the biopsy technique, the slow- and fast-twitch types of muscle cells have been clearly identified.

Each type of fiber has several unique characteristics. The slow-twitch fiber contracts more slowly than the fast-twitch fiber. The slow-twitch has many mitochondria and a high aerobic capacity and, therefore, is fatigue-resistant. Slow-twitch fibers, also referred to as red fibers, are smaller in cross section than fast-twitch fibers. Fast-twitch fibers, also called white fibers, are divided into two major sub-groups — type IIa and type IIb. Type IIa fibers are called fast-twitch oxidative because they have more mitochondria than type IIb, which are referred to as fast-twitch glycolytic. However, type IIa fibers do not have the aerobic capability of slow-twitch fibers.

In terms of the distribution of fast- and slow-twitch fibers, there are two general considerations. First, in a given individual, the distribution of fast- and slow-twitch fibers is different in different muscles. For example, there is a different percentage of fast- and slow-twitch fibers in the biceps compared to the quadriceps, and in the deltoids compared to the triceps. Second, the percentage of fast- and slow-twitch fibers of a given muscle varies from person to person. For example, one person may have a high percentage of fast-twitch fibers in the quadriceps muscles, whereas another person will have a lower percentage.

As a general rule, those people who are world-class power athletes, such as power weight lifters, have a distribution of approximately 60 percent to 90 percent fast-twitch fibers in those muscles that are used in their activity. In comparison, world-class endurance athletes, such as long-distance runners and cross-country ski racers, would likely have 60 percent to 90 percent slow-twitch fibers in the muscles used in their events.

You need to understand that while endurance training does not change fast-twitch fibers (type II) to slow-twitch fibers (type I), research shows that it is possible to increase the aerobic capacity of the type II fast-twitch fibers, especially the type IIa. Furthermore, power training does not change slow-twitch fibers to fast-twitch fibers. Fiber type characteristics and responses to training are complex, involving more than is necessary for the purposes of this manual. As long as it is clear that a client's fiber type distribution is apparently genetically determined, and training will not change one fiber type to the other, you can design individual programs and understand the reasons why different clients respond differently to the same training program.

There are no differences between males and females with respect to fiber type distribution. In fact, there is no physiological difference between the muscle fibers in a male and a female; there is no such thing as a "male muscle cell" and a "female muscle cell." A muscle fiber is a muscle fiber, and fast- and slow-twitch fibers are found in both females and males, with the same distribution and fiber performance characteristics.

Basic Skeletal Muscle Anatomy and Physiology

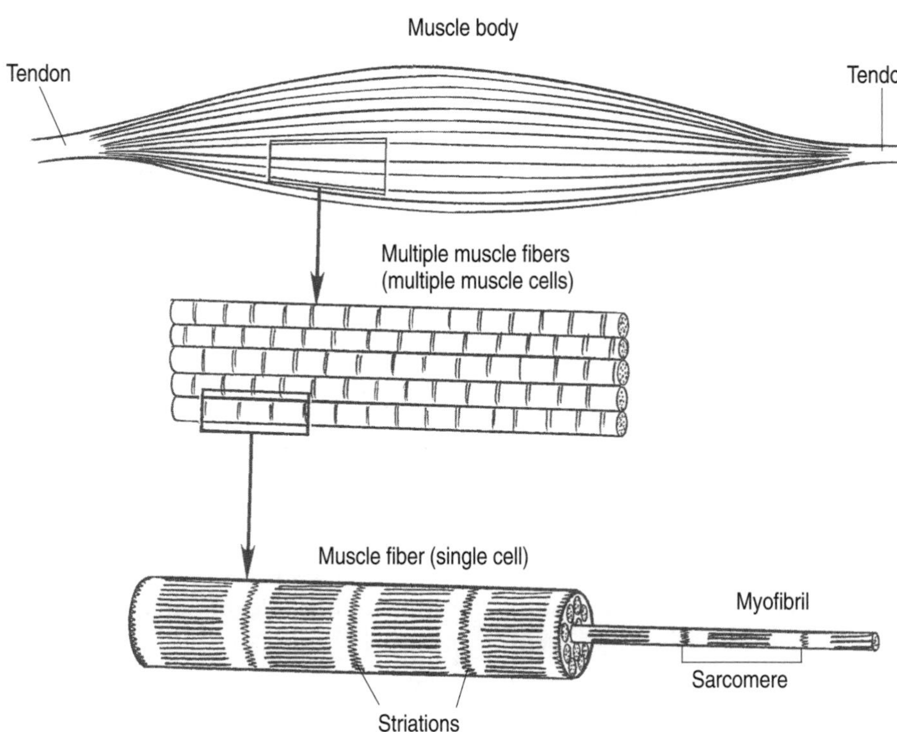

FIGURE 1.6
Anatomy of skeletal muscle: muscle, muscle fiber, myofibrils and sarcomere.

Skeletal Muscle Anatomy

Muscle cells, whether fast- or slow-twitch fibers, contract by the same basic mechanism. Functionally, the fast-twitch fibers simply contract to maximum force more rapidly than the slow-twitch fibers, but the process of contraction is the same. A fast-twitch fiber is a single muscle cell, as is a slow-twitch fiber. The contractile process and anatomy are the same for both. Refer to Figure 1.6 for an illustration of basic skeletal muscle anatomy.

Muscles are composed of many individual muscle fibers. Running the length of each muscle fiber are strands of protein known as **myofibrils**. There are several proteins in a myofibril. The proteins **actin** and **myosin**, also known as contractile proteins, are the two primary proteins related to the process of muscle contraction.

Looking at a muscle fiber under a microscope shows it is made of several repeating units called **sarcomeres** along the length of the muscle cell. Running through all the sarcomeres, from one end of the cell to the other, are the myofibrils (of which actin and myosin are a part). Within each sarcomere of the muscle cells, the proteins actin and myosin are located in different areas. The myosin protein is located in the middle of each sarcomere; each actin portion of the myofibril overlaps a portion of one end of the myosin, and extends through the sarcomere boundary into the adjacent sarcomere, where it overlaps one end of the myosin in that sarcomere.

Muscle Contraction

In order for muscle contraction to occur, there must be sufficient ATP near the actin and myosin proteins, and there must be a nervous impulse from the central nervous system. According to the **sliding filament theory** of muscle contraction, when these two factors are present, the tiny projections from the myosin (myosin heads) attach to the actin, forming an actinmyosin cross bridge. Figure 1.7 illustrates this process.

The energy from ATP causes the myosin heads on each end of the myosin to swivel toward the center of the sarcomere, pulling

Basic Skeletal Muscle Anatomy and Physiology

on the attached actin filament so that the actin slides inward toward the center of the sarcomere. This process causes each sarcomere along the entire length of the muscle fiber to shorten. Since all of the sarcomeres shorten at the same time, the overall length of the muscle fiber is decreased. When a multitude of fibers contract, the result is muscle contraction, which is really nothing more than the simultaneous shortening of many of the fibers in the whole muscle.

Even though individual fibers attempt to shorten when they contract, muscle contraction does not always involve a shortening in the length of the whole muscle. A **concentric (positive) contraction** shortens the muscle. However, an **eccentric (negative) contraction** lengthens the muscle. An eccentric contraction occurs when individual fibers contract, but the resistance is greater than the force generated, so the muscle actually lengthens. **Isometric contraction** describes a contraction of individual fibers, but no change in the length of the whole muscle.

To review, muscle contraction is an interaction between the actin and myosin proteins causing an attempted shortening of individual muscle fibers. If the force of contraction is greater than the external resistance, a concentric contraction occurs. If the external resistance is greater than the force of contraction, an eccentric contraction occurs. It is important to remember that sufficient ATP (energy) must be present, as well as a continued nervous impulse, in order to sustain this contraction process.

Force of Contraction (Strength). When a muscle fiber contracts, it exerts force. Skeletal muscle tissue functions according to an all-or-none principle. This means that when a single muscle fiber shortens, it generates its maximum force capability. A skeletal muscle fiber has no ability to grade its force of contraction (as cardiac muscle cells do); when it is stimulated to contract, it does so maximally. The amount of force that is generated during contraction in the whole muscle depends

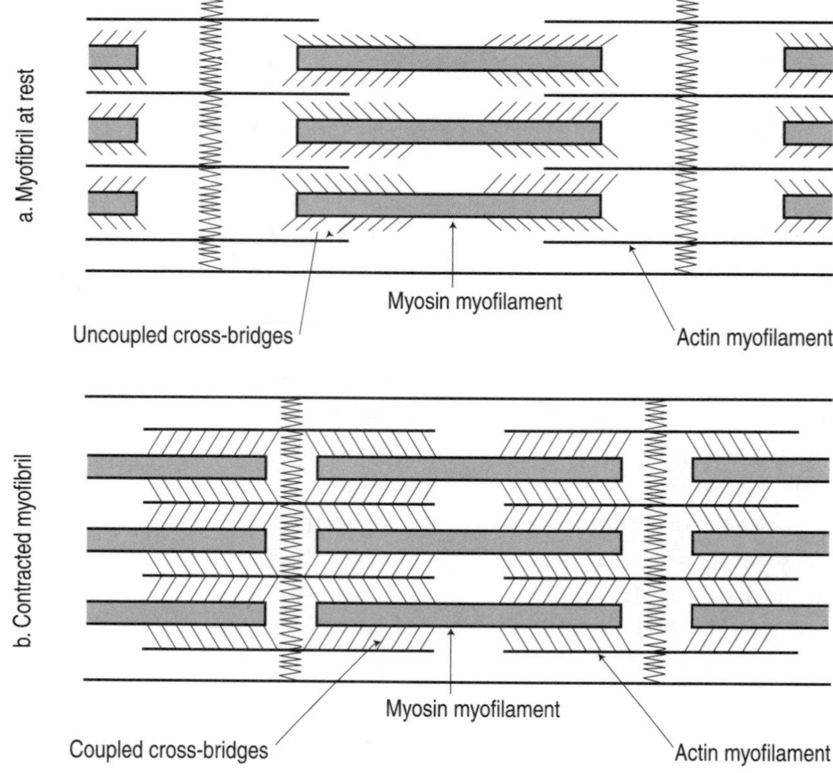

FIGURE 1.7
Anatomy of a muscle:
a. resting myofibril.
b. contracted myofibril.

on two factors: 1) the size of the individual fibers contracting (a larger fiber is a stronger fiber), and 2) the number of muscle fibers that contract simultaneously (to generate more force, more fibers are recruited).

The force generated by muscle contraction is related to the speed of movement at the associated joint, as well as the initial length of the muscle belly. The "force-velocity" relationship suggests that, in general, the faster the speed of movement, the lower the force generated by the contracting muscle. For example, the biceps muscle will generate more force during a maximal contraction when the elbow joint is flexing at 60 degrees of movement per second than when the elbow is flexing at 180 degrees of movement per second.

The "length-tension" relationship demonstrates that a muscle generates maximum force when it begins its contraction at 1.2 times its resting length. This relationship helps explain why athletes such as baseball batters and golfers slightly stretch the appropriate muscles before beginning the swinging movement.

Muscle Fiber Size. The force the fiber generates is related to its cross-sectional area. A larger fiber exerts more force than a smaller one. Note that the strength of a given cross-sectional area of muscle tissue from males and females is the same. Males are generally stronger because of a greater amount of muscle tissue. Women respond to a strength-training program in many of the same ways men do. Therefore, strength training is an important part of a physical fitness program for both genders.

Motor Units. In a given muscle, muscle fibers are stimulated in units or groups. A single motor nerve (from the spinal cord) and all the muscle fibers it stimulates is called a **motor unit.** Motor units come in different sizes. Those made up of a single nerve stimulating just five to 10 fibers are responsible for fine, delicate movements like moving the eye, blinking the eyelid and drawing intricate detail in a picture. On the other hand, motor units consisting of one motor nerve and 500 to 1,000 fibers are called on for forceful tasks like lifting, kicking or jumping. Regardless of the size, motor units are made of either all fast-twitch fibers or all slow-twitch fibers. When the fibers of a motor unit are called on to contract, all of the muscle fibers in the unit contract together, and they contract with maximum force (remember the all-or-none principle). So the amount of force generated at any one time depends on how many motor units are called on to contract simultaneously.

To exert minimal force — like picking up a pencil — only a few motor units in the forearm muscles are recruited. To pick up a dumbbell, many more motor units in these muscles would be stimulated to contract. To exert maximum muscle force, the nervous system will attempt to contract as many motor units in the muscle as possible. Since the number of motor units (fibers) and the size of the fibers in those contraction motor units determine how much force will be generated on contraction, you need to understand how muscle fibers respond to a strength-training program.

ADAPTATIONS TO STRENGTH TRAINING

Describing adaptations to strength training is not as straightforward as the discussion of adaptations to aerobic training. There are many variables that influence strength-training adaptations, including the relationship of resistance and repetitions in the lifting program, the distribution of fast- and slow-twitch fibers in the muscles being trained, and the level of the hormone testosterone. It is important to understand that individual differences in the above-mentioned variables can dramatically influence specific response in a given client.

The specific overload to cause strength gains is a progressive increase in the amount

Adaptations to Strength Training

of resistance (weights, elastic bands, water) used in the training program. To continue to increase strength, one must continue to increase overload. This section describes those changes that occur in the body as a result of strength training, that account for an increased ability to generate force.

Muscle Fiber Adaptation

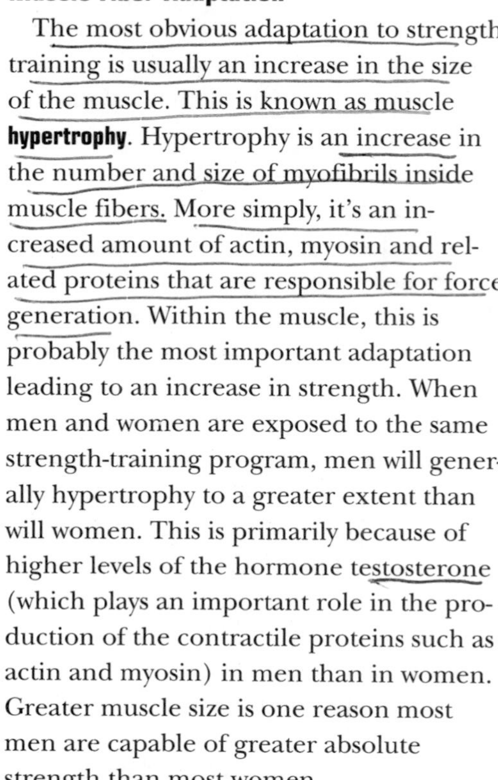

The most obvious adaptation to strength training is usually an increase in the size of the muscle. This is known as muscle **hypertrophy**. Hypertrophy is an increase in the number and size of myofibrils inside muscle fibers. More simply, it's an increased amount of actin, myosin and related proteins that are responsible for force generation. Within the muscle, this is probably the most important adaptation leading to an increase in strength. When men and women are exposed to the same strength-training program, men will generally hypertrophy to a greater extent than will women. This is primarily because of higher levels of the hormone testosterone (which plays an important role in the production of the contractile proteins such as actin and myosin) in men than in women. Greater muscle size is one reason most men are capable of greater absolute strength than most women.

While hypertrophy will generally result as an adaptation to strength training, the relationship of repetitions (rep) and resistance to hypertrophy is clear. A high-resistance (6 to 10 RM) program will usually lead to significant hypertrophy in most males. Most females, because of naturally low levels of testosterone, will not generate significant hypertrophy even with this type of program. Conversely, a low-resistance, high-rep program will generally lead to little hypertrophy even in males. Many women shy away from strength training because of a fear of the "body-builder" hypertrophy. You can allay their fears by using lower resistance (12 to 15 RM) programs.

Besides increasing fiber size, training also will increase the number of sarcomeres in trained fibers. The increase in size enhances the amount of contractile protein in the fibers as well, adding to the strength potential of the fiber. Further, some research with animals suggests that the use of extremely high resistance might possibly increase the number of muscle fibers (hyperplasia) in the muscle. Evidence for muscle fiber hyperplasia in humans has not been found. For now, the conclusion is that the change in the muscle is an increase in protein content, and often in diameter, of existing fibers, not an increase in the number of muscle fibers.

Connective Tissue Adaptation

In addition to changing muscle tissue itself, training also changes the **connective tissues** of the body. There are three basic types of connective tissue: **cartilage**, which serves as padding between the bones that meet at a joint in the skeleton; **ligaments**, which connect bones to bones at a joint; and **tendons**, which connect skeletal muscles to the bones, transmitting the force of muscle contraction to the bones. The tendons are an extension of tendinous connective tissue, which weaves a network of support around and between the muscle fibers of a muscle, giving strength and stability to the belly of the muscle by holding the fibers of the motor units together.

In response to strength training, the connective tissues associated with muscle become stronger by becoming thicker, and are thus able to withstand the increase in force of contraction generated by the strength-trained muscle. The increased strength of connective tissue is thought to play a highly significant role in the total strength gain which results from a regular resistance training program.

Increased Nervous System Activity

A third change in response to strength training is the stimulation of motor units that were previously inactive. Part of strength generation depends on the number of motor units contracting. When untrained, and not working against much resistance, some fibers (motor units) are never used. But the need to generate more force in a strength-training program stimulates activation of some inactive fibers (motor units).

When an untrained client begins a carefully designed strength program, gains in strength can often be noted in just a couple of weeks. Clearly, there will not be noticeable hypertrophy in such a short period. What accounts for the initial gains? Most likely, the recruitment of previously inactive motor units is responsible for much of the initial increase in strength. In addition, the brain increases its ability to coordinate the recruitment of individual motor units.

Decreased Nervous Inhibition

One of the most important adaptations to strength training is that we can overcome, or decrease, nervous inhibition to the muscles. Nervous inhibition is both psychological and physiological. In a psychological sense, confidence increases, allowing lifts never before thought possible. This is especially true in non-athletes who think themselves weaker than they actually are.

Physiological (functional) adaptation also is important. In the tendons, which connect the muscle to the bones, there is a sensor called a muscle tendon organ, or a **Golgi tendon organ**. This tendon organ is a part of the nervous system, a protection against generating too much contractile force. When the muscle tendon organ is stimulated by too much contractile force, its associated muscle will relax to prevent injury to the muscle itself or to its associated connective tissues. Under normal circumstances, maximal contraction is prevented; that is, all of the motor units in a muscle will not contract simultaneously because of the inhibitory protection of the muscle tendon organ.

It is possible, however, to override the physiological Golgi protective inhibition. Two examples can illustrate the consequences of overriding the Golgi inhibition. The first is that of a woman who finds that the jack has slipped while her husband was working under the car and the car has fallen on him. She reaches under the bumper of the car, generates a maximum muscular contraction in several muscle groups, and miraculously lifts the car off her husband's body. In so doing, however, she undoubtedly has suffered injury to some of her connective tissues because she overrode the threshold protection of the Golgi tendon organs.

A second example is the weight lifter who attempts to lift more weight than he has trained himself to lift, and physiologically (or pharmacologically) pumps himself up to the point where he is able to overcome the threshold protection of the tendon organ. In attempting the lift, the weight lifter can actually tear the tendon, causing severe injury. The biceps tendon and the quadriceps tendon are two connective tissue structures often injured by overriding their associated tendon organ protection.

Strength training raises the threshold of force generation at which the Golgi tendon organ is stimulated, probably because the overload of training causes more connective tissue protein to be added to the tendon. The associated muscle can then generate greater contractile force before the tendon organ is stimulated.

In summary, the ability to exert more force after strength training is not solely owing to muscle fiber adaptations, but involves extremely important adaptations in connective tissue and the nervous system as well. Many scientists argue that the connective tissue and nervous system adaptations are probably more important to overall strength gains than the changes in the muscle fibers. Clearly, many successful strength athletes follow significantly different training protocols. Without a doubt, it will take continued research in the area of strength adaptations to elucidate the specific details of the current theories.

GUIDELINES FOR STRENGTH TRAINING

With an idea about how the body adapts to the progressive overload of a strength-training program, you need an understanding of general concepts in order to develop a strength-training program. (Please refer to Chapter 8 for a detailed discussion of the variables to be considered when developing and supervising such programs.) Strength training is a highly individualized procedure. Well-trained and highly successful power and endurance athletes have all established their own most effective training regimens. And frequently, two equally successful strength athletes will have very different training routines. However, as with any aspect of fitness development, you must assist your clients in challenging the factors responsible for strength with an appropriate and specific overload.

Types of Strength Overloads

For many years, strength-training programs have been described as being isometric, isotonic or isokinetic, based on the type of muscle contraction involved during the exercise. (The prefix "iso" means "same.")

Isometric (same length) refers to exercises that develop high-intensity contractions in the muscle with no change in muscle length. Generally, isometric exercises call for a maximal effort against an immovable object, like a wall or desk. Isometric training clearly increases muscle strength, but only at the joint angle where the contraction occurs.

Isotonic (same tone or tension) refers to exercises that use a given amount of external resistance which is challenged through the entire range of motion. The tension in the muscle is not constant throughout the range of motion. The actual amount of force generated by a muscle will change throughout the movement because of the biomechanics at the joint or joints involved. For example, even though a 10-pound dumbbell is obviously a constant weight throughout a biceps curl, the biceps does not generate a constant 10 pounds of force throughout its entire contraction. (The biomechanics of this concept are presented in Chapter 3.)

Several exercise physiologists now suggest that strength exercises using a fixed amount of external resistance be referred to as "**dynamic constant** external **resistance**" training, not isotonic training. Exercises that use machines with a shaped cam can be called "**dynamic variable** external **resistance**." These descriptions accurately suggest that even though the weight is constant throughout the movement, the amount of force generated by the overloaded muscles changes throughout the movement.

Isokinetic (same speed) refers to a type of resistance exercise that causes the exercising muscles to generate a maximum amount of force throughout the entire range of movement, while keeping the speed of movement constant. Isokinetic and dynamic resistance exercises are performed with either concentric or eccentric muscle contractions, or both. Concentric (shortening) movements are often referred to as the positive phase of a lift. Eccentric (lengthening) movements, on the other hand, are referred to as the negative phase. The type of contractions involved during strength training appears to have an impact on the degree of muscle soreness which occurs one to three days after training.

Muscle Soreness and Fatigue

Muscle Soreness. There are two general

types of exercise-related muscle soreness. One is the immediate soreness felt while, or immediately after, exercising. The other type of soreness is that which persists for one to three days following a session.

Immediate soreness appears to be most directly related to the build-up of lactic acid (and other byproducts) in the muscle that have leaked out of the muscle cells and stimulated sensitive nerve endings near them. This excess lactic acid is removed quite rapidly when the exercise session is completed, generally within 30 to 60 minutes. Much of the excess lactic acid is metabolized in the muscle cell in which it was produced during exercise. The lactic acid not used is carried to the liver as lactate where it is metabolized. Immediate soreness may involve minor muscle or connective tissue tears, so don't ignore it. Refer to Chapter 15 for a discussion of a wide range of exercise-related injuries and sources of soreness during exercise.

The explanation of latent soreness, the soreness unnoticed during exercise, but present from one to three days following exercise, is the subject of much research and some controversy. The most current research indicates that delayed soreness (delayed onset muscle soreness, DOMS) is most likely the result of very small tears in the connective tissues that hold individual muscle fibers together within the belly of the muscle, as well as some tearing of the membrane of the muscle cells.

Furthermore, research suggests that this latent soreness is closely associated with the eccentric, or negative, phase of muscular effort. During negative work, the muscle fibers are contracting and attempting to cause a shortening of the muscle. But the resistance is greater than the force developed, so the muscle and associated connective tissue is actually lengthening. This lends credibility to theories that implicate microscopic tears within the muscle cell membrane and/or connective tissues during aggressive negative effort. Studies investigating concentric overloads report little or no delayed soreness, compared with the significant soreness usually reported with heavy eccentric work.

Muscle Fatigue. The reasons for fatigue also are varied, but they relate primarily to the intensity and duration of the exercise bout. For instance, the fatigue felt when performing a power event or other maximum effort that lasts from 0 to 30 seconds to exhaustion occurs because the active muscle cells run out of ATP at the site of the actin-myosin crossbridge, which is part of the mechanism of muscle fiber contraction. Without ATP present, the fibers can no longer contract.

Muscle fatigue that results during heavy exercise, lasting anywhere from about 30 seconds up to about 40 to 60 minutes to exhaustion, is generally thought to be related to lactic acid accumulation. Clearly this is a broad range, and several other factors may be involved in varying degrees, but lactic acid accumulating from intense effort ultimately inhibits the ability of the muscle cell to contract.

Finally, the fatigue felt in prolonged endurance activities lasting 60 to 180 minutes or longer occurs primarily because **glycogen** — the storage form of glucose — becomes depleted in the exercising muscles. Without a source of glucose, muscle cells cannot contract even with an adequate supply of oxygen and fat. In other words, when glycogen is depleted (a marathoner calls this "hitting the wall"), the muscles being used are unable to maintain the required intensity. Other factors also implicated in fatigue during prolonged activities include **dehydration**, increased body temperature, by-products other than lactic acid, and boredom with the activity.

FLEXIBILITY TRAINING

Flexibility is defined as the range of motion about a joint. Therefore, flexibility training is designed to increase the range of motion in a specific area, such as the low back, the hamstrings or the shoulder girdle. Flexibility is primarily limited by four factors: 1) the elastic limits of the ligaments and tendons crossing the joint, 2) the **elasticity** of the muscle tissue itself, 3) the bone and joint structure and 4) the skin.

Many types of exercises can increase flexibility. As every system must be overloaded to generate specific gains, so must the connective and skeletal muscle be overloaded to generate increased flexibility. It appears that one of the safest overloads for flexibility training is a slow, sustained stretch. Bobbing and bouncing activities are not generally recommended. They can lead to injury in the muscle fibers and connective tissues, since there is an increased likelihood of the connective tissues being overstretched.

Only general guidelines for stretching are presented here. A detailed discussion of specific guidelines for increasing flexibility is presented in Chapter 10. Slowly stretch to the point where tension (tightness) is felt in the muscles being stretched. Do not stretch to the point of pain. Hold the stretch for about 10 seconds, being sure not to hold your breath. Some research suggests that four sets of 10- to 15-second stretches can lead to significant improvements in flexibility.

Just as the Golgi tendon organ serves as a protection against generating too much contractile force, fibers in the muscle tissue protect against too much stretch. These fibers are called **muscle spindles**. In **ballistic** (rapid, bouncing) stretching, the muscle spindle is likely stimulated, causing the muscle to contract as a protection against the excessive stretch. On the next rapid bob or bounce, when we stretch against a contracted muscle, there is a high risk of tearing in the muscle or connective tissues. Slow, sustained stretching that does not cause pain apparently does not stimulate the muscle spindles as quickly.

SUMMARY

This chapter gives you a basic introduction to the principles of exercise physiology. First, you must develop a sound understanding of the relationships between exercise intensity and energy production in exercising muscles. Then you can apply the principles of specificity and overload to design the most appropriate program for any client.

The amount of information on exercise physiology is growing at a rapid pace. This chapter is, by necessity, geared to present the basics of many areas of the science of exercise. All fitness professionals must recognize the responsibility of becoming students of the literature in this field to keep abreast of the constant flow of information.

REFERENCE

Bergstrom, J., Harris, R.C., Hultman, E. & Nordensjo, L.O. (1971). Energy-rich phosphagens in dynamic and static work. In B. Pernow & B. Saltin (Eds.) *Muscle Metabolism During Exercise* (p. 341). New York: Plenum Press.

SUGGESTED READING

Alter, M.J. (1988). *The Science of Stretching.* Champaign: Human Kinetics.

Katch. F.L. & McArdle, W.D. (1988). *Nutrition, Weight Control and Exercise* (3rd ed.) Philadelphia: Lea & Febiger.

McArdle, W.D., Katch, F.I. & Katch, V.L. (1991). *Exercise Physiology: Energy, Nutrition and Human Performance.* (3rd ed.) Philadelphia: Lea & Febiger.

Sharkey, B. J. (1990). *Physiology of Fitness.* (3rd ed.) Champaign: Human Kinetics.

Costill, D.L. & Wilmore, J.H. (1994). *Physiology of Sport & Exercise.* Champaign: Human Kinetics.

CHAPTER 2

Human Anatomy

2

IN THIS CHAPTER:

Rod A. Harter, Ph.D., ATC/R, is an associate professor and program director of athletic training education in the department of exercise and sport science at Oregon State University in Corvallis. He specializes in sports medicine and biomechanics. Dr. Harter is a fellow of the American College of Sports Medicine and serves on the editorial boards of the Journal of Athletic Training *and the* Journal of Sport Rehabilitation.

Rod A. Harter

Anatomy is a broad science concerned with the study of the structure of the body and the relationships of the body parts to one another. A fundamental understanding of human anatomy is essential for you to be able to meet your responsibilities as a personal trainer and identify appropriate activities and exercises to help clients achieve their personal fitness goals. This chapter provides a brief description of the functional anatomy of five major systems operating within the human body: the cardiovascular system, the respiratory system, the nervous system, the skeletal system and the muscular system.

Anatomical Terminology

ANATOMICAL TERMINOLOGY

When studying anatomy for the first time, you may encounter descriptive terms that are unfamiliar. Use of the correct anatomical terms for position, location and direction is essential when describing a particular movement, exercise or activity to a client or fitness professional.

Most anatomical terms have their roots in the Latin and Greek languages and are usually quite descriptive. For example, many muscle names tell of the muscle's location, shape or action. To illustrate, let's use the **posterior** tibialis muscle. For our purposes, posterior means "toward the rear." The rest of "tibialis" refers to the tibia, the larger of the two bones that connect the knee to the ankle. In this case, by knowing the meanings of the root words, you can understand both the anatomical term and the location of the muscle — the posterior tibialis muscle is found on the back of the tibia. Other important terms that describe anatomical positions are defined in Table 2.1. To help you avoid having to refer continually to a medical dictionary to define the terms used throughout this chapter, a summary of commonly used anatomical and medical terms is presented in Table 2.2. A representation of anatomical position is given in Figure 2.1, along with the anatomical planes of motion.

There are five major human body systems pertinent to physical activity: the cardiovascular system, the respiratory system, the nervous system, the skeletal system and the muscular system.

Table 2.1
Anatomical, Directional and Regional Terms

Term	Definition
Anterior (ventral)	Toward the front
Posterior (dorsal)	Toward the back
Superior	Toward the head
Inferior	Away from the head
Medial	Toward the midline of the body
Lateral	Away from the midline of the body
Proximal	Toward the attached end of the limb, origin of the structure, or midline of the body
Distal	Away from the attached end of the limb, origin of the structure, or midline of the body
Superficial	External; located close to or on the body surface
Deep	Internal; located further beneath the body surface than the superficial structures
Cervical	Regional term referring to the neck
Thoracic	Regional term referring to the portion of body between the neck and the abdomen; also known as the chest (thorax)
Lumbar	Regional term referring to the portion of the back between the abdomen and the pelvis
Plantar	The sole or bottom of the foot
Dorsal	The top surface of the foot and hands
Palmar	The anterior or ventral surface of the hands
Sagittal Plane	A longitudinal (imaginary) line that divides the body or any of its parts into right and left sections
Frontal Plane	A longitudinal (imaginary) section that divides the body into anterior and posterior parts; lies at a right angle to the sagittal plane
Transverse Plane	Also known as the horizontal plane; an imaginary line that divides the body or any of its parts into superior and inferior sections

CARDIOVASCULAR SYSTEM

Oxygen is required for energy production and, thus, sustains cellular activity (cellular metabolism) in the human body. A by-product of this activity is carbon dioxide. Since high levels of carbon dioxide in the cells produce

Anatomical Terminology

Table 2.2
Common Anatomical (Medical) Terminology

Root	Meaning	Term	Definition
arthro	joint	arthritis	inflammation in a joint
bi	two	biceps	two-headed muscle
brachium	arm	brachialis	muscle of the arm
cardio	heart	cardiology	the study of the heart
cephalo	head	cephalic	pertaining to the head
chrondro	cartilage	chondro-ectomy	excision of a cartilage
costo	rib	costo-chondral	pertaining to a rib and its cartilage
dermo	skin	dermatitis	inflammation of the skin
hemo, hemat	blood	hemorrhage	internal or external bleeding
ilio	ilium	ilium	the wide, upper part of the pelvic bone
myo	muscle	myocitis	inflammation of a muscle
os, osteo	bone	osteomalacia	softening of the bone
pulmo	lung	pulmonary artery	vessel that brings blood to the lungs
thoraco	chest	thorax	chest
tri	three	triceps brachii	three-headed muscle on arm

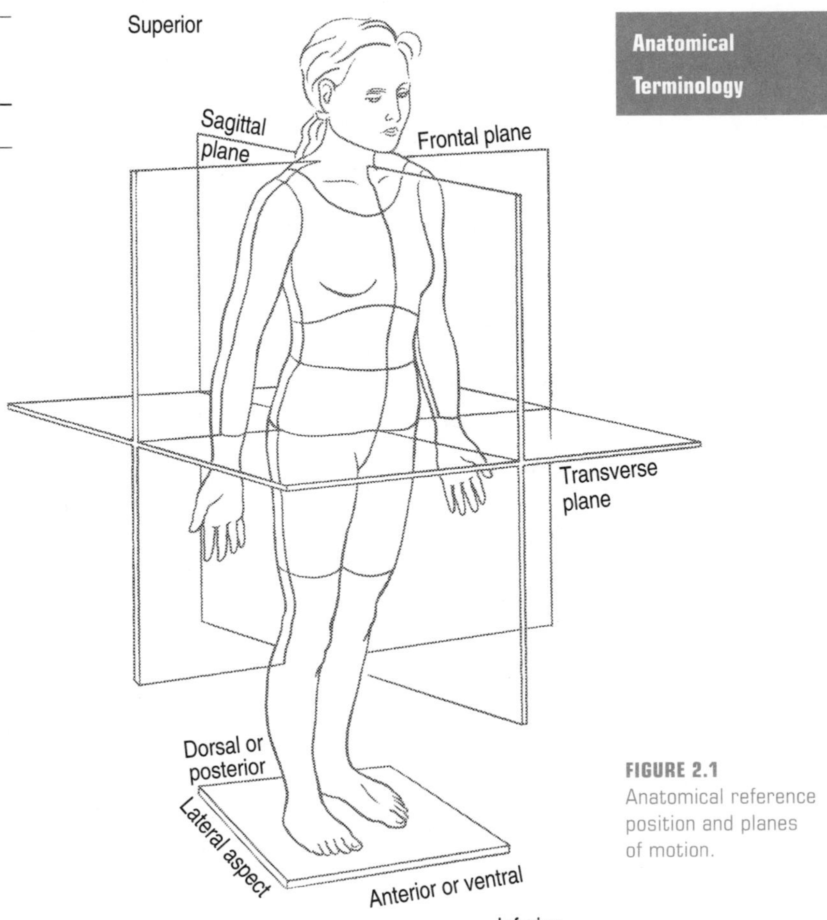

FIGURE 2.1
Anatomical reference position and planes of motion.

acidic conditions that are poisonous to cells, excess carbon dioxide must be eliminated rapidly. The cardiovascular and respiratory systems are primarily responsible for this function. The cardiovascular system is comprised of blood, the blood vessels and the heart. The cardiovascular system distributes oxygen and nutrients to the cells, carries carbon dioxide and metabolic wastes from the cells, protects against disease, helps regulate body temperature and prevents serious blood loss after injury through the formation of clots.

Blood is the only fluid tissue in the body and is composed of two parts: formed elements, which include different types of living blood cells (white blood cells, red blood cells, platelets) and plasma, the nonliving liquid portion of blood. Plasma is about 92 percent water and 8 percent dissolved solutes. There are more than 100 different types of dissolved solutes in plasma; the most abundant of these are plasma proteins. In adults, blood accounts for about 8 percent of body weight; an average-sized healthy woman has about 4 to 5 liters, while an average-sized healthy man

Anatomical Terminology

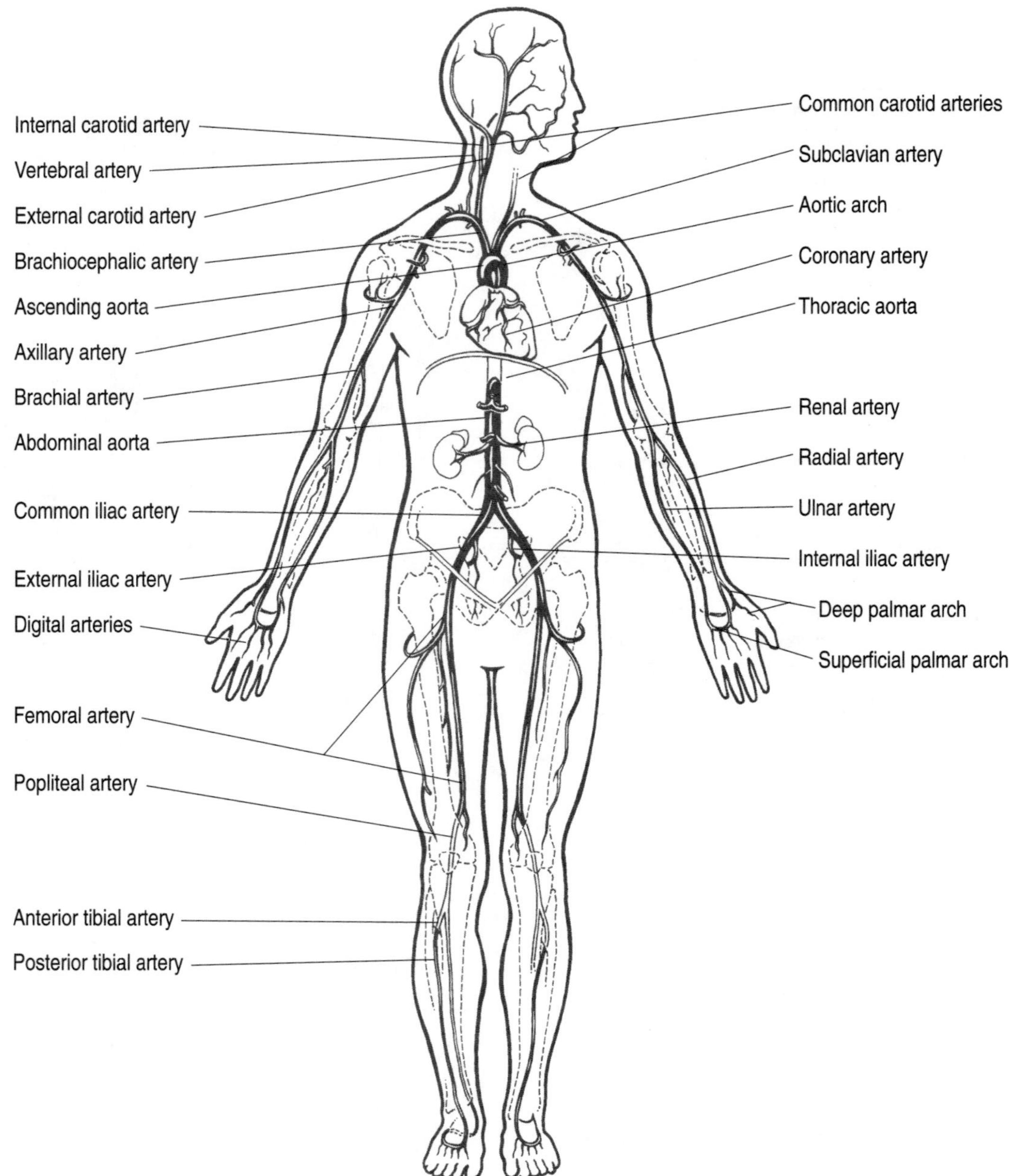

FIGURE 2.2
a. Major arteries of the body (anterior view).

has about 5 to 6 liters of blood.

There are two types of blood vessels: **arteries**, which carry blood away from the heart; and **veins**, which transport blood toward the heart. Arteries are stronger and thicker than veins, and their muscular walls help propel blood (Figure 2.2a). Unlike arteries, veins contain valves to prevent the blood from flowing backward. The largest arteries are those nearest the heart; as blood flows further away from the heart, the arteries branch into smaller vessels called **arterioles** that deliver the blood to the even smaller **capillaries**. These are microscopic blood vessels that branch to form an extensive network throughout the distal tissues. It is in the capillary beds that the critical exchange of nutrients and metabolic waste products takes place. Depleted of its oxygen and nutrients on the way from the heart to the periphery, capillary blood now begins the journey back

Anatomical Terminology

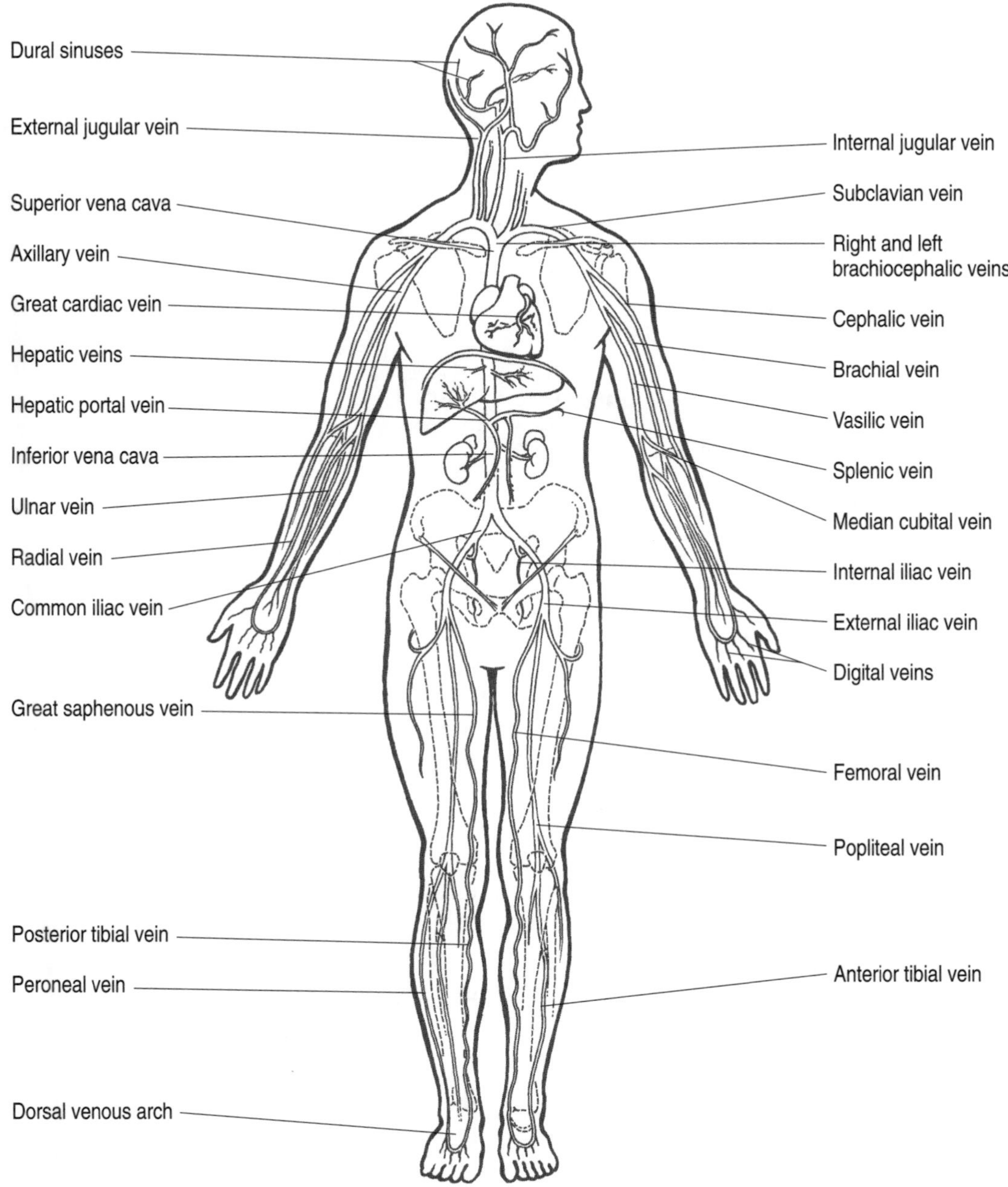

FIGURE 2.2 continued
b. Major veins of the body (anterior view).

to the heart via small vessels called **venules**. The venules are a continuation of the capillaries, and join together to form veins. As the blood is transported back to the heart, the veins become larger, carrying a greater volume of blood (Figure 2.2b).

The human heart, a hollow, muscular organ that pumps blood throughout the blood vessels, is at the center of the cardiovascular system. In the adult, the heart is about the same size as a closed fist, and lies to the left of center, behind the sternum and between the lungs. The heart itself is divided into four chambers that receive circulating blood. The two upper chambers are called the right **atrium** and left atrium; the two lower chambers of the heart are known as the right and left **ventricles** (Figure 2.3).

The heart is a series of four separate pumps: the two primer pumps, the atria, and the two power pumps, the ventricles.

Respiratory System

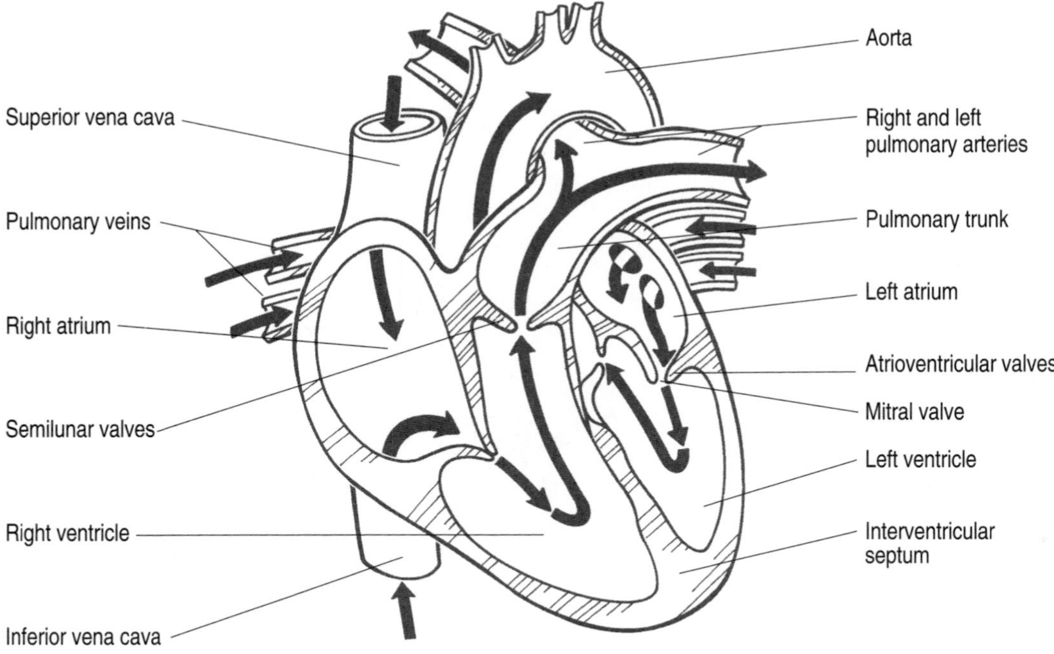

FIGURE 2.3
Structure of the heart and flow of blood within it.

Knowledge of the sequence of blood flow through the heart is fundamental to understanding the cardiovascular system. The right atrium receives blood from all parts of the body, except the lungs. The superior vena cava, a large vein that drains blood from body parts above or superior to the heart (head, neck, arms), and the inferior vena cava, which brings blood from the parts of the body below or inferior to the heart (legs, abdominal region), transport blood to the right atrium. During contraction of the heart, blood accumulates in the right atrium. When the heart relaxes, blood from the right atrium flows into the right ventricle, which during contraction pumps it into the pulmonary trunk. The pulmonary trunk then divides into right and left pulmonary arteries, which transport blood to the lungs, where carbon dioxide is released and oxygen is acquired. This newly oxygenated blood returns to the heart via four pulmonary veins that empty into the left atrium. The blood then passes into the left ventricle, which during contraction pumps the blood into the ascending aorta. From this point the blood is distributed to all body parts (except the lungs) by several large arteries.

RESPIRATORY SYSTEM

The respiratory system supplies oxygen, eliminates carbon dioxide, and helps regulate the acid-base balance (pH) of the body. The respiratory system is comprised of the lungs and a series of passageways leading to and from them (mouth, throat, trachea, bronchi). Respiration is the overall exchange of gases (oxygen, carbon dioxide, nitrogen) between the atmosphere, the blood and the cells. There are three general phases of respiration: external, internal and cellular. External respiration is the exchange of oxygen and carbon dioxide between the atmosphere and the blood within the large capillaries in the lungs. Internal respiration involves the exchange of those gases between the blood and the cells of the body. Cellular respiration involves the utilization of oxygen and the production of carbon dioxide by the metabolic activity within cells. When the body is at rest, air

Respiratory System

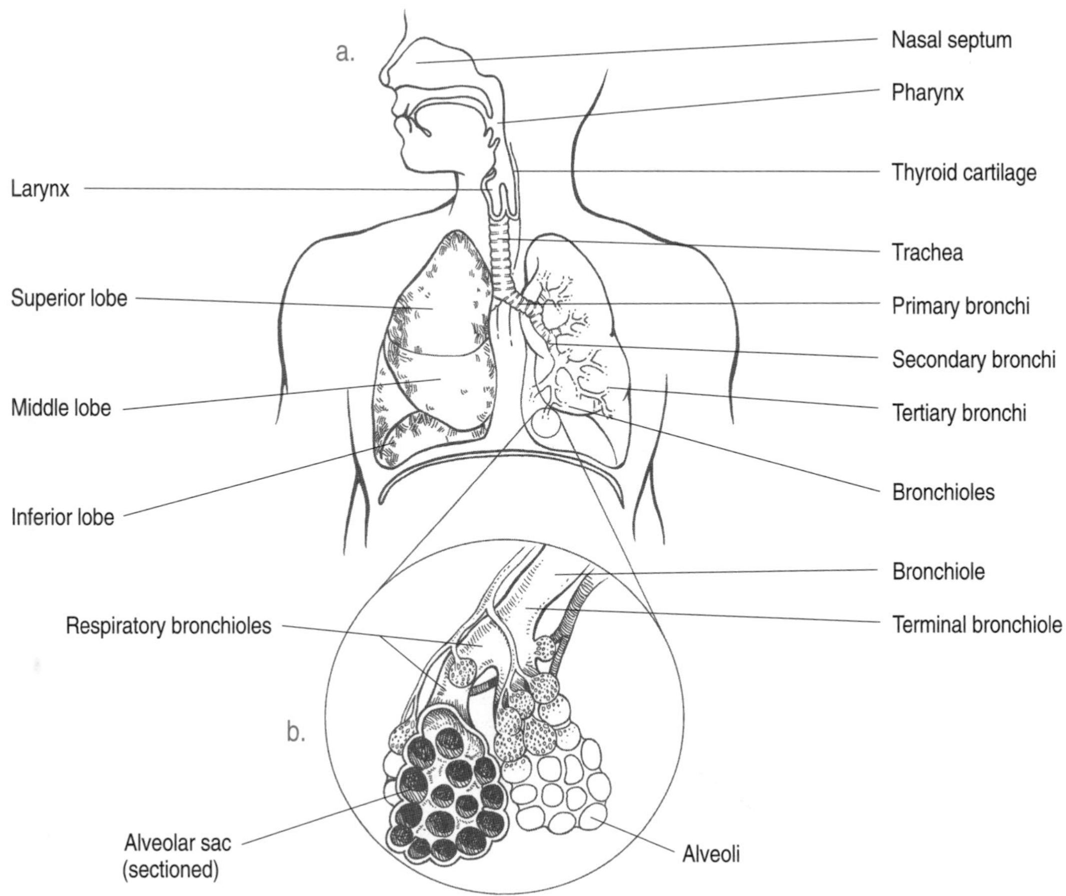

FIGURE 2.4
a. Upper and lower respiratory pathways.

b. Enlargement of transition from terminal bronchiole into alveoli.

enters the respiratory system via the nostrils of the nose, and is warmed as it passes through a series of nasal cavities lined by the mucous membrane. This membrane is covered with cilia (small hairs) that filter out small particles (Figure 2.4). From the nasal cavity, inspired air next enters the pharynx (throat), which lies just posterior to the nasal and oral (mouth) cavities. The pharynx serves as a passageway for air and food, and also provides a resonating chamber for speech sounds. During vigorous physical activity, mouth breathing tends to predominate, and air taken in via the mouth is not filtered to the same extent as air taken in through the nostrils.

The larynx (the organ of voice) is the enlarged upper (proximal) end of the trachea (windpipe). The larynx conducts air to and from the lungs via the pharynx. An easy landmark for locating the larynx is the thyroid cartilage, or Adam's apple. The trachea is a tubular airway approximately 12 centimeters long (about 4.5 inches) kept open by a series of C-shaped cartilages that function in a manner similar to the wire rings in the hose of a vacuum cleaner. The trachea extends from the larynx to approximately the level of the fifth thoracic vertebra, where it divides into the right and left primary bronchi. After the trachea divides into the right and left primary bronchi, each primary bronchus then enters a lung and divides into smaller secondary bronchi, one for each lobe of the lung (five in total). The secondary bronchi branch into many tertiary bronchi, and these branch several times further, eventually forming tiny terminal **bronchioles**. The terminal bronchioles have microscopic branches called respiratory bronchioles that, in turn,

Nervous System

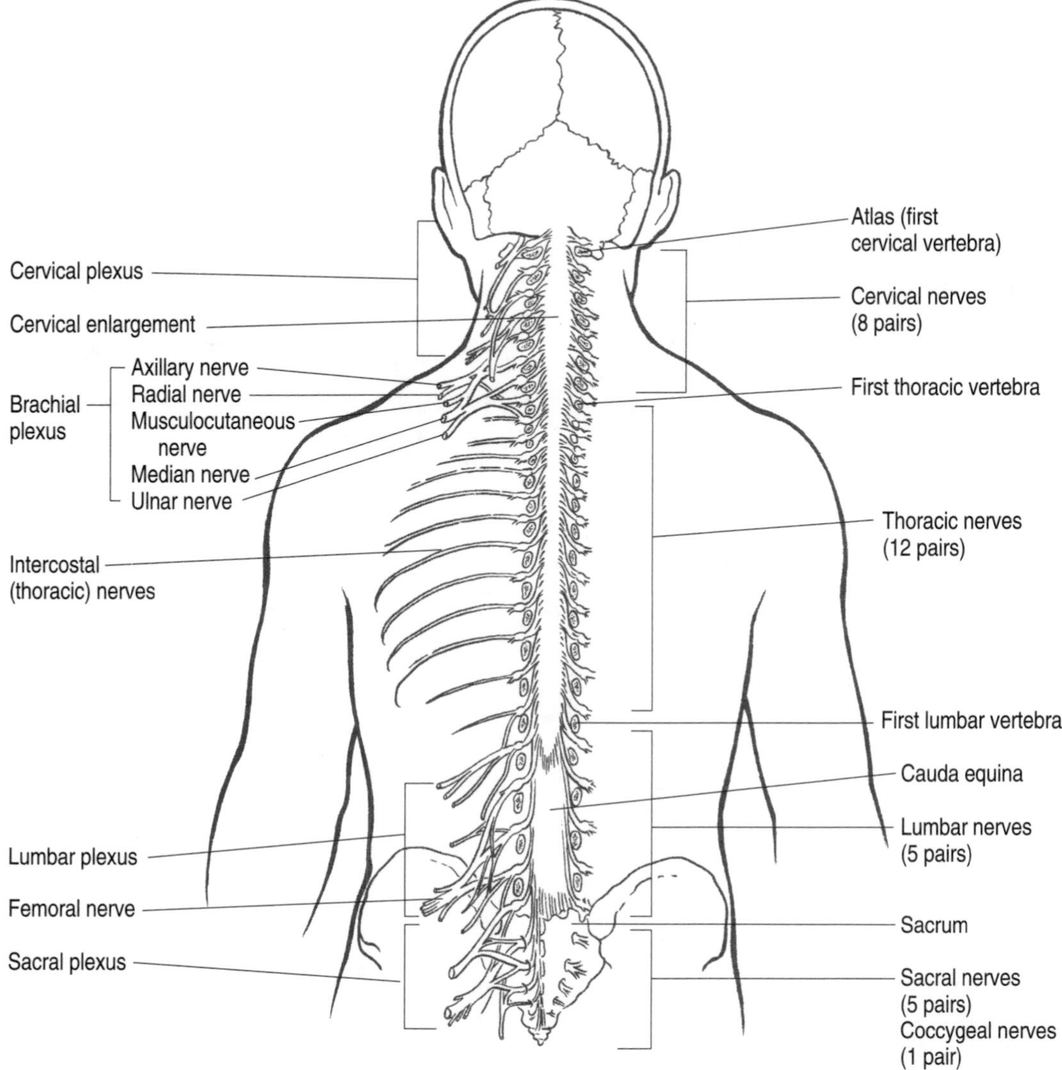

FIGURE 2.5
Spinal cord and spinal nerves (posterior view).

subdivide into several alveolar ducts (plural = alveoli). The actual exchange of respiratory gases, such as oxygen and carbon dioxide, between the lungs and the blood occurs at this anatomic level. The lungs contain an estimated 300 million alveoli that provide an extremely large surface area (approximately 70 square meters or 230 square feet) for the exchange of gases. The continuous branching of the trachea resembles a tree trunk and its branches and is commonly referred to as the bronchial tree.

The final components of the respiratory system are the lungs — paired, cone-shaped organs lying in the thoracic cavity. The right lung has three lobes; the left lung has only two. The diaphragm, the muscle that forms the floor of the thoracic cavity, contracts during inspiration and relaxes to allow expiration. The lungs are separated by a space known as the mediastinum which contains, most notably, the heart, the esophagus (the tube that connects the throat with the stomach) and a portion of the trachea.

NERVOUS SYSTEM

The nervous system is the body's control center and network for internal communication. As a personal trainer, you must understand the nervous system's role in stimulating

Nervous System

and controlling movement. A skeletal muscle cannot contract until it is stimulated by a nerve impulse. Without central control, coordinated human movements are impossible.

The nervous system is divided into two parts according to location: the central nervous system and the peripheral nervous system. The central nervous system (CNS), comprised of the brain and the spinal cord, is completely enclosed within bony structures. The brain is protected by the skull, while the spinal cord is protected by the vertebral canal of the spinal column. The CNS is the control center of the nervous system, since it receives and integrates information from the peripheral nervous system, and formulates appropriate responses to the information. The peripheral nervous system is made up of nerves that connect the outlying parts of the body (the extremities) and their receptors within the CNS. The peripheral nervous system includes: 12 pairs of cranial nerves, two of which arise from the brain, while the remaining 10 pairs originate in the brain stem; and 31 pairs of spinal nerves that arise from the spinal cord. The spinal nerves include eight cervical pairs, 12 thoracic pairs, five lumbar pairs, five sacral pairs and one coccygeal pair (Figure 2.5). These nerves are named and numbered according to region and the vertebral level at which they emerge from the spinal cord. For example, the first lumbar nerve (written L1) exits the spinal cord at the level of the first lumbar vertebra.

The anterior branches of the second through 12th thoracic spinal nerves (written T2 through T12) innervate muscles and other structures, such as the internal organs, individually. In all other cases, the anterior branches of the spinal nerves join with adjacent nerves to form a plexus, or a network of nerve branches. There are four main plexuses in the human body: the cervical plexus (spinal nerves C1 through C4) whose nerves supply the head, neck, upper chest and shoulders; the brachial plexus (spinal nerves C5 through T1) supplying from the shoulder down to the fingers of the hand; the lumbar plexus (spinal nerves L1 through L4) innervating the abdomen, groin, genitalia and antero-lateral aspect of the thigh; and the sacral plexus (spinal nerves L4 through S4), which supplies the large muscles of the posterior thigh and the entire lower leg, ankle and foot. Table 2.3 provides a summary of the primary spinal nerve roots that supply the major muscles innervated by

Table 2.3
Selected Spinal Nerve Roots and Major Muscles Innervated

Nerve Root	Muscles Innervated
C5	Biceps brachii, deltoid, supraspinatus, infraspinatus
C6	Brachioradialis, supinator, extensor carpi radialis longus and brevis, extensor carpi ulnaris
C7	Triceps brachii, flexor carpi radialis, flexor carpi ulnaris
C8	Extensor pollicis longus and brevis, adductor pollicis longus
T1	Intrinsic muscles of the hand (lumbricals, interossei)
L2	Psoas major and minor, adductor magnus, adductor longus, adductor brevis
L3	Rectus femoris, vastus lateralis, vastus medialis, vastus intermedius, psoas major and minor
L4	Tibialis anterior, tibialis posterior
L5	Extensor hallucis longus, extensor digitorum longus, peroneus longus and brevis, gluteus maximus, gluteus medius
S1	Gastrocnemius, soleus, biceps femoris, semitendinosus, semimembranosus, gluteus maximus
S2	Gluteus maximus, flexor hallucis longus, flexor digitorum longus
S4	Bladder, rectum

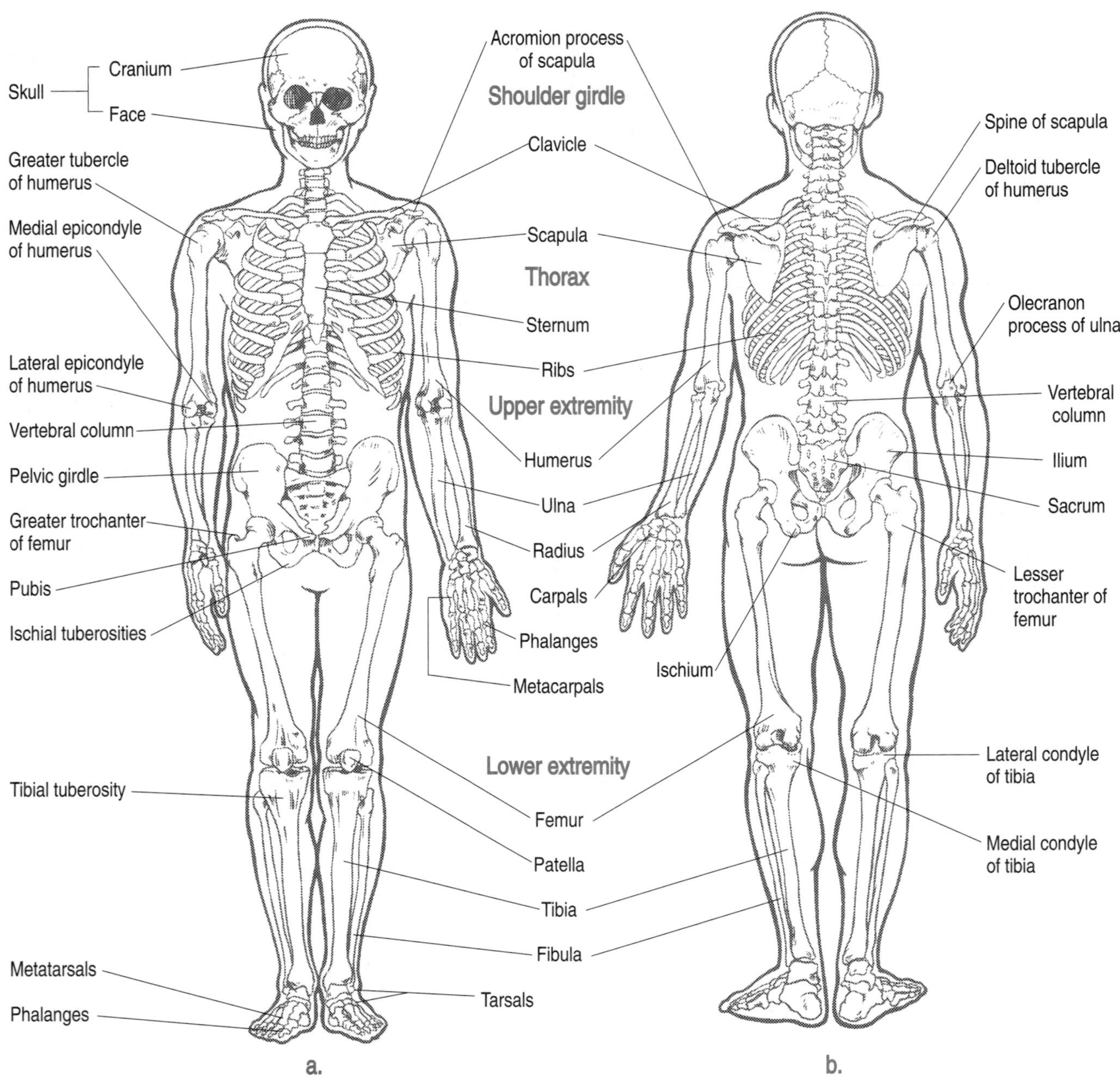

FIGURE 2.6
Skeletal system.
a. anterior view.

b. posterior view.

each of these plexuses.

The nerve cells that comprise the nervous system carry messages called nerve impulses that originate in either the central nervous system (brain or spinal cord) or in specialized nerve cells called receptors. Receptors are located throughout the body. Different types of receptors are sensitive to pain, temperature, pressure and changes in body position. Sensory nerve cells carry the impulses from the peripheral receptors to the spinal cord and brain. Motor nerve cells carry impulses away from the CNS to respond to the perceived changes in the body's internal or external environment.

An example of how this system works is the withdrawal reflex. If the hand encounters a very hot stimulus, such as an open flame, receptors in the skin of the hand send impulses to the spinal cord that communicate extreme heat and pain. In a matter of milliseconds, the appropriate muscles are activated to withdraw the hand from the fire. Similarly, when performing a complex physical activity, such as an inclined bench press, the central and peripheral nervous systems work in unison to initiate, guide and monitor all aspects of the specific activity. In this example, the nerve receptors in the periphery, located in the arm and shoulder region, provide continuous information (feedback) to the CNS regarding the amount of resistance encountered, limb position, pressure sensed on the palms of the hands and so on. This communication between the central and peripheral nervous systems utilizing the motor and sensory nerves is essential for us to learn, modify and successfully perform both simple and complex physical activities.

Feeling the "burn" of fatigue in a muscle or group of muscles being heavily exercised is another example of how the feedback provided by our nervous system functions to protect us. While many individuals judge the quality or quantity of a workout by the "burn" they feel in their muscles, the intense burning sensation that often accompanies muscle fatigue should be taken as a warning of an increased risk of muscle or tendon injury through overexertion, as well as a clear signal to lower the intensity level of the particular activity or workout.

SKELETAL SYSTEM

The human skeletal system consists of 206 bones (Figure 2.6) that can be divided into two sections: the axial skeleton, the 80 bones that comprise the head, neck and trunk; and the appendicular skeleton, the 126 bones that form the extremities (Table 2.4). The bones that form the skeleton combine to provide five basic yet important functions. First, the skeletal system provides protection for many of the vital organs, such as the heart, brain and spinal cord. Second, the skeleton provides support for the soft tissues so that erect posture and the form

Table 2.4
Bones in the Axial and Appendicular Skeletons

Axial Skeleton	Number of Bones
Skull	
Cranium	8
Face	14
Hyoid	1
Vertebral Column	26
Thorax	
Sternum	1
Ribs	24
(Auditory ossicles)*	6
	80

Appendicular Skeleton	Number of Bones
Lower Extremity	
Phalanges	28
Metatarsals	10
Tarsals	14
Patella	2
Tibia	2
Fibula	2
Femur	2
Pelvic Girdle	
Hip or pelvis (os coxae = ilium, ischium & pubis)	2
Shoulder Girdle	
Clavicle	2
Scapula	2
Upper Extremity	
Phalanges	28
Metacarpals	10
Carpals	16
Radius	2
Ulna	2
Humerus	2
	126

*NOTE: The auditory ossicles, three per ear, are not considered part of the axial or appendicular skeletons, but rather a separate group of bones. They were placed in the axial skeleton group for convenience.

Skeletal System

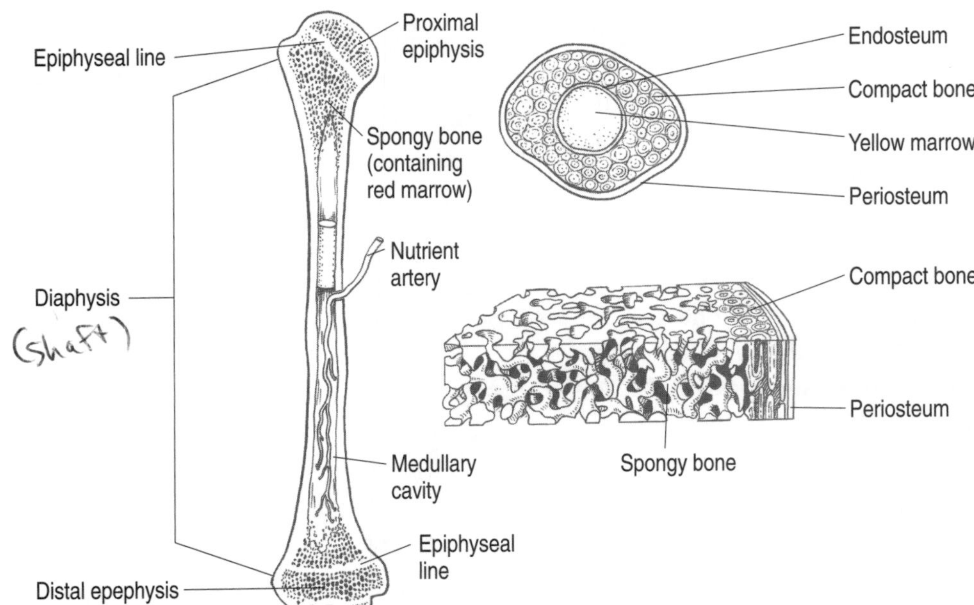

FIGURE 2.7
Long bone gross anatomy.

of the body can be maintained. Third, the bones provide a framework of levers to which muscles are attached. When particular muscles contract, long bones typically act as levers to produce movement. Fourth, the red marrow of bone is responsible for the production of certain blood cells, namely red blood cells, some types of white blood cells and platelets. Fifth, bones serve as storage areas for calcium, phosphorus, potassium, sodium and other minerals. Due to their high mineral content, bones remain intact for many years after death. Fat also is stored within the middle section of long bones in the medullary cavity (Figure 2.7).

Bones may also be classified according to their shape: long, short, flat or irregular. Long bones are those in which the length exceeds the width and the thickness. Most of the bones in the lower and upper extremities are long bones, including the femur, tibia, fibula and metatarsals in the lower limbs, and the humerus, radius, ulna and metacarpals in the upper extremity. Each long bone has a shaft called a diaphysis and two ends, known as epiphyses, that are usually wider than the shaft (singular = epiphysis). The diaphysis of a long bone is surrounded by a connective tissue sheath called the periosteum (Figure 2.7). The periosteum has two layers: an outer layer that serves as an attachment site for muscles and tendons, and an inner layer that, when disrupted by fracture, signals the release of osteoblasts (bone-forming cells) to repair the fracture.

Short bones have no long axis but are approximately equal in length and width. They are found in the hands (carpals) and the feet (tarsals). Flat bones are partially described by their name; they are thin, but usually bent or curved rather than flat. Examples include the bones of the skull, the ribs, the sternum and the scapulae (shoulder blades). Irregular bones are bones of various shapes that do not fall into the other three categories. The hip bones (os coxae), the vertebrae and many of the bones of the skull are examples of irregular bones.

Bone is composed of an organic component made of **collagen**, a complex protein that is found in various forms within bone and other **connective tissues**; and an inorganic component comprised of mineral salts, primarily calcium and potassium. According to Wolff's Law, bone is capable of adjusting its strength in proportion to the amount of stress placed on it. When healthy people participate in resistance-training programs for extended periods, their bones will become more dense through increases in collagen fibers and mineral salts. On the other hand, if bones are not subjected to stress, as in individuals with **sedentary** lifestyles or in the absence of gravity (as in space flight), bones will become less dense over time as mineral salts are withdrawn. An easy way to remember this important law is with the dictum, "Form follows function." Simply stated, the form that bone will take (strong or weak) is in direct response to the recent function of that bone.

It is important to keep this in mind when developing specific conditioning and resistance exercise programs for your clients. Since the low levels of the hormone estrogen that accompany **amenorrhea** (two or less menstrual periods per year) and menopause in women lead to substantial bone mineral loss, it is important that you assist your clients in developing strength-building programs.

Axial Skeleton

As previously stated, the axial skeleton consists of the 80 bones that form the skull, the vertebral column and the thorax (chest). This portion of the skeletal system provides the main structural support for the body and also protects the central nervous system and vital organs in the thorax (heart, lungs, etc.). Of primary importance is the adult vertebral column, consisting of 33 vertebrae divided into five groups according to the region of the body in which they are located. The upper seven are cervical vertebrae, followed in descending order by 12 thoracic vertebrae, five lumbar vertebrae, five sacral vertebrae fused into one bone as the sacrum and four coccygeal vertebrae fused together into one bone called the coccyx. The sacral vertebrae and coccygeal vertebrae become fused in the adult, so there are only 26 movable vertebrae (Figure 2.8).

Skeletal System

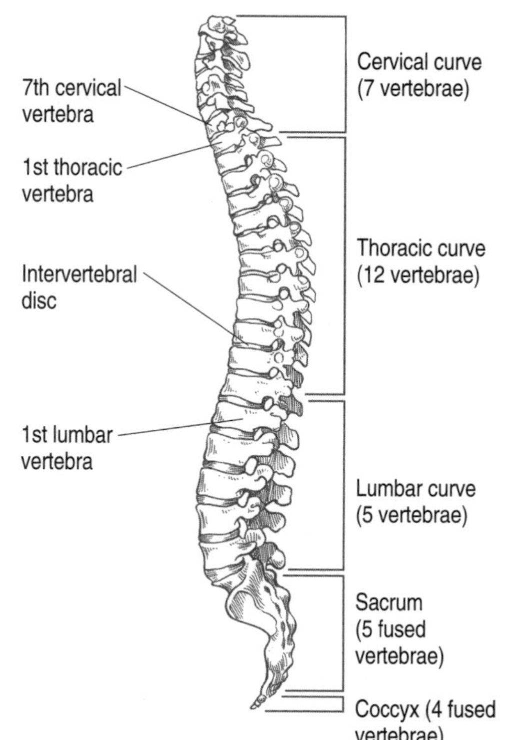

FIGURE 2.8
Vertebral column (lateral view).

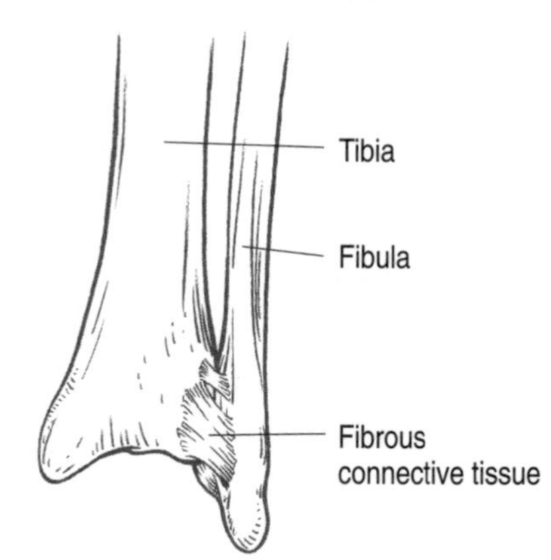

FIGURE 2.9
Example of a fibrous (syndesmotic) joint.

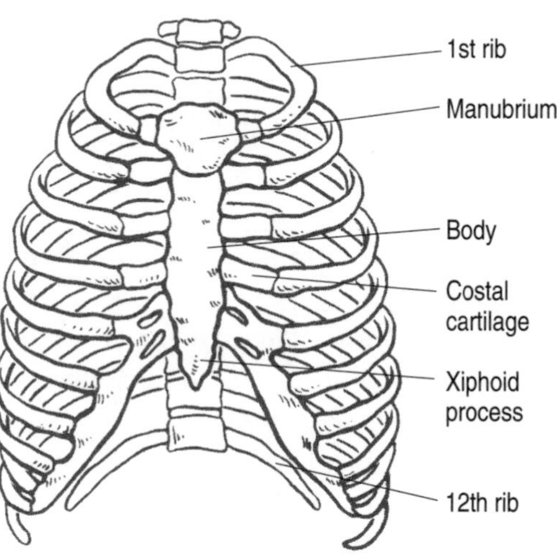

FIGURE 2.10
Example of a cartilaginous (synchrondrotic) joint.

Skeletal System

Appendicular Skeleton

The appendicular skeleton is comprised of the bones of the lower and upper limbs and the bones that attach the legs and arms to the axial skeleton — the pelvic (hip) and pectoral (chest) girdles. The pelvic girdle consists of two large hip bones known collectively as the os coxae, with each side comprised of an ilium, an ischium and a pubis (Figure 2.6). Much of the weight supported by the os coxae is transferred to the bones of the lower limbs. Conversely, the two pectoral girdles, each consisting of a clavicle (collarbone) and scapula (shoulder blade), attach the bones of the upper extremities to the axial skeleton at the sternum. Since this is the only attachment to or link between the upper extremities and the axial skeleton, several tradeoffs result from this configuration. Most importantly, the pectoral girdle does not provide very strong support for the upper extremity; however, the girdle does permit a wide range of movements at the shoulder, making it the most mobile joint in the body.

Articulations (Joints)

An **articulation**, or joint, is the point of contact or connection between bones, or between bones and cartilage. The stability and integrity of all joints are maintained by **ligaments**, the dense, fibrous strands of connective tissue that link together the bony segments. Some joints permit a large range of motion in several directions, whereas other joints permit virtually no motion at all. The various joints in the body can be classified into two general categories according to: 1) the structure of the joints; and 2) the type of movement allowed by the joints.

Structural Classification of Joints. When classifying joints according to their structure, two main characteristics differentiate the types of joints: 1) the type of connective tissue that holds the bones of the joint together; and 2) the presence or absence of a joint cavity. There are three major structural categories of joints: fibrous, cartilaginous and synovial. Fibrous joints (syndesmoses) have no joint cavity and include all joints in which bones are held tightly together by fibrous connective tissue. Very little space separates the ends of the bones of these joints; as a result, little or no movement occurs. Examples include the joints, or sutures, between the bones of the skull, the joint between the distal tibia and fibula, and the joint between the radius and ulna (Figure 2.9).

In cartilaginous joints (synchondroses), the bones are united by cartilage. No joint cavity exists and, as with fibrous joints, little or no motion occurs. Familiar examples include the joints formed by the hyaline cartilages that connect the ribs to the sternum (breastbone), and fibrocartilages that separate the bodies of vertebrae in the spinal column (Figure 2.10).

Most of the joints in the body are synovial joints (diarthroses). These joints all have a space, or joint cavity, between the bones that form them. The movement of synovial joints is limited only by the shapes of the bones of the joint and the soft tissues (ligaments, joint capsules, tendons, muscles) that surround the joint. Synovial joints have four distinguishing features that set them apart structurally from the other types of joints. First, the ends of the bones in synovial joints are covered with a thin layer of articular cartilage. The articular cartilage of synovial joints is hyaline cartilage, and although it covers the surfaces of the articulating bones, the hyaline cartilage does not attach the bones together. Second, all synovial joints are surrounded by an articular or joint capsule made of dense, fibrous connective tissue. Third, the inner surface of the joint capsule is lined with a thin synovial membrane. The primary function of the synovial membrane is the secretion of synovial fluid – the fourth unique characteristic of synovial joints. Synovial fluid acts as a lubricant for the

Table 2.5
Major Joints in the Body

Region/Joint	Type	Number of Axes of Rotation	Movement(s) Possible
Lower Extremity			
Metatarsophalangeal	Synovial (condyloid)	2	Flexion & extension; abduction & adduction; circumduction
Ankle	Synovial (hinge)	1	Plantarflexion & dorsiflexion
Between distal tibia & fibula	Fibrous	0	Slight movement possible
Knee (tibia & femur)	Synovial (modified hinge)	2	Flexion & extension; internal & external rotation
Hip	Synovial (ball & socket)	3	Flexion & extension; abduction & adduction; circumduction; internal & external rotation
Upper Extremity			
Metacarpophalangeal	Synovial (condyloid)	2	Flexion & extension; abduction & adduction; circumduction
Thumb	Synovial (saddle)	3	Flexion & extension; abduction & adduction; circumduction; opposition
Wrist	Synovial	2	Flexion & extension; abduction & adduction; circumduction
Proximal radioulnar	Synovial (pivot)	1	Pronation & supination
Elbow (ulna & humerus)	Synovial (hinge)	1	Flexion & extension
Shoulder	Synovial (ball & socket)	3	Flexion & extension; abduction & adduction; circumduction; internal & external rotation
Ribs and sternum	Cartilaginous	0	Slight movement possible

joint, and provides nutrition to the articular cartilage. Normally, only a very small amount of synovial fluid is present in even the largest joints, such as the knee and shoulder. However, acute injury to, or overuse of, a synovial joint can stimulate the synovial membrane to secrete excessive fluid, typically producing swelling and decreasing the pain-free range of motion.

In addition to these four features, some synovial joints have articular disks called menisci (singular = meniscus) that are made of fibrocartilage. In a weight-bearing joint like the knee, these cartilages help to absorb shock, increase joint stability, aid in joint nutrition by directing the flow of synovial fluid, and increase the joint contact area, thereby decreasing the pressure (load per unit area) on the weight-bearing structures. A torn cartilage or meniscus, one of the most common knee injuries in sports, is simply a tearing of one of the articular disks in the joint.

Functional Classification of Joints. The functional classification of joints is based on the degree and type of movement they allow. Fibrous joints are classified as synarthroses (syn = together, arthro = joint; "an immovable joint;" (Figure 2.9). Cartilaginous joints, which fall into the category of amphiarthroses (amphi = both sides, arthroses = joints; "cartilage on both

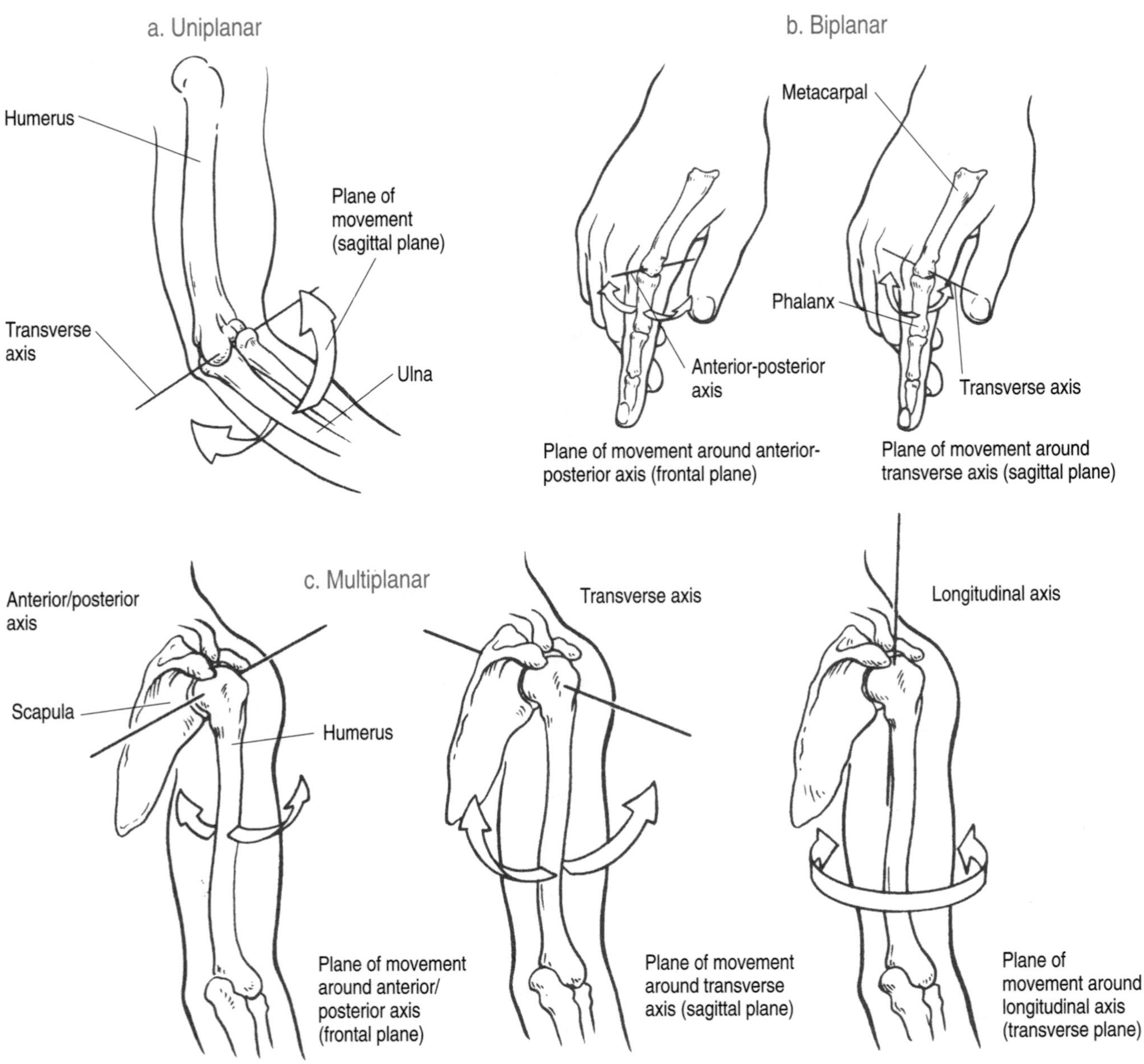

FIGURE 2.11
Movement of synovial (diarthrodial) joints.

sides of the joint"), are slightly movable (Figure 2.10). Finally, the largest functional category of joints, diarthrodial (di = apart, arthro = joint; "apart joint"), is that of the synovial joints. Diarthroses are freely movable joints; typically, many different movements are possible at these joints.

Unlike joints classified according to the material that connects the bones together, synovial joints are classified by the movements they allow. Typically, the shapes of the bony structures forming a synovial joint are the primary factors limiting the movement of a joint. Other factors that limit motion in synovial joints areas are as follows: 1) ligament and/or joint capsular tension; 2) poor muscle/tendon flexibility; and 3) apposition (touching) of the soft tissues, such as the calf against the hamstrings. A summary of the major joints in the body, classified by type and movements, is presented in Table 2.5.

Movement of Synovial Joints. Recall the earlier discussion of the anatomical planes of motion used to describe the actions of the body (Figure 2.1). In order for a joint

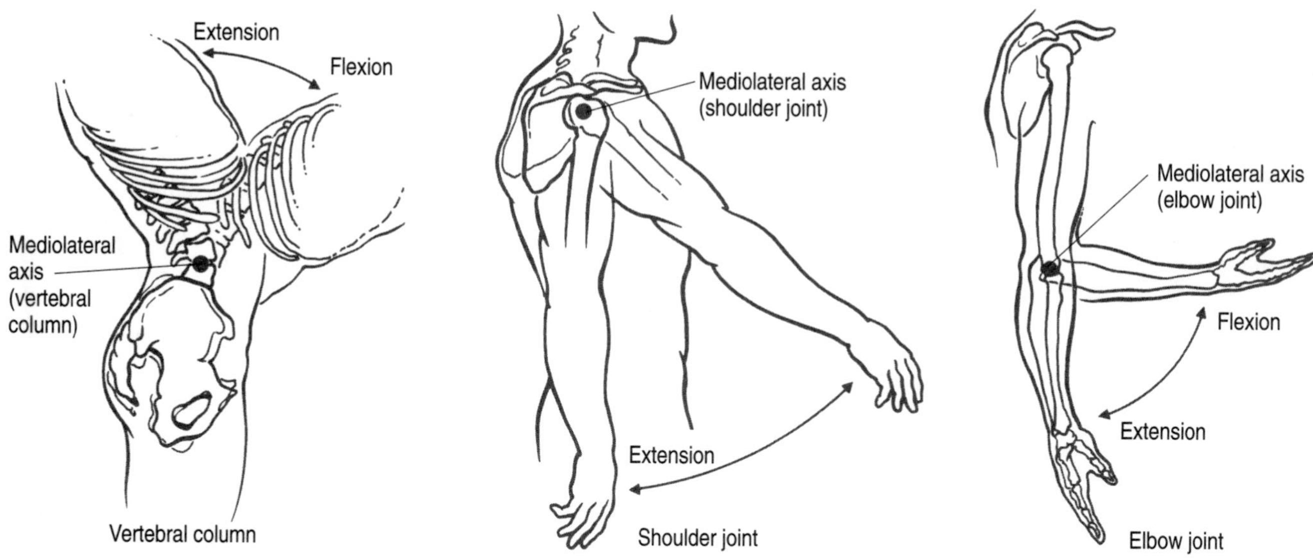

to move in a given plane, there must be an axis of rotation. An **axis of rotation** is an imaginary line perpendicular to (at a right angle to) the plane of movement about which a joint rotates. Due to their configuration, many joints have several axes of rotation, enabling bones to move in the various planes.

Joints with one axis of rotation can only move in one plane, and are known as uniplanar joints. Uniplanar joints also are known as "hinge" joints, since hinges only work in one plane. The ankle (talocrural) and the elbow (ulnohumeral) joints are examples of uniplanar joints. Some joints have two axes of rotation, permitting motion in two planes that are at right angles to one another. These biplanar joints, common throughout the body, include the knee (tibiofemoral) joint, a modified hinge joint; the joints of the hand and fingers (metacarpal/phalangeal), condyloid joints; and the joints of the feet and toes (metatarsal/phalangeal joints), also condyloid joints. Multiplanar joints have three axes of motion and permit movement in three planes. Examples include the hip joint and the shoulder (glenohumeral), both of which are ball-and-socket joints, and the thumb (the first metacarpal/phalangeal joint), which is a saddle joint (Figure 2.11).

There are two basic types of movements in the various synovial joints: angular and circular. Angular movements increase or decrease the angle between bones, and include primarily **flexion, extension, abduction** and **adduction**. Flexion and extension occur in the **sagittal** (anterior/posterior) **plane.** Flexion usually involves a decrease in the angle between the **anterior** surfaces of articulating bones, whereas extension most often describes an increase in this angle. Exceptions are the knee and toe joints, where the reference points for flexion and extension are the **posterior** articulating surfaces of the joints (Figure 2.12).

Abduction and adduction movements always occur in the **frontal** (medial/lateral) **plane** and are defined with respect to the midline of the body. When an arm or leg is moved away from the midline of the body, abduction occurs. Adduction is the return motion from abduction, and involves movement of the body part toward the midline of the body, to regain **anatomical position.** Abduction and adduction movements are possible at many joints, some of which are presented in Figure 2.13.

In addition to the four primary angular movements, there are four circular movements possible at some of the synovial

FIGURE 2.12 Segmental movements in the sagittal plane. (Redrawn from Kreighbaum and Barthels, 1985, pp. 43-44).

Skeletal System

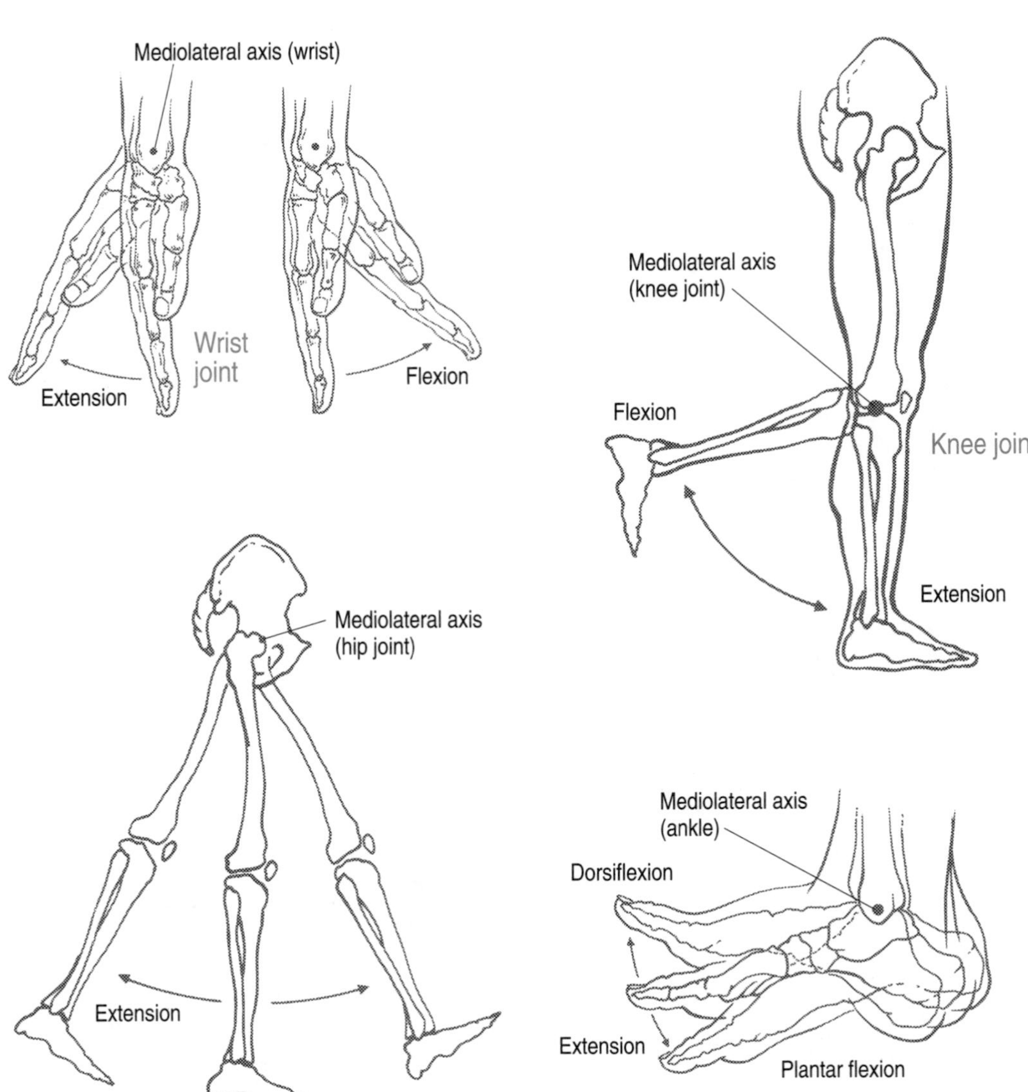

FIGURE 2.12 continued Segmental movements in the sagittal plane. (Redrawn from Kreighbaum and Barthels, 1985, pp. 45-46).

joints. Rotation is the motion of a bone around a central axis, and is described as being either internal or external rotation of the anterior surface of the bone involved. The femur at the hip joint and the humerus at the shoulder (glenohumeral) joint are among the most frequently rotated bones (Figure 2.14).

From the anatomical position, forearm supination and pronation are motions in the transverse or horizontal plane. Supination is a term that specifically describes the external rotation of the forearm which causes the palm to face anteriorly. The radius and the ulna are parallel in this position, which is the anatomical or reference position for the forearms (Figure 2.1). Pronation describes the internal rotation of the forearm that causes the radius to cross diagonally over the ulna and the palms to face posteriorly. The fourth circular movement, circumduction, is a sequential combination of flexion, abduction, extension and adduction. Similar to rotation, circumduction commonly occurs at the hip and shoulder joints. At some synovial joints, the fundamental movements are given specialized names to clarify their action. These, together with the primary angular and circular movements, are summarized in Table 2.6.

MUSCULAR SYSTEM

The anatomical system most directly affected by exercise is the muscular system. While bones and joints provide the framework for the body, it is the contraction (and relaxation) of specific muscles that enables us to move. There are three types of muscle tissue: skeletal, cardiac and visceral. Skeletal muscle tissue is attached to bones by **tendons**, and is typically named according to its location. Skeletal muscle is voluntary muscle; that is, it can be made to contract by conscious effort. Cardiac muscle tissue forms the walls of the heart and is involuntary by nature. The third type of muscle, visceral muscle, is found in the walls of internal organs like the stomach and intestines and in blood vessels. The contraction of visceral muscle also is involuntary and, thus, is not under conscious control. While all three types of muscle have vital functions, the structure and function of skeletal muscles warrant further discussion. Both ends of a skeletal muscle are attached to bone via tendons (a cord of connective tissue). In some cases, skeletal muscles are attached to bone by an **aponeurosis,** a broad, flat type of tendon. The wide, flat insertion of the rectus abdominis is an excellent example of an aponeurosis.

While there are more than 600 muscles within the human body, only the major muscles will be discussed in this chapter. Muscles are named according to:

- ✔ location (posterior tibialis, rectus abdominis)
- ✔ shape (deltoid, trapezius, serratus anterior, rhomboid)
- ✔ action (various muscle names include the terms extensor, flexor, abductor, adductor)
- ✔ number of divisions (biceps brachii, triceps brachii, quadriceps femoris)
- ✔ bony attachments (coracobrachialis, iliocostalis)
- ✔ size relationships (pectoralis major, pectoralis minor)

Muscular System

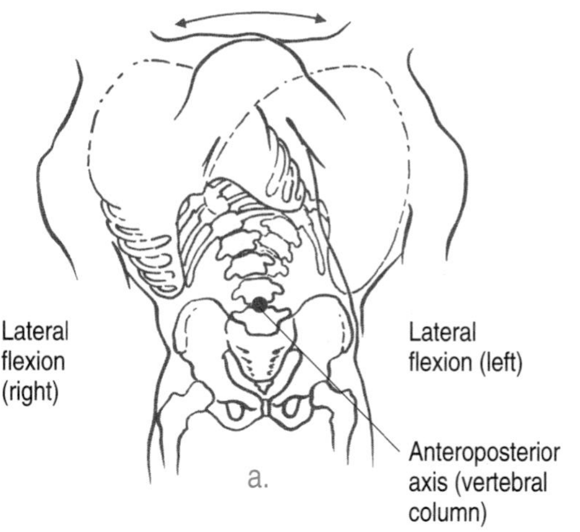

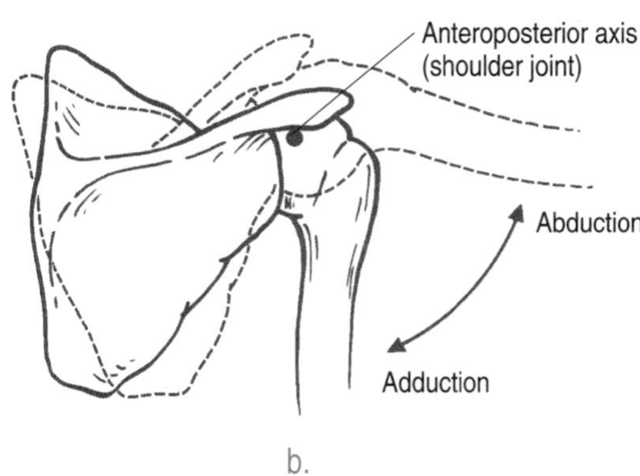

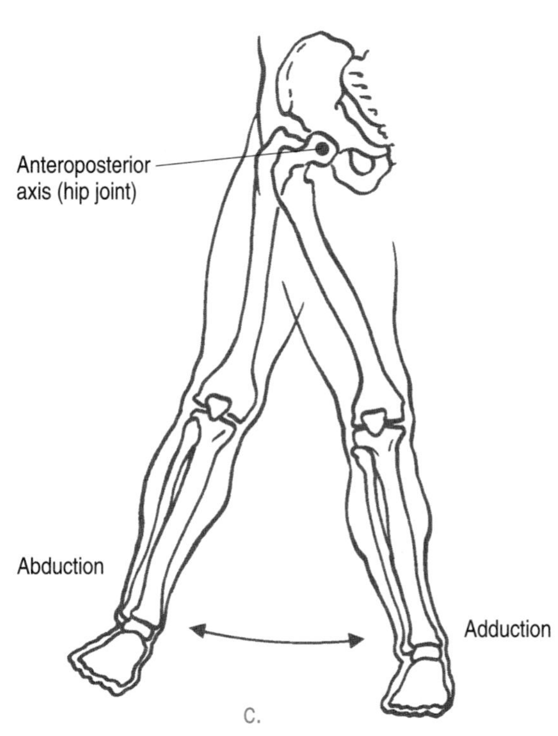

FIGURE 2.13 Segmental movements in the frontal plane. (Redrawn from Kreighbaum and Barthels, 1985, pp 45-46.)

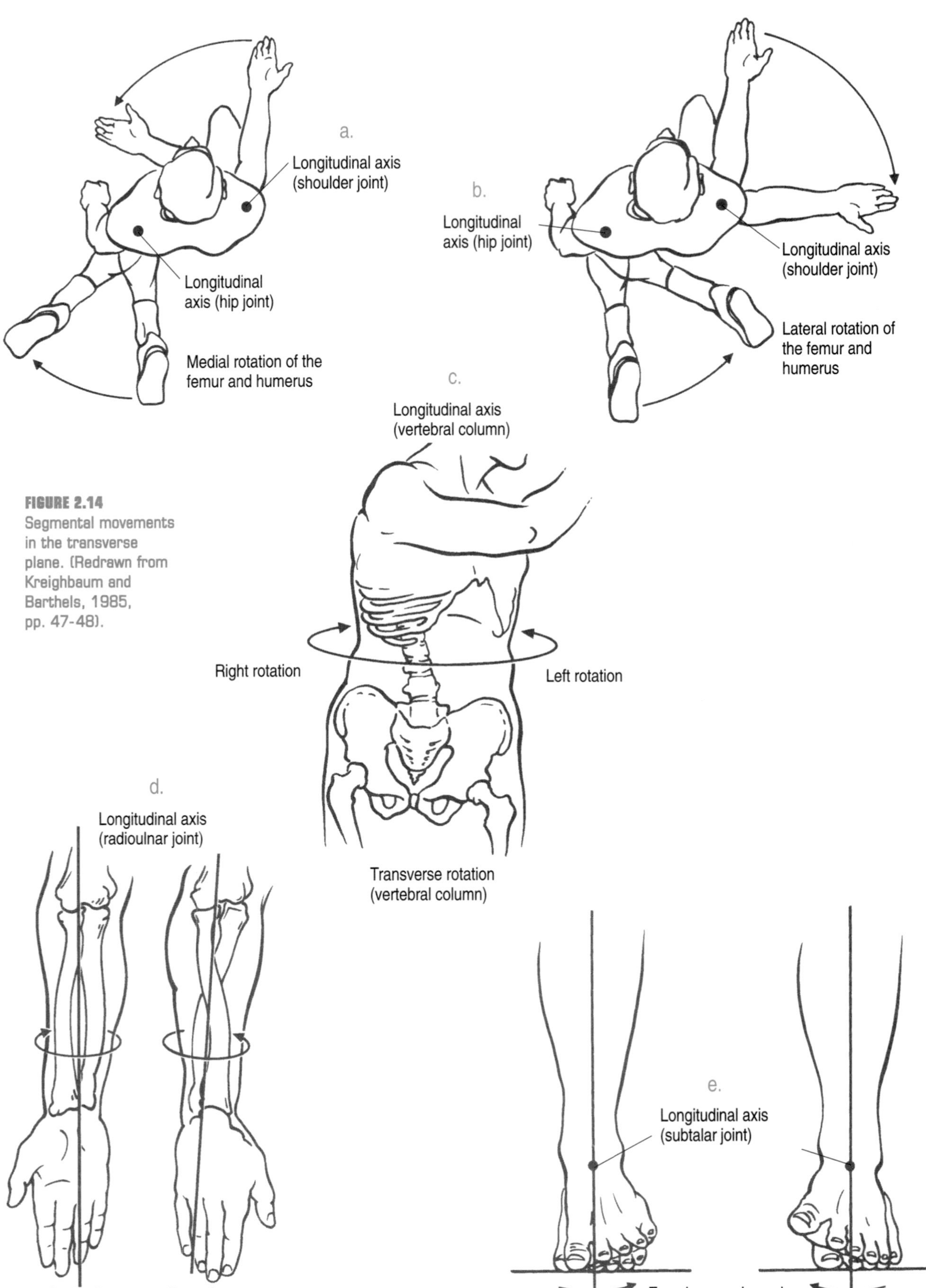

FIGURE 2.14
Segmental movements in the transverse plane. (Redrawn from Kreighbaum and Barthels, 1985, pp. 47-48).

Table 2.6
Fundamental Movements (from Anatomical Position)

Plane	Action	Definition
Sagittal	Flexion	Decreasing the angle between two bones
	Extension	Increasing the angle between two bones
	Dorsiflexion	Moving the top of the foot toward the shin (only at the ankle joint)
	Plantarflexion	Moving the sole of the foot downward; "pointing the toes" (only at the ankle)
Frontal	Abduction	Motion away from the midline of the body (or part)
	Adduction	Motion toward the midline of the body (or part)
	Elevation	Moving to a superior position (only at the scapula)
	Depression	Moving to an inferior position (only at the scapula)
Transverse	Inversion	Lifting the medial border of the foot (only at the subtalar joint)
	Eversion	Lifting the lateral border of the foot (only at the subtalar joint)
	Rotation	Internal (inward) or external (outward) turning about the vertical axis of bone
	Pronation	Rotating the hand & wrist medially from the elbow
	Supination	Rotating the hand & wrist laterally from the elbow
	Horizontal flexion	From a 90-degree abducted arm position, the humerus is flexed in, toward the midline of the body in the transverse plane
	Horizontal extension	The return of the humerus from horizontal flexion
Multiplanar	Circumduction	Motion that describes a "cone"; combines flexion, abduction, extension and adduction in sequence
	Opposition	Thumb movement unique to humans and primates

In addition, several muscles include the terms "longus" (long) and "brevis" (short) in their names.

Muscle tissue has the ability to receive and respond to input from the nervous system that may cause the muscle to contract (shorten and thicken) or relax. Muscle tissue also has elasticity so that, with proper techniques, muscles may be safely stretched. From a functional perspective, it is important to understand that most muscles of the trunk and extremities are arranged in opposing pairs. That is, when one muscle is contracting to achieve a desired movement (the **agonist**), its opposite muscle (the **antagonist**) is being stretched. For example, when the abdominal muscles are contracted during a bent-knee sit-up, the erector spinae muscles are being stretched. At most joints, several muscles help (combine) to perform the same anatomical function; these muscles are functionally known as **synergists.** For example, the synergistic contractions of the gastrocnemius, soleus and six other muscles of the leg produce plantarflexion at the ankle joint.

Muscular contraction results in motion,

Table 2.7
Actions of Major Lower-extremity Multi-joint Muscles

Muscle	Hip	Knee	Ankle
Rectus Femoris	Flexion	Extension	———
Biceps Femoris	Extension (long head) External rotation	Flexion External rotation	———
Semitendinosus	Extension Internal rotation	Flexion Internal rotation	———
Semimembranosus	Extension Internal rotation	Flexion Internal rotation	———
Gracilis	Adduction Internal rotation	Flexion Internal rotation	———
Sartorius	Flexion External rotation	Flexion Internal rotation	———
Gastrocnemius	———	Flexion	Plantarflexion

the maintenance of posture and heat production. Locomotion (walking, running) is the result of the complex, combined functioning of the bones, joints and muscles. Muscle contraction also enables the maintenance of posture in stationary positions, such as sitting and standing. Through regular contraction, muscles produce heat, which plays an important role in maintaining normal body temperature.

Muscles of the Lower Extremity

The major links of the lower extremity are the: 1) ankle joint formed by the distal tibia, distal fibula and talus; 2) knee joint comprised of the tibiofemoral and patellofemoral joints; and 3) hip joint linking the femur with the hip (coxal) bone. When compared to the muscles of the upper extremity, the muscles of the lower extremity tend to be larger and more powerful. Many of the muscles of the lower extremity cross two joints (either the hip and the knee, or the knee and the ankle). The major muscles of the lower extremity that act at more than one joint are listed in Table 2.7.

Muscles That Act at the Ankle and the Foot. The muscles of the leg are grouped into four compartments that are divided by interosseous membranes (inter = between, os = bone) between the tibia and fibula. The anterior tibial compartment muscles contract to extend the toes and dorsiflex (flex) the ankle. These muscles include the anterior tibialis, extensor digitorum longus and extensor hallucis longus (Figure 2.15a). The muscles of the lateral tibial compartment are known as the peroneals (peroneus longus and peroneus brevis), and act to cause **eversion** (abduction) of the foot and **plantarflexion** of the ankle (Figure 2.15b). The posterior muscles of the leg are contained in two separate spaces — the **superficial** and **deep** posterior tibial compartments. The largest muscles of the calf (soleus and gastrocnemius), along with the smaller plantaris, are located in the superficial post- erior tibial compartment. The deep posterior tibial compartment contains the popliteus, posterior tibialis, flexor hallucis longus and flexor digitorum longus (Figure 2.16). The primary functions of these posterior muscles include plantarflexion (extension) of the ankle, flexion of the toes and

Muscular System

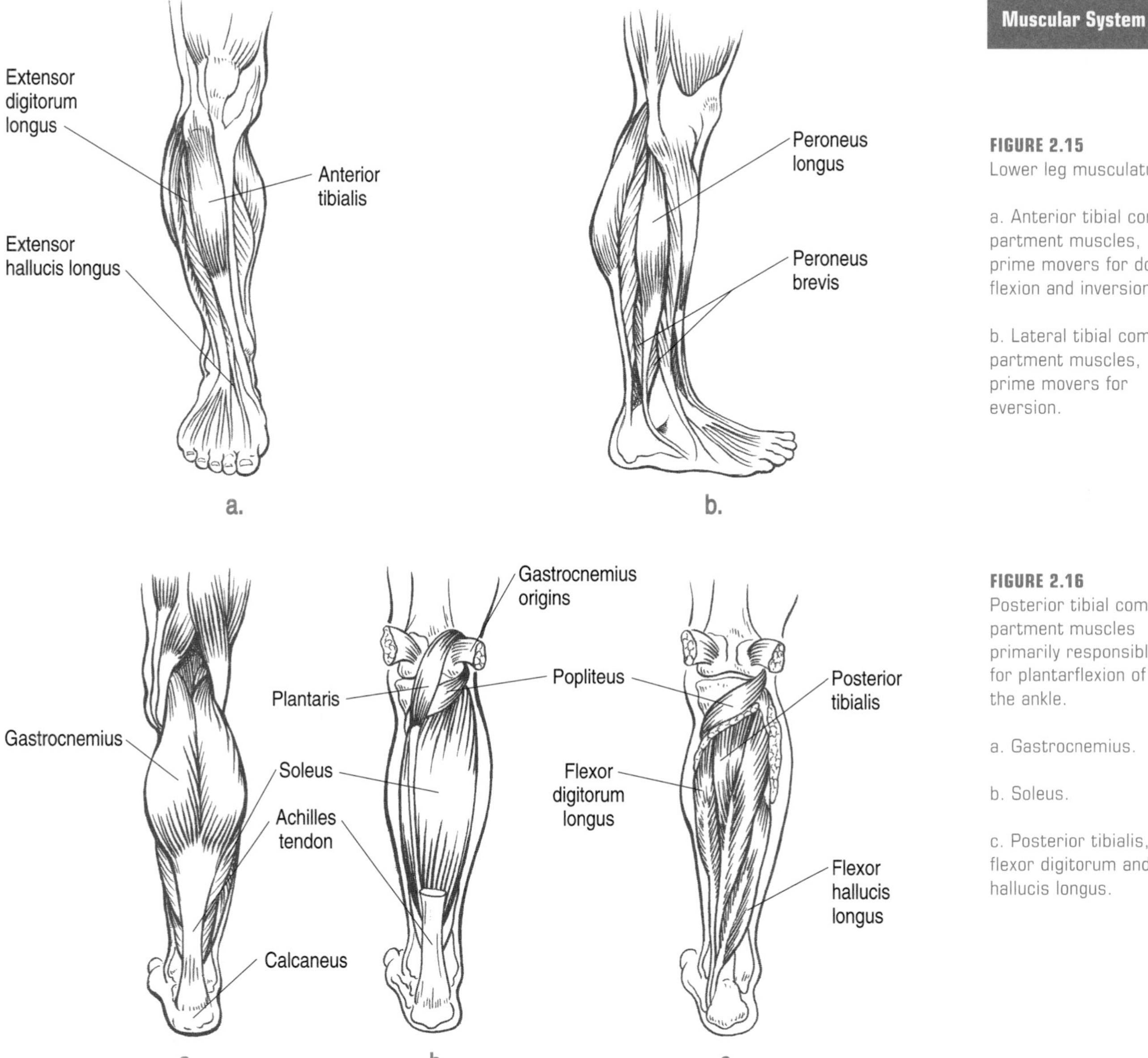

FIGURE 2.15
Lower leg musculature.

a. Anterior tibial compartment muscles, prime movers for dorsiflexion and inversion.

b. Lateral tibial compartment muscles, prime movers for eversion.

FIGURE 2.16
Posterior tibial compartment muscles primarily responsible for plantarflexion of the ankle.

a. Gastrocnemius.

b. Soleus.

c. Posterior tibialis, flexor digitorum and hallucis longus.

inversion (adduction) of the foot. The largest tendon in the body, the Achilles tendon is found in the posterior compartment and attaches the gastrocnemius and soleus via one common tendon to the calcaneus (heel bone). The origins, insertions, primary functions, and examples of exercises to develop the muscles that act at the ankle and the foot are presented in Table 2.8.

Muscles that Act at the Knee Joint. The muscles that cross the knee joint to act on the leg (tibia and fibula) can be divided into three separate groups. The four major muscles on the front of the thigh are located in the anterior, or extensor, compartment. The primary function of these muscles is to extend the leg. They are typically grouped together and referred to as the quadriceps femoris, although each muscle has its own individual name: rectus femoris, vastus medialis, vastus intermedius and vastus lateralis (Figure 2.17). The quadriceps insert via a common tendon known as the patellar tendon, which attaches to the tibial tuberosity (Figure 2.6).

Table 2.8
Major Muscles that Act at the Ankle and Foot

Muscle	Origin	Insertion	Primary Function(s)	Selected Exercises
Anterior Tibialis	Proximal ⅔ of lateral tibia	Medial aspect of 1st cuneiform and 1st metatarsal	Dorsiflexion at ankle; inversion at foot	Cycling with toe clips; resisted inversion (with dorsiflexion)
Peroneus Longus	Head of fibula and proximal ⅔ of lateral fibula	Inferior aspects of medial tarsal (1st cuneiform) and 1st metatarsal	Plantarflexion at ankle; eversion at foot	Resisted eversion of foot; walking on inside of foot
Peroneus Brevis	Distal ⅔ of lateral fibula	Base of the 5th metatarsal	Plantarflexion at ankle; eversion at foot	Resisted eversion of foot with rubber tubing; walking on inside of foot
Gastrocnemius	Posterior surfaces of femoral condyles	Posterior surface of calcaneus via Achilles tendon	Plantarflexion at ankle	Hill running, jumping rope, calf raises with barbell on shoulder, cycling, stair-climber machine, in-line skating
Soleus	Proximal ⅔ of posterior surfaces of tibia and fibula	Posterior surface of calcaneus via Achilles tendon	Plantarflexion at ankle	Virtually the same as for gastrocnemius; bent-knee toe raises with resistance
Posterior Tibialis	Posterior surface of tibia-fibular interosseous membrane	Lower medial surfaces of medial tarsals and metatarsals	Plantarflexion at ankle; inversion at foot	Resisted inversion of foot with surgical tubing, with plantarflexion

Table 2.9
Major Muscles that Act at the Knee Joint

Muscle	Origin	Insertion	Primary Function(s)	Selected Exercises
Rectus Femoris	Anterior-inferior spine of ilium	Superior aspect of patella and patellar tendon	Extension (most effective when the hip is extended)	Cycling, leg press machine, squat, vertical jumping, stair climbing, jumping rope, plyometrics
Vastus Lateralis, Intermedius, and Medialis	Proximal ⅔ of anterior femur at midline	Patella and tibial tuberosity via the patellar tendon	Extension (particularly when the hip is flexed)	Same as for rectus femoris, resisted knee extension, in-line skating, cross-country skiing
Biceps Femoris	Ischial tuberosity	Lateral condyle of tibia and head of fibula	Flexion and external rotation	Jumping rope, hamstring curls with knee in external rotation
Semitendinosus	Ischial tuberosity	Proximal anterior medial aspect of tibia	Flexion and internal rotation	Essentially the same as for biceps femoris; hamstring curls with knee in internal rotation
Semimembranosus	Ischial tuberosity	Posterior aspect of medial tibial condyle	Flexion and internal rotation	Same as semitendinosus

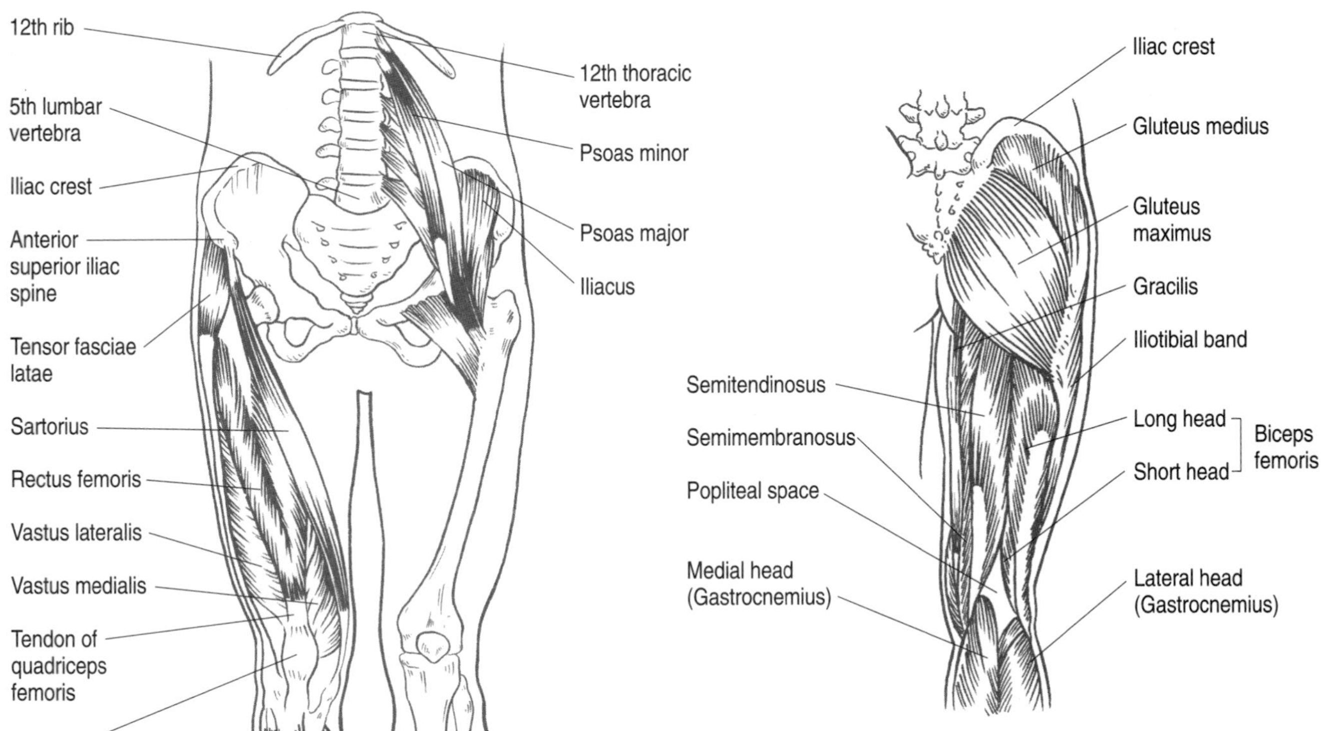

FIGURE 2.17 Anterior musculature of the hip and knee, prime movers for hip flexion (iliacus, psoas major and minor) and knee extension.

FIGURE 2.18 Posterior musculature of the hip and knee, prime movers for hip extension (gluteus maximus and hamstrings) and knee flexion (hamstrings and gastrocnemius).

The muscles in the posterior, or flexor, compartment of the thigh are the biceps femoris, semitendinosus and semimembranosus. These muscles, collectively known as the hamstrings, cross the knee joint and cause flexion of the leg. This large group of muscles has a common origin at the ischial tuberosity (Figure 2.6). Below the knee, the biceps femoris attaches **laterally**, while the semitendinosus and semimembranosus attach on the medial aspect of the tibia. Between these tendons lies the popliteal space, a triangular area on the posterior aspect of the knee joint (Figure 2.18).

The third major group of muscles that act on the leg is the pes anserine group, which includes the previously mentioned semitendinosus as well as the sartorius and the gracilis (Figures 2.17 and 2.18). These muscles are grouped together because of their common site of insertion on the **medial** tibia, just below the knee. The sartorius, the longest muscle in the body, originates on the ilium and courses diagonally across the anterior aspect of the thigh to its insertion on the **proximal** tibia. Even though the sartorius is an anterior muscle, its contraction causes flexion of the leg. As a group, the three pes anserine muscles internally rotate the leg (tibia) when the knee is flexed. The origins, insertions, primary functions, and examples of exercises to develop the major muscles that act on the leg are presented in Table 2.9.

Muscles that Act at the Hip Joint. Most of the muscles that cross the hip joint and act on the thigh (femur) have their origins on the pelvis. Located on the anterior aspect of the hip, the psoas major and the psoas minor muscles arise from the five lumbar vertebrae. These two muscles, along with the iliacus, have a common attachment on the lesser trochanter of the femur and work together as powerful flexors of the thigh. This group of three muscles is commonly referred to as the iliop- soas muscle. The rectus femoris is the only muscle of the quadriceps femoris group that crosses the hip joint. It also causes flexion of the thigh (Figure 2.17).

Posteriorly, three large muscles combine

Table 2.10
Major Muscles that Act at the Hip Joint

Muscle	Origin	Insertion	Primary Function(s)	Selected Exercises
Iliacus	Inner surface of the ilium and base of sacrum	Lesser trochanter of femur	Flexion and external rotation	Straight-leg sit-ups, running with knees lifted up high, leg raises
Psoas Major and Psoas Minor	Transverse processes of all 5 lumbar vertebrae	Lesser trochanter of femur	Flexion and external rotation	Essentially same as iliacus
Rectus Femoris	Anterior-inferior spine of ilium	Superior aspect of patella and patellar tendon	Flexion	Running, leg press, squat, jumping rope
Gluteus Maximus	Posterior ¼ of iliac crest and sacrum	Gluteal line of femur and iliotibial band	Extension and external rotation	Cycling, plyometrics, jumping rope, squat, stair-climbing machine
Biceps Femoris	Ischial tuberosity	Lateral condyle of tibia and head of fibula	Extension	Cycling, hamstring curls with knee in external rotation
Semitendinosus	Ischial tuberosity	Proximal anterior-medial aspect of tibia	Extension	Essentially the same as for biceps femoris; hamstring curls with knee in internal rotation
Semimembranosus	Ischial tuberosity	Posterior aspect of medial tibial condyle	Extension	Same as semitendinosus
Gluteus Medius and Minimus	Lateral surface of ilium	Greater trochanter of femur	Abduction	Side-lying leg raises, walking, running
Adductor Magnus	Pubic ramus and ischial tuberosity	Medial aspects of femur	Adduction and external rotation	Side-lying bottom leg raises; manual resistance adduction exercises
Adductor Brevis and Longus	Pubic ramus and ischial tuberosity	Medial aspects of femur	Adduction, flexion and internal rotation	Side-lying bottom leg raises, resisted adduction

to give shape to the buttocks and serve as powerful mobilizers of the hip joint. The gluteus maximus, the largest and most superficial of the three, extends and externally rotates the thigh. Underlying the gluteus maximus, are the gluteus medius and the gluteus minimus, which combine to abduct and internally rotate the femur. Also on the posterior aspect of the thigh are the hamstring muscles (biceps femoris, semitendinosus, semimembranosus), whose action at the hip joint is to extend the thigh (Figure 2.18).

The muscles located on the medial aspect of the thigh are named for both their function and their size. The adductor magnus, adductor longus and adductor brevis work in concert to adduct the femur (Figure 2.19). The adductors also are synergists for internal and external rotation of the thigh. The origins, insertions, primary actions, and examples of exercises to develop the major muscles that act at the hip joint are presented in Table 2.10.

Muscles that Act on the Trunk. For our discussion, the muscles of the trunk will include only the major muscles associated with the spinal column and the wall of the abdomen. Contraction of these muscles, in their agonist/antagonist relationships, results primarily in sagittal plane motion (i.e., flexion and extension of the trunk.) There are three major muscles responsible for movement of the vertebral column: the iliocostalis, the longissimus and the spinalis, better known by their functional

Muscular System

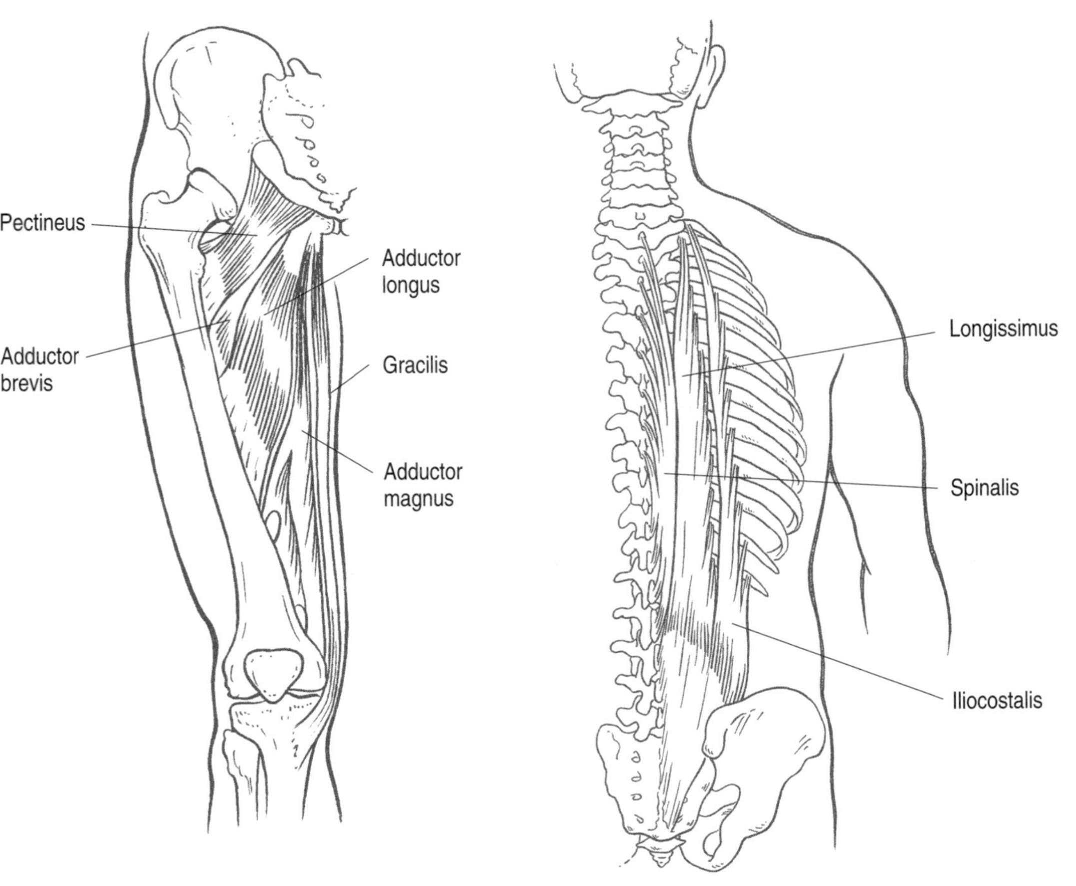

FIGURE 2.19
Medial muscles of the hip that are responsible for adduction.

FIGURE 2.20
The erector spinae muscles (posterior view). Redrawn from Daniels & Worthingham (1986).

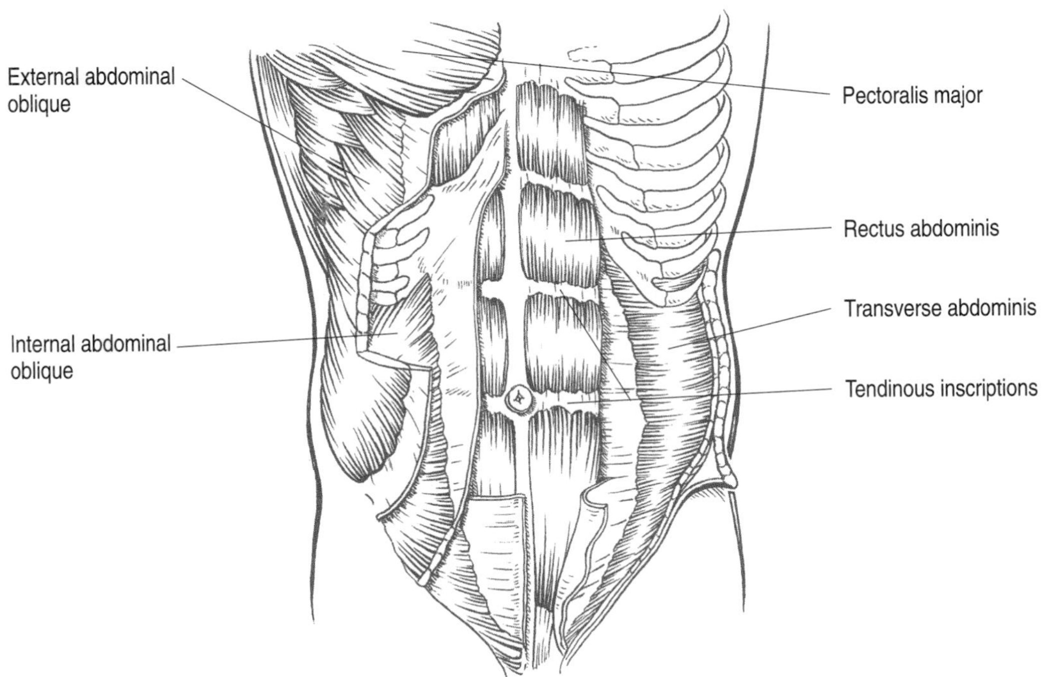

FIGURE 2.21
Muscles of the abdominal wall.

Table 2.11
Major Muscles that Act at the Trunk

Muscle	Origin	Insertion	Primary Function(s)	Selected Exercises
Rectus Abdominis	Pubic crest	Cartilage of 5th through 7th ribs and xiphoid process	Flexion and lateral flexion of the trunk	Bent-knee sit-ups, partial curl-ups, good posture, pelvic tilts
External Oblique	Anteriolateral borders of lower 8 ribs	Anterior ½ of ilium, pubic crest, and anterior fascia	Lateral flexion of the trunk	Twisting bent-knee sit-ups (rotation opposite), and curl ups
Internal Oblique	Iliac crest	Cartilage of last 3 to 4 ribs	Lateral flexion of the trunk	Twisting bent-knee sit-ups (rotation same side), and curl ups
Transverse Abdominis	Iliac crest, lumbar fascia, and cartilages of last 6 ribs	Xiphoid process of sternum, anterior fascia, and pubis	Compresses abdomen	No motor function
Erector Spinae	Posterior iliac crest and sacrum	Angles of ribs, transverse processes of all ribs	Extension of trunk	Squat, dead lift, prone back extension exercises, good standing posture

Table 2.12
Actions of Major Upper Extremity Multijoint Muscles

Muscle	Shoulder	Elbow	Forearm	Wrist
Biceps Brachii	Flexion	Flexion	Supination	—
Brachioradialis	—	Flexion	Pronation & supination	—
Triceps Brachii	Extension (long head)	Extension	—	—
Flexor Carpi Radialis	—	Flexion	—	Flexion, abduction
Flexor Carpi Ulnaris	—	Flexion	—	Flexion, adduction
Extensor Carpi Radialis (longus and brevis)	—	Extension	—	Extension
Extensor Carpi Ulnaris	—	Extension	—	Extension, adduction

group name, the erector spinae. Each of the three muscles in this group has a subdivision name based on the particular portion of the spinal column to which it attaches. For example, there are three divisions of the iliocostalis muscle: the iliocostalis lumborum, iliocostalis thoracis and iliocostalis cervicis. In addition to extending the vertebral column, unilat- eral contraction of the iliocostalis muscle will produce lateral flexion to that side (Figure 2.20).

The walls of the abdominal cavity are supported entirely by the strength of surrounding muscles since there are no bones that provide support for this region. To make up for the lack of skeletal support, the three layers of muscles in the abdominal wall run in different directions (Figure 2.21). In the outermost (superficial) layer

Muscular System

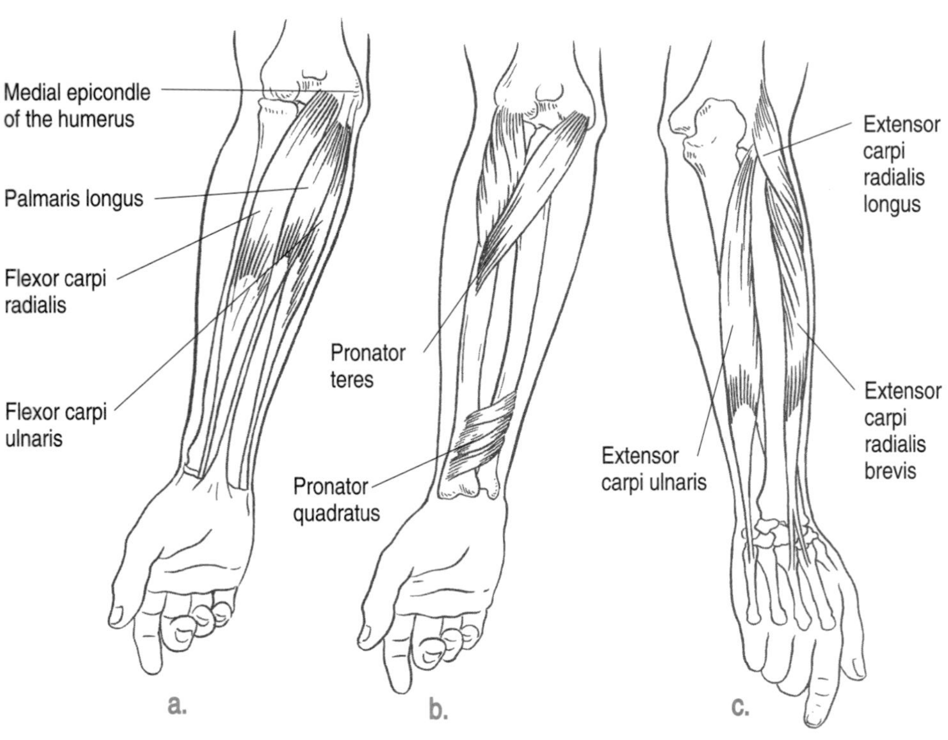

FIGURE 2.22
Muscles of the wrist:

a. Flexors.

b. Pronators.

c. Extensors.

Table 2.13
Major Muscles that Act at the Wrist

Muscle	Origin	Insertion	Primary Function(s)	Selected Exercises
Flexor Carpi Radialis	Medial epicondyle of humerus	2nd and 3rd metacarpals	Flexion	Wrist curls against resistance; grip strengthening exercises for humerus; baseball and softball; racquet sports, particularly racquetball and badminton
Flexor Carpi Ulnaris	Medial epicondyle of humerus	5th metacarpal	Flexion	Same as flexor carpi radialis
Extensor Carpi Radialis Longus	Lateral epicondyle of humerus	2nd metacarpal	Extension	"Reverse" wrist curls; racquet sports, particularly tennis
Extensor Carpi Ulnaris	Lateral epicondyle of humerus	5th metacarpal	Extension	Same as extensor carpi radialis longus

is the external oblique muscle, whose fibers run anteriorly downward and toward the midline. In the second layer, the fibers of the internal oblique muscle run posteriorly and downward. An easy way to remember the orientations of these two muscles is to picture the fibers of the external oblique running into the front pockets of your slacks and the fibers of the internal oblique running diagonally into the rear pockets. Unilateral (one side) contraction of the lateral fibers of the obliques (external and internal) produces lateral flexion of the spinal column on that side. Trunk rotation is produced by contraction of an external oblique and an internal oblique muscle on opposite sides. Bilateral (both sides) contraction of the external and internal obliques compresses the abdominal cavity; these muscles are commonly

Muscular System

Table 2.14
Major Muscles that Act on the Elbow and Forearm

Muscle	Origin	Insertion	Primary Function(s)	Selected Exercises
Biceps Brachii	Long head from tubercle above glenoid cavity; short head from coracoid process of scapula	Radial tuberosity and bicipital aponeurosis	Flexion at elbow; supination at forearm	"Curling" with barbell, chin-ups, rock climbing, upright "rowing" with barbell
Brachialis	Anterior humerus	Ulnar tuberosity and coronoid process of ulna	Flexion at elbow	Same as for biceps brachii
Brachioradialis	Distal ⅔ of lateral condyloid ridge of humerus	Radial styloid process	Flexion at elbow	Same as for biceps brachii
Triceps Brachii	Long head from lower edge of glenoid cavity of scapula; lateral head from posterior humerus; short head from distal ⅔ of posterior humerus	Olecranon process of ulna	Extension at elbow	Push-ups, dips on parallel bars, bench press, military press
Pronator Teres	Distal end of medial humerus and medial aspect of ulna	Middle ⅓ of lateral radius	Flexion at elbow; pronation at forearm	Pronation of forearm with dumbbell

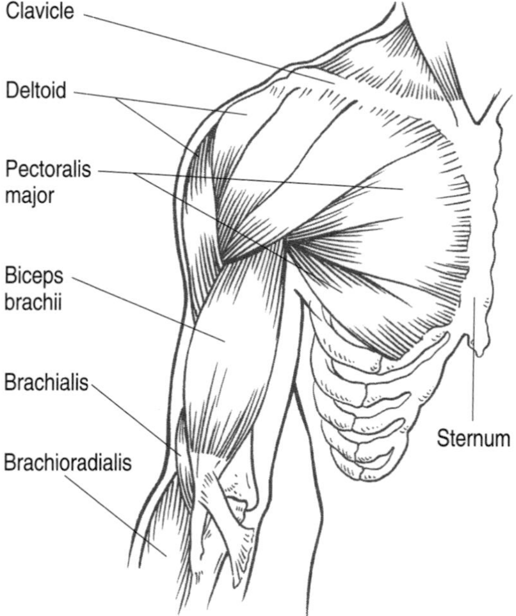

FIGURE 2.23
Superficial musculature of the anterior chest, shoulder and arm (humerus).

activated during forced exhalation, defecation and urination.

In the deepest muscular layer in the abdominal wall lies the transverse abdominis muscle. The fibers of this thin muscle run horizontally, encircling the abdominal cavity. Contraction of this muscle also compresses the abdomen (Figure 2.21). The rectus abdominis is a narrow, flat muscle on the anterior aspect of the abdominal wall that flexes the vertebral column; its fibers run vertically from the pubis to the rib cage. The rectus abdominis is crossed by three transverse fibrous bands called tendinous inscriptions (Figure 2.21). The origins, insertions, primarily functions, and examples of exercises to develop the muscles that act on the trunk are presented in Table 2.11.

Muscles of the Upper Extremity

In studying the musculature of the upper extremity, you should concentrate on understanding the motions (and muscles responsible for producing motion) at the four major links: the wrist joint, comprised of the **distal** radius, ulna and proximal carpal bones; the elbow joint, formed by the union of the olecranon process of the

Muscular System

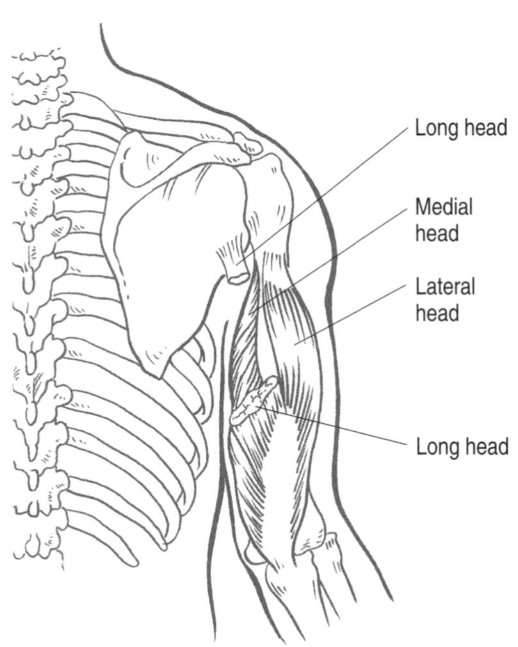

FIGURE 2.24
Triceps brachii muscle, responsible for elbow extension.

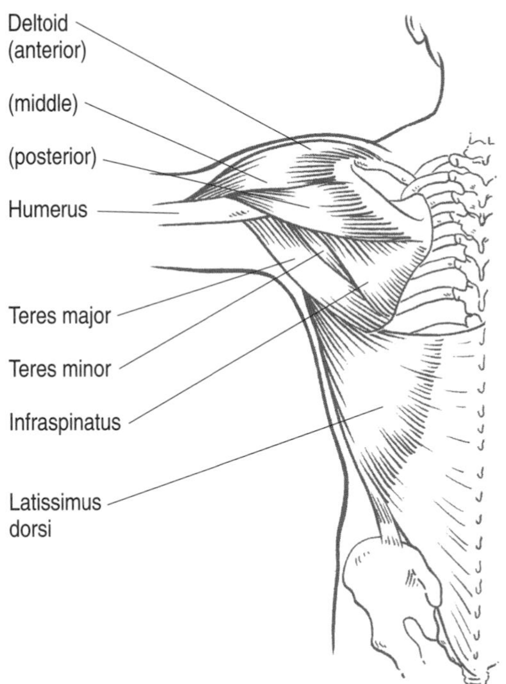

FIGURE 2.25
Superficial musculature of the superior and inferior shoulder joint, prime movers for shoulder abduction (deltoid) and adduction (latissimus dorsi and teres major). Redrawn from Luttgens (1992).

ulna and the distal humerus; the shoulder joint, consisting of the proximal humerus and the glenoid fossa of the scapula; and the scapulothoracic articulation. The connection between the scapula and the thorax is not a bony joint, per se, but more an important functional, soft tissue (muscle and fascia) link between the scapula and the trunk. Similar to the lower extremity, there are many muscles in the upper extremity that act at two joints. These muscles are identified in Table 2.12.

Muscles that Act at the Wrist. The muscles that act at the wrist joint can be grouped according to their origin and function. The flexor-pronator muscles originate on the medial epicondyle of the humerus, and cause flexion of the wrist and pronation of the forearm (radius and ulna). The major wrist flexors include the flexor carpi radialis, palmaris longus and flexor carpi ulnaris (Figure 2.22a). The major pronators of the forearm are the pronator teres at the elbow and the pronator quadratus at the wrist (Figure 2.22b). The antagonist muscles to the flexor-pronators are the extensor-supinators which arise from a common tendon on the lateral humeral epicondyle and, as their names indicate, cause extension of the wrist and supination of the forearm. The major wrist extensors are the extensor carpi radialis longus and the extensor carpi ulnaris (Figure 2.22c). Simply enough, the supinator muscle (with synergistic help from the biceps brachii) is responsible for supination of the forearm (Figure 2.22b). The origins, insertions, primary functions and examples of exercises to develop the muscles that act at the wrist and forearm are presented in Table 2.13.

Muscles that Act at the Elbow Joint. The muscles that act at the elbow joint produce motion of the forearm (radius and ulna), and are easily remembered by the motions that their contractions produce. As you recall, the elbow (ulnohumeral) joint is a hinge joint and permits motion in only one plane. In the case of the elbow, that one plane is the sagittal plane, and the only motions in the sagittal plane are flexion and extension. The flexors of the elbow, the biceps brachii, brachialis and brachioradialis are located on the anterior aspect of the arm (humerus) (Figure 2.23). The triceps brachii is the

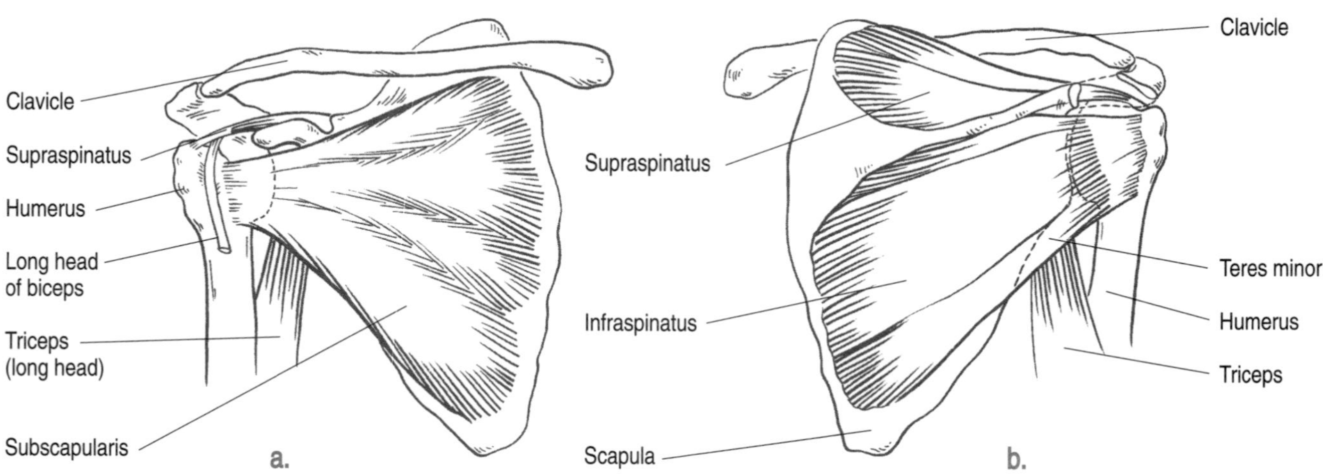

FIGURE 2.26
Rotator cuff muscles. Redrawn from Luttgens (1992).

a. Anterior view (subscapularis).

b. Posterior view (supraspinatus, infraspinatus, teres minor).

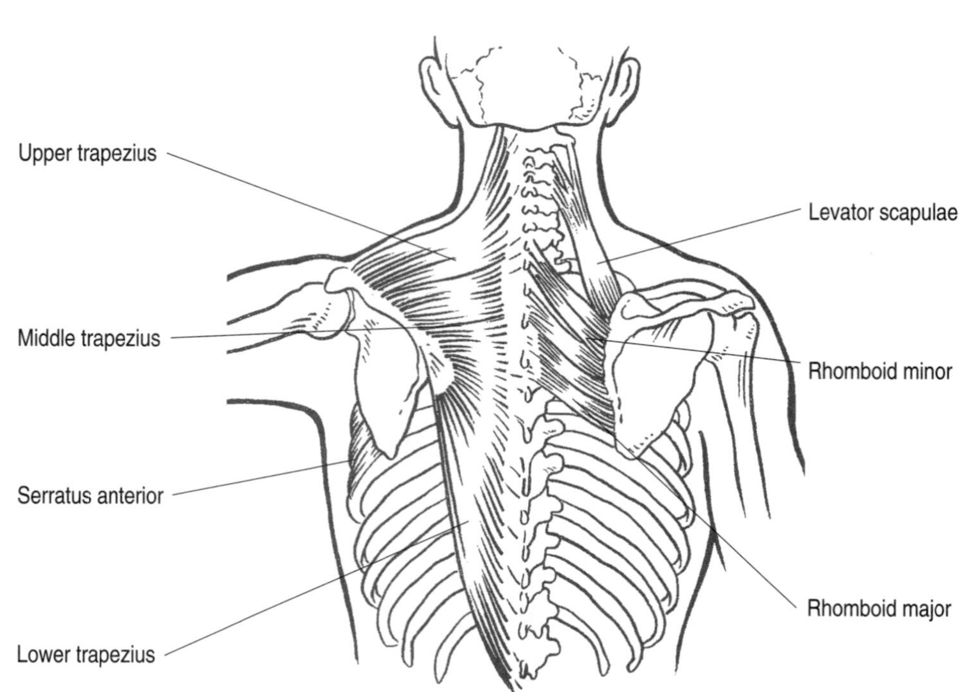

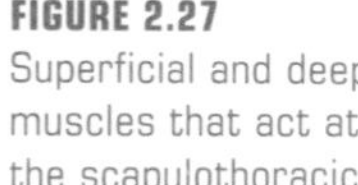

FIGURE 2.27
Superficial and deep muscles that act at the scapulothoracic articulation.

major extensor of the elbow joint and is located on the posterior aspect of the arm. As its name suggests, the triceps has three heads, or origins: one on the scapula and two on the proximal humerus. All three heads converge and insert, via a common tendon, into the olecranon process of the ulna (Figure 2.24). The origins, insertions, primary functions, and examples of exercises to develop muscles at the elbow joint are listed in Table 2.14.

Muscles that Act at the Shoulder Joint. As mentioned, the shoulder (glenohum-eral) joint is the most mobile joint in the body. We will concern ourselves here with only the nine major muscles that cross the shoulder joint and act on the arm (humerus). The two largest muscles, the pectoralis major and the latissimus dorsi have their origins on the thorax. The pectoralis major has several important functions at the shoulder: flexion in the sagittal plane, adduction in the frontal plane and internal rotation in the transverse plane (Figure 2.23). The latissimus dorsi arises posteriorly from the pelvis and the lumbar

Table 2.15
Major Muscles that Act at the Shoulder

Muscle	Origin	Insertion	Primary Function(s)	Selected Exercises
Pectoralis Major	Clavicle, sternum, and first six costal cartilages	Greater tubercle of humerus	Flexion; adduction; internal rotation	Push-ups, pull-ups, incline bench press, regular bench press, climbing a rope, all types of throwing, tennis serve
Deltoid	Anterolateral clavide, border of the acromion, and lower edge of spine of the scapula	Deltoid tubercle of humerus on mid-lateral surface	Abduction: entire muscle; anterior fibers: flexion, internal rotation; posterior fibers: extension, external rotation	Lateral "butterfly" (abduction) exercises with dumbbells; anterior deltoid has similar functions as the pectoralis major
Latissimus Dorsi	Lower six thoracic vertebrae, all lumbar vertebrae, crests of ilium and sacrum, lower four ribs	Medial side of intertubercular groove of humerus	Extension; adduction; internal rotation	Chin-ups, rope climbing, dips on parallel bars, rowing, any exercise that involves pulling the arms downward against resistance, e.g.,"lat" pulls on exercise machine
Rotator Cuff	Various aspects of scapula	All insert on greater tubercle of humerus except for the subscapularis, which inserts on the lesser tubercle of humerus	Infraspinatus and teres minor external rotation; subscapularis internal rotation; supraspinatus: abduction	Exercises that involve internal and external rotation, e.g., tennis serve, throwing a baseball, internal and external rotation exercises from prone position with dumbbells

and lower thoracic vertebrae. Interestingly, due to its medial insertion on the arm, the latissimus shares two functions with the pectoralis major. While the latissimus dorsi is a prime extensor of the shoulder joint, it complements the pectoralis as an adductor and internal rotator of the arm (Figure 2.25).

The remaining muscles that act at the shoulder joint have their origins on the scapula itself. The deltoid muscles, superficial muscles located on the superior aspect of the shoulder joint, resemble their name in several ways. The deltoid is shaped like a triangle (Greek letter delta = Δ), and is also divided into three functional sections. The anterior deltoid fibers flex and internally (inwardly) rotate the arm. The middle portion of the deltoid is a primary abductor of the arm. The posterior deltoid fibers extend the arm as well as produce external rotation when activated (Figures 2.23 and 2.25).

The rotator cuff muscles, a group of four small muscles, are functionally very important. These muscles act against the pull of gravity to hold the arm in the transverse plane. These muscles are frequently injured due to errors in training, such as general overuse, improper or insufficient warm-up, or excessive repetitions of shoulder abduction with internal rotation. Inflammation of the rotator cuff muscles commonly results in a painful condition known as impingement syndrome in which the swollen rotator cuff muscles and the bursa are "pinched" by the scapula when the arm is abducted. If you recommend exercise regimens that include repeated overhead arm motions, such as swimming, weight training, racquet sports and gymnastics, you should closely monitor your client's performance to avoid inducing shoulder impingement syndrome. The rotator cuff muscles are easily remembered as the SITS muscles: the supraspinatus, which abducts the arm; the infraspinatus and teres minor, which externally rotate the arm; and the subscapularis, which, as its name implies,

Table 2.16
Major Muscles that Act at the Shoulder Girdle

Muscle	Origin	Insertion	Primary Function(s)	Selected Exercises
Trapezius	Occipital bone, spines of cervical and thoracic vertebrae	Acromion process and spine of scapula	Upper: elevation of scapula middle: adduction of scapula lower: depression of scapula	Upright rowing, shoulder shrugs with resistance
Levator Scapulae	Upper four or five cervical vertebrae	Vertebral border of scapula	Elevation of scapula	Shoulder shrugs with resistance
Rhomboid Major and Minor	Spines of seventh cervical through fifth thoracic vertebrae	Vertebral border of scapula	Adduction and elevation of scapula	Chin-ups, supported dumbbell bentover rows

is located on the inferior surface of the scapula, and internally rotates the arm (Figure 2.26). The origins, insertions, primary functions, and examples of exercises designed to develop the muscles that cross the shoulder joint are presented in Table 2.15.

Muscles that Act at the Scapulothoracic Articulation. The primary function of the muscles and fascia that make up the soft tissue "joint" between the scapula and the trunk is to stabilize the scapula during movement of the arm (humerus). The four major muscles that anchor the scapula are named according to their shape (trapezius, rhomboid major and rhomboid minor) and function (levator scapulae) (Figure 2.27). Due to its shape and the varied directions of its fibers, the superficial trapezius has several different functions. The upper portion of the trapezius is responsible for elevation of the scapula (example: shrugging the shoulders). The middle section of the trapezius has horizontally directed fibers, resulting in adduction of the scapula when stimulated. The fibers of the lower portion of the trapezius angle downward toward their attachment on the thoracic vertebrae. Contraction of the lower trapezius primarily results in depression and adduction of the scapula.

Deep to the trapezius are the rhomboids (major and minor), which work in unison to produce adduction and slight elevation of the scapula (Figure 2.27). Good muscle tone in the rhomboids will help maintain good upper-back posture and, thereby, avoid the "rounded shoulders" posture. The levator scapulae muscle runs from the upper cervical vertebrae to the medial border of the scapula and, together with the upper part of the trapezius, elevates the scapula. The origins, insertions, primary functions and examples of exercises to develop the muscles of the scapulothoracic "articulation" are listed in Table 2.16.

SUMMARY

As a personal trainer, you are required to design programs that are safe and effective and that accomplish the desired fitness and/or personal goals of your clients. Without a fundamental understanding of human anatomy, this task is nearly impossible. Anatomical terminology and the five major anatomical systems — cardiovascular, respiratory, nervous, skeletal and muscular — were presented. With this information, you have sufficient information to identify specific exercises and physical activities that will efficiently accomplish the fitness goals of your clients.

REFERENCES

Gardner, E., Gray, D. & O'Rahilly, R. (1975). *Anatomy: A Regional Study of Human Structure.* (4th ed.) Philadelphia: W. B. Saunders.

Guyton, A. (1991). *Textbook of Medical Physiology.* (8th ed.) Philadelphia: W. B. Saunders.

Hamill J. & Knutzen K. (1995). *Biomechanical Basis of Human Movement.* Baltimore: Williams and Wilkins.

Kreighbaum, E. (1987). *Anatomy and Kinesiology.* In Van Gelder, N. & Marks, S. (Eds.) *Aerobic Dance-Exercise Instructor Manual.* (pp.35-88), San Diego: American Council on Exercise.

Marieb, E. (1995). *Human Anatomy and Physiology.* (3rd ed.) Redwood City: Benjamin-Cummings.

Rasch, P. (1989). *Kinesiology and Applied Anatomy.* (7th ed.) Philadelphia: Lea and Febiger.

Smith, L., Weiss, E. & Lehmkuhl, L. (1996). *Brunnstrom's Clinical Kinesiology.* (5th ed.) Philadelphia: F. A. Davis.

Tortora, G. (1983). *Principles of Human Anatomy.* (3rd ed.) New York: Harper & Row.

SUGGESTED READING

Clemente, C. (1975). *A Regional Atlas of the Human Body.* Philadelphia: Lea & Febiger.

Snow-Harter, C. & Marcus, R. (1991). Exercise, bone mineral density, and osteoporosis. In Holloszy, J. (Ed.) *Exercise and Sport Science Reviews,* 19, 351-388.

Thompson, C. & Floyd, R. (1994). *Manual of Structural Kinesiology* (12th ed.) St. Louis: Mosby.

CHAPTER 3

Biomechanics and Applied Kinesiology

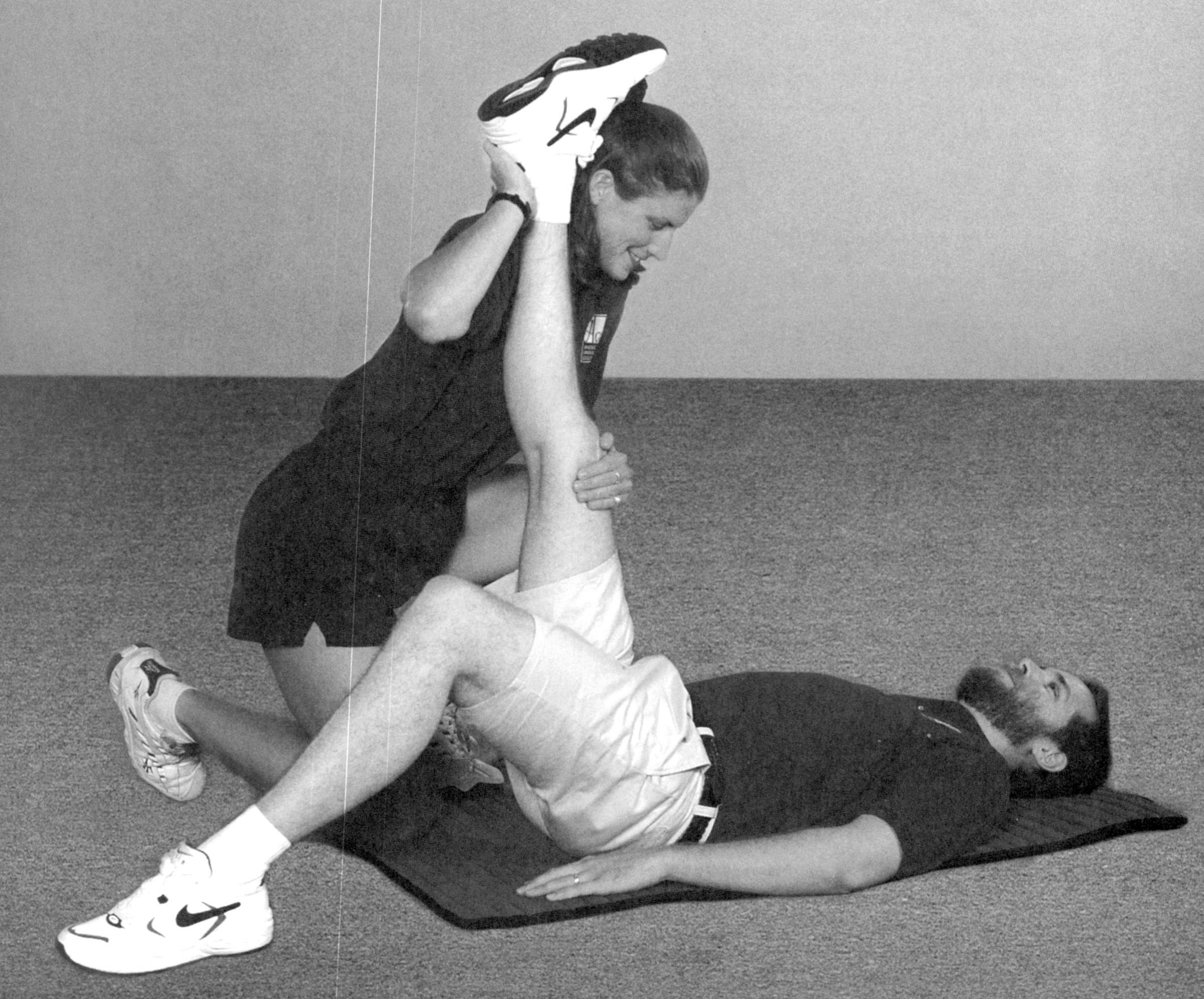

IN THIS CHAPTER:

Deborah Ellison

Deborah Ellison, P.T., is a registered physical therapist and personal trainer. Her company, Movement That Matters, provides exercise design consultation and instructor training. She has worked with the American Council on Exercise as director of education, an item-writer for certification exams, chair of the Accreditation Commission, and she is currently participating in the design of the personal trainer practical training course. She is a regular contributor to SHAPE *magazine,* IDEA Today *magazine and* ACE Fitness*Matters®. She has also published several books on exercise design, including* Advanced Exercise Design for the Lower Body *and* Advanced Exercise Design for the Upper Body.

The human body is a magnificent, extremely sophisticated machine. Its many parts (bones, joints, muscles, connective tissue, nerves, vessels and organs) can produce an infinite number of movements, positions and postures. Kinesiology is the study of those movements and postures and is grounded in the principles of two sciences: anatomy and mechanics. To understand human movement, you must know the physical structure of the component parts (bones, joints, muscles) and how the physical laws of motion govern that structure (mechanics). The goal is to understand how the component parts work together to provide the stability and mobility needed for effective human performance in sports and the activities of daily living. Applying the principles of biomechanics (mechanics applied to living things) and **kinesiology** will enable you to design exercise programs that are safe, effective and compatible with the body's function and design.

BIOMECHANICS

Motion is a change in an object's position in relation to another object. It is necessary to choose a reference point to determine whether an object is moving or at rest. For example, a sleeping baby in a car traveling 30 mph is at rest if the car seat is the reference point. If the road is the reference point, however, the baby is in motion.

To avoid confusion it also is necessary to choose a reference point to analyze the motion of the body and its parts. We use two primary reference points in the body: the joints and segments. Segments are body parts between two joints (bones). For example, the upper arm segment is between the shoulder and elbow, the lower leg segment is between the knee and ankle joints.

Four Types of Motion

There are four basic types of motion: translatory, rotary, curvilinear and general plane motion (Figures 3.1 and 3.2).

When an object in motion is not tied down anywhere and moves in a straight line, it moves in translatory or linear motion; all parts move in the same direction and at the same speed.

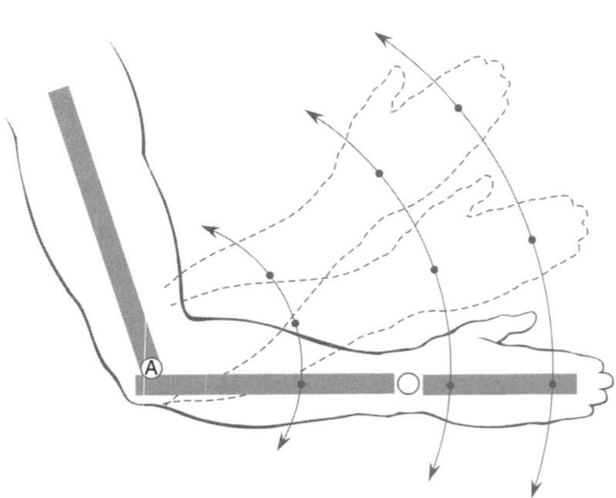

FIGURE 3.1
Rotary motion. Each point in the forearm/hand segment follows the same angle, at a constant distance from the axis of rotation (A), and at the same time.

If the object is tied down at a fixed point, it turns around that fixed point in rotary (angular) motion, much like a tetherball. Body segments generally move in rotary motion as they rotate around the joint at one end (the fixed point). However, many human movements combine translatory and rotary movements to accomplish such a task as reaching for an object. In this case, the forearm and hand move straight forward because of rotary motion at the shoulder and elbow. This creates a third type of motion: curvilinear motion, which is similar to the path of a ball thrown through the air. A small gliding motion within the joint (linear or translatory) combines with the more obvious rotary motion of the segment. The gliding within the joint slightly changes the axis of rotation throughout the movement, particularly at the knee and shoulder, and is an important part of normal movement patterns.

When motions at various joints are sim-

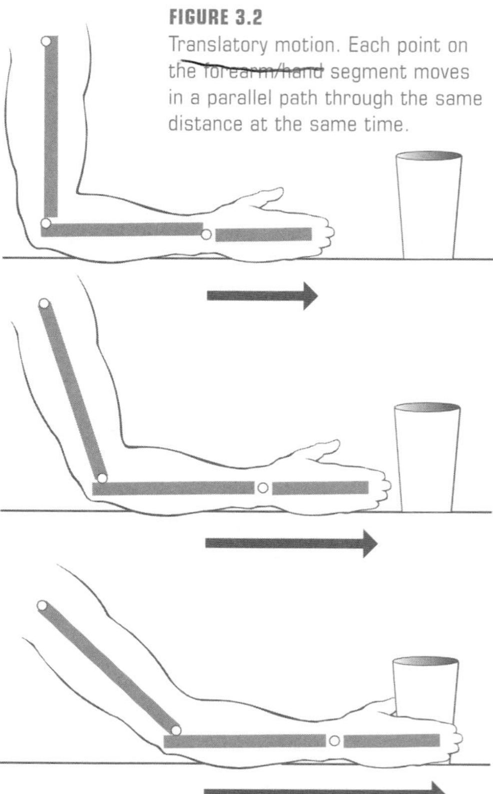

FIGURE 3.2
Translatory motion. Each point on the forearm/hand segment moves in a parallel path through the same distance at the same time.

Table 3.1
Fundamental Movements (from Anatomical Position)

Plane	Action	Definition
Sagittal	Flexion	Decreasing the angle between two bones
	Extension	Increasing the angle between two bones
	Hyperextension	Increasing the angle between two bones beyond anatomical position (continuing extension past neutral)
	Dorsiflexion	Moving the top of the foot toward the shin (ankle only)
	Plantarflexion	Moving the sole of the foot downward (ankle only)
Frontal	Abduction	Motion away from the midline of the body (or body part)
	Adduction	Motion toward the midline of the body (or body part)
	Elevation	Moving the scapula to a superior position
	Depression	Moving the scapula to an inferior position
	Inversion	Lifting the medial border of the foot (subtalar joint only)
	Eversion	Lifting the lateral border of the foot (subtalar joint only)
Transverse	Rotation	Medial (inward) or lateral (outward) turning about the vertical axis of bone in the transverse plane
	Pronation	Rotating the hand and wrist from the elbow to the palm down position (elbow flexed) or back (elbow extended)
	Supination	Rotating the hand and wrist from the elbow to the palm up position (elbow flexed) or forward (elbow extended)
	Horizontal flexion (horizontal adduction)	From a 90-degree abducted arm position, the humerus moves toward the midline of the body in the transverse plane
	Horizontal extension (horizontal abduction)	The return of the humerus from horizontal flexion (adduction) to 90-degree abduction
Multiplanar	Circumduction	Motion that describes a "cone"; combines flexion, abduction, extension and adduction in sequential order
	Opposition	Thumb movement unique to primates and humans that follows a semicircle toward the little finger

ultaneously linear and rotary, "general plane motion" occurs. The whole body is in linear motion when we ride a bicycle, some body segments also experience rotary motion around the joints (hips, knees, ankles). The body as a whole undergoes rotary motion during a somersault or a cartwheel. At the same time, we are in linear motion across the floor.

Forces and Motion

A force is something that tends to cause motion. Simply stated it is a push or pull exerted by one object or substance on another. A force can be external to the body, such as gravity (the pull of the earth on a body), water, air (wind), other objects or other people. Muscular forces are considered internal forces when the body as a

Biomechanics

whole is the reference point. However, when the joint or joint axis is the reference point, muscular forces are classified as "external" because they act outside the joint itself.

In describing human movement, we often refer to motive and resistive forces. A **motive force** causes an increase in speed or a change in direction. A **resistive force** resists the motion of another external force.

In weight training the contracting muscle may be the motive force (tending to cause motion) and gravity (acting on the body segment and the dumbbell) is the resistive force (resists the motion of the motive force). This occurs in the up-phase of a lifting motion such as a "biceps curl." The contraction of the elbow flexors tends to cause upward motion of the forearm, and the force of gravity of the dumbbell and the arm tend to resist the upward movement. In the return phase of the same biceps curl the opposite occurs: the motive force is gravity which tends to cause downward motion. The elbow flexor contraction in the return phase tends to resist the downward motion and is the resistive force.

There are several terms used in kinesiology to describe the various muscular actions described above. When the muscle acts as the motive force, it shortens as it creates muscle tension. This is called a **concentric action**. When the muscle acts as the resistive force, it lengthens as it creates muscle tension. This is called **eccentric action**. When muscle tension is created but no apparent change in length occurs, the muscle action is called **isometric**. These terms are explained further on pages 77 and 80-81 (see Terms for Type of

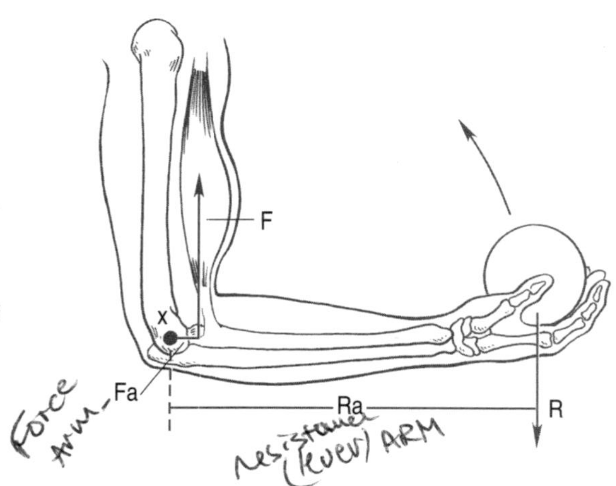

FIGURE 3.3
Example of a lever system in the human body.
X = axis of rotation; F (biceps contraction) = motive force; R (weight in hand) = resistance; Fa (biceps force x distance of biceps attachment from axis) = lever arm of the motive force; Ra (weight x distance from axis) = lever arm of the resistance.

Sample Torque Calculation

A client holding a weight in their hand is asked to hold it steady at 90 degrees of elbow flexion. The force of the weight and the arm segment is considered to be 10 pounds. The elbow flexors are considered to act at a perpendicular distance from the elbow joint of 2 inches. The lever arm length of the weight + the arm segment is 15 inches. What is the torque of the elbow flexors in a balanced system? To calculate the torque of the elbow flexors, solve the following equation:

R x Ra = F x Fa

10 pounds x 15 inches = 150 pound-inches

In the balanced system the torque of the resistance and the torque of the elbow flexors would be equal at 150 pound-inches.

To answer the question of how much force must be created by the elbow flexors to hold the 10 pound weight steady, solve for F:

R x Ra = F x Fa

10 pounds x 15 inches = F x 2 inches

150 pound-inches = 2F

150 pound-inches / 2 inches = F

75 pounds = F

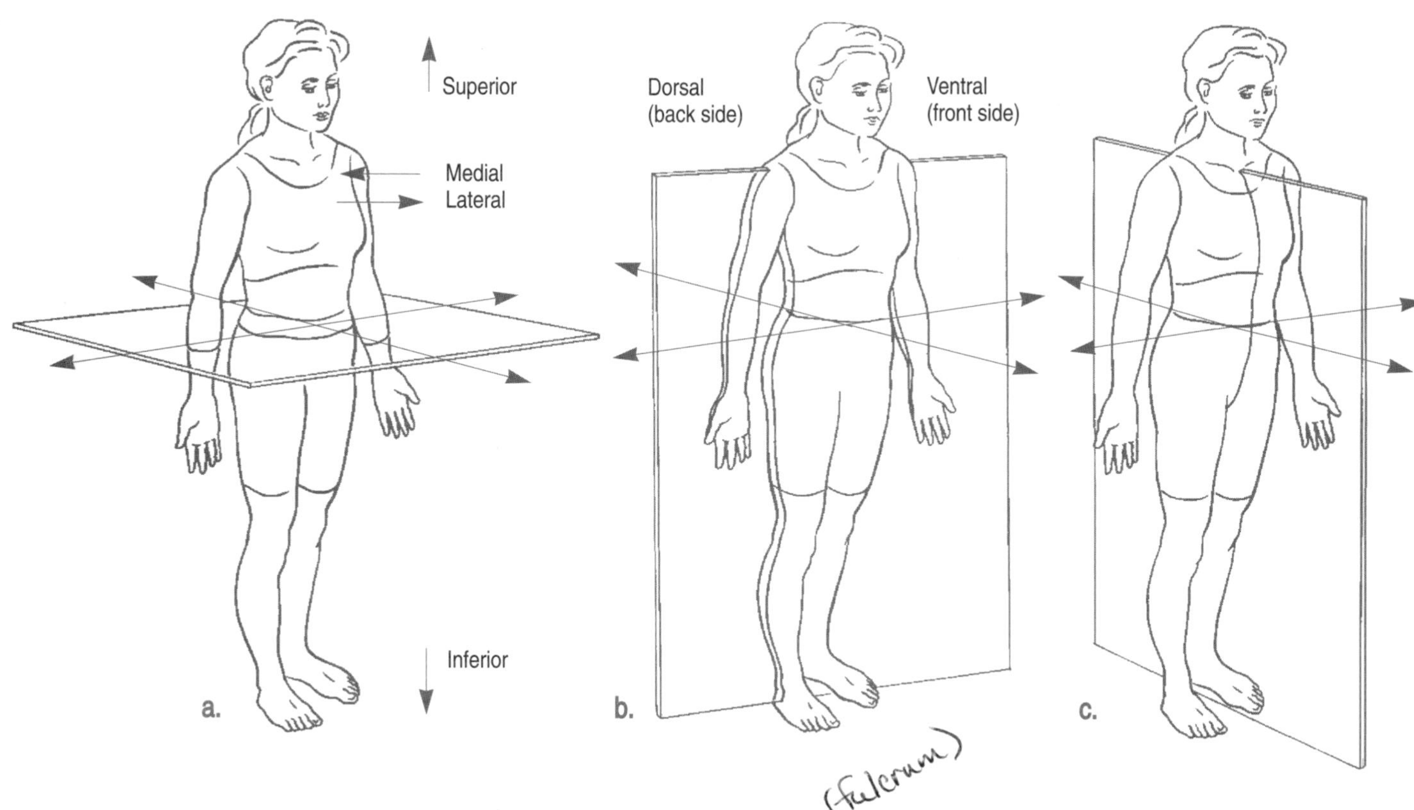

FIGURE 3.4
a. Transverse plane.
b. Frontal plane.
c. Sagittal plane.

Muscular Action).

We often refer to the tools we use in strength training, such as free weights, variable-resistance machines, elastic bands or tubing, manual resistance and body weight, as "resistance." It is important to remember, though, that they are the resistive force in one phase of the movement and the motive force in the other phase.

Levers and Torque

Body segments work as a system of levers as they rotate around the joints. A **lever** is a rigid bar with a fixed point around which it rotates when an external force is applied. The fixed point is called its **fulcrum**. In general, the center of a joint acts as a fulcrum for rotary motion of the body segments.

Rotary motion occurs in one of three planes of motion (Figure 3.4). When the body is in anatomical position **flexion** and **extension** occur in the sagittal plane, **abduction** and **adduction** occur in the frontal plane, and internal and external rotation occur in the transverse plane.

The **axis of rotation** is the imaginary line or point about which the lever rotates. It intersects the center of the joint (Figure 3.3) and is perpendicular to the plane of movement. The axis of rotation is in the frontal or coronal plane (side-to-side) for movements occurring in the sagittal plane. The axis of rotation is in the sagittal plane (anterior-posterior) for movements occurring in the frontal plane. The axis of rotation is called longitudinal (superior-inferior) for movements occurring in the transverse plane.

For rotation to occur, the motive force must contact the lever at some distance from the axis of rotation. If the motive force passes through the axis of rotation no movement will occur.

The perpendicular distance from the axis of rotation to the line of applied force is called a **lever arm**. The lever arm length of the motive force (F) is the force arm (Fa). The lever arm length of the resistance (R) is the resistance arm (Ra). Equilibrium occurs (the lever is in balance) if the force times the force arm equals the resistance times the resistance arm (F x Fa = R x Ra).

When a force acts on a lever at some distance from the axis of rotation a turning effect occurs. This turning effect is called **torque**. The magnitude of torque is found by multiplying the amount of force by the length of the lever arm (perpendicular distance from the axis of rotation). Therefore, F x Fa is the torque of the motive force, and R x Ra is the torque of the resistance. Rotation occurs in the direction of the greater torque.

PHYSICAL LAWS AFFECTING MOTION

To understand forces and their effects on human movement, it helps to know the physical laws formulated by Sir Isaac Newton that govern the motion of all objects. They are the law of inertia, the law of acceleration and momentum, and the law of impact and reactive forces.

Inertia

The **law of inertia** states: A body at rest stays at rest, and a body in motion stays in motion with the same velocity and direction unless acted upon by an unbalanced force. In other words, force is required to start an object into motion and to decelerate or stop an object that is already moving.

A body's inertia is proportional to its mass. For example if you are lifting weights, a heavier weight requires more force both to set it in motion and to slow down or stop its motion than a light weight does.

Acceleration and Momentum

Newton's second law is the **law of acceleration**. It states that the force (F) acting on a body moving in a given direction is equal to the body's mass (m) multiplied by the body's acceleration (a): F = ma. From this we can see that the acceleration of a body is proportional to the magnitude of the force applied: a = F/m. So, a body's acceleration depends on how hard you push it, divided by its mass. The harder you push or pull something, the faster it will accelerate in the direction of the force.

The second law also relates to a moving body's momentum. Linear or angular momentum is the quantity of motion which a moving body possesses, and is equal to its mass times its velocity. This means that a body's momentum can increase in two ways: by increasing its mass or increasing its velocity. So, when lifting a 10-pound weight and then a 20-pound weight at the same velocity, the 20-pound weight will have more momentum. If you lift a 10-pound weight at a slow speed, then a faster speed, the lift with the faster speed requires more force than the slower one even though the resistance is the same. As momentum increases, more force is also required to stop or change the motion.

Momentum can be a positive force when playing sports like football in which a player is racing down the field, hoping the opponents cannot match their momentum. However, in a progressive fitness-training program, your own body must be able to stop the momentum you create. Excessive momentum can cause injury, especially when working with weights, so strength training should occur at velocities that are under complete muscular control.

In other words, if you "cheat" by initiating a movement with momentum from a body part other than the one you are focusing on, the momentum of the moving weight may be greater than the muscle's ability to decelerate and stop it. The "stopping muscles" may not be strong enough to match the forces involved. If momentum resulting from an external force, rather than muscular force (internal), is used to lift a weight that's too heavy, the opposing muscles may not be strong enough to stop the motion. This may expose the ligaments, fascia and joints to over-stress and injury.

Physical Laws Affecting Motion

Impact and Reactive Forces

Newton's third law states that for every force applied by one body to a second, the second applies an equal force on the first, but in the opposite direction. Thus, for every action there is an equal and opposite reaction.

The third law applies to the impact forces that the body must absorb during activities such as running, jumping and high-impact aerobics. According to the **law of impact and reaction forces**, the earth exerts a force against the body that is equal to the force applied to the earth as one runs or jumps.

Overuse and stress injuries can result from the body's inability to withstand impact and reaction forces. Impact on the feet and body mounts quickly during impact activities, especially in larger people or during activities with high acceleration. Landing impact is the body's mass (m) multiplied by its acceleration (a). The body exerts a force (m • a) on the earth; the earth exerts an equal reactive force on the body that must be dissipated through its shock-absorbing structures. Injuries often occur when the body is misaligned so that the forces are not evenly distributed, or are concentrated in the tissues that were not designed to absorb such strong forces.

This further explains why overuse and stress injuries can also occur in weight-training activities which involve momentum: the force of the tissues involved in stopping the motion must match the mass of the weight and body segment multiplied by the acceleration of the weight and body segment.

Lever Classes

As mentioned previously, the body operates as a system of levers (rigid bars rotating around fixed points). If you possess knowledge of the types and mechanics of levers, you will better understand the motion and workings of the human body.

There are three classes of levers, each determined by the relative location of its axis, force and resistance. The first two classes are demonstrated primarily outside the body (Figure 3.5). Levers such as the crow bar and the wheelbarrow enable us to lift or push heavy objects with relatively small forces. In these levers, the motive force acts further away from the axis of rotation than the resistive force, allowing smaller forces to easily move large amounts of resistance. A mechanical advantage is utilized with a long lever arm. We use a relatively small amount of force at the end of a long lever arm to move a relatively large force at the end of a short lever arm.

Internally the body operates primarily as a series of third-class levers in which the force (F) acts between the axis (X) and the resistance (R), as in the example of the biceps action at the elbow in Figure 3.3. That is, the motive force has a short lever arm and the resistance has a long lever arm. In a third-class lever system, the motive force muscles are at a mechanical disadvantage and must create a strong force to lift small amounts of resistance.

Since muscle attachments are typically close to the joint and use a short lever arm, and the bones are relatively long, with resistance applied at the end (long lever arm), the forces necessary to lift even small weights are larger than we might imagine. For example, to abduct the arm to

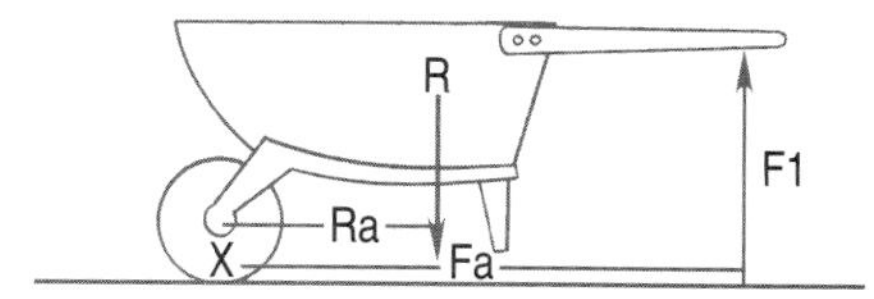

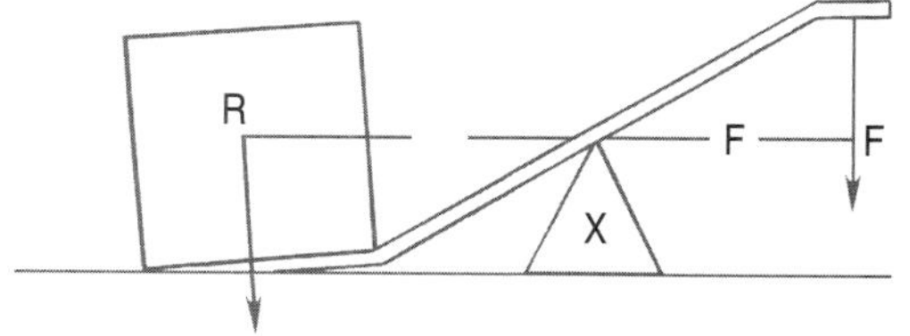

FIGURE 3.5
The first two classes of levers. X = axis of rotation (fulcrum); R = resistance load; F = effort force; Fa = lever arm distance from the force to the axis (force arm); Ra = lever arm distance from the resistance to the axis (resistance arm). The product of force and force lever arm balances the product of the resistance and resistance lever arm in this example (F x Fa = R x Ra); therefore, the resulting torques (turning effects) are equal.

Physical Laws Affecting Motion

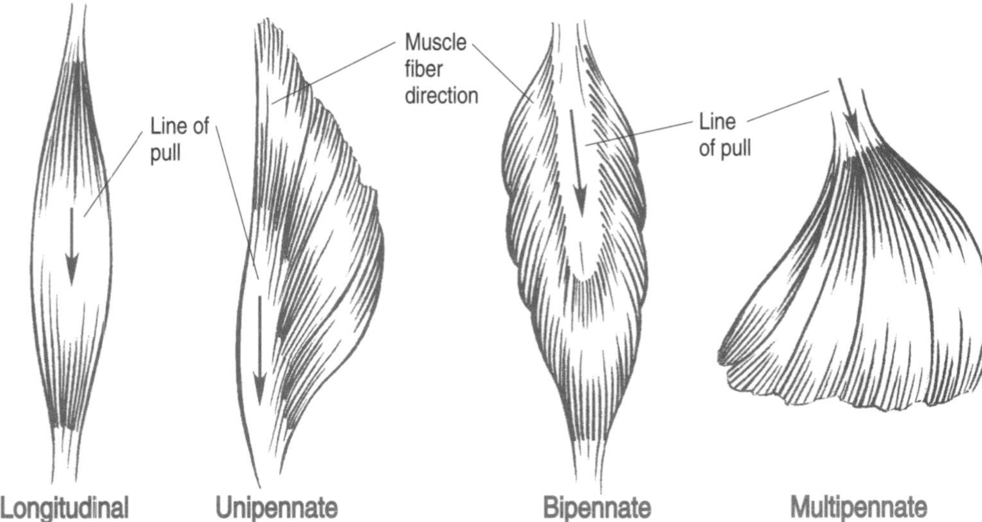

FIGURE 3.6
Muscle fiber arrangements.

80 degrees (lateral raise) with a 10-pound weight in the hand may require up to 300 pounds of tension in the deltoid. If the deltoid connected one inch farther down (longer lever arm for the motive force) and the arm were two inches shorter (shorter lever arm for the resistance), it would take much less muscular force to lift the same weight. This is why world-class weight lifters usually have relatively short arms and legs.

This is also why a lateral raise (abducting the shoulder to 80 degrees) is easier if we bend the elbow slightly or attach the weight higher on the arm. When the lever arm of the resistance is shortened, we can move it with much less tension in the deltoid. You can use the principles of levers when varying resistance for a client. To create more resistance with the same amount of weight, move the weight further from the working joint. To lessen the resistance as fatigue occurs, move the weight closer to the working joint.

Muscles and Force Production

Although the body's lever system puts the muscles at a mechanical disadvantage in terms of force production for lifting heavy weights, it is very conducive to force production when high velocities of motion are involved. Since force equals mass times acceleration, muscular forces of the shoulders and arms can create significant striking or throwing forces but relatively small lifting forces. A strong contraction of upper body muscles can provide considerable acceleration of the hand. With tools that extend the lever arm beyond the hand, such as an ax, significant forces can be achieved to accomplish a task such as splitting wood.

There also are anatomical and physiological factors that influence a muscle's ability to create force, such as the number and size of muscle fibers, fiber type and arrangement, as well as neurological training and recruitment.

There are several kinds of muscle fiber arrangements, including penniform (unipennate, bipennate, multipennate) and longitudinal (Figure 3.6). Penniform muscles are designed for higher force production than longitudinal muscles. Most muscles in the body are penniform muscles, in which the fibers lie diagonally to the line of pull. (The line of pull is generally thought of as a straight line between the muscle's two points of attachment.) A penniform muscle allows a greater number of fibers to be packaged into a given cross-sectional area, making it possible for more fibers to contribute to force production. The quadriceps is an example of a penniform muscle that can produce significant amounts of force. (Its attachments also are relatively far from the moving joints.)

Longitudinal muscles are long and thin and have parallel fibers that run in the same direction as the length of the muscle. This type of fiber arrangement allows for speed of contraction. However, since the cross section of a longitudinal muscle is small, its force of contraction is small. The sartorius and the rectus abdominis are examples of longitudinal muscles.

Anatomical, physiological and biomechanical factors play an important role in determining the appropriate resistance for a client and in designing their conditioning program. A muscle's structure will tell you much about its primary function and how it should be trained.

BALANCE AND ALIGNMENT

In order to understand human motion and design appropriate exercises, you must understand several other mechanical principles that relate to the body's balance and alignment: center of gravity, the line of gravity and base of support.

Center of Gravity

To track an object's motion we look at its center of gravity. In a rigid object of uniform density, like a baseball, this point is at its geometric center. The location of the center of gravity in the ever-changing human body is more difficult to find. The body's center of gravity is the point at which its mass is considered to concentrate and where it is balanced on either side in all planes (frontal, sagittal, transverse). We also consider gravity as enacting its constant downward pull through this point. Thus, a body's center of mass is considered to be its center of gravity.

In an average person this point is generally located at the level of the second sacral vertebra, but it changes from person to person, depending on their build. It also changes with a person's position in space and depends on whether they are supporting external weight. See Figures 3.7 a-d for various locations of a person's center of gravity.

Balance and Alignment

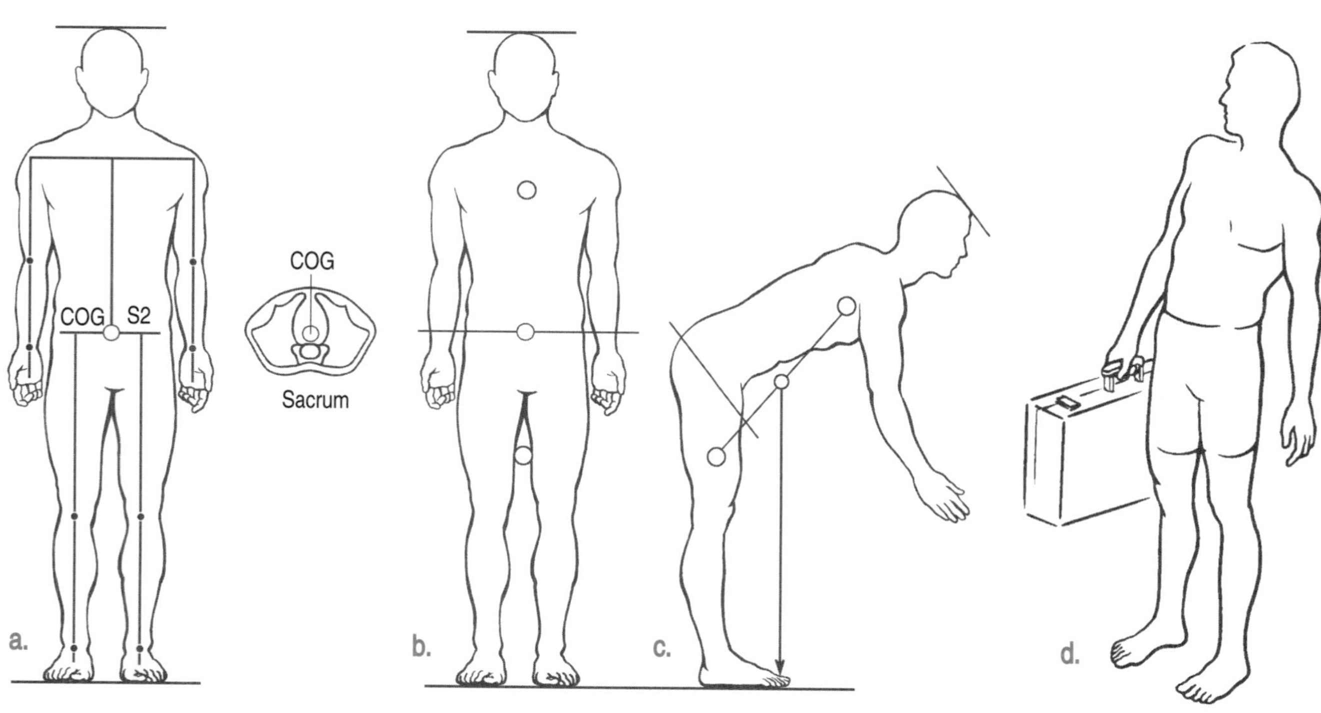

FIGURE 3.7
a. The center of gravity (COG) of the human body lies approximately at point S2, anterior to the sacrum (see inset).

b. and c. Location of the center of gravity in the upper trunk and lower limb segments.

d. The added weight of the suitcase to the shoulder girdle causes the center of gravity to shift up and to the right. The man leans laterally to the left to bring the line of gravity back to the middle of her base of support.

Line of Gravity and Base of Support

Gravity acts on a body in a straight line through its center of gravity toward the center of the earth. This line of gravitational pull is the line of gravity (Figure 3.8). To maintain balance without moving, a person's line of gravity must fall within the base of support. This is the area beneath the body that is encompassed when you connect, via one continuous line, all points of the body that are in contact with the ground (e.g., the space between the feet if a person is standing). A large, wide base of support is more stable than a small, narrow one. Thus, standing with one's feet apart and toes turned out is more stable than placing them parallel and close together. This is why a person with balance problems will automatically stand and walk with their feet apart. If you want to work on balance with a client, make their base of support more narrow to stimulate adaptation to the imposed demand.

To stand without excessive muscular effort or strain, the body parts must be equally distributed about the line of gravity (within the base of support). Such balanced, neutral alignment prevents excessive stress on muscles and ligaments. An important goal of exercise and training is to stimulate and reinforce neutral, symmetrical alignment about the line of gravity (static balance).

Linear and rotary motion of the whole body (walking, running, doing a flip or a dive) involve shifting the line of gravity beyond the base of support, then moving to re-establish a new base of support beneath it. The muscles exert forces to rotate and move, then re-establish equilibrium (dynamic balance).

POSTURE AND MUSCLE IMBALANCE

Neutral alignment occurs when the parts of the body are balanced and symmetrical around the line

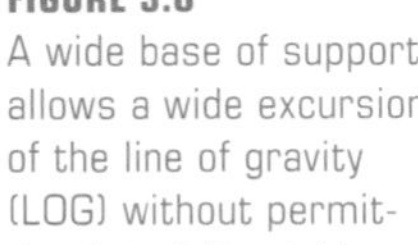

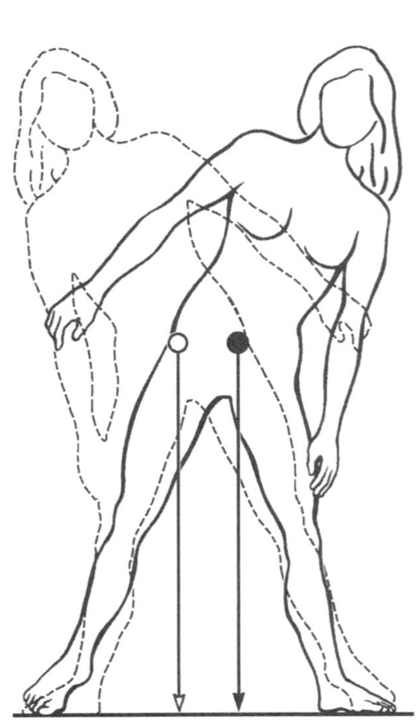

FIGURE 3.8
A wide base of support allows a wide excursion of the line of gravity (LOG) without permitting it to fall outside the base of support.

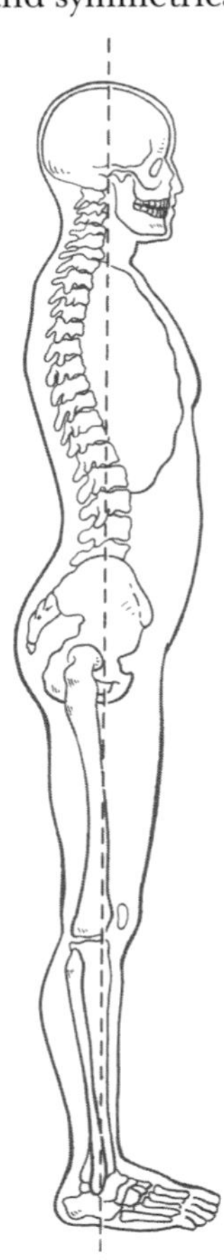

FIGURE 3.9
Ideal (neutral) alignment.

of gravity: the right and left halves of the body are mirror images of each other, and the body is balanced from the front to the back allowing the spine to display its natural curves. The ankles, knees, hips and shoulders are even and parallel to the floor (Figure 3.9), and there is a slight inward curve of the spine at the lumbar level, a slight outward curve of the spine at the thoracic level, and a slight inward curve at the cervical level. In neutral alignment the line of gravity is considered to pass just anterior to the ankle, through the center of the knee, hip and shoulder joints and through the external meatus of the ear. A client's alignment may be assessed by comparing it to the straight vertical line of a plumb line. A plumb line follows the line of gravity and is made by tying a weight to a string that is suspended from the ceiling.

Neutral alignment is an important consideration when working as a personal trainer. It is the position in which the spine is best equipped to deal with external stress and strain, so it is the safest position for lifting heavy objects, including weights and other tools used in strength training.

The ability to assume and maintain neutral alignment is an important neuromuscular skill that comes with repeated practice. Most acute and chronic injuries are caused by a person's inability to maintain neutral alignment during various activities. Therefore, building the strength, endurance and flexibility necessary to attain and hold neutral in all activities is the cornerstone to an effective and functional training program. It requires static and dynamic balance and coordination as well as muscular balance in all aspects of fitness: flexibility, strength and endurance, especially when adding resistance in various body positions and in various sports maneuvers.

Posture and Muscle Imbalance

Muscular imbalances manifest themselves in a person's posture and alignment, and are frequently influenced by work and standing, sitting and moving habits. For example, if a person sits most of the day (working, eating, driving, watching TV) they spend many hours with their back and shoulder blades in an unbalanced, (stretched) position, and their chest, hips and shoulders in an unbalanced, shortened position.

Habitual postures also influence a

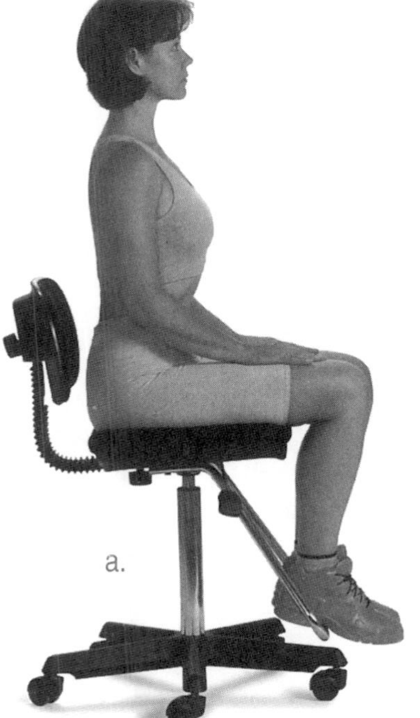

a.

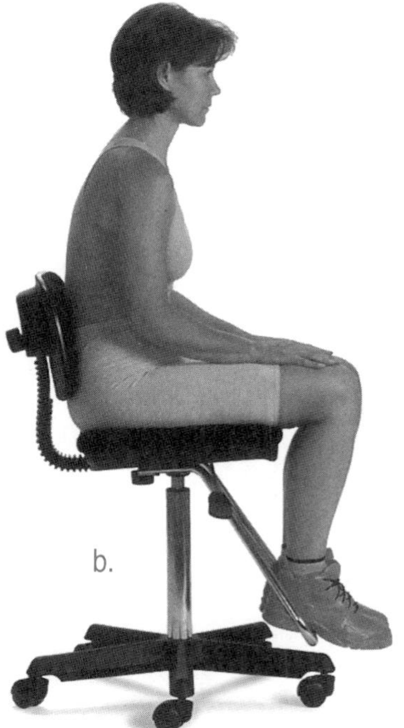

b.

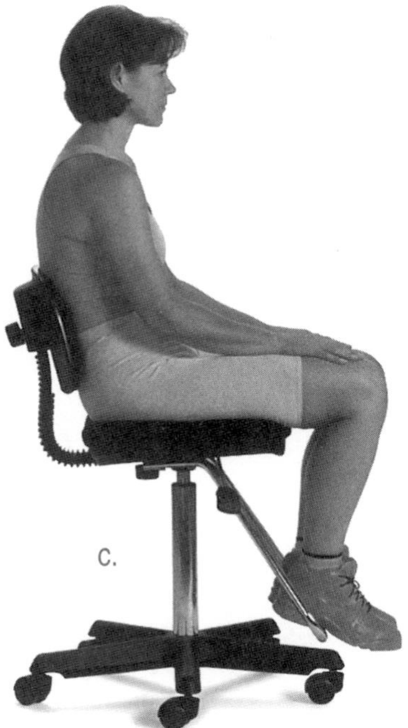

c.

FIGURE 3.10
Good alignment of the body in the sitting position can reduce or prevent pain associated with posture-related problems. Figure a. shows good alignment which allows for the greatest ease since it requires the least amount of muscle energy. Figure b. is sometimes mistaken for the correct sitting position, but in reality, the low back is in a lordosis, causing the muscles to fatigue. This position can only be maintained with effort. The slumped position in figure c. gives no support to the low back and results not only in strain, but also faulty position of the upper back, neck and head.

Posture and Muscle Imbalance

person's kinesthetic awareness, or their ability to know where their body is in space without looking. For example, many people sit with their head forward and chest collapsed (Figure 3.10). This position "feels right" to them, while correct alignment feels "unnatural." Their awareness of their own body alignment is inaccurate.

Allowing clients to observe their movements in a mirror or on video will help increase their awareness of correct and incorrect postures, and going through the full range of motion of the exercise several times, ending in the neutral position, can sharpen kinesthetic awareness.

There are several classic postural deviations that you should be able to recognize and describe: kyphosis-lordosis, flat back posture, sway-back posture, forward head posture and scoliosis. **Kyphosis-lordosis** (Figure 3.11) is an increase in the normal inward curve of the low back, often accompanied by a protruding abdomen and buttocks, increased flexion (outward curve) of the thoracic spine, rounded shoulders and a forward-tilted head. Flat back posture (Figure 3.12) is a decrease in the normal inward curve of the lower back, with the pelvis in posterior tilt. Sway-back posture (Figure 3.13) is a long outward curve of the thoracic spine with an an accentuated lumbar curve and a backward shift of the upper trunk. It is often accompanied by rounded shoulders, a sunken chest and a forward-tilted head. **Scoliosis** (Figure 3.14) is a lateral curve of the spine. There are usually two curves, on opposite sides of the spine, which compensate for each other.

Table 3.2 lists several common muscle imbalances that accompany postural misalignment. Use it after you are familiar with the various muscle groups and

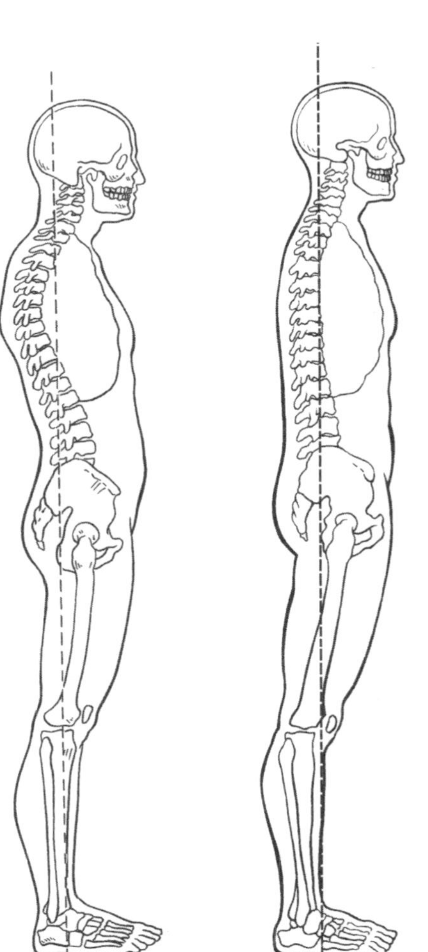

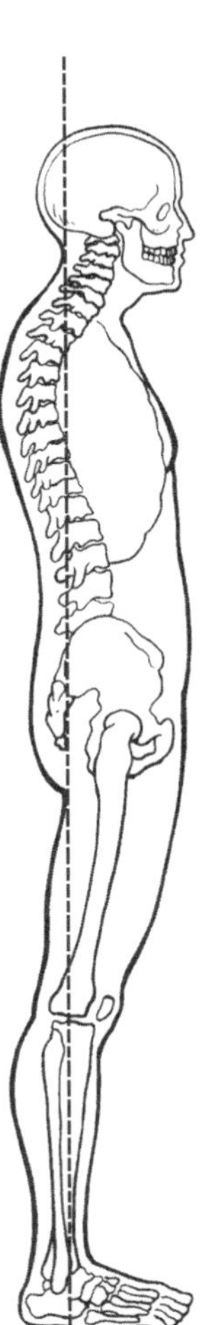

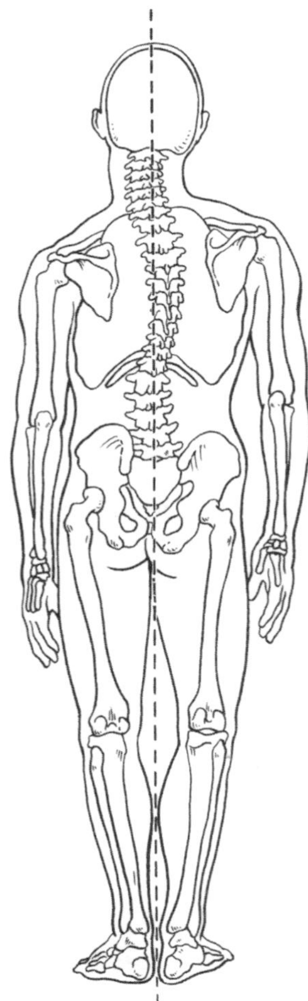

FIGURE 3.11
Kyphosis-lordosis posture.

FIGURE 3.12
Flat back posture.

FIGURE 3.13
Sway-back posture.

FIGURE 3.14
Scoliosis.

Table 3.2
Postural Deviations and Associated Muscle Imbalances

Malalignment	Possible Tight Muscles	Possible Weak Muscles
Lordosis	Lower back (erectors), hip flexors	Abdominals (especially obliques), hip extensors
Flat-back	Upper abdominals, hip extensors	Lower back (erectors), hip flexors
Sway-back	Upper abdominals, hip flexors	Oblique abdominals, hip extensors
Kyphosis	Internal oblique, shoulder adductors (pectorals and latissimus), intercostals	Erector spinae of the thoracic spine, scapular adductors (mid and lower trapezius)
Forward Head	Cervical extensors, upper trapezius	Neck flexors

their functions.

Postural deviations may be temporary or permanent. They can be changed with exercise if they are temporary and caused by muscle or **connective tissue** imbalances. However, if the deviations are due to abnormalities of the bones, exercise will not have a primary impact. Attention to postural deviations is important because over time, the tissues, including the bones, adapt to these postures, and cause the deviations to become irreversible. Clients with any of these conditions should be referred to a physician or therapist.

HUMAN MOTION TERMINOLOGY

Several terms are important to know when discussing human motion. They are usually one-word descriptions of movements, directions, relationships and positions, so that discussions can be concise. See Chapter 2 for a discussion of these terms.

There also are terms for muscle functions and the roles they play during movement. An **agonist** is a muscle that causes a desired motion and may also be called the prime mover. **Antagonists** are muscles that have the potential to oppose the action of the agonist. For example, if shoulder flexion is the desired action (without gravity as a factor), the shoulder flexors are the agonists and the shoulder extensors are the antagonists.

Synergist muscles assist the agonist in causing a desired action. They may act as joint stabilizers, or may neutralize rotation or come in when the external resistance increases, or the agonist becomes fatigued. The term **co-contraction** describes when the agonist and antagonists contract together and occurs when a joint must be stabilized. It is an important component of functional or usable strength because the torso muscles must be able to stabilize the spine to safely move external resistance. The muscles that co-contract to protect a joint and maintain alignment are called **stabilizers**. Stimulating strength and endurance of the stabilizers is a vital component of effective fitness training.

Terms for Types of Muscular Action

When a muscle contracts it develops tension or force as cross-bridges within muscle fibers are formed and broken. There are several types of muscle actions, named after the muscle's apparent length during the action. A muscle may actually shorten (come together), lengthen (away from the middle) or remain the same.

Static (Isometric) Action. In an **isometric action** no visible movement occurs, and the resistance matches the muscular tension. The resistance may come from the

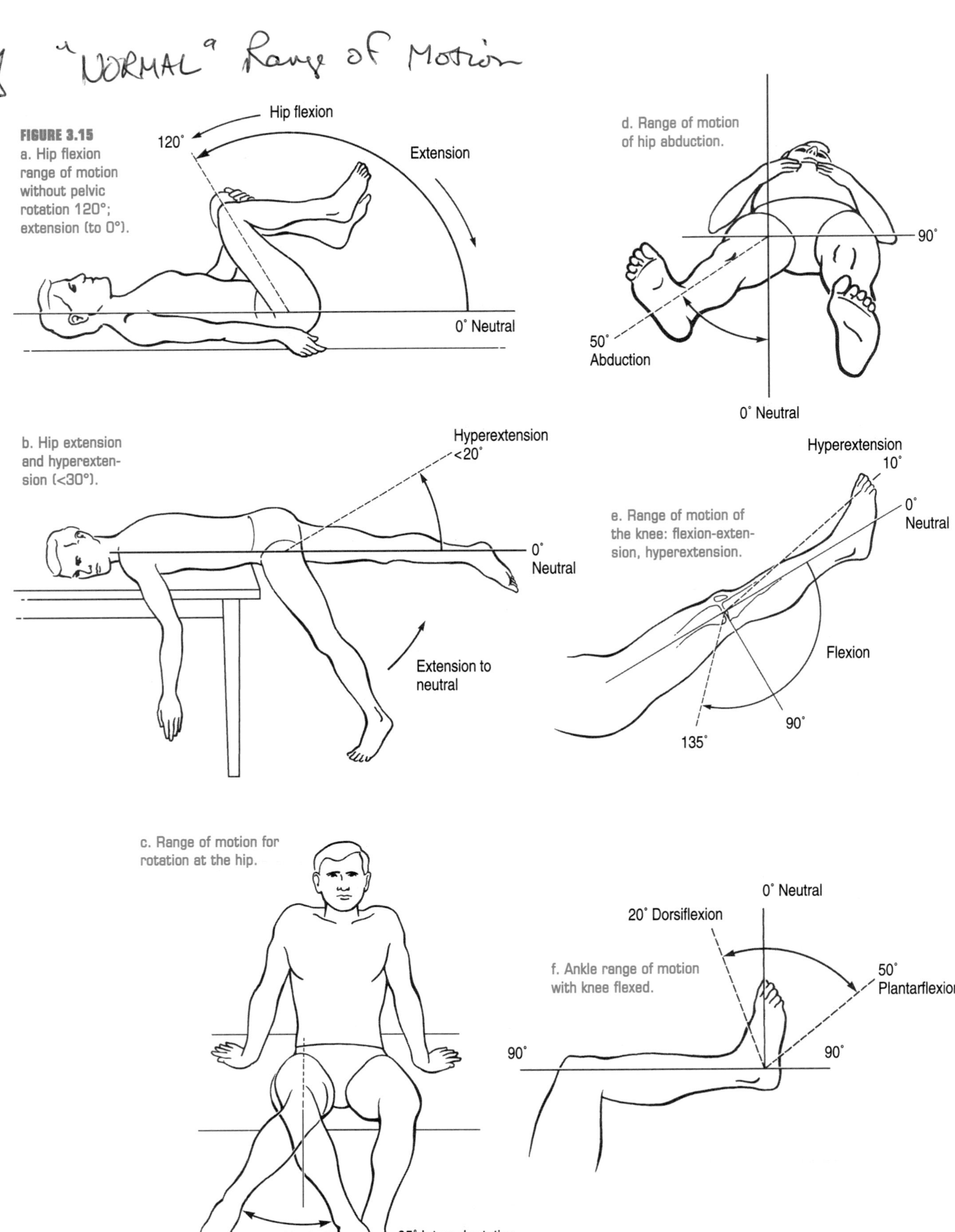

FIGURE 3.15
a. Hip flexion range of motion without pelvic rotation 120°; extension (to 0°).

Human Motion Terminology

Table 3.3
Lower Body Muscles — Functions and Selected Exercises

Muscle	Primary Function	Selected Exercises
Erector Spinae	Trunk extension, hyperextension, lateral flexion	S/E: Prone back hyperextension (Figure 3.17), squats, return to good sitting posture from flexion F: Supine knees to shoulders (Figure 3.18)
Rectus Abdominis	Flexion and lateral flexion of the spine	S/E: Standing and supine pelvic tilts with resistance, supine abdominal curl-ups, straight reverse abdominal curls, abdominal crunches
External Oblique	Lateral flexion of the spine	S/E: Holding neutral "press and reach," oblique abdominal curls, straight and oblique reverse abdominal curls, resisted pelvic tilts, straight abdominal curls with feet away from buttocks
Internal Oblique	Lateral trunk flexion	S/E: Holding neutral "press and reach," side-lying torso raises, supine pelvic tilts, oblique abdominal curls, reverse abdominal curls
Transverse Abdominis	Compresses abdominal viscera	S/E: Forceful expiration while lifting
Iliopsoas	Hip flexion and lateral rotation	S/E: Straight leg raises, bench-stepping, knee lifts F: Forward lunge with back knee bent, posterior pelvic tilt (Figure 3.24b)
Rectus Femoris	Hip flexion and knee extension	S/E: Squats, bench-stepping, lunges, lunge walk, standing straight-leg raise F: Standing, passive knee flexion holding to ankle, posterior pelvic tilt
Sartorius	Hip flexion, abduction and lateral rotation; knee flexion and medial rotation	S/E: Knee lift with hip external rotation, wide stance onto bench
Tensor Fasciae Latae	Hip flexion, medial rotation, abduction	S/E: Side-lying leg lifts with the hip slightly flexed and internally rotated F: Side-lying, hips extended; let top leg drop behind
Gluteus Maximus	Hip extension and lateral rotation	S/E: Bench-stepping, squats, lunges, resisted hip extension in standing, jumping
Biceps Femoris (hamstring)	Hip extension and knee flexion	S/E: Squat, lunge, dead lift F: (Figure 3.26) Standing stretch
Semitendinosus	Hip extension and knee flexion	S/E: Squat, lunge, dead lift
Semimembranosus	Hip extension and knee flexion	S/E: Same as for semitendinosus
Hip External Rotators	Hip lateral rotation	S/E: Maintain hips in neutral with arches of feet lifted F: (Figure 3.29) Supine crossover stretch
Adductor Magnus, Brevis and Longus	Hip adduction and rotation	S/E: Walking lunges

continued on next page

Human Motion Terminology

Table 3.3 continued

Muscle	Primary Function	Selected Exercises
Gracilis	Hip adduction, knee flexion and medial rotation	S/E: Same as for adductors
Pectineus	Hip flexion and internal rotation	S/E: Sitting, lift flexed knee toward opposite shoulder
Gluteus Medius and Minimus	Hip abduction, medial rotation	S/E: Standing leg raises to the side with elastic resistance
Quadriceps: Vastus Medialis, Intermedius and Lateralis	Knee extension	S/E: Resisted knee extension, straight leg raises, squats, one-legged squats, lunges, bench-stepping F: Same as rectus femoris
Gastrocnemius	Ankle plantarflexion and assists with knee flexion	S/E: Bilateral heel raises, unilateral heel raises F: Sitting hamstring stretch position + active dorsiflexion
Soleus	Ankle plantarflexion	S/E: Same as for gastrocnemius, bent-knee resisted heel raises, bi- & unilateral F: Same as for gastrocnemius with knee flexed
Posterior Tibialis	Foot inversion, assists with ankle plantarflexion	S/E: Resisted inversion with plantarflexion using elastic resistance
Anterior Tibialis	Ankle dorsiflexion, foot inversion	S/E: Resisted dorsiflexion with inversion, toe-tapping side to side
Peroneus Longus	Plantarflexion and eversion	S/E: Resisted eversion, alternate toe-and-heel lifts moving right and left
Peroneus Brevis	Plantarflexion and eversion	Same as for peroneus longus

S/E (Strength/Endurance): Exercises to improve strength and/or endurance of the muscle, depending upon the resistance and repetitions. Each exercise is not isolated to that particular muscle, as muscles work in groups to cause movement; however, the exercises listed would include the designated muscle as a prime mover.

F (Flexibility): Exercises to improve the flexibility of the designated muscle. Flexibility exercises do not stretch the muscle fiber itself, but are designed to lengthen the connective tissue associated with each particular muscle group. For maximum effectiveness, they should be performed after the muscle group is thoroughly warmed.

opposing muscle group (co-contraction) or from another force such as gravity, an immovable object or weight-training equipment. Bodybuilders use isometric action when striking a pose to show their muscle development, and physical therapists use isometrics in rehabilitation following an injury when a joint must not move. Isometric action also is used in PNF stretching techniques (see Chapter 10). Isometric muscle action can be used in balance and stabilization training and may be included in strengthening programs. Holding the torso upright in neutral position during a V-sit exercise, or a brief hold at the top of a push-up are good examples. If isometric methods are used, the client must be able to take deep, fluid breaths throughout the individual muscle action. (See Chapter 8 for further discussion on isometric action.)

Concentric (Shortening) Action. In a **concentric action** the muscle shortens and overcomes the resistive force. For example, the biceps brachii acts concentrically in the upphase of a biceps curl with a dumbbell.

Eccentric (Lengthening) Action. In an **eccentric action** the muscle is producing force and is "lengthening," or returning to its resting length from a shortened position. The muscle "gives in" to, or is overwhelmed by, the external force, and it can be thought of as "putting on the brakes," or slowing the descent of a weight, like lowering a piano out of a second-story window with a rope.

An eccentric action occurs when an external force exceeds the contractile force generated by a muscle. For example, the biceps brachii acts eccentrically in the return phase of a biceps curl performed with a dumbbell.

An understanding of muscle actions is crucial to exercise analysis. Joint motion alone does not accurately reveal the muscle causing that motion.

MUSCLES AND MOVEMENTS OF THE PELVIS AND LOWER EXTREMITY

Movements of the lower body include motion of the lumbar spine, pelvis, hip, knee and ankle joints. Figure 3.15 represents the movements of the lower body and the "normal" range of motion at each joint. The range of motion required for specific sports or activities such as dance, martial arts or gymnastics may vary greatly and go beyond what is considered the "normal" range of motion.

The normal ranges of motion pictured in Figure 3.15 serve as the functional range of motion for most people, but when working with clients, you will find that the range of possible movement varies from person to person. It is determined by their individual bone and joint structure, muscle mass and soft tissue flexibility. If an individual's range is less than average, they probably need to work on flexibility.

Table 3.3 summarizes the muscles and movements of the lower body along with selected exercises for each.

Pelvis and Lumbar Spine

To teach a client to maintain neutral

Muscles and Movements of the Pelvis and Lower Extremity

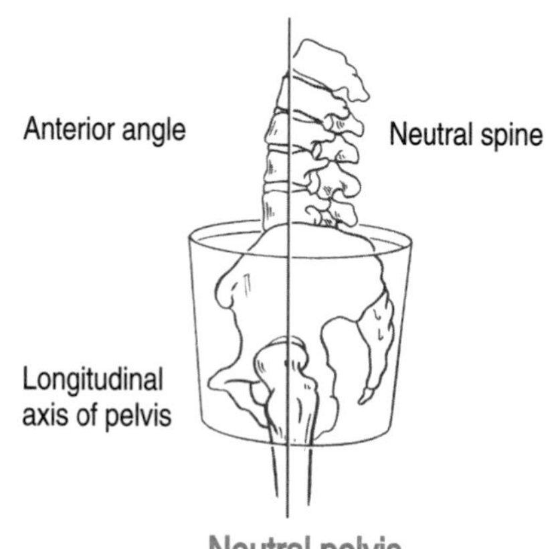

FIGURE 3.16
a. Neutral lumbar spine with neutral pelvis.

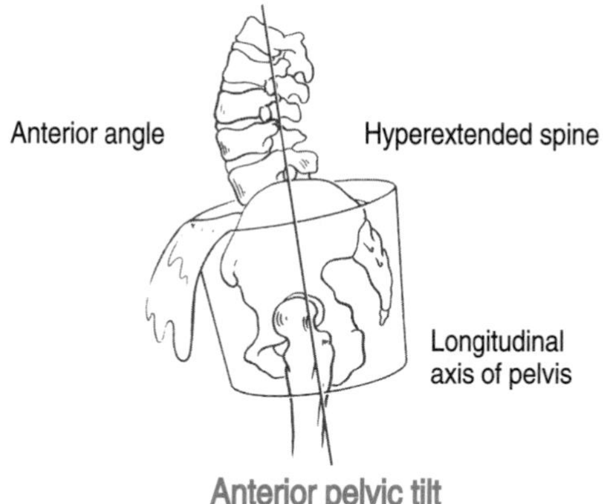

b. Lumbar hyperextension with anterior pelvic tilt.

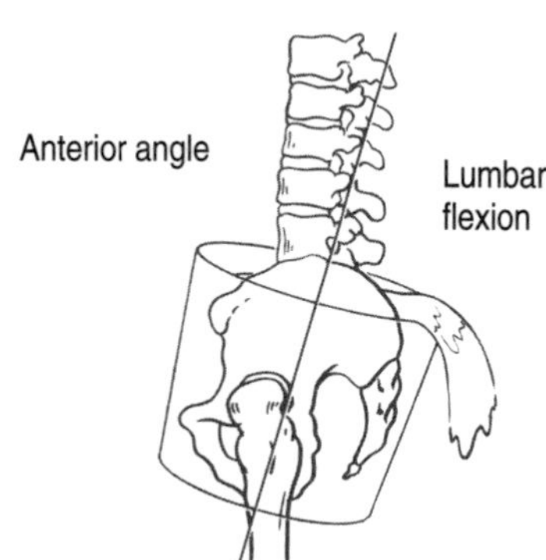

c. Slight lumbar flexion with posterior pelvic tilt.

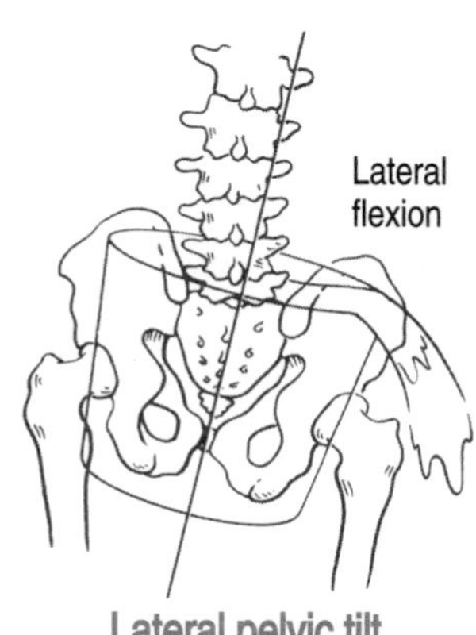

d. Lateral lumbar flexion with lateral pelvic tilt.

Muscles and Movements of the Pelvis and Lower Extremity

alignment you must understand pelvis and lower back movements and how the two relate. Neutral position of the lumbar spine and pelvis is the central position, not flexed, extended, tilted or rotated.

Pelvic motion is called tilt and can be anterior, posterior or lateral (Figure 3.16). If we think of the pelvis as a bucket, then the anterior tilt is like tipping the bucket forward and spilling the water in front. It is associated with increased hip flexion and low-back **hyperextension**. The posterior tilt is tipping the bucket backward and spilling the water behind. It is associated with hip hyperextension and flexion of the low back at the lumbosacral joint. A lateral tilt is like lifting the hip to walk with a stiff knee; the pelvis would be tipped to the side. In neutral, the bucket would be straight up, not tipped in any direction. The pelvis can also rotate, which is important to normal walking. Pelvic rotation is like grasping the rim of the bucket and twisting back and forth.

Motion of the lumbar spine includes flexion, extension, hyperextension, lateral flexion and rotation. Flexion is bending forward; extension is the return to neutral; hyperextension is further extension backward past the neutral position; lateral flexion is bending toward the side, away from the midline; and rotation is a twist, clockwise or counterclockwise, around the axis of the spine. Motion of the pelvis and the lumbar spine occur together. Therefore, the muscles responsible for lumbar motion also will cause pelvic motion. For example, the abdominals flex the spine, and posteriorly tilt the pelvis. It is important to include all these lumbar spine and pelvis motions in a training program, but progressive loads must be carefully integrated.

There is nothing inherently wrong or unsafe about any spinal motion under normal circumstances. It is when static positions are maintained for long periods of time, such as sitting forward flexed at your desk all day, week after week, that problems occur. For example, constant spinal flexion loads the discs unevenly, overstretches the posterior ligaments of the back and causes poor alignment of the upper body as well (upper spine, head, neck and shoulders). The likeliness of problems increases if the spine is overloaded (lifting weights) when it is out of the neutral position. The spine is designed to bear loads and stresses in neutral; if it is not aligned properly those loads and stresses are transmitted unevenly and transferred to structures which were not designed for load-bearing.

Pelvic and lower back movement can also be caused by hip muscles that attach to the pelvis. If the hamstrings (hip extensors) are tight, they can cause the pelvis to tilt posteriorly and the lumbar spine to flex. Likewise, if the hip flexors are tight, they can cause the pelvis to tilt anteriorly and the lumbar spine to hyperextend (Figures 3.11 and 3.12). Therefore, an effective training program for the lower back and pelvis must also include strength and flexibility training for the hip muscles: flexors, extensors, abductors, adductors and rotators. Weak or tight hip/pelvic

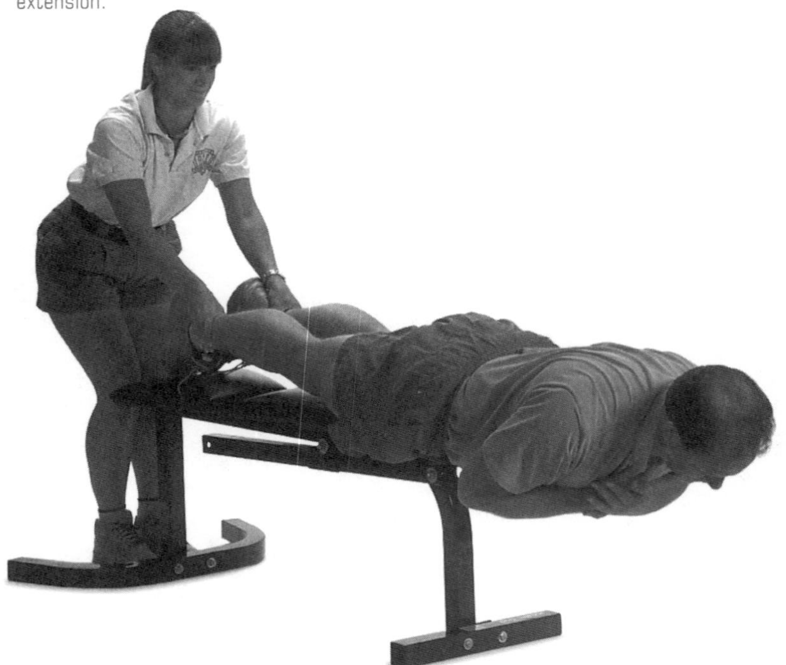

FIGURE 3.17
Active spinal extension.

muscles can have a significant impact on the spine.

Lumbar Extensors: Erector Spinae

The erector spinae group has three main divisions (lateral, medial and intermediate) and extends from the sacrum to the occiput. These muscles attach to the transverse and spinous processes of all vertebrae. The muscle is large in the lumbosacral region, but divides into several segments (iliocostalis, longissimus and spinalis) as it continues upward toward the head. The erector spinae muscles extend, hyperextend and laterally flex the spine. When standing in neutral alignment, the activity of this muscle is very low, but it is active in the upright position as the spine flexes forward (eccentric contraction) and when it extends again to neutral (concentric contraction).

To strengthen the erector spinae muscles, use an extension machine, or have the client flex forward over the edge of a bench or table for full range of motion (Figure 3.17); you will have to help them stabilize their legs in the prone position. Begin with the client's arms at the side (short lever arm), and progress to crossing them on the chest or overhead (increases lever arm length). Slowly hyperextend the spine from the prone (face down) position.

To stretch the erector spinae, have the client lie supine with their hips and knees flexed toward the shoulders. You may gently assist them by pressing upward from beneath the hips (Figure 3.18).

An important part of training the lumbar muscles is holding the lower back in

Muscles and Movements of the Pelvis and Lower Extremity

FIGURE 3.18
Erector spinae stretch.

a. Stand close to the object with a wide stance. Bend knees to lower yourself to the object and keep the curve in the low back.

b. Lean back to keep your balance and lift by straightening the knees. Do not jerk up.

c. When upright, pivot with your feet; do not twist your low back.

FIGURE 3.19
Correct lifting technique.

neutral when lifting heavy objects and when performing squats and lunges, particularly when using resistance. When the lower back is in neutral during a lift the spinal muscles co-contract with other torso muscles to stabilize the back, keeping the load evenly distributed over the spinal structures. The actual lifting is performed by the larger, more powerful hip and knee extensors (Figure 3.19).

If the spine is flexed while lifting a heavy object, the erector spinae muscles must generate tremendous force. Consider the biomechanics of lifting with the spine in flexion: the weight held by the arms is relatively far from the fulcrum of motion, the lumbar spine (long lever arm). The spinal extensors are very close to the fulcrum of motion (short lever arm). The spinal extensors are small muscles with a relatively small cross-section and are not designed for high force production. Let's say a person must lift a large box and the combined weight of the box and the upper body is 100 pounds. If the box is held where the total lever arm length is 10 inches long, the torque of the resistance is 1,000. If the spinal extensors act with a lever arm of 2 inches, their force production must be more than 500 pounds in order to lift the box by themselves. These muscles are easily strained in such a lift. The discs and posterior ligaments also are at high risk. For safety, keep the spine neutral and use the larger thigh muscles to lift heavy loads.

Lumbar Flexors: Posterior Tilters of the Pelvis

Various abdominal muscles are responsible for trunk flexion and stabilization. Let's consider the structure and location of the various abdominal muscles which relates to their purpose and effective training.

The most **superficial** of the abdominal muscles are the external obliques. They arise from the outer surfaces of ribs 5 through 12, extend toward the midline of the abdomen and insert into a broad, flat **aponeurosis**. This aponeurosis forms the outer layer of the connective-tissue sheath that covers the rectus abdominus muscle. The attachments to the ribs reach around the torso toward the back. The uppermost fibers interdigitate with the serratus anterior. The direction of the anterior fibers is diagonal, like putting your hands in your pockets, forward and downward toward the center, but ending several centimeters from it. This muscle also has **lateral** fibers that are more vertically aligned, between the ribs and the iliac crests (Figure 3.20).

The internal obliques are beneath the external obliques. Their fibers also run

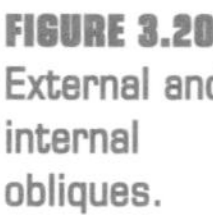
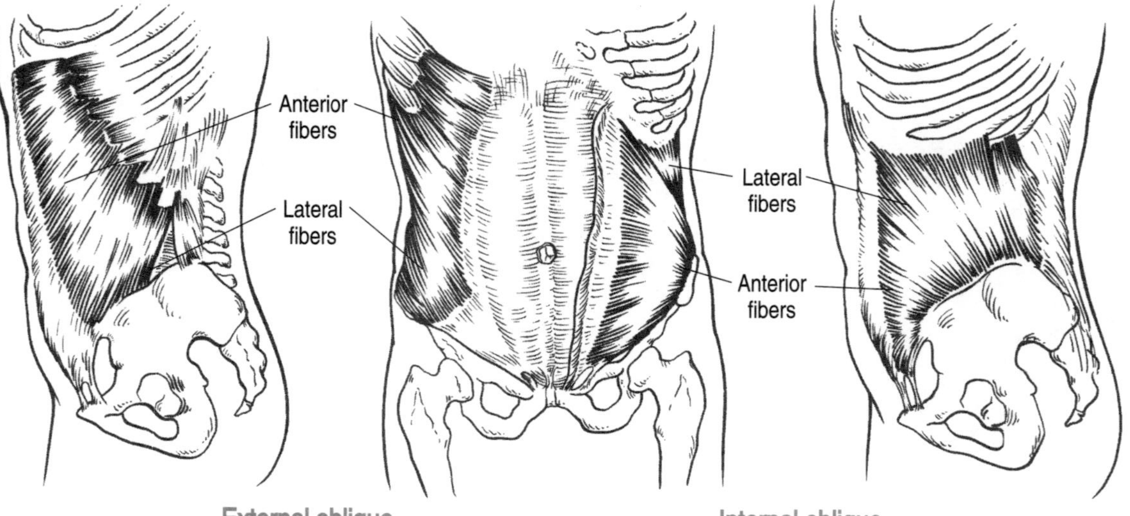

FIGURE 3.20 External and internal obliques.

diagonally, but in the opposite direction, like an inverted V. The muscles arise from various parts of the pelvis: the inguinal ligaments, iliac crests and the lumbar aponeurosis. The fibers attach to the lower ribs and into the aponeurosis which forms the connective-tissue sheath around the rectus abdominis.

The obliques are thin muscles, not designed for high force production. The right and left sides of the internal and external obliques connect into the same aponeurosis, and with their other connections to the back and pelvis they essentially form a continual wrap around the torso, enclosing the internal structures, including the vertebrae, in a protective support.

The fibers of the rectus abdominus run vertically from the sternum and upper ribs to the pubic bone. The rectus abdominis is a longitudinal, or "strap-like" muscle, designed for long, smooth movement.

The deepest abdominal muscle is the transversus abdominis. Its fiber direction is essentially horizontal, extending from the inner surfaces of the lower 6 ribs, the thoracolumbar fascia, internal surfaces of the iliac crest, and the inguinal ligaments to the linea alba by means of an aponeurosis. Its primary function is forced expiration such as coughing or sneezing, and it acts as a girdle to flatten the abdominal wall and compress the abdominal viscera.

We usually think of the abdominals as serving two functions: flexing the spine and providing support for the lower back. The rectus is the primary spinal flexor, however, it only flexes the spine in the **supine** position or in returning the torso to the upright position from hyperextension. In the upright posture, flexion is controlled by eccentric contraction of the back extensors as they lower the weight of the torso in the same direction as gravity. The rectus is seldom used in the upright position. According to electromyograph (EMG) studies, it is not active when straining or lifting. What seems to be a rectus abdominis contraction during these activities (except coughing) is just a passive bulging of the muscles and their sheaths (Basmajian, Floyd and Silver).

EMG studies show that the active muscles in such lifting and straining actions are the obliques. The pattern is the same with forced expiration and singing: the obliques are active, the rectus is quiet. The obliques also have a function in upright movement because as you lean or twist sideways the obliques on the opposite side contract to control the motion.

It is the obliques and the sheath of the rectus (formed by the aponeuroses of the external and internal obliques and the transversus), that protects the abdominal area during the functions of straining, lifting, bearing down, sneezing and forced expiration. It seems logical, then, to focus training time on the obliques as well as the rectus abdominis.

Injuries occur when we fail to stabilize the torso as we push, pull or lift or move large objects. We need "torso-stabilizing strength," not "torso-moving strength," to keep gravity from constantly pulling us out of neutral while sitting or standing.

One way to train the abdominals to stabilize the pelvis against the changing resistance of moving arms and legs is the press-and-reach exercise (Figure 3.21). Have the

a. Lie supine with the back flat and the shoulders and hips flexed.

b. Raise both arms overhead and straighten one leg toward the floor.

FIGURE 3.21
Abdominal training.

Muscles and Movements of the Pelvis and Lower Extremity

client lie supine with their back flat, and shoulders and hips flexed to 90 degrees. Focus on keeping the back flat during the arm and leg movement (which will tend to pull the back off the floor). Simultaneously raise both arms overhead and straighten one leg toward the floor; the movements should be slow and smooth. Return to the starting position and repeat, lifting both arms and straightening the opposite leg. Continue as long as the abdominals can keep the back flat. To overload, use enough resistance to fatigue the abdominals in one to two minutes.

Muscles Acting to Tilt the Pelvis

Active anterior pelvic tilt is achieved by contraction of the iliopsoas muscle and/or the lower back muscles, depending on the body's position relative to gravity. The fact that the iliopsoas originates on the lumbar vertebrae tells us that it exerts a force on the pelvis as well as on the hip joint. When the hips are extended, as when standing, this muscle is too short and it passively pulls the pelvis into an anterior tilt.

The antagonists to the iliopsoas at the pelvis are those muscles that tilt the pelvis posteriorly, primarily the abdominals.

If tightness exists in the hip flexors, clients may wish to flex the hips slightly during abdominal strengthening exercises such as trunk curls (the hips should be flexed only enough to accommodate the existing muscle shortness). With their hips slightly bent and feet on the floor, the shortened iliopsoas won't pull the pelvis forward (Figure 3.23). It will be stabilized in a position of posterior tilt by an active abdominal contraction. Meanwhile, work on flexibility training for the iliopsoas. Perform torso curls at the limit of hip flexor length, so that the back is actively stabilized on the floor by abdominal action. Avoid doing this exercise when the hips are fully flexed with the feet near the buttocks, since the back is stabilized passively with no abdominal action required. Use

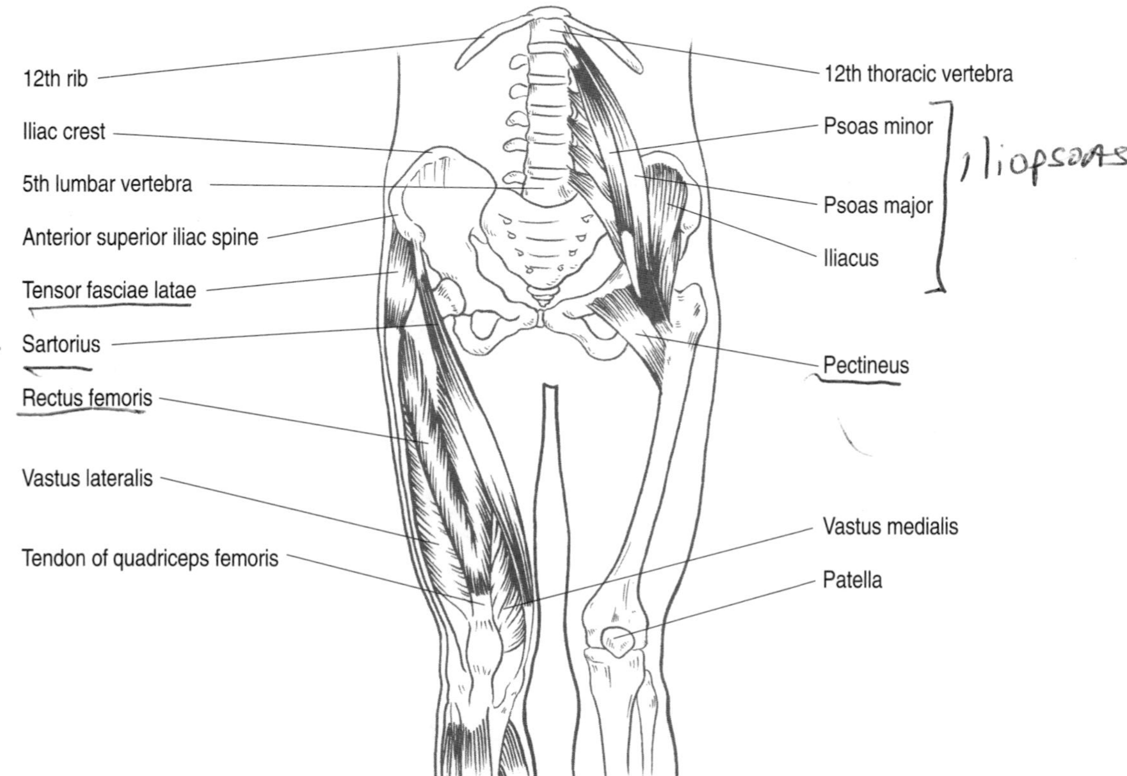

FIGURE 3.22
Anterior muscles of the hip and knee.

Muscles Acting at the Hip Joint

the tilt-and-curl to train the abdominals to actively stabilize, as well as flex, the spine (Figure 3.23).

MUSCLES ACTING AT THE HIP JOINT

The hip joint is a triaxial joint which allows motion to occur in several planes. The hip has inherent stability in its bone and ligament structure and its movements include flexion and extension, hyperextension, abduction and adduction, **circumduction**, internal and external rotation, and the hybrid horizontal abduction and adduction. All the hip muscles connect the lower extremity with the pelvis, except the psoas which attaches the femur to the lumbar spine. It does, however, have action at the pelvis since it crosses it.

Anterior Hip Muscles: Hip Flexors

The anterior hip muscles cause the hip to flex. They include the iliopsoas, rectus femoris, sartorius, tensor fasciae latae and the pectineus (Figure 3.22). Hip flexion can occur by lifting the thigh toward the torso as in a knee lift or straight leg raise, or by lifting the torso toward the thigh as in a full sit-up. The flexors also contract eccentrically to control hip extension, as in the return phase of a straight leg raise.

Iliopsoas. The iliopsoas is actually three muscles — the psoas major, the psoas minor and the iliacus — that function as one. It flexes the hip when the lumbar spine is stabilized, such as in a straight leg raise performed while lying face-up on the floor. It moves the trunk toward the thighs if the femur is stabilized, as in a sit-up done with the legs held down.

There is another condition that must be met for the iliopsoas to move the trunk toward the thighs: the movement must occur against gravity or another external resistance. Thus, bending forward from the standing position does not involve the hip flexors, but is controlled by an eccentric contraction of the hip and/or lower back extensors.

Rectus Femoris. The rectus femoris is one of four parts of the quadriceps muscle. It attaches to the anterior inferior iliac spine and to the tibia via the patellar tendon (ligament). The concentric action of the muscle against resistance is to flex the hip and/or extend the knee. It also works eccentrically to control knee flexion in a weight-bearing position, such as a squat or lunge.

Sartorius. The sartorius also originates on the anterior superior iliac spine and inserts on the medial side of the tibia below the knee. It is a **synergist** to flex, abduct and externally rotate the hip, and to flex and inwardly rotate the knee.

Tensor Fasciae Latae. The origin of this muscle is on the outer surface of the anterior superior iliac spine and the front part of the iliac crest. It inserts into the iliotibial band about one third of the way down the femur. It acts to flex, internally rotate and abduct the hip, and it may also contribute to the stability of the extended knee.

Pectineus. This muscle originates on the pubic bone and inserts along the anteriomedial surface of the femur. It is a

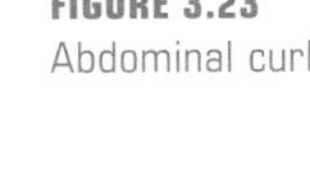

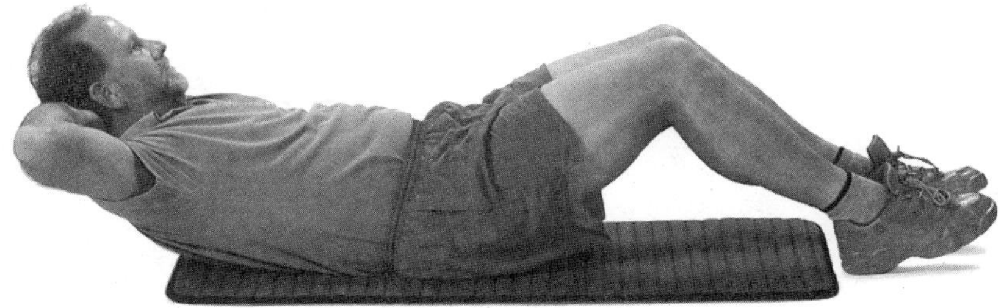

FIGURE 3.23
Abdominal curl.

Muscles Acting at the Hip Joint

synergist to hip flexion and adduction.

As a group the hip flexors are often short and tight. (See Chapter 6 for specific flexibility tests.) Tight hip flexors are not identified by hip flexion in a standing position. The tightness is seen as a forward tilt of the pelvis and lordosis of the lower back and results from the hip extension that occurs while standing. The short iliopsoas pulls the lumbar spine forward as a result of being put in a stretched position.

Stretching the hip flexors is a priority in an exercise program. Figure 3.24 demonstrates an effective hip flexor stretch that will be safe for most clients. Assume a semi-lunge position with the back knee bent and back heel off the floor. Use the abdominals to tilt the pelvis backward, stretching the iliopsoas. Add a stretch of the rectus femoris by dipping into a deep lunge position and adding increased flexion of the back knee.

Posterior Hip Muscles: Hip Extensors

The hip extensor muscles include the gluteus maximus and hamstrings (biceps femoris, semimembranosus and semitendinosus). They extend the hip against gravity, as when lifting your leg behind you, and they also control hip flexion by contracting eccentrically, as in the down phase of a squat or lunge. In weight-bearing positions, they work with the knee extensors (quadriceps) to move the torso up and down.

Gluteus Maximus. The largest and most superficial of the **posterior** hip muscles is the gluteus maximus. It attaches to the pelvic rim at one end and broadly along the iliotibial tract (IT band) at the other (Figure 3.25).

This muscle is a good example of why we can seldom assign a single purpose to a muscle. Its function depends on how the fibers cross the joint. Most of the fibers in the gluteus maximus cross behind the joint, so its primary role is to extend the hip. There are other fibers, though, that synergistically contribute to abduction and adduction, and external rotation, depending on the position of the hip joint at the time.

In daily living activities the gluteus max-

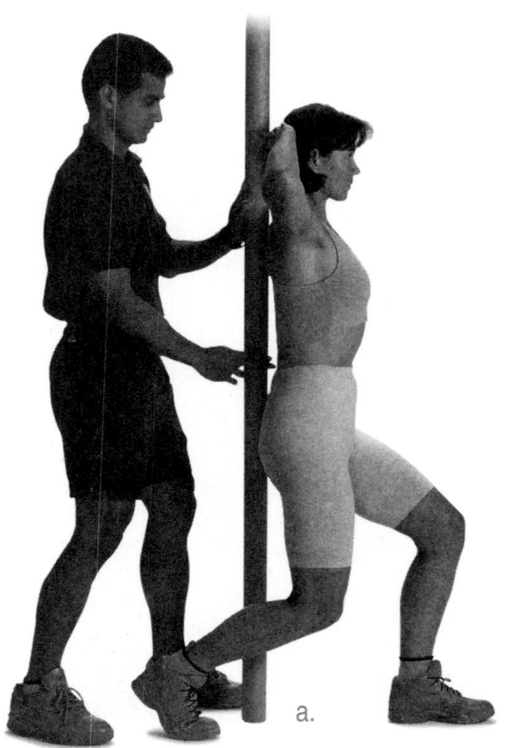

FIGURE 3.24
Hip flexor stretch.

a. Incorrect anterior pelvic tilt.

b. Posterior pelvic tilt.

imus plays its greatest role during walking up an inclined plane, stair climbing, jumping and hyperextending the hip against resistance from the erect standing position.

Hamstrings. The hamstrings cross the hip and the knee and originate (except the short head of the biceps femoris) on the ischial tuberosity (Figure 3.25). The semimembranosus and semitendinosus attach medially to the tibia, and the biceps femoris attaches laterally to the fibular head. The hamstrings extend the hip and flex the knee against resistance and are important knee stabilizers. They also help to control hip flexion in a weight-bearing position by contracting eccentrically when the flexion occurs in the same direction as gravity, such as in a "dead-lift," or hip-hinge position as you bend to sit down.

Many clients have tight hamstrings. As with hip flexor tightness, you will observe it as a pelvic tilt rather than as hyperextended hips or flexed knees. Very tight hamstrings can cause the pelvis to tilt posteriorly which shows up as a "flat-back" posture.

To effectively stretch the hamstrings combine an anterior tilt of the pelvis with hip flexion and knee extension (Figure 3.26). Place one foot on a step with a straight knee and bend forward from the hip keeping the back straight and sternum lifted. Turn the tailbone toward the ceiling, as if sliding the buttocks up a wall. This tilts the pelvis forward and gives the hamstrings a better stretch. To increase the stretch, rotate the leg slightly in then out. This isolates the medial or lateral hamstrings.

The hamstrings may be weak as well, particularly in relation to quadriceps strength. It is important to include strengthening exercises in weight-bearing positions that use the muscle in the same way it is used in sports or in everyday life. Squats and lunges are good examples of hamstring strengthening exercises in weight-bearing positions. Isolated hamstring curls can also be used in cases of imbalance.

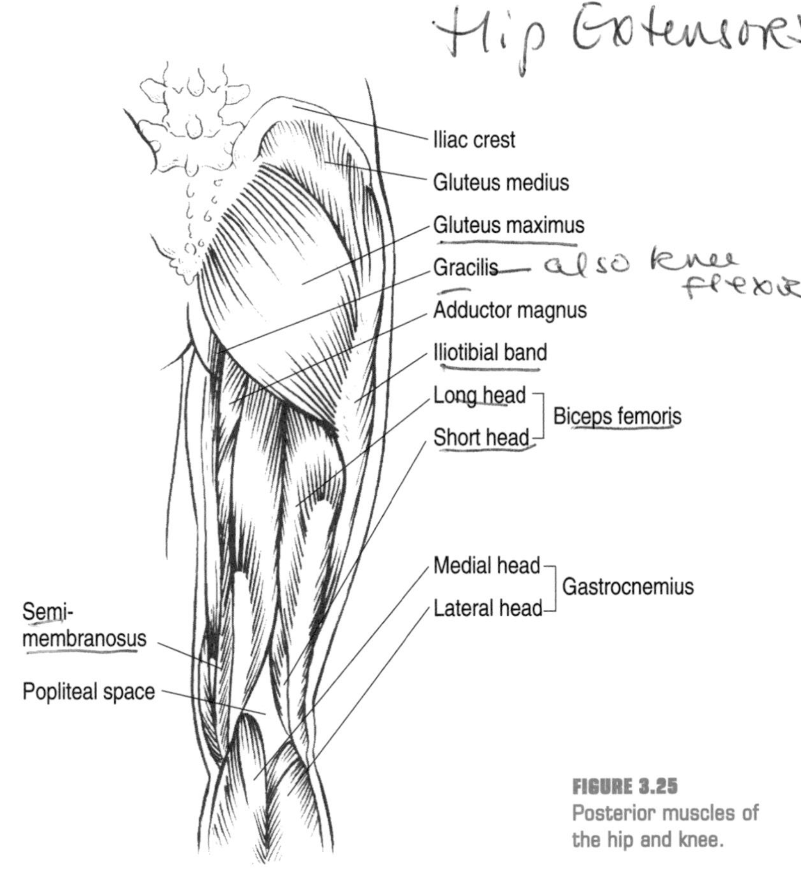

FIGURE 3.25
Posterior muscles of the hip and knee.

FIGURE 3.26
Standing hamstring stretch.

Muscles Acting at the Hip Joint

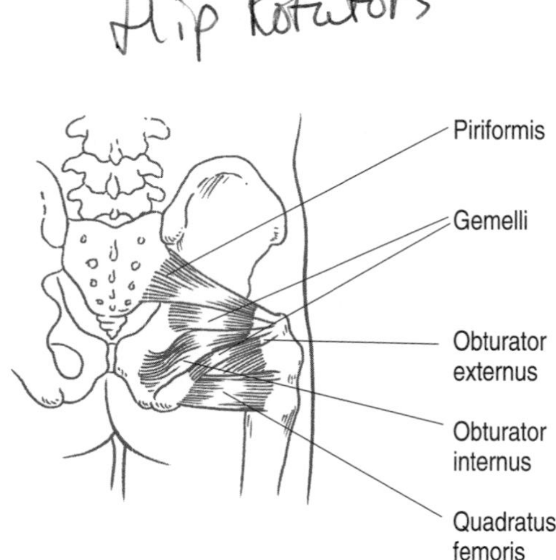

FIGURE 3.27
Deep rotators of the hip. Avoid overloading these muscles with long lever arm exercises.

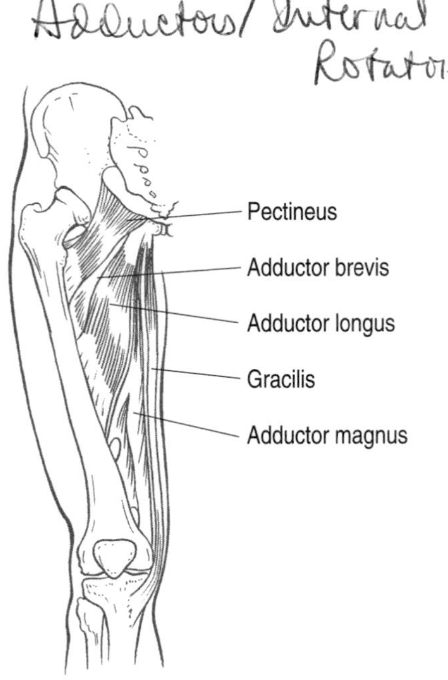

FIGURE 3.28
Adductor muscles of the hip.

Deep External Rotators

The six primary hip rotators are located beneath the gluteus maximus. (Figure 3.27) Their order, from top to bottom, is: piriformis, gemelli superior, obturator internus, gemelli inferior, obturator externus and quadratus femoris. They have horizontal fibers that cross behind the joint. Their attachment to the femur is very close and behind the joint, meaning they rotate the hip externally and help the femoral head to stay in its socket. Because of their small size and short lever arm, they are not designed to resist large forces. Their primary function seems to be stabilization and alignment of the hip.

Tightness or spasm in these muscles, particularly the piriformis, can lead to hip and leg pain, since the sciatic nerve passes through the piriformis and can become irritated. These muscles frequently become tight in runners. To stretch and relax the rotators, have the client position their hip in internal rotation (opposite to the muscles' concentric function). Greater range of motion can be achieved if the client flexes the hip (Figure 3.29).

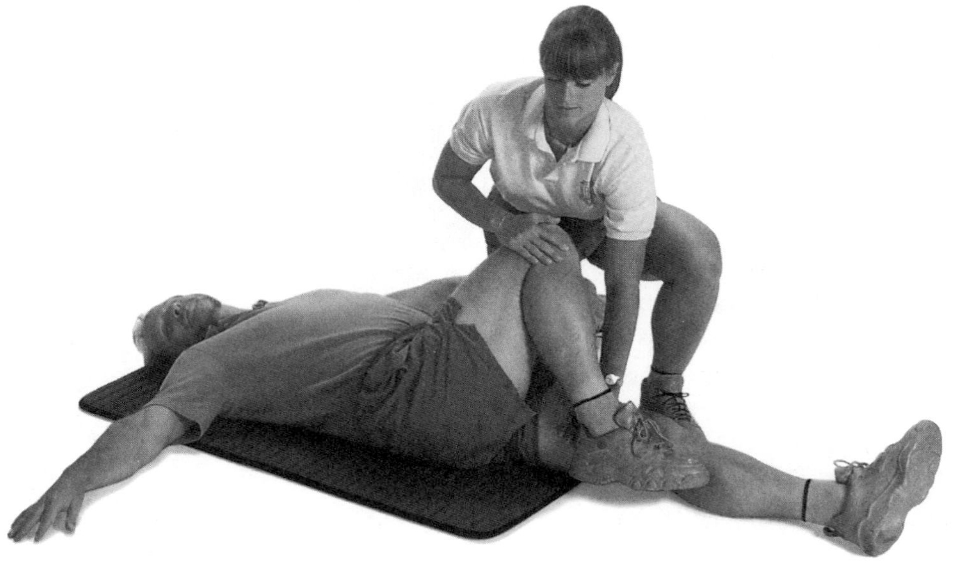

FIGURE 3.29
Rotator stretch with trainer assistance.

Muscles Acting at the Hip Joint

Medial Hip Muscles: Adductors and Internal Rotators

The muscles located **medial** to the hip joint adduct and internally rotate the hip. They include the pectineus (see hip flexors), and the adductor magnus, minimus, longus and brevis (Figure 3.28). The last adductor, the gracilis, crosses the knee joint as well as the hip joint.

These muscles seem to function primarily as thigh stabilizers, especially during movements such as walking lunges. Their stabilizing function can also be trained by doing squats with the knees held together or by placing a ball between the knees (Figure 3.30). Figure 3.31 shows an effective stretch for these muscles.

Many female clients may want to eliminate the fat deposits and "tone" the inner thigh. You will have to teach them that spot-reducing does not work and that they must exercise aerobically to decrease body fat stores. Muscles will become "toned" if they are functioning correctly. Performing the adductors' stabilizing function in squats and lunges will effectively "shape and tone" them.

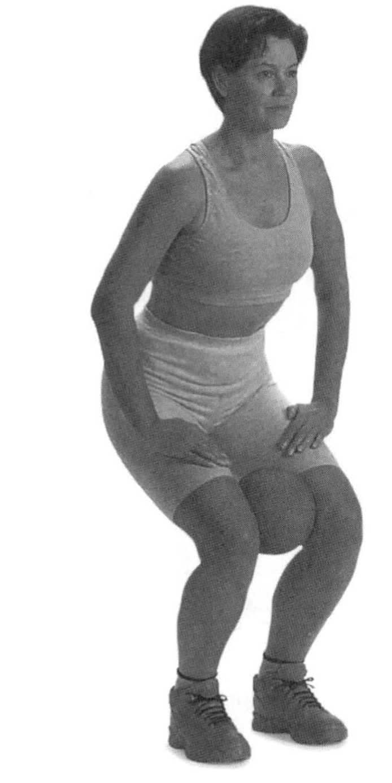

FIGURE 3.30
Adductor muscles help to stabilize the body in a variety of weight-bearing movements.

FIGURE 3.31
Adductor stretch.

Lateral Hip Muscles: Hip Abductors

The muscles which abduct the hip include the gluteus medius and minimus and the tensor fasciae latae (Figure 3.32).

Gluteus Medius and Minimus. These muscles are located high on the hip, not the outer thigh, and their origin is the external surface of the ilium. They insert laterally (medius) and anteriorly (minimus) on the greater trochanter of the femur. In addition to abduction, these muscles internally rotate the hip. This can occur as movement of the leg around the hip joint, but more often occurs as movement or stabilization of the pelvis (ilium) around the hip joint.

Like the hip adductors, the primary function of the abductors is that of stabilizing the hip and pelvis. Abduction occurs when the muscles contract but is

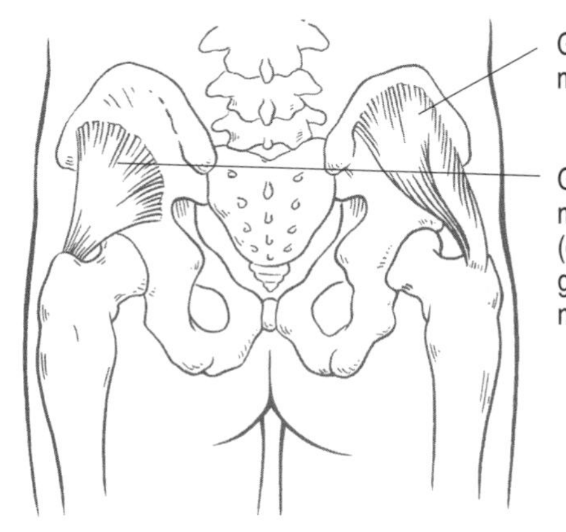

FIGURE 3.32
Abductors of the posterior hip.

Muscles Acting at the Knee Joint

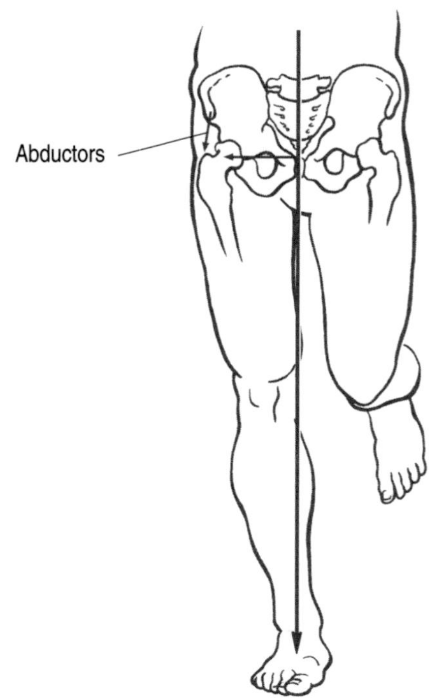

FIGURE 3.33
Action of the abductors during walking.

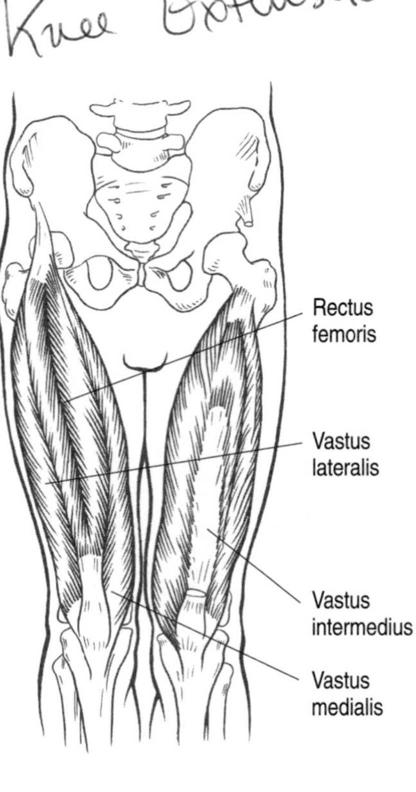

FIGURE 3.34
Quadriceps muscles.

not evidenced as a side leg lift. Instead it prevents adduction and keeps the pelvis even during locomotion. To clarify this function let's think about walking (Figure 3.33). As the left leg is lifted during walking, the left side of the pelvis is unsupported and would drop toward the ground if nothing stabilized it. The right hip abductors contract and pull down on the upper right rim of the pelvis to hold it even and keep the left side from dropping. So, the right hip abductors function to prevent right hip adduction and lateral tilt of the pelvis during walking.

Again, many clients are concerned about reducing the fat deposits in the upper thigh. Specific exercises for the hip abductors will not diminish body fat; only systematic aerobic exercise and proper nutrition will accomplish that goal.

MUSCLES ACTING AT THE KNEE JOINT

The knee is a hinge joint, so the primary motions, for general training purposes, are flexion and extension. The knee is supported medially and laterally by ligaments. The muscles controlling knee motion are located anteriorly (the extensors) and posteriorly (the flexors).

Anterior Muscles: Knee Extensors

The knee extensors are the four quadriceps muscles: rectus femoris (see hip flexors), vastus medialis, vastus intermedius and vastus lateralis. As penniform muscles, they have a large cross section and are capable of producing significant force. The fibers converge at the patella, wrap around it, and attach to the tibia by way of the patellar ligament, sometimes called the patellar tendon (Figure 3.34). The patella acts like a pulley, enabling the muscle to have a favorable angle of pull even when the knee is flexed past 90 degrees.

Strong knee extensors are needed to lift heavy objects, climb stairs, and walk downhill. Therefore, weight-bearing exercises such as squats, lunges, lifting or stair-climbing will probably be the most effective means of preparing them for optimum function. It is important to maintain an appropriate progression of resistance and proper alignment in these activities, especially since there is controversy among experts regarding safe strengthening exercises for the quadriceps. Knee and lower back safety is important when performing a squat or deep knee bend. During a squat the hip and knee extensors contract eccentrically to control hip and knee flexion in the down-phase of the movement. The motive forces are the weight of the torso and upper body; the resistive forces are the eccentric contractions of the hip and knee extensors (Figure 3.35). Although the muscles are able to sustain large forces, problems can occur with muscle imbalance and poor alignment of the knee joint. There also is potential for the patella to slip out of its track if the quadriceps' line of pull is not balanced, resulting in damage to the cartilage on the underside.

Experts suggest that the best way to avoid knee injury in squats and lunges is to limit the degree of knee flexion to no more than 90 degrees. It may, however, be necessary to flex more than 90 degrees to lift objects from the floor in daily life.

Posterior Muscles: Knee Flexors

The primary knee flexors are the hamstrings, which were previously discussed with the hip extensors. Secondary knee flexors include the gastrocnemius, sartorius, gracilis and popliteus (see Figures 3.22, 3.25, and 3.26). The popliteus is a stabilizer that prevents knee dislocation when a squatting position is maintained. It also unlocks the knee by inwardly rotating from the anatomical position. The gastrocnemius, though primarily an ankle muscle, acts in certain instances to stabilize or flex the knee.

Muscles Acting at the Knee Joint

FIGURE 3.35
Squat.

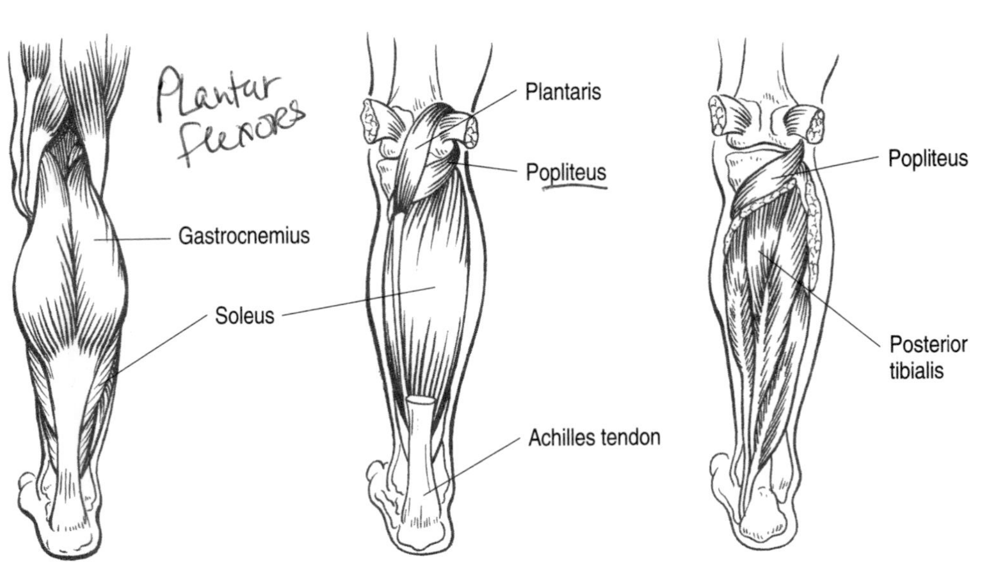

FIGURE 3.36
Posterior calf muscles.

FIGURE 3.37
Calf stretch.

Posterior Muscles Acting at the Ankle: Plantarflexors

The gastrocnemius and soleus group make up the bulk of the muscles on the **posterior** calf (Figure 3.36). They both cross posterior to the ankle joint so they plantarflex the ankle. Their primary function is to rotate the leg (and everything above it) around the ankle. This is a massive muscle group, designed to lift and propel the full body weight forward, not just rotate the foot at the ankle.

Gastrocnemius. This is a two-joint muscle, with a penniform fiber arrangement and a large angle of pull. It is capable of creating very large forces. Overload by performing multiple sets of heel raises on both feet, progressing to one foot. Varying the speed of contraction can progress toward training the muscle for power.

Soleus. The soleus acts with the gastrocnemius to plantarflex the ankle. It does not cross the knee. It is designed to plantarflex with the knee flexed or straight. To isolate the soleus from the gastrocnemius flex the knee to strengthen or stretch it.

Posterior Tibialis. This muscle is located between the tibia and fibula and connects to several bones of the foot. It is deep below the gastrocnemius and soleus muscles. It inverts the foot and participates in plantarflexion, and it also is important in maintaining the longitudinal arch of the foot.

These calf muscles are often shortened and tight. You can help your clients stretch them effectively by utilizing the stretch in Figure 3.37.

Anterior Muscles Acting at the Ankle: Dorsiflexors

Figure 3.38 shows the **anterior** muscles of the lower leg, primarily the tibialis anterior, whose function is to **dorsiflex** the foot

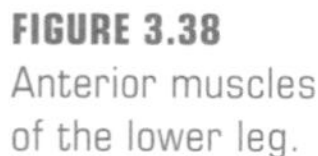

FIGURE 3.38
Anterior muscles of the lower leg.

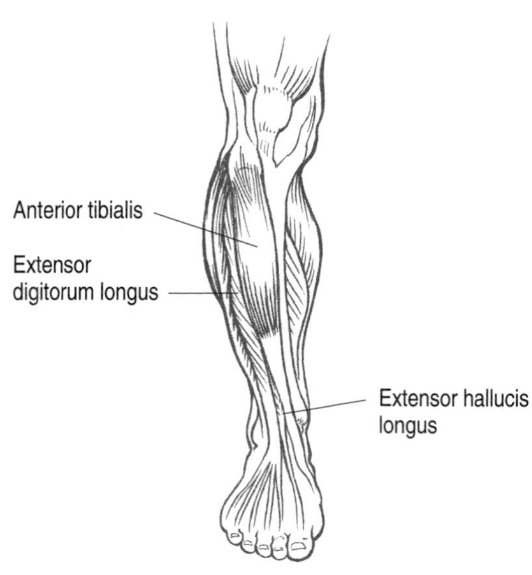

FIGURE 3.39
Lateral muscles of the lower leg.

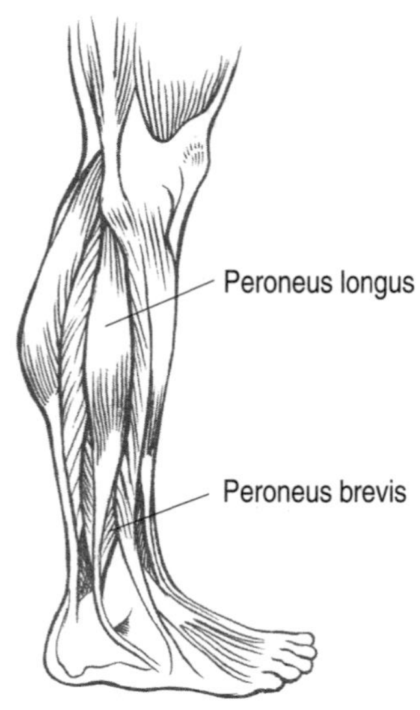

around the ankle. These muscles located along the shin are the first line of defense in high-impact activities with regard to shock absorption. They also control the foot movements important to balance during walking and running, particularly on uneven ground. Toe tapping will provide a thorough warm-up of these muscles prior to impact activities.

When you compare the mass of the gastrocnemius and soleus group with that of the anterior muscles, their respective functions become more apparent. The small anterior muscle is designed to move the foot (small load); the large posterior muscles are designed to move the body (large load). It is easy to see how the anterior muscles become injured with the impact and momentum of running when they are not adequately conditioned.

Lateral Muscles Acting at the Ankle and Foot

The peroneus longus and brevis are the muscles that compose the lateral compartment of the lower leg (Figure 3.39). Their tendons curve around the lateral malleolus of the ankle and attach to the first and fifth metatarsal, respectively. They are designed for plantarflexion and **eversion**, so they are active in walking and also are important in maneuvering on uneven ground. Strengthen these muscles with manual resistance, or by laterally dragging a weighted towel (Figure 3.40).

UPPER BODY MUSCLES: MOVEMENTS, FUNCTIONS AND EXERCISE IMPLICATIONS

Upper body motion includes movement of the head and neck, scapulae, shoulders, elbows, wrists and hands, as well as of the cervical and thoracic spine. Table 3.4 summarizes the muscles, movements and selected exercises for the upper body. For the purposes of this text, we will not discuss the intricate, complex muscles and functions of the hand and wrist.

Shoulder and upper arm movements are the result of a combination of movements of several joints, primarily the scapulae and the glenohumeral joint. For example,

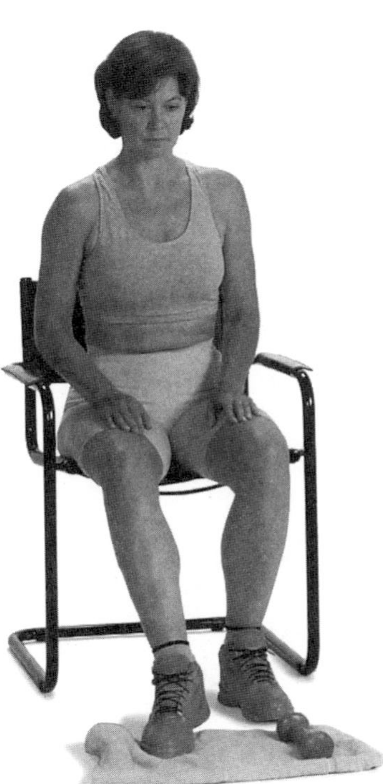

FIGURE 3.40 Lateral lower leg strengthener.

Upper Body Muscles: Movements, Functions and Exercise Implications

Table 3.4
Upper Body Muscles — Functions and Selected Exercises

Muscle	Primary Function	Selected Exercises
Trapezius: Upper	Scapular elevation, stabilizer for scapular adduction, upward rotation of the scapula, with insertion fixed, acting bilaterally, head and neck extension; unilaterally, head extension, lateral flexion and rotation to the opposite side	S/E: Lateral raises, overhead presses. Emphasize scapular rotation function to balance with lower and middle. Decrease emphasis on isolated function F: Depress shoulder, tilt head diagonally to opposite side (Figure 3.44)
Trapezius: Middle	Scapular adduction, stabilizer for upward rotation	S/E: Prone or simulated prone for antigravity position; bilateral or unilateral scapular adduction (double- or single-arm row) (Figure 3.45); Standing scapular adduction against elastic resistance pull-up (Figure 3.48) F: Often already overstretched
Trapezius: Lower	Scapular depression, stabilizer for scapular adduction, upward rotation	S/E: Pull scapulae down and toward the middle (Figure 3.47). Prone overhead lifts, pull-up (Figure 3.48)
Rhomboids (Major and Minor)	Scapular adduction and elevation, downward rotation of scapula	S/E: Prone or simulated prone for antigravity position: arms extended and adducted; pull scapulae up and together upright, same motion with elastic resistance under feet
Levator Scapulae	Scapular elevation, downward rotation; with insertion fixed – rotates and laterally flexes the cervical vertebrae to the same side	S/E: Prone: rotate head to the side and extend neck while lifting head off the ground F: In supine position depress scapulae, tuck chin and flex head forward
Serratus Anterior	Upward rotation of scapula, holds scapula flat on thorax, scapular abduction	S/E: Modified wall push-ups (Figure 3.50), scapular abduction at end of supine pectoral fly or press; upright anterior shoulder press against elastic resistance around midback
Pectoralis Minor	Tilts scapulae anteriorly; with scapulae stabilized in adduction may lift chest and assist with forced inspiration	S/E: Squeeze scapulae together, then lift chest F: Manual stretch with trainer assistance
Deltoid (anterior)	Shoulder flexion and internal rotation, stabilizer for shoulder abduction	S/E: Diagonal raise: abduct arm halfway between front and side
Deltoid (middle)	Shoulder abduction	S/E: Lateral shoulder raises with weights or elastic resistance under feet Avoid abduction with internal rotation to protect the rotator cuff from impingement
Deltoid (posterior)	Shoulder extension and external rotation, stabilizer for shoulder abduction	S/E: Forward lunge position: arms down toward the floor. Abduct, extend and externally rotate the arm, also seated manual resistance (Figure 3.53)
Supraspinatus (rotator cuff)	Shoulder abduction, stabilizes humeral head in glenoid fossa	S/E: Lateral shoulder raises in neutral rotation

Table 3.4 continued

Muscle	Primary Function	Selected Exercises
Infraspinatus (rotator cuff)	Shoulder external rotation, stabilizes humerus in glenoid fossa during shoulder motion	S/E: Holding elastic resistance in front at waist level, arms adducted, pull hands apart, rotating back
Teres Minor (rotator cuff)	Shoulder external rotation, stabilizes humeral head in glenoid fossa during shoulder motion	S/E: Same as for infraspinatus
Subscapularis (rotator cuff)	Shoulder internal rotation, stabilizes humeral head in glenoid fossa during shoulder motion	S/E: Holding elastic resistance in back at waist level, arms adducted and elbows flexed, cross hands in front, rotating inwardly at the shoulder
Latissimus Dorsi	Shoulder adduction, extension and internal rotation	S/E: Pulling the arms downward against elastic resistance held overhead, "dips" on bench with arms abducted, lat "pull-down" to chest with neutral head, neck and spine
Teres Major	Shoulder adduction, extension and internal rotation	S/E: Same as for latissimus dorsi
Pectoralis Major	Shoulder adduction and internal rotation; upper fibers: shoulder flexion and horizontal adduction to opposite shoulder; lower fibers horizontal adduction toward opposite iliac crest	S/E: Push-ups, (Figure 3.54a) standing horizontal adduction against elastic resistance around midback, supine "bench press" or "fly"; incline bench press or fly large ball F: Pole stretch
Coracobrachialis	Shoulder flexion and adduction	S/E: Shoulder flexion and adduction with elbow flexed and forearm supinated
Biceps Brachii	Shoulder flexion; long head assists with shoulder abduction if the humerus is externally rotated; elbow flexion and forearm supination	S/E: Biceps curls adding supination, with weights or elastic resistance under feet; use in conjunction with scapular retraction
Brachialis	Elbow flexion	S/E: Biceps curls without supination, with weights or elastic resistance under feet
Brachioradialis	Elbow flexion; assists with supination to midposition; assists with pronation to midposition	S/E: "Hammer curls": curls with forearm in neutral position (not prorated or supinated)
Triceps Brachii	Elbow extension; long head may assist in shoulder adduction and extension	S/E: Push-ups; dips from bench; bench press; triceps kickback with scapular stabilization
Pronator Teres	Forearm pronation; assists with elbow flexion	Curls with pronation and supination

S/E (Strength/Endurance): Exercises to improve strength and/or endurance of the muscle, depending upon the resistance and repetitions. Each exercise is not isolated to that particular muscle, as muscles work in groups to cause movement; however, the exercises listed would include the designated muscle as a prime mover.

F (Flexibility): Exercises to improve the flexibility of the designated muscle. Flexibility exercises do not stretch the muscle fiber itself, but are designed to lengthen the connective tissue associated with each particular muscle group. For maximum effectiveness, they should be performed after the muscle group is thoroughly warmed.

Upper Body Muscles: Movements, Functions and Exercise Implications

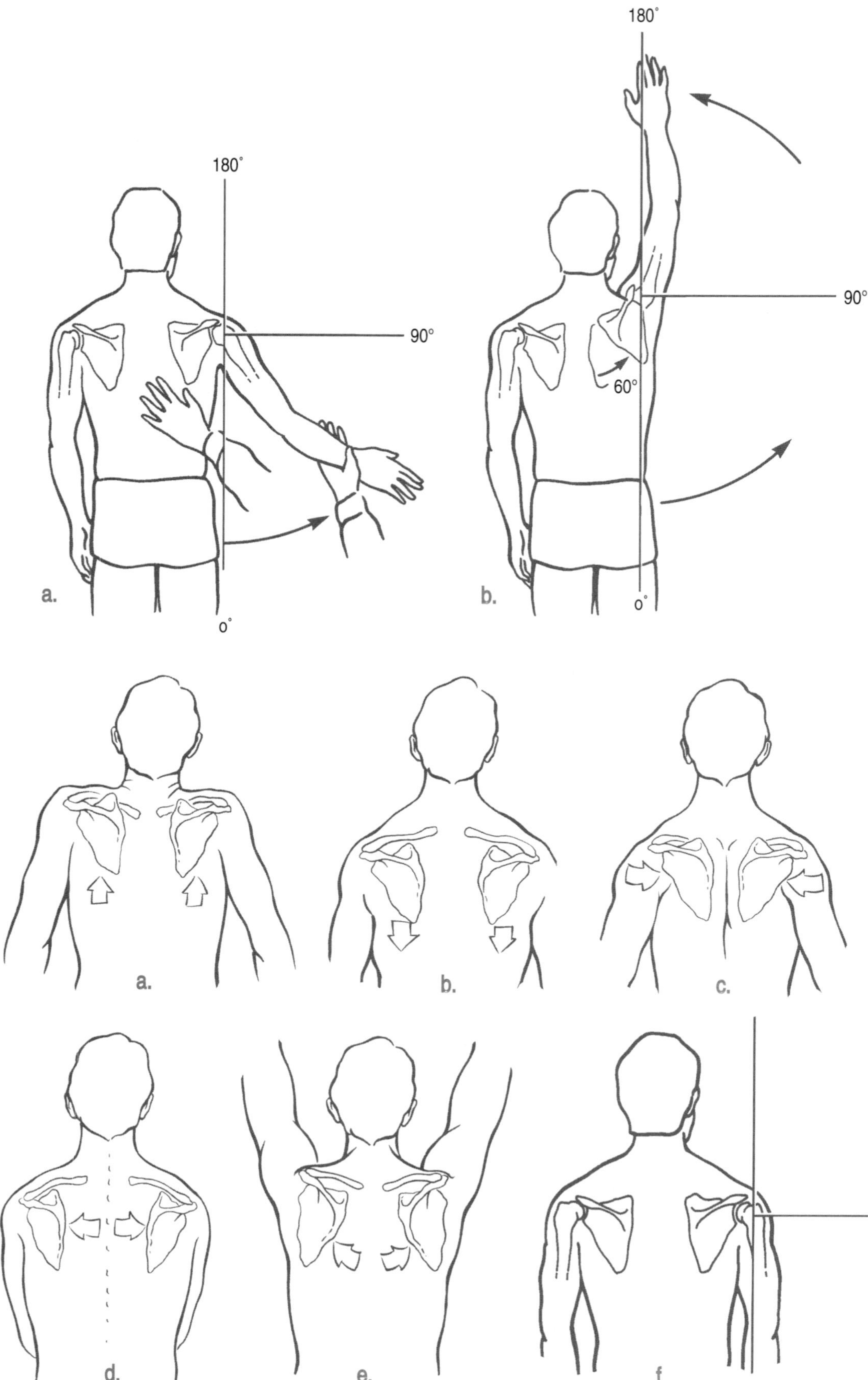

FIGURE 3.41
Scapulohumeral rhythm.

a. Shoulder joint abduction to 90° is 30° scapular rotation and 60° abduction of the glenohumeral joint.

b. As the arm is abducted overhead, the scapula outwardly (upwardly) rotates to 60°.

FIGURE 3.42
Scapular movements.

a. Elevation.

b. Depression.

c. Adduction (retraction).

d. Abduction (protraction).

e. Upward rotation.

f. Downward rotation (return to neutral position).

Upper Body Muscles: Movements, Functions and Exercise Implications

shoulder abduction to 90 degrees is a combination of 30 degrees of upward rotation of the scapula and 60 degrees of abduction at the shoulder joint. This synchronization of movement is known as scapulohumeral rhythm (Figure 3.41).

Scapular movements controlled by the shoulder girdle muscles are pictured in Figure 3.42. They include **retraction** and **protraction** (also known as scapular adduction and abduction), elevation and depression, and upward and downward rotation. These movements describe scapulae motion alone; do not confuse them with shoulder joint motion.

Scapular muscles are classified into two groups according to their location: posterior shoulder girdle and anterior shoulder girdle muscles. In activities of daily living the scapular muscles move and stabilize. They hold the upper body in position so that we can reach, flex, push or pull with our arms and hands. Some also stabilize the humerus in its socket. Proper training techniques can add power to arm and shoulder motions by strengthening the scapulo-humeral rhythm.

Posterior Shoulder Girdle Muscles

Posterior shoulder girdle muscles earned their name because of their stabilizing function. They connect the scapula to the back of the head and torso, particularly to the spine, and they include the trapezius, rhomboids major and minor, and the levator scapulae.

Trapezius. The largest and most superficial of the posterior shoulder girdle muscles is the trapezius (Figure 3.43). One end attaches along the base of the skull, at all the cervical vertebrae, and at all the thoracic vertebrae, and to the scapular spine at the other end.

Because the muscle's origin is very broad, the fibers actually travel in three very different directions; as such, they almost function as three different muscles. But it is very important to seek balance among the three parts for proper upper-body functioning and injury prevention.

If contracting alone, the upper trapezius will elevate and retract the scapula (the scapula would move up and toward the spine). When the middle trapezius contracts alone, the scapula retracts, or moves toward the spine. The lower trapezius, acting alone, will depress and retract the scapula (the scapula moves down and in).

The trapezius, however, is designed to function not in isolated segments, but together with the other scapular muscles and muscles of the shoulder (scapulo-humeral rhythm). The upper and lower trapezius, along with the serratus anterior, upwardly rotate the scapula, which occurs each time the arm is raised to the front or

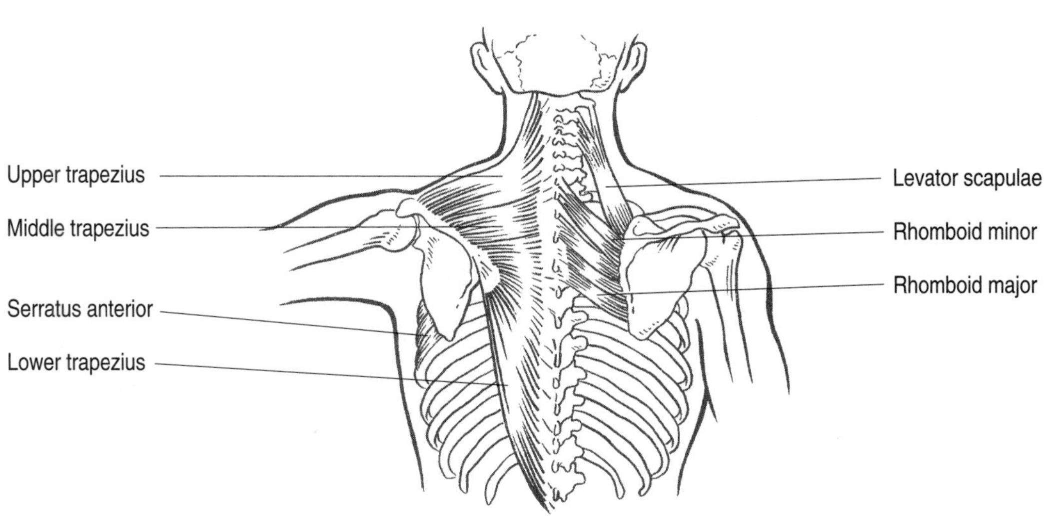

FIGURE 3.43
Posterior shoulder girdle muscles.

Upper Body Muscles: Movements, Functions and Exercise Implications

FIGURE 3.44
Upper trapezius stretch.

to the side. Downward rotation of the scapula occurs with action of the middle trapezius and rhomboids.

Imbalance of the scapular muscles can produce problems such as impingement at the shoulder joint and has also been implicated in some cases of headache and carpal tunnel syndrome. It is important to correct any imbalance that exists among the scapular muscles and to prevent its progression. Imbalances typically exist in clients before they begin a training program.

The upper trapezius is often imbalanced with the middle and lower regions of the muscle. To help create balance, concentrate more training time on the middle and lower portions of the muscle (low rows), and less time on isolated upper trapezius work (shrugs, upright rows). Design and cue exercises so that the stronger upper trapezius can not take over for the weaker areas and reinforce the existing imbalance.

The upper trapezius may also be short and tight because of habitual postures and everyday stress. It needs stretching. Habitual forward head posture with hyperextended cervical vertebrae causes the upper trapezius muscles to adapt over time to the restricted range of motion. This is especially true if work is done with the arms in front and unsupported.

To effectively stretch the upper trapezius, the muscle should be positioned with the shoulder depressed and the head tilted slightly forward and to the other side (opposite of a shoulder shrug) (Figure 3.44).

If working with free weights, strengthen

FIGURE 3.45
Middle trapezius strengthener.

FIGURE 3.46
Incorrect row technique that results from fatigue.

Upper Body Muscles: Movements, Functions and Exercise Implications

the middle trapezius in antigravity positions (Figure 3.45). Have the client lie face down with arms out to the sides and elbows bent. Squeeze the shoulder blades together and lift the arms, keeping them parallel to the floor. Start with a short lever arm (arms bent), progress to a long lever arm (arms straight), and then progress to holding weights, first with elbows bent, then straight.

If using machines such as a seated row, try elastic around the feet, or held in both hands at chest level; the client sits upright. Watch carefully for fatigue — it shows as the upper trapezius takes over and the shoulders begin to elevate (Figure 3.46).

A latissimus pull-down machine can be used to strengthen the lower trapezius: grip the bar and pull only the shoulder blades down and together (the elbows remain extended and the shoulders flexed) (Figure 3.47).

An advanced exercise for the lower and middle fibers is a pull-up (Figure 3.48). In the starting position, the scapulae are abducted and upwardly rotated due to the arm position. To perform a pull-up, the lower and middle fibers of the trapezius must strongly contract to stabilize the scapulae (retract, depress and downwardly rotate) so that the arms can adduct and lift the body to clear the chin over the bar. The muscles are having to lift the body weight against gravity.

Rhomboids. The major and minor rhomboids are located beneath the middle and upper trapezius (Figure 3.43). They connect the entire medial border of the scapula to the spine and their function is to retract and elevate the scapula. They also participate in downward scapula rotation. The fibers are diagonal.

Levator Scapulae. This muscle connects the scapula to the transverse processes of

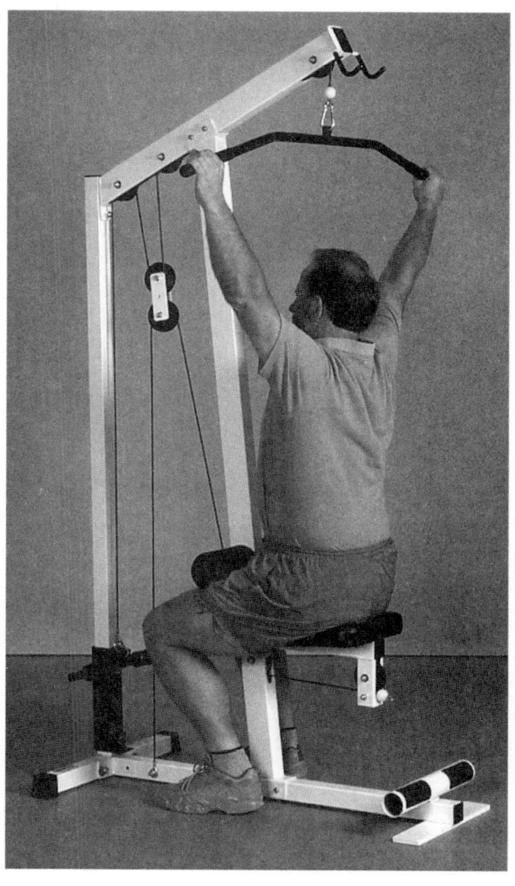

FIGURE 3.47
Lower trapezius strengthener, pull only the shoulder blades down and together.

FIGURE 3.48
Pull-up, an advanced exercise for the middle and lower trapezuis fibers.

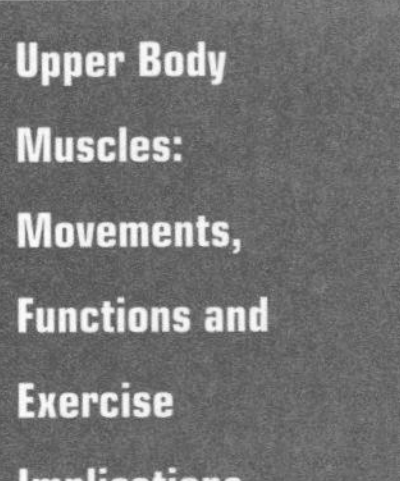

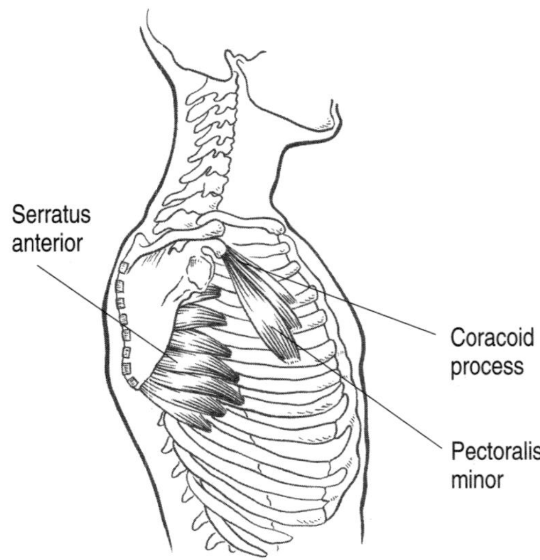

FIGURE 3.49
Anterior shoulder girdle muscles.

the cervical vertebrae with a vertical line of pull (Figure 3.43). Its function is scapular elevation and downward scapular rotation.

Anterior Shoulder Girdle. The anterior shoulder girdle muscles attach the scapulae to the front of the chest. They include the serratus anterior and the pectoralis minor (Figure 3.49).

FIGURE 3.50
Wall push-up.

Serratus Anterior. The serratus anterior connects the medial border of the scapulae on its underside to the front of the rib cage (ribs one through nine). The muscle interdigitates with the external oblique. Its function is protraction and upward rotation of the scapula and it also participates in reaching motions, such as a jab or punch in boxing.

If this muscle is weak, the shoulder blade may protrude from the surface of the back, particularly along the medial border and will be clearly visible during a push-up. This muscle will become relatively weaker as others substitute for its weakened function. To strengthen the serratus, work it alone by having the client do "wall push-ups" (Figure 3.50). Spot carefully to make sure the shoulder blades stay flat.

People whose shoulder blades are protracted (pulled forward, away from the spine), may also have a tight serratus. At rest the medial border of the scapula should be about 2 inches from the spine.

Pectoralis Minor. This muscle connects the coracoid process of the scapula to the third, fourth and fifth ribs. It can have a positive or negative effect on posture, depending on the condition of the scapular retractors. If the middle and lower trapezius are weak or overstretched, the pectoralis minor can become shortened and tilt the scapulae (and the whole upper body) forward and down. If the scapular retractors are properly stabilizing the scapulae, the pectoralis minor can lift the chest by pulling the ribs upward.

Muscles of the Shoulder and Elbow

The shoulder is called the glenohumeral joint. It is the **articulation** between the glenoid fossa of the scapula and the humerus, and it is a multiaxial joint.

The movements and normal ranges of motion of the shoulder are pictured in Figure 3.51, a-j. They include: flexion and extension in the sagittal plane, abduction and adduction in the frontal plane, exter-

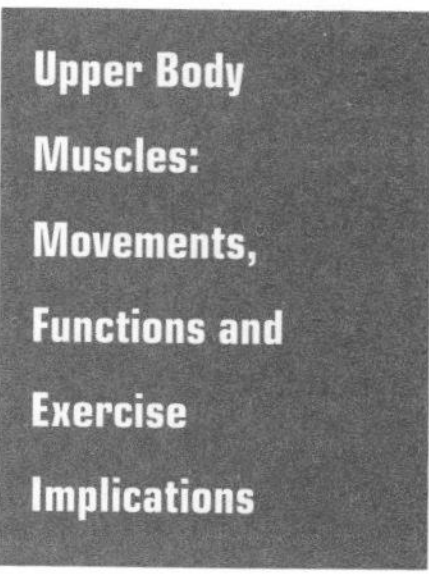

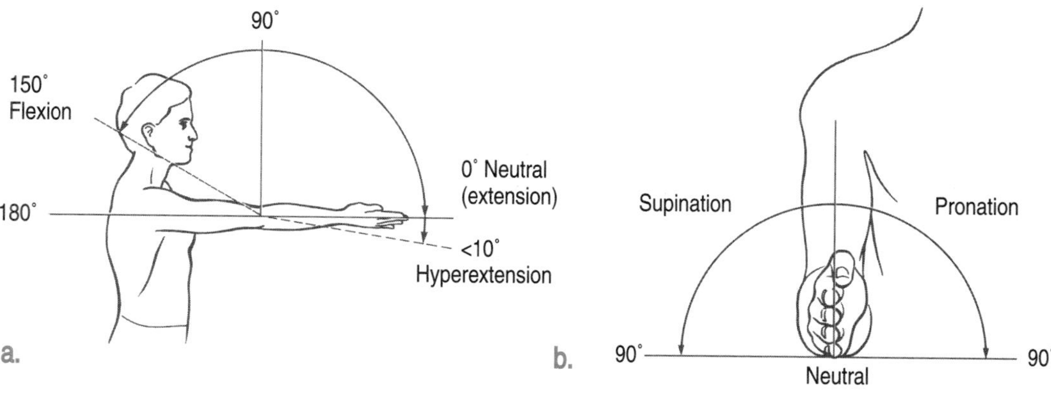

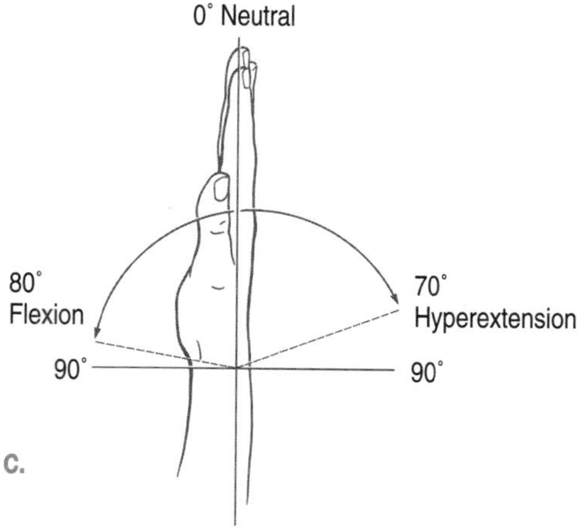

Radial deviation 20° 0° 30° Ulnar deviation

d.

FIGURE 3.51
Upper extremity movements and ranges of motion.

a. Elbow range of motion: flexion 150°; extension (to 0°); hyperextension (<10°).

b. Forearm range of motion: pronation 90°; supination 90°.

c. Wrist range of motion: flexion 80°; extension (to 0°); hyperextension 70°.

d. Range of motion of the wrist: radial deviation 20°; ulnar deviation 30°.

continued on next page

nal and internal rotation, and horizontal flexion and extension in the transverse plane, and circumduction in a combination of planes.

The muscles acting at the glenohumeral joint attach the humerus to the scapula and cause movement of the upper arm. Remember that the shoulder girdle muscles act as stabilizers during all arm movements, so scapular motion and stabilization occurs simultaneously with shoulder movements. If there is a problem with arm movement, it may stem from weakness or tightness either of the arm or shoulder girdle or both.

Each muscle acting at the shoulder has many functions depending on the shoulder's current angle. The muscles include the deltoid, coracobrachialis, latissimus dorsi and teres major, as well as the group called the rotator cuff (supraspinatus, infraspinatus, teres minor and subscapularis).

Deltoid. The deltoid is identified by three names, relative to fiber location around the joint (Figure 3.52). The muscle is multipenniform and attaches a good distance from the joint, making it a powerful mover of the shoulder joint.

The anterior deltoid originates along the lateral third of the clavicle and inserts on the deltoid tuberosity of the humerus. It acts with the posterior deltoid as a stabilizer and synergist during shoulder abduction and also flexes, horizontally adducts and internally rotates the arm at the shoulder. Front raises and many traditional pectoral exercises work the anterior deltoid.

The middle deltoid originates on the acromion and inserts on the deltoid tuberosity. With shoulder girdle muscles acting as synergists, the middle deltoid abducts the arm at the shoulder, as in a lateral raise. It also controls the down-phase of a lateral raise (shoulder adduction in the same direction as gravity) (Figure 3.52).

Perform a lateral raise with the shoulder

Upper Body Muscles: Movements, Functions and Exercise Implications

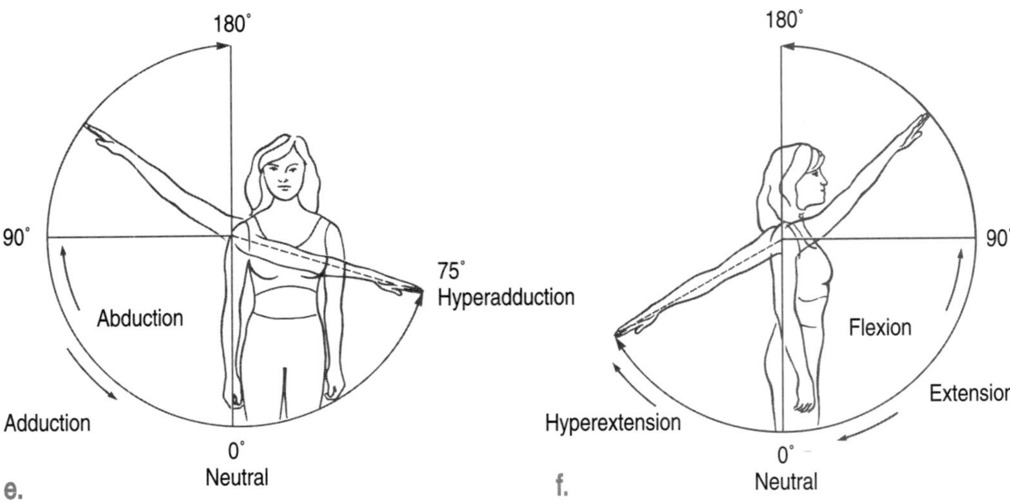

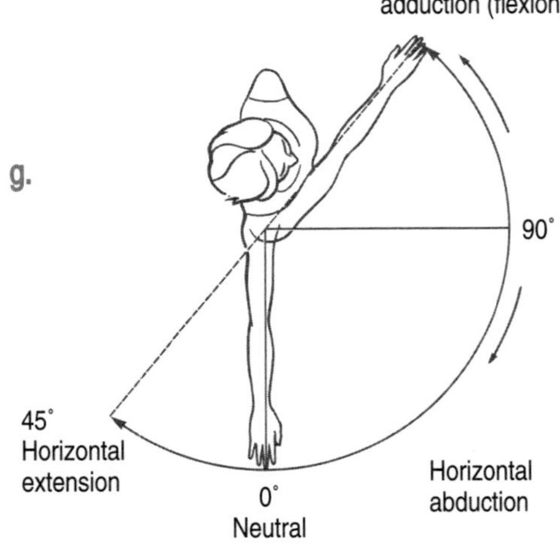

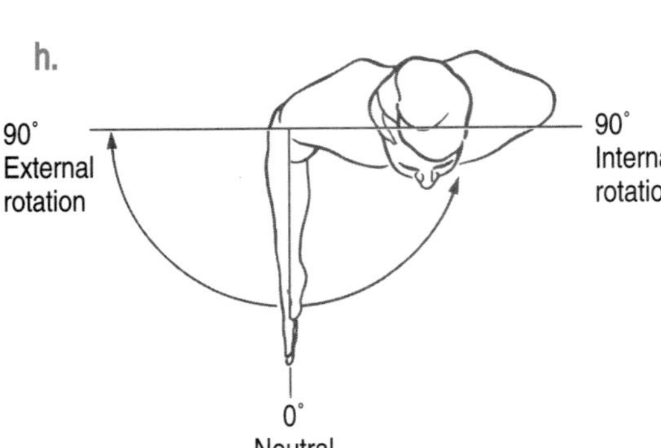

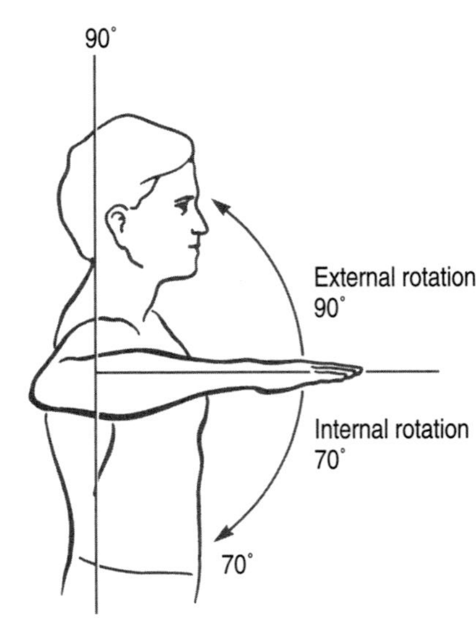

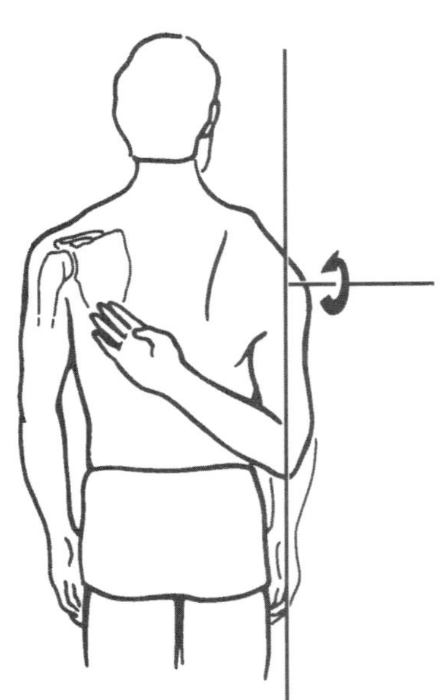

FIGURE 3.51 continued

e. Shoulder abduction 180°; adduction (to neutral); hyperadduction 75° (frontal plane).

f. Shoulder range of motion in sagittal plane: flexion 180°; extension (to 0°); hyperextension 60°.

g. Shoulder range of motion in the transverse plane: horizontal adduction (flexion) 130°; horizontal abduction (to 0°); horizontal extension 45° past neutral.

h. Shoulder rotation range of motion in the transverse plane (shoulder is adducted to neutral); extend rotation 90°; internal rotation 90°.

i. Shoulder rotation range of motion in sagittal plane external (outward) rotation 90°; internal rotation 70° (shoulder joint is abducted to 90°).

j. Rotation with arm at side; rotation with arm in abduction; internal rotation posteriorly.

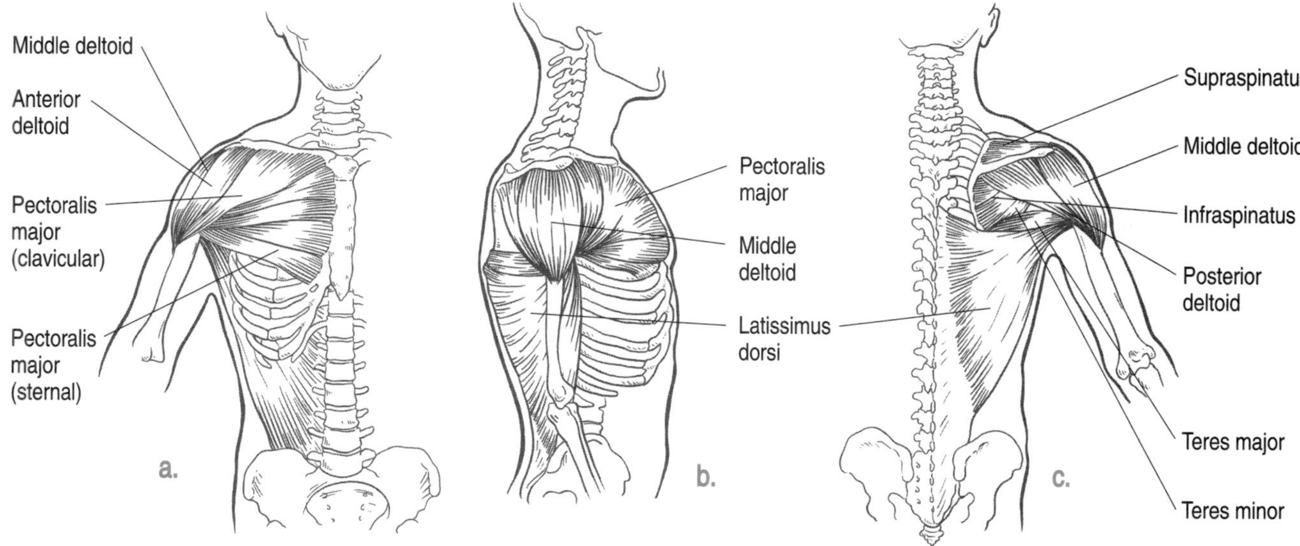

FIGURE 3.52
Superficial shoulder muscles.

a. Anterior deltoid and pectoralis major.

b. Latissimus dorsi pectoralis and deltoid, lateral view.

c. Posterior muscles of the shoulder (gleno-humeral) joint.

in neutral rotation to prevent injury. Forcing a lateral raise with internal rotation at the shoulder can impinge and damage the rotator cuff. Impingement also can occur if the raise is performed in poor alignment, such as with rounded shoulders or protracted scapulae.

The posterior deltoid originates on the posterior border of the scapular spine, and passes behind the shoulder joint to insert on the deltoid tuberosity. It functions as a shoulder extensor and horizontal abductor. If using free weights when exercising the posterior deltoid, position the client prone on an incline bench. Use dumbbells or apply manual resistance to the rear of the upper arm (Figure 3.53).

Latissimus Dorsi and Teres Major. The position and fiber direction of these two muscles are very similar (Figure 3.52). The teres major attaches to the lower corner of the scapula. The latissimus dorsi is much larger with a broad attachment along the lower thoracic and lumbar spine, sacrum and pelvis. They both insert on the anterior surface of the upper humerus, and their function is to extend, adduct and internally rotate the arm on the torso at the shoulder. They also act to propel the torso forward and upward on the arms such as in swimming, rowing, cross-country skiing, pull-ups or to pull the body along the ground as one might do on a military obstacle course.

The most common strengthening exercise for these muscles is the "lat pull-down." To achieve the maximum effectiveness of this exercise, pull the bar down to the

FIGURE 3.53
Manual resistance for posterior deltoid.

Upper Body Muscles: Movements, Functions and Exercise Implications

chest rather than the back of the shoulders. Pulling to, and lifting the chest toward, the bar also engages the lower trapezius and does not compromise the shoulder or head and neck positions. Keep the chest lifted and the back in neutral throughout the exercise.

In the absence of variable-resistance equipment, a good way to provide progressive resistance to these muscles is to have clients perform a lat pull-down against elastic bands or tubing that is held in a door jamb. Swimming, rowing and lifting the body up on parallel bars also will strengthen these muscles.

Pectoralis Major. The origin of the pectoralis major is broad and ranges from the medial half of the clavicle, anterior surface of the sternum, cartilages of the first six or seven ribs and the aponeurosis of the external oblique (Figure 3.52). It inserts near the latissimus dorsi on the anterior surface of the upper humerus and functions as a shoulder adductor and internal rotator. It also participates in shoulder flexion and horizontal adduction.

The push-up is an important exercise to strengthen the pectorals. The pectoralis major, serratus anterior and triceps contract eccentrically to lower the weight of the body toward the floor. The same muscles contract concentrically to lift the body up from the floor. For maximum effectiveness, use the torso stabilizers to maintain neutral alignment of the head, neck, spine, and hip joints as shown in Figure 3.54a. Figure 3.54b shows unsatisfactory alignment during a push-up with the head jutting forward and the low back in lordosis.

To stretch the pectoralis major effectively, the client should lie supine on a bench with their back pressed against it. The hands touch the head just behind the ears with the elbows flexed. You may assist with the stretch by applying slow, mild, downward pressure just above the elbows.

There are several common training errors related to the latissimus dorsi and pectoralis major. One occurs when swimmers and bodybuilders work hard to build up

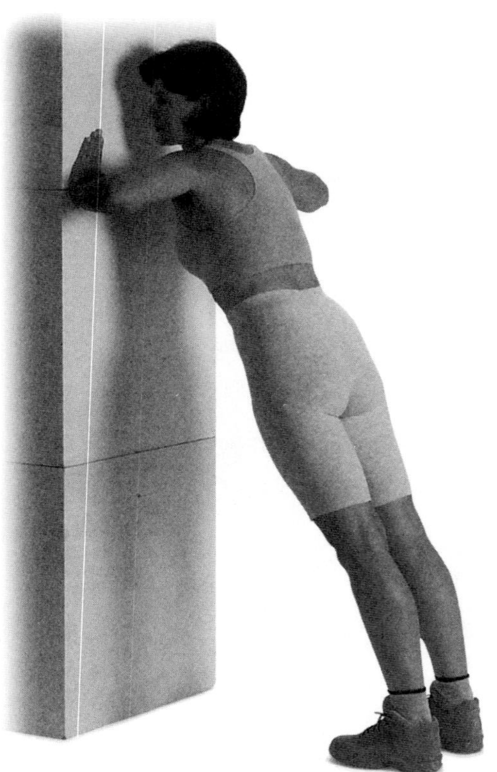

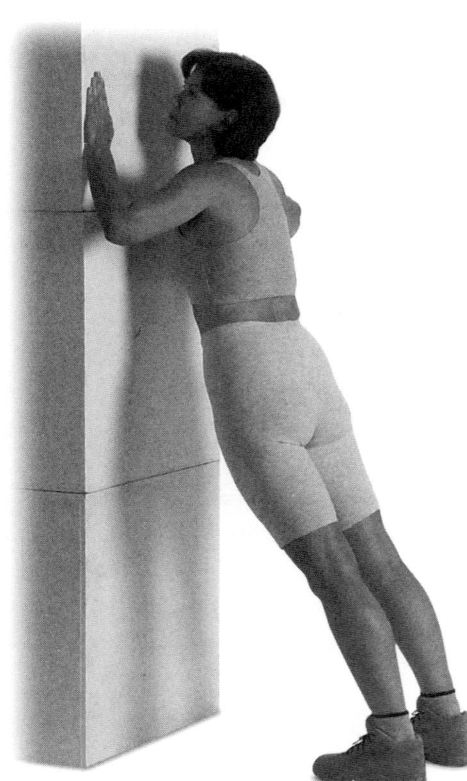

FIGURE 3.54
a. Correct push-up alignment.

b. Incorrect push-up alignment.

Upper Body Muscles: Movements, Functions and Exercise Implications

their pectorals and latissimus but fail to stretch those muscles. Their shoulders are always internally rotated (Figure 3.55), possibly because the pecs and lats are too short. A less severe version of this standing posture is evidenced by shoulders that are rounded forward and hands that face backward instead of toward each other during relaxed standing. In an undeveloped individual, this may be due to weak, overstretched scapular retractors and shoulder external rotators that passively allow the shoulder to fall forward into internal rotation. The scapular retractors become overstretched because, in a habitually poor sitting and standing posture, the scapulae passively slide away from the spine, keeping the muscles that connect the scapulae to the spine in a state of perpetual stretch. This may be accompanied and accentuated by a tight pectoralis minor that exerts a downward pull on the upper front part of the scapula (Figure 3.55).

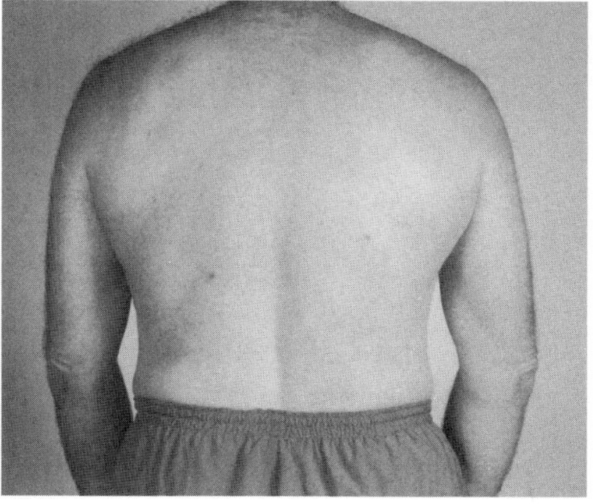

FIGURE 3.55
Internal rotation of the shoulders.

Training time is often spent strengthening the pectoralis major and latissimus dorsi without stretching. Trainers must be sure to consider muscular balance when planning time with a client.

Sometimes the motion shown in Figure 3.56a is recommended as a pectoral stretch. However, this isn't very effective for this muscle since the position opposes only one of its functions and may even reinforce a tight pectoralis minor. For a better pectoral stretch, the arm should be in a combined position of abduction, external rotation and some hyperextension as

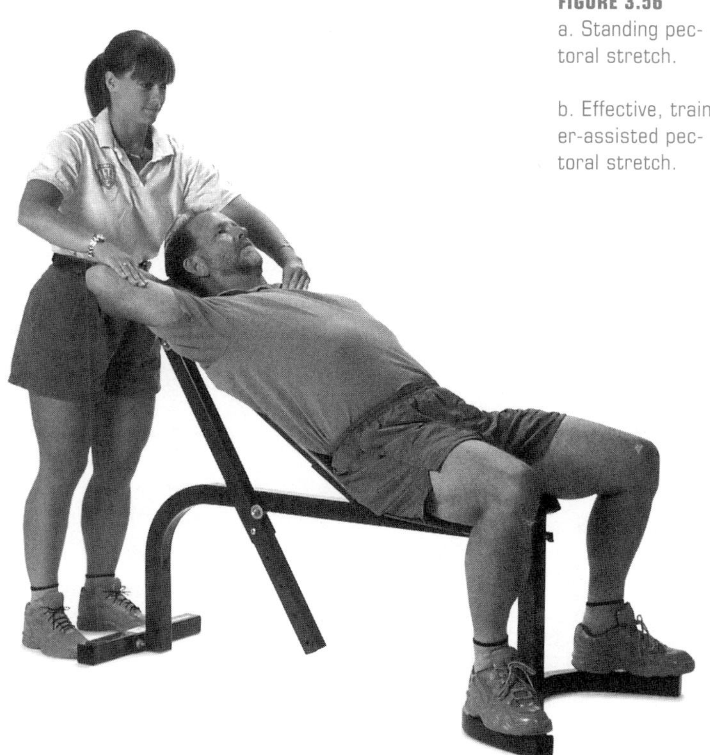

FIGURE 3.56
a. Standing pectoral stretch.

b. Effective, trainer-assisted pectoral stretch.

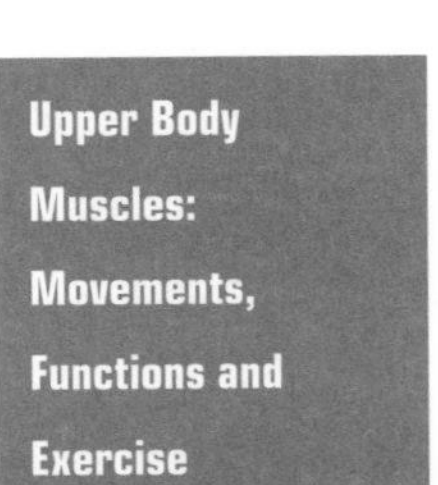

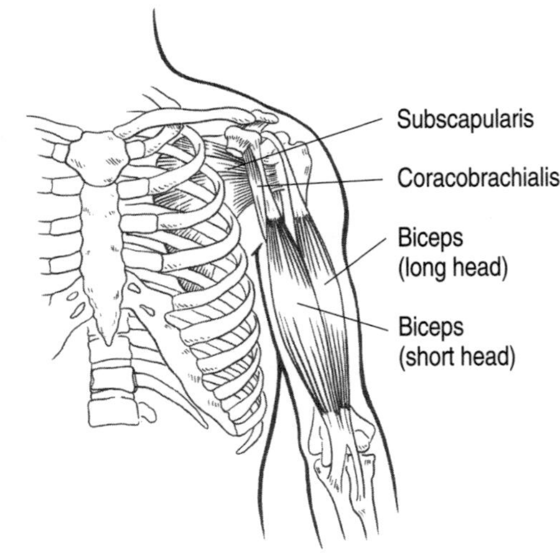

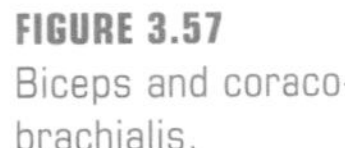
FIGURE 3.57
Biceps and coraco-brachialis.

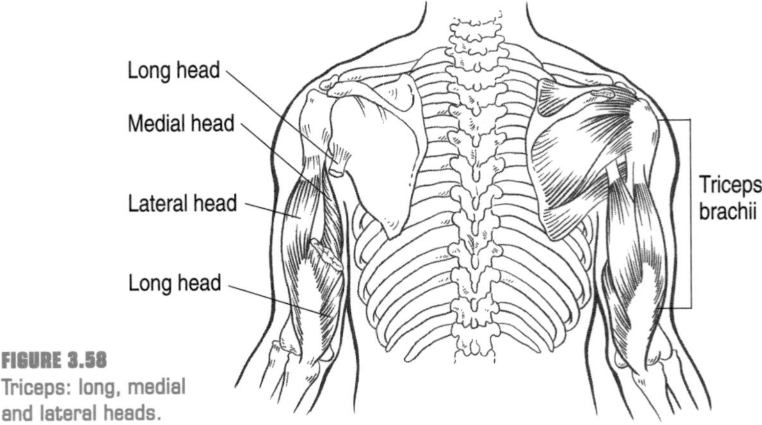

FIGURE 3.58
Triceps: long, medial and lateral heads.

in Figure 3.56b. Varying the angle of abduction would stretch different parts (sternal and clavicular) of the muscle. The posterior scapular muscles should actively contract to stabilize the scapulae in a depressed, retracted position.

Coracobrachialis and Biceps Brachii. The coracobrachialis and biceps brachii originate on the top front of the scapula and insert on the humerus (coracobrachialis) and radius (biceps) (Figure 3.57). They are **anterior** to the joint, so they flex the shoulder. The biceps brachii has two heads that attach to the scapula; if the shoulder is externally rotated, the long head moves laterally and will assist with shoulder abduction.

In addition to shoulder motion, the biceps flexes the elbow and **supinates** the forearm. The biceps curl is commonly used to strengthen this muscle. Incorporating supination with the curl will utilize both functions at the elbow.

However, the biceps is not the prime mover when the forearm is **pronated** (palms face down). The brachialis is the "pure flexor of the elbow." It is the prime mover for all positions of the forearm. This is demonstrated by feeling the biceps muscle as we first flex the elbow with the palm up, then down. Feeling it once more as we pull up against the bottom of a table with the back of the hand (resisted elbow flexion with pronation), we see that the biceps is a synergist when there is resistance. Because the biceps brachii is wrapped around the radius when the forearm is pronated, it cannot provide as much force for elbow flexion as it can when the forearm is supinated.

Triceps. The triceps also is a two-joint muscle, crossing posterior to the shoulder and elbow (Figure 3.58), attaching to the scapula proximally and the forearm distally. It therefore extends the shoulder and elbow joints. If using free weights as resistance, place the client's arm into an antigravity position. For example, the client could stand in a slight forward lunge and hold the shoulder in hyperextension, then extend the elbow. Or they could lie supine, pointing their elbow toward the ceiling, and then lift the hand toward the ceiling. The client could also hold the shoulders abducted to 70 degrees, then flex and extend the elbows.

Rotator Cuff Muscles. The muscles that rotate the shoulder joint are located on the scapula. They are stabilizers as well as movers. Their tendons form a cuff around the upper and posterior part of the joint. You may remember them better as S.I.T.S. muscles: supraspinatus, infraspinatus, teres minor and subscapularis. They attach to the humerus in that order, starting at the top and moving toward the back and then

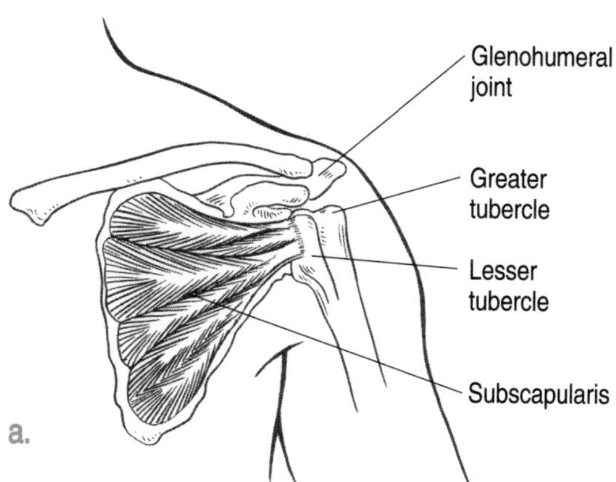

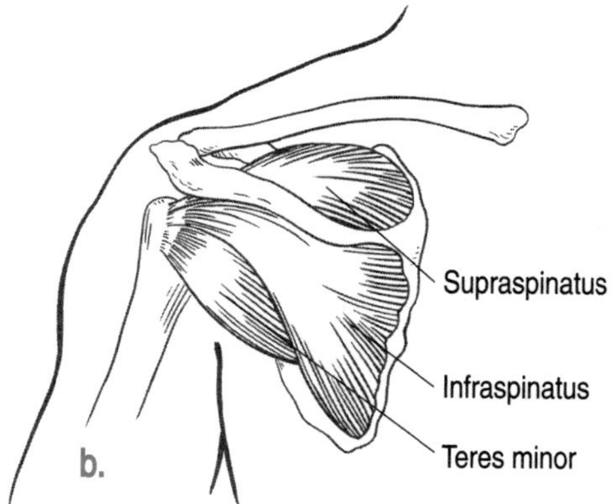

FIGURE 3.59
Rotator cuff muscles. Avoid shoulder abduction with internal rotation to prevent impingement.

a. Anterior view.

b. Posterior view.

around and underneath to the front (Figure 3.59). The supraspinatus is above (supra) the spine (spinatus) of the scapula. It does not rotate the shoulder in neutral, but helps abduct and stabilize the head of the humerus in the socket. The infraspinatus is below (infra) the scapular spine and the teres minor is located inferior to the infraspinatus. These muscles externally rotate the shoulder. The subscapularis is located on the anterior side, or beneath (sub) the scapula (scapularis), and attaches to the front of the humerus. It internally rotates the shoulder.

Impingement of these muscles can occur when the shoulder is abducted and internally rotated simultaneously. In this position, the humerus contacts the acromion, pinching the tendons, and they may fray and become inflamed. To prevent injury, abduct the shoulder when it is neutral or externally rotated.

Forearm and Wrist

The muscles located along the forearm act to control wrist and finger motion. The forearm muscles are usually exercised in all movements of the shoulder and elbow when a machine or gripping a weight is involved. They may also benefit from individual strengthening since restricted grip strength is sometimes the limiting factor for other exercises such as pull-ups or lunges performed while holding heavy dumbbells.

Applied Kinesiology

APPLIED KINESIOLOGY

The purpose of learning the location and functions of various muscles, as well as the mechanical principles of movement, is to enhance your ability to analyze movement and design effective exercises.

The body's position and the direction of gravity's pull often are clues to which muscle is contracting and how. If the movement occurs against the pull of gravity, the agonist which normally performs that joint action is contracting concentrically. If the movement is slow and controlled and occurs in the same direction as the pull of gravity, the agonist muscle is contracting eccentrically. (The motion must be slower than the segment during free fall with no muscle action. An eccentric contraction then provides a "braking" action on the movement.) If the motion occurs in the direction of gravity, but is faster than the acceleration of gravity or occurs against external resistance, the cause is a concentric contraction of the agonist. When the movement occurs perpendicular to the pull of gravity, it is usually due to alternating concentric contractions of the expected muscle groups.

As an illustration, analyze hip abduction and adduction in several body positions. In Figure 3.60a (side-lying leg raise), the joint action is hip abduction, against gravity. The hip abductors (agonists) are contract-

Examples of Exercise Analysis

ing concentrically. In the return phase, the joint action is hip adduction. However, since the motion occurs slowly in the same direction as gravity, hip adduction is controlled by the hip abductors contracting eccentrically. In Figure 3.60b (lying supine, hips flexed to 90 degrees, feet toward the ceiling), the joint action is horizontal abduction of the hip as the legs move apart. The movement occurs in the same direction as gravity and is controlled by the hip adductors contracting eccentrically. To lift the legs again, adduction occurs against gravity, by concentric contraction of the adductors. In Figure 3.60c (lying supine, legs extended on the floor), the joint actions are hip abduction and adduction. In this case, gravity is not a factor; the muscular action is what one would expect: the hip abductors contract concentrically as the hip abducts, and the hip adductors contract concentrically as the hip adducts.

FIGURE 3.60
Hip abduction and adduction.

a. Side-lying leg raise, hip adduction against gravity.

b. Supine with feet toward ceiling, legs are pulled apart and then together.

c. Supine with legs extended on the floor.

Exercise Analysis

The following questions may guide you in analyzing and designing effective exercises:

1. What movements occur at each joint?
2. Is the movement slow or fast, against resistance or not?
3. Is the motion occurring against gravity or in its same direction? Against some other resistance (pulleys, elastic)?
4. What muscles are causing the joint movement?
5. Is the contraction concentric, eccentric or isometric?
6. Which muscles are movers and which are stabilizers?
7. Does the movement achieve the stated goal of the exercise?
8. Does the exercise train the primary function of the muscle?
9. Does the movement compromise the safety of other body parts? Are non-moving joints stabilized adequately in neutral?
10. How can the exercise be adapted to meet the specific needs of the client (made more difficult or less difficult)?

EXAMPLES OF EXERCISE ANALYSIS

Having reviewed the locations and functions of most of the major muscles of the trunk and extremities, and having applied biomechanical principles pertinent to each muscle group and analyzed the type of muscle contractions involved in many joint movements, let's put it all together to analyze two exercises commonly employed by personal trainers: the push-up and the seated lat pull-down.

Push-up

Up-phase. To press the torso away from the floor, the body is raised by extending the elbows and horizontally flexing the shoulders. (Horizontal flexion occurs if the elbows are wide, but not if the elbows are held close to the sides.) Motion occurs at the shoulders, shoulder girdle, elbows and wrists. And, though no movement occurs, critical stabilization happens at the neck, lumbar spine and hips.

Shoulders: The joint movement is horizontal flexion and internal rotation. The movement occurs against gravity, so it is controlled by concentric contraction of the shoulder flexors and internal rotators: pectoralis major, anterior deltoid, coracobrachialis and subscapularis.

Shoulder girdle: The motion is scapular abduction and upward rotation controlled by concentric contraction of the agonists: pectoralis minor, serratus anterior, upper and middle trapezius and rhomboids.

Elbows: The movement is extension against gravity, so muscular action is concentric contraction of the extensors: triceps.

Wrists: Hyperextension occurs here by concentric contraction of the wrist extensors.

Head and neck: Cervical vertebrae are maintained in neutral alignment by isometric contraction of the cervical extensors. (When there is no movement, we can imagine what would happen if all muscles relaxed, then decide which muscles are contracting to prevent that motion.)

Lumbar spine: A neutral spine is maintained by isometric contraction of the abdominals.

Hips: No movement occurs, but the joint is stabilized by isometric contraction of the flexors since gravity, acting unresisted, would tend to cause hip extension.

Down-phase. In the down-phase of the movement, the opposite movements occur at the shoulder, shoulder girdle, elbows and wrists. Since the down-phase movements occur in the same direction as gravity, they are controlled by eccentric contractions of the muscles just listed. The head, spine and hips are maintained in a neutral position by the same muscles contracting isometrically.

Lat Pull-down

Next, analyze the "lat pull-down" pictured in Chapter 9 (page 275).

Down-phase. In the down-phase the resistance of the machine is lifted by adducting and extending the shoulders. The prime motion occurs at the shoulders, shoulder girdle and elbows. Stabilization occurs at the wrist, neck, lumbar spine and hips. In the analysis of an exercise performed against an external resistance other than gravity, the direction of the movement in relation to gravity is a lesser consideration.

Shoulders: The primary joint movements are adduction and extension. The movement occurs against the external resistance of the machine, so it is controlled by concentric contractions of the agonists: shoulder adductors (pectoralis major, latissimus dorsi and teres major), and extensors (latissimus, teres major, posterior deltoid and triceps). Also, some internal rotation may occur depending on the exact start and end positions, so the subscapularis also contracts concentrically.

Shoulder girdle: The motion is scapular adduction, depression and downward rotation occurring against the external resistance of the machine (the resistance is being lifted against gravity). Therefore, it is controlled by concentric contraction of the agonists: primarily the lower and middle trapezius muscles and the rhomboids.

Elbows: The movement is flexion against the resistance of the machine. (It occurs in the same direction as gravity, but we must remember that the resistance is being lifted against gravity.) The muscular action is concentric contraction of the biceps, and because the forearm is pronated, the brachialis also contracts concentrically.

Wrists: Ideally, the wrists should be stabilized in neutral by isometric co-contraction of the flexors and extensors.

Head and neck: Cervical vertebrae are maintained in neutral, with minimal muscle contraction if they are properly aligned.

Lumbar spine: In sitting, gravity tends to pull the pelvis into a posterior tilt. Neutral position is achieved by isometric contraction of the spinal extensors.

Hips: No movement occurs ordinarily, though a slight forward lean at the hip may occur, controlled by eccentric contraction of the hip extensors.

Return Phase. In the return phase of the exercise, the opposite motions occur at the shoulder, shoulder girdle and elbows. They are controlled by eccentric contractions of the muscles just listed for those three joints.

EXERCISE DESIGN, INSTRUCTION AND CORRECTION

The effective personal trainer applies the principles of biomechanics and kinesiology to analyze and design exercises appropriate for each individual client. It is important for you to begin the exercise program at the proper level and to progress slowly to prevent risk of injury.

To progressively overload muscles, use the principles of biomechanics presented earlier in this chapter: First, the body position can be changed from one in which gravity is not a factor to an antigravity position. Second, the trainer can utilize a series of concentric, eccentric and (when appropriate) isometric contractions of the same muscle group. Third, the lever arm of the resistance can be increased, as in a lateral raise with the elbow extended instead of flexed. External resistance can be added in the form of either your own manual resistance, elastic bands or tubing, or free weights applied with various lever arm lengths.

Injury prevention should be a major consideration when designing exercise programs. Body parts such as the neck and low back should not be put at risk for injury in order to gain advantage for another muscle group. Progressive resistance should be added gradually. Decrease the resistance if form is not perfect. Thorough instruction and continual reminders also are important.

Spotting is particularly crucial when working with large amounts of resistance. You should be able to recognize muscle substitution patterns that occur as muscles fatigue and approach failure. This will show as subtle variations in body position that allow other muscles to substitute. The client may be focused on more reps and often will not even realize that their form has changed. You must take responsibility for recognizing these substitutions and signs of fatigue so that the spine and surrounding structures are not injured.

In correcting a client's position, there are two effective methods. First, place your hand in the desired position and ask the client to touch it. For example, if the client has a forward head posture, put your hand where their head would be with good alignment and instruct them to glide their head back to touch your hand. An alternative is to place your hand in the undesired position and instruct them to avoid contact with your hand. For example, if the client is allowing their knees to go forward past the toes in a squat, place your hand even with the toes and instruct the client to keep the knees behind your hand. These techniques encourage the person to actively assume the correct position. They set up the desired neurological pathways and recruitment patterns, improving kinesthetic awareness of the correct position.

Pushing or pulling a person's body into a desired position will usually produce a reflex response in the opposite direction and may actually interfere with their ability to actively return to the desired position.

Summary

SUMMARY

The body is like an incredible machine. Its function actually improves with use if its movement is compatible with its design and the physical laws of motion. However, if repetitive movement occurs that is incompatible with the body's design, a breakdown results, either as an acute injury or degeneration over time. It is vital that the exercises and activities you employ as a personal trainer not only enhance the body's performance, but also prevent its injury in the gym and in real life.

Use the tools and knowledge base of kinesiology to prepare your clients for the physical activities of their lives. Consider the body's daily activities, postures and the physical stresses it undergoes in those positions. Next, identify possible areas of weakness or tightness caused by those habitual positions and activities. Then design activities to improve the body's function under those performance conditions. The result will be a balanced fitness program which not only includes cardiovascular endurance, but also muscular balance, neutral alignment and good body mechanics.

REFERENCES

Basmajian & Deluca. (1985). *Muscles Alive.* (5th ed.) Baltimore: Williams and Wilkins.

Ellison, D. (1993). Biomechanics and Applied Kinesiology. In Richard T. Cotton, (Ed.) *Aerobics Instructor Manual: The Resource for Fitness Professionals.* San Diego: American Council on Exercise.

Ellison, D. (1993). *Advanced Exercise Design for Lower Body.* San Diego: E & C Productions.

Ellison, D. (1995). *Advanced Exercise Design for Upper Body.* San Diego: E & C Productions.

Enoka, R. (1994). *Neuromechanical Basis of Kinesiology.* Champaign: Human Kinetics.

Luttgens, K., Deutsch, H. & Hamilton, N. (1992). *Kinesiology: Scientific Basis of Human Motion.* Dubuque: Brown and Benchmark.

Kapit, W. & Elson, L. (1977). *The Anatomy Coloring Book.* New York: Harper & Row.

Kendall, McCreary & Provance. (1993). *Muscles: Testing and Function.* Baltimore: Williams & Wilkins.

Kreighbaum, E. & Barthels, K. (1981). *Biomechanics.* Minneapolis: Burgess.

Norkin & Levangie. (1992). *Joint Structure and Function.* Philadelphia: F.A. Davis.

Rasch, P. (1989). *Kinesiology and Applied Anatomy.* Philadelphia: Lea & Febiger.

CHAPTER 4 Nutrition

4

IN THIS CHAPTER:

Jacqueline R. Berning

Jacqueline R. Berning, Ph.D., R.D., holds a master's degree in exercise science from the University of Colorado-Boulder and a doctorate in nutrition from Colorado State University. Currently she is associate professor in the department of biology at the University of Colorado in Colorado Springs, and is the co-author of TRAINING NUTRITION: The Diet and Nutrition Guide for Peak Performance *with Ed Burke, Ph.D. She is the nutrition consultant for United States Swimming, the University of Colorado Athletic Department in Boulder, the Denver Broncos and the Cleveland Indians minor league teams.*

Over the past 10 years, nutrition research and education have become a priority for many Americans. We now recognize that a lack of nutrition knowledge and poor eating habits can contribute to poor fitness, low energy stores and the development of such lifestyle-related diseases as heart disease, some types of cancer and obesity. The time is right for Americans to start making wise food choices and commit to an exercise program. Eating well is not difficult in principle. All that is needed is to eat a selection of foods that supplies appropriate amounts of the essential nutrients and energy. Yet to put this into practice may be extremely difficult for some. As a personal trainer, you will help your clients commit to fitness programs, and make appropriate food selections for good health. You should

Why is it so Hard to Make Wise Food Choices?

become knowledgeable about nutrition so you can provide sound, credible nutrition information to your clients in terms they can understand and follow, as well as know when to refer them to a registered dietitian or physician. Find a local resource in nutrition, possibly a registered dietitian capable of giving sensible responses to your questions, or a group of dietitians who practice in sports and cardiovascular nutrition (SCAN). To locate local SCAN dietitians, contact the American Dietetic Association and ask for the SCAN referral list. And most important, be a role model and practice healthful eating habits to show a commitment to good nutrition.

WHY IS IT SO HARD TO MAKE WISE FOOD CHOICES?

Why are we so tempted to eat foods that we know we should avoid? What triggers our eating habits? Why do we like high-fat, high-calorie foods?

Many factors influence our eating patterns, including hunger, habits, economics, marketing, availability, convenience and nutritional value. Probably the strongest reason we choose to eat certain foods is for taste. We like the taste of sweet and salty foods and, as a result, we tend to eat too many of them. We also like foods that have happy associations, such as those we eat at family gatherings or on holidays.

Social pressure has a very powerful influence on food choices and it is at work in every culture and social circle. Many of us have been programmed to feel that it is rude not to accept food in certain social situations, and we've all felt the pressure of being forced to eat at office celebrations even though we are not hungry or are trying to watch caloric intake. Availability, convenience and economics also play a role in choosing the foods we do. You cannot eat foods that are unavailable or unaffordable. In addition, because we are all so busy, we tend to pick foods based on convenience. We are more likely to choose foods that we can pop in the microwave and eat in five minutes, than take the time to prepare a meal from scratch. Both physical and emotional stress affect our eating habits. Some people respond to stress, whether positive or negative, by eating; others may use food to ward off loneliness, boredom or anxiety.

As you can see, there are a variety of reasons for choosing the foods we do. So how do you get your clients, and perhaps yourself, to select foods with good nutritional value? To do so successfully, you need to help your clients learn about the nutrients that the body needs and, specifically, what foods supply them in adequate amounts for optimal health and fitness.

NUTRIENTS

Nutrients are life-sustaining substances found in food. They work together to supply the body with energy and structural materials, and to regulate growth, maintenance and repair of the body's tissues.

Protein, carbohydrate, fat, vitamins, minerals and water are the six major classes of nutrients. Table 4.1 lists the nutrient classes and their major functions. While the amounts of nutrients that a body needs varies widely from one nutrient to another, there are guidelines for making sure that the body receives enough **nutrients** to sustain a healthy and active lifestyle.

Essential Nutrients

The body can make certain nutrients from other nutrients. For example, it can convert some amino acids into carbohydrates, and it can manufacture some vitamins from amino acids as well. However, certain compounds that the body cannot make for itself, called **essential amino acids**, are absolutely indispensable to bodily functions. There are about 40 essential nutrients to be concerned about, so it may be a relief to discover that diet planning can be reduced to a few simple principles to ensure that we take in all the nutrients in the appropriate amounts without having to count and weigh each one.

Recommended Nutrient Intakes

Normal, healthy adults of average size who engage in physical activity should consume the following amounts of nutrients daily to remain in optimal health.

- ✔ Protein — approximately 50 to 70 grams, depending on body size, or 12 percent to 20 percent of caloric intake as protein
- ✔ Carbohydrate — a minimum of 125 grams, optimal 350 to 400 grams, or 55 percent to 65 percent of caloric intake as carbohydrate
- ✔ Fat — approximately 30 to 65 grams, depending on caloric consumption, or 25 percent to 30 percent of caloric intake from fat
- ✔ Vitamins — specific amounts are listed in the Recommended Dietary Allowances (RDA)
- ✔ Minerals — specific amounts are listed in the RDA
- ✔ Water — 2 to 3 quarts per day

Table 4.1
The Six Classes of Nutrients and Their Major Functions

Nutrient	Function
Protein	✔ Builds and repairs body tissue ✔ Major component of enzymes, hormones and antibodies
Carbohydrate	✔ Provides a major source of fuel to the body ✔ Provides dietary fibers
Lipids	✔ Chief storage form of energy in the body ✔ Insulate and protect vital organs ✔ Provide fat-soluble vitamins
Vitamins	✔ Help promote and regulate various chemical reactions and bodily processes ✔ Do not yield energy themselves, but participate in releasing energy from food
Minerals	✔ Enable enzymes to function ✔ A component of hormones ✔ A part of bone and nerve impulses
Water	✔ Enables chemical reactions to occur ✔ About 60 percent of the body is composed of water ✔ Essential for life as we cannot store it, nor conserve it

RECOMMENDED DIETARY ALLOWANCE

The **Recommended Dietary Allowances (RDAs)** are nutrient recommendations designed to meet the needs of essentially all people of similar age and gender. Established by the Food and Nutrition Board of the National Academy of Science, they are a general guide for estimating your nutritional needs. RDAs are expressed as an optimal amount with upper and lower limits — meaning too little is not good and too much also may present problems. Many Americans mistakingly believe that if a little is good, more has to be better. In nutrition, however, that kind of thinking may lead to toxicities, especially with some **fat-soluble** vitamins.

The RDA is to be used as a guide — a ballpark figure. It does not mean that if you do not consume the RDA for a certain vitamin or mineral that you will come down with a deficiency disease. On the contrary, symptoms of nutritional deficiencies may be subtle and develop over a long period of time. The opposite also is true. Taking large amounts of specific vitamins or minerals also may lead to toxicity problems. The RDAs are not minimums. Be careful when assessing a client's diet using the RDA. Use it to see if your clients are getting the nutrients they need. If a client is consistently three quarters below the RDA for a particular nutrient for a long period, they may be at risk for certain

Dietary Guidelines

FIGURE 4.1
The Food Guide Pyramid.

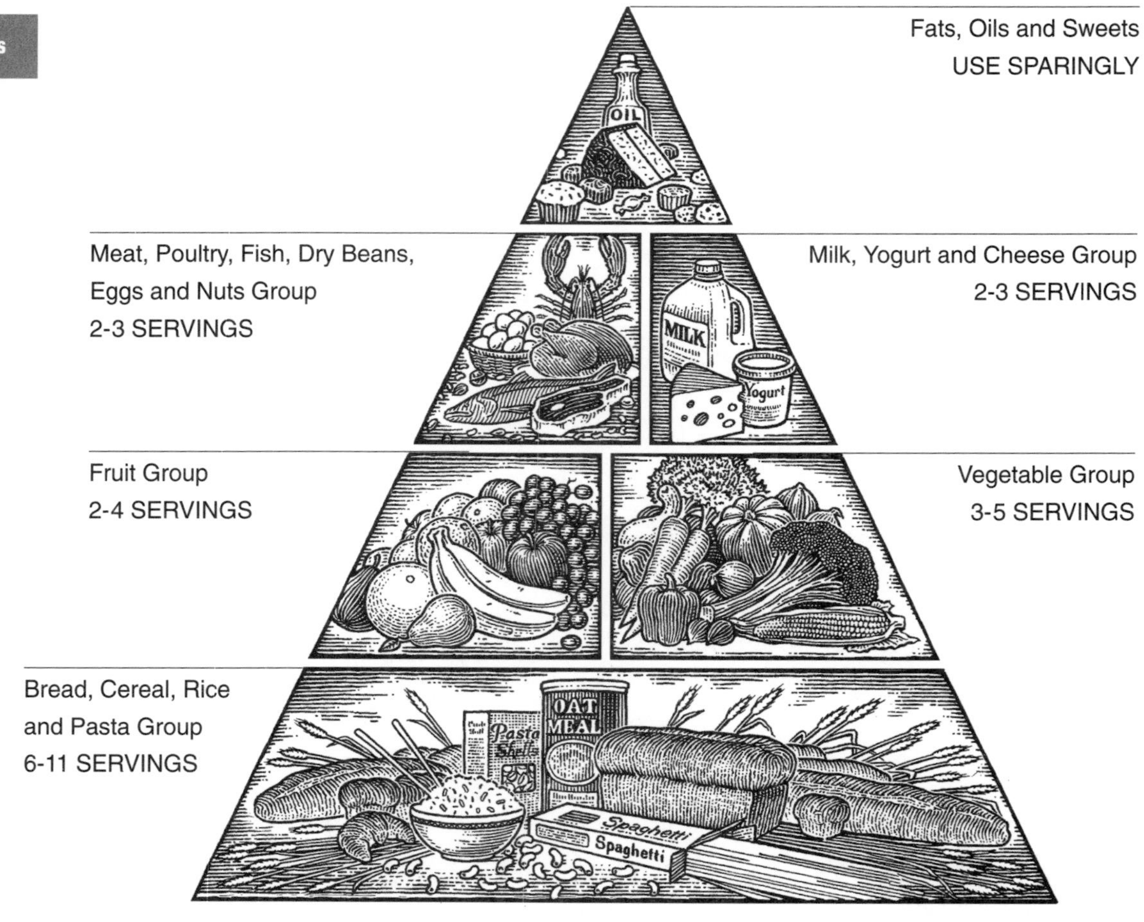

Use the Food Guide Pyramid to help you eat better every day ... the Dietary Guidelines way. Start with plenty of Breads, Cereals, Rice and Pasta; Vegetables; and Fruits. Add two to three servings from the Milk group and two to three servings from the Meat group.

Each of these food groups provides some, but not all, of the nutrients you need. No one food group is more important than another — for good health you need them all. Go easy on fats, oils and sweets, the foods in the tip of the Pyramid.

Source: U.S. Department of Agriculture.

nutritional deficiencies. You should consult with the client's physician and/or a registered dietitian rather than diagnose dietary deficiencies. You can make diet- ary suggestions by using the Food Guide Pyramid approach, emphasizing variety and moderation.

DIETARY GUIDELINES

In response to the fact that overindulgence of either fat, sugar and sodium are risk factors in the leading causes of death in the United States and other developing countries, the federal government issued the Dietary Guidelines — seven principles that all Americans should know in order to make wise food choices. By adapting these seven principles, people can reduce their risk of such diet-related diseases as cancer, heart disease, diabetes, hypertension and **obesity**, to name a few. The Dietary Guidelines for Americans are as follows:

1. Eat a variety of foods.
2. Balance the food you eat with physical

Table 4.2
The Food Guide Pyramid — A Summary

Food Group	Servings	Major Contributions	Food and Serving Size
Milk, Yogurt, Cheese	2-3 adult; 3-4 children, teens, pregnant, or lactating	Calcium Carbohydrate Riboflavin Protein Zinc Potassium	1 cup of milk 1½ ounce of cheese 1 cup yogurt 2 cups cottage cheese 1 cup pudding
Meat, Poultry, Fish, Dry Beans, Eggs and Nuts	2-3	Protein Niacin Iron Vitamin B_6 Zinc Thiamin Vitamin B_{12}	2-3 ounces of meat, poultry or fish 1½ cups beans 2 Tbsp. peanut butter 2 eggs ½-1 cup nuts
Fruits	2-4	Carbohydrate Vitamin C Fiber	¼ cup dried fruit ½ cup cooked fruit ¾ cup juice 1 whole piece of fruit
Vegetables	3-5	Carbohydrate Vitamin A Vitamin C Folate Magnesium Dietary Fiber	½ cup raw or cooked 1 cup leafy greens ½ cup vegetable juice
Bread, Cereals Rice and Pasta	6-11	Carbohydrate Thiamin Iron Niacin Folate Magnesium Fiber Zinc	1 slice of bread 1 ounce of ready-to-eat cereal ½ - ¾ cup cooked cereal, pasta or rice
Fats, Oils and Sweets	Foods from this group should not replace any from the other groups. Amounts consumed should be determined by individual energy needs.		

activity to maintain or improve your weight.

3. Choose a diet low in total fat, saturated fat and cholesterol.

4. Choose a diet with plenty of vegetables, fruits and grain products.

5. Choose a diet moderate in sugars.

6. Choose a diet moderate in salt and sodium.

7. If you drink alcoholic beverages, do so in moderation.

Specifically, experts say to reduce your intake of all fats to no more than 30 percent of total calories. The current consumption of fat in this country is around 34 percent. Saturated fat should provide no more than 10 percent of total daily calories, and cholesterol should not exceed 300 milligrams daily. More breads, rice, pasta, cereals, bagels, fruits and vegetables should be consumed, and salts and sugars should be eaten in moderation. There may be possible benefits to moderate consumption of alcoholic beverages, such as a reduced risk of heart disease, but your clients should discuss appropriate alcohol intake with their physician. Women should also be

Food Guide Pyramid

reminded not to drink alcohol when they are pregnant.

FOOD GUIDE PYRAMID

While the RDA lists specific amounts of nutrients to consume, they only make general statements about energy, and little or no recommendations about fat, sugar, cholesterol, salt or alcohol consumption. For this reason, the United States Department of Agriculture (USDA) developed the **Food Guide Pyramid,** a guide to daily food choices comprised of six food groups. The Food Guide Pyramid serves three main purposes: it graphically displays the dietary guidelines, replaces the Basic Four Food Groups that most individuals learned back in third grade, and reflects contemporary nutrition knowledge (Figure 4.1). The Food Guide Pyramid is a practical way to turn the RDAs and the Dietary Guidelines into food choices. You can get all the essential nutrients by eating a balanced variety of foods each day from the food groups listed in the pyramid. The minimum number of servings of each food group provides approximately 1,600 to 1,800 calories. Table 4.2 lists serving sizes, recommended servings per day and major nutrient contributions of each group in the Food Guide Pyramid. Other points to keep in mind when using the Food Guide Pyramid:

1. The guide does not apply to infants or children under the age of two.

2. Variety is the key to the plan, and is guaranteed by choosing foods from all groups and selecting different foods within each group.

3. Consuming moderate amounts of calories from fat and sugar will help.

The Food Guide Pyramid is a helpful tool in teaching clients how to make wise food choices, plan menus for nutritious meals, grocery shop and assess a diet to determine if it's nutritionally sound. Advise clients to follow three easy steps:

Step 1: Eat foods from each food group every day. The five food groups in the pyramid will supply more than 40 nutrients that the body needs to stay healthy.

Step 2: Include a variety of foods from each food group. Foods within each group in the pyramid are usually good sources of the same nutrients, and by eating different foods within each food group, clients have a good chance of getting all the nutrients they need. You can suggest to clients that yogurt be substituted for milk because it supplies protein, calcium and riboflavin in about the same amounts. Dried beans and peas, as well as nuts, are alternative choices for meats.

Each food group is a source of leader nutrients.

- ✔ Try lowfat milk, cheeses and yogurt from the Milk Group. They supply the body with calcium, protein and riboflavin as leader nutrients. The recommended number of servings per day is two to three with a serving size of 8 ounces of fluid or 1 ounce of cheese (Table 4.2).
- ✔ Experiment with new recipes for chicken, fish, beef, eggs, dried beans and peas from the Meat Group. These supply leader nutrients such as protein, niacin, iron and thiamine. The recommended number of servings is two to three of a 2- to 3-ounce serving size (Table 4.2).
- ✔ Find creative ways to include servings from the Fruit Group. The recommended number of servings from this group has increased to two to four per day and can be met by adding fruit to breads and cereals, or using it in place of high-fat, high-sugar snacks. One serving is one fresh piece, or ½ cup cooked fruit.
- ✔ Consume more foods from the Vegetable Group. Try adding spinach, carrots, broccoli, mushrooms and green peppers to salads and casseroles. This group provides vitamins A and C as

leader nutrients. It is recommended that people eat five servings of vegetables daily, as demonstrated by the new slogan "Five Alive," meaning five servings of vegetables a day for a healthy lifestyle. One serving is ½-cup cooked vegetables.

- ✔ Enjoy new tastes from the Grain Group. Try bagels, tortillas, and rye, pita or cracked-wheat bread for sandwiches. The Grain Group supplies carbohydrates, thiamine, iron and niacin as leader nutrients. One serving is one slice of bread or ½ cup cereal, pasta or rice.

Step 3: Practice moderation. Individuals can get the nutrients they need without getting additional, unnecessary amounts of fat and/or sodium by eating moderate amounts of food. Help your clients do this by suggesting they:

- ✔ Eat at least the recommended number of servings from each food group in the Pyramid every day.
- ✔ Pay attention to how many servings they eat from the group at the top of the pyramid. Foods that do not fit into any of the Food Groups are listed together at the top of the pyramid. Although some of them do contribute nutrients, they are either not classified as foods or their nutrient content is not significant enough to characterize them with other food groups. Many years ago, health professionals labeled these foods "empty calories," meaning they contain more calories than nutrients. Today, most nutritionists use the concept of **nutrient density.** This is a measure of nutrients per calorie. A nutrient-dense food provides more nutrients at a low-caloric cost, whereas a non-nutrient-dense food, such as potato chips, cake, cookies and soda pop, is one that contains more calories and/or fat and fewer nutrients.
- ✔ Eat servings of food in the portions listed in Table 4.2.

As you can see, the Food Guide Pyramid can be used with great flexibility. The plan can be adapted to casseroles and other mixed dishes and can be used to assess different national and cultural cuisines. Oriental dishes that have vegetables, chicken and rice supply three of the five groups. Spanish and Mexican dishes, such as tamales with beans, rice, cheese and salsa have four out of the five groups; by adding a banana, all five food groups will be included in one meal. The pyramid is especially useful for clients who exercise or train regularly. Eating the higher number of recommended servings from the grain group, and eating more servings from the fruits and vegetables group will provide additional carbohydrates so that athletes and active individuals can meet their energy requirements.

VEGETARIANS

The vegetarian faces a special problem in diet planning — obtaining the needed nutrients from fewer food groups. There are two major classes of vegetarians (with many variations): the **lacto-ovo vegetarian** eats milk and eggs but excludes meat, fish and poultry from the diet, whereas a pure vegetarian, or **vegan,** eats only foods from plant sources.

For both types, it is necessary to know how to combine foods to obtain the nutrients for health, as well as performance. Foods derived from animal sources like chicken, fish, beef, milk and eggs contain all the essential amino acids and are called **complete proteins.** Plant sources of food contain incomplete proteins because they are missing one or more amino acids. **Incomplete proteins** can be made complete by combining them either with other foods that are complete proteins, such as cereal with milk, and rice with cheese, or with other incomplete proteins, such as beans with rice, and peanut butter with bread. Many cultures have dishes or food

Nutrient Needs for the Physically Active Adult

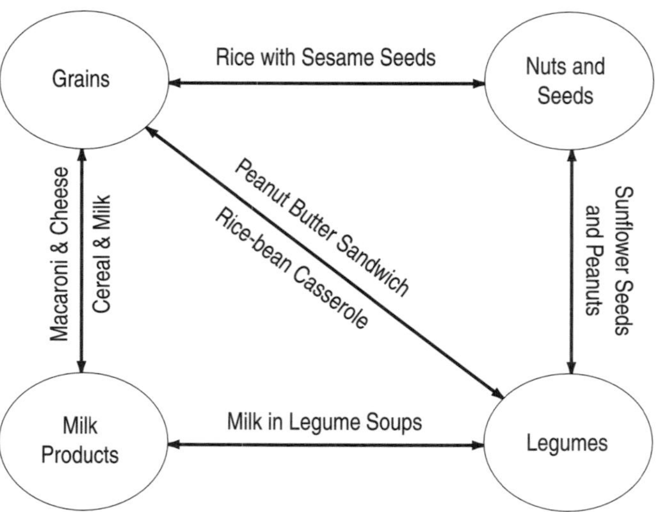

FIGURE 4.2
Protein complementarity chart. Adapted from *Diet for a Small Planet* by Frances M. Lappé.

combinations that meet the requisite amino acid combinations. In most cases, these dishes have been served for many generations. For example, Mexicans serve beans and tortillas and/or rice; Indians eat lentils and rice; Lebanese prepare humus tahini (garbanzo beans and sesame seed paste) with pita bread; and cornbread and beans are served in the southern United States. Figure 4.2 gives examples of how to combine incomplete proteins to make a complete protein. Eating extra servings of grains, nuts and seeds will supply the necessary quantities of riboflavin, iron and zinc.

For the lacto-ovo vegetarian, the Food Guide Pyramid can be adapted by making a change in the meat group and by using non-meat proteins such as eggs, dairy products, legumes and nuts. The strict vegetarian who doesn't eat dairy products or animal protein should take a vitamin B_{12} supplement, or use soy or rice milk fortified with vitamin B_{12} and calcium.

NUTRIENT NEEDS FOR THE PHYSICALLY ACTIVE ADULT

Carbohydrates

Carbohydrates are the most important nutrient for exercising muscles. Adequate amounts of carbohydrates are essential not only for muscular performance, but for the brain and central nervous system. The principle functions of carbohydrates are to:

- ✔ serve as the primary energy source for working muscles
- ✔ ensure that the brain and nervous system function properly
- ✔ help the body use fat more efficiently

Stored carbohydrates, in the form of **glycogen,** are the primary fuel for exercise. If your clients are having a hard time maintaining normal workout intensities, they may have inadequate muscle carbohydrate or glycogen stores. Unless adequate glycogen levels are restored, exercise performance will continue to deteriorate to the point where even a low-intensity workout causes fatigue.

Carbohydrate Recommendations

Clients should consume at least 55 percent to 65 percent of their total calories from carbohydrates. Those who exercise more than one hour every day should consume close to 65 percent of their calories as carbohydrates. Those who work out every other day should consume around 55 percent to 60 percent of calories from carbohydrates. Current consumption of carbohydrates for Americans is about 45 percent, and much of this is in the form of simple carbohydrates or sugars rather than complex carbohydrates such as breads, cereal, rice and pasta. Complex

Table 4.3
Foods Listed by Groups with Carbohydrate and Fat Content

	Calories	Carbohydrate (gm)	Fat (gm)
Milk Group			
2% Milk, 1 cup	121	12	5
Skim Milk, 1 cup	86	12	0
Lowfat Yogurt, 1 cup	225	42	3
Cottage Cheese, 1 cup	164	7	2
Lowfat Cheddar Cheese	80	8	5
Lowfat American Cheese	72	6	4
Lowfat Mozzarella Cheese	79	8	5
Meat Group			
Lean Ground Beef, 3 oz.	214	0	14
Flank Steak, 3 oz.	209	0	12
Chicken, Light Meat w/o Skin, Roasted, 3 oz.	148	0	4
Chicken, Dark Meat, w/o Skin, Roasted, 3 oz.	176	0	8
Turkey, Light Meat, w/o Skin, Roasted, 3 oz.	135	0	3
Turkey, Dark Meat, w/o Skin, Roasted, 3 oz.	160	0	6
Turkey Sandwich Slices, 1 oz.	44	0	1
Tuna, Spring Water, 1 oz.	60	0	1
Rainbow Trout, Broiled, 3 oz	129	0	4
Salmon, 3 oz.	99	0	3
Beans, Refried, 1 cup	270	47	3
Kidney Beans, 1 cup	216	40	1
Ham, Lean, 3 oz.	124	1	5
Peas, Blackeye, 1 cup	198	36	1
Peanut Butter, 1Tbsp.	95	2	8
Fruits			
Apple, Medium	80	20	1
Applesauce, ½ cup	53	14	0
Apricots, Dried, 4 halves	33	9	0
Banana, Medium	105	27	0
Cantaloupe, 1 cup pieces	57	13	0
Cherries, Sweet, 10	49	11	0
Dates, Dried, 10	228	61	0
Grapefruit, 1 half	39	10	0
Grapes, 1 cup	58	16	0
Orange	65	16	0
Peach	37	10	0
Pear	98	25	0
Pineapple, 1 cup pieces	77	19	0
Raisins, ⅔ cup	300	79	0
Strawberries, 1 cup	45	11	0
Watermelon, 1 cup	50	12	0
Vegetables			
Asparagus, 6 spears	22	4	0
Green Beans, ½ cup	22	5	0
Broccoli, ½ cup	23	4	0
Carrots, 1 medium	31	7	0
Cauliflower, ½ cup	15	3	0
Celery, 1 stalk	6	2	0
Corn, ½ cup	89	21	0
Green Peas, ½ cup	67	13	0
Baked Potato	220	51	0
Mushrooms, ½ cup	9	2	0
Spinach, ½ cup	6	1	0
Tomato	24	5	0
Grain Group			
Bagel	163	31	1

continued on next page

Nutrient Needs for the Physically Active Adult

Table 4.3 continued

	Calories	Carbohydrate (gm)	Fat (gm)
Whole Wheat Bread, 1 slice	61	11	1
White Bread, 1 slice	64	12	1
French Bread, 1 slice	81	15	1
Bread Sticks, 2	77	15	1
Graham Crackers, 2 squares	60	11	1
Saltines, 10	125	20	4
Oatmeal, Quaker, ¾ cup	105	18	2
English Muffin	135	26	1
Life Cereal, Quaker, ⅔ cup	111	19	2
Pancake, 4" diameter	61	9	2
Pasta, ½ cup	100	19	1
Rice, ½ cup	112	25	0
Flour Tortilla, 8"	105	18	3

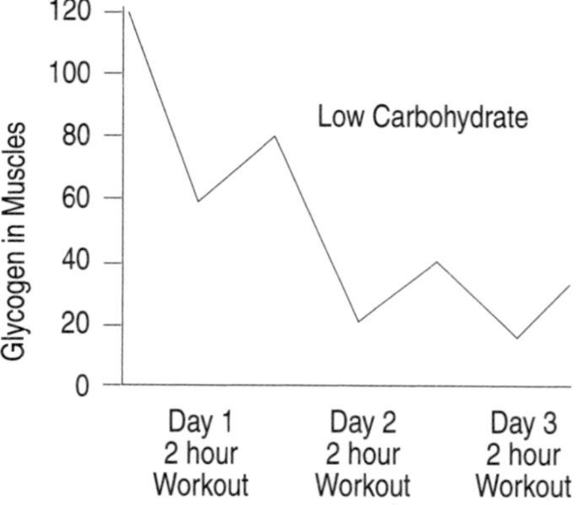

FIGURE 4.3
After 3 days of training, individuals can use most of their muscle glycogen. A low-carbohydrate diet does not replace the glycogen quickly enough.

carbohydrates also contain ample amounts of B vitamins and fiber, and some trace minerals. While telling a client to consume 65 percent of their total calories from carbohydrates is excellent advice, most individuals have no idea how much carbohydrate that is or what foods they should be eating to reach that goal. It appears that most consumers find it easier to count grams of carbohydrate than calculate percentages. The recommended carbohydrate intake in gram weight is 8 to 10 grams of carbohydrate per kilogram of body weight. By giving your client a list of common carbohydrate foods in grams weight, they can calculate how many servings and what carbohydrate foods they should be eating more of (Table 4.3).

Carbohydrate Loading

Muscle glycogen depletion is a well-recognized limitation to endurance exercise that exceeds 90 minutes (Figure 4.3). **Carbohydrate loading** can nearly double an individual's muscle glycogen stores. Obviously, the greater the pre-exercise glycogen content, the greater the endurance potential.

The classic study on carbohydrate loading compared exercise time to exhaustion. Subjects exercised at 75 percent of VO_2 max after consuming diets with varying amounts of carbohydrate — a low-carbohydrate diet, a normal diet and a high-carbohydrate diet. The low-carbohydrate diet sustained only an hour of exercise; the mixed diet sustained 115 minutes of exercise; and the high-carbohydrate diet sustained 170 minutes of the high-intensity exercise (Bergstrom, 1991).

Following additional research, the carbohydrate-loading sequence developed into a week-long regimen, beginning with an exhaustive training session one week before competition. For the next three days, the athlete consumed a low-carbohydrate diet, yet continued exercising to lower muscle glycogen stores even further. Then, for three days prior to competition, the athlete rested and consumed a high-carbohydrate diet to promote glycogen supercompensation. For many years, this week-long sequence was considered the optimal way to achieve maximum glycogen storage. However, it has many drawbacks. The three days of reduced carbohydrate intake can cause **hypoglycemia** (low blood sugar) and **ketosis** (increased blood acids), which is associated with nausea, fatigue, dizziness and irritability. These dietary manipulations prove to be too cumbersome for many athletes, and an exhaustive training session the week before competition may predispose the athlete to injury.

A revised method of carbohydrate loading eliminates many of the problems associated with the old regimen. Six days before the competition, the athlete exercises hard (70 percent to 75 percent of aerobic capacity for 90 minutes) and consumes a diet of 60 percent carbohydrates. On the second and third days, training is decreased to 40 minutes at 70 percent to 75 percent of aerobic capacity and, again, the athlete consumes the same diet. On the next two days, the athlete consumes a high-carbohydrate diet providing 70 percent carbohydrate (about 550 grams, or 10 grams per kilogram) and reduces training to 20 minutes at 70 percent to 75 percent of aerobic capacity. On the last day, the athlete rests while maintaining the high-carbohydrate diet. The modified regimen results in muscle glycogen stores equal to those provided by the classic low-carbohydrate regimen (Table 4.4).

Today, most athletes no longer practice the full technique of carbohydrate loading simply because they train and need to have glycogen stores maximized every day. It appears that most exercising individuals are now concerned about reloading muscle glycogen stores following heavy training to minimize fatigue associated with repeated days of it. This means that most individuals need to consume adequate amounts of carbohydrates every day.

Table 4.4
Modified Carbohydrate Loading Technique

Day	Exercise Duration	Dietary Carbohydrate %
1	90 minutes	60
2	40 minutes	60
3	40 minutes	60
4	20 minutes	70
5	20 minutes	70
6	rest	70
7	competition	70

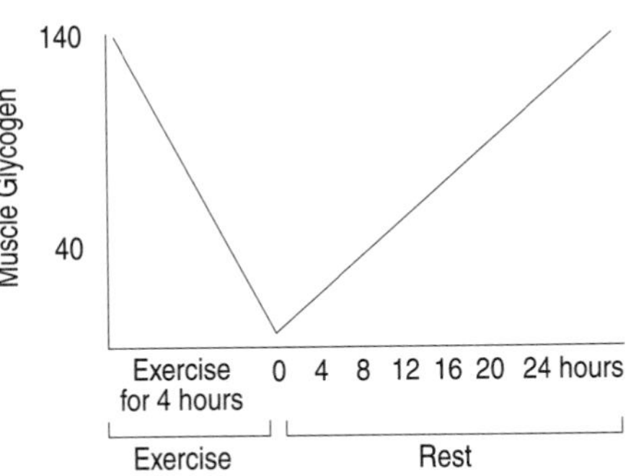

FIGURE 4.4
It takes 24 hours to replenish muscle glycogen after strenuous exercise.

Glycogen Resynthesis

It takes about 24 hours before muscle glycogen is fully restored (Figure 4.4). However, some individuals may exercise again in 12 hours or less. It appears that *when* carbohydrate is consumed, relative to exercise, is important for refilling muscle glycogen. Studies have shown that when carbohydrate consumption is delayed after exercise, muscle glycogen storage is reduced and recovery is impaired. Ivy and associates found that individuals who consume about 1.5 grams of carbohydrate per kilogram of body weight (about 100 grams) within 30 minutes after a moderate- to high-intensity exercise session, followed by an additional 1.5 grams of carbohydrate per kilogram of body weight every two hours, maximizes muscle glycogen levels (Ivy, 1988). Keep in mind that these guidelines are for highly fit exercisers; glycogen resynthesis is less of a concern for moderate exercisers.

Recently, Zawadzki and colleagues found that combining protein with carbohydrates induced a faster rate of glycogen resynthesis in four hours than either the carbohydrates or protein alone. They found significantly higher blood glucose and insulin levels, factors that stimulate glucose uptake by the muscles and activation of the enzyme that converts glucose to glycogen (Zawadski, 1992). Table 4.5 lists foods that

Table 4.5
Foods with Protein and 100 Grams of Carbohydrate

- ✔ One bagel with peanut butter and ⅔ cup of raisins
- ✔ One cup lowfat yogurt, one banana and a cup of orange juice
- ✔ One turkey sandwich on whole wheat bread with one cup of applesauce
- ✔ Spaghetti with meat sauce and garlic bread
- ✔ 8 ounces of skim milk, one apple, one orange, two slices of bread and three pancakes
- ✔ 12 ounces of a carbohydrate-loading drink and a bagel

contain 100 grams of carbohydrates as well as some protein.

Glycemic Index

A number of different types of carbohydrates have been studied to determine which might be optimal for glycogen resynthesis. Carbohydrates that quickly empty into the blood stream (high glycemic) are recommended immediately after exercise. High-glycemic foods such as simple carbohydrates raise blood glucose and insulin levels, and facilitate glycogen synthesis. The remaining carbohydrates should be derived from other natural resources, such as the complex and simple carbohydrates found in fruits, vegetables, breads, cereals, pasta and rice. Table 4.6 lists foods with different glycemic indices.

Table 4.6
Glycemic Index of Various Food

High Glycemic Foods (greater than 85)
Honey, Corn Syrup
Bagel, White Bread
Cornflakes
Raisins
Potato (baked, boiled or mashed)
Sweet Corn
Moderate Glycemic Foods (60-85)
Spaghetti, Macaroni
Oatmeal
Banana, Grapes, Oranges
Rice
Yams
Baked Beans
Low Glycemic Foods (less than 60)
Apple, Applesauce
Cherries, Dates, Figs, Peaches, Pears, Plums
Kidney Beans, Chick Peas, Green Peas, Navy Beans, Red Lentils
Whole Milk, Skim Milk, Plain Yogurt

PROTEIN

The principle role of protein in the body is to build and repair body tissues, including muscles, ligaments and tendons. Protein also is important for the synthesis of hormones, enzymes and antibodies, as well as for fluid transport and energy. Contrary to popular belief, protein is not a primary source of energy, except when you don't consume enough calories or carbohydrates. If your clients fail to eat enough calories or put themselves on restricted-energy diets, then protein is broken down and used as an energy source instead of being used for its intended job of building tissue, enzymes, hormones, etc.

Proteins are structural and regulatory molecules made up of specific combinations of 20 different amino acids. Eight of these amino acids cannot be synthesized in the body and therefore must be supplied by the diet. Generally, the dietary intake of most individuals exceeds even the highest recommendation. Whenever you consume more protein than the body can use, the excess amino acids are stored as fat in the body. Research suggests that an adult needs about 0.8 to 1.0 grams of protein per kilogram of body weight. This would mean that a 45-year-old male who weighs 155 pounds (2.2 pounds = 1 kilogram) needs 56 to 70 grams of protein per day. Use the following equation to determine protein requirements:

Your weight in lbs. ______
÷ 2.2 = _______ weight in kilograms
your weight in kilograms ______
x 0.8 = ______ protein requirement per day

To determine the amount of protein in food, use the following as a guide:

- ✔ 8 grams of protein are found in 1 cup of milk or yogurt
- ✔ 8 grams of protein are found in 1 ounce of cheese
- ✔ 8 grams of protein are found in ¾ cup of cottage cheese
- ✔ 7 grams of protein are found in 1 ounce of meat (chicken, fish, pork, beef) and in one egg
- ✔ 3 grams of protein are found in ½ cup of pasta, rice, corn, beans or 1 slice of bread

Table 4.7 lists the specific amounts of protein in some common protein-rich foods.

Table 4.7
Protein in Common Foods

Food	Portion Size	Protein (grams)
Milk (skim, 2%, whole)	1 cup	8
Yogurt (nonfat, lowfat)	1 cup	8
Cheese (any variety)	1 ounce	8
Lean Hamburger Patty	3 ounces	26
Egg/Egg White	1	7
Lean Steak	3 ounces	21
Chicken Breast	3.5 ounces	30
Taco	1	11
Pizza	2 slices	32
Tuna	3 ounces	24
Peanut Butter	1 tablespoon	4
Whole Wheat Bread	1 slice	2
Pasta	1 cup	4

Protein Requirements for Exercising Individuals

Because protein is used as a metabolic fuel during exercise, much controversy surrounds the need for protein in exercising individuals. There is now sufficient data in the literature to suggest that protein requirements do vary with the type and intensity of exercise performed, and the total energy consumed.

In general, protein recommendations for athletes are about 1.2 to 1.7 grams of protein per kilogram of body weight. Current research suggests that the protein requirements of resistance athletes fall near the end of this range, while endurance athletes need slightly more. Reports of food intake in athletes and nonathletes consistently indicate that protein represents from 12 percent to 20 percent of total energy intake or 1.2 to 2 grams of protein per kilogram of body weight per day. The exception to the rule will be the small, active woman who may consume a low energy intake in conjunction with an exercise or training program. These women may consume close to the RDA for protein which may be inadequate to maintain lean mass.

Consuming more protein than the body can use should be avoided. When athletes consume diets that are high in protein, they compromise their carbohydrate status, possibly affecting their ability to train and compete at peak performance. The National Research Council also points out that because protein foods are often high in fat, eating too much protein makes it difficult to maintain a low-fat diet. In addition, the **hypercalciuric effect** of high-protein diets is still considered by some a significant factor in calcium balance and, until the controversy is settled, a conservative approach is advised.

Amino Acid Supplementation

Protein or amino acid supplementation in the form of powders or pills is not necessary and should be discouraged. Taking large amounts of these supplements can lead to dehydration, loss of urinary calcium, weight gain and kidney and liver stress. Taking single amino acids or combinations, such as arginine and lysine, may interfere with the absorption of certain essential amino acids (Slavin, 1991). An additional concern is that substituting amino acid supplements for food may cause deficiencies of other nutrients found in protein-rich foods such as iron, niacin and thiamin. Amino acid imbalances and toxicities are possible if single amino acid supplements, such as arginine and ornithine, are consumed in large quantities to achieve growth hormone release and muscle development. Because single amino acid supplements have not been routinely consumed by humans in the past, little scientific data is available. You need to realize that amino acid supplements taken in large doses have not been tested in human subjects, and no margin of safety is available. They are essentially drugs with unknown physiological effects. It is important for you to develop a strategy to effectively approach and discuss supplement use with clients.

FAT

Fat is the major, if not most important, fuel for light- to -moderate-intensity exercise. It is the most concentrated source of food energy and supplies more than twice as many calories by weight (9 kcal/gram) as protein (4 kcal/gram) or carbohydrate (4 kcal/gram). Fat provides **essential fatty acids,** and is necessary for the proper functioning of **cell membranes,** skin and hormones, and for transporting fat-soluble vitamins. The body has total glycogen stores (both muscle and liver) equaling about 2,500 calories, whereas each pound of body fat supplies 3,500 calories. This means that an athlete weighing 74 kg (163 pounds) with 10 percent body fat has 16.3 pounds of fat, which equals 57,000 calories.

Although fat performs many important functions in the body and is a valuable metabolic fuel for muscle activity during long-term aerobic exercise, no attempt should be made to consume more fat, especially since individuals consuming a high-fat diet typically consume fewer carbohydrate calories. Recently, Simonsen et al had elite rowers consume either 40 percent or 20 percent of their calories from fat, and then compared the two diets for power output and speed. After taking a biopsy of the rowers' muscle, they found that those who consumed the low-fat, high-carbohydrate diet had more muscle glycogen. Rowers on the high-fat, low-carbohydrate diet had moderate levels of muscle glycogen and actually were able to complete the workout sets. However, when it came to power output and faster speeds, those athletes who consumed the lower-fat, higher-carbohydrate diets had significantly higher power and speed (Simonsen, 1991). This has implications for individuals who participate in muscular endurance sports that require bursts of power, such as rowing, swimming, gymnastics, figure skating, judo, boxing or any other sport that needs energy generated by the anaerobic pathway (see Chapter 1). Following a low-fat, high-carbohydrate diet is important for health reasons as well, since a high-fat diet has been associated with cardiovascular disease, obesity, **diabetes** and some types of cancers (Krause, 1984).

You need to recognize the many sources of hidden fat in foods. Fat is present, but not visible, in dairy products such as cheese, ice cream and whole milk, and in bakery items, granola bars, french fries, avocados, chips, nuts and many processed foods. Fat is more clearly visible in margarine, butter, mayonnaise, salad dressing, oil and highly-

Fat

Table 4.8
Fat Substitutions

Instead of	Try
Whole milk	Skim milk
Cheddar, jack or swiss cheese	Part-skim mozzarella, string or lowfat cottage cheese, other cheeses that contain less than 5 grams of fat per ounce
Ice cream	Ice milk or lowfat/nonfat frozen yogurt
Butter or margarine	Jam, yogurt, ricotta cheese, light or nonfat cream cheese, lowfat yogurt, light sour cream, blender-whipped cottage cheese dressing
Bacon	Lowfat turkey bacon, Canadian bacon or bacon bits
Ground beef	Extra lean ground beef or ground turkey
Fried chicken	Baked chicken without the skin
Doughnuts and pastries	Bagels, whole-grain breads, homemade breads, muffins and quick breads
Apple pie	Baked or raw apples
Chocolate candy or bars	Jelly beans, hard candy, licorice
Cookies, cakes, brownies	Vanilla wafers, gingersnaps, graham crackers, fig bars

marbled meats.

Most athletes should consume 20 percent to 30 percent of their calories from fat. Aside from decreasing overall calories, limiting consumption of dietary fat is the first step toward losing excess body fat. Doing so eliminates excess calories, but not nutrients as long as the client consumes nutritious, low-fat foods. Suggestions for reducing fat intake are listed in Table 4.8.

HEART DISEASE

There are nearly two million deaths in this country each year and almost 30 percent of them are the result of **coronary heart disease.** Most coronary heart disease is due to blockages in the arteries that supply blood to the heart muscle. Fat, saturated fat and **cholesterol** that circulate in the blood are deposited on the inner walls of the arteries. Over time, scar tissue builds up as more fat and cholesterol are deposited, and the arteries become progressively narrower. This process is known as **atherosclerosis.**

Cholesterol

Human and animal studies have shown that elevated levels of blood cholesterol lead to early development of coronary heart disease. Research also shows that individuals with high blood cholesterol have a greater chance of developing heart disease than do people with lower levels of cholesterol, and that the chances of developing coronary heart disease increase in proportion to the amount the cholesterol is elevated. The National Cholesterol Education Programs (NCEP) has set standards to determine an individual's risk for cardiovascular disease. The NCEP suggests that blood cholesterol levels should be classified as follows:

Desirable	Less than 200 mg/dl
Borderline high	200-239 mg/dl
High	240 mg/dl and above

These categories apply to all adults over age 20, regardless of age or sex.

Heart Disease

Table 4.9
Risk Factors for Heart Disease

Risk Factors for Heart Disease
High blood pressure
Cigarette smoking
Obesity
Diabetes
Gender (males are at higher risk)
Family history of heart disease before the age of 55
Low HDL-cholesterol (less than 35mg/dl)
Circulation disorders of blood vessels to legs, arms and brain

A physician can assess a person's risk for heart disease, offer advice on how to make dietary changes and monitor progress toward cholesterol reduction. Persons with very high cholesterol levels might need a prescribed cholesterol-lowering drug.

Clients with desirable blood cholesterol levels (less than 200 mg/dl) are advised to have a serum cholesterol test again within three years. Clients with cholesterol levels of 200 mg/dl or greater should repeat the test to confirm the value and use the average as a guide.

Those who have high blood cholesterol (240 mg/dl or greater) should undergo **lipoprotein** analysis. Clients with borderline high blood cholesterol (200-239 mg/dl) who are considered high risk because they have coronary heart disease, or two other risk factors, should also have their lipoprotein levels analyzed. See Table 4.9 and Chapter 5 for a discussion of risk factors.

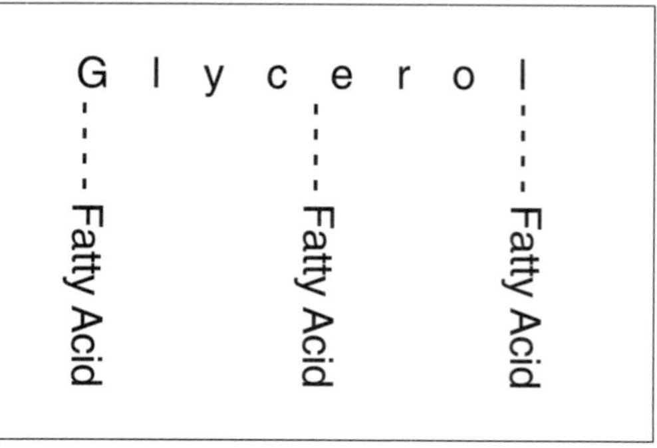

FIGURE 4.5
Structure of a triglyceride.

Lipoproteins

Low-density lipoproteins (LDLs) and **high-density lipoproteins (HDLs)** are made by the body to transport fat and cholesterol through the blood. LDLs contain the greatest amounts of cholesterol, and may be responsible for depositing it on the artery walls. For this reason, they are sometimes called "bad" cholesterol. The NCEP also has set standards for LDLs:

Desirable	below 130 mg/dl
Borderline high	130-159 mg/dl
High	160 mg/dl and above

LDL cholesterol can be lowered by exercising, weight loss, incorporating more monounsaturated and polyunsaturated fats into the diet, and decreasing the overall percentage of fat calories consumed. Clients with extremely high LDL levels may need medication to control LDL cholesterol.

HDLs contain more protein than cholesterol. They remove cholesterol from the cells in the arteries and transport it back to the liver for repackaging and removal from the body. Studies have shown that individuals with higher levels of HDL have a lower incidence of heart disease. Thus, HDLs have become known as the "good" cholesterol. HDL cholesterol levels below 35 mg/dl are considered a risk factor for coronary heart disease. Several factors, including regular consistent exercise, have been found to raise HDLs. One study showed that persons who ran just eight miles per week saw an increase in HDL levels. Moderate alcohol consumption also appears to raise HDL levels, but most health professionals recommend exercise as a better method.

With the technology available today, you can easily provide initial cholesterol screening for your clients. However, if lipoprotein analysis is desired, which involves a 12-hour fast and a venipuncture blood draw, a referral to a medical professional is necessary. All clients with an LDL cholesterol level greater than 160 mg/dl, or a level of 130-159 mg/dl combined with high-risk status, should be clinically evaluated by a physician.

Triglycerides

The bulk of dietary fat is ingested in the form of **triglycerides,** which are made up of a glycerol backbone with three **fatty acids** attached (Figure 4.5). The fatty acids attached to the glycerol may differ from one another in either chain length and degree of saturation, or in chemical structure. A **saturated fatty acid** is one that carries the maximum number of hydrogen atoms, leaving no points unsaturated. There are two types of unsaturated fatty acids: **monounsaturated** and **polyunsaturated.** Food fats contain a mixture of the three kinds of fatty acids.

When a fat contains predominantly saturated fatty acids, it is said to be a saturated fat. Similarly, when a fat or oil contains a large proportion of monounsaturated or polyunsaturated fatty acids, it is called a monounsaturated fat or a polyunsaturated fat, respectively. The more saturated fat an individual eats, the higher their blood cholesterol will be. The major sources of saturated fatty acids in the diet come from animal products such as meats and whole milk dairy products. Lowfat dairy products are lower in saturated fats and are recommended for adults who need to lower their levels of saturated fats and cholesterol. A few vegetable fats are quite high in saturated fatty acids: coconut oil, palm kernel oil, palm oil and the cocoa fat found in chocolate. While these four oils are not available for consumer purchase, they are often used in commercial baked goods and other processed foods.

Since saturated fats raise blood cholesterol, eating less of them is recommended. Remember:

- ✔ Reducing total fat can reduce saturated fat as well.
- ✔ Most animal fats contain high proportions of saturated fat, whereas vegetable foods provide a higher proportion of polyunsaturated fatty acids.
- ✔ Vegetable oils from palm kernel, coconut, palm and cocoa fat contain large proportions of saturated fat.
- ✔ Some margarines are lower in saturated fat and higher in unsaturated fats than butter.

Hydrogenation

Hydrogenation is the chemical process by which hydrogen atoms are added to unsaturated and polyunsaturated fats. This reduces the number of double bonds and makes them more saturated and more resistant to rancidity.

When fatty acids are hydrogenated, their shapes change (Figure 4.6). A cis-fatty acid has its hydrogen atoms on the same side, whereas a trans-fatty acid has them on opposite sides. The cis- configuration is typical of the fatty acids found in natural foods, but during hydrogenation, some hydrogen atoms shift and form trans-fatty acids. Trans-fatty acids are more stable, but their safety is questionable. Some studies have found that diets rich in trans-fatty acids raise LDLs and lower HDLs, at least to the same extent as saturated fatty acids do. Clients need to be educated about finding hydrogenated fats in their foods and margarines, and they should know that food processors can control the ex-

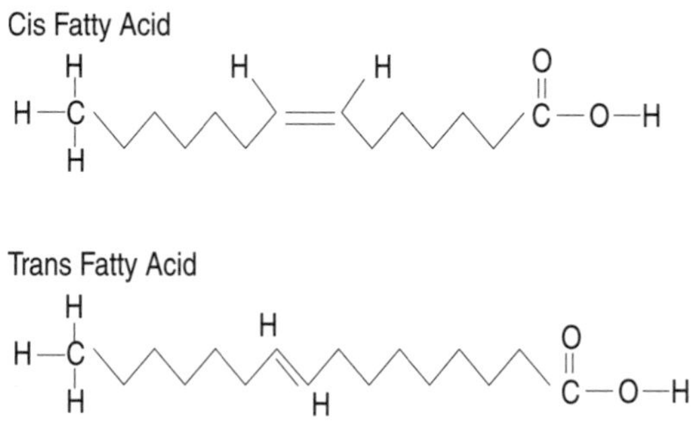

Cis Fatty Acid

Trans Fatty Acid

FIGURE 4.6
Transformation of a fatty acid as a result of hydrogenation.

tent of hydrogenation — they do not have to automatically convert all unsaturated fatty acids to saturated ones. Any margarine that lists hydrogenated fats first on the label is going to have more trans-fatty acids than cis-fatty acids. It seems desirable to take advantage of all opportunities to select foods and design meals that are low in both fat and hydrogenated fat.

VITAMINS AND MINERALS

Vitamins and minerals are food components that serve as coenzymes in the metabolic reactions that release energy, transport and consume oxygen and maintain cell integrity. Because of these important functions, their use as **ergogenic aids** has been highly touted, even though there is little scientific evidence to document their effect. The need for vitamins and minerals for exercise has been reviewed recently by Haymes and Clarkson, and resulted in the consensus that unless an individual is deficient in a given nutrient, supplementation of that nutrient does not have a major effect on performance (Haymes, 1991; Clarkson, 1991).

Nutrient Deficiencies

Nutrient deficiencies for the exercising population are similar to those of the general population. In other words, just because you exercise does not mean that you need special amounts of any vitamin or mineral. The nutrients that people often don't get enough of include folate, vitamin B_6, **antioxidants,** calcium and zinc. Because many women exercisers also are vegetarians, iron and vitamin B_{12} may be of specific concern to this subgroup.

Vitamin/Mineral Supplementation

Because consumers experience a lot of confusion over what makes up a nutritionally balanced diet, and because most individuals don't understand the RDA, many Americans turn to vitamin and mineral supplementation as nutritional insurance. But should most people be taking a supplement? Generally, no, although the consumer who takes a simple one-a-day type of vitamin or mineral supplement that does not exceed the nutrient levels of the RDA is probably not doing any harm. It may even be appropriate to suggest a multiple one-a-day to clients who limit their food selection and calories, since they may have a difficult time getting the recommended levels of nutrients. Of greater concern is the client who has a whole medicine cabinet full of supplements. These individuals take a handful of supplements for breakfast, perhaps several tablespoons of nutritional yeast, assorted pills containing trace minerals, powdered protein and herbs. They are asking the pills and supplements to play a role that is better delegated to food.

Many athletes, in search of a competitive edge, also turn to supplements in the form of pills, powders or magical elixirs in an effort to make the body perform at its best. They listen to self-claimed "experts" who try to convince the athletes that their product will elevate their performance by improving muscle contractions, preventing fat gain, enhancing strength or supplying energy. These "experts" may insist that fatigue and muscle soreness is due to a vitamin or mineral deficiency when, in fact, if there is a nutritional reason for fatigue, it is usually a lack of calories and/or carbohydrates.

Takers of self-prescribed supplements need a warning about the risks of overdosing. There are two types of vitamins: **water-soluble** and fat-soluble. Concern should be expressed if individuals are taking high doses of fat-soluble vitamins (A, D, E and K). These particular vitamins are stored in body fat, principally in the liver, and toxic levels have been found in people who take megadoses of these nutrients.

The water-soluble vitamins (B complex and C) are not stored by the body, and any

Table 4.10
Vitamin Facts

Vitamin	U.S. RDA*	Best Sources	Functions
A (carotene)	5,000 IU/day	Yellow or orange fruits and vegetables, green leafy vegetables, fortified oatmeal, liver, dairy products	Formation and maintenance of skin, hair and mucous membranes; helps you see in dim light; bone and tooth growth
B_1 (thiamine)	1.5 mg/day	Fortified cereals and oatmeals, meats, rice and pasta, whole grains, liver	Helps body release energy from carbohydrates during metabolism; growth and muscle tone
B_2 (riboflavin)	1.7 mg/day	Whole grains, green leafy vegetables, organ meats, milk and eggs	Helps body release energy from protein, fat and carbohydrates during metabolism
B_6 (pyridoxine)	2 mg/day	Fish, poultry, lean meats, bananas, prunes, dried beans, whole grains, avocados	Helps build body tissue and aids in metabolism of protein
B_{12} (cobalamin)	6 mcg/day	Meats, milk products, seafood	Aids cell development, functioning of the nervous system and the metabolism of protein and fat
Biotin	0.3 mg/day	Cereal/grain products, yeast, legumes, liver	Involved in metabolism of protein, fats and carbohydrates
Folate (folacin, folic acid)	0.4 mg/day	Green leafy vegetables, organ meats, dried peas, beans and lentils	Aids in genetic material development and involved in red blood cell production
Niacin	20 mg/day	Meat, poultry, fish, enriched cereals, peanuts, potatoes, dairy products, eggs	Involved in carbohydrate, protein and fat metabolism
Pantothenic Acid	10 mg/day	Lean meats, whole grains, legumes, vegetables, fruits	Helps in the release of energy from fats and carbohydrates
C (absorbic acid)	60 mg/day	Citrus fruits, berries and vegetables — especially peppers	Essential for structure of bones, cartilage, muscle and blood vessels; helps maintain capillaries and gums and aids in absorption of iron
D	400 IU/day	Fortified milk, sunlight, fish, eggs, butter, fortified margarine	Aids in bone and tooth formation; helps maintain heart action and nervous system
E	30 IU/day	Fortified and multi-grain cereals, nuts, wheat germ, vegetable oils, green leafy vegetables	Protects blood cells, body tissue and essential fatty acids from harmful destruction in the body
K	**	Green leafy vegetables, fruit, dairy and grain products	Essential for blood clotting functions

* For Adults and Children over four. IU = international units; mg = milligrams; mcg = micrograms.
** There is no U.S. RDA for vitamin K, however the Recommended Dietary Allowance is 1 mcg/kg of bodyweight.

excesses are excreted in the urine. It was once thought that a toxic level of water-soluble vitamins was impossible. But recent research shows that if consumers ingest **megadoses** of water-soluble vitamins, they, too, can reach toxic levels. Table 4.10 lists all of the vitamins, their physiologic function and major food sources.

Vitamin toxicity usually affects the nervous system. Both vitamins A and B_6 are known to produce adverse neurologic reactions (such as nerve transmission) when ingested in megadoses, rather than the Recommended Dietary Allowances (RDAs). The RDA is the daily amount of a nutrient recommended for practically all healthy individuals to promote optimal health. It is not a minimal amount needed to prevent disease symptoms — a large margin of safety is included. The symptoms of vitamin or mineral toxicity are vague at best; diarrhea, vomiting, skin rashes, and overall "just not feeling right" have been reported. Because these symptoms could describe any disease or illness, it is best for you not to make recommendations about vitamin toxicity to clients. You should, however, suggest that such clients seek professional medical advice about the symptoms. Encourage them to take their supplements to the physician and/or dietitian for assessment.

Because consumers may have strong beliefs in their vitamin supplement program, several strategies can be used to avoid upsetting them. Acknowledge their feelings and the values that underlie their practice, and then distinguish between practices that are dangerous and those that are not. For example, clients using supplements at pharmacological doses (greater than 100 times the RDA) are headed for toxic levels, unlike those who are just taking a multivitamin/mineral supplement once a day. Confront only the dangerous practices; ignore the harmless ones. Try to wean such clients off of their supplements gradually instead of asking them to quit all at once, and encourage them to get their nutrients from foods. Let your clients know that there is a lot of information that scientists have not yet discovered about nutrients and the effects of their combinations in foods, and teach them to attain nutritional adequacy and balance by adopting the principles of the Food Guide Pyramid.

While it has been shown that a severely inadequate intake of certain vitamins can impair performance, it is unusual for individuals who exercise to have such deficiencies. Even marginal deficiencies do not appear to markedly affect the ability to exercise efficiently. Most individuals can meet the RDA by making wise food selections from the Food Guide Pyramid.

The Antioxidant Vitamins

Antioxidants are compounds that preserve and protect other compounds in the body from free radical damage. Five nutrients have been identified as having antioxidant properties: beta carotene, vitamin C, vitamin E, and the minerals sulfur and selenium.

Free radicals are oxygen molecules with a single electron. Oxygen is composed of two atoms that are bound together, but occasionally these oxygen atoms split and create two individual or singlet oxygen atoms. It is these molecules that cause damage to tissues and create health problems. Sometimes these singlet oxygen molecules will attach to other compounds in the body, particularly polyunsaturated fats, and start chain reactions that create even more free radicals and further health problems. Free radicals have been linked to the development of cancer, atherosclerosis, cataracts and the aging process.

Out of all the antioxidant nutrients, vitamin E appears to be the most promising. Research has confirmed that vitamin E helps protect LDL cholesterol from becoming oxidized, thus preventing plaque from forming in veins and arteries.

Clients may ask about adding vitamin E

Table 4.11
Minerals

Mineral	U.S. RDA	Best Sources	Functions
Calcium	1,000 mg/day	Milk and milk products	Strong bones, teeth, muscle tissue; regulates heart beat, muscle action and nerve function; blood clotting
Chromium	No RDA	Corn oil, clams, whole grain cereals, brewer's yeast	Glucose metabolism (energy); increases effectiveness of insulin
Copper	2 mg/day	Oysters, nuts, organ meats, legumes	Formation of red blood cells, bone growth and health; works with vitamin C to form elastin
Iodine	150 mcg/day	Seafood, iodized salt	Component of hormone thyroxine, which controls metabolism
Iron	18 mg/day	Meats & organ meats, legumes	Hemoglobin formation; improves blood quality; increases resistance to stress and disease
Magnesium	No RDA	Nuts, green vegetables, whole grains	Acid/alkaline balance; important in metabolism of carbohydrates, minerals and sugar
Manganese	No RDA	Nuts, whole grains, vegetables, fruits	Enzyme activation; carbohydrate and fat production; sex hormone production; skeletal development
Phosphorus	1,000 mg/day	Fish, meat, poultry, eggs, grains	Bone development; important in protein, fat and carbohydrate utilization
Potassium	No RDA	Lean meat, vegetables, fruits	Fluid balance; controls activity of heart muscle, nervous system, kidneys
Selenium	50-200 mcg/day provisional RDA	Seafood, organ meats, lean meats, grains	Protects body tissues against oxidative damage from radiation, pollution and normal metabolic processing
Zinc	15 mg/day	Lean meats, liver, eggs, seafood, whole grains	Involved in digestion & metabolism, important in development of reproductive system, aids in healing

Source: American Institute for Cancer Research

to their diets. A typical low-fat diet may provide as much as 25 milligrams of vitamin E per day, roughly three times the RDA, and by adding a bowl of fortified cereal to their diet, clients could more than double that level. If they do decide to take a vitamin E supplement, it is wise to stay within a modest range (65 to 260 mg, or 100 to 400 IUs).

MINERALS

Minerals perform a variety of functions in the body. While some are used to build tissue, such as calcium and phosphorus for bones and teeth, others are important components of hormones, such as iodine in thyroxine. Iron is critical for the formation of hemoglobin, which carries oxygen within the red blood cells. Minerals also are important for regulating muscle contractions and body fluids, conducting nerve impulses and regulating normal heart rhythm.

Minerals are divided into two groups. The first are referred to as macro minerals and are needed in amounts from 100 mg to 1 gram. These include calcium, phosphorus, magnesium, sodium, potassium, chloride and sulfur. The others fall under the category of trace minerals and include copper, iodine, zinc, cobalt, fluoride and

Minerals

selenium. Food sources and the physiologic functions for each mineral are listed in Table 4.11.

Iron

Iron is present in all cells of the body and plays a key role in numerous reactions. It is vital to the transport and activation of oxygen, and is present in several pathways that create energy. Various studies have found some women's diets to be deficient in iron, a result of dieting and limiting calories. Due to the fact that women face a potentially greater chance of lacking iron because of increased physiological need, low-calorie intakes and increased iron loss through menstruation, it has been suggested that they consider routine use of iron supplements, particularly during periods of heavy training. In one report, 42 percent of the female distance runners studied were modified vegetarians and consumed fewer than 200 grams of meat per week (Brooks, 1984). Iron supplementation in non-anemic women, however, has not been shown to be useful, and may even be potentially harmful. Clearly, there is some hazard from prolonged administration of large doses of iron to persons who are not iron deficient. They are needlessly exposed to hemosiderosis, a disorder of iron metabolism in which large deposits of iron are made in the liver. Routine screening tests for women should be performed by medical professionals to detect early stages of iron depletion. Those women found to be iron-deficient or **anemic** should receive professional dietary counseling from a physician or dietitian. Supplemental iron may be indicated in individual cases; however, routine use of iron supplements by all females is not warranted.

While dietary intake of iron is tied to caloric intake, iron absorption depends upon the bioavailabilty, or rate of absorption, of the iron. Meats contain heme-iron, which is a highly bioavailable source of iron. Heme-iron also enhances the absorption of the non-heme-iron found in plant foods like leafy greens, legumes, cereals, whole grains and enriched breads. Combining these foods with a source of vitamin C can significantly enhance the absorption of iron, (for example, combine orange juice with an iron-enriched cereal, pasta with broccoli, or tomatoes and green peppers).

Regular monitoring of iron levels in physically active individuals, including biochemical evaluations and dietary assessments, is recommended to ensure optimal health and performance.

To ensure an adequate iron intake you should encourage the following for your clients:

- ✔ Eat foods high in vitamin C at each meal to help the body absorb iron. For example, eat salsa and/or chili peppers with a bean burrito.
- ✔ Include meat, preferably lean red meat and the dark meat of chicken and turkey, as part of the training diet. These foods provide the body with heme-iron.
- ✔ To enhance the absorption of non-heme-iron (vegetable and grain sources of iron), combine vegetable proteins with meat. For example, split pea soup with ham, tuna noodle casserole, turkey vegetable soup, chicken soup with lentils, or chili beans with lean ground turkey or hamburger.
- ✔ To increase iron and carbohydrate intake, eat cereals, breads and pastas labeled "enriched" or "fortified."

Calcium

Osteoporosis is a major health concern, especially for women. Although the disease has been regarded as an elderly women's problem, young females, especially those who have had interrupted menstrual function, may be at risk for decreased bone mass. There is still much to be discovered about the cause of osteoporosis, but three major risk factors have been identified: hormonal status (particularly estrogen deficiency), calcium consumption and physical activity.

Bone mass is developed until the ages of 35 to 40 years. Peak bone mass, however, is obtained between the ages of 14 to 24. The amount of bone mass a woman has by age 35 will strongly influence her susceptibility to fractures in later years. Therefore, it is important that young women consume calcium throughout early life and all through the peak bone mass years and into early adulthood.

The National Institutes of Health (NIH) recommends that **premenopausal** adult women consume 1,000 mg of calcium per day. **Postmenopausal** women who are not taking estrogen should consume 1,500 mg of calcium per day. Unfortunately, though specific calcium levels have been recommended for women, the Health and Nutrition Examination Survey (NHANES) found that 50 percent of all females age 15 and older consume less than 75 percent of the RDA of 1,200 mg, and that 75 percent of women over 35 consume less than the RDA of 800 mg.

Lowfat and nonfat dairy products, such as milk, buttermilk, yogurt, cheese and cottage cheese, are excellent sources of dietary calcium.

You can recommend that your clients try the following to incorporate more calcium into their diet:

- ✔ Prepare canned soup with skim milk instead of water.
- ✔ Add nonfat dry milk to soups, stews, casseroles and even cookie recipes.
- ✔ Add grated lowfat cheese to salads, tacos and pasta dishes.
- ✔ Eat yogurt as a snack, or use it to make low-calorie dressings.
- ✔ Choose calcium-rich desserts, such as lowfat cheese and fruit, frozen nonfat or lowfat yogurt and puddings made with skim milk.
- ✔ Drink hot chocolate made with skim milk.

Athletic Amenorrhea

Some women who exercise strenuously stop menstruating due to a condition known as athletic **amenorrhea.** It is associated with many factors, such as nutritional inadequacy, physical stress, energy drain and acute and chronic hormonal alterations (Sanborn, 1987).

Although the specific cause of athletic amenorrhea is unknown and may vary among women, it appears to coincide with decreased estrogen production. Since estrogen deficiency also is an important risk factor for the development of osteoporosis, amenorrhea may predispose female athletes to early-onset osteoporosis and fractures.

Spinal bone mass has been found to be lower in amenorrheic women runners compared to **eumenorrheic** women runners (Drinkwater, 1984). What is especially disturbing about this is that further follow-up of these women indicated that bone mineral density remained well below the average for their age group four years after the resumption of normal menses (Drinkwater, 1986).

Women with athletic amenorrhea should consult a physician to rule out any serious medical problems, and all amenorrheic women should be consuming 1,500 mg of calcium per day. A physician may suggest several strategies to promote the resumption of menses, including estrogen replacement therapy, weight gain, diet modification and reduced training.

Regardless of menstrual history, most female athletes need to increase their calcium intake to meet the RDA for calcium.

Lactose Intolerance

One of the more common problems of the gastrointestinal tract is lactose intolerance. Lactase is the enzyme responsible for breaking down lactose, a carbohydrate commonly found in dairy products. Without lactase, lactose cannot be digested and absorbed. As individuals get

Table 4.12
Comparison of Sport Drinks

Beverage	Type of Carbohydrate	Carbohydrate Concentration Per 8 oz
Gatorade	Sucrose and glucose	6%
PowerAde	High fructose corn syrup and maltose dextrin	8%
Exceed	Glucose polymers, fructose	7%
AllSport	High fructose corn syrup	8% to 9%
Hydra Fuel	Glucose polymers, fructose, glucose	7%
Cytomax	Fructose corn syrup and sucrose	7% to 11%
10K	Sucrose, glucose, fructose	6.3%
Breakthrough	Maltodextrin, fructose	8.5%

older, lactase activity appears to decrease and can cause bloating, gas, diarrhea and sometimes nausea.

It seems that lactose intolerance is not an "all or nothing phenomena." A person with lactose intolerance does not need to give up all dairy products. Some individuals with lactose intolerance may be able to handle small amounts of lactose throughout the day, and others can tolerate fermented dairy products because the bacteria in the products provide their own lactase activity. Have clients try yogurt, buttermilk, some cheeses and frozen yogurt. For those who are very sensitive to lactose in dairy products, a product called Lactaid can be added to milk and will, in most cases, reduce symptoms.

FLUID AND HYDRATION

Maintaining hydration is by far the greatest concern for regular exercisers. Clients who are **dehydrated** will fatigue earlier and lose coordination skills. Their performance can suffer when they lose as little as 2 percent of body weight due to dehydration. To prevent this from happening, exercising individuals must drink plenty of fluids before, during and after a workout. Relying on thirst as an indicator of how much fluid is lost is not an accurate method. If your clients relied on thirst, they would only put back 50 percent to 75 percent of the fluid they have lost, and would start their next workout already in a state of dehydration. Don't wait until you're thirsty to drink, and don't stop drinking once your thirst has been quenched. Most people have no idea how much fluid they need, let alone how much they have lost during the day or during exercise. In order to gain insight into fluid losses, have your clients self-monitor their fluid levels by one of two methods:

- ✔ Weigh in before and after a workout. Consume two cups of fluid for each pound of body weight lost.
- ✔ Check the color of their urine. A dark gold color means the client is dehydrated. A pale yellow, or no color, means the client is headed toward a state of hydration. Clients who consume a lot of caffeine, which is a **diuretic,** will have pale or clear urine even though they are, in fact, dehydrated. Alcohol also is a very powerful diuretic.

Sports Drinks

Most experts will now recommend sports drinks to exercising individuals, especially if their workout lasts longer than 45 minutes. The fear that sports drinks impair fluid absorption is unfounded, and it has been shown that sports drinks formulated with 6 percent to 8 percent carbohydrates plus sodium replace fluids faster than water, improve performance, and help ensure optimal rehydration. They also maintain physiological function as well as, if not better than, water.

Dispelling Sport Nutrition Myths

Remind your clients to pay attention to the percentage of carbohydrates in each drink. Those containing less than 5 percent carbohydrate do not provide enough energy to enhance performance, and beverages containing 10 percent carbohydrate or more (fruit juices and soda) are associated with intestinal cramping, nausea and diarrhea.

Guidelines for Fluid Replacement 

- ✔ Consume one to two cups (8 to 16 ounces) of fluid at least one hour before the start of exercise. If possible, consume 8 ounces of fluid 20 minutes before the start of exercise.
- ✔ Consume 4 to 8 ounces of fluid every 10 to 15 minutes during the workout.
- ✔ Consume two cups of fluid for every pound of body weight lost after exercise.

DISPELLING SPORT NUTRITION MYTHS

Myth: Large amounts of protein will increase muscle strength and size.

Reality: There is no evidence to show that consuming excess amounts of protein will increase muscle strength or size. In fact, protein consumed in excess of what the body needs will be converted to fat. It is true that athletes in heavy training (muscular endurance training lasting 60 to 90 minutes) may need to allocate a slightly greater percentage of their calories from protein, while nonathletes require only 12 percent to 15 percent. This is because the body may have reduced protein stores during heavy training periods. People don't, however, necessarily need to consume excess amounts of protein to meet this increased requirement since it can be met by eating a well-balanced diet with protein-rich foods during periods of heavy training.

Myth: Eating honey, candy bars, soft drinks or sugar before competing will provide a quick burst of energy.

Reality: Studies have shown that these foods have a high sugar content and eating them within an hour of competition causes the amount of insulin in the blood to rise and, consequently, the sugar in the blood is removed too quickly. The exerciser may feel tired and weak as a result of low blood sugar. More recent evidence suggests, however, that high-carbohydrate foods consumed two to three hours prior to competition may improve performance since the exerciser is no longer compensating for low blood sugar, and the food can serve as a source of fuel. Does this mean that endurance athletes should load up on soft drinks and candy bars a few hours before they exercise? A comparison of the results of the old and new studies suggests that individuals differ in their susceptibility to a lowering of blood glucose during exercise. The physiological basis for this difference has not been determined, so at this time, you should advise your clients that consuming sugar-containing foods three to 45 minutes prior to exercise could harm their performance if they are sensitive to a lowering of their blood glucose level.

Myth: Drinking water prior to and during exercise causes upset stomach and cramps.

Reality: Water is the most important nutrient to an exercising individual. Restricting fluids during exercise, especially in hot weather, can cause severe dehydration and limit performance. Remind your clients to drink 4 to 8 ounces of water every 10 to 15 minutes during exercise to help replace body fluids lost through perspiration. They should monitor water losses and rehydrate with the appropriate amount (see *Guidelines for Fluid Replacement*).

Myth: Drinking milk causes cotton mouth and reduces speed.

Reality: There is no evidence that cotton mouth results from drinking milk. In fact, it is believed to be caused by emotional

Dispelling Sport Nutrition Myths

stress and a loss of body fluids. Milk consumption should not be restricted since it is an important source of calcium, which is necessary for the proper development of bones and teeth. Advise your clients to drink milk as part of their daily meal plan.

Myth: Muscle cramps are caused by inadequate salt intake.

Reality: Cramps are caused by excess water loss through perspiration. Ingesting salt tablets can aggravate existing dehydration by drawing water out of body tissues and into the stomach. Water should be consumed before, during and after exercise to prevent dehydration.

Myth: Taking vitamin supplements will provide more energy.

Reality: Not one of the 14 vitamins has been shown to supply energy; their role is to release the energy from food. Some vitamins are involved in energy production, but taking excess amounts or megadoses of them will not result in increased energy. You should stress to your clients that all 14 vitamins can be supplied by a well-balanced diet.

Myth: Tea and coffee are the best precompetition beverages.

Reality: Tea and coffee contain caffeine, which is a stimulant. Some research suggests that caffeine can improve endurance performance by increasing the use of fat as an energy source, thus sparing muscle glycogen, but not all individuals will experience this effect. In fact, a hypersensitive response resulting in increased heart rate and anxiety is a more likely occurrence. There also is evidence of increased urine production, which can lead to dehydration.

Myth: Crash diets are the fastest, most effective way to lose weight.

Reality: Though crash dieting can result in large amounts of weight loss, it is muscle mass, glycogen stores and water, not excess body fat, that is lost. This can impair an individual's endurance and cause poor performance. Other problems associated with crash diets include electrolyte imbalances, calcium deficiency, iron deficiency anemia, and vitamin and mineral deficiencies. It is important to be sensible about modifying a diet to lose weight. A person should lose no more than two pounds per week. If they reduce their caloric intake by 500 calories per day and increase their activity to burn an additional 500 calories per day, they will likely lose two pounds by the end of one week. (See Chapter 12 for more information on weight control.)

Myth: Special supplements such as aspartic acid, brewer's yeast, ginseng, chromium picolinate, bee pollen and strawberry extract improve athletic performance.

Reality: There is no scientific evidence to show that these expensive compounds contribute anything to performance, and some of them may even be harmful.

SUMMARY

Fortunately, the same diet that enhances good health also will maximize performance for most people. A basic knowledge of nutrition should aid you in helping your clients make wise food choices that will contribute to their health. Clients should be aware of the nutrients they are consuming and the effect those nutrients are having on their body. Because carbohydrates are the main fuel for the exercising muscle, it is extremely important that at least 55 percent to 65 percent of total daily calories come from carbohydrates. Consuming excess protein may result in a gain in fat weight. Being aware of fat in the diet and recognizing heart-healthy foods will help reduce the risk of cardiovascular disease.

Help your clients integrate the dietary guidelines into their nutrition plans to reduce their risk for diet-related diseases. The food guide pyramid will enable clients to visualize contemporary ways they can combine foods to meet the guidelines and recommended dietary allowances.

Summary

Probably one of the most important nutritional concerns for exercising individuals is fluids and hydration. A 2-percent decrease in body weight due to perspiration will decrease performance, so exercisers must monitor their water losses. It also is important to closely monitor calcium and iron intake, especially for female and adolescent male athletes, since performance can be impaired with even a mild iron deficiency. Though most people aren't aware of it, they can consume the RDAs of most nutrients by eating a balanced diet (except iron and calcium for women). Instead, many choose to supplement their diets with vitamins and minerals and often believe that the more they take the better. Make clients aware that megadoses of vitamins and minerals will not boost their performance. If they still feel the need to take a supplement, a multiple-type vitamin is recommended.

REFERENCES

Bergstrom, J., Hermanson, L., Hultman, E. & Saltin, B. (1967). Diet, muscle glycogen and physical performance. *Acta Physiology Scandinavia,* 71, 140-150.

Brooks, S.M., Sanborn, C.F., Albrecht, B.H. & Wagner, W.W. (1984). Diet in athletic amenorrhea. *Lancet.* 1, 559.

Clarkson, P.M. (1991). Vitamins and trace minerals in: *Perspectives in exercise science and sports medicine, Vol 4: Ergogenic enhancement of performance in exercise and sport,* 123-182. Lamb, D.R. & Williams, M.H., (Eds.) Ann Arbor: Brown and Benchmark.

Drinkwater, B.L., Nilson, K. & Chestnut, C.H. (1984). Bone mineral content of amenorrheic and eumenorrheic athletes, *New England Journal of Medicine,* 311, 277-281.

Drinkwater, B.L., Nilson, K., Ott, S. & Chestnut, C.H. (1986). Bone mineral density after resumption of menses in amenorrheic athletes. *Journal of the American Medical Association*, 256, 380-382.

Haymes, E.M. (1991). Vitamin and mineral supplementation to athletes. *International Journal of Sport Medicine,* 1, 146-169.

Ivy J.L., Datz, A.L., Cutler, C.L., Sherman, W.M. & Coyle E.F. (1988). Muscle glycogen synthesis after exercise effect of time of carbohydrate ingestion. *Journal of Applied Physiology,* 64, 1480-1485.

Krause, M.E & Mahan, C.K. (1984). *Food Nutrition and Diet Therapy.* (7th ed.) Philadelphia: Saunders.

Sanborn, C.F., Albrech, B.H. & Wagner, W.W. (1987). Athletic amenorrhea, lack of association with body fat. *Medicine and Science in Sports and Exercise,* 19, 207-212.

Simonsen, J.C., Sherman, W.M., Lamb, D.L., Dernbach, A.R., Doyle, J.A. & Strauss, R. (1991). Dietary carbohydrate, muscle glycogen, and power output during rowing training. *Journal of Applied Physiology,* 70, 4, 1500-1505.

Slavin, J. (1991). Protein needs for athletes in: Berning and Steen, (eds.) *Sports Nutrition for The Nineties: The Health Professionals Handbook.* Gaithersberg, MD: Aspen Publishers.

Zawadski, K.M., Yaspelkis, B.B. & Ivy J.L. (1992). Carbohydrate-protein complex increases the rate of muscle glycogen storage after exercise. *Journal of Applied Physiology,* 72950, 1854-1859.

SUGGESTED READING

Bernadot, D. (Ed.) (1994). *Sports Nutrition: A Guide for the Professional Working with Active People.* (2nd ed.) Chicago: American Dietetic Association.

Brouns, F. (1993). *Nutritional Needs of Athletes.* New York: John Wiley and Sons.

Burke, E.R. & Berning, J.R. (1996). *Training Nutrition: The Diet and Nutrition Guide for Peak Performance.* Carmel, IN: Cooper Publishing.

Burke, L. & Deakin, V. (Eds.) (1995). *Clinical Sports Nutrition.* New York: Mcgraw-Hill.

Clark, N. (1994). *The New York City Marathon Cookbook.* Nashville: Rutledge Hill Press.

Coleman, E. (1989). *Eating for Endurance.* Palo Alto: Bull Publishing.

Houtkooper, L. (1994). *Winning Sports Nutrition: Training Manual.* Tucson: University of Arizona.

Jackson, C.G. (Ed.) (1995). *Nutrition for The Recreational Athlete.* Boca Raton: CRC Press.

Kies, C.V. & Driskell, J. (Eds.) (1995). *Sports Nutrition: Minerals and Electrolytes.* Boca Raton: CRC Press.

National Dairy Council. (1990). *Food Power: A Coach's Guide to Improving Performance.* Rosemont: National Dairy Council.

Simopoulos, A.P. & Knostantinous, N.P. (1993). *Nutrition and Fitness for Athletes.* Farmington: S. Krager Publishers.

Tribole, E. (1992). *Eating on the Run.* Champaign: Leisure Press.

Williams, M.H. (1995). *Nutrition for Fitness and Sport.* (4th ed.) Dubuque: William C. Brown.

Wolinsky, I. & Hickson, J. F. (1993). *Nutrition in Exercise and Sport.* Boca Raton: CRC Press.

VIDEOS

Gatorade Sports Science Institute. (1994). *Smart Choices.* Chicago: Norman Graphics.

Portland Public Schools Nutrition Services. (1992). *Training Table: Your Competitive Advantage.* Portland.

Western Dairy Council. (1993). *The Inside Edge.* Colorado: Western Dairy Council.

PART II

II

Screening and Evaluation

CHAPTER 5 Health Screening

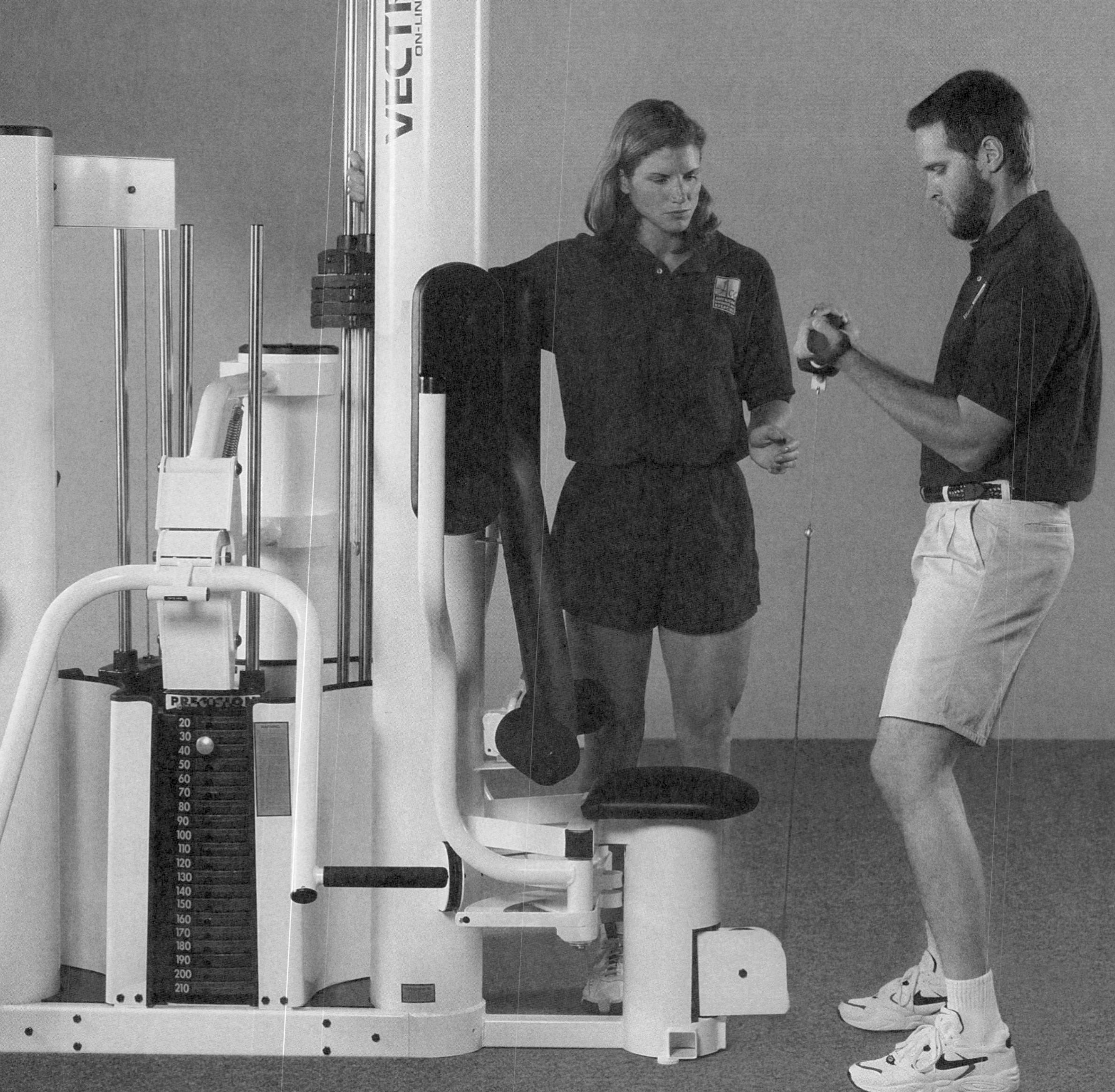

5

IN THIS CHAPTER:

- **Health Screening Forms**
- **Health Conditions that Affect Physical Activity**
  - Cardiovascular Disease
  - Respiratory
  - Musculoskeletal
  - Metabolic
  - Other Conditions
- **Medications**
  - Antihypertensives
  - Bronchodilators
  - Cold Medications
- **Client's Preferences, Expectations and Lifestyle Information**
- **Physical Screen**

Jeff Anthony

Jeff Anthony, D.O., is a team physician at San Diego State University and for the USA Men's Olympic Volleyball teams. He is a staff physician at the San Diego Family Practice & Sports Medicine Center and lectures on sports medicine at colleges and medical conferences. He is a member of the IDEA Advisory Board.

Health screening is a vital first step in the personal trainer/client relationship. Not only does it give you essential information that will assure safety and effectiveness in exercise programming, but it also raises the quality and professionalism of your services. Health screening allows you to: 1) identify health conditions and risk factors that may necessitate referral or place the client at risk when participating in certain activities; 2) identify possible contraindicated activities; 3) assist in designing an exercise program that includes safe activities and/or appropriate modifications; 4) fulfill legal and insurance requirements for you or the health club and 5) open lines of communication between you and physicians that will help you to gain a reputation as a concerned professional and ally in health

Health Screening Forms

promotion. This chapter will outline the components of an effective health screening and will identify some conditions that may require modifications to an exercise program and/or healthcare professional participation.

Because the primary purpose of a physical activity program is to improve one's quality of life, aggravating an existing medical condition is counterproductive. To set up the most effective program, you need to evaluate your clients' health conditions and their goals. If a significant health condition or risk factor for injury exists, a client may need medical clearance or specific recommendations from a physician. This should not deter you from working with a client if you possess the appropriate training and experience. With proper modifications to the exercise program, almost everyone can, and should, engage in physical activity. Your client and their physician should work with you to coordinate the most effective program, giving careful consideration to the risks, benefits and goals of exercise.

Intensity Defined

The American College of Sports Medicine (ACSM) has defined what is considered moderate and vigorous exercise in order to assist in determining the need for referral and/or physician clearance for certain individuals.

Moderate exercise is defined as an intensity of 40 percent to 60 percent **VO_2 max**. If you are not able to accurately determine the intensity of an activity, moderate exercise also can be defined as "an intensity well within the individual's current capacity that can be sustained for a prolonged period of time, that is, 60 minutes, which has a gradual initiation and progression, and is generally noncompetitive."

Vigorous exercise is defined as an intensity greater than 60 percent VO_2 max or "exercise intense enough to represent a substantial cardiorespiratory challenge, or if it results in fatigue within 20 minutes" (ACSM Guidelines, 1995, p.25). Keep in mind your client and the activity they want to pursue when deciding on the need for referral or physician clearance.

It is only in the last two decades that exercise has truly been appreciated as a medical necessity. In the early 1900s, the average life expectancy was 50 years; most people died of infections or **acute** diseases. With the advent of antibiotics, immunizations and better health care, people are now living much longer. The average life expectancy today approaches 80 years and statistics tell us that at the end of this century, 80 percent of the deaths in the United States will be from **chronic** diseases that are largely a result of lifestyle (Rosenstein, 1987). This is exciting because by taking responsibility for how we live, we may be able to gain some control over our health and mortality.

For the human body, the key components to a healthy life are:

- ✔ Physical activity
- ✔ Good nutrition
- ✔ Stress alleviation/management
- ✔ Psychological balance
- ✔ Routine check-ups

As a personal trainer, you focus on the importance of physical activity, which positively influences the other components. A **sedentary** lifestyle is now recognized as a health hazard (Paffenbarger et al., 1993; ACSM Guidelines, 1995; Blair, 1993) and everyone can benefit from some form of physical activity. However, before beginning to work with a client, you must take a health and exercise history to assess client goals, their commitment to an active lifestyle and their fitness level. Please refer to Table 5.1 for a flowchart of specific health screening procedures, results and decisions based on these results.

HEALTH SCREENING FORMS

A client's health history is your primary tool for setting up a safe and effective training program. The necessary components of a health history form include: 1) demographic information, such as age, sex and occupation;

Table 5.1
Health Screening Flowchart

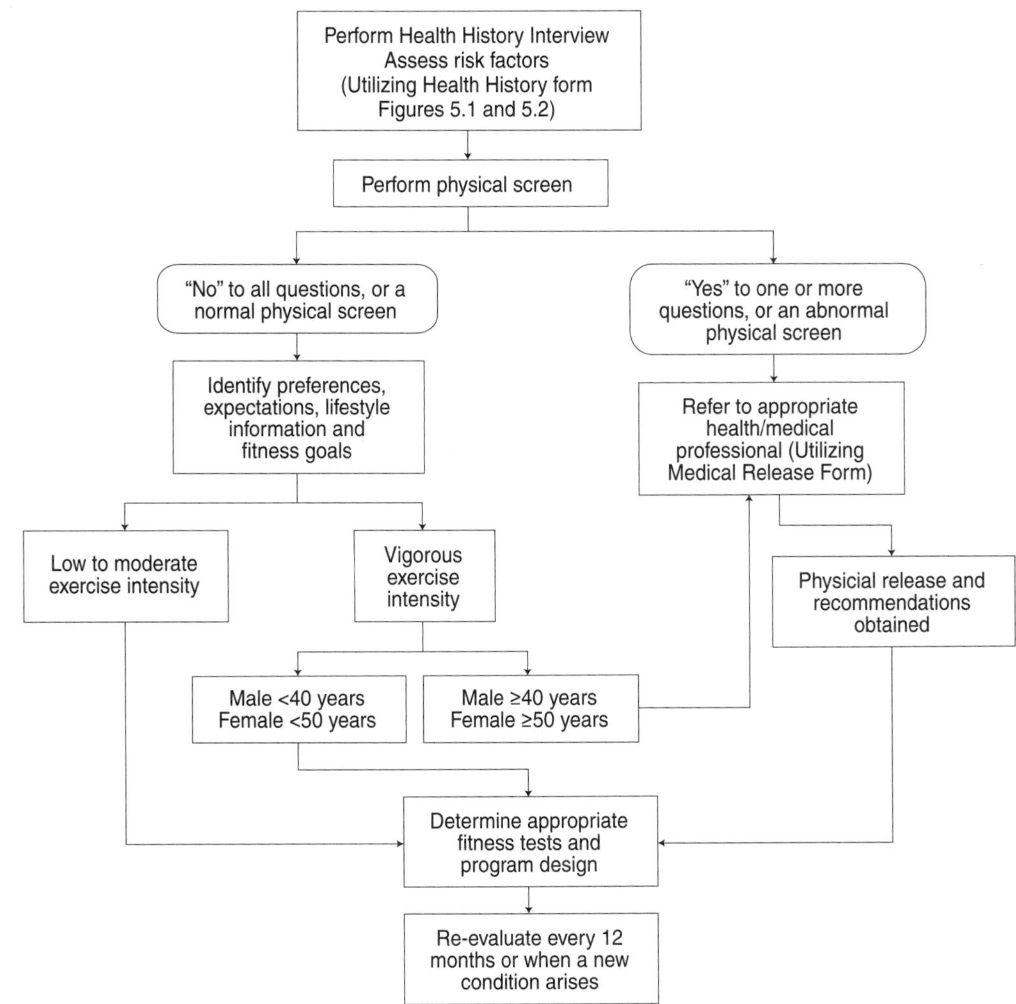

2) past and present exercise history; 3) health risk factors; 4) medications; 5) recent or current illness and injuries; 6) surgery and injury history and 7) family medical history. Demographic information is important because gender, age and occupation all bring risks, needs, expectations and referral differences to programming. Information on activity patterns will help to identify the client's current fitness level and the most appropriate type and progression of the exercise program. It also will help you to identify the risks of activity for that individual. Cardiovascular **risk factors**, medications and illness/injury information all have a tremendous impact on both referral and programming issues. And family medical history is important for determining risk as well. The Physical Activity Readiness Questionnaire (PAR-Q) has been recommended as a minimal prerequisite for beginning a low- to moderate-intensity exercise program (Figure 5.1). A sample of a more comprehensive health history form is shown in Figure 5.2 and serves as a model that you can modify as needed. Listing common conditions that affect the ability to exercise enables you to identify the major health risks for clients beginning a program. The information on the form should be updated every year or any time a new condition arises.

The Physical Activity Readiness Questionnaire - PAR-Q

(revised 1994)

PAR Q & YOU (A Questionnaire for People Aged 15 to 69)

Regular physical activity is fun and healthy, and increasingly more people are starting to become more active every day. Being more active is very safe for most people. However, some people should check with their doctor before they start becoming much more physically active.

If you are planning to become much more physically active than you are now, start by answering the seven questions in the box below. If you are between the ages of 15 and 69, the PAR-Q will tell you if you should check with your doctor before you start. If you are over 69 years of age, and you are not used to being very active, check with your doctor.

Common sense is your best guide when you answer these questions. Please read the questions carefully and answer each one honestly: check YES or NO.

YES	NO	
☐	☐	1. Has your doctor ever said that you have a heart condition and that you should only do physical activity recommended by a doctor?
☐	☐	2. Do you feel pain in your chest when you do physical activity?
☐	☐	3. In the past month, have you had chest pain when you were not doing physical activity?
☐	☐	4. Do you lose your balance because of dizziness or do you ever lose consciousness?
☐	☐	5. Do you have a bone or joint problem that could be made worse by a change in your physical activity?
☐	☐	6. Is your doctor currently prescribing drugs (for example, water pills) for your blood pressure or heart condition?
☐	☐	7. Do you know of any other reason why you should not do physical activity?

If you answered Yes to one or more questions:

✔ Talk with your doctor by phone or in person BEFORE you start becoming much more physically active or BEFORE you have a fitness appraisal. Tell your doctor about the PAR-Q and which questions you answered YES.

✔ You may be able to do any activity you want — as long as you start slowly and build up gradually. Or, you may need to restrict your activities to those that are safe for you. Talk with your doctor about the kinds of activities you wish to participate in and follow his/her advice.

✔ Find out which community programs are safe and helpful for you.

If you answered NO honestly to all PAR-Q questions, you can be reasonably sure that you can:

✔ Start becoming much more physically active — begin slowly and build up gradually. This is the safest and easiest way to go.

✔ Take part in a fitness appraisal — this is an excellent way to determine your basic fitness so that you can plan the best way for you to live actively.

FIGURE 5.1
The Physical Activity Readiness Questionnaire.

continued on next page

DELAY BECOMING MUCH MORE ACTIVE:

✔ If you are not feeling well because of a temporary illness such as a cold or a fever — wait until you feel better; or

✔ If you are or may be pregnant — talk to your doctor before you start becoming more active.

Please note: If your health changes so that you then answer YES to any of the above questions, tell your fitness or health professional. Ask whether you should change your physical activity plan.

Informed Use of the PAR-Q: The Canadian Society for Exercise Physiology, Health Canada, and their agents assume no liability for persons who undertake physical activity, and if in doubt after completing this questionnaire, consult your doctor prior to physical activity.

You are encouraged to copy the PAR-Q but only if you use the entire form.

Note: If the Par-Q is being given to a person before he or she participates in a physical activity program or a fitness appraisal, this section may be used for legal or administrative purposes.

I have read, understood and completed this questionnaire. Any questions I had were answered to my full satisfaction.

____

Name

____

Signature   Date

____

Signature of Parent
or Guardian (for participants under the age of majority)   Witness

Supported by: Health Canada Santé Canada

FIGURE 5.1 continued

Sample Health History Form

Name____________________________ Date____________

Age____________________________ Sex ☐ M ☐ F

Physician's Name ____________________________

Physician's Phone (______) ____________________________

Person to contact in case of Emergency:

Name ____________________ Date _________ Phone________________

Are you taking any medications or drugs? If so, please list medication, dose and reason.

____

____

Does your physician know you are participating in this exercise program?

____

____

Describe any physical activity you do somewhat regularly.

____

____

Do you now, or have you had in the past:	Yes	No
1. History of heart problems, chest pain or stroke	☐	☐
2. Increased blood pressure	☐	☐
3. Any chronic illness or condition	☐	☐
4. Difficulty with physical exercise	☐	☐
5. Advice from physician not to exercise	☐	☐
6. Recent surgery (last 12 months)	☐	☐
7. Pregnancy (now or within last 3 months)	☐	☐
8. History of breathing or lung problems	☐	☐
9. Muscle, joint or back disorder, or any previous injury still affecting you	☐	☐
10. Diabetes or thyroid condition	☐	☐
11. Cigarette smoking habit	☐	☐
12. Obesity (more than 20 percent over ideal body weight)	☐	☐
13. Increased blood cholesterol	☐	☐
14. History of heart problems in immediate family	☐	☐
15. Hernia, or any condition that may be aggravated by lifting weights	☐	☐

Please explain any "yes" answers on the back.

Comments:

____

____

____

____

FIGURE 5.2
Sample Health History Form.

Sample Medical Release Form

Date ____________________

Dear Doctor:

Your patient ____ wishes to start a personalized training program. The activity will involve the following:

(type, frequency, duration and intensity of activities)

If your patient is taking medications that will affect their heart rate response to exercise, please indicate the manner of the effect (raises, lowers or has no effect on heart-rate response):

Type of medication ____

Effect ____

Please identify any recommendations or restrictions that are appropriate for your patient in this exercise program:

____

____

____

Thank you.
Sincerely,

Fred Fitness
Personalized Gym
Address
Phone

____ has my approval to begin an exercise program with the recommendations or restrictions stated above.

Signed ____ Date _______________ Phone ____________

FIGURE 5.3
Sample Medical Release Form.

Health Conditions That Affect Physical Activity

Clients who answer "yes" to one or more of the questions on either form may be at increased risk for injury during exercise, and should obtain a physician's release before becoming more physically active or having a fitness assessment. Also, if a client has a medical condition you are not thoroughly equipped to handle, you should obtain recommendations from their physician or, preferably, refer the client to a more qualified professional.

The physician's release provides you with clarification of a client's status and explains any limitations to physical activity. It also enables the physician to direct modifications to the exercise program. Figure 5.3 is an example of a physician release form, which outlines the planned exercise program for the physician and enables them to return their consent and recommendations, if any.

Once the health history has been obtained, the information should be used, not just filed away. This information is crucial to designing a safe and effective exercise program and can provide support and guidance for the client's overall health and fitness program.

It is your responsibility to be familiar with appropriate local healthcare professionals for referral. These professionals may include psychotherapists, registered dietitians, physical therapists, athletic trainers and clinical exercise physiologists among others. When making referrals, it is imperative that the professionals you recommend be degreed, licensed, boarded and/or otherwise qualified in their area of expertise. It also is important that you recommend at least two professionals in order to avoid bias and allow your clients a choice in their care.

Classification of Cholesterol Levels

An increased blood cholesterol level, specifically a high concentration of **low-density lipoprotein (LDL)** cholesterol or a low concentration of high-density lipoprotein (HDL) cholesterol, increases risk for CAD. The National Cholesterol Education Program (NCEP) has developed guidelines to determine risk (NCEP, 1993; ACSM Guidelines, 1995). Generally, desirable total cholesterol is less than 200 mg/dL and high total cholesterol is more than 240 mg/dL. Anything in between is considered borderline high cholesterol. Desirable LDL cholesterol is less than 130 mg/dL, high is 160 mg/dL or greater and 130-159 mg/dL is classified as borderline high. Low HDL cholesterol is anything less than 35 mg/dL.

HEALTH CONDITIONS THAT AFFECT PHYSICAL ACTIVITY

The benefits of regular physical activity are well established (ACSM Guidelines, 1995). But there also are risks inherent in physical activity. Identifying these risks is the first step in preventing them. Regular physical activity increases the risk of both musculoskeletal injury and cardiovascular problems, such as cardiac arrest. While your clients need to be informed of these risks (see Chapter 17 for more information on informed consent), they also should know that the overall absolute risk in the general population is low, especially when weighed against the health benefits of regular exercise (ACSM Guidelines, 1995). Injuries related to physical activity usually come from:

- ✔aggravating an existing condition (either known or unknown by the client); or
- ✔precipitating a new condition.

The primary systems of the body that experience stress during physical activity are the cardiovascular, respiratory and musculoskeletal systems. Certain metabolic and other medical conditions also will be affected by regular physical activity. Obtaining a complete health history provides you with essential information in these areas that will ensure your client gets the most benefit from an exercise program with the lowest degree of risk. The following are health conditions that may affect your clients benefit-to-risk ratio and should be considered when developing a physical activity program:

Health Conditions That Affect Physical Activity

Cardiovascular Disease

Atherosclerosis is a process in which fatty deposits of **cholesterol** and calcium accumulate on the walls of the arteries, causing them to harden, thicken and lose elasticity. When this process affects the arteries that supply the heart, it is called **coronary artery disease (CAD)**. As with other muscles, the heart contracts when we exercise. The increased contraction of the heart muscle occurs because of an increased supply of oxygen-rich blood that provides necessary nutrients. The greater the exercise intensity, the larger the demand for blood and oxygen to the heart muscle. If the vessels that supply this blood to the heart are narrowed from atherosclerosis, the blood supply is limited, and the increased oxygen demand by the heart cannot be met. This can result in chest discomfort, called **angina**, and possibly a **myocardial infarction,** or heart attack.

Angina is usually described as a pressure or tightness in the chest, but can also be experienced in the arm, shoulder or jaw. This pain may be accompanied by shortness of breath, sweating, nausea and palpitations (pounding or racing of the heart). Although regular exercise may be an important part of the treatment and rehabilitation for CAD, limitations may be necessary. Anyone with a history of CAD or chest pain should have a physician's release, along with a description of any specific limitations, before beginning an exercise program.

Risk Factors. Unfortunately, many people with CAD have no known symptoms and are unaware of their potential risk for a heart attack. Long-term studies have helped researchers identify several factors that correlate with an increased risk for CAD. The ACSM has identified the following as positive (increased risk) coronary artery disease risk factors (ACSM Guidelines, 1995, p.18):

1. Age: Men older than 45 years; women older than 55 years
2. Family history: Myocardial infarction or sudden death before age 55 in father or other first-degree male relative, or before

Classification of Blood Pressure for Adults

The Fifth Report of the Joint National Committee on Detection, Evaluation and Treatment of High Blood Pressure (JNC V Report), offers new classifications for blood pressure, an expanded section on primary prevention and the role of lifestyle modification, and a section on special populations that includes recommendations regarding hypertension in women.

In a blood pressure reading, the systolic (top) number is the maximum pressure in the vessels during contraction of the heart. The diastolic (bottom) number represents the pressure that remains in the arteries when the heart relaxes. According to the JNC V Report classification, normal blood pressure is classified as less than 130 mmHg systolic and less than 85 mmHg diastolic for an adult that is not taking antihypertensive drugs and not acutely ill. High-normal is 130 to 139 mmHg systolic and 85 to 89 mmHg diastolic. Blood pressure readings of 140/90 or higher, based on an average of two or more readings taken on two or more visits, fall into four stages of hypertension ranging from mild to very severe. You should refer any client demonstrating blood pressure readings of 140/90 or greater to their physician for evaluation and recommendations. Be aware that when systolic and diastolic pressures fall into different categories, the higher category should be selected. Therefore, a client with an average blood pressure reading of 136/95 would need to be referred to their physician. Optimal blood pressure, with respect to cardiovascular risk, is less than 120 mmHg systolic and less than 80 mmHg diastolic. Unusually low readings also should be referred for medical evaluation.

age 65 in mother or other female first-degree relative

3. Current cigarette smoking

4. **Hypertension**: Blood pressure higher than 140/90 mmHg, confirmed by measurements on at least two separate occasions, or if on antihypertension medication

5. **Hypercholesterolemia**: Total serum cholesterol greater than 200 mg/dL or **HDL** less than 35 mg/dL (see sidebar, *Classification of Cholesterol Levels*)

6. **Diabetes mellitus**: Persons with **insulin-dependent diabetes mellitus (IDDM)** who are greater than 30 years of age, or have had IDDM more than 15 years, and persons with **noninsulin-dependent diabetes mellitus (NIDDM)** who are over 35 years of age

7. Sedentary lifestyle: Persons physically inactive as defined by the combination of sedentary jobs with no regular exercise or active recreational pursuits

The ACSM also has defined the following negative (decreased risk) risk factor: High serum **high-density lipoprotein (HDL) cholesterol** greater than 60 mg/dL.

Note: It is common to add up, or sum, risk factors in determining increased risk. If HDL is high, subtract one risk factor from the sum of positive risk factors, since high HDL reduces CAD risk. **Obesity** is not listed as an independent positive risk factor because its effects are exerted through other risk factors such as hypertension, **hyperlipidemia** and diabetes (ACSM Guidelines, 1995, p.18).

The more risk factors a person has, the greater their chance of having or developing CAD. An important goal of any exercise program should be to minimize these risk factors as much as possible to reduce the risk of heart disease. Any client with two or more risk factors should be referred to a physician before beginning an exercise program (see sidebar, *Intensity Defined*). In addition, the ACSM recommends that males over age 40 and females over age 50 have a medical evaluation, including a maximal exercise test, before beginning vigorous exercise programs. You and the physician can then work together to develop an ideal program. If low-to-moderate exercise is the goal, only those persons diagnosed with cardiopulmonary disease, or those with one or more major signs or symptoms suggestive of cardiopulmonary disease, need to have a medical examination and clinical exercise test prior to beginning an exercise program (ACSM Guidelines, 1995, pp.17, 25).

Hypertension. Hypertension, or high blood pressure, is more prevalent among the elderly and the African-American population. An individual's risk of CAD, **stroke** and kidney disease increases progressively with higher levels of **systolic** and **diastolic blood pressure** (Young, 1995). This is important information for you as a personal trainer because blood pressure increases with exercise, especially in activities involving heavy resistance, such as weight lifting, or isometric exercises. If a person's resting blood pressure is already high, it may elevate to dangerous levels during exercise, increasing the likelihood of a stroke.

Respiratory

The lungs (respiratory system) extract oxygen from the air we breathe and deliver it to the body's tissues via the cardiovascular system. Oxygen is essential to all body tissues for survival. A problem in the respiratory system will interfere with the body's ability to provide enough oxygen for the increasing demand that occurs during aerobic exercise. Bronchitis, **asthma** and **chronic obstructive pulmonary disease** are some of the more common respiratory problems. Each of these conditions may result in **dyspnea** (difficult breathing), making exercise difficult. Regular exercise may aggravate the condition for some people, and may improve it for others. Anyone with a disorder of the respiratory system should have a physician's clearance and recommendations before beginning or continuing an exercise program. More information on respiratory conditions and programming concerns can be found in Chapter 12.

Musculoskeletal

The musculoskeletal system consists of the muscles, bones, **tendons** and **ligaments** that support and move the body. This is the system most commonly injured during exercise. Aside from the pain and discouragement of an injury, there are other factors to contend with. Client motivation and your **scope of practice** create concerns when working with a client with previous or current musculoskeletal injuries. Changes or modifications in the exercise program are necessary to accommodate the injury. For these reasons, it is important to be cognizant of potentially hazardous situations before they occur. Most minor sprains and strains are easily managed, but a persistent problem or a more serious injury requires physician referral for appropriate treatment.

The health screening evaluation is crucial to identifying both old injuries and risk factors for potential new injuries. Asking the client about current conditions, previous injuries and pain that comes and goes is critical in detecting potential problems. The most common type of injury sustained by persons participating in physical activity is the **overuse injury**. These injuries are usually the result of poor training techniques, poor body mechanics, or both. Examples of overuse injuries include runner's knee (a painful knee condition), swimmer's shoulder (pain in the shoulder), tennis elbow (epicondylitis), shin splints (pain in the anterior lower leg) and iliotibial (IT) band syn- drome (pain along the outside of the thigh and knee). To avoid aggravating an existing injury, and to allow for healing to occur, modify the client's exercise program using a **cross-training** strategy.

Other common conditions to screen for in the health history interview are **sprains** (ligament) or **strains** (muscle or its tendon), **herniated disc**, **bursitis**, **tendinitis** and **arthritis**. Information on arthritis and low-back disorders can be found in Chapter 12. These conditions must be recognized before implementing an exercise program to avoid worsening the condition. Guidelines for recognizing and preventing injuries can be found in Chapter 15. Any musculoskeletal disorder that you are not qualified to deal with should be referred to an appropriate health professional, and a client with an injury more severe than a simple sprain or strain must have a physician's approval before beginning an exercise program. If a specific muscle weakness or joint looseness exists, medical referral is recommended, and appropriate accommodations to their program are necessary.

A client who has recently undergone orthopedic surgery may not be ready for a standard exercise program. Depending on the type of surgery performed, it may take up to one year (in the case of knee reconstruction, for example) for the tissues to heal completely. Also, disuse **atrophy** of the muscles surrounding an injury may begin after just two days of inactivity. Properly rehabilitating the weakened area requires knowledge of the type of surgery as well as the indicated rehabilitation program. This information can be obtained from the client's surgeon and physical therapist. Beginning an exercise program before complete rehabilitation may lead to biomechanical imbalances that could predispose the client to other injuries. Communication with their physician is paramount, particularly for clients who have had surgery within the last year.

Metabolic

There are many metabolic diseases that may interfere with metabolism, or the utilization of energy. Two of the more common types are **diabetes mellitus** and thyroid disorders. A client with either condition requires physician approval before initiating an exercise program. Exercise, both as a means to regulate blood glucose and to facilitate fat loss, is an important component of the lifestyle of an individual with diabetes mellitus. Your diabetic client should discuss their situation and exercise program with their physician before working with you. Physician referral is especially important if the client is receiving insulin. Diabetes mellitus types and exercise programming concerns are discussed further in Chapter 12.

The thyroid is a small gland in the neck that secretes a hormone that regulates the rate of metabolism. Hyperthyroid persons have an increased level of this hormone and a higher metabolic rate. Hypothyroid persons have a reduced level of this hormone and require thyroid medication to increase their metabolism to a normal rate. Because exercise also increases the metabolism, it could be dangerous in a person with uncontrolled thyroid disease.

Other Conditions

Hernia. Another condition that needs consideration, especially when incorporating weight lifting into a program, is a history of an inguinal or abdominal **hernia**. This is a protrusion of the abdominal contents into the groin or through the abdominal wall, respectively. Pain is usually present, but may not be in some cases. During an activity involving increased abdominal pressure, such as the **Valsalva maneuver**, the hernia may be further aggravated. A hernia is a relative contraindication for weight lifting unless cleared by a physician. If there is a history of a hernia, it is very important to instruct and educate the client on proper breathing and lifting techniques.

Pregnancy. Optimum fitness levels during pregnancy are beneficial to both the mother's and the unborn infant's health. This is not a good time to pursue maximum fitness goals, but rather to focus on maintaining a good fitness level. A client should have a physician's approval for exercise during pregnancy and until three months after delivery. Please refer to Chapter 12 for more information on modifying an exercise program during pregnancy.

Illness or Infection. A recent history of illness or infection may impair a client's ability to exercise. Moderate exercise may be acceptable during a mild illness such as a cold. A more serious condition, however, requires more of the body's energy reserves, and exercise would be contraindicated until the client improves. Our bodies have a given amount of available energy that must be balanced between the body's physiological requirements, which includes fighting infections, and the energy used during exercise. This balance varies from person to person, but it is generally not advisable to start a new exercise program during an illness. To distinguish between a minor and a major illness, you may need to consult with the client's physician.

MEDICATIONS

Medication or drug use is another important topic to cover when taking a health history. These substances alter the biochemistry of the body and may effect a client's ability to perform or respond to exercise. The properties of these drugs must be understood and discussed with your client. In designing and supervising an exercise program, it is important to realize that many over-the-counter medications and prescription or illicit drugs affect the heart's response to exercise. There are hundreds of thousands of different drugs on the market and each may be referred to by the manufacturer's brand name (e.g., Inderal) or by the scientific generic name (e.g., propranolol). Table 5.2 lists many medication categories that may affect a person's response to exercise. To use the table, consult the participant, the participant's physician or a medical reference to find the correct category for the medication. Then refer

Medications

Table 5.2
Effects of Medication on Heart-rate (HR) Response

Medications	Resting HR	Exercising HR	Maximal Exercise HR	Comments
Beta-adrenergic Blocking Agents	↓	↓	↓	Dose-related response
Diuretics	↔	↔	↔	
Other Antihypertensives	↑, ↔ or ↓	↑, ↔ or ↓	Usually ↔	Many antihypertensive medications are used. Some may decrease, a few may increase and others do not affect heart rates. Some exhibit dose-related response.
Calcium Channel Blockers	↑, ↔ or ↓	↑, ↔ or ↓	Usually ↔	Variable and dose-related responses
Antihistamines	↔	↔	↔	
Cold medications:				
without Sympathomimetic Activity (SA)	↔	↔	↔	
with Sympathomimetic Activity (SA)	↔ or ↑	↔ or ↑	↔	
Tranquilizers	↔, or if anxiety reducing may ↓	↔	↔	
Antidepressants and some Antipsychotic Medications	↔ or ↑	↔	↔	
Alcohol	↔ or ↑	↔ or ↑	↔	Exercise prohibited while under the influence; effects of alcohol on coordination increase possibility of injuries
Diet Pills:				Discourage as a poor approach to weight loss; acceptable only with physician's written approval
with SA	↑ or ↔	↑ or ↔	↔	
Containing Amphetamines	↑	↑	↔	
without SA or Amphetamines	↔	↔	↔	
Caffeine	↔ or ↑	↔ or ↑	↔	
Nicotine	↔ or ↑	↔ or ↑	↔	Discourage smoking; suggest lower target heart rate and exercise intensity for smokers

↑ = increase ↔ = no significant change ↓ = decrease

Note: Many medications are prescribed for conditions that do not require clearance. Don't forget other indicators of exercise intensity, e.g., participant's appearance, rating of perceived exertion.

Medications

to the general category under which each drug is grouped, such as **beta blockers**, antihistamines or **bronchodilators**. The drugs in each group are thought to have a similar effect on the average person, although individual responses will vary.

A particular response is usually dose dependent; the larger the dose, the greater the response. An important factor to consider in this dose-related response is the time when the medication is taken. As medications are metabolized, their effects diminish. If you have any questions concerning a client's medications, discuss them with the client and their physician. Any client taking a prescription medication that could potentially have an effect on exercise should have a physician's clearance for physical activity. The following are some of the most common categories of medications that you should be aware of:

Antihypertensives

High blood pressure, or hypertension, is common in our society, and there are many medications used for its treatment. Most antihypertensives primarily affect one of four different sites: the heart, to reduce its force of contraction; the peripheral blood vessels, to open or dilate them to allow more room for the blood; the brain, to reduce the sympathetic nerve outflow; or the kidneys, to deplete body water and decrease blood volume. The site that the medication acts upon helps to determine its effect on the individual as well as any potential side effects. The following are common anti-hypertensives:

Beta blockers. Beta-adrenergic blocking agents, or beta blockers, are commonly prescribed for a variety of cardiovascular and other disorders. These medications block beta-adrenergic receptors and limit sympathetic nervous system stimulation. In other words, they block the effects of catecholamines (epinephrine and norepinephrine) throughout the body, and reduce resting, exercise and maximal heart rates. This reduction in heart rate requires modifying the method used for determining exercise intensity. Using the Borg Scale of Perceived Exertion, for example, would be appropriate for a safe and effective aerobic exercise program for someone on beta blockers (see Chapter 12).

Calcium channel blockers. Calcium channel blockers prevent calcium-dependent contraction of the smooth muscles in the arteries, causing them to dilate and lower blood pressure. These agents also are used for angina and heart dysrhythmias (rapid or irregular heart rate). There are several types of calcium blockers on the market, and their effect on blood pressure and heart rate depends on the specific agent. Notice in Table 5.2 that calcium channel-blocking drugs may either increase, decrease or have no effect on the heart rate. Therefore, while it is important to know the general effects of a category of medication, remember that individual responses can vary.

Angiotensin-converting Enzyme (ACE) inhibitors. ACE inhibitors block an enzyme secreted by the kidneys, preventing the formation of a potent hormone that constricts blood vessels. If this enzyme is blocked, the vessels dilate, and blood pressure decreases. ACE inhibitors should not have an effect on heart rate, but will cause a decrease in blood pressure at rest and during exercise.

Diuretics. **Diuretics** are medications that increase the excretion of water and electrolytes through the kidneys. They are usually prescribed for high blood pressure, or when a person is accumulating too much fluid, as occurs with congestive heart failure. They have no primary effect on the heart rate, but they can cause water and **electrolyte** imbalances, which may lead to dangerous cardiac **arrhythmias**. Since diuretics can decrease blood volume, they may predispose an exerciser to dehydration. A client taking diuretics needs to maintain adequate fluid intake before, after and dur-

Lifestyle Information Form

Name ______________________ Date __________

Physical Activity

1. In the past year, how often have you been engaged in physical activity?
   - ☐ Regularly (3 to 4 times/week)
   - ☐ Semiregular (1 to 2 times/week)
   - ☐ Sporadic (1 to 2 times/month)
   - ☐ None
2. What types of physical activity do you consider "fun?" ______________________
3. What are your personal barriers to exercise (i.e., your reasons for not exercising)? __________
4. What physical activity have you been successful with in the past (liked and participated in regularly)? ______________________
5. How do you think your weight affects your daily activities? ______________________

Support

6. Do you feel any family, friends or co-workers have negative feelings (i.e., disapproval, resentment) toward your efforts at physical activity? ______________________
7. Is your significant other or a close friend involved in any regular physical activity? ______________________

Occupation/Leisure

8. What is your present occupation? ______________________
9. Does your occupation require much activity (i.e., walking, getting up and down, carrying things)? ______________________
10. What are your usual leisure activities? ______________________

Stressors

11. What types of things make you feel stressed? ______________________
12. How do you deal with your stress normally? ______________________

Dietary Patterns

13. How many meals and/or snacks do you have per day? ______________________
14. What would you estimate your caloric intake to be per day? ______________________
15. Do you feel you eat healthy "most of the time?" ______________________

Expectations

16. Specifically describe what you would like to accomplish through your fitness program during the next:
    1 month ______________________
    4 months ______________________
    1 year ______________________

FIGURE 5.4
Lifestyle Information Form.

ing exercise, especially in a warm, humid environment. Diuretics are sometimes used by athletes to try to lose weight for sport. This is a dangerous practice and should not be condoned by a responsible trainer.

Bronchodilators

Asthma medications, also known as **bronchodilators**, relax or open the air passages in the lungs, allowing better air exchange. There are many different types, but the primary action of each is to stimulate the **sympathetic nervous system**. Bronchodilators increase exercise capacity in persons limited by bronchospasm.

Cold Medications

Decongestants act directly on the smooth muscles of the blood vessels to stimulate **vasoconstriction**. In the upper airways, this constriction reduces the volume of the swollen tissues and results in more air space. Vasoconstriction in the peripheral vessels may raise blood pressure and increase heart rate both at rest and possibly during exercise.

Antihistamines block the histamine receptor, which is involved with the mast cells and the allergic response. These medications do not have a direct effect on the heart rate or blood pressure, but they do produce a drying effect in the upper airways and may cause drowsiness.

Most cold medications are a combination of decongestants and antihistamines and may have combined effects. However, they are normally taken in low doses and have minimal effects on exercise.

CLIENTS' PREFERENCES, EXPECTATIONS AND LIFESTYLE INFORMATION

A simple questionnaire that you can use with your clients in an interview format will give you invaluable information about what they want and need from you. Figure 5.4 is an example of a Lifestyle Information questionnaire that can be quickly administered in an orientation session. This information not only serves as an important adjunct to the health history (past musculoskeletal injuries resulting from past activity), but allows you to personalize the physical activity program to the highest degree and avoid potential errors. This interview also serves as a stepping stone for assisting the client in establishing realistic goals. The important components of a lifestyle information form are: 1) physical activity feelings, barriers, preferences and history; 2) family and social support; 3) occupation; 4) stressors; 5) dietary patterns and 6) hobbies and leisure activities. Information on the client's expectations of you and/or physical activity will help you develop their program wisely.

PHYSICAL SCREEN

The medical history is very important, but it has the limitation of defining only the conditions that a client is aware of and remembers to report. A client may be completely unaware of a significant risk factor. The purpose of a physical evaluation is to identify these unknown conditions and to further delineate a known condition. The physical screen also establishes an initial baseline and can uncover specific areas that need work. Finally, it communicates to clients that you are interested in them and are designing an individualized program to meet their needs.

Two important components of the screening are resting blood pressure and resting heart rate. Optimal blood pressure with respect to cardiovascular risk is 120/80. However, as stated earlier, a blood pressure reading below 130/85 is considered normal. There are many factors that can elevate blood pressure, including atherosclerosis, medications, obesity and stress. Exercise training can be a form of treatment if performed correctly. However, exercise in a person with uncontrolled hypertension can be dangerous and should be postponed until the condition is treated. A blood pressure greater than 140/90 in an adult is classified as hypertension and needs the attention of a physician (see sidebar, *Classification of Blood Pressure for Adults*). Normal blood pressure for children varies depending on age and body mass (Kaplan, 1986).

Resting heart rate in adults is usually 60 to 100 beats per minute and is regular in rhythm. Well-trained endurance athletes have developed an efficient cardiovascular system and often have resting heart rates in the low 40s. If an untrained client's resting heart rate is greater than 100, or less than 60, or if the heart rate is irregular, medical referral is recommended.

Observation is the next part of the physical screen and should begin as soon as you meet a client. You should look for shortness of breath at rest, perform a simple postural analysis, check for muscle tightness imbalances and observe their **gait**. Be aware of any physical characteristics or limitations that may influence the design of the program.

SUMMARY

Summary

Exercise is a vital component of good health. An effective exercise program improves a client's quality of life without aggravating or precipitating an injury or illness. Health screening is a crucial first step in working with a client and requires recognizing any significant medical conditions or risk factors for injury so a program can be modified accordingly.

The medical history is an important component of the health screening and should pay particular attention to the cardiovascular and musculoskeletal systems. It also is important to address risk factors for different diseases, as the client may not be aware of a potential or underlying problem. Finally, medications should be evaluated because they can alter exercise per- formance and increase risk factors.

Comprehensive health screening for the personal trainer involves the following steps and tools:

- ✔ Health history form and interview
- ✔ Assessment of risk factors and need for referral and/or physician clearance
- ✔ Assessment of any medications and their affect on exercise response
- ✔ Identification of lifestyle factors that may affect program design
- ✔ Physical screening

In many cases, a safe and appropriate exercise program requires a coordinated effort by you, your client and their physician to safely achieve the desired goals.

REFERENCES/SUGGESTED READING

American College of Sports Medicine (1995). ACSM's *Guidelines for Exercise Testing and Prescription.* 5th ed. Media, PA: Williams & Wilkins.

Blair, S.N. (1993). 1993 C.H. McCloy *Research Lecture: Physical Activity, Physical Fitness, and Health. Research Quarterly for Exercise and Sport,* 64(4):365-378.

Expert Panel on Detection, Evaluation and Treatment of High Blood Cholesterol in Adults (1993). Summary of the Second Report of the National Cholesterol Education Program (NCEP) Expert Panel on Detection, Evaluation and Treatment of High Blood Cholesterol in Adults (Adult Treatment Panel II). *Journal of the American Medical Association* 269:3015-23.

Kaplan, N. (1986). Clinical Hypertension (4th ed.). Baltimore: Williams & Wilkins.

Paffenbarger, R.S., Hyde, R.T., Wing, A.L., Lee, I.M., Jung, D.L. & Kampert, J.B. (1993). The association of changes in physical activity level and other lifestyle characteristics with mortality among men. *New England Journal of Medicine,* 328:538-45.

Physician's Desk Reference (1995). 49th ed. Montvale, NJ: Medical Economics Data Production Company.

Rosenstein, A. (1987). The benefits of health maintenance. *The Physician and Sportsmedicine,* 15:57-69.

Van Camp, S. (1993). Health Screening in R. Cotton (Ed.), *Aerobics Instructor Manual,* pp. 147-155. San Diego: American Council on Exercise.

Young, J.M. (1995). The Fifth Report of the Joint Committee on Detection, Evaluation and Treatment of High Blood Pressure. *AAOHN Journal,* 43(6):301-305.

CHAPTER 6

Testing and Evaluation

IN THIS CHAPTER:

6

Richard T. Cotton

Richard T. Cotton, M.A., is the vice president of publications for the American Council on Exercise in San Diego, Calif. He is an ACE-certified Personal Trainer, and is certified as both a Preventive and Rehabilitative Exercise Program Director and Exercise Specialist by the American College of Sports Medicine.

The testing and evaluation of a client is an essential first step in the training process and provides valuable information for both you and your client. Fitness testing and evaluation offers an opportunity to gather information related to a client's current level of physical fitness. The purpose may be any or all of the following:

- ✓ to assess current fitness levels relative to age and sex
- ✓ to aid in the development of an exercise program
- ✓ to identify areas of health and injury risks with possible referral to the appropriate health professional
- ✓ to establish goals and provide motivation
- ✓ to evaluate progress

While the specific tests administered may vary from client to client, a comprehensive

Required vs. Optional Evaluation Components

assessment measures the following four components:

- ✔ cardiorespiratory efficiency (at rest and during exercise)
- ✔ muscular strength and endurance
- ✔ muscle and joint flexibility
- ✔ body composition

A sound fitness testing battery should assess the function of the heart, blood vessels, lungs and muscles according to the physical demands of the individual's optimal lifestyle. Many clients desire a level of fitness that supports daily activities, an active lifestyle and the ability to confront unforeseen emergencies. Others desire a level of physical fitness that is more athletic and will want to achieve more competitive levels of **cardiovascular endurance, muscular strength** and **endurance, flexibility** and **body composition.**

REQUIRED VS. OPTIONAL EVALUATION COMPONENTS

Not all clients need or desire comprehensive exercise testing, but some form of evaluation is necessary to obtain the health-screening information you need to assess their cardiovascular risk and suitability for any level of testing and training.

Cardiovascular risk and the consequent necessity of physician referral are determined by applying the cardiovascular **risk factor** guidelines developed by the American College of Sports Medicine; these are explained in detail in Chapter 5. Additionally, a client's exercise history and attitudes toward exercise must be considered. Figure 6.1, the exercise history and attitude questionnaire, is an example of a pre-exercise assessment tool. It can be used in conjunction with comprehensive fitness testing and also as a minimum evaluation for a client, who, for whatever reason, is not being tested.

While many of your clients will look forward to testing and evaluation, it is important to understand that others are very uncomfortable with the process, and that in these cases, it may actually be counterproductive to the success of an exercise program. Some may be embarrassed of their physical condition and would rather be tested at a later date or perhaps not at all. Others are extremely competitive with themselves and understand that poor test results might be too much to tolerate when attempting to make such an important lifestyle change. The minimum evaluation you should require is the assessment of health-risk factors (see Chapter 5), and the completion of an exercise history and attitude questionnaire (Figure 6.1). The risk factor assessment must be completed in order to determine the necessity of physician clearance and/or physician-supervised exercise testing. The history and attitude questionnaire is necessary to help you design a unique program geared to each client's habits and motivation.

Pretest and Safety Procedures

While the **submaximal aerobic exercise test** and other tests outlined in this chapter carry a relatively low risk of cardiovascular or other medical complications, it is essential that you follow accepted procedure in the assessment of cardiovascular and other medical risks before testing or training a client. Before a client is tested, the cardiovascular risk assessment should be administered and reviewed. The American College of Sports Medicine (ACSM) recommends that men over 40 and women over 50 with two or more positive cardiovascular risk factors have a physician-supervised maximal graded exercise test before taking part in any vigorous exercise (i.e., greater than 60 percent of capacity). The cardiovascular risk assessment should include questions related to all the cardiovascular risk factors recognized by the ACSM and outlined in Chapter 5.

Written Consent. All clients should read and sign an **informed consent** before being

Required vs. Optional Evaluation Components

Exercise History and Attitude Questionnaire

Name ______________________________ Date __________

General Instructions: Please fill out this form as completely as possible. If you have any questions, DO NOT GUESS; ask your trainer for assistance.

1. Please rate your exercise level on a scale of 1 to 5 (5 indicating very strenuous) for each age range through your present age:
   15-20 _____ 21-30 _____ 31-40 _____ 41-50 _____ 50+_____

2. Were you a high school and/or college athlete?
   ☐ Yes ☐ No If yes, please specify ______________________

3. Do you have any negative feelings toward, or have you had any bad experience with, physical activity programs?
   ☐ Yes ☐ No If yes, please explain ______________________

4. Do you have any negative feelings toward, or have you had any bad experience with, fitness testing and evaluation?
   ☐ Yes ☐ No If yes, please explain ______________________

5. Rate yourself on a scale of 1 to 5 (1 indicating the lowest value and 5 the highest). Circle the number that best applies.

   Characterize your present athletic ability.
   1 2 3 4 5

   When you exercise, how important is competition?
   1 2 3 4 5

   Characterize your present cardiovascular capacity.
   1 2 3 4 5

   Characterize your present muscular capacity.
   1 2 3 4 5

   Characterize your present flexibility capacity.
   1 2 3 4 5

6. Do you start exercise programs but then find yourself unable to stick with them?
   ☐ Yes ☐ No

7. How much time are you willing to devote to an exercise program?
   _______ minutes/day _______ days/week

8. Are you currently involved in regular endurance (cardiovascular) exercise?
   ☐ Yes ☐ No If yes, specify the type of exercise(s) ______________
   _______ minutes/day _______ days/week

   Rate your perception of the exertion of your exercise program (circle the number):
   (1) Light (2) Fairly light (3) Somewhat hard (4) Hard

continued on next page

FIGURE 6.1 A sample exercise history and attitude questionnaire.

Required vs. Optional Evaluation Components

FIGURE 6.1 continued

9. How long have you been exercising regularly?
   ________ months ________ years

10. What other exercise, sport or recreational activities have you participated in?
    In the past 6 months? ____________________
    In the past 5 years? ____________________

11. Can you exercise during your work day?
    ☐ Yes ☐ No

12. Would an exercise program interfere with your job?
    ☐ Yes ☐ No

13. Would an exercise program benefit your job?
    ☐ Yes ☐ No

14. What types of exercise interest you?

☐ Walking	☐ Jogging	☐ Swimming
☐ Cycling	☐ Dance exercise	☐ Strength training
☐ Stationary biking	☐ Rowing	☐ Racquetball
☐ Tennis	☐ Other aerobic	☐ Stretching

15. Rank your goals in undertaking exercise:
    What do you want exercise to do for you? ____________________
    ____
    ____

    Use the following scale to rate each goal separately:

Extremely important				Somewhat important					Not at all important
1	2	3	4	5	6	7	8	9	10

    a. Improve cardiovascular fitness ______
    b. Body-fat weight loss ______
    c. Reshape or tone my body ______
    d. Improve performance for a specific sport ______
    e. Improve moods and ability to cope with stress ______
    f. Improve flexibility ______
    g. Increase strength ______
    h. Increase energy level ______
    i. Feel better ______
    j. Enjoyment ______
    k. Other ______

16. By how much would you like to change your current weight?
    (+) ________ lbs (-) ________ lbs

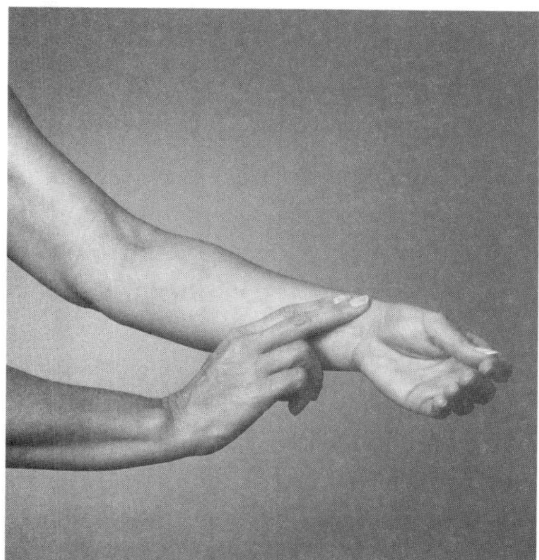

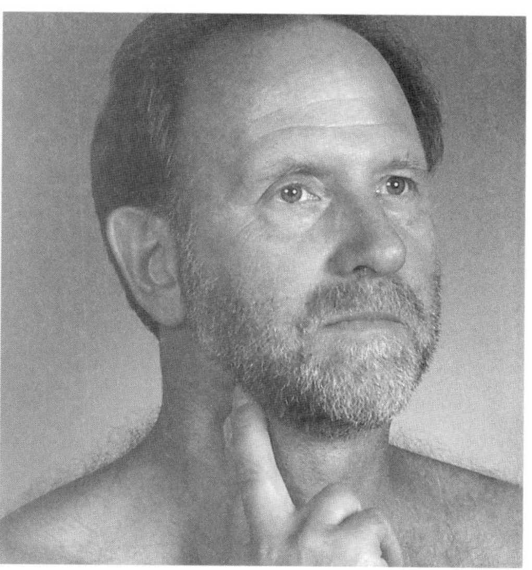

Cardiorespiratory Testing and Evaluation

FIGURE 6.2
Radial pulse is palpated with two fingers on the wrist at the base of the thumb.

FIGURE 6.3
To palpate the carotid pulse, place the fingertips on the neck, just to the side of the larynx.

tested. This consent should explain the purpose and process of the testing and include a statement of the potential for discomfort, pain or even death associated with its implementation. While this may sound extreme, it is your legal responsibility to adequately inform your clients of even the most unlikely occurrences that could take place during a procedure. In the event of an incident, properly written emergency procedures and consents may help to protect you or the exercise facility (see Chapters 16 and 17).

Written Emergency Procedures. All trainers and exercise facilities should have written emergency procedures that include everything from how to report an emergency and what to do for minor injuries in the gym, to how to respond to an apparent cardiovascular event. All procedures should include a detailed delineation of responsibilities and documentation in the event of an incident (see Chapter 16).

CARDIORESPIRATORY TESTING AND EVALUATION

Cardiorespiratory testing can give you valuable information to aid in both the development and maintenance of your client's program. Regular **resting heart rate** and **blood pressure** checks provide some basic cardiovascular health status and program progress information. Aerobic fitness testing not only helps you develop your client's exercise program, but periodic testing can be motivating as improvements are documented.

Measuring Heart Rate

The resting heart rate may be measured indirectly by placing the fingertips on a pulse site (**palpation**), or directly by listening through a stethoscope (**auscultation**). Resting heart rate is most accurately measured just before the client gets out of bed in the morning. Accuracy is further enhanced by averaging three separate morning readings. To determine the number of beats per minute, take the resting pulse rate for a full minute, or for 30 seconds and then multiply by two. One of the points at which the resting pulse can be accurately measured by palpation is at the radial pulse on the wrist, in line with the base of the thumb (Figure 6.2). Place the tips of your index and middle fingers (not the thumb, which has a pulse of its own) over the artery and lightly apply pressure.

The resting pulse, as well as the exercise pulse, also is accurately palpated from the larger carotid artery on the side of the larynx (Figure 6.3). Heavy pressure should not be applied to the carotid arteries

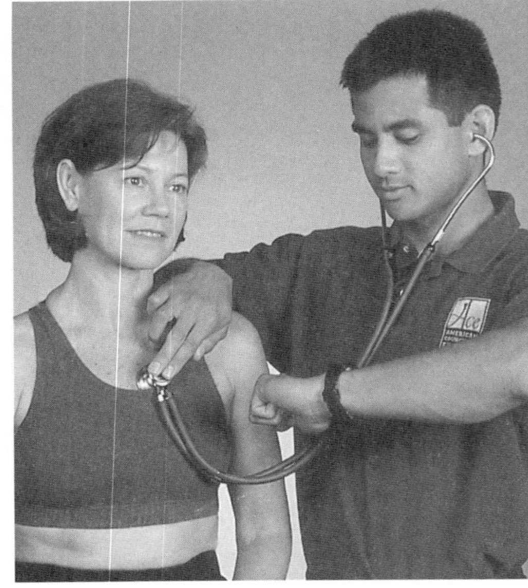

FIGURE 6.4
Correct stethoscope position for measuring resting and exercise heart rates.

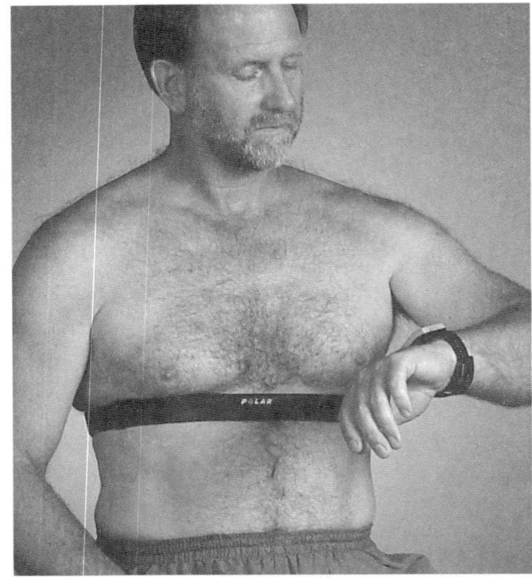

FIGURE 6.5
Chest-strap heart-rate monitor.

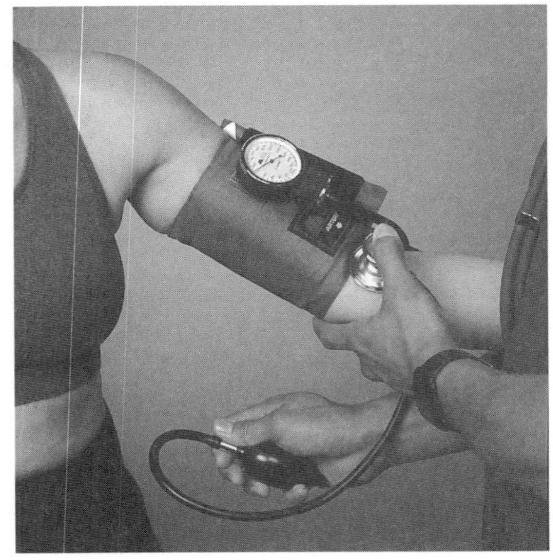

FIGURE 6.6
Correct cuff position for measuring blood pressure.

because they contain **baroreceptors** that sense increases in pressure and respond by slowing the heart rate. Exercise pulse should be taken for 10 seconds, counting the first pulse beat as zero at the start of the 10-second period. When measuring by auscultation, place the bell of the stethoscope to the left of the sternum just above the nipple line (Figure 6.4).

Another very accurate and easy method of measuring heart rate, for both testing and training, uses one of the portable heart-rate monitors currently on the market. These consist of a chest strap that contains electrodes that pick up the actual heart rate (not pulse rate) and transmit the signal to a digital readout on a wrist receiver (Figure 6.5). These monitors currently cost between $40 and $350 and are an indispensable tool for personal trainers.

Interpreting resting heart rate as it relates to cardiovascular fitness is difficult. A normal resting heart rate can vary from as low as 40 beats per minute to as high as 100 beats per minute. Men average about 70 beats per minute and women average about 75 beats per minute. Endurance-trained persons generally have a lower resting heart rate due to the increased amount of blood that the heart pumps with each beat (**stroke volume**). Resting heart rate can vary widely for both endurance-trained athletes and deconditioned subjects. It can be used to measure improvements in cardiovascular fitness because it usually decreases as cardiovascular fitness improves. Also, an elevated resting heart rate can be an indication that a client may not quite be recovered from the previous workout. A chronically elevated resting heart rate in a vigorous exerciser is a sign of overtraining.

Measuring Blood Pressure

Blood pressure reflects the force of the heartbeat and the resistance of the arteries to the pumping action of the heart. It is measured in millimeters of mercury (mmHg). The higher number, **systolic blood pressure**, represents the pressure created by the heart as it pumps blood (via ventricular contraction) to the body; this is the maximum pressure created by the heart during a complete cardiac cycle. The lower number, **diastolic blood pressure**, represents the pressure that remains in the arteries during the filling phase of the **cardiac cycle**, when the heart relaxes. It is the minimum pressure within the arteries during a complete cardiac cycle.

Blood pressure is measured using a medical grade sphygmomanometer and stethoscope after a client has been seated with both feet flat on the floor for two full minutes. The cuff should be smoothly and firmly wrapped around the arm with its lower margin about one inch above the **antecubital space**. (Use an appropriate-sized cuff as very obese clients may have falsely elevated blood pressure readings with small, standard-sized cuffs.) The arm should be comfortably supported on either an arm chair, or by you, at an angle of 10 to 45 degrees (Figure 6.6). Place the stethoscope over the brachial artery using a minimal amount of pressure so as not to distort the artery. The stethoscope should not touch the cuff or its tubing. Rapidly inflate the cuff to 20 to 30 mmHg above the point when the pulse can no longer be felt at the wrist. Release the pressure at a rate of about 2 mmHg per second, listening for sounds. The systolic pressure is determined by the first perception of sound. The diastolic pressure is determined when the sounds cease to be heard or when they become muffled. A duplicate measurement should be made using the other arm. Normative values for blood pressure readings are presented in Table 6.1.

If a blood pressure reading needs to be repeated, allow 30 to 60 seconds between trials so normal circulation can return. Record each of the results for comparison with subsequent measurements. If abnormal readings result, repeat the measurement on the opposite arm. If there is a significant discrepancy between readings from arm to arm, it could represent a circulatory problem, and the client should be referred to their physician for a medical evaluation.

Table 6.1
Classification of Blood Pressure for Adults

Systolic Reading*	Diastolic Reading*	Category
< 130	< 85	Normal
130-139	85-89	High normal
140-159	90-99	Mild hypertension
160-179	100-109	Moderate hypertension
180-209	110-119	Severe hypertension

*In mmHg.

Source: Fifth Report of the Joint Committee on Detection, Evaluation and Treatment of High Blood Pressure (JNCV), *Archives of Internal Medicine*, 153,154-183. (1993).

Cardiorespiratory Fitness Testing

Cardiorespiratory fitness is directly assessed by measurement of oxygen uptake during a **maximal graded exercise test**, or indirectly by estimating **maximal oxygen uptake (VO_2 max)** from the heart rate response to a submaximal workload. The direct measurement of maximal oxygen uptake is by far the most accurate method, but it requires specialized equipment. Depending on the age and cardiovascular risk of the client, this method is often limited to clinical or research facilities and is usually performed in the presence of a physician trained in advanced cardiac life support. Depending on the type of submaximal test administered, the submaximal exercise test provides a reasonably accurate estimation of maximal oxygen uptake (±10 to 20 percent). In order to keep the test submaximal, the intensity should not exceed 85 percent of **heart rate reserve** (Karvonen

Table 6.2
Norms for Relative Maximal Oxygen Uptake - Men (ml/kg/min)

Relative Maximal O_2 Uptake	Age (years) 18-25	26-35	36-45	46-55	56-65	65+
Excellent	> 60	> 56	> 51	> 45	> 41	> 37
Good	52-60	49-56	43-51	39-45	36-41	33-37
Above average	47-51	43-48	39-42	35-38	32-35	29-32
Average	42-46	40-42	35-38	32-35	30-31	26-28
Below average	37-41	35-39	31-34	29-31	26-29	22-25
Poor	30-36	30-34	26-30	25-28	22-25	20-21
Very poor	< 30	< 30	< 26	< 25	< 22	< 20

Source: Adapted from Golding, et al. (1986). *The Y's Way To Physical Fitness* (3rd ed.). Reprinted with permission of the YMCA of the USA.

formula) or maximal oxygen uptake.

While there may be some error in the estimation of maximal oxygen uptake, the heart rates measured at equivalent submaximal workloads can be very informative. Therefore, it is the comparison of the heart rates at equivalent workloads during follow-up testing that will show a relative change in aerobic fitness. Even though the maximal oxygen uptake estimated from the test may be somewhat inaccurate, if the heart rates are precise and the testing procedures are correct and consistent, a change in estimated maximal oxygen uptake will be a valid measurement of relative change in aerobic fitness.

Perceived Exertion Scale

6
7 Very, Very Light
8
9 Very Light
10
11 Fairly Light
12
13 Somewhat Hard
14
15 Hard
16
17 Very Hard
18
19 Very, Very Hard
20

FIGURE 6.7
Perceived exertion scale.

It also is very important for you to record perceived exertions during submaximal fitness tests (Figure 6.7). **Ratings of perceived exertion** give you an indication of your clients' status during a test and will be valuable in the determination of a **training heart rate range** following the test.

Absolute vs. Relative Maximal Oxygen Uptake

Because cycling is non-weight-bearing, the maximal oxygen consumption figures measured from bike tests will usually be given in liters per minute (l/min) so weight is not a factor in the measurement. Maximal oxygen uptake measurements that are taken from weight-bearing activities like walking, jogging and stepping are usually given in milliliters of oxygen per kilogram of bodyweight per minute ($mlO_2/kg_{BW}/min$).

You can convert absolute oxygen uptake to relative oxygen uptake using the following formula:

$$\text{Relative } O_2 \text{ uptake} = \frac{O_2 \text{ uptake (L/min) x } 1{,}000}{\text{bodyweight (kg)}}$$

Calculate oxygen uptake in $mlO_2/kg_{BW}/min$ by multiplying the oxygen uptake in l/min by 1,000 to convert to ml/min. Divide this figure by the subject's weight, in kilograms, to determine relative oxygen uptake in $mlO_2/kg_{BW}/min$.

The calculation of relative oxygen uptake allows for comparison to others of differ-

Cardiorespiratory Testing and Evaluation

Table 6.3
Norms for Relative Maximal Oxygen Uptake - Women (ml/kg/min)

Relative Maximal O_2 Uptake	Age (years) 18-25	26-35	36-45	46-55	56-65	65+
Excellent	> 56	> 52	> 45	> 40	> 37	> 32
Good	47-56	45-52	38-45	34-40	32-37	28-32
Above average	42-46	39-44	34-37	31-33	28-31	25-27
Average	38-41	35-38	31-33	28-30	25-27	22-24
Below average	33-37	31-34	27-30	25-27	22-24	19-22
Poor	28-32	26-30	22-26	20-24	18-21	17-18
Very poor	< 28	< 26	< 22	< 20	< 18	< 17

Source: Adapted from Golding, et al. (1986). *The Y's Way To Physical Fitness.* (3rd ed.).
Reprinted with permission of the YMCA of the USA.

ent body weights. A heavy person may have a somewhat high absolute maximal oxygen uptake (l/min) when compared to a lighter person, but when expressed in relative terms (ml/kg/min), the lighter person may show a higher level of cardiovascular fitness.

	Subject A	Subject B
Weight	231 lb (105 kg)	132 lb (60 kg)
Absolute VO_2 max	3.8 l/min	3.2 l/min
Relative VO_2 max	3.8 x 1,000/ 105 = 36.1 ml/kg/min	3.2 x 1,000/ 60 = 53.3 ml/kg/min

The norms for relative maximal oxygen uptake are given in Table 6.2 for men and Table 6.3 for women. These describe "aerobic fitness" of adults and are not based on health-related measures. Table 6.4 gives health-related minimums for maximal oxygen consumption for both men and women. In order to realize the health benefits of aerobic activity, your clients should aim for these levels. For those interested in optimizing both health and aerobic fitness the figures given in Tables 6.2 and 6.3 can become the basis for goal setting.

YMCA Submaximal Bicycle Test

The YMCA adapted a submaximal bicycle ergometer test from the tests developed by Sjostrand (1947) to evaluate **physical working capacity**, and by Astrand and Rhyming (1954) to estimate maximal oxygen

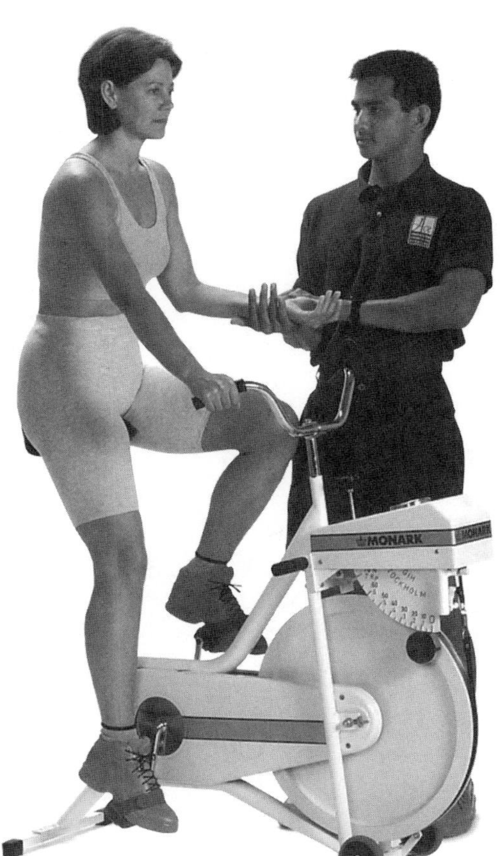
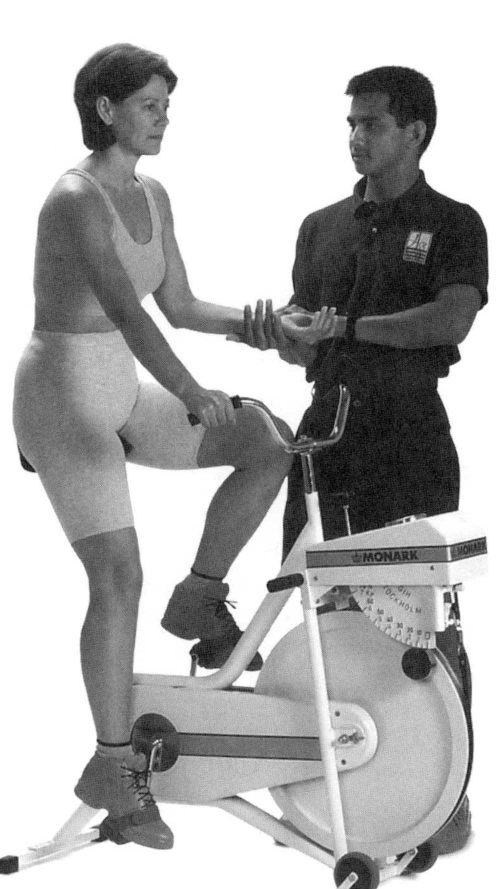

FIGURE 6.8
Basic positioning for bicycle ergometer submaximal testing.

Cardiorespiratory Testing and Evaluation

uptake. The YMCA uses the bicycle ergometer instead of the treadmill because it is less expensive, requires little space, is easily transported and makes it easier to take a heart rate. And, because its external work is known (treadmill workload must be calculated from rate and grade), it requires little training or practice. The ergometer used should be accurate, easily calibrated and have a range of 1 to 2,100 kilogram-meters per minute (kgm/ min). The two most commonly used ergometers are manufactured by either Monark (Figure 6.8) or Bodyguard. The test also requires the use of a metronome to time the test duration, a stethoscope and stopwatch

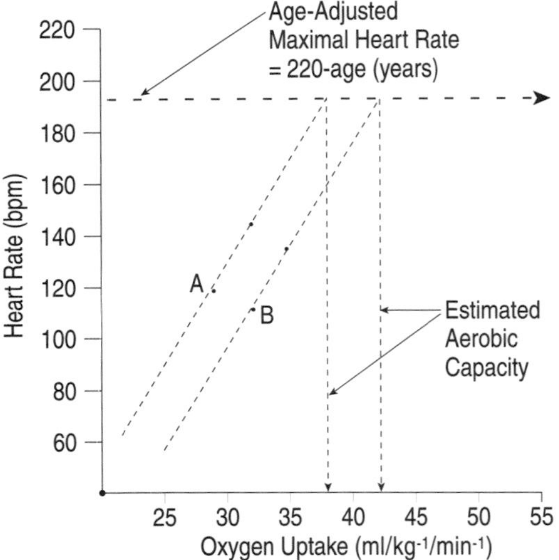

FIGURE 6.9 Extrapolating submaximal heart rates to age-adjusted maximal heart rate to estimate aerobic capacity. Note that in this example, a 25-year-old has heart rates plotted and extrapolated on two different occasions. This results in a 12-percent error.

to measure heart rate (or a heart-rate monitor), and the proper form on which to record data.

In order to estimate maximal oxygen uptake you must record two steady-state submaximal heart rates between 110 and 150 beats per minute. Heart rate is considered to be at a steady state in this test when it is measured within five beats at the end of the second and third minute of each stage. Each workload/heart-rate point is plotted on a graph and connected to form a line segment (Figure 6.9). This line segment is then extended up and to the right to the point of intersection with the horizontal line extending from the predicted maximal heart rate (220 minus age). A vertical line perpendicular to the maximal heart rate line is then drawn down from that point to the baseline. The point of intersection with the baseline marks the estimated maximal oxygen uptake. Maximal oxygen uptake estimates that are the result of bicycle ergometer testing are given in liters per minute (absolute measurement). In order to calculate the relative maximal oxygen uptake you will need to convert the liters to milliliters and divide that figure by the client's weight in kilograms. The result can then be used for comparison to established norms (Tables 6.1, 6.2 and 6.3).

Ross Submaximal Treadmill Protocol

The Ross Submaximal Treadmill Protocol given in Table 6.5 is an easy-to-use alternative to bicycle ergometer testing. The treadmill speed is held constant at a comfortable walk of 3.4 mph, and the elevation is increased every 3 minutes. The change is 4 percent per stage for men, and 3 percent per stage for women. Submaximal heart rate is measured during the last 15 seconds of every minute. Since the movement produced by walking on a treadmill makes it difficult to measure heart rate by palpitation, electronic equipment is necessary to measure exercise heart rate for treadmill tests. Individual heart rate responses to the power output will vary according to fitness levels. The submaximal heart rate at any stage should not exceed 150 to 155 beats per minute. The following guidelines are offered to ensure that submaximal exercise is achieved:

- ✔ Do not go to Stage II if the heart rate exceeds 140 at Stage I; this person is unfit.
- ✔ Stages IV and V should only be used for individuals under age 50.
- ✔ Never go to the next stage if the heart rate exceeds 145 beats per minute.

Cardiorespiratory Testing and Evaluation

Table 6.4
Aerobic Fitness Standards for Health
VO_2 max ($mlO_2/kg_{BW}/min$)

Age Group	Men	Women
<45	36	32
50	34	31
55	32	29
60	31	28
>65	30	27

Source: Baumgartner, T.A. & Jackson, A.S. (1995). *Measurement for Evaluation.* Madison: Brown & Benchmark.

Table 6.5
Ross Submaximal Treadmill Protocol

Stage	Minutes	MPH	Percent Grade	VO_2 (ml/kg/min)	METs
Women					
I	1-3	3.4	0	14.9	4.25
II	4-6	3.4	3	18.4	5.27
III	7-9	3.4	6	22.0	6.29
IV	10-12	3.4	9	25.6	7.31
V	13-15	3.4	12	29.2	8.33
Men					
I	1-3	3.4	0	14.9	4.25
II	4-6	3.4	4	19.6	5.61
III	7-9	3.4	8	24.4	6.97
IV	10-12	3.4	12	29.2	8.33
V	13-15	3.4	16	33.9	9.09

Source: Baumgartner, T.A. & Jackson, A.S. (1995). *Measurement for Evaluation.* Madison: Brown & Benchmark.

Table 6.5 lists the submaximal oxygen uptake and **MET** levels for each stage. The submaximal oxygen uptake estimations and their associated heart rates are used to estimate maximal oxygen uptake by using the formulas given below. If maximal heart rate is known, substitute it for the 220-minus-age portion of the formula.

Formulas for estimating VO_2 max from Ross Submaximal Treadmill Protocol:

Women

$$VO_2\ (ml/kg/min) = \frac{(VO_2 \text{ from Table 6.5}) \times (220 - Age - 73)}{ExHR - 73}$$

Men

$$VO_2\ (ml/kg/min) = \frac{(VO_2 \text{ from Table 6.5}) \times (220 - Age - 63)}{ExHR - 63}$$

Note: Exercise heart rates for this test must be within the range of 45 percent to 70 percent of heart rate reserve (Karvonen formula).

YMCA Submaximal Step Test

The three-minute step test developed by Dr. Fred Kasch of San Diego State University also is used by the YMCA. The aerobic stimulus is controlled by stepping to a standardized cadence. This type of test is easier to administer than the bicycle ergometer test. It requires less equipment, costs less and can be used in mass testing situations. A disadvantage of this test is that it does not result in an estimation of maximal oxygen consumption. The comparison to established norms are based on a one-minute recovery heart rate.

The following equipment is needed to administer the test:

- ✔ a 12-inch-high step bench
- ✔ a metronome for accurate pacing (96 bpm)
- ✔ a timer for timing the three-minute test and the one-minute recovery
- ✔ test forms on which to record data

Before beginning the test, demonstrate the stepping procedure. With the metronome set to 96 bpm (24 stepping cycles per minute), start stepping to a four-beat cycle — up, up, down, down (Figure 6.10). It does not matter which foot begins the cycle, although both feet must touch the top of the bench on the up portion of the cycle, and both feet must touch the floor during the down portion. The lead foot may change during the test.

Remind the client that they will step for three minutes and be seated immediately afterward for a one-minute pulse count. Have the client face the bench and step in place, in time with the metronome. Start timing the three minutes when the client begins stepping. Check stepping rhythm throughout the test, announcing when one minute, two minutes, and two minutes and 40 seconds have elapsed. You may want to provide additional verbal cues by clapping your hands or saying "up, up, down, down" in cadence with the metronome. At the end of the three-minute stepping period, immediately begin counting the heart rate of the seated subject for one minute. The one-minute post-exercise heart rate is used to score the test and can be compared to both the norms in Tables 6.6 and 6.7 and previous test results if appropriate.

McArdle Step Test

An alternative test developed by McArdle and colleagues may be useful for more fit clients. Though this test results in an estimation of maximal oxygen uptake, the standard error of estimation of ±16 percent is still comparable to other submaximal tests. You will need a 16.25-inch-high step (41.28 cm). Men should step at a 24-step per minute rate (96 bpm), while women step at 22 steps per minute (88 bpm).

Have the client step for three minutes and remain standing. Wait five seconds and take a 15-second pulse. Multiply the 15-second pulse by four to convert it to beats per minute. The maximal oxygen uptake in ml/kg/min is estimated using the following equations:

Men: VO_2 max = 111.33 - (0.42 x HR)
Women: VO_2 max = 65.81 - (0.1847 x HR)

These results can then be compared to the norms in Tables 6.2-6.4.

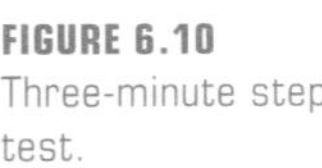
FIGURE 6.10
Three-minute step test.

The Rockport Fitness Walking Test (1-Mile Walk)

The Rockport Fitness Walking Test is routinely used to assess the cardiovascular fitness of those with a low-to-moderate aerobic fitness level. The test involves a timed 1-mile walk on a smooth and level surface (preferably a ¼-mile running track). The only other equipment necessary is a timing device and a form for recording results.

Whereas lab tests measure parameters (e.g., estimated VO_2 workload or heart rate) that give a very good indication of how well an individual will perform during aerobic activity, the Rockport Fitness Walking Test evaluates performance directly. This test also is excellent for mass testing. It does, however, have its limits. Pacing ability and body-fat weight may adversely affect performance, and since the test requires the mile to be walked as fast as possible, lack of motivation may result in an underestimation of cardiovascular fitness.

Before beginning the test, have clients warm up by walking and performing light stretching exercises. Explain that while this test requires a near maximal effort, clients should not walk to exhaustion and should stop at any time if necessary. Elapsed times should be announced with every lap. After completing the test, take a 10-second exercise pulse. This 10-second value and its corresponding per-minute pulse (the 10-second pulse times six) should be recorded along with the time it took to complete the mile walk. After test completion, all participants should walk for at least five minutes to cool down.

In addition to completion time and immediate post-exercise heart rate, the highest rating of perceived exertion (Figure 6.7) should also be recorded to provide an indication of effort and a comparison

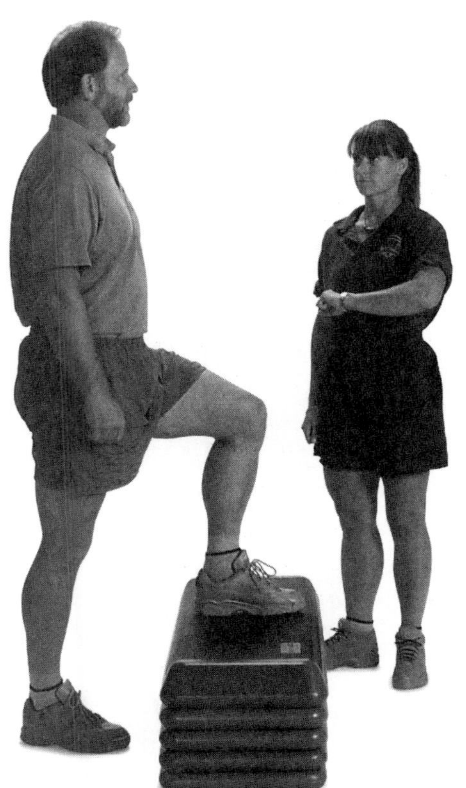

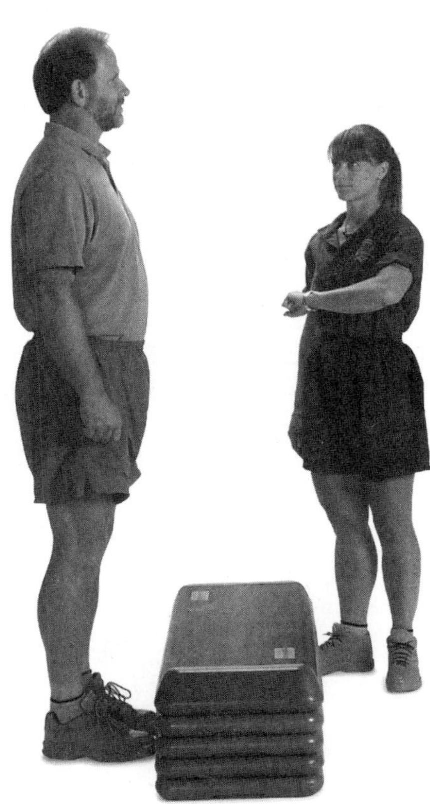

FIGURE 6.10 continued

Table 6.6
Post-exercise Heart Rate Norms for 3-minute Step Test (Men)

Fitness Category	Age (years) 18-25	26-35	36-45	46-55	56-65	65+
Excellent	<79	<81	<83	<87	<86	<88
Good	79-89	81-89	83-96	87-97	86-97	88-96
Above average	90-99	90-99	97-103	98-105	98-103	97-103
Average	100-105	100-107	104-112	106-116	104-112	104-113
Below average	106-116	108-117	113-119	117-122	113-120	114-120
Poor	117-128	118-128	120-130	123-132	121-129	121-130
Very poor	>128	>128	>130	>132	>129	>130

Source: Adapted from Golding, et al. (1986). *The Y's Way To Physical Fitness.* (3rd ed.). Reprinted with permission of the YMCA of the USA.

to subsequent tests. Completion time and minute pulse rate are used to estimate maximal oxygen uptake using the following formulas:

Women
VO_2 (ml/kg/min) = 132.85 - (0.388 x Age) - (0.077 x $Weight_{lbs}$) - (3.265 x Mile Walk $Time_{min}$) - (0.156 x Exercise HR)

Men
VO_2 (ml/kg/min) = 139.168 - (0.388 x Age) - (0.077 x $Weight_{lbs}$) - (3.265 x Mile Walk $Time_{min}$) - (0.156 x Exercise HR)

The standard error of the estimate of maximal oxygen uptake from the Rockport walking test is 5.0 $mlO_2/kg_{BW}/min$. This is about 1.0 $mlO_2/kg_{BW}/min$ better than most submaximal bike, treadmill or step tests.

BYU Jog Test

Researchers at Brigham Young University (BYU) have developed a test similar to the Rockport test by replacing walking with jogging. It is a good test for more fit clients. The test requires a 1-mile jog at a steady pace, and exercise heart rate is measured immediately after the run.

Your client should first take a two- to three-minute warm-up jog. The goal is to jog the mile at a steady and suitable pace. Remind your client that this is a submaximal test and they should not run at an "all-out" rate. Set run time and exercise limits to ensure a submaximal effort. Clients' exercise heart rates should be less than 180 beats per minute, and men should not jog at a pace faster than eight minutes per mile, and women should not exceed nine minutes per mile. Use the following equations to estimate maximal oxygen uptake:

Women
VO_2 = 100.5 - (0.164 x $Weight_{kg}$) - (1.438 x Mile Jog $Time_{min}$) - (0.193 x Exercise HR)

Men
VO_2 = 108.44 - (0.164 x $Weight_{kg}$) - (1.438 x Mile Jog $Time_{min}$) - (0.193 x Exercise HR)

Note: The standard error of this test (SE = 3.0 ml/kg/min) is half that of the submaximal bike, treadmill and step tests.

BODY COMPOSITION TESTING AND EVALUATION

Excess body fat has been associated with a number of health risks, including heart disease, **diabetes,**

Table 6.7
Post-exercise Heart Rate Norms for 3-minute Step Test (Women)

Fitness Category	Age (years) 18-25	26-35	36-45	46-55	56-65	65+
Excellent	<85	<88	<90	<94	<95	<90
Good	85-98	88-99	90-102	94-104	95-104	90-102
Above average	99-108	100-111	103-110	105-115	105-112	103-115
Average	109-117	112-119	111-118	116-120	113-118	116-122
Below average	118-126	120-126	119-128	121-126	119-128	123-128
Poor	127-140	127-138	129-140	127-135	129-139	129-134
Very poor	>140	>138	>140	>135	>139	>134

Source: Adapted from Golding, et al. (1986). *The Y's Way To Physical Fitness.* (3rd ed.)
Reprinted with permission of the YMCA of the USA.

hypertension, arthritis, gall bladder disease, cirrhosis of the liver, **hernia**, intestinal obstruction and sleep disorders. It also is associated with reduced endurance performance and an increased risk for injury. The primary reason most adults begin exercise programs is to reduce body weight, so it is important to be able to assess body composition in order to determine a reasonable body weight goal and to develop a safe and effective exercise program to reach it. Body composition refers to the quality or makeup of total body mass, which can be divided into **fat-free mass** and fat mass. Fat-free mass is composed of bone, muscle and organs, and fat mass is composed of **adipose tissue**. Body composition assessment determines the relative percentages of fat-free and fat mass.

Ideal body weight has historically been determined without concern for body composition, and involved the use of the standardized height-weight tables. Ideal body weight is estimated only from height and frame size without consideration of the composition of the weight. Therefore, a well-muscled bodybuilder would most likely be considered overweight, while another person could fall within the accepted range and actually be over-fat by body-composition standards. It is not uncommon for an exerciser to lose fat weight and gain muscle weight without any change in total body weight. Without an assessment of body composition, this favorable change could go undetected and possibly lead to frustration on the part of the exerciser.

The four most common methods of assessing body composition are hydrostatic weighing, circumference measurements, bioelectrical impedance and skinfold measurements.

Hydrostatic Weighing

Hydrostatic weighing, also known as underwater weighing, is considered the "gold standard" of body composition assessment. The test involves suspending a client, seated in a chair attached to a scale, in a tank of water. Body density is calculated from the relationship of normal body weight to underwater weight. Body-fat percentage is calculated from body density. This method is most accurate when combined with a measurement of **residual volume** (the amount of air left in the lungs after a complete expiration). When residual volume is estimated from a formula, the accuracy of the hydrostatic method can be significantly decreased. Though hydrostatic weighing is accurate, it is often impractical in terms of expense, time and equipment.

Table 6.8
Body Mass Index

	19	20	21	22	23	24	25	26	27	28	29	30	35	40
Height (inches)							Weight (pounds)							
58	91	95	100	105	110	115	119	124	129	134	138	143	167	191
59	94	99	104	109	114	119	124	128	133	138	143	148	173	198
60	97	102	107	112	118	123	128	133	138	143	148	153	179	204
61	100	106	111	116	121	127	132	137	143	148	153	158	185	211
62	104	109	115	120	125	131	136	142	147	153	158	164	191	218
63	107	113	118	124	130	135	141	146	152	158	163	169	197	225
64	110	116	122	128	134	140	145	151	157	163	169	174	203	233
65	114	120	126	132	138	144	150	156	162	168	174	180	210	240
66	117	124	130	136	142	148	155	161	167	173	179	185	216	247
67	121	127	134	140	147	153	159	166	172	178	185	191	223	255
68	125	131	138	144	151	158	164	171	177	184	190	197	230	263
69	128	135	142	149	155	162	169	176	182	189	196	203	237	270
70	132	139	146	153	160	167	174	181	188	195	202	209	243	278
71	136	143	150	157	165	172	179	186	193	200	207	215	250	286
72	140	147	155	162	169	177	184	191	199	206	213	221	258	294
73	144	151	159	166	174	182	189	197	204	212	219	227	265	303
74	148	155	163	171	179	187	194	202	210	218	225	233	272	311
75	152	160	168	176	184	192	200	208	216	224	232	240	279	319
76	156	164	172	180	189	197	205	213	221	230	238	246	287	328

Bioelectrical Impedance

Bioelectrical impedance is a popular method for determining body composition. It is based on the principle that the conductivity of an electrical impulse is greater through lean tissue than through fatty tissue. An imperceptible electrical current is passed through pairs of electrodes, which are placed on the hand and foot. The analyzer, essentially an ohmmeter and a computer, measures the body's resistance to electrical flow and computes body density and body-fat percentage. The subject must lie still, with wrist and ankle electrodes accurately placed. The client should be well-hydrated and not have exercised in the past six hours or consumed any alcohol in the past 24 hours. Some research has shown the impedance method to be as accurate as the skinfold method, depending on the quality of the analyzer, the formula used to compute body density and the adherence of the client to the aforementioned restrictions. Assessing body composition via bioelectrical impedance is both fast and easy and requires minimal technical training. The cost of the analyzers ranges from \$300 to \$5,000 depending on design and report-generation capabilities (from simple digital readouts to elaborate multi-page reports).

Body Mass Index

More useful estimates of body composition can be obtained by adjusting weight for height or stature and calculating a height-normalized index. The most commonly used index is the **Body Mass Index (BMI)**, which is calculated as follows:

$$\text{BMI} = \frac{\text{Weight (kg)}}{\text{Height}^2\text{(m)}}$$

Example:

Convert weight from pounds to kilograms by dividing by 2.2:

Weight = 209.5 pounds

$$\frac{209}{2.2} = 95.2 \text{ kg}$$

Convert height from inches to centimeters, and then to meters, by multiplying by 2.54 and then dividing by 100:

Height = 67.7 inches

$$67.7 \times 2.54 = 172 \text{ cm}$$

$$\frac{172}{100} = 1.72 \text{ m}$$

$$\text{BMI} = \frac{95.2}{(1.72)^2} = 32.2$$

Use Table 6.8 to determine body mass index. Find your client's height in the far left column, and move across the row to the weight that is closest to their own. Their body mass index will be at the top of that column.

People in a normal weight range usually have a BMI between 19 and 25. Individuals who are considered mildly overweight make up approximately 90 percent of the overweight population, are up to 20 percent above their normal weight and tend to have BMIs between 25 and 30. Moderately overweight people make up 9.5 percent of the overweight population, are considered 21 percent to 40 percent over their normal weight, and have BMIs between 30 and 35. Finally, severely overweight individuals are more than 40 percent above their normal weight, make up .5 percent of overweight people and have BMIs greater than 35 (Table 6.9).

Table 6.9
BMI Reference Chart

Weight Category	BMI Range
Normal weight	19 to <25
Overweight	25 to <30
Obese	30 to <35
Seriously obese	≥ 35

Table 6.10
Anatomic Locations of Circumference Measurement Sites

Circumference	Anatomic Site
Abdomen	At the level of the umbilicus
Hips	The largest circumference below the umbilicus
Iliac	Level with the iliac crests
Waist	The narrowest part of the torso

Since BMI uses total body weight (i.e., not estimates of fat and lean body mass separately) in the calculation, it does not discriminate between the overfat and the athletic, more muscular body type. Therefore, BMI should ideally be used in conjunction with other body composition assessments.

Anthropometry

Anthropometric assessments of body

Body Composition Testing and Evaluation

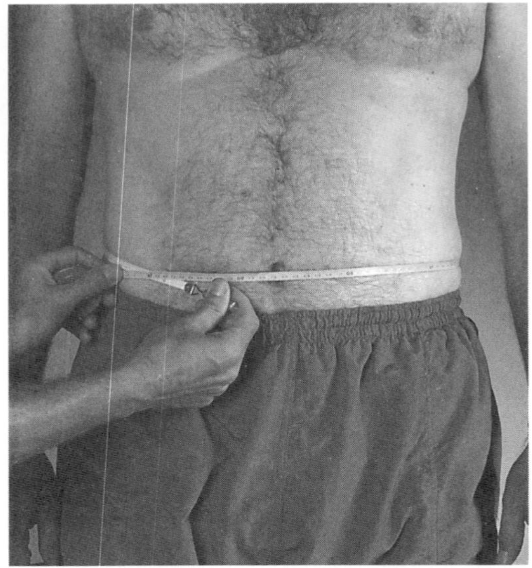

FIGURE 6.11
Abdominal circumference.

Table 6.11
Waist to Hip Ratios and Associated Level of Health Risks

Classification	Men	Women
High risk	>1.0	>0.85
Moderately high risk	0.90 - 1.0	0.80 - 0.85
Lower risk	<0.90	<0.80

Adapted from Van Itallie (1988).

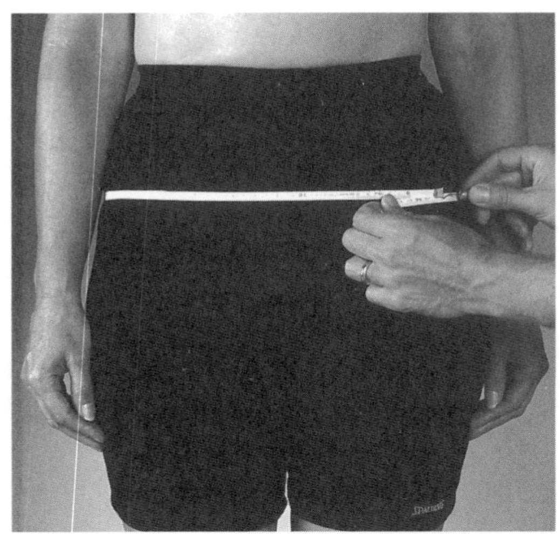

FIGURE 6.12
Hip circumference.

composition are perhaps the easiest and least expensive methods for assessing body composition. These include circumference and skinfold measures, which are readily used in the field. Anthropometric measures also can be used to estimate body fat and its distribution (i.e., central vs. peripheral, or upper vs. lower body).

Circumference Measures. Circumference measures can easily be used to assess body composition, even with significantly overweight clients. However, to ensure accuracy, you must use exact anatomical landmarks for taking each circumference measurement (Table 6.10 and Figures 6.11-6.14). A thorough review of anthropometric measurement sites and techniques for optimizing accuracy are presented in

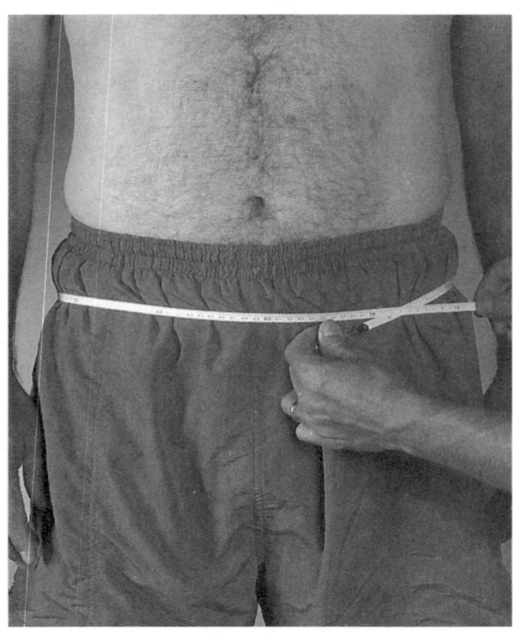

FIGURE 6.13
Iliac circumference.

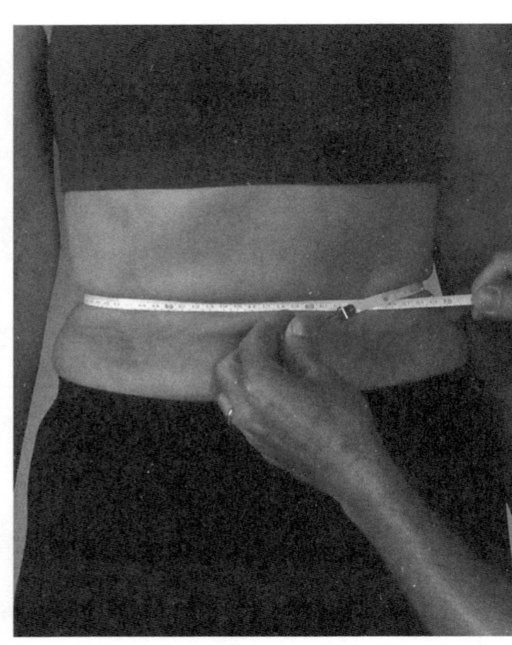

FIGURE 6.14
Waist circumference.

Body Composition Testing and Evaluation

Lohman et al. (1988).

A cloth or fiberglass (i.e., non-elastic) metric measurement tape must be used. The tape should be periodically calibrated against a meter stick to ensure it hasn't been stretched. When assessing significantly overweight clients, be sure to use a long enough tape. Pull the tape tight enough to keep it in position without causing an indentation of the skin. There are tapes available that have a gauge that indicates the correct tension.

Estimating Body Fat from Circumference Measures. Body density (BD) for women and men can be predicted from generalized equations which use girth measurements (Tran and Weltman, 1989; Tran et al., 1988):

$$\text{BD for women} = 1.168297 - (0.002824 \times \text{abdomen}_{cm}) + (0.0000122098 \times \text{abdomen}^2_{cm}) - (0.000733128 \times \text{hips}_{cm}) + (0.000510477 \times \text{height}_{cm}) - (0.000216161 \times \text{age})$$

$$\text{BD for men} = 1.21142 + (.00085 \times \text{weight}_{kg}) - (.00050 \times \text{iliac}_{cm}) - (.00061 \times \text{hip}_{cm}) - .00138 \times \text{abdomen}_{cm})$$

Body density can then be converted to percent fat by using the following formula:

$$\text{Percent fat} = \left(\frac{495}{\text{BD}}\right) - 450$$

Estimating Body-Fat Distribution. Upper-body or abdominal obesity is known to increase health risk, so it is important to assess your client's body-fat distribution. A quick and reliable technique is the **waist-to-hip circumference ratio (WTH)**. To calculate the WTH ratio, divide the waist measurement by the hip measurement. Table 6.11 illustrates the relative risk ratings for WTH ratios.

Skinfold Measurements. Skinfold measurements are a relatively inexpensive way to assess body composition, and, if the mea-

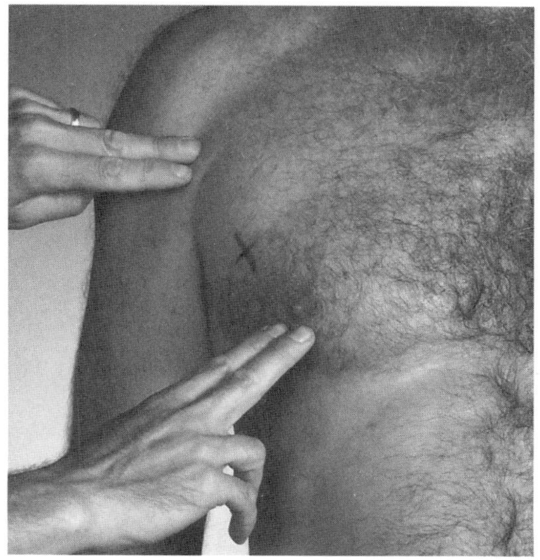

FIGURE 6.15
Chest skinfold measurement for men:

a. Locate the site midway between the anterior axillary line and the nipple.

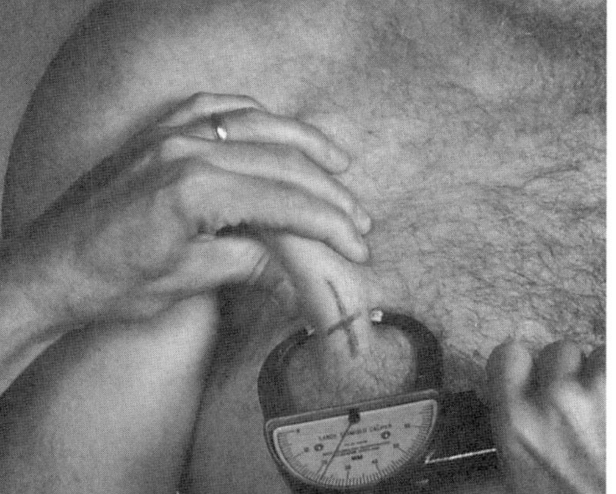

b. Grasp a diagonal fold and pull it away from the muscle.

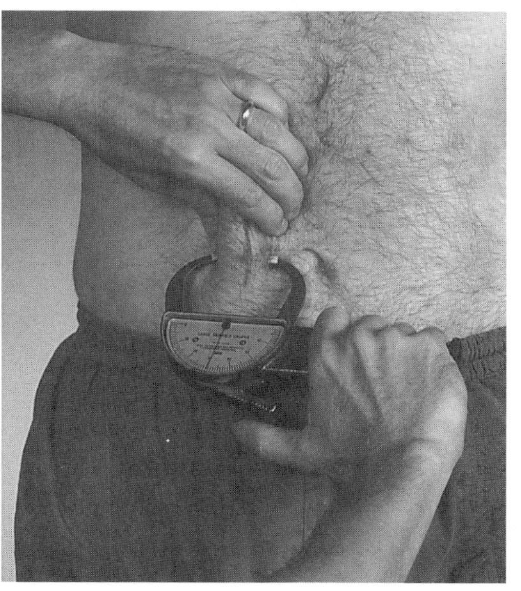

FIGURE 6.16
Abdominal skinfold measurement for men: Grasp a vertical skinfold one inch to the left of the umbilicus.

Body Composition Testing and Evaluation

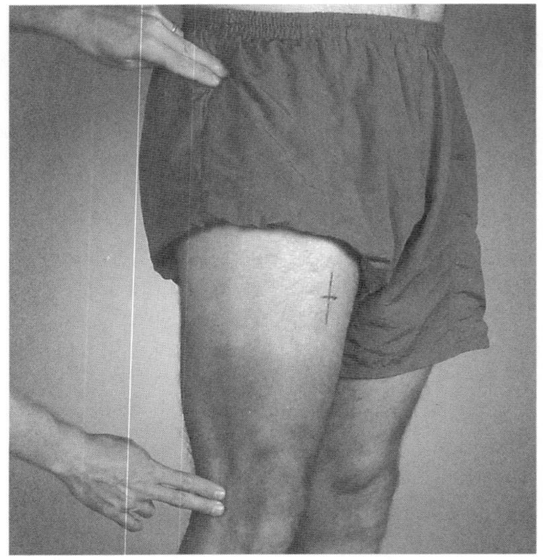

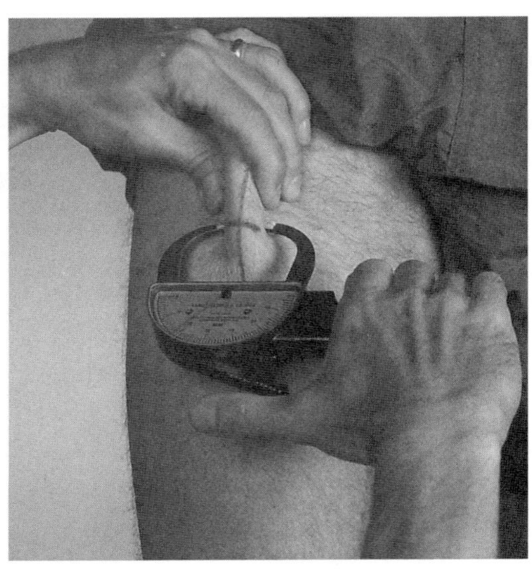

FIGURE 6.17
Thigh skinfold measurement for men:

a. Locate the hip and the knee joints and find the midpoint on the top of the thigh.

b. Grasp a vertical skinfold and pull it away from the muscle.

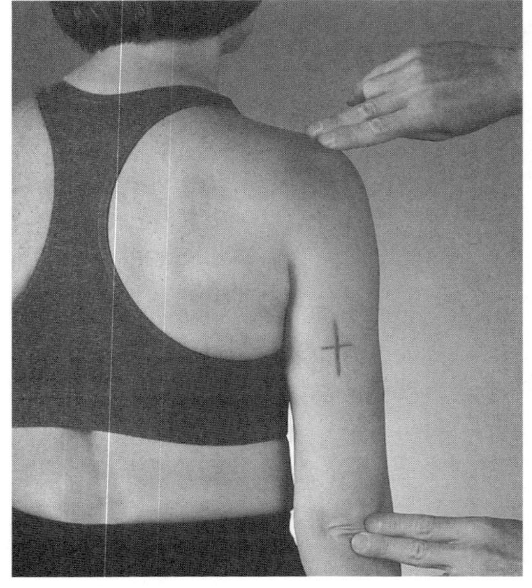

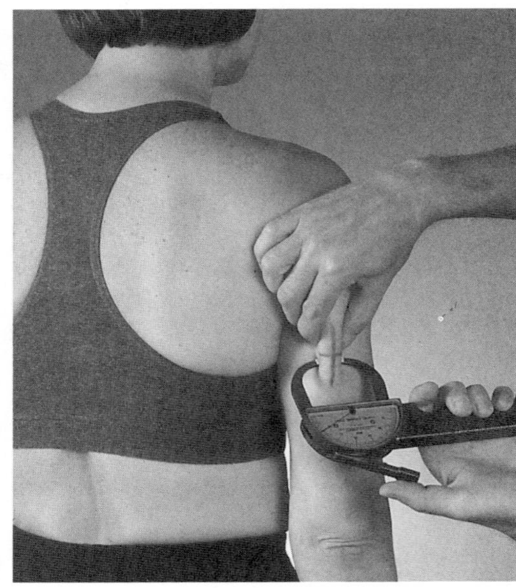

FIGURE 6.18
Triceps skinfold measurement for women:

a. Locate the site midway between the acromial (shoulder) and olecranon (elbow) processes.

b. Grasp a vertical fold on the posterior midline and pull it away from the muscle.

surements are taken properly, the results are both valid and reliable. The standard error associated with this method is 3.5 percent, depending on the equation applied. This is compared to a 2.7 percent error for a hydrostatically determined measurement. Skinfold measurement is based on the belief that approximately 50 percent of total body fat lies under the skin, and involves measuring the thickness of the skinfolds at standardized sites. These measurements are summed and applied to one of many equations available. For the most part, the equations calculate body density, with percent fat being calculated from the same formula used for hydrostatic weighing. Calculation is often simplified through the use of a table or nomogram. Calipers specifically designed for skinfold measurement are the only equipment needed for this method of body-fat assessment, and range in cost from $3 to $300.

The procedure for measuring skinfolds is as follows:

1. Identify the anatomical location of the skinfold. Take all measurements on the right side of the body. (Optional: Mark the site with a common eyebrow pencil to expedite site relocation in

repeated measures).

2. Grasp the skinfold firmly with the thumb and index finger of the left hand.

3. Holding the calipers perpendicular to the site, place the pads of the calipers approximately one-quarter inch from the thumb and forefinger.

4. Approximately one or two seconds after the trigger has been released read the dial to the nearest 0.5 millimeter.

5. A minimum of two measurements should be taken at each site, with at least 15 seconds between measurements to allow the fat to return to its normal thickness.

6. Continue to take measurements until two measurements vary by less than 1 millimeter.

Improper site determination and measurement are the two primary sources of error when using this method. The technique is best learned by locating and measuring the standard sites numerous times and comparing results with those of a well-trained associate. Skinfold measurements should not be taken after exercise because the transfer of fluid to the skin could result in overestimations.

Of the many equations for estimating body composition, two developed by Jackson and Pollock (1985) have the smallest margin of error for the general population. These equations are based on the sum of measurements taken at three sites.

For men the skinfold sites are as follows:

1. Chest (Figure 6.15): a diagonal skinfold taken midway on the anterior axillary line (crease of the underarm and the nipple.)

2. Abdomen (Figure 6.16): a vertical skinfold taken 1 inch lateral to the umbilicus.

3. Thigh (Figure 6.17): a vertical skinfold taken midway between the hip and knee joints on the front of the thigh.

For women, the skinfold sites are as follows:

1. Triceps (Figure 6.18): a vertical fold on the back of the upper arm taken half-

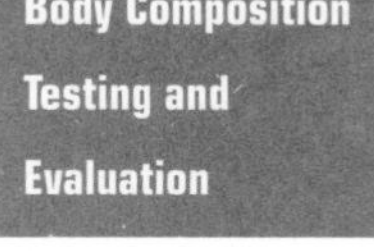

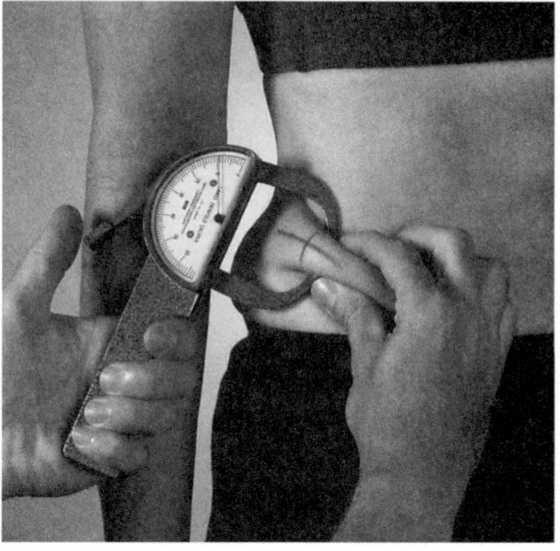

FIGURE 6.19 Suprailium skinfold measurement for women: Grasp a diagonal skinfold just above, and slightly forward of, the crest of the ilium.

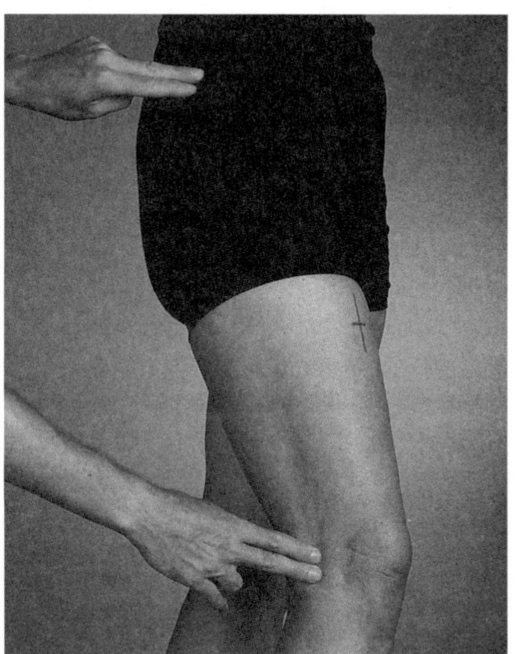

FIGURE 6.20 Thigh skinfold measurement for women:

a. Locate the hip and the knee joints and find the midpoint on the top of the thigh.

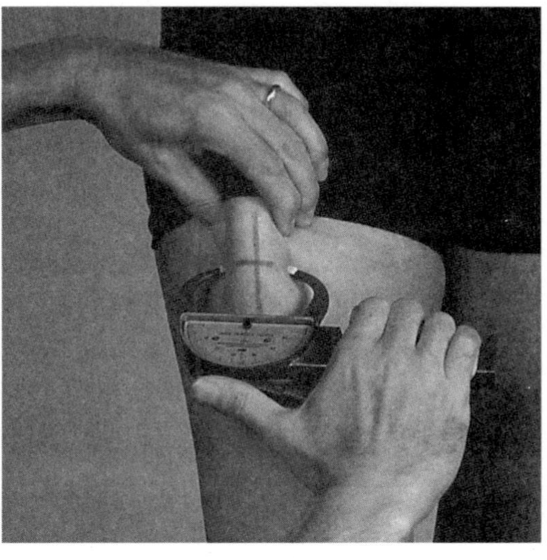

b. Grasp a vertical skinfold and pull it away from the muscle.

Table 6.12
Percent Body Fat Estimations for Men — Jackson and Pollock Formula

Sum of Skinfolds (mm)	Age Groups Under 22	23-27	28-32	33-37	38-42	43-47	48-52	53-57	Over 57
8-10	1.3	1.8	2.3	2.9	3.4	3.9	4.5	5.0	5.5
11-13	2.2	2.8	3.3	3.9	4.4	4.9	5.5	6.0	6.5
14-16	3.2	3.8	4.3	4.8	5.4	5.9	6.4	7.0	7.5
17-19	4.2	4.7	5.3	5.8	6.3	6.9	7.4	8.0	8.5
20-22	5.1	5.7	6.2	6.8	7.3	7.9	8.4	8.9	9.5
23-25	6.1	6.6	7.2	7.7	8.3	8.8	9.4	9.9	10.5
26-28	7.0	7.6	8.1	8.7	9.2	9.8	10.3	10.9	11.4
29-31	8.0	8.5	9.1	9.6	10.2	10.7	11.3	11.8	12.4
32-34	8.9	9.4	10.0	10.5	11.1	11.6	12.2	12.8	13.3
35-37	9.8	10.4	10.9	11.5	12.0	12.6	13.1	13.7	14.3
38-40	10.7	11.3	11.8	12.4	12.9	13.5	14.1	14.6	15.2
41-43	11.6	12.2	12.7	13.3	13.8	14.4	15.0	15.5	16.1
44-46	12.5	13.1	13.6	14.2	14.7	15.3	15.9	16.4	17.0
47-49	13.4	13.9	14.5	15.1	15.6	16.2	16.8	17.3	17.9
50-52	14.3	14.8	15.4	15.9	16.5	17.1	17.6	18.2	18.8
53-55	15.1	15.7	16.2	16.8	17.4	17.9	18.5	19.1	19.7
56-58	16.0	16.5	17.1	17.7	18.2	18.8	19.4	20.0	20.5
59-61	16.9	17.4	17.9	18.5	19.1	19.7	20.2	20.8	21.4
62-64	17.6	18.2	18.8	19.4	19.9	20.5	21.1	21.7	22.2
65-67	18.5	19.0	19.6	20.2	20.8	21.3	21.9	22.5	23.1
68-70	19.3	19.9	20.4	21.0	21.6	22.2	22.7	23.3	23.9
71-73	20.1	20.7	21.2	21.8	22.4	23.0	23.6	24.1	24.7
74-76	20.9	21.5	22.0	22.6	23.2	23.8	24.4	25.0	25.5
77-79	21.7	22.2	22.8	23.4	24.0	24.6	25.2	25.8	26.3
80-82	22.4	23.0	23.6	24.2	24.8	25.4	25.9	26.5	27.1
83-85	23.2	23.8	24.4	25.0	25.5	26.1	26.7	27.3	27.9
86-88	24.0	24.5	25.1	25.7	26.3	26.9	27.5	28.1	28.7
89-91	24.7	25.3	25.9	26.5	27.1	27.6	28.2	28.8	29.4
92-94	25.4	26.0	26.6	27.2	27.8	28.4	29.0	29.6	30.2
95-97	26.1	26.7	27.3	27.9	28.5	29.1	29.7	30.3	30.9
98-100	26.9	27.4	28.0	28.6	29.2	29.8	30.4	31.0	31.6
101-103	27.5	28.1	28.7	29.3	29.9	30.5	31.1	31.7	32.3
104-106	28.2	28.8	29.4	30.0	30.6	31.2	31.8	32.4	33.0
107-109	28.9	29.5	30.1	30.7	31.3	31.9	32.5	33.1	33.7
110-112	29.6	30.2	30.8	31.4	32.0	32.6	33.2	33.8	34.4
113-115	30.2	30.8	31.4	32.0	32.6	33.2	33.8	34.5	35.1
116-118	30.9	31.5	32.1	32.7	33.3	33.9	34.5	35.1	35.7
119-121	31.5	32.1	32.7	33.3	33.9	34.5	35.1	35.7	36.4
122-124	32.1	32.7	33.3	33.9	34.5	35.1	35.8	36.4	37.0
125-127	32.7	33.3	33.9	34.5	35.1	35.8	36.4	37.0	37.6

Source: Jackson, A.S. & Pollock, M.L.: Practical Assessment of Body Composition. (May 1985). Reprinted with permission of McGraw-Hill.

Table 6.13
Percent Body Fat Estimations for Women — Jackson and Pollock Formula

Sum of Skinfolds (mm)	Age Groups								
	Under 22	23-27	28-32	33-37	38-42	43-47	48-52	53-57	Over 57
23-25	9.7	9.9	10.2	10.4	10.7	10.9	11.2	11.4	11.7
26-28	11.0	11.2	11.5	11.7	12.0	12.3	12.5	12.7	13.0
29-31	12.3	12.5	12.8	13.0	13.3	13.5	13.8	14.0	14.3
32-34	13.6	13.8	14.0	14.3	14.5	14.8	15.0	15.3	15.5
35-37	14.8	15.0	15.3	15.5	15.8	16.0	16.3	16.5	16.8
38-40	16.0	16.3	16.5	16.7	17.0	17.2	17.5	17.7	18.0
41-43	17.2	17.4	17.7	17.9	18.2	18.4	18.7	18.9	19.2
44-46	18.3	18.6	18.8	19.1	19.3	19.6	19.8	20.1	20.3
47-49	19.5	19.7	20.0	20.2	20.5	20.7	21.0	21.2	21.5
50-52	20.6	20.8	21.1	21.3	21.6	21.8	22.1	22.3	22.6
53-55	21.7	21.9	22.1	22.4	22.6	22.9	23.1	23.4	23.6
56-58	22.7	23.0	23.2	23.4	23.7	23.9	24.2	24.4	24.7
59-61	23.7	24.0	24.2	24.5	24.7	25.0	25.2	25.5	25.7
62-64	24.7	25.0	25.2	25.5	25.7	26.0	26.7	26.4	26.7
65-67	25.7	25.9	26.2	26.4	26.7	26.9	27.2	27.4	27.7
68-70	26.6	26.9	27.1	27.4	27.6	27.9	28.1	28.4	28.6
71-73	27.5	27.8	28.0	28.3	28.5	28.8	29.0	29.3	29.5
74-76	28.4	28.7	28.9	29.2	29.4	29.7	29.9	30.2	30.4
77-79	29.3	29.5	29.8	30.0	30.3	30.5	30.8	31.0	31.3
80-82	30.1	30.4	30.6	30.9	31.1	31.4	31.6	31.9	32.1
83-85	30.9	31.2	31.4	31.7	31.9	32.2	32.4	32.7	32.9
86-88	31.7	32.0	32.2	32.5	32.7	32.9	33.2	33.4	33.7
89-91	32.5	32.7	33.0	33.2	33.5	33.7	33.9	34.2	34.4
92-94	33.2	33.4	33.7	33.9	34.2	34.4	34.7	34.9	35.2
95-97	33.9	34.1	34.4	34.6	34.9	35.1	35.4	35.6	35.9
98-100	34.6	34.8	35.1	35.3	35.5	35.8	36.0	36.3	36.5
101-103	35.3	35.4	35.7	35.9	36.2	36.4	36.7	36.9	37.2
104-106	35.8	36.1	36.3	36.6	36.8	37.1	37.3	37.5	37.8
107-109	36.4	36.7	36.9	37.1	37.4	37.6	37.9	38.1	38.4
110-112	37.0	37.2	37.5	37.7	38.0	38.2	38.5	38.7	38.9
113-115	37.5	37.8	38.0	38.2	38.5	38.7	39.0	39.2	39.5
116-118	38.0	38.3	38.5	38.8	39.0	39.3	39.5	39.7	40.0
119-121	38.5	38.7	39.0	39.2	39.5	39.7	40.0	40.2	40.5
122-124	39.0	39.2	39.4	39.7	39.9	40.2	40.4	40.7	40.9
125-127	39.4	39.6	39.9	40.1	40.4	40.6	40.9	41.1	41.4
128-130	39.8	40.0	40.3	40.5	40.8	41.0	41.3	41.5	41.8

Source: Jackson, A.S. & Pollock, M.L.: Practical Assessment of Body Composition. (May 1985). Reprinted with permission of McGraw-Hill.

Body Composition Testing and Evaluation

Table 6.14
General Body-Fat Percentage Categories

Classification	Women (% fat)	Men (% fat)
Essential fat	10-13%	2-5%
Athletes	14-20%	6-13%
Fitness	21-24%	14-17%
Healthy	25-31%	18-24%
Obese	32% and higher	25% and higher

way between the acromial (shoulder) and olecranon (elbow) processes.

2. Suprailium (Figure 6.19): a diagonal fold taken at, or just anterior to, the crest of the ilium.

3. Thigh (Figure 6.20): a vertical skinfold taken midway between the hip and knee joints on the front of the thigh.

After obtaining three satisfactory measurements, add them and refer to Table 6.12 for men and Table 6.13 for women.

For example, a 47-year-old man has the following measurements: chest, 20; abdomen, 30; thigh, 17; for a total measurement of 67. According to Table 6.12, at the intersection of the row corresponding to the sum of the skinfolds and the column corresponding to the age, his estimated body-fat percentage is 21.3 percent. Table 6.14 contains various ranges of body-fat for optimal health, fitness or competitive athletics. This man is 5 percent above the upper limit of the 14 percent to 17 percent range for men desiring optimal fitness. In order to calculate this man's weight for the desired range, his lean body weight must first be calculated. Since 21.3 percent of his body weight is fat weight, subtract 21.3 percent from 100 percent, which equals 78.7 percent of his weight as lean body mass. Assuming a total body weight of 212 pounds, we then use the decimal form of the percentage figure to derive a lean body weight of 166.8 pounds. To summarize:

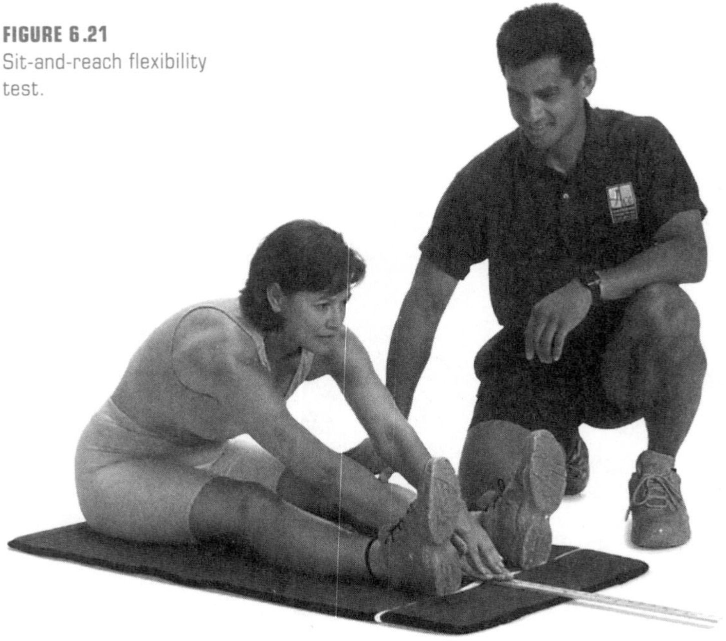

FIGURE 6.21
Sit-and-reach flexibility test.

Step 1: 100 percent - fat percentage = lean body percentage
100 percent - 21.3 percent = 78.7 percent

Step 2: body weight x lean body percentage = lean body weight
212 x .787 = 166.8 pounds

A body weight for a desired percent fat is then calculated by first subtracting the desired percent fat from 100 percent and then dividing the lean body weight by the decimal form of this percentage:

Step 3: 100 - desired percent fat = desired lean percent

Upper limit: 100 percent - 17 percent = 83 percent

Lower limit: 100 percent - 12 percent = 88 percent

Step 4: lean body weight / desired lean percentage = desired body weight

$$\frac{167}{0.83} = 201 \text{ pounds}$$

$$\frac{167}{0.88} = 190 \text{ pounds}$$

The weight range corresponding to a desired body fat of 12 percent to 17 percent is 190 to 201 pounds. With regular aerobic activity, resistance training and dietary management, this man would need to lose a minimum 11 pounds of fat weight (212 - 201 = 11).

It is important to understand that muscle weight can increase even when exercise participation is limited to aerobic activity. Body composition should be assessed periodically throughout an exercise program. This can provide motivating information, especially when fat weight loss appears to have plateaued.

Girth Measurements

Girth measurements may be used alone or with skinfold measurements to assess body composition. While this method of assessment has been shown to be no more accurate than skinfolds alone, it is valuable in the evaluation of girth changes that result from resistance training and provides a good check on skinfolds and other methods of assessment as body composition changes.

The two primary sources of error in measuring girth are inconsistent tape placement during repeated measures, and variations in the tension placed on the tape during the measurement. You can minimize the first error by using the standardized sites described below. You can overcome the second error by using a cloth tape specifically designed for girth measurement. These tapes have a scale that standardizes the tension applied to the tape as each site is measured.

Take the measurements at these sites:

1. Chest — at the nipple line during the midpoint of a normal breath
2. Waist — at the narrowest point, below the rib cage and just above the top of the hip bones
3. Hips — with feet together, at the level of the symphysis pubis in front, at the maximal protrusion of the buttocks in the back
4. Thigh — at the crotch level and just below the fold of the buttocks
5. Calf — at the maximal circumference
6. Ankle — at the minimal circumference, usually just above the ankle bone
7. Upper arm — at the maximal circumference; arm extended, palm up
8. Wrist — at the minimal circumference; arm extended, palm up

Record the measurements for comparison each time body composition is assessed.

FLEXIBILITY TESTING AND EVALUATION

Flexibility is defined as the range of motion of a given joint. It is often associated only with muscular flexibility, the extent to which range of motion is limited by muscles and tendons surrounding the joint. But flexibility also is influenced by the amount of freedom allowed by the ligaments connecting the bones that make up a given joint. Flexibility affects both health and fitness.

Inflexibility increases risk for joint and muscle injury. Low-back inflexibility, which relates to low-back pain and injury, is a common example. In order for athletes to perform at optimal levels, they must be able to move through motions that are specific to their sport with ease and fluidity. Limitations to movement in sports affect both performance and musculoskeletal health.

As with strength testing, there is no single flexibility test that predicts the range of motion of other joints of the body. Each joint must be assessed individually with a specifically designed test. While it is not the purpose of this chapter to explain the assessment of multiple joints throughout the body, tests of shoulder, hip and low-back range of motion will be highlighted.

Trunk Flexion

Trunk flexion is measured with the sit-and-reach test, which is administered with a yardstick and tape, and has well-established norms for comparison. There is a

Table 6.15
Norms for Trunk Flexibility Test (Men)

Flexibility	Age (years) 18-25	26-35	36-45	46-55	56-65	65+
Excellent	>20	>20	>19	>19	>17	>17
Good	18-20	18-19	17-19	16-17	14-17	13-16
Above average	17-18	16-17	15-17	14-15	12-14	11-13
Average	15-16	15-16	13-15	12-13	10-12	9-11
Below average	13-14	12-14	11-13	10-11	8-10	8-9
Poor	10-12	10-12	9-11	7-9	5-8	5-7
Very poor	<10	<10	<8	<7	<5	<5

Source: Adapted from Golding, et al. (1986). *The Y's Way To Physical Fitness.* (3rd ed.). Reprinted with permission of the YMCA of the USA.

Table 6.16
Norms for Trunk Flexibility Test (Women)

Flexibility	Age (years) 18-25	26-35	36-45	46-55	56-65	65+
Excellent	> 24	> 23	> 22	> 21	> 20	> 20
Good	21-23	20-22	19-21	18-20	18-19	18-19
Above average	20-21	19-20	17-19	17-18	16-17	16-17
Average	18-19	18	16-17	15-16	15	14-15
Below average	17-18	16-17	14-15	14-15	13-14	12-13
Poor	14-16	14-15	11-13	11-13	10-12	9-11
Very poor	<13	<13	<10	<10	<9	<8

Source: Adapted from Golding, et al. (1986). *The Y's Way To Physical Fitness.* (3rd ed.). Reprinted with permission of the YMCA of the USA.

FIGURE 6.22
Final position for trunk-extension assessment. Note where the bending takes place.

slight risk of muscle strain or pull if a forward movement is attempted that is too vigorous. Therefore, all participants should warm up with gentle stretching of the low back and hamstrings, and the test should be performed slowly and cautiously. Place the yardstick on the floor, and put a piece of tape at least 12 inches long at a right angle to the stick between the legs, with the zero mark toward the body. The client's feet should be approximately 12 inches apart and their heels aligned with the tape at the 15-inch mark on the yardstick (Figure 6.21). Have the client place one hand on top of the other, with the tips of the fingers aligned, then exhale and slowly lean forward by dropping the head toward or between the arms. The client's fingers should maintain contact with the yardstick while you keep their knees straight.

The score is the farthest point reached after three trials. Scores can be compared to norms in Tables 6.15, 6.16 and 6.17. The quality of the trunk flexion can be evaluated further by observing where along the spine the bending is taking place while the subject is in the flexed position.

Trunk Extension

The trunk-extension test evaluates the amount of backward bend (extension) available to the lumbar spine. As flexibility in the lumbar spine is lost, the risk for low-back pain and injury increases significantly. Have your client lie face down with their hands in position for a push-up (Figure 6.22). The client then pushes their upper body up while letting the lower back relax as much as possible and attempting to keep their hip bones in contact with the floor. Although this movement is commonly used as a therapeutic exercise for low-back-pain patients, it is still important to avoid injury by making sure the extension is not forced and the movement stops when the hip bones begin to lose contact with the floor. Note the location along the spine where the bending is taking place. Evaluate trunk extension using Table 6.18.

Hip Flexion

Hip flexion tests evaluate range of motion in the hips and hamstring tightness. Limitations to hip flexion place undue stress on the low back, increasing risk for low-back pain and injury. To assess hip flexion, have the client lie flat on their back. Hold their left leg down with your right hand to stabilize the pelvis, and use

Table 6.17
Evaluation of Trunk Flexion

Flexion	Characteristics
Good	The trunk is able to move forward onto the thighs, and motion occur at the hips and low back.
Fair	Bending forward causes some restriction in the low back so that bending occurs more in the lumbar spine.
Poor	Bending forward results in the lumbar spine remaining straight, and the bending occurs in the upper areas of the spine.

Source: Adapted from Krepton, D., & Chu, D. (1984). *Everybody's Aerobics Book* (1st ed.). Oakland: Star Rover House. Reprinted with permission.

Table 6.18
Evaluation of Trunk Extension

Extension	Characteristics
Good	The hips remain in contact with the floor while the arms are fully extended.
Fair	The hips rise from the ground up to two inches.
Poor	The hips rise from the ground two inches or more.

Source: Adapted from Krepton, D., & Chu, D. (1984). *Everybody's Aerobics Book* (1st ed.). Oakland: Star Rover House. Reprinted with permission.

Table 6.19
Evaluation of Shoulder Flexibility

Flexibility	Characteristics
Good	The fingers can touch.
Fair	The fingertips are not touching, but are less than two inches apart.
Poor	The fingertips are more than two inches apart.

Source: Adapted from Krepton, D., & Chu, D. (1984). *Everybody's Aerobics Book* (1st ed.). Oakland: Star Rover House. Reprinted with permission.

your left hand to passively raise their right leg to an angle of 80 to 85 degrees. Normal range of motion will allow for this amount of hip flexion (Figure 6.23). Tight hamstrings and other limitations to a normal range of motion are demonstrated when the client's leg raises to less than 80 degrees of hip flexion (Figure 6.24). All ranges should be measured without pain in the back of the leg or bending at the knee.

To test for hip flexor length, have the client maintain a flat low back on the table while grasping behind their left knee and pulling the leg toward their chest. Normal length is demonstrated when the right leg stays flat to the table (Figure 6.25). Shortened hip flexors are indicated when the right leg raises off the table (Figure 6.26).

Shoulder Flexibility

Swimming, racquet and throwing sports all require flexibility in the shoulders for good performance and avoidance of injury. The test of shoulder flexibility measures the multi-rotational components of the shoulder joints. Test the left shoulder by having the client sit or stand with their right arm straight up, letting the elbow bend so the hand comes to rest, palm down, between the shoulder blades. The client should reach back with the left arm so the palm is up. Have the client attempt to touch hands with their fingers (Figure 6.27). Evaluate shoulder flexibility using Table 6.19, and repeat the procedure for the opposite shoulder.

Poor shoulder flexibility also can affect a client's postural alignment. If the shoulder adductors are excessively tight, the client may assume a posture with shoulders depressed and rotated forward, with their arms medially rotated, often called the "gorilla stance." To test for poor shoulder adductor flexibility, have the client lie on their back with knees bent, back flat and arms overhead. Adequate flexibility is demonstrated if the arms lie flat overhead (Figure 6.28). If the arms do not lie flat (Figure 6.29), a shortness in the pectoralis

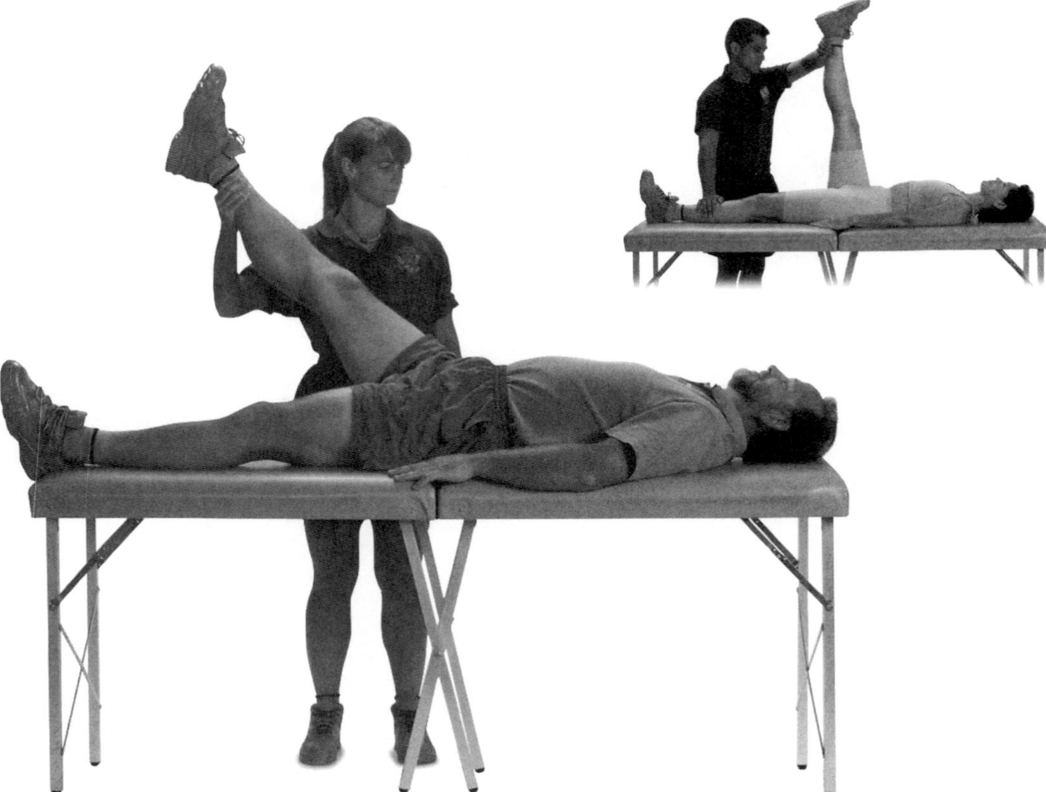

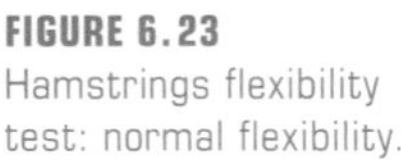

FIGURE 6.23
Hamstrings flexibility test: normal flexibility.

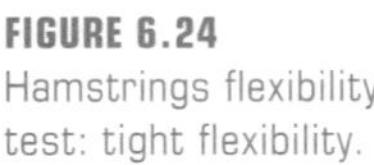

FIGURE 6.24
Hamstrings flexibility test: tight flexibility.

Muscular Strength and Endurance Testing and Evaluation

major, teres major and latissimus dorsi is indicated.

MUSCULAR STRENGTH AND ENDURANCE TESTING AND EVALUATION

Two components of muscular fitness testing are muscular strength and muscular endurance. Muscular strength is the greatest amount of force that muscles can produce in a single maximal effort. Muscular endurance refers to the muscle's ability to exert a submaximal force either repeatedly or statically over time. Adequate muscular strength and endurance are necessary for both optimal health and athletic performance. They allow people to take part in activities of daily living without injury or undue fatigue, and also enhance life at a desired level of human functioning. Strength and muscular endurance requirements for athletics vary significantly according to the requirements of each sport. Both are necessary for good performance in competitive and most recreational sports, and muscular strength training is even a subject of increased interest among distance runners.

One reason for performing fitness evaluations is to compare a client's physical ability to established standards of performance. A more useful application is to determine a client's appropriate exercise starting point and to show progressive personal improvement as a result of the training program. A basic premise of fitness assessment is to use similar exercise modes for testing and training. Although this should generally be the case, strength testing may offer occasional exceptions to the rule.

Isometric Strength Testing

Any strength test that involves movement will either underestimate or overestimate maximum force output. This is because internal muscle friction decreases effective force output during **concentric** muscle **contractions,** and increases effective force output during **eccentric** muscle

FIGURE 6.25
Test for hip flexor length: normal length.

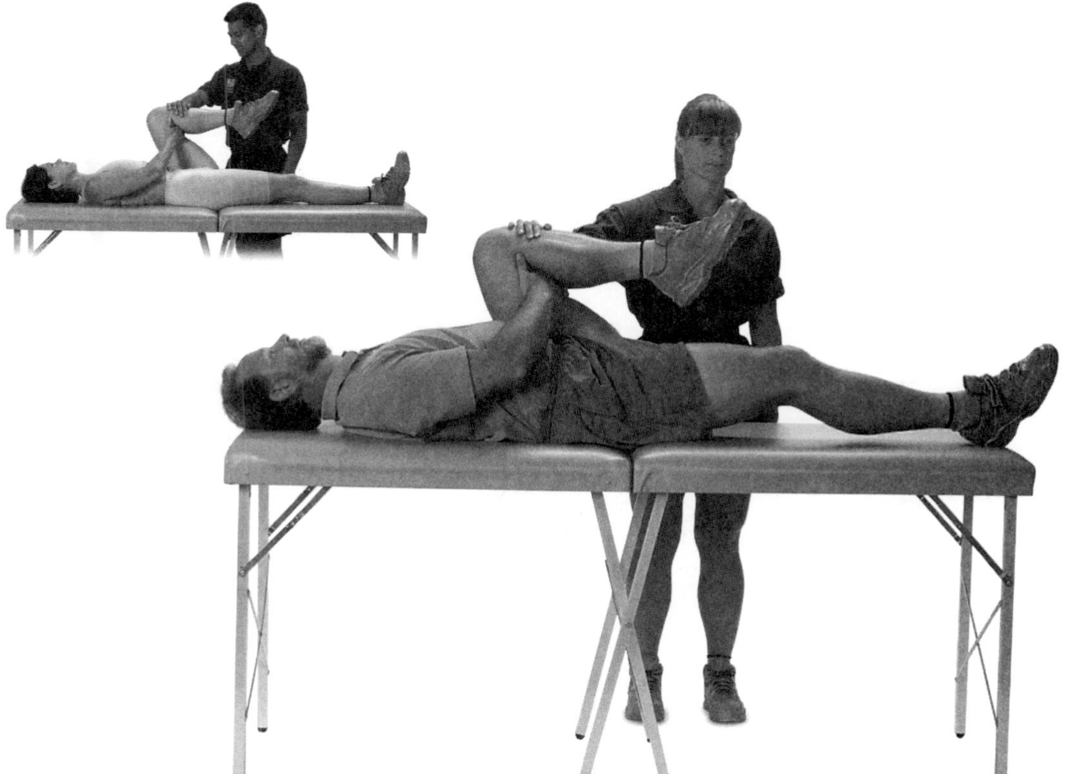

FIGURE 6.26
Test for hip flexor length: shortened length.

FIGURE 6.27
Assessing flexibility of the right shoulder.

contractions. To complicate matters further, faster movement speeds produce more internal muscle friction. Consequently, because **isometric** (static) strength testing entails muscle contraction without movement, it is the most accurate means for assessing actual muscle strength.

One disadvantage of isometric strength testing is that it tends to elicit a higher blood pressure response. It also requires testing at a variety of positions because effective muscle strength varies throughout the range of joint movement.

Isokinetic Strength Testing

Isokinetic strength testing measures effective muscle force output at every point in the movement range using a computer. However, for isokinetic strength comparisons to be valid, the tests must be performed with identical technique and movement speed. Even then, the damping controls smooth out the actual force recording curves. While the data collected from isokinetic strength assessments may provide more information than isometric

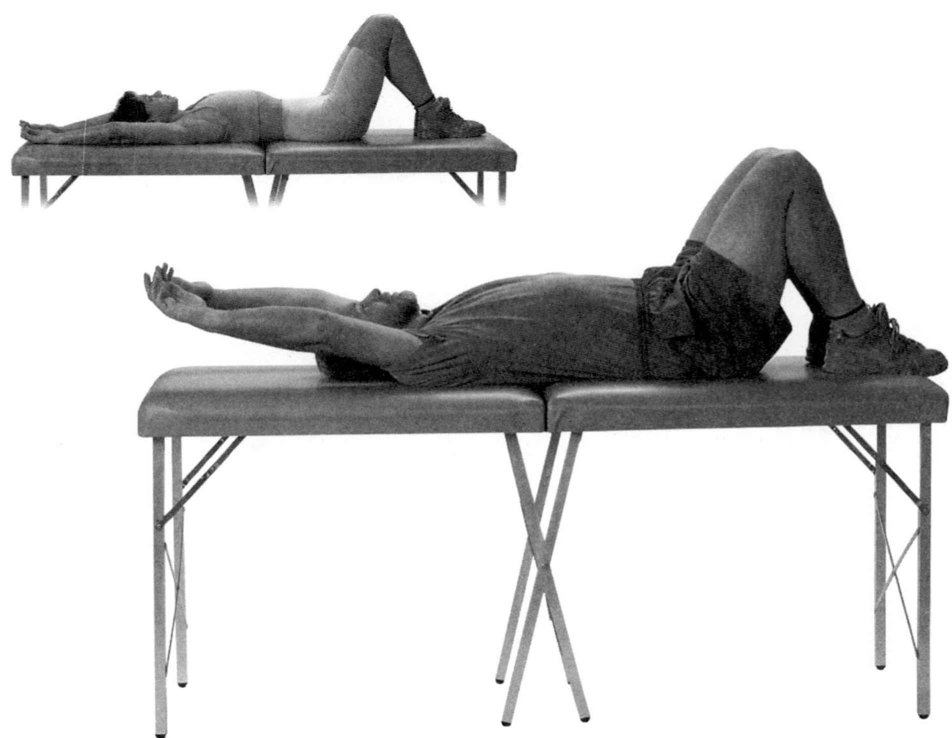

FIGURE 6.28
Test for shoulder flexibility: adequate flexibility.

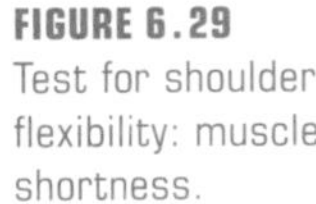

FIGURE 6.29
Test for shoulder flexibility: muscle shortness.

Table 6.20
Leg Strength (Men)*

1 Repetition Maximum Leg Press.
Leg Press Weight Ratio = Weight Pushed/Body Weight

	%	Age <20	20-29	30-39	40-49	50-59	60+
Superior	95	2.82	2.40	2.20	2.02	1.90	1.80
Excellent	80	2.28	2.13	1.93	1.82	1.71	1.62
Good	60	2.04	1.97	1.77	1.68	1.58	1.49
Fair	40	1.90	1.83	1.65	1.57	1.46	1.38
Poor	20	1.70	1.63	1.52	1.44	1.32	1.25
Very Poor	5	1.46	1.42	1.34	1.27	1.15	1.08

*Data provided by the Institute for Aerobics Research, Dallas, TX, (1994).

Table 6.21
Leg Strength (Women)*

1 Repetition Maximum Leg Press.
Leg Press Weight Ratio = Weight Pushed/Body Weight

	%	Age <20	20-29	30-39	40-49	50-59	60+
Superior	95	1.88	1.98	1.68	1.57	1.43	1.43
Excellent	80	1.71	1.68	1.47	1.37	1.25	1.18
Good	60	1.59	1.50	1.33	1.23	1.10	1.04
Fair	40	1.38	1.37	1.21	1.13	.99	.93
Poor	20	1.22	1.22	1.09	1.02	.88	.85
Very Poor	5	1.06	.99	.96	.85	.72	.63

*Data provided by the Institute for Aerobics Research, Dallas, TX, (1994).

Table 6.22
Upper Body Strength (Men)*

1 Repetition Maximum Bench Press
Bench Press Weight Ratio = Weight Pushed/Body Weight

	%	Age <20	20-29	30-39	40-49	50-59	60+
Superior	95	1.76	1.63	1.35	1.20	1.05	.94
Excellent	80	1.34	1.32	1.12	1.00	.90	.82
Good	60	1.19	1.14	.98	.88	.79	.72
Fair	40	1.06	.99	.88	.80	.71	.66
Poor	20	.89	.88	.78	.72	.63	.57
Very Poor	5	.76	.72	.65	.59	.53	.49

*Data provided by the Institute for Aerobics Research, Dallas, TX, (1994).

Table 6.23
Upper Body Strength (Women)*

1 Repetition Maximum Bench Press
Bench Press Weight Ratio = Weight Pushed/Body Weight

	%	Age <20	20-29	30-39	40-49	50-59	60+
Superior	95	.88	1.01	.82	.77	.68	.72
Excellent	80	.77	.80	.70	.62	.55	.54
Good	60	.65	.70	.60	.54	.48	.47
Fair	40	.58	.59	.53	.50	.44	.43
Poor	20	.53	.51	.47	.43	.39	.38
Very Poor	5	.41	.44	.39	.35	.31	.26

*Data provided by the Institute for Aerobics Research, Dallas, TX, (1994).

and isotonic testing, the necessary computer equipment is very expensive. Consequently, the accessibility of isokinetic strength evaluations may be a practical consideration.

Dynamic Strength Testing

Perhaps the most popular form of strength testing is **dynamic (isotonic)** assessments using free-weights or weight-stack machines. Examples include the **one-repetition maximum (1 RM)** bench press, squat, overhead press and dead-lift. Although these are reasonably good indicators of strength performance, it is not advisable to test beginners with maximum resistance lifts. Because most people can complete 10 repetitions with 75 percent of their maximum resistance, the 10-repetition-maximum (10 RM) test may be a safer means for evaluating muscle strength.

Because of momentum, isotonic strength

Muscular Strength and Endurance Testing and Evaluation

tests must be conducted with strict form and slow movement speed. While not as comprehensive as isokinetic assessments, properly performed isotonic tests can provide valid strength comparisons at considerably less cost.

For meaningful strength assessments in men and women of different sizes, it is essential to make comparisons on a pound-for-pound basis. For this reason it is best to use a ratio of weight lifted to body weight to accurately account for differences in body size and muscle mass.

Tables 6.20 through 6.23 give the one-repetition maximum ratios for men and women for one upper body exercise, a bench press, and one lower body exercise, the leg press. These tests were performed on Universal® resistance training equipment, so the data is really only valid for use on this brand of equipment. Since there are so many different brands of resistance-training equipment, one of the only options open to a personal trainer is to begin collecting data on each of your clients and determine your own percentiles based on age and gender. Undergraduate level physical education testing and evaluation texts explain how to do this basic statistical analysis (see *References and Suggested Reading*). You would need at least 30 clients of each gender to begin to have some statistical significance. As each age group reaches about 30 clients you can begin to divide the data into age ranges. You can give the results to your clients simply as percentiles, or you can add the descriptive "Excellent," "Good," "Fair" and "Poor" classifications. The challenge to adding the classifications is that your clients may not represent a cross-section of adults, and those in the lower categories may be unfairly labeled.

If you have access to Universal® equipment you can use a 10 RM test to estimate a 1 RM weightload and determine a strength ratio using the following procedure:

1. Determine the heaviest weightload the client can perform for 10 good repetitions (10-repetition maximum weightload).
2. Convert the 10 RM weightload to a 1 RM estimation by dividing the weight load by .75.
3. Divide the 1 RM estimated weightload by the client's body weight to attain the strength ratio.
4. Compare the client's strength ratio to the strength fitness classifications in Tables 6.20 through 6.23.

For example, a 120-pound 35-year-old woman who completes 10 leg presses with 120 pounds would have an estimated 1 RM of 160 pounds (120 lbs. divided by .75). Her leg press weight ratio would be 1.33 (160 divided by 120) which places her in the "Good" category of strength fitness.

FIGURE 6.30
Push-up test:

a. Modified bent-knee position.

b. Standard push-up position.

Table 6.24
Push-up Norms for Men and Women by Age Groups Using Number Completed

Age (Years)	(15-19)		(20-29)		(30-39)		(40-49)		(50-59)		(60-69)	
Gender	M	F	M	F	M	F	M	F	M	F	M	F
Excellent	>39	>33	>36	>30	>30	>27	>22	>24	>21	>21	>18	>17
Above average	29-38	25-32	29-35	21-29	22-29	20-26	17-21	15-23	13-20	11-20	11-17	12-16
Average	23-28	18-24	22-28	15-20	17-21	13-19	13-16	11-14	10-12	7-10	8-10	5-11
Below average	18-22	12-17	17-21	10-14	12-16	8-12	10-12	5-10	7-9	2-6	5-7	1-4
Poor	<17	<11	<16	<9	<11	<7	<9	<4	<6	<1	<4	<1

Source: CSTF Operations Manual. (3rd ed.) *Ottawa, Fitness and Amateur Sport,* 1986.
The Canadian Standardized Test of Fitness was developed by, and is reproduced with the permission of, Fitness Canada, Government of Canada.

Muscular Endurance Testing

While the assessment of muscular strength can be independent of muscular endurance, the assessment of muscular endurance also measures strength to some degree. Careful consideration of client health and fitness should be made before specific muscular fitness tests are chosen. The lower-weight/high-repetition muscular endurance tests are more appropriate for less-fit clients and those with health-related exercise-strength goals, especially if they have previously been inactive. Two muscle endurance tests that are both reliable and easy to administer are the one-minute timed sit-up test and the push-up test. Both measure relative muscular endurance, since their results are relative to body weight. Another option is the bench-press test, a muscular endurance test only. The weight used is standardized, so results do not vary as a function of body weight.

Push-up Test

The purpose of the push-up test is to evaluate muscular strength and endurance of the upper body, including the triceps, anterior deltoid and pectoralis muscles. Men use the standard push-up position with only the hands and toes in contact with the floor (Figure 6.30a). Women use the modified push-up position (Figure 6.30b). Although the positions are different for each sex, the procedures for administering the test are similar.

Required items:

- ✔ Record sheet with name of the client and space for recording the number of push-ups completed

Before test day:

- ✔ Explain the purpose of the test to the client (to determine how many push-ups can be completed to reflect muscular strength and endurance).
- ✔ Review standard and bent-knee positions, making sure that the hands are shoulder-width apart.
- ✔ Review the test counting procedure. The push-up is complete when the chest touches the fist of a partner and returns to the start position with arms fully extended.
- ✔ Allow clients to practice if desired.
- ✔ Inform clients of proper breathing technique — to exhale with the effort (when pushing away from the floor).

Administration:

- ✔ Have the client assume the standard (for men) or bent-knee (for women) position while you take a position in front with your fist below their chest.
- ✔ When ready, the client can begin.

Count the total number of push-ups the client completes before reaching the point of exhaustion.

- ✔ Remind the client that rest is allowed in the UP position only.
- ✔ The client's score is the total number of push-ups performed.

You can classify your client's muscular strength and endurance by comparing their results to Table 6.24. For example, a 52-year-old man who performs 18 push-ups is classified as "above average" for his age.

Bent-knee Curl-up Test

The purpose of the bent-knee curl-up test is to evaluate abdominal muscle strength and endurance. Previously used sit-up tests have been unsatisfactory because the hip flexor involvement during sit-up motion is potentially harmful to the low back. This is particularly true when the feet are held motionless, since increased stress is placed on the lumbar vertebrae. Even though modifications to the traditional sit-up have been instituted, including a bent-knee position, stress to the low back is still present during the motion. Consequently, the bent-knee curl-up test was recently modified to eliminate potential low-back problems and better assess abdominal muscle function. Additionally, the curl-up test remains inexpensive and easy to administer, is valid and reliable, and affords standards for comparing men and women of similar ages.

The procedures for administering the bent-knee curl-up test are as follows:

Required items:

- ✔ padded flooring or mat
- ✔ metronome or cadence device set at 40 bpm
- ✔ recording sheet

Before test day:

- ✔ Explain the purpose of the test to each client (to determine how many curl-ups can be completed at a set cadence without time constraints).
- ✔ Review and demonstrate the curl-up test and allow the client to practice if desired.
- ✔ Inform the client of proper clothing requirements.

Administration:

- ✔ Place two strips of tape parallel to each other and 8 centimeters apart.
- ✔ Have the client warm-up before

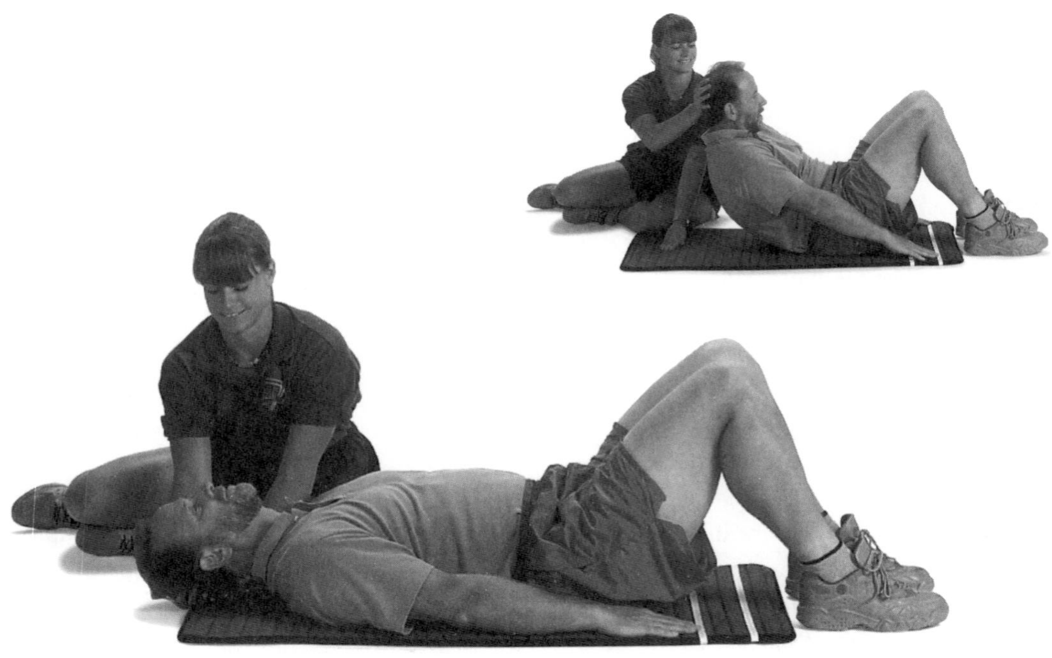

FIGURE 6.31
a. Curl-up test, up position.

b. Curl-up test, down position. Head support is optional.

taking the test.

- ✔ Have the client assume a lying position with feet flat on the floor and knees bent at about 90 degrees. They should place their hands palms-down at their sides, with fingertips touching the first strip of tape. Place your hands behind their head (Figure 6.31).
- ✔ Begin the metronome cadence of 40 bpm — equal to three seconds per curl-up, or 20 curl-ups per minute.
- ✔ When ready the client slowly flattens their lower back and curls their upper spine until the fingertips touch the second strip of tape.
- ✔ The client then returns to the original position with the back of their head touching your hands.
- ✔ One curl-up is counted each time the client's head touches your hands.
- ✔ The client should perform as many curl-ups as possible without stopping, up to a maximum of 75.
- ✔ The test is terminated if the cadence is broken.

Compare your client's results to Table 6.25 to classify their abdominal muscle strength and endurance.

Table 6.25
Curl-up Standards Using Number Completed

Category	Men / Age			Women / Age		
	<35	35-44	45	<35	35-44	45
Excellent	60	50	40	50	40	30
Good	45	40	25	40	30	15
Marginal	30	25	15	25	15	10
Needs work	15	10	5	10	6	4

Source: Faulkner et al. (1988).

Muscular Strength and Endurance Testing and Evaluation

Bench-press Test

The bench-press test developed by the YMCA is a good method of testing the endurance and strength of the chest and shoulders. The main disadvantage of the test is that it uses a fixed weight, which places lighter clients at a disadvantage. The bench-press test should be administered as follows:

1. Use a 35-pound barbell for women, or an 80-pound barbell for men. A spotter should be present during the test. If one spotter is unable to safely lift the weight, two spotters should be present.
2. Set a metronome to 60 bpm.

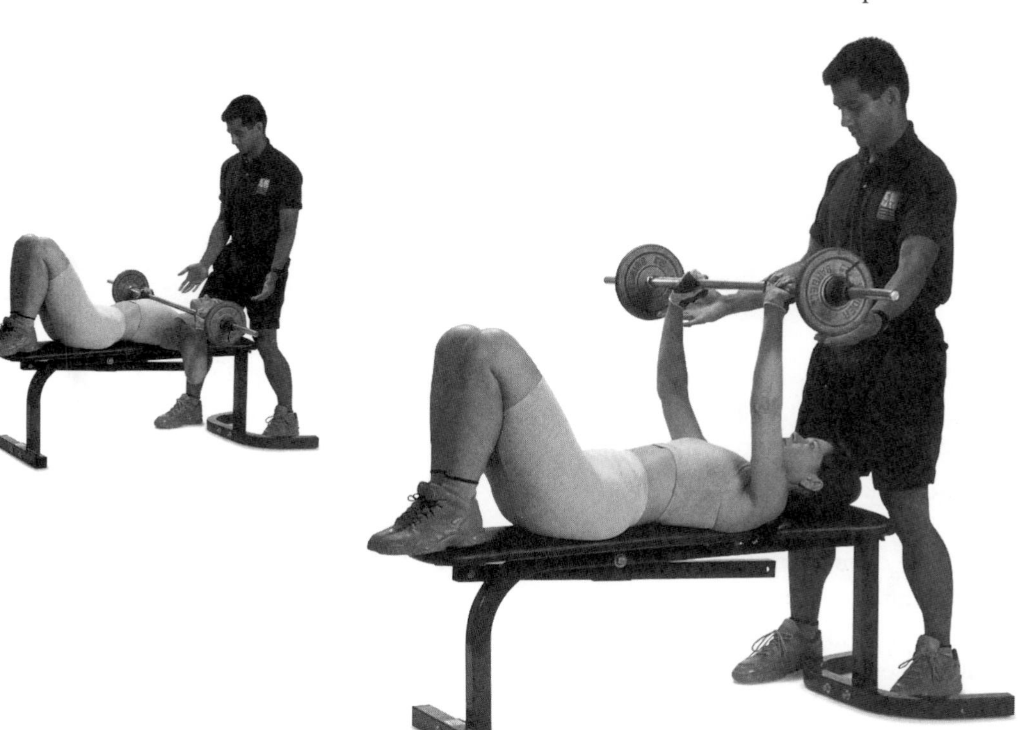

FIGURE 6.32
Bench press test:

a. Starting (down) position.

b. Completion of one repetition.

Table 6.26
Norms for Bench-press Test (Men)

Fitness	Age (years) 18-25	26-35	36-45	46-55	56-65	65+
Excellent	>37	>33	>29	>23	>21	>17
Good	29-37	26-33	23-29	19-23	14-21	10-17
Above average	24-28	22-25	19-22	14-18	10-13	8-9
Average	21-23	18-21	15-18	10-13	7-9	5-7
Below average	15-20	13-17	11-14	7-9	4-6	3-4
Poor	9-14	6-12	6-10	3-6	1-3	1-2
Very poor	<9	<6	<6	<3	<1	0

Source: Adapted from Golding, et al. (1986). *The Y's Way To Physical Fitness.* (3rd ed.) Reprinted with permission of the YMCA of the USA.

Table 6.27
Norms for Bench-press Test (Women)

Fitness	Age (years) 18-25	26-35	36-45	46-55	56-65	65+
Excellent	>35	>32	>27	>25	>21	>17
Good	27-35	24-32	21-27	19-25	16-21	12-17
Above average	22-26	19-23	16-20	13-18	11-15	9-11
Average	17-21	15-18	12-15	10-12	8-10	5-8
Below average	13-16	11-14	9-11	6-9	4-7	2-4
Poor	7-12	4-10	3-8	2-5	1-3	0-1
Very poor	<7	<4	<3	<2	0	0

Source: Adapted from Golding, et al. (1986). *The Y's Way To Physical Fitness.* (3rd ed.) Reprinted with permission of the YMCA of the USA.

3. The spotter should hand the weight to the client in the down position with the elbows flexed and hands shoulder-width apart (Figure 6.32a).

4. A repetition is counted when the elbows are fully extended (Figure 6.32b). After each extension the bar should be lowered to touch the chest.

5. Up or down movements should be in time to the 60-bpm rhythm, which would be 30 lifts per minute.

6. The test is terminated when the client is unable to come to full extension or falls behind the 60-bpm rhythm.

Count the number of successful repetitions, and use Tables 6.26 and 6.27 to compare the results to norms.

FOLLOW-UP

Consultation

When testing is completed, present the results to the client. Ideally, this consultation should take place in a private area with comfortable seating around a desk or table. The communication of test results is an art in and of itself. Try to get to know your clients so you can gauge how to effectively convey their results.

Testing

The frequency of follow-up testing will depend on the quality and quantity of exercise training, and on the design of the testing and training packages offered by you or the fitness center. While many clients will begin to feel the positive effects of training in as little as one week, measurable changes will usually take about four weeks. Therefore, the first follow-up tests will usually be administered four to 12 weeks following the onset of training.

SUMMARY

The foundation of a well-designed fitness program is determined, in part, by the acquisition and analysis of baseline fitness information. This chapter provides you with a number of ways to test and evaluate a client's fitness level. You should assess the client's cardiorespiratory efficiency, body composition, flexibility and muscular strength and endurance in order to design a quality fitness program and, most importantly, to evaluate the program's effectiveness over time, you should retest the client and measure how their results change.

REFERENCES

Astrand, P.O. & Rhyming, J. (1954). A nomogram for calculation of aerobic capacity (physical fitness) from pulse rate during submaximal work. *Journal of Applied Physiology,* 7, 218-221.

Faulkner, R.A., Syringings, E.S., McQuarrie, A. & Bell, R.D. (1988). Partial Curl-up Research Project Final Report. Report submitted to the *Canadian Fitness and Lifestyle Research Institute.*

Golding, L.A., Meyers, C.R. & Sinning, W. E. (Eds.) (1986). *The Y's Way to Physical Fitness.* (3rd ed.) Champaign: Human Kinetics.

Jackson, A.S. & Pollock, M.L. (1985). Practical assessment of body composition. *The Physician and Sportsmedicine,* May, 76-90.

Sjostrand, T. (1947). Changes in the respiratory organs of workmen at an ore melting works. *Acta Medica Scandinavia,* 128, (suppl. 196), 687-699.

Tran, Z. & Weltman, A. (1989). Generalized equation for predicting body density of women from girth measurements. *Medicine and Science in Sports and Exercise,* 21, 101-104.

Tran, Z., Weltman, A. & Seip, R. (1988). Predicting body composition of men from girth measurements. *Human Biology,* 8- 60, 167-176.

SUGGESTED READING

American College of Sports Medicine. (1995). *Guidelines for Exercise Testing and Prescription.* (5th ed.) Philadelphia: Lea & Febiger.

American College of Sports Medicine. (1993). *Resource Manual for Guidelines for Exercise Testing and Prescription.* (2nd ed.) Philadelphia: Lea & Febiger.

Baumgartner, T. A. & Jackson, A. S. (1995). *Measurement for Evaluation.* (5th ed.) Madison: Brown and Benchmark.

Cotton, Richard T., (Ed.) (1993). *Aerobics Instructor Manual.* San Diego: American Council on Exercise.

Hassard, T. H. (1991). *Understanding Biostatistics.* St. Louis: Mosby.

Heyward, V. H. (1991). *Advanced Fitness Assessment & Exercise Prescription.* Champaign: Human Kinetics.

Howley, E. & Franks, D. (1992). *Health Fitness Instructor's Handbook.* Philadelphia: Lea & Febiger.

Lohman, T. G., Roche, A. F. & Martorell, R. (Eds.) (1988). *Anthropometric Standardization Reference Manual.* Champaign: Human Kinetics.

MacDougall, J. D., Wenger, H.A. & Green, H.J. (Eds.) (1991). *Physiological Testing of the High-Performance Athlete.* Champaign: Human Kinetics.

Morrow, J. R., Jackson, A. W., Disch, J. G. & Mood, D. P. (1995). *Measurement and Evaluation in Human Performance.* Champaign: Human Kinetics.

Nieman, D. C. (1990). *Fitness and Sports Medicine, An Introduction.* Palo Alto: Bull Publishing.

Ross, R. M. & Jackson, A. S. (1990). *Exercise Concepts Calculations & Computer Applications.* Carmel, IN: Benchmark.

PART III

Principles and Methods of Training

CHAPTER 7

Cardiorespiratory Fitness and Exercise

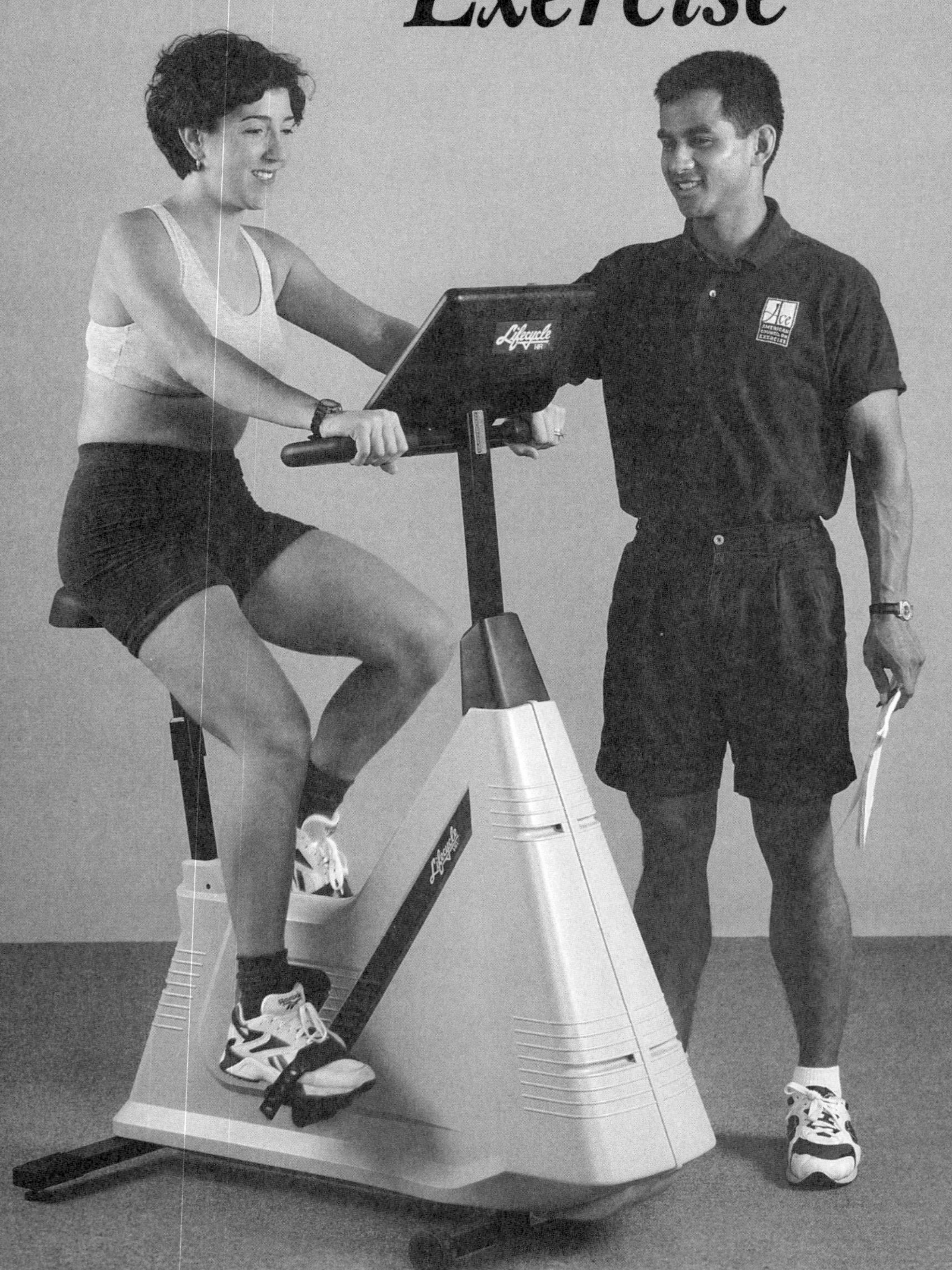

IN THIS CHAPTER:

7

Ralph La Forge

Ralph La Forge, M.S., is a clinical exercise physiologist with 20 years experience working in clinical cardiology and 12 years experience teaching exercise physiology at the University of California, San Diego. He is currently working with the University of North Carolina, Chapel Hill, department of medicine in the cardiology division. He also is the acting director of the Lipid Clinic Preceptorship Training Program at the San Diego Cardiac Center Medical Group, and has developed and implemented numerous programs in exercise science, applied psychobiology and cardiac rehabilitation.

Cardiorespiratory fitness continues to receive high acclaim as a centerpiece of physical fitness and cardiovascular health. For health and fitness applications, the terms cardiorespiratory fitness, cardiovascular fitness and aerobic endurance are synonymous. Cardiorespiratory fitness best describes the health and function of the heart, lungs and circulatory system, and is related to cardiorespiratory endurance, which is the ability to persist or sustain activity for prolonged periods. Cardiorespiratory fitness also describes the capacity of the lungs to exchange oxygen and carbon dioxide with the blood, and the circulatory system's ability to transport blood and nutrients to metabolically active tissues for sustained periods without undue fatigue.

Benefits of Cardiovascular Fitness

BENEFITS OF CARDIOVASCULAR FITNESS

The numerous benefits of cardiorespiratory fitness (Table 7.1) are related to a variety of adaptive physiologic responses to aerobic exercise. Physiologic responses to training — such as an increase in body-fat utilization, a decrease in **peripheral vascular resistance** and an increase in **maximal oxygen consumption** — help decrease the risk of cardiovascular disease by favorably modifying **risk factors** like **obesity**, **hypertension**, and elevated **triglycerides** and **LDL**-cholesterol. When such risk factors are removed from clients' health profiles, they can attain an acceptable level of cardiovascular health. Cardiovascular health goes beyond merely attaining aerobic fitness. It defines the status of the heart muscle, its blood vessels and the circulatory system it serves. Acquiring and maintaining cardiorespiratory fitness is one of the primary pathways to cardiovascular health.

Likewise, aerobic endurance activities have been effective in other conditioning and clinical therapies, such as cardiac and pulmonary rehabilitation, sleep disorder treatment, diabetic treatment, prenatal/post-partum and renal dialysis conditioning, and anxiety- and depression-management programs. In such clinical settings, aerobic exercise must be prescribed and managed carefully by trained exercise specialists or other qualified clinicians. Experienced and qualified personal trainers may form adjunct relationships with such clinicians in order to effectively manage the patient. Referrals from such programs depend on your relationship and knowledge of local clinical rehabilitation programs and/or affiliated health-care institutions.

Cardiorespiratory fitness also serves as a foundation for other fitness programs. The conditioning and health of the heart, lungs and blood vessels are prime ingredients in the safety and performance of nearly all sports and recreational programs. Activities such as tennis, golf, skiing, dancing, skating, basketball, volleyball, boxing and nearly all muscular strength-training programs will benefit from attaining acceptable levels of cardiorespiratory fitness. Clients with adequate cardiorespiratory fitness generally have more stamina, which translates to less fatigue and fewer risks for certain types of injuries.

COMPONENTS OF AN AEROBIC EXERCISE PROGRAM

It is imperative for you to understand the physiologic rationale and application of each component of the cardiorespiratory exercise program. The essential components of the written plan are:

1. Warm-up and cool-down
2. Primary cardiorespiratory activity criteria:
   a. Mode of exercise
   b. Frequency of exercise session
   c. Duration of exercise session
   d. Intensity of exercise session
3. Supportive conditioning exercise (e.g., strength and flexibility)
4. Progression plan
5. Safety and cautions

Each of these components must be discussed with the client and presented in a legible and succinct written form. Chapters 11 and 12 will provide examples of formats to use in various settings.

Warm-up and Cool-down

Although most fitness professionals teach a variety of warm-up and cool-down techniques, few fully understand their psychological and physiological rationales (Table 7.2). Graduated low-level aerobic exercise is essential for maximizing safety and economy of movement during the cardiorespiratory conditioning phase of an exercise session. The warm-up should gradually increase the heart rate, blood pressure, oxygen consumption, dilation of the blood vessels, elasticity of the active muscles and the heat produced by the active muscle groups. The warm-up should consist of two distinct components:

1. Graduated aerobic warm-up activity (e.g., walking or slow tempo rhythmic calisthenic movements)
2. Flexibility exercise specific to the biomechanical nature of the primary conditioning activity (e.g., calf, quadriceps and Achilles stretching prior to running or hiking).

Because a warm muscle is more easily stretched than a cold muscle, the flexibility component should be preceded by five to eight minutes of low-level aerobic activity using the same muscle groups. For instance, a 10-minute walk will increase muscle temperature and circulation of the legs, thereby promoting easier and safer stretching of the same muscle groups.

Table 7.3 lists sample warm-up activities for a variety of aerobic exercises. The intensity of the warm-up should be well below that of the primary conditioning activity. The warm-up duration depends on the level and intensity of the primary conditioning activity, as well as the fitness level of the client.

The cool-down is an integral part of the exercise program. The purpose of the cool-down is to slowly decrease the heart rate and overall metabolism, both of which have been elevated during the conditioning phase. Low-level aerobic exercise, similar to that of the conditioning exercise, is recommended (Table 7.3). Walking, slow jogging, cycling with little or no resistance, and slow aquatic activity or swimming are good examples. Cool-down helps prevent the sudden pooling of blood in the veins and ensures adequate circulation to the skeletal muscles, heart and brain. Cool-down may aid in preventing delayed muscle stiffness and reduces any tendency toward post-exercise fainting and dizziness.

For high cardiovascular risk clients, a gradual decrease in the intensity of exercise is crucial. Sudden cessation of exercise without cool-down may adversely affect cardiac function because a relatively high concentration of adrenaline remains in the blood from the conditioning exercise. Sudden exercise cessation also may adversely affect filling pressures of the heart, putting a weak heart at risk. The length of the cool-down phase is prop. tional to the intensity and length of the conditioning phase. A typical 30- to 40-minute conditioning phase at 70 percent of maximum heart rate would warrant a five- to 10-minute

Table 7.1
Reported Benefits of Cardiorespiratory Exercise

Health benefits
Reduction in blood pressure
Increased HDL-cholesterol
Decreased total cholesterol
Decreased body fat stores
Increased aerobic work capacity
Decreased clinical symptoms of anxiety, tension and depression
Reduction in glucose-stimulated insulin secretion
Increased heart function
Reduction in mortality in post myocardial infarction patients
Adaptive physiologic responses
Increased lactate threshold
Decreased resting heart rate
Increased heart volume
Increased resting and maximum stroke volume
Increased maximum cardiac output
Increased maximum oxygen consumption
Increased capillary density and blood flow to active muscles
Increased total blood volume
Increased maximal ventilation
Increased lung diffusion capacity
Increased mobilization and utilization of fat
Reduced all-cause mortality
Decreased anxiety and depression
Decreased incidence of some cancers

Source: Adapted from ACSM's *Guidelines for Exercise Testing and Prescription.*

Components of an Aerobic Exercise Program

Components of an Aerobic Exercise Program

Table 7.2
Physiological and Psychological Rationale for Warm-up and Cool-down

Warm-up

1. Permits a gradual metabolic adaptation (e.g., oxygen consumption), which enhances cardiorespiratory performance (e.g., a higher maximum cardiac output and oxygen uptake).
2. Prevents the premature onset of blood lactic acid accumulation and fatigue during higher level aerobic exercise.
3. Causes a gradual increase in muscle temperature which decreases the work of contraction and reduces the likelihood of muscle injury.
4. Facilitates neural transmission for motor unit recruitment.
5. Improves coronary blood flow in early stages of the conditioning exercise, lessening the potential for myocardial ischemia.
6. Allows a gradual redistribution of blood flow to active muscles.
7. Increases the elasticity of connective tissue and other muscle components.
8. Provides a screening mechanism for potential musculoskeletal or metabolic problems that may increase at higher intensities.
9. Provides a psychological warm-up to higher levels of work (i.e., increases arousal and focus on exercise).

Cool-down

1. Prevents post-exercise venous blood pooling and too rapid a drop in blood pressure, thereby reducing the likelihood of post-exercise lightheadedness or fainting.
2. Reduces the immediate post-exercise tendency for muscle spasm or cramping.
3. Reduces the concentration of exercise hormones (e.g., norepinephrine) that are at relatively high levels immediately after vigorous aerobic exercise. This reduction will lower the probability of post-exercise disturbances in cardiac rhythm.

Source: Adapted from McArdle, et al. 1991.

cool-down. The aerobic component of the cool-down phase should be followed by several minutes of stretching those muscle groups active in the conditioning phase.

Primary Cardiorespiratory Exercise Criteria

For maximum effectiveness and safety, the cardiorespiratory exercise program must include specific instructions on the mode, frequency, duration and intensity of exercise. Most of these criteria originate from the American College of Sports Medicine (ACSM) exercise guidelines and position statements to ensure standardization and validity in the broad field of exercise science (ACSM, 1995).

To avoid confusion, the exercise criteria listed in this section are those needed for measurable improvements in cardiorespiratory fitness (e.g., increase in **VO_2 max**). This is an important clarification, since the exercise threshold criteria for health enhancement are generally lower (ACSM, 1995; Haskell, 1994). For instance, the minimum duration and intensity of physical activity required for health enhancement is 15 minutes at 40 percent of VO_2 max. Here, health enhancement refers to reduced risk of degenerative disease, such as cardiovascular disease.

Exercise Mode. Selection of the exercise mode is made on the basis of the client's **functional capacity**, interests, time availability, equipment and facilities, and personal goals. Any activity that uses large muscle groups, is rhythmical and cardiorespiratory in nature, and is maintained continuously can be used. The American College of Sports Medicine classifies **cardiorespiratory endurance** activities into three groups:

GROUP 1: Physical activities in which exercise intensity is easily maintained at a constant level, and interindividual variation in energy expenditure is relatively low. Examples are walking and cycling, especially treadmill and cycle ergometry.

GROUP 2: Physical activities in which energy expenditure is related to skill, but

Components of an Aerobic Exercise Program

Table 7.3
Sample Warm-up and Cool-down Activities (including stretching exercise)

Primary Conditioning Exercise	Warm-up/Cool-down Activity
Aerobics (group exercise)	Graduated low-level aerobic activity utilizing same muscle groups
Circuit weight training	Low-level aerobic activity (e.g., walking or cycling, and/or beginning the circuit training session with a set of relatively high repetition, low-resistance exercises)
Hiking	Graduate from relatively flat terrain at minimal altitudes to steeper terrain and higher altitudes
Jogging and running	Walking, walk-jogging, or jogging at a slower pace
Outdoor cycling	Begin with relatively flat terrain in lower gears; gradually shift to higher gears and steeper terrain
Racquetball, handball or squash	Walk-jog and/or graduated tempo volleying
Rope skipping	Graduated walking or walk-jogging pace and/or slow tempo rope skipping pace
Sprinting	Jogging and graduated pace in running intervals
Stationary cycling	Start with cycling against little or no resistance at ⅔ of the pedal crank rpm used in the conditioning phase
Stationary exercise devices	Begin with 50 percent to 60 percent of intended conditioning workload or speed; the duration of submaximal graduated warm-up should be proportional to the peak intensity of the conditioning work load
Step exercise (e.g., stair climber, rowing)	Low-level aerobic activity (e.g., walking or cycling and/or relatively low-tempo step exercise)
Swimming	Begin with slow crawl and gradually increase arm stroke and pace, and/or begin with short 1- or 2-lap slow intervals
Tennis (competitive)	Walk-jog and/or graduated tempo volleying proportional to the level of the game

for a given individual can provide a constant intensity: aerobic dance, aerobic step exercise, slide exercise, swimming, skating and cross-country skiing.

GROUP 3: Physical activities that are quite variable in both skill and intensity: soccer, basketball and racquet sports.

Group 1 activities are recommended when precise control of the exercise intensity is necessary, as in the beginning stages of a conditioning program. These activities can be performed in a continuous or discontinuous (interval) format, depending upon the client's fitness level and personal preference, and are useful during all stages of conditioning. Group 2 activities are useful because of the enjoyment provided by group exercise and settings other than an exercise gym. Adding Group 2 exercise to a training program helps foster compliance and reduce boredom. Because of the skill and variable intensity nature of Group 3 activities, they require a base level of conditioning using Group 1 activities. Group 3 activities tend to be group- or team-sport oriented and, therefore, provide greater interest and compliance for many individuals. Group 3 activities should be cautiously considered for high-risk, deconditioned or symptomatic individuals.

Exercise Frequency. Frequency refers to the number of exercise sessions per week

Components of an Aerobic Exercise Program

Table 7.4
Relationship Between Percent Maximal Aerobic Capacity (VO_2max) and Percent Maximal Heart Rate

Percent Max Heart Rate	Percent VO_2max
50	28
60	40
70	58
80	70
90	83
100	100

Source: McArdle, W., Katch, F., and Katch, V. (1986). *Exercise*

included in the program. The frequency of exercise depends on the duration and intensity of the exercise session. Lower-intensity exercise performed for shorter periods can warrant more sessions per week. To improve both cardiorespiratory fitness and maintain body fat at near optimum levels, a client should exercise at least three days per week with no more than two days between sessions. The American College of Sports Medicine recommends three to five days per week for most aerobic programs. When a client starts an aerobic exercise program, exercising every other day for at least the first eight weeks is appropriate. For those with a poor functional capacity, one to two daily sessions may be recommended. Those with an average functional capacity should exercise at least three times per week on alternate days. In general, clients who are just beginning weight-bearing exercise, such as aerobic dancing, aerobic step exercise and jogging, should have at least 36 to 48 hours of rest between workouts to prevent **overuse injuries** and promote adequate bone/joint stress recovery. This is especially true with those who are overweight.

Exercise Duration. Duration refers to the number of minutes of exercise during the conditioning period. The conditioning period, exclusive of the warm-up and cool-down, may vary from as little as five to 60 or more minutes. The duration required for cardiorespiratory benefits is dependent upon the exercise intensity. Take a given intensity of exercise, for example 75 percent of functional capacity, and compare it to an exercise duration of five minutes versus 20 minutes at this intensity. Obviously, more total energy is expended during the 20-minute exercise session. The conditioning response to an exercise session is the result of the product of the intensity and duration of exercise (total energy expenditure). Beginners who are in the lower cardiorespiratory fitness classifications should begin with 10 to 20 minutes of aerobic conditioning. Very deconditioned individuals may be more suited for multiple sessions of short duration, such as five to 10 minutes. Those in the average classification should go for 15 to 45 minutes, and those in the high fitness classification can go for 30 to 60 minutes.

Intensity of Exercise. Intensity refers to the speed or exercise workload. As a rule, the American College of Sports Medicine (ACSM, 1995) recommends a range of 60 percent to 90 percent of **maximal heart rate (MHR)**. This range approximates 50 percent to 85 percent of heart rate reserve (Karvonen formula) and maximal oxygen uptake (functional capacity or aerobic capacity). It is important for you to understand that for any given percentage of maximum oxygen uptake, except for maximum exercise intensities, the percentage of maximum heart rate will be somewhat higher (Table 7.4).

From a physiologic point of view, this 50 percent to 85 percent of maximum oxygen uptake range is the goal for cardiorespiratory training benefits. Lower intensities, such as 50 percent to 60 percent of maximal oxygen consumption and **heart rate maximum reserve**, are advised for beginners in the lower cardiorespiratory fitness levels. Persons with very low fitness levels, however, can benefit from training intensities as low as 40 percent to 50 percent of maximal oxygen uptake. Exercise intensities as high as 75 percent to 85 percent of maximal oxygen uptake and heart rate reserve may be more appropriate for those who are apparently healthy and in the higher fitness classifications. Overall, the average exercise intensity for apparently healthy adults is usually between 60 percent and 70 percent of their maximum oxygen uptake.

Exercise intensity and health-related outcomes. Years of research on exercise and health has made it clear that such health-related outcomes as increased HDL-cholesterol, decreased blood pressure, improved glucose tolerance, reduced blood clotting tendency (fibrinolysis) and reduced anxiety can result from moderate intensities of exercise (i.e., 40 percent to 60 percent of maximum oxygen uptake). In some cases, even lower intensities are recommended (Haskell, 1994).

Table 7.5
Ratings of Perceived Exertion

RPE	Newer Rating Scale
6	0 Nothing at all
7 Very, very light	0.5 Very, very weak
8	1 Very weak
9 Very light	2 Weak
10	3 Moderate
11 Fairly light	4 Somewhat strong
12	5 Strong
13 Somewhat hard	6
14	7 Very strong
15 Hard	8
16	9
17 Very hard	10 Very, very strong
18	Maximal
19 Very, very hard	
20	

Source: Borg, G.V. (1982). Psychological basis of perceived exertion. *Medicine and Science in Sports and Exercise*, 14, 377-381. American College of Sports Medicine.

Monitoring Exercise Intensity

Of the numerous methods for monitoring exercise intensity, five have been somewhat standardized and are recommended for the personal trainer. The method you choose will depend on your client's exercise program and level of fitness, your access to exercise test data (e.g., treadmill stress test heart rates, work loads, functional capacity) and your experience. The following are the primary methods of monitoring exercise intensity:

1. Heart Rate
   a. Percentage of maximal heat rate
   b. Percentage of heart rate reserve
2. Rating of Perceived Exertion
3. The "talk test" method
4. By METS

Percentage of Maximal Heart Rate. This method of monitoring intensity of exercise calculates the exercise heart rate as a percentage of maximal heart rate. Maximal heart rate can be determined by a maximal functional capacity test, using a bicycle or treadmill ergometer, or by age-predicted maximal heart rate tables, which frequently use the 220-minus-age formula. If this method of estimating maximal heart rate is used, the following formula applies:

Training Heart Rate
= Maximal measured or predicted heart rate
x 60 percent to 90 percent (desired percent of maximal H.R.)

For example:

A 40-year-old man for whom an intensity of 70 percent of maximal heart rate is desired:

220 - 40 = 180 (predicted max H.R.)
180 (predicted max H.R.)
x .70 (70 percent exercise intensity)
= 126 exercise heart rate)

You should use caution when using age-group average maximal heart rate tables because these tables only estimate a "rule of thumb" maximal heart rate, usually

Table 7.6
Classification of Intensity of Exercise Based on 30 to 60 Minutes of Endurance Training

HR max*	Relative Intensity (%) Rating of VO_2 max* or HR max reserve	Perceived Exertion	Classification of Intensity
< 35%	< 30%	< 10	Very light
35-59%	30 - 49%	10 - 11	Light
60-79%	50-74%	12-13	Moderate (somewhat hard)
80-89%	75-84%	14-16	Heavy
> 90%	> 85%	>16	Very heavy

* VO_2 max = maximum oxygen uptake; HR max = maximum heart rate.

Source: Pollock, M.L., Fox, S. & Wilmore, J.H. (1990).

from the 220-minus-age formula. This method has a variability of plus or minus 10 to 12 beats per minute (Durstine, 1993). In addition, women generally have a higher heart rate response than men to the same absolute work output. Recent research has also demonstrated that older individuals (older than age 65) may have significantly higher maximal heart rates than predicted by the 220 minus age formula (Whaley, 1992).

It is essential for you to understand the relationship between exercise heart rate and aerobic capacity (maximal oxygen consumption). An important point is often overlooked in aerobic exercise: For nearly all levels of submaximal exercise, the percentage of heart rate maximum does not equal the same percentage of aerobic capacity unless the heart rate maximum reserve method (**Karvonen formula**) is used. As described in Table 7.4, for any given percentage of maximal heart rate, the corresponding percentage of maximal oxygen consumption (aerobic capacity) is five percent to 10 percent less.

Percentage of Heart Rate Reserve (Karvonen Formula). The heart rate reserve method is similar to the percentage of maximal heart rate method, except resting heart rate is factored in:

Training Heart Rate
= (Maximum heart rate
- Resting heart rate)
x Desired intensity
(50 percent to 85 percent)
\+ Resting heart rate

For example: What is the target heart rate for a 40-year-old client with a resting heart rate of 80 bpm at an intensity of 70 percent?

T.H.R. = (Max H.R. - R.H.R.)
x Intensity + R.H.R.

220-40 = 180 (Predicted max H.R.)

180 (predicted maximal heart rate)
-80 (Resting heart rate)
100 (Heart rate reserve)
x.70 (70% intensity)
70
+80 (Resting heart rate)
150 (Target heart rate at 70 percent of heart rate reserve)

Note that this exercise heart rate of 150 bpm is 24 bpm higher than the straight percentage of maximum heart rate method illustrated previously. Therefore, you must be careful when recommending exercise intensity using only the heart rate reserve (Karvonen) method.

The physiological basis for the heart rate reserve method is that the difference between resting and maximal heart rates for a given client represents the reserve of the heart for increasing cardiac output. Like the percentage of maximal heart rate method, the accuracy of the Karvonen Formula is somewhat compromised when the predicted maximal heart rate is estimated from tables or 220-minus-age, rather than determined from an actual functional capacity test. Still, this method is one of the most popular for determining exercise heart rates.

Rating of Perceived Exertion. Exercise intensity also can be measured by assigning a numerical value (6 to 20 or 1 to 10) to subjective feelings of exercise exertion. The popular name for this method is the **ratings of perceived exertion (RPE).** Originally designed by Dr. Gunnar Borg, it is sometimes called the Borg Scale. RPE takes into account all that the exercising client is perceiving in terms of exercise fatigue, including psychological, musculoskeletal and environmental factors. The RPE response also correlates very well with cardiorespiratory and metabolic factors such as heart rate, breathing rate, oxygen consumption and overall fatigue. This level of perceived physical effort is assigned a rating from either of the two rating scales in Table 7.5. For instance, using the Borg Scale, an RPE of 12 to 13 corresponds to approximately 60 percent to 70 percent of maximal heart rate, or 50 percent to 74 percent of maximal oxygen consumption or heart rate reserve (Table 7.6). An RPE of 16 would correspond to about 90 percent of maximal heart rate or 85 percent of maximal oxygen consumption or heart rate reserve. Thus, as a rule, most clients would exercise between 12 and 16 on the Borg Scale. The Borg Scale begins at 6 because originally it was used to approximate exercise heart rate. For example, an RPE of 6 would approximate a heart rate of 60; an RPE of 15 would approximate a heart rate of 150.

In recent years, a revised Borg Scale (see the Newer Rating Scale in Table 7.5) has made it easier to use because of its simpler 0 to 10 rating. On this revised RPE Scale, a client should exercise between an RPE of 4 (somewhat strong) and an RPE of 5 or 6 (strong) (Carlton, 1985). Perhaps the most appropriate use of RPE is as an adjunct to heart-rate monitoring. Ideally, the trainer or exercising client will monitor and record both intensities to ensure close observation of the cardiac and physiological exercise response.

Dishman (1994) believes that the standard scales can be prone to error, and he is currently researching an alternative approach known as "preferred exertion." In this method the exercise participant self-selects exercise intensity (e.g., power output on a stationary cycle) according to their own volition, as long as the selected intensity is within an effective exercise intensity range. It has been suggested that complimentary use of "preferred intensities" may be safer and may better promote long-term exercise adherence than a strict exercise prescription based on more precise physiological criteria, especially if those criteria conflict with a person's intensity preference.

The Talk-test Method. Another means of evaluating the intensity of exercise is the talk test. Like the RPE method, the talk test is subjective, but it is quite useful in determining a "comfort zone" of aerobic intensity. Clients should be able to breathe comfortably and rhythmically throughout all phases of a workout to ensure a safe and comfortable level of exercise, especially for those just beginning an exercise program. Those who progress to higher functional capacities and higher-level workouts may find this technique somewhat conservative, especially at intensities greater than 80 percent of functional capacity.

In summary, you can modify criteria such as the mode, frequency, duration and

Components of an Aerobic Exercise Program

Table 7.7
Training Method Selection

Cardiorespiratory Fitness Level	Aerobic Capacity (METS)	Training Method
Poor	1-3.9	Low-level (2-3 METS) aerobic interval training
Low	4-6.9	Aerobic interval training at 3-5 METS
Average	7-10.9	Aerobic interval training at 6-8 METS; continuous training at 5-8 METS
Good	11-13.9	Aerobic interval training at 9-12 METS; continuous training at 8-12 METS; aerobic composite training at 8-12 METS; moderate anaerobic interval training
High	14+	Aerobic interval training at 10-13+ METS; continuous training at 9-13+ METS; aerobic composite training at 9-13+ METS; anaerobic or Fartlek training

intensity of exercise to suit the client's level of fitness, program goals and schedule. As a rule, however, building a foundation of endurance at a relatively low-to-moderate intensity prior to performing higher-intensity workouts or competition is clearly justified for safety and comfort. This may mean moving the client, for the first few weeks, through gradual increases in duration, while holding intensity nearly constant until an acceptable level of endurance, such as 20 to 30 minutes, has been achieved. Within each of these criteria, you have an enormous range of choices, such as variations in modes and intensities, with which to vary the exercise stimulus and maximize the client's interest and adaptation to increasing levels of exercise.

Intensity Measured by METs. Exercise intensity can be assessed by a graded exercise test (bicycle or treadmill) (Figure 7.7). Based on the time the client stays on the treadmill or bicycle ergometer, the maximal oxygen consumption (i.e., functional capacity) can be estimated and converted to a **MET** equivalent. A MET is a multiple of resting oxygen consumption. One MET equals a person's oxygen uptake at rest, which is equal to approximately 3.5 milliliters of oxygen per kilogram of body weight per minute (3.5 ml/kg/min). The intensity of exercise may be determined as a specified percentage of the client's maximal oxygen consumption or functional capacity (e.g., 50 percent to 85 percent), and then choosing activities that are known to require energy expenditure at the desired level (Table 7.8). For example, if a client has a functional capacity of 10 METS and you recommend they begin at 60 percent of functional capacity, then 60 percent times 10 METS equals 6 METS beginning intensity.

10 METS (functional or aerobic capacity)
x .60 (60 percent recommended exercise intensity)
= 6 METS (beginning exercise intensity)

Exercise intensity determined by METS has some disadvantages. Environmental influences such as wind, hills, heat, humidity, altitude, air pollution and a variety of mechanical factors, such as the mechanical efficiency of a bicycle, can alter the energy cost of the activity. In addition, as the client improves cardiorespiratory endurance, higher MET levels will be required to ensure an adequate training stimulus. As a rule, training by heart rate and perceived exertion may be an easier and more accurate method for determining effective aerobic exercise.

Table 7.8
Approximate Energy Expenditure, in METS, of Various Activities

METs	Activity Category	Specific Activity
8.5	Bicycling	Bicycling, BMX or mountain
4.0	Bicycling	Bicycling, <10 mph, general, leisure, to work or for pleasure
6.0	Bicycling	Bicycling, 10-11.9 mph, leisure, slow, light effort
8.0	Bicycling	Bicycling, 12-13.9 mph, leisure, moderate effort
10.0	Bicycling	Bicycling, 14-15.9 mph, racing or leisure, fast, vigorous effort
12.0	Bicycling	Bicycling, 16-19 mph, racing/not drafting or >19 mph drafting, very fast, racing general
16.0	Bicycling	Bicycling, >20 mph, racing, not drafting
5.0	Bicycling	Unicycling
5.0	Conditioning exercise	Bicycling, stationary, general
3.0	Conditioning exercise	Bicycling, stationary, 50 W, very light effort
5.5	Conditioning exercise	Bicycling, stationary, 100 W, light effort
7.0	Conditioning exercise	Bicycling, stationary, 150 W, moderate effort
10.5	Conditioning exercise	Bicycling, stationary, 200 W, vigorous effort
12.5	Conditioning exercise	Bicycling, stationary, 250 W, very vigorous effort
8.0	Conditioning exercise	Calisthenics (e.g., pushups, pullups, situps), heavy, vigorous effort
4.5	Conditioning exercise	Calisthenics, home exercise, light or moderate effort, general (example: back exercises), going up & down from floor
8.0	Conditioning exercise	Circuit training, general
6.0	Conditioning exercise	Weight lifting (free weight, nautilus or universal-type), power lifting or body building, vigorous effort
5.5	Conditioning exercise	Health club exercise, general
6.0	Conditioning exercise	Stair-treadmill ergometer, general
9.5	Conditioning exercise	Rowing, stationary ergometer, general
3.5	Conditioning exercise	Rowing, stationary, 50 W, light effort
7.0	Conditioning exercise	Rowing stationary, 100 W, moderate effort
8.5	Conditioning exercise	Rowing, stationary, 150 W, vigorous effort
12.0	Conditioning exercise	Rowing, stationary, 200 W, very vigorous effort
9.5	Conditioning exercise	Ski machine, general
6.0	Conditioning exercise	Slimnastics
4.0	Conditioning exercise	Stretching, hatha yoga
6.0	Conditioning exercise	Teaching aerobic exercise class
4.0	Conditioning calisthenics exercise	Water aerobics, water
3.0	Conditioning exercise	Weight lifting (free, nautilus or universal-type), light or moderate effort, light workout, general
1.0	Conditioning exercise	Whirlpool, sitting
6.0	Dancing	Aerobic, ballet or modern, twist
6.0	Dancing	Aerobic, general
5.0	Dancing	Aerobic, low impact
7.0	Dancing	Aerobic, high impact
4.5	Dancing	General
5.5	Dancing square)	Ballroom, fast (disco, folk,
3.0	Dancing	Ballroom, slow (e.g., waltz, foxtrot, slow dancing)
5.0	Fishing and hunting	Fishing, general
5.0	Fishing and hunting	Fishing from river bank and walking
2.5	Fishing and hunting	Fishing from boat, sitting
3.5	Fishing and hunting	Fishing from river bank, standing
6.0	Fishing and hunting	Fishing in stream, in waders
2.0	Fishing and hunting	Fishing, ice, sitting
2.5	Fishing and hunting	Hunting, bow and arrow or crossbow
6.0	Fishing and hunting	Hunting, deer, elk, large game
2.5	Fishing and hunting	Hunting, duck, wading
5.0	Fishing	Hunting, general

Table 7.9
Reasons to Temporarily Defer Exercise

Recurrent illness
Progression of cardiac disease
Abnormally elevated blood pressure
Recent changes in symptoms
Orthopedic problem
Emotional turmoil
Severe sunburn
Alcoholic hangover
Cerebral dysfunction — dizziness or vertigo
Sodium retention — edema or weight gain
Dehydration
Environmental factors
Weather (excessive heat or humidity)
Air pollution (smog or carbon monoxide)
Heavy, large meal within two hours
Coffee, tea, cola (xanthine and other stimulating beverages)
Drugs
Illicit drugs (e.g., tobacco, amphetamines, cocaine, marijuana)
Decongestants
Bronchodilators
Atropine
Weight-reduction agents

Source: Adapted from *Resource Manual for Guidelines for Exercise Testing and Prescription.*

Supportive Conditioning Exercise

All cardiorespiratory exercise programs must be supported by flexibility, strength and even neuromuscular fitness exercise in order to enhance the efficiency of aerobic exercise (exercise economy) and minimize musculoskeletal injury. Although some of this supportive exercise, such as stretching, can be part of the warm-up and/or cool-down, it is prudent to add several separate sessions per week that improve the strength of the back, legs and abdomen. Stretching and range-of-motion exercises are fundamental to a successful cardiorespiratory fitness program. Incorporating various neuromuscular relaxation activities into the cool-down phase of the program is appropriate for those coming from high-stress work environments who need more than just aerobic exercise. You can help your clients relax both mentally and physically by teaching them easy stretching and mental relaxation skills simultaneously. Chapters 9 and 10 describe strength and flexibility exercises in more detail.

Cardiorespiratory Fitness Goals

The goals of cardiorespiratory exercise must be clearly stated in the written exercise plan to reinforce compliance and motivation and for assessment during follow up. The client's implementation and progression plan must reflect these goals and depict means of achieving them safely and realistically. Chapter 11 contains an excellent discussion of goal formulation. The following are examples of areas that can be addressed in the formulation of cardiorespiratory exercise and activity goals:

1. Overall acquisition and maintenance of cardiorespiratory fitness (e.g., kcal/day energy expenditure, mastery of jogging, 20 pound weight loss)
2. Cardiovascular risk factor modification
   a. Body composition
   b. Blood pressure reduction
   c. Cholesterol control
   d. Stress and anxiety reduction
3. Performance objectives
   a. Personal accomplishment (e.g., 10K run, 1-mile swim, or 6-mile hike)
   b. Increase physical stamina

Progression Plan

A written progression plan with periodic reevaluation is crucial. This plan must provide details for a graduated progression in the frequency, duration and intensity of exercise. There must be sufficient flexibility in the rate of progression so that the plan comfortably adjusts to the client's cardiorespiratory and musculoskeletal response. The rate of progression depends upon a number of factors (Figure 7.9):

- individual level of fitness (aerobic capacity)
- age
- health status
- cardiorespiratory response to exercise
- individual preferences and goals
- social and family support
- level of exercise initiative and motivation
- access to appropriate facilities and equipment

Three stages of progression for the cardiorespiratory endurance exercise plan are identified in the American College of Sports Medicine guidelines (ACSM, 1995): the initial conditioning stage, the improvement conditioning stage and the maintenance conditioning stage.

Initial Conditioning Stage. This stage usually lasts four to six weeks or longer and includes low-level aerobic activities, stretching and light calisthenics. Exercise frequency should begin with every other day. Depending upon initial level of fitness and functional capacity, duration should start with 10 to 20 minutes and gradually increase according to the client's cardiorespiratory and musculoskeletal response. For those with low functional capacity (4 to 7 METS or less), it may be appropriate to prescribe low-level aerobic interval exercise of two to five minutes at a time. The most important thing to remember during the initial conditioning stage is to be conservative with the exercise intensity. For example, if the individual has a 9 MET functional capacity (31.5 ml/kg/min VO_2 max), begin at a conservative 40 percent to 60 percent of this value or at about 4 METS. Here, exercise heart rate should begin at approximately 40 percent to 60 percent of heart rate reserve (Karvonen). This initial intensity range is lower than that stated by the 1991 edition of the *ACE Personal Trainer Manual* because of enhanced safety and the number of health benefits that can be realized from lower-intensity activities.

Improvement Conditioning Stage. This is the primary conditioning stage for most aerobic training programs. It may last from eight to 20 weeks, and the rate of progression in intensity is more rapid. The exercise intensity can be increased to the next highest level than that completed in the initial conditioning stage, and within the 60 percent to 90 percent of maximal heart rate (50 percent to 85 percent of $V0_2$ max or heart rate reserve) depending on fitness level and age. Exercise duration should be increased every two to three weeks according to the client's response and goals. It is important to periodically review progress at two- to four-week intervals during this stage, either by direct monitoring or by assessing self-report data (RPE, heart rate, symptoms, caloric expenditure).

Maintenance Stage. When clients reach their target functional capacity or primary goals, the maintenance stage begins. This stage is usually reached after the first six months of training, but it may be delayed as long as 12 months, depending upon goals. In any case, it is important to reassess goals at the beginning of this stage. Maintenance of a particular level of cardiorespiratory fitness can be derived from an exercise program that has similar energy requirements to that of the conditioning program. Cardiorespiratory fitness can often be maintained by regularly engaging in a variety of endurance-related sports activities that are fun and enjoyable.

Cautions

The last component of an exercise plan involves using individual information to ensure each client's exercise safety with specific precautions. List any personal or environmental information that reduces the risk of exercise injury or that may compromise exercise safety. Individualized comments such as those describing hot, humid environments or avoiding musculoskeletal symptoms specific to the client should be included. Another useful format is to list several cautions that are standard for nearly all exercise programs:

- ✔ Do not exercise for at least 90 minutes after a meal.
- ✔ Avoid continuing exercise with chest discomfort, lightheadedness or dizziness.
- ✔ Reduce exercise intensity in response to very hot or humid environments or to altitudes above 5,000 feet.
- ✔ Avoid exercise with tenderness in a joint (for example, a knee or foot) that tends to worsen with activity.
- ✔ Avoid strenuous aerobic exercise during viral infections such as the flu or upper-respiratory tract infection.

TRAINING METHODS

Once the mode, frequency, duration and intensity of exercise has been established, you must choose the appropriate training method. The choice provides the foundation for the exercise progression plan. Selection requires understanding the physiological response to various training methods and, preferably, personal experience with each of those methods. As with exercise intensity and progression, the training method depends on the functional fitness level and the goals of the participant. There are five major training meth- ods (Heyward, 1984; Wells & Pate, 1988):

1. Continuous training
   a. Intermediate slow distance
   b. Long slow distance
2. Interval training
   a. Aerobic interval training
   b. Anaerobic interval training
3. Fartlek training
4. Circuit training
5. Aerobic cross training

Continuous Training

Continuous training involves conditioning stage exercise, such as walking, jogging, cycling, swimming and aerobic dancing. The prescribed intensity is maintained continuously between 50 percent and 85 percent of functional capacity (maximal oxygen uptake). For those with initially low functional capacities, continuous training may be initiated at 40 percent of functional capacity and is usually preceded by four to six weeks of interval training in the initial conditioning stage. In practice, continuous training is divided into two types:

- ✔ Intermediate slow distance: Generally from 20 to 60 minutes of continuous aerobic exercise — the most common type of sustained aerobic exercise for fitness improvement. Body-fat reduction, improvement in cardiorespiratory fitness and cardiovascular risk factor management all are responsive to this type of continuous training.
- ✔ Long slow distance (LSD): 60 or more minutes of continuous aerobic exercise, usually employed for athletic training in such sports as cycling and long-distance running. Cardiorespiratory and metabolic demands are great for LSD training. At least six months of successful intermediate slow distance training should precede LSD training. Increased risk of musculoskeletal injury (e.g., Achilles tendinitis) accompanies this type of prolonged aerobic training.

Interval Training

Interval training involves the alternating of relatively more intense bouts of cardiovascular exercise with those that are relatively less intense. Interval training has useful applications for beginning exercisers, as well as experienced, conditioned clients who wish to improve aerobic power. You can use two types of interval training: aerobic and anaerobic. For aerobic or anaerobic interval training the following four variables should be considered when designing an interval training program:

- ✔ intensity of work interval (e.g., speed)
- ✔ duration of work interval (e.g., distance or time)
- ✔ duration of rest or recovery interval
- ✔ number of repetitions or repeat intervals

Aerobic Interval Training. Aerobic interval training is best suited for those beginning in the poor- or low-cardiorespiratory fitness classifications (Table 7.10) because it is less intense. Generally, aerobic interval training uses exercise bouts of two to 15 minutes at an intensity between 60 percent and 80 percent of functional capacity (modified from Wells & Pate). Those with poor- or low-functional capacity should start with two- to three-minute exercise intervals at 60 percent to 70 percent of functional capacity. Rest intervals should take approximately the same time as a complete exercise interval. Intervals can be repeated five to 10 times depending on the client's response and program goals; for example, stationary bicycling for three minutes at a work load intensity of 60 percent to 70 percent of functional capacity with a two-minute "rest period" of cycling at zero resistance or load. Hypothetically, this would be repeated five to 10 times or for a total workout of 25 to 50 minutes. Higher-intensity and longer-duration aerobic interval training (e.g., five- to 15-minute bouts at 70 percent to 90 percent of functional capacity) should be reserved for those in higher cardiorespiratory fitness classifications seeking increased aerobic endurance and speed.

Anaerobic Interval Training. Anaerobic interval training is primarily reserved for those in the higher cardiorespiratory fitness classifications who desire to increase speed, lactate threshold and overall aerobic power. Such training usually results in greater lactic acid concentrations in exercising muscles, and is accompanied by greater muscular discomfort. Because of the relatively high metabolic and cardiorespiratory demands, beginners or those below a 10-MET aerobic capacity should refrain from anaerobic interval training. Although there are many derivations of anaerobic interval training, the training stimulus is usually between 30 seconds and four minutes at an intensity of 85 percent to greater than 100 percent of functional capacity (maximal oxygen uptake). The probability of musculoskeletal injury is greater because of high muscle contraction velocities and forces. The client, frequently an athlete, should engage in substantial low-level aerobic warm-up and stretching before vigorous activity.

Table 7.10
Cardiorespiratory Fitness Level Classifications*

	Oxygen Consumption	
Fitness Level	ml/kg/min	METS
Poor	3.5-13.9	1.0-3.9
Low	14.0-24.9	4.0-6.9
Average	25.0-38.9	7.0-10.9
Good	39.0-48.9	11.0-13.9
High	49.0-56.0	14.0-16.0

*For 40-year-old males. Adjustments are appropriate to apply these standards to others.

Source: ACSM. (1991). *Guidelines for Exercise Testing and Prescription* (4th ed.). Philadelphia: Lea and Febiger. Reprinted with permission.

Fartlek Training

Fartlek training is similar to interval training, however, the work-rest intervals are not systematically or accurately measured. Work-rest intervals and intensity are usually determined by how the participant feels. Over the years, Fartlek training has blossomed in many aerobic-training regimens, primarily to prevent boredom and to enhance aerobic endurance. One of its most useful applications is in running, where the warm up consists of running for 10 to 20 minutes, then the pace is significantly varied every five to 10 minutes. Like long, slow distance aerobic training, this form should be reserved for those in the average or above-average cardiorespiratory fitness levels because of the relatively high demand on the cardiorespiratory system.

Circuit Training

Circuit training takes the participant through a series of exercise stations, with relatively brief rest intervals between each station. The number of stations may range from four to 10. Historically, circuit training was designed for enhancing muscular endurance and incorporated mostly muscular endurance exercises such as sit-ups, the bench press and the leg press. A circuit of four to 10 stations with a low-level aerobic warm-up and cool-down station (for example, the stationary bicycle) could be followed by exercise stations using either free weights and/or single-station weight machines. A good example of circuit training in a more natural environment is par course exercise. This method intersperses walking or jogging with a variety of flexibility, muscular endurance and strength exercises.

For the last decade or so, aerobic circuit training programs have become popular. Between four and eight aerobic exercise stations with one to five minutes per station and a 15-second rest break between stations constitute a circuit. Stations may include stationary cycling, treadmill exercise, moderate stair climbing and rowing. Depending on the number of stations, the number of circuits completed would be equivalent to 20 to 50 minutes of aerobic exercise. One key to success is to avoid excessive workloads at each station. Each station should be set at 50 percent to 70 percent of the client's functional capacity.

Aerobic Cross Training

Aerobic **cross training** is an individualized combination or composite of all aerobic-training methods, and is characterized by a variety of intensities and modes. It is primarily for those in the maintenance phase of conditioning who want variety and an intensity corresponding to how they feel during a given exercise workout. A good example is a 50-minute workout where the client warms up by jogging 15 minutes to a nearby pool, then swims for 20 minutes, and then jogs 15 minutes back home. Another example is bicycling 20 minutes to a track or running course and, after 20 minutes of running, cycling back home. Combining a group of aerobic activities into one workout at steady or various intensities is an excellent method of cross-training to fight boredom from the same daily workout mode and intensity. This method can also be applied to circuit training in a gym by combining a continuous, relatively low-level aerobic session, such as 20 minutes of stationary cycling, with 10 to 20 minutes of a variety of higher-intensity aerobic intervals on various aerobic ergometers, and concluding with a 5- to 10-minute cool-down of stationary cycling. The many obvious permutations of this method should begin and end with a continuous low-level cardiorespiratory exercise effort for effective physiological warm-up. This method instills variety and is a mini-version of a "training triathlon."

GUIDELINES FOR CARDIORESPIRATORY ACTIVITY

The best resources for detailed aerobic activities are those that adopt sensible progression guidelines with adequate instruction for each form of exercise (e.g., Greenberg & Pargman, 1989; Howley & Franks, 1992; and Nieman, 1990). Following are guidelines for popular aerobic and sport activities.

Walking

Walking is the easiest aerobic-conditioning activity and is often preferred because of its low injury rate, relative simplicity and adaptability to busy schedules. Although

Guidelines for Cardiorespiratory Activity

nearly anyone can incur significant health benefits from walking, several types of clients will respond particularly well to a graduated walking program:

- ✔ Those with low functional capacity (2 to 7 METS) who need an initial low-intensity workout.
- ✔ Those over 60 years of age who have been sedentary and are just beginning an exercise program.
- ✔ Those who are 20 or more pounds overweight.

The energy cost of walking is relatively low compared to that of jogging because of slower speeds; however, at walking speeds of five miles per hour and faster, the oxygen and caloric cost per minute approaches that of jogging or running (Table 7.11). There still exists an abundance of misinformation regarding the energy costs of walking versus running. Despite the long-standing claim that walking 1 mile is equivalent to running 1 mile, this is not the case, with the exception of very fast walking speeds of greater than five miles per hour (Howley & Franks, 1992; Howley & Glover, 1974). In general, the **net caloric cost** per mile* of walking is 50 percent to 60 percent of that for running 1 mile. This is an important point if you intend to prescribe and quantify walking mileage for weight management purposes.

Table 7.11
Energy Costs of Walking (kcal/min)

Body Weight (lb)	Miles Per Hour/METS 2.0/ 2.5	2.5/ 2.9	3.0/ 3.3	3.5/ 3.7	4.0/ 4.9	4.5/ 6.2	5.0/ 7.9
110	2.1	2.4	2.8	3.1	4.1	5.2	6.6
120	2.3	2.6	3.0	3.4	4.4	5.6	7.2
130	2.5	2.9	3.2	3.6	4.8	6.1	7.8
140	2.7	3.1	3.5	3.9	5.2	6.6	8.4
150	2.8	3.3	3.7	4.2	5.6	7.0	9.0
160	3.0	3.5	4.0	4.5	5.9	7.5	9.6
170	3.2	3.7	4.2	4.8	6.3	8.0	10.2
180	3.4	4.0	4.5	5.0	6.7	8.4	10.8
190	3.6	4.2	4.7	5.3	7.0	8.9	11.4
200	3.8	4.4	5.0	5.6	7.4	9.4	12.0
210	4.0	4.6	5.2	5.9	7.8	9.9	12.6
220	4.2	4.8	5.5	6.2	8.2	10.3	13.2

Source: Franks, D., & Howley, E. (1992). *Health Fitness Instructor's Handbook.*

**The net cost of exercise is the exercise energy expenditure minus resting energy expenditure. The net cost measures the energy expenditure used over that when just sitting around.*

Walking is generally less intense than jogging or running, thus longer sessions can be maintained with less likelihood of musculoskeletal injury. When hilly terrain is gradually added to the walking program, there is greater energy expenditure. Perhaps the safest and most effective cardiorespiratory weight-control exercise for those who are 20 to 30 pounds overweight is progressive variable-terrain walking. This walking protocol graduates from walking approximately 2 miles on flat terrain to walking up to 5 or more miles over a variety of grades, such as those found on many urban and rural park and nature trails. It is not difficult to achieve and maintain the walking intensity and duration necessary for acceptable cardiorespiratory fitness. As a general rule, achieving acceptable fitness will require at least 20 minutes (preferably 30 or more minutes) of fast-paced, flat-ground walking or slightly slower variable-terrain walking. When prescribing walking exercise, three things are important:

1. When walking is the primary activity, footwear is important. Specialized walking or hiking shoes are available from many stores, although many walkers will prefer a good pair of running shoes.

2. Always warm up and cool down. Begin each session by walking for about five minutes and then stretch the Achilles tendon, calf and low-back muscles. After the primary conditioning phase, cool down by walking at a slower pace and stretching the muscles that were previously stretched.

3. Give special emphasis to graduating

Table 7.12
Energy Costs of Jogging and Running (kcal/min)

	Miles Per Hour/METS							
Body weight (lb)	**3.0/ 5.6**	**4.0/ 7.1**	**5.0/ 8.7**	**6.0/ 10.2**	**7.0/ 11.7**	**8.0/ 13.3**	**9.0/ 14.8**	**10.0/ 16.3**
110	4.7	5.9	7.2	8.5	9.8	11.1	12.3	13.6
120	5.1	6.4	7.9	9.3	10.6	12.1	13.4	14.8
130	5.5	7.0	8.6	10.0	11.5	13.1	14.6	16.1
140	5.9	7.5	9.2	10.8	12.4	14.1	15.7	17.3
150	6.4	8.1	9.9	11.6	13.3	15.1	16.8	18.5
160	6.8	8.6	10.5	12.4	14.2	16.1	17.9	19.8
170	7.2	9.1	11.2	13.1	15.1	17.1	19.1	21.0
180	7.6	9.7	11.8	13.9	15.9	18.1	20.2	22.2
190	8.1	10.2	12.5	14.7	16.8	19.1	21.3	23.5
200	8.5	10.8	13.2	15.4	17.7	20.1	22.4	24.7
210	8.9	11.3	13.8	16.2	18.6	21.1	23.5	25.9
220	9.3	11.8	14.5	17.0	19.5	22.2	24.7	27.2

Source: Franks, D., & Howley, E. (1992). *Health Fitness Instructor's Handbook.*

the duration — for example, from 15 to 60 minutes — over the length of the program. Progression in intensity should follow successful duration progression. Emphasize duration first, then gradually add faster-paced walking. Keep in mind that adding hilly terrain increases the intensity, so be sure that the terrain is within the client's capacity.

Jogging and Running

Jogging and running are superb cardiorespiratory endurance activities. The essential difference between the two is that jogging is "slower running," or as some authorities define it, jogging is running slower than eight minutes per mile. For beginners, a natural sequence of progression might be:

1. Walk/jog intervals: walk 50 yards, jog 50 yards, repeat 10 to 20 times; over time, gradually increase the jogging interval to 2 or more miles.
2. Jogging: gradually increase jogging distance to desired distance or energy expenditure.
3. Running: as jogging endurance improves, increase stride frequency and stride length to a comfortable running style.

It is not necessary to graduate to running if desired goals can be achieved by jogging. However, running is a natural progression for those who orthopedically and psychologically respond well to jogging. Table 7.12 shows the energy cost in calories per minute for jogging and running. Note that the energy cost increases proportionately with increasing speed. These proportional increases in energy cost mean that a client who runs a mile at nine miles an hour (6.6 minutes per mile) will finish the mile twice as fast as when jogging 4.5 miles per hour (13.3 minutes per mile), but energy cost per mile is about the same. Numerous benefits can be obtained from successful jogging and running programs that are adequately balanced with appropriate muscular strength and flexibility exercises. Some of these benefits include increased maximum oxygen uptake, improved **body composition** (decrease in body-fat stores), coronary risk reduction, increased bone strength and enhanced psychological well-being.

Four things are important when prescribing jogging or running exercise:

1. Wear appropriate footwear. A comfortable pair of running shoes designed for distance jogging/running should have adequate sole cushion, good heel support and sufficient sole flexibility.
2. Always accompany jogging or running exercise with appropriate flexibility exercise. Stretching the Achilles tendon, calf, hamstrings, quadriceps, foot and low-back muscles will help improve jogging and running efficiency (see Chapter 10).
3. For beginners, jog every other day or no more than four days per week with a day of rest between workouts to allow for

adequate recovery of the weight-bearing joints, ligaments and tendons. Limit the initial duration to no more than 25 to 30 minutes per workout for the first six to eight weeks.

4. Increase jogging pace and add hills only gradually. Emphasize a gradual increase in distance at a relatively slow pace, and then slowly increase pace or speed. Aerobic interval training will facilitate a safe and gradual increase in distance.

Cycling

Cycling is another excellent cardiorespiratory activity with benefits similar to jogging and running. It is a good alternative for those who do not like to jog or run, or who have orthopedic limitations to weight-bearing exercise. Two types are outdoor cycling and indoor stationary cycling. Both have advantages and disadvantages; however, with sufficient frequency, duration and intensity, both can be an excellent stimulus to cardiorespiratory fitness.

Outdoor Cycling. The benefits of outdoor cycling are sunlight, fresh air, adequate cooling and variety of terrain and scenery. And it can be a good source of inexpensive transportation. Most clients find cycling outdoors makes it easier to prolong duration of exercise because of distances between destinations and more interesting environments. Disadvantages include inclement weather, nightfall and some unsafe city environments. However, convenient outdoor cycling, combined with indoor stationary cycling, can be a stimulating year-round program.

Guidelines for outdoor bicycling include the following:

1. Use a bicycle with at least 10 speeds so that the cyclist can easily adapt to nearly any change in grade or wind.

2. For beginners, keep a relatively constant pedal crank speed by adjusting the gears to variable grades and headwinds. This pedal crank speed can vary depending on fitness and comfort, but will usually be between 70 rpm and 90 rpm per leg. This will help minimize fatigue and maximize blood flow and nutrients to the legs.

3. Bicycle seat height should be high enough so that the leg that is on the downstroke is not quite completely extended when the ball of the foot is on the pedal.

4. Use toe clips, especially with significant hill climbing. Toe clips improve pedaling efficiency by delivering more muscular power to the pedal crank axis throughout the entire revolution.

5. Wear bicycling apparel. Always wear a cycling helmet. Padded shorts and gloves will increase comfort for cycling lasting longer than 45 minutes.

Indoor Stationary Cycling. The advantages of indoor stationary cycling include its convenience and relative safety. Most health clubs and fitness centers have two types of stationary cycles: those with mechanically braked flywheels and those that are electronically braked. Either type will provide a good aerobic or anaerobic workout; however, the electronically controlled cycles generally display digital workload information that may be helpful to motivate clients. On electronically controlled cycles, some beginners do not always get an adequate warm-up when selecting certain exercise programs on the display monitor. Regardless of the type of cycle, always warm up by cycling against low pedal crank resistance for at least six to eight minutes. Many stationary cycles are not accurately calibrated, so there may be noticeable differences in pedal crank resistances for similarly indicated workloads between cycles.

The following guidelines apply to stationary cycling machines:

1. Ensure proper ventilation. If necessary, a fan gives adequate cross ventilation to enable good evaporative heat loss. Cooling the body by the evaporation of sweat is necessary to prevent a rapid rise in body temperature. Unlike outdoor bicycling, indoor cycling requires adequate ventilation

for prolonged exercise.

2. As in outdoor bicycling, adjust seat height for a slight bend in the knee at the downstroke position.

3. Adjust the handlebars so that the client is relaxed and leaning slightly forward.

4. Hold pedal crank speed relatively constant for beginners in the range of 70 rpm to 90 rpm per leg.

5. Always warm up and cool down with five to 10 minutes of low resistance cycling.

Swimming

Swimming activities are another excellent form of cardiorespiratory endurance exercise. Swimming is a good alternative for those with chronic orthopedic problems or a recent musculoskeletal injury. Relatively experienced swimmers generate a lower heart-rate response for any level of effort compared to cyclists and runners. The diminished cardiac work is due to the prone position and the effect of immersion in a relatively cool environment. This is important when determining a target heart-rate range, which may be as much as 10 beats per minute lower with lap swimming than with cycling or running. This does not mean that swimming is not a significant cardiorespiratory stimulus. However, swimming generally requires a higher level of motor skill that may take significantly longer to learn than that of cycling or running. Several factors determine swimming efficiency and early success with any swimming program, including body buoyancy, swimming skill and style, and body dimensions. Women are generally more efficient swimmers than men, partly because of greater body-fat stores and a more even distribution of body fat, which improves buoyancy. For an efficient swimmer, the energy cost of swimming 1 mile has been estimated to be more than 400 kcal. Unskilled swimmers may require twice the energy expenditure for a given velocity compared to skilled swimmers, and often fatigue early.

The following guidelines should be followed for swimming:

1. Assess swimming or aquatic exercise skill by evaluating exercise history or by observation. If skill level (i.e., stroke efficiency and style) is low, supervision and swimming lessons should precede swimming as a cardiorespiratory conditioning exercise.

2. Keep pool temperature for lap swimming at 76 degrees to 84 degrees (F).

3. Ideally, use a lap pool with, at the most, 80 lengths per mile to enable the swimmer to attain a reasonable stroke rhythm before turning.

4. Use interval training for the beginning swimmer. For example, swimming either the width or length of the pool one to two times may be appropriate. Each of these would constitute a set with a rest interval of walking one or two widths in waist-high water. This could be repeated four to 10 times, depending on skill and cardiorespiratory fitness.

5. For the beginner, include a good warm-up and cool-down exercise, such as walking the width of the pool in waist- or chest-high water for five to 10 minutes.

6. For those who are not comfortable in the pool and perhaps cannot swim, flotation devices can help (e.g., small life-vests, kick-boards, pull-buoys, triathlon wet-suits).

Rowing

Rowing machines have become popular in gyms and fitness centers for cardiorespiratory exercise, as well as for attaining a reasonable degree of arm, back and thigh muscular endurance. As with any stationary aerobic exercise device, a fan should provide air circulation to facilitate sweat evaporation and prevent overheating. There are numerous manufacturers of rowing machines, some very basic and some quite sophisticated with hydraulic action of the arm movement and workload display monitors. However, most operate on the principle of coordinated effort of lower extremity muscular work with arm rowing action. Rowing intensity (rowing motion resistance) can be varied in most machines by changing the force angle of the rowing arm of the machine, by changing the hydraulic pressure in the pressure cylinder, or via electronic programming. Intensity also can be varied by increasing the rowing rate or number of rows per minute. Those just learning should note that several sessions are required to learn how to perform repetitive, efficient rowing motions that require synchronizing the arms, back and legs. Several guidelines may be helpful:

1. Secure feet in the anchors on the front part of the machine.
2. Use a smooth rowing action (coordinate arm and back rowing movements with leg extensions).
3. Begin with a relatively low intensity (low resistance) with approximately eight to 10 rows per minute for hydraulic rowers, for five to 10 minutes.
4. Graduate the speed to approximately 15 to 30 rows per minute and gradually increase duration to 15 to 30 minutes.
5. Gradually increase intensity according to heart rate and perceived exertion.

Stair Climbing

Stair climbing can be an effective means of attaining cardiorespiratory fitness. The client may use either a staircase or one of the electrically braked stair-climbing machines that are popular in fitness centers. The advent of computer-interactive, electrically braked stair-climbing machines has brought effective and well-controlled stair climbing to the health club and fitness center. They allow for a more effective warm-up and cool-down as well as a variety of training intensities because most of these devices regulate the intensity of climbing based on step rate and training method. You should also note that many people incorrectly support their weight by holding on to guard rails so the actual work performed is less than that indicated on the monitor. Most people find these machines fun, and they can provide an interesting addition to circuit training programs or be a primary means of attaining cardiorespiratory fitness.

Safety precaution: A fan or other means of convective cooling should always be used because of the tendency to overheat on stationary exercise machines.

Because the energy cost of actual stair climbing is largely dependent upon body weight, a large anaerobic component is possible for those who are overweight or unaccustomed to regular stair climbing. Adequate warm-up and cool-down periods must be incorporated due to the potentially large energy costs. Walking for five to 10 minutes on relatively flat terrain, either on a track or treadmill, usually provides adequate warm-up or cool-down. Interval-training methods are best when beginning a program with regular stairs or steps in a stadium. After warming up, repeating a sequence of walking four flights of stairs and taking a 60-second walk on flat ground four to 10 times is one example of an interval approach.

Aerobic Dance

Studies on the effects of aerobic dance show it to be an excellent form of cardiorespiratory endurance exercise. To gain significant benefits, the client must maintain the aerobic phase for at least 20 to 30 minutes, three to four times per week. The tempo (speed or pace) should be adjusted to fit the desired intensity or heart-rate range. Like swimming, aerobic dance requires a degree of motor skill and coordination, and may take more time to learn than walking, jogging or cycling. For those who are significantly overweight or have a history of orthopedic injuries, this type of exercise may create undue demands on the cardiorespiratory and musculoskeletal systems.

For aerobic-dance exercise, the following guidelines apply:

Guidelines for Cardiorespiratory Activity

1. Wear appropriate footwear. An aerobic shoe should adhere to four standards: cushion, support, flexibility and traction compatibility.

2. For beginners, recommend low-impact aerobics—a form of aerobic dance that features one foot on the ground at all times, reducing the risk of musculoskeletal injury, and may include the use of light weights.

3. For beginners, recommend a class that will adapt appropriately to the beginner's functional capacity and skill level.

4. Lower the target heart rate slightly, because aerobic-dance exercise may elicit heart rates 10 to 15 beats per minute higher than running or cycling for the same percentage of aerobic capacity (Parker, et al., 1989). This disproportionate relationship between oxygen consumption and heart rate is generally true for most aerobic-exercise routines using upper-body muscle groups.

Refer to the *ACE Aerobics Instructor Manual,* published by the American Council on Exercise (1993), for more information on aerobic instruction techniques.

Step Aerobics

Step aerobic exercise has gained wide popularity in fitness centers and health clubs across the United States and many parts of Asia and Europe. More than 30 studies now confirm that the energy cost of step aerobic training (7 to 11 METs) is commensurate with that of traditional aerobic exercise, such as running and cycling, and is an adequate stimulus of aerobic endurance. Choices of step bench height generally range from 4 to 10 inches, with a standard stepping rate of 120 to 130 steps per minute. Beginners should be advised to begin with smaller step heights of 4 to 6 inches with a goal of 8 inches after four to eight weeks of successful training. The addition of hand-held weights should be discouraged for beginners and those who are coronary-prone, because of the increased blood pressure response for any given step rate and step height. For more information on step aerobics, refer to the *ACE Aerobics Instructor Manual,* published by the American Council on Exercise (1993).

Tennis, Racquetball and Handball

Tennis, racquetball and handball are all popular sports and deserve special attention for their ability to increase cardiorespiratory fitness. Each requires various motor skills and neuromuscular coordination, and the level and duration of play depend on these skills. For the beginner, racquet sports demand more from anaerobic energy systems than aerobic. However, as one becomes more skilled and efficient with movement and play, it is easier to prolong the activity and obtain more cardiorespiratory benefits. Improvements in cardiorespiratory fitness are dependent upon several factors:

- ✔ skill level and style of the player
- ✔ level of competition (intensity)
- ✔ total duration of each point played
- ✔ time interval between points and games
- ✔ total duration of entire exercise session

As the intensity and duration of these sports meet the criteria for cardiorespiratory endurance fitness (that is, 50 percent to 85 percent of maximal oxygen uptake for 20 to 60 minutes), they become more of a cardiorespiratory stimulus.

Racquetball and handball often are played in hot, unventilated environments, and require more attention to regular fluid intake and signs of dehydration. Generally, these racquet sports require at least average cardiorespiratory fitness and are excellent activities for developing and maintaining fitness.

Hiking and Backpacking

Hiking and backpacking activities can require high levels of cardiorespiratory endurance. Although most clients do not engage in these activities more than once a week, they are an excellent adjunct to

Monitoring Cardiorespiratory Exercise

a cardiorespiratory fitness program using fundamental aerobic activities such as jogging, cycling or aerobics. The energy cost (oxygen uptake and calories expended) per minute is lower for hiking and backpacking, depending on grade, packloads and altitude. The duration of such activity is usually prolonged (two to eight hours) and, therefore, the total energy cost is well above most routine aerobic workouts. It is important to be in at least average cardiorespiratory fitness, preferably the "good" classification (Table 7.10), before attempting prolonged variable-terrain hiking. One of the most important concerns with prolonged hiking is dehydration. Be sure to carry adequate water and glucose replacement on trips lasting longer than 60 minutes.

Many factors govern the cardiorespiratory and metabolic cost of hiking and backpacking. The following are among the most important:

- ✔ body weight of hiker
- ✔ duration of the hike
- ✔ number and size of the grades
- ✔ altitude at which the hike occurs
- ✔ speed of movement
- ✔ pack load
- ✔ air temperature

MONITORING CARDIORESPIRATORY EXERCISE

Monitoring cardiorespiratory exercise performance is necessary for assessing exercise response, regulating exercise intensity, documenting progress and assuring safety. Essentially, three techniques are used to monitor cardiorespiratory exercise: heart rate, ratings of perceived exertion and laboratory monitoring techniques.

Monitoring Heart Rates

As mentioned earlier, heart rate is a good guide for exercise intensity and cardiorespiratory responsiveness. The heart rate can be obtained by palpating (feeling) the pulse or by using a cardiotachometer or electrocardiogram. From a practical standpoint, palpation or feeling the pulse is the easiest method to assess heart rate. The pulse may be palpated in the neck (carotid artery), the head (temporal artery), the wrist (radial artery) or the chest (apical). For example, the carotid pulse may be felt by gently placing the index and middle finger over a carotid artery in the neck on either side of the larynx. It is important not to apply too much pressure as there are carotid sensors in these arteries that are sensitive to pressure and may induce a sudden drop in heart rate. Assessing the radial pulse in the wrist is done by placing the first two fingers (index and middle) on the underside and thumb side of the wrist. See Chapter 6 for a complete discussion on heart rate monitoring.

Heart Rate Response to Training. There are two trends to look for when monitoring the heart rate response to cardiorespiratory exercise training. First is the tendency of the heart rate, for any given level of exercise, to decrease with training. This tendency primarily applies to submaximal exercise, such as that between 60 percent and 80 percent of maximum functional capacity. For example, expect a decrease in heart rate for the same submaximal work load on a stationary cycle after several weeks of training. The actual decrease in exercise heart rate and the length of time required to elicit this change is variable between clients, but is primarily dependent upon age, initial level of fitness, length of the training program, and the exercise program intensity. Resting heart rate also tends to decrease with training along with the decrease in submaximal exercise heart rate. You must understand that there are other physiological reasons why resting heart rate may be low beyond that induced by endurance exercise training. A low resting pulse rate by itself is not by any means a perfect predictor of fitness.

Special Considerations and Safety

Required Time for Expected Increases in Aerobic Capacity

For young and middle-aged adults, the usual improvement in aerobic capacity will be 15 percent to 20 percent over 10 to 20 weeks of training (Pollock). However, aerobic capacity may increase up to 45 percent to 50 percent depending upon the following factors:

- ✔ initial level of fitness
- ✔ age
- ✔ frequency of training
- ✔ intensity of training

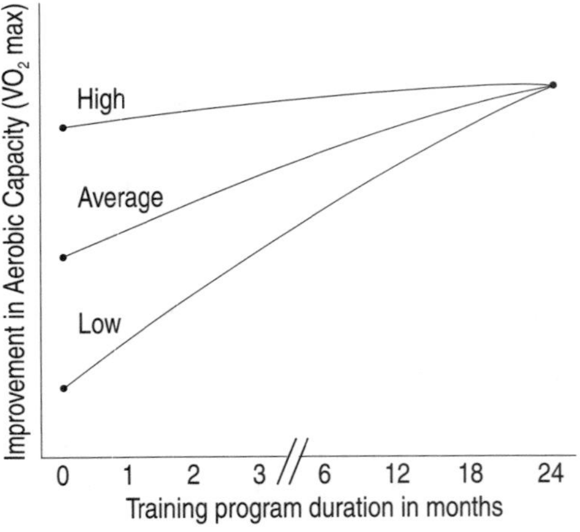

FIGURE 7.1
Hypothetical relationship between training program duration and improvements in aerobic capacity for three cardiorespiratory fitness levels (in healthy individuals).

- ✔ duration of exercise and total training programs
- ✔ genetics (oxidative processes, muscle fiber type ratio, etc.)

Those who begin a moderately intense cardiorespiratory conditioning program with a relatively high aerobic capacity can expect little improvement in aerobic capacity compared to those with initially low capacities. Age is not a detriment to increasing aerobic capacity in itself; however, training generally shows smaller improvements in aerobic capacity because of lower exercise intensities.

Overall, you can expect greater improvements with greater intensity and/or duration of exercise up to a point. This range for aerobic improvement is reflected in the mode, frequency, duration and intensity standards previously mentioned. For most clients, cardiorespiratory changes, including aerobic capacity, continue to take place over many months, perhaps up to 24, as depicted in Figure 7.1. This figure illustrates the relationship between initial functional capacity represented by three cardiorespiratory fitness levels and approximate times required to increase aerobic capacity (Pollock, 1973; Saltin et al., 1977; & McArdle et al., 1991). This will provide you with a general estimate of expected aerobic capacity changes compared to program duration. Note that endurance performance (increasing exercise duration) may increase with little or no further increase in aerobic capacity. This is more likely to occur during the latter stages of training, such as the maintenance stage. The time required for other changes to occur, such as body-fat reduction and coronary risk modification, will vary considerably.

SPECIAL CONSIDERATIONS AND SAFETY

You are responsible for determining current health status, developing an exercise program and following up on a variety of clients. Two areas of special importance are understanding and differentiating the various sources of cardiorespiratory exercise fatigue, and maximizing exercise safety.

The ability to recognize and differentiate exercise fatigue is especially helpful when evaluating self-report progress and teaching exertion limitation and safety precautions. Chapter 1 covers the physiology of aerobic and anaerobic capacity. This chapter will discuss only basic sources of endurance exercise fatigue and list their basic characteristics. These sources often overlap. For example, during longer exercise bouts, there may be heat fatigue, glycogen depletion and lactic acid accumulation. Becoming cognizant of each source of fatigue will better enable you to understand the spectrum of exercise res-

Special Considerations and Safety

ponses. Following are six basic sources and manifestations of fatigue observed in cardiorespiratory exercise programs:

1. Exercise fuel depletion. Liver and muscle glycogen (storage forms of carbohydrate) are at relatively low levels after 60 to 80 minutes of intense cardiorespiratory exercise, depending on the level of endurance fitness. This form of fatigue is focused in the exercising muscle groups and, if exercise continues, leads to increasing anaerobic work.

2. **Anaerobic** accumulation of **lactic acid**. This form of fatigue usually comes with over-pacing at too high an intensity, usually at levels of greater than 80 percent of maximal oxygen consumption or as a result of inadequate warm-up. Anaerobic accumulation of lactic acid may also occur with exercise in hot weather or exercise at relatively high altitudes (more than 5,000 feet). This fatigue has a relatively fast onset. It is characterized by the inability to sustain a pace or intensity, shortness of breath and by transient muscular weakness.

3. Hyperthermia-dehydration. This is a gradual increase in body temperature from prolonged aerobic exercise in hot, humid conditions and/or inadequate water replenishment during prolonged exercise. Elevated body temperatures, high heart rates, inability to sustain usual aerobic exercise intensities and mental confusion can characterize this form of exercise fatigue.

4. Musculoskeletal (orthopedic). Musculoskeletal discomfort exhibits "fatigue-like" qualities. This discomfort is often the result of overuse, with prolonged repetitive movements or unusual stress on a joint or bone from weight-bearing exercise, such as jogging. This form of fatigue is nearly always focused on the muscle, ligament, tendon or joint that is stressed, and is characterized by increasing joint or muscular tenderness that tends to worsen with repeated activity.

5. General overtraining syndrome or staleness. This syndrome refers to the final stage in a proposed continuum of increasingly severe chronic fatigue states that develop as a result of overtraining, especially high-volume endurance overtraining. Overtraining syndrome is characterized by persistent plateau or worsening in performance that is not improved by short-term rest periods or reduced training. It also is associated with disturbances in mood and sleep, loss of appetite and weight, muscle soreness, a propensity for overuse injuries or increased resting heart rate. Chapter 15 of this manual will address injury prevention in much greater depth. Refer to Raglin (1993) for a current and detailed review of overtraining and staleness syndrome monitoring. Ketner & Mellion (1995) have also written an excellent review of the pathophysiology of overtraining and treatment strategies.

6. Abnormal cardiac symptoms or chest discomfort (angina). Although uncommon, this form of "fatigue" would represent a contraindication to continued exercise and justify a physician referral. This symptom usually characterizes coronary artery disease and someone who is prone to heart attack. Symptoms include chest discomfort (aching, pressure, burning or tightness), that tends to come with physical effort and is relieved by rest. You should always ensure the client understands the seriousness of the symptoms and discontinues exercise, and should require the client to report these symptoms to a physician without delay.

Maximizing Exercise Safety

You should be aware of and understand the behavioral and environmental factors that can either alter the response to exercise or predispose the client to increased risk of injury or cardiovascular complications. These factors include post-meal exercise, thermal stress, air pollutants, drugs and other substances, and the presence of unusual symptoms.

Exercise Following Meals. Vigorous aerobic exercise soon after a full meal can cause the heart to work harder, compromise oxygen and nutrient delivery to the working muscles and cause gastric discomfort. Consequently, you should advise waiting at least 90 minutes after a full meal before beginning to engage in moderate- and higher-level aerobic exercise. The level of exercise and the amount and type of food ingested both affect the amount of time required for digestion to be completed before beginning exercise. The higher the exercise level and/or the greater the number of calories of food ingested, the longer the individual should wait between eating and exercise.

Thermal Stress. Exercise in hot, humid environments can place the client at risk for heat injury, as well as affect the usual intensity of exercise. Heat injury treatment is discussed in Chapter 16. Methods recommended by the American College of Sports Medicine and others (Vogel et al., 1993) can prevent thermal or heat stress.

1. Allow 10 to 14 days for acclimatization to a hot, humid environment.
2. Defer exercise if the heat index is in the "high risk" zone. (See Vogel et al., 1993).
3. Avoid training during the hottest part of the day, usually between 10 a.m. and 2 p.m., during summer months.
4. Drink 8 ounces of cold water about 20 minutes before exercising, and 4 to 8 ounces every 10 to 15 minutes during activity. Before and during exercise, fluid replacement should be accomplished with either water or approximately 6-percent glucose solution.
5. Wear loose-fitting clothing that will allow for the evaporation of sweat.
6. Adjust training intensity down by monitoring heart rate.
7. Incorporate compulsory rest periods of at least 10 minutes for every 45 to 50 minutes of physical activity.
8. Closely monitor daily body weight. If losses are greater than 3 percent of body weight they should be replaced by drinking before the next training session.
9. Give special consideration to, and use caution with, the following heat-susceptible persons: those unacclimatized to the heat, the obese, the unfit (low cardiorespiratory fitness classifications), the dehydrated and those with a previous history of heat stroke.

Air Pollutants. The principal air pollutants that may concern those who exercise outdoors in or near big cities are ozone, carbon monoxide and sulfur dioxide. The major factors in determining the dose are the concentration of the pollutant, the duration of the exposure and the volume of air inhaled. Since ventilation increases with the level of exercise, the effects of the pollutant will also depend on the intensity of exercise. See the ACSM *Resource Manual for Guidelines for Exercise Testing and Prescription* (1993) for a more detailed description of air pollution hazards and exercise.

Perhaps the most problematic of these pollutants is ozone or smog (not stratospheric ozone) that is formed by the reaction of a combination of ultraviolet light and emissions from internal combustion engines. The level of ozone we breathe is a function of weather patterns, traffic density and industrial output. Ozone exposure may impair lung function during moderate aerobic exercise at concentrations as low as .08 parts per million, which is at or below most air quality standards.

Carbon monoxide is another common air pollutant that can substantially reduce aerobic capacity. A 10 percent increase in carbon monoxide in the blood results in an approximate 10 percent reduction in maximal oxygen consumption. Moderate submaximal exercise in healthy individuals does not appear to be significantly affected by a 10 percent to 15 percent increase in blood carbon monoxide. Cardiac and pulmonary patients are generally affected by as little as a 5 percent increase in this pollutant. It also is noteworthy that because of the relatively slow removal of carbon monoxide from the blood (the clearance half-time is two to four hours), exposures that occur hours before an exercise session, on crowded freeways or in smoke-filled rooms, could influence aerobic performance.

Sulfur dioxide is most frequently produced in smelters, refineries and other stationary sources and is not a major irritant for most apparently healthy individuals. However, those persons with asthma or bronchospasm tendencies may be quite sensitive to sulfur dioxide.

Particulate matter (e.g., dust and smoke) are minute particles that are generally 3 to 10 microns in size that may arise from dust in windy conditions, or smoke from burning firewood. Smaller particles of 3 to 5 microns can easily penetrate the upper respiratory track whereas those less than 3 microns can settle in the alveoli. Such particulate inhalation can cause bronchoconstriction (asthma symptoms) and inflammation and congestion of the lower respiratory track.

You should be aware of the environmental air quality in your county. An excellent resource for local trends and standards of air quality is the county Air Quality Board or local Environmental Protection Agency. In most cities, one of these agencies or the weather bureau will periodically measure these pollutants and combine them into a Pollution Standards Index (PSI) that ranges from 0 to 500. Generally, PSI levels above 100 will affect those who are very unfit or who have cardiovascular or pulmonary disease, while levels greater than 150 are required to impair cardiorespiratory performance in healthy normal clients. By understanding environmental air quality standards and being knowledgeable of resources for more information, you can minimize unnecessary fatigue and respiratory distress in clients.

Drugs and Other Substances. There are a number of substances that, when combined with moderate to high level aerobic exercise, can increase the risk of cardiovascular complications and/or affect the response to exercise. These substances are certain prescription medications, alcohol, tobacco, strong stimulants and over-the-counter medications. Although each is briefly discussed here, refer to a comprehensive review of drugs and substances and their effects on exercise performance in the ACSM *Resource Manual for Guidelines for Exercise Testing and Prescription* (1993).

Virtually all beta-blocking drugs and some of the calcium-channel blocking medications prescribed for a variety of hypertensive and cardiac disorders lower the heart rate response to exercise (see Chapter 5). Although these medications may, in fact, increase the client's ability to perform safe exercise, it is important to understand that the heart rate response to both submaximal and maximal exercise will be blunted. Psychological medications can have side effects that could make exercise more difficult. Some anti-anxiety medications, such as phenothiazines, can reduce blood pressure and cardiac output, each of which can reduce exercise capacity.

One of the most prevalent categories of drugs employed in medicine, and one that you are likely to at least occasionally observe in your clients, is antihypertensive drugs (ie. blood pressure-lowering drugs). The major categories of anti-hypertensive drugs include diuretics, beta- and alpha-blockers, calcium channel blockers and ACE inhibitors. Within limitations, all of these antihypertensive agents can make exercise safer for the patient with high blood pressure. Diuretic drugs (e.g., thiazides) can induce a relative depletion of blood volume which can increase the vulnerability of a patient to hypotension in the post-exercise period. This side effect

Summary

of diuretics is of greater concern after prolonged exercise when dehydration may compound the problem.

Alcohol consumption before, during or after exercise can impair normal exercise heat exchange in prolonged exercise in hot weather. Smoking tobacco in any form increases blood carbon monoxide levels, which will decrease the oxygen consumption of the heart and skeletal muscles. Stimulants such as nicotine, amphetamines and especially cocaine all have the potential to induce abnormal cardiac rhythms and decrease coronary blood flow. These substances also may mask important signs of exercise fatigue which are important for the client to discern in order to adjust exercise intensity. Mixing these or combining any of these substances with near maximal or maximal aerobic exercise markedly increases risk of cardiovascular complications, even sudden cardiac death.

Over-the-counter medications such as decongestants, antihistamines and aspirin products are not contraindications to exercise by themselves but warrant attention because of the infections or ailments for which they are taken. You should caution clients who have viral infections to abstain from prolonged and/or intense aerobic exercise because of the potential for complications and cardiac rhythm disturbances.

Unusual Symptoms. Chest discomfort, musculoskeletal pain, dizziness, lightheadedness or malaise are indications to discontinue exercise and, in some cases, consult a physician. Exceptional chest discomfort (not necessarily chest "pain") such as aching, pressure, tightness or burning in the chest is always an indication to consult a physician. The client should never exceed the exercise threshold necessary to cause chest discomfort.

When a client experiences overall listlessness and/or recent onset lethargy (feelings of no energy) for no apparent reason, you should either have the client abort exercise or significantly decrease exercise intensity and duration. Such vague symptoms can precede viral infections and even be prodromal to cardiovascular complications.

Musculoskeletal pain or tenderness in a muscle or joint which tends to increase with increasing exercise intensity or duration is an indication to discontinue that particular mode and/or intensity of exercise (see Chapter 15). The beginner should be told to expect some minor muscle soreness and general post-exercise fatigue. These minor symptoms usually resolve themselves in several weeks; however, those musculoskeletal symptoms which tend to reproduce themselves over the course of several weeks warrant special attention.

Exercise during viral infections, such as the flu and upper respiratory infections, may lead to complications including worsening of the infections, an increase in body temperature and cardiac rhythm disturbances. You should advise rest and the usual recuperative recommendations as long as malaise, congestion or fever persist.

SUMMARY

Cardiorespiratory fitness, or the ability of the lungs to provide oxygen to the blood, and of the heart and circulatory system to transport blood and its nutrients to the tissues, is basic to all fitness programs. You must understand the physiology and application of each component of a cardiorespiratory exercise program: warm-up and cool-down; mode, frequency, duration and intensity of an exercise session; importance of supporting cardiorespiratory exercise with flexibility and strength exercise; development of a written exercise progression plan that is updated on a regular basis; and information and guidance necessary to ensure each client's safety, including when to defer exercise.

You have a variety of training methods and cardiorespiratory activities with which

Summary

to develop an exercise program that meets the needs of each client. You must be familiar with the application of, and the physiological response to, five basic training methods: continuous training, interval training, Fartlek training, circuit training and aerobic composite training. You also must provide guidelines for such popular aerobic and sport activities as walking, jogging, indoor and outdoor cycling, swimming, rowing, aerobics, stair-climbing, racquet sports and hiking. These guidelines include teaching clients to monitor their exercise intensity using such self-monitoring techniques as heart rate and/or ratings of perceived exertion. Finally, you must understand the various sources of cardiorespiratory exercise fatigue, environmental considerations, effects of a variety of drugs and medications, and take proactive steps to maximize exercise safety for each client.

REFERENCES/SUGGESTED READING

American Council on Exercise. (1993). Richard T. Cotton (Ed.) *Aerobics Instructor Manual.* San Diego.

American College of Sports Medicine. (1995). ACSM's *Guidelines for Exercise Testing and Prescription* (5th ed.) Baltimore: Williams and Wilkins.

American College of Sports Medicine. (1993). ACSM'S *Resource Manual for Guidelines for Exercise Testing and Prescription.* (2nd ed.) Philadelphia: Lea & Febiger.

American College of Sports Medicine. (1990). The recommended quantity and quality of exercise for developing and maintaining fitness in healthy adults. ACSM position statement. *Medicine and Science in Sports and Exercise,* 22, 265-274.

American Heart Association. January 15, 1995. Exercise standards: A statement for healthcare professionals from the American Heart Association. *Circulation,* 91, 2.

Astrand, P.O. & Rodahl, K. (1977). *Textbook of Work Physiology.* New York: McGraw-Hill.

Borg, G.B. (1982). Psychological basis of perceived exertion. *Medicine and Science in Sports and Exercise,* 14, 377-381.

Bouchard, C., Shepard, R., Stephens, T., Sutton, J. & McPherson, B. (1990). *Exercise Fitness and Health: A Consensus of Current Knowledge.* Champaign: Human Kinetics.

Carlton, R. & Rhodes, E. (1985). A critical review of the literature on the ratings scales of perceived exertion. *Sports Medicine,* 2, 198-222.

Dishman, R., Farquhar, R. & Cureton, K. (1994). Responses to preferred intensities of exertion in men differing in activity levels. *Medicine and Science in Sports and Exercise,* 26, 783.

Durstine, L. & Pate, R. (1993). Cardiorespiratory responses to acute exercise. ACSM's *Resource Manual for Guidelines for Exercise Testing and Prescription* (2nd ed.) Philadelphia: Lea & Febiger.

Folinsbee, L. (1990). Exercise and the environment. Brochard, C., Shepard R., Stephens T., Sutton J. & McPherson B. (Eds.) *Exercise Fitness and Health.* Champaign: Human Kinetics.

Franks D. & Howley, E. (1989). *Fitness Facts.* Champaign: Human Kinetics.

Greenberg, J. & Pargman, D. (1989). *Physical Fitness: A Wellness Approach* (2nd ed.) Englewood Cliffs, NJ: Prentice-Hall.

Haskell, W.L. (1994). Health consequences of physical activity: Understanding and challenges regarding dose-response. *Medicine and Science in Sports and Exercise,* 26, 649-660.

Herbert, W., & Herbert, D. *The Exercise Standards and Malpractice Reporter,* 1987 to present.

Heyward, V.H. (1984). *Designs for Fitness.* Minneapolis: Burgess Publishing.

Howley, E. & Franks, D (1992). *Health Fitness Instructor's Handbook* (2nd ed.) Champaign: Human Kinetics.

Howley, E. & Glover, M. (1974). The caloric costs of running and walking 1 mile for men and women. *Medicine and Science in Sports and Exercise,* 6, 235-237.

Ketner, J.B. & Mekkion, M.B. (1995). The overtraining syndrome: A review of presentation, pathophysiology, and treatment. *Medical Exercise Nutrition Health,* 4, 136-145.

McArdle, W., Katch, F. & Katch, V. (1991). *Exercise Physiology* (3rd ed.) Philadelphia: Lea & Febiger.

Nieman, D. (1990). *Fitness and Sports Medicine: An Introduction.* Palo Alto: Bull Publishing.

Ockene, I. & Ockene, J. (1992). *Prevention of Coronary Heart Disease.* Boston: Little Brown & Company.

Painter, P. & Haskell, W. (1993). Decision making in programming exercise. In American College of Sports Medicine's *Resource Manual for Guidelines for Exercise Testing and Prescription.* (2nd ed.) Philadelphia: Lea & Febiger.

Parker, S., Hurley, B., Hanlon, D. & Vaccaro, P. (1989). Failure of target heart rate to accurately monitor intensity during aerobic dance. *Medicine and Science in Sports and Exercise,* 21, 230.

Pollock, M. (1973). The quantification of endurance training programs. *Exercise and Sport Science Reviews,* 1, 155-188.

Pollock, M., Wilmore, J. & Fox, S. (1984). *Exercise in Health and Disease.* Philadelphia: Saunders.

Raglin, J.S. (1993). Overtraining and Staleness: Psychometric Monitoring of Endurance Athletes. *Handbook of Research on Sport Psychology.* Singer, R.B., Murphey, M. & Tennant L. (Eds.) New York: Macmillan.

Richie, D. (1989). Medical and legal implications of dance exercise leadership: The role of footwear. *Exercise Standards and Malpractice Reporter,* 3, 61.

Saltin, B, et al. (1977). Fiber types and metabolic potentials of skeletal muscles in sedentary men and endurance runners. *Annals of the New York Academy of Science,* 301, 3.

Shapiro, U. & Seidman, D. (1990). Field and clinical observations of exertional heat stroke patients. *Medicine and Science in Sports and Exercise,* 22, 1.

Van Camp, S. (1993). Pharmacologic factors in exercise and exercise testing. In American College of Sports Medicine's *Resource Manual for Guidelines for Exercise Testing and Prescription.* (2nd Ed.) Philadelphia: Lea & Febiger.

Vogel, J., Rock, P.B., Jones, B.H. & Havenith G. (1993). Environmental considerations in exercise testing and training. In American College of Sports Medicine's *Resource Manual for Guidelines for Exercise Testing and Prescription.* (2nd Ed.) Philadelphia: Lea & Febiger.

Whaley, M., Kaminsky, L., Dwyer, G., Getchell, L. & Norton, J. (1992). Questioning the routine use of 220 - AGE heart rate formula. *Medicine and Science in Sports and Exercise,* 24, 1173.

Wells, C. & Pate, R. (1988). Training for performance in prolonged exercise. Lamb, D. & Murray, R. (Eds.) *Prolonged Exercise* (Vol.1), 357-389. Carmel, IN: Benchmark Press.

Wilmore, J. H. & Costill, D. (1994) *Physiology of Sport and Exercise.* Champaign: Human Kinetics.

CHAPTER 8

Muscular Strength and Endurance

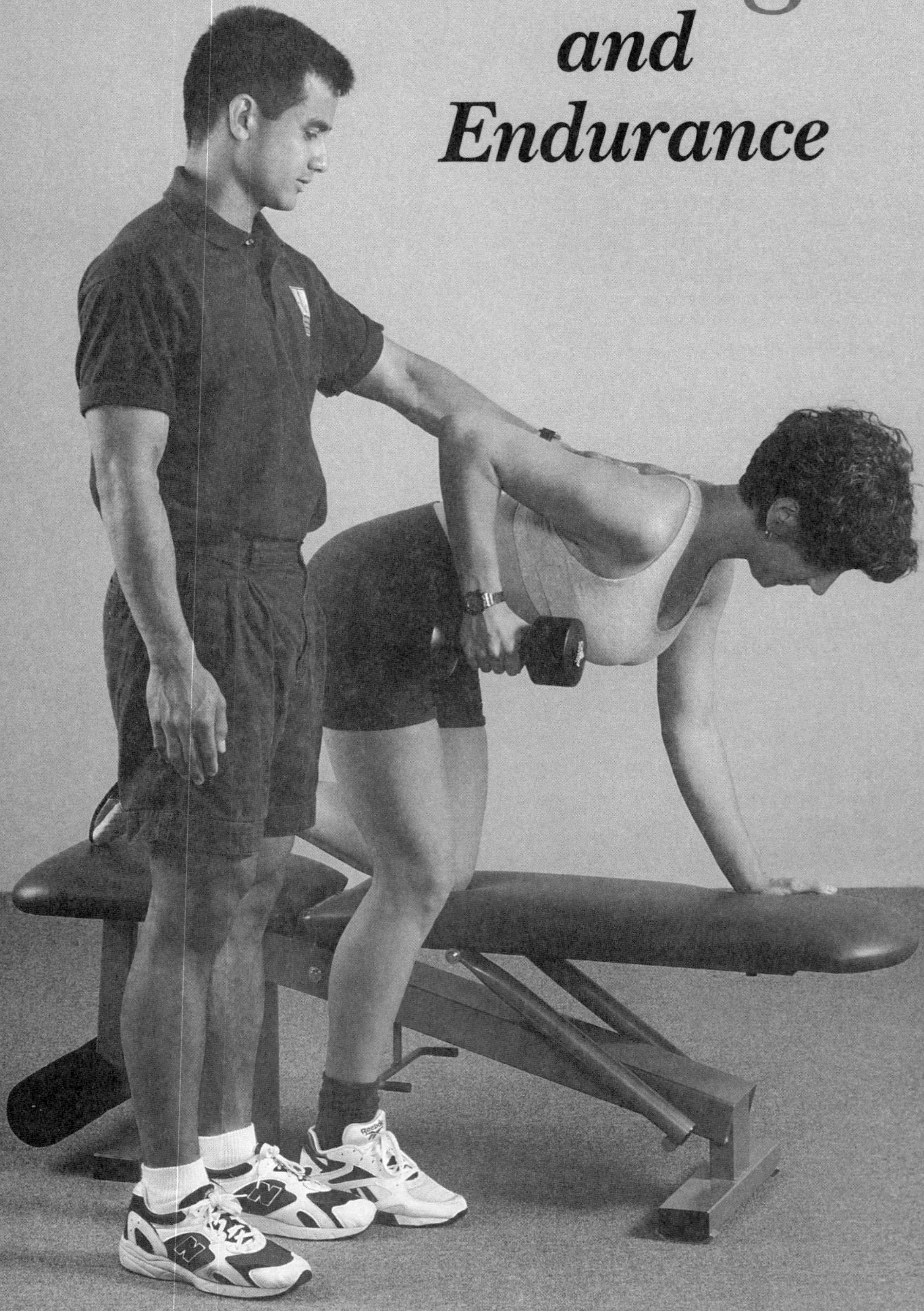

8

IN THIS CHAPTER:

Wayne L. Westcott

Wayne L. Westcott, Ph.D., is the Fitness Research Director for the South Shore YMCA in Quincy, Mass., and the author of numerous texts and articles on strength fitness. He has served as a strength training consultant for the YMCA of the USA, the President's Council on Physical Fitness and Sports, the American Council on Exercise, IDEA and Prevention, Men's Health, Fitness *and* Club Industry *magazines. Dr. Westcott has received both the Healthy American Fitness Leader and the IDEA Lifetime Achievement awards for service to the fitness profession.*

Every movement we make involves our muscular system. Muscles are unique in their ability to relax, contract and produce force. In addition, this metabolically active tissue is highly responsive to training stimuli. With appropriate exercise, muscles become larger and stronger; without appropriate exercise, muscles become smaller and weaker. This chapter presents information about the benefits of sensible strength training and the recommended procedures for safe, effective and efficient muscle development.

Strength Benefits

STRENGTH BENEFITS

Strength training is the process of exercising with progressively heavier resistance for the purpose of strengthening the musculoskeletal system. Physiologically, regular strength training results in the following positive adaptations:

- ✔ increased muscle fiber size
- ✔ increased muscle contractile strength
- ✔ increased tendon tensile strength
- ✔ increased bone strength
- ✔ increased ligament tensile strength

These beneficial changes within the musculoskeletal tissue have a profound influence on our physical capacity, physical appearance, metabolic function and injury risk.

Physical Capacity

Physical capacity may be loosely defined as one's ability to perform work or exercise. Muscles utilize energy to produce movement and generate strength, functioning as the engines of our bodies. Specifically, strength training increases the size and strength of our muscle fibers, resulting in a greater physical capacity to perform work. Stronger muscles enable us to lift a heavier weight once (muscle strength), and to lift a lighter weight more than once (muscle endurance).

Research indicates that previously untrained men and women gain about 2 to 4 pounds of muscle and 40 percent to 60 percent more strength after two months of regular strength exercise. The rate of muscle gain and strength development slows down after the initial training period, but typically continues for several months.

Physical Appearance

Our skeletal muscles have a lot to do with our overall physique. Consequently, strength training can play a major role in enhancing our **body composition** and physical appearance. Consider a 114-pound woman who is 24 percent fat (27 pounds fat weight, 87 pounds lean weight). If she loses 4 pounds of fat and adds 4 pounds of muscle she will still weigh 114 pounds but will be only 20 percent fat (23 pounds fat weight, 91 pounds lean weight). Although her body weight remains the same, she has less fat and more muscle for a leaner, firmer and fitter appearance.

Our physical appearance and capacity can be positively influenced by muscle gain or negatively influenced by muscle loss. Unfortunately, unless we perform regular strength exercise, we lose more than one-half pound of muscle every year of life after age 25. Without an appropriate training stimulus, our muscles gradually decrease in size and strength (atrophy). Strength training is essential for preventing the muscle loss that normally accompanies the aging process.

Metabolic Function

Muscle is very active tissue with high energy requirements for maintenance and rebuilding processes. Even while we sleep, our skeletal muscles are responsible for more than 25 percent of our calorie use. An increase in muscle tissue causes a corresponding increase in our metabolic rate; likewise, a decrease in muscle tissue causes a corresponding decrease in our metabolic rate.

The gradual loss of muscle tissue in nontraining adults leads to a 5-percent reduction in metabolic rate every decade of life. This gradual decrease in metabolism is closely related to the gradual increase in body fat that typically accompanies the aging process. When less energy is required for daily metabolic function, calories that were previously used by muscle tissue are stored as fat. Although our metabolism eventually slows down with age, this and other degenerative processes can be markedly delayed through regular strength training.

Injury Risk

In addition to functioning as the engines of the body, our muscles also serve as shock absorbers and balancing agents. Strong muscles help dissipate the repetitive landing forces experienced in weight-bearing activities such as running and aerobic dance. Balanced muscle development reduces the risk of overuse injuries that result when one muscle group is much stronger than its opposing muscle group. Jogging, for example, places more stress on the **posterior** leg muscles than the **anterior** leg muscles, creating a muscle imbalance that may cause knee injuries.

To reduce the risk of unbalanced muscle development, trainers should address opposing muscle groups such as the gastrocnemius and anterior tibialis muscles of the leg, quadriceps and hamstring muscles of the thigh, low-back and abdominal muscles of the midsection, pectoralis, latissimus dorsi and deltoid muscles of the torso, biceps and triceps muscles of the arm, and flexor and extensor muscles of the neck.

A comprehensive strength-training program that addresses all of the major muscle groups may be the most effective means for reducing the risk of injury and many degenerative diseases. Although four out of five Americans experience low-back discomfort, 80 percent of low-back problems are muscular in nature and appear to be preventable by strengthening the low-back muscles. Strength training also has been shown to increase bone mineral density, improve glucose metabolism, reduce gastrointestinal transit time, lower resting blood pressure, improve blood lipid levels and ease arthritic pain.

STRENGTH PRODUCTION

When a muscle is signaled to contract, it develops tension and attempts to shorten. The resulting movement, or lack of movement, depends on the relationship between muscular forces and resistive forces.

Isometric Contraction. When the muscular force is equal to the resistive force, there is no movement. This is known as an **isometric** contraction and is most representative of one's actual strength production. For example, if Ralph can hold a maximum weight of 50 pounds at 90 degrees of elbow flexion, his effective isometric force output is 50 pounds.

Concentric Contraction. When the muscular force is greater than the resistive force, the muscle shortens, resulting in a **concentric** (positive) contraction. Concentric contractions are not as strong as isometric contractions because internal muscle friction decreases the effective force output by about 20 percent. For example, Ralph can hold a maximum weight of 50 pounds at 90 degrees of elbow flexion (isometric contraction), but he can lift a maximum weight of 40 pounds in the biceps curl exercise (concentric contraction). Ralph's actual strength production is still 50 pounds, but internal muscle friction subtracts about 20 percent from his effective concentric force output.

Eccentric Contraction. When the muscular force is less than the resistive force, the muscle lengthens, resulting in an **eccentric (negative) contraction**. Eccentric contractions are stronger than isometric contractions because internal muscle friction increases the effective force output by about 20 percent. For example, Ralph can hold a maximum weight of 50 pounds at 90 degrees of elbow flexion (isometric contraction), but he can lower a maximum weight of 60 pounds in the biceps curl exercise (eccentric contraction). Ralph's actual strength production is still 50 pounds, but internal muscle friction adds about 20 percent to his effective eccentric force output.

Prime Mover Muscles. Muscles that are principally responsible for a given joint movement are called **prime mover muscles**. For example, the biceps muscles are prime movers, contracting concentrically during the lifting phase and eccentrically during the lowering phase of the biceps curl exercise.

Antagonist Muscles. Muscles that produce the opposite joint movement are referred to as antagonist muscles. For example, the triceps muscles responsible for elbow extension serve as **antagonists** to the biceps muscles. Antagonist muscles work cooperatively with prime mover muscles to produce smooth and controlled joint movements.

Stabilizer Muscles. Muscles that stabilize one joint so that the desired movement can occur at another joint are known as **stabilizer** muscles. For example, during the biceps curl exercise, the pectoralis major and latissimus dorsi muscles contract isometrically to stabilize the shoulder joint so that the desired movement can occur at the elbow joint.

Fiber Types. Muscles are composed of two primary fiber types: **slow-twitch (Type I)** and **fast-twitch (Type II).** The smaller slow-twitch fibers are better suited for aerobic energy utilization, and can produce relatively low levels of force for relatively long periods of time. The larger fast-twitch fibers are suited for anaerobic energy utilization, and can produce relatively high levels of force for relatively short periods of time. During a typical set of a strength exercise, both slow-twitch and fast-twitch muscle fibers actively participate in force production. The more fatigue-resistant slow-twitch fibers are recruited first. As resistive forces increase, the less fatigue-resistant fast-twitch fibers are recruited.

Motor Unit. A motor unit consists of a single motor nerve and all of the muscle fibers to which it attaches. A typical slow-twitch motor unit contains about 100 muscle fibers, and a typical fast-twitch motor unit contains about 500 muscle fibers. When activated, all of the muscle fibers in a motor unit maximally contract simultaneously. This is known as the **all or none principle.** Therefore, curling a 5-pound dumbbell requires only a few (slow-twitch) motor units, but curling a 35-pound dumbbell requires many (slow-twitch and fast-twitch) motor units. Much of the performance improvement during the initial weeks of strength training is due to more efficient motor unit utilization. This is known as the **motor learning effect.**

Muscle Fatigue. The temporary muscle fatigue encountered during an exercise set is most likely due to a variety of physiological changes within the working muscle. These factors may include lactic acid accumulation, increased tissue acidity, nerve impulse interference and chemical energy depletion. Temporary muscle fatigue and discomfort pass quickly upon cessation of the exercise.

Muscle Soreness. A more lasting form of muscle discomfort is known as **delayed onset muscle soreness (DOMS)**. DOMS is usually experienced 24 to 48 hours following a demanding strength-training session. It is typically associated with eccentric muscle contractions, and is most likely the result of microscopic tears in the muscle or connective tissue. DOMS indicates that a few non-training days may be required for the tissue repair and building processes that lead to stronger muscles.

STRENGTH FACTORS

We have little control over a number of factors that affect our strength performance. These include gender, age, limb length, muscle length, tendon insertion and muscle fiber type.

Gender. Gender does not affect the quality of our muscle, but it does influence the quantity. Although male and female muscle tissue is essentially the same, men typically have more muscle than women because muscle size is positively influenced by the presence of testosterone, a male sex hormone. Because most human muscles produce approximately 1 to 2 kilograms of force per square centimeter of cross-sectional area, larger muscles are stronger muscles. However, when evaluated on a pound-for-pound basis, men and women demonstrate similar strength performance. For example, one study evaluated quadriceps strength in more than 900 men and women. The average male performed 10 strict leg extensions with 62 percent of his body weight, and the average female completed 10 strict leg extensions with 55 percent of her body weight. However, when assessed in terms of lean body weight, average strength performances for the men and women were almost identical.

Age. Recent research has revealed that men and women of all ages can increase their muscle size and muscle strength through progressive strength training. However, the rate of strength gain appears to be greater during the years of normal growth and development, generally considered to be from ages 10 to 20.

Limb Length. There are several reasons for avoiding strength comparisons with other individuals. One of these is related to limb length. Other things being equal, people with short limbs may use more exercise resistance than people with long limbs because favorable leverage factors enhance effective force output. For example, Jim and John have identical strength capacity in their biceps muscles. However, because Jim has a shorter forearm he can hold more weight at 90 degrees of elbow flexion due to his leverage advantage.

Muscle Length. Muscles are attached to bones by **connective tissue** called tendons. Relative to bone length, some people have long muscles with short tendon attachments, while others have short muscles with long tendon attachments. Other things being equal, people with relatively long muscles have a greater potential for developing size and strength than people with relatively short muscles.

Tendon Insertion. Another factor that influences effective muscle strength is the point of tendon insertion. For example, Susan and Gayle both have the same forearm length and biceps strength. However, Susan's biceps tendon attaches to her forearm a little farther from her elbow joint than Gayle's. This gives Susan a biomechanical advantage that enables her to use more resistance than Gayle in elbow flexion exercises.

Muscle Fiber Type. Most men and wo- men have a fairly even mix of slow-twitch and fast-twitch fibers in the majority of their skeletal muscles. However, some people inherit a high percentage of slow-twitch muscle fibers, which enhances their performance potential for endurance exercise. For example, world-class distance runners are born with a preponderance of slow-twitch muscle fibers that, given appropriate training programs, enable them to be successful in their events. Other people inherit a high percentage of fast-twitch muscle fibers that enhances their performance potential for power activities. For example, world-class sprinters are born with a preponderance of fast-twitch muscle fibers that, given appropriate training programs, enable them to be successful in their events.

Although both fiber types respond positively to progressive resistance training, the fast-twitch fibers experience greater increases in size and strength (hypertrophy). Consequently, people with a preponderance of fast-twitch muscle fibers may obtain better results from their strength-training program.

Strength/ Endurance Relationships

STRENGTH/ENDURANCE RELATIONSHIPS

Muscle strength is defined as one's ability to perform a single repetition with maximum resistance. Muscle endurance is one's ability to perform many repetitions with a sub-maximum resistance. Muscle endurance may be evaluated at any point beyond the first repetition on the strength-endurance continuum.

Strength-Training Equipment

Although one may train specifically for muscle strength or muscle endurance, there is an inherent relationship between these abilities. Research indicates that most people can perform about 10 repetitions with 75 percent of their maximum resistance. For example, if Kim's maximum bench press is 100 pounds, she can most likely complete 10 repetitions with 75 pounds. If she increases her maximum bench press to 120 pounds, she should be able to complete 10 repetitions with 90 pounds. In other words, Kim's 10-repetition maximum resistance changes in direct proportion to her **one-repetition maximum.**

People with a high percentage of fast-twitch (low endurance) muscle fibers typically perform fewer repetitions with 75 percent of their maximum resistance, whereas people with a high percentage of slow-twitch (high endurance) muscle fibers typically perform more repetitions with 75 percent of their maximum resistance. Because the ratio of fast-twitch to slow-twitch muscle fibers is unaffected by training protocol, it appears that genetics largely determines our muscle endurance with a given percentage of maximum resistance.

STRENGTH-TRAINING EQUIPMENT

There are basically four categories of strength-training equipment. These include devices that provide isometric resistance, isokinetic resistance, dynamic constant resistance and dynamic variable resistance.

Isometric Equipment

Although **isometric (static) equipment** is frequently used for testing muscle strength, it is seldom recommended for developing muscle strength. This is because isometric muscle contractions restrict blood flow and may trigger unacceptable increases in blood pressure. Whenever possible, it is best to avoid isometric (static) forms of strength training. However, if isometric exercises are used, encourage the client to breathe continuously during each contraction.

The advantages of isometric exercise include little equipment, low cost, space efficiency and time efficiency. Disadvantages include blood pressure escalation, increases in strength only at specifically exercised positions in the movement range, training monotony and lack of performance feedback.

Isokinetic Equipment

Isokinetic equipment is characterized by a constant movement speed and a matching resistive force. That is, the amount of muscle force applied determines the amount of resistive force encountered. A greater muscle force produces a greater resistive force, and vice versa.

There are various types of isokinetic equipment, including hydraulic resistance machines and electronic resistance machines. Hydraulic machines provide resistance only during concentric muscle contractions. Some electronic machines provide resistance only during concentric muscle contractions, while others offer resistance during both the concentric and eccentric movements.

The advantages of isokinetic exercise include accommodating resistance forces, speed regulation and detailed performance feedback. Disadvantages include cost of equipment, inconsistent force regulation and lack of eccentric muscle contractions.

Dynamic Constant Resistance Equipment

Barbells are an example of **dynamic (isotonic) constant resistance equipment.** First, the amount of resistive force encountered determines the amount of muscle force applied. A greater resistive force requires a greater muscle force, and vice-versa. Second, the resistive force remains constant throughout the exercise movement.

However, due to the mechanics of human movement, the effective muscle force is higher in some positions and lower in other positions. As a result, the muscle effort varies throughout the exercise movement.

The advantages of dynamic constant resistance exercise include low cost of equipment, similarity to most work and exercise activities, variety of training movements, tangible evidence of improvement and easy accessibility. Disadvantages include the inability to train through a full range of joint motion in some exercises, and inconsistent matching of resistive forces and muscular forces throughout the exercise movements.

Dynamic Variable Resistance Equipment

Dynamic (isotonic) variable resistance equipment is similar to dynamic constant resistance equipment in that the amount of resistive force encountered determines the amount of muscle force applied. It is different in that the resistive force changes throughout the exercise movement. By the use of moving levers, cams or linkage systems, dynamic variable resistance machines provide proportionally less resistive force in weaker muscle positions and proportionally more resistive force in stronger muscle positions. Consequently, the muscle effort remains relatively constant throughout the exercise movement. Dynamic variable resistance is provided by specially designed weight stack machines and air pressure equipment.

The advantages of dynamic variable resistance exercise include the ability to train through a full range of joint motion on most exercises, reasonably consistent matching of resistive forces and muscular forces throughout the exercise movements and, in most cases, tangible evidence of improvement. Disadvantages include equipment expense, limited number of training movements and lack of accessibility.

STRENGTH-TRAINING GUIDELINES

Strength-Training Guidelines

There are as many ways to develop muscle strength as there are strength trainers. In fact, almost any form of progressive resistance exercise will stimulate some degree of strength gain. Unfortunately, many strength-training programs have a high rate of injury and a low rate of muscle development. The following exercise guidelines are basic to safe, effective and efficient strength training. While they may not be fully representative of advanced bodybuilding or weight-lifting routines, they provide a sensible approach for achieving high levels of strength fitness.

Exercise Selection. It is important to select at least one exercise for each major muscle group to ensure comprehensive muscle development. Training only a few muscle groups leads to muscle imbalance and increases the risk of injury. The major muscle groups include the quadriceps, hamstrings, hip adductors, hip abductors, low-back, abdominals, pectoralis major, rhom- boids, trapezius, latissimus dorsi, deltoids, biceps, triceps, neck flexors and neck extensors. Other muscle groups that should be trained regularly are the gluteals, obliques, gastrocnemius, anterior tibialis, forearm flexors and forearm extensors.

Exercise Sequence. When performing a series or circuit of strength exercises, it is advisable to proceed from the larger muscle groups of the legs to the smaller muscle groups of the torso, arms and neck. This allows you to perform the most demanding exercises when you are the least fatigued.

Exercise Speed. Exercise speed plays a major role in both injury risk and strength development. Lifting at a fast pace places a high level of stress on the muscles and connective tissue at the beginning of each movement. Lifting at a slower pace requires a more even application of muscle force throughout the movement range.

In addition, slow movement speeds are characterized by less momentum and less internal muscle friction. Although control is the major objective, a reasonable training recommendation is one to two seconds for each lifting movement (concentric contraction) and three to four seconds for each lowering movement (eccentric contraction).

Exercise Sets. An exercise set is usually defined as a number of successive repetitions performed without resting. The number of sets per exercise is largely a matter of personal preference. Several studies have shown similar strength gains from one, two or three sets of exercise. Clients who prefer single-set exercise usually continue to the point of momentary muscle failure, which is referred to as high-intensity training. Those who choose multiple-set exercise typically rest one to three minutes between sets. Multiple-set training may be advisable for clients who prefer not to push themselves hard on single-set exercise routines. Regardless of the number of sets performed, each repetition should be done using proper exercise form and control.

An advantage of multiple-set strength training is the higher-calorie use for the longer exercise session. An advantage of single-set strength training is the lower time requirement for the shorter exercise session.

Exercise Resistance and Repetitions. There is an inverse relationship between exercise resistance and exercise repetitions as you will note below.

Reps	% IRM
1	100
6	85
8	80
10	75
12	70
14	65

Training above 85 percent of maximum resistance increases the injury risk, and training below 65 percent of maximum resistance decreases the strength stimulus. Consequently, eight to 12 repetitions with 70 percent to 80 percent of maximum resistance is a sound training recommendation for safe and productive strength development. When performed in a controlled manner, eight to 12 repetitions with 70 percent to 80 percent of maxi-mum resistance require about 50 to 70 seconds of high-intensity (anaerobic) muscle effort.

Exercise Range. It is important to perform each exercise through a full range of joint movement, with emphasis on the completely contracted position. Full-range exercise movements are advantageous for strengthening the prime-mover muscles and for stretching the antagonist muscles, thereby enhancing both muscle strength and joint flexibility.

Exercise Progression. The key to strength development is progressive resistance. As the muscles adapt to a given exercise resistance, it must be gradually increased to stimulate further strength gains. Of course, the increase in resistance is usually accompanied by a temporary decrease in the number of repetitions performed with the heavier weightload.

A double progressive program, in which the client alternately increases repetitions and resistance, is recommended for safe and systematic muscle strengthening. The client begins with a resistance that can be performed at least eight times. When 12 repetitions can be completed, the resistance is increased by 5 percent or less. For example, when Mary works up to 12 repetitions with 50 pounds, she increases the resistance to 52.5 pounds. When she achieves 12 repetitions with 52.5 pounds, she increases the resistance to 55 pounds. Under some circumstances it may not be practical to increase the resistance by 5 percent or less. Although each case must be evaluated individually, it is not advisable to increase the resistance by more than 10 percent between successive training sessions.

Exercise Frequency. High-intensity resistance exercise may produce tissue microtrauma that temporarily reduces strength output and causes varying degrees of muscle soreness. This is why ample rest time between successive training sessions is so important. During this recovery period, the muscles synthesize proteins and build slightly higher levels of strength. Because the muscle rebuilding process typically requires about 48 hours, strength workouts should be scheduled on an every-other-day basis. Clients who prefer to train more frequently should avoid working the same muscle groups on consecutive days.

STRENGTH PROGRAM CONSIDERATIONS

These strength-training guidelines address those factors most essential for a safe and productive exercise session. However, there are additional considerations that may affect the overall training program.

Common Training Mistakes

The most common and critical training mistakes are related to exercise technique. The tendency to use too much resistance typically results in poor form, which decreases the training stimulus and increases the injury risk. Examples of unacceptable exercise form include rebounding the bar off the chest in the bench press, bouncing at the bottom of the squat, using hip/back extension to initiate barbell curls, bending backward under barbell presses and using momentum and fast training speeds.

Warm-up

It is always prudent to warm up prior to a strength-training workout. A few minutes of progressive warm-up exercise physiologically and psychologically prepares the body for higher levels of effort and energy utilization. Although warm-up routines may take many forms, it is advisable to include some light aerobic activity such as stationary cycling or stairclimbing. It also is important to perform stretching exercises for the major muscle groups, paying particular attention to the low back area.

Because many clients are pressed for time, they often eliminate or abbreviate the warm-up exercises. You should encourage clients to take full advantage of a progressive warm-up to reduce their risk of injury and enhance training responsiveness.

Cool-down

Blood tends to accumulate in the lower body when a vigorous exercise session is stopped abruptly. With reduced blood return, cardiac output decreases and lightheadedness may occur. Because muscle movement helps squeeze blood back to the heart, it is important to continue lower-level physical activity after the last exercise set is completed. Easy cycling and walking are appropriate cool-down activities. A few stretching exercises are recommended at the conclusion of the cool-down. Because of possible cardiovascular complications, you must not permit clients to omit the cool-down portion of their workout. As a general guideline, the last five to 10 minutes of the training session should be dedicated to cool-down activity.

Circuit Training

Circuit training is a form of strength training in which the participant performs a series of strength exercises with little rest between exercise stations. One popular system of circuit training involves a line of 10 to 12 exercise machines that work each major muscle group, from largest to smallest. This type of training is effective for strength development and is efficient in terms of time commitment. Generally, a 10 to 12 station strength circuit can be completed in 20 to 25 minutes. Although not the recommended means of cardiovascular conditioning, positive physiological adaptations result from maintaining a target-zone heart rate throughout a 20- to 25-minute circuit strength-training session.

Bodybuilding Routine

Some clients have the genetic potential and personal motivation to pursue competitive bodybuilding. The major objective in bodybuilding is to develop larger muscles. Bodybuilders typically perform several sets (four to six) of moderate repetitions (eight to 12) in each exercise, with brief rests (15 to 45 seconds) between sets. This produces blood accumulation within the muscles and is referred to as a muscle pump. Furthermore, bodybuilders generally perform three to five exercises per muscle group to maximize fiber involvement. Because bodybuilding routines are very demanding in terms of time and energy, many bodybuilders follow a six-day training schedule. For example, to provide ample rebuilding time they may train their legs, low back and abdominals on Mondays and Thursdays, their chest, shoulders and triceps on Tuesdays and Fridays, and their upper back, biceps and neck on Wednesdays and Saturdays.

Weight-lifting Routine

Some clients have the genetic potential and personal motivation to pursue competitive weight lifting. The main objective in weight lifting is to develop stronger muscles, particularly those involved in the competitive lifts. Olympic lifters compete in two explosive lifts — the clean and jerk, and the snatch. Power lifters compete in three slow lifts — the squat, the bench press and the dead lift.

Because strength maximization and sport specificity require the use of relatively heavy weightloads, weight lifters usually take long rests (three to six minutes) between sets. They generally perform several sets (six to eight) of low repetitions (two to six) in the competitive lifts and a few sets of supplementary exercises. Because the training programs may be very demanding and time consuming, some weight lifters perform different exercises on different days with ample rebuilding time for individual muscle groups.

Spotting

In terms of performance enhancement, few things work as well as a conscientious trainer who demands proper technique and full effort on every exercise set. An effective trainer gives plenty of encouragement and just enough assistance to permit completion of a final repetition. One of your most important functions as a trainer is to provide protection in high-risk barbell exercises such as squats, bench presses and incline presses. These lifts should not be performed without proper spotting, since failure to complete the final repetition could trap the client under a heavy barbell. During the squat, you should stand behind the client ready to help them to a standing position (arms around upper torso) if necessary. During the bench press and incline press, you should stand behind the bench ready to grasp the barbell and help lift it back to the standards when needed.

In addition to reducing the risk of injury, you can assist your clients by observing and modifying their training technique. Consequently, you provide an essential service for both free-weight and machine strength training.

Supplements

Muscle tissue is composed of approximately 75 percent to 80 percent water and about 20 percent **protein**. Protein has been emphasized as a muscle-building **nutrient**, and numerous protein supplements are available for the purpose of enhancing muscle growth. This is unfortunate for several reasons:

✔ The normal diet in modern nations

Strength Program Considerations

provides considerably more protein than the relatively small amount required for muscle development. In fact, a 175-pound adult requires only 80 grams of protein per day (1 gram of protein for every 2.2 pounds bodyweight), which is less than 3 ounces of protein daily.

- ✔ Protein consumption does not increase muscle size. After the growth years, muscles must be stimulated by progressive resistance exercise to increase their size and strength. In fact, even though American adults ingest plenty of protein, they lose more than one-half pound of muscle every year unless they perform regular strength training.
- ✔ Too much protein consumption can be physically harmful. Extra protein must be broken down metabolically, and the waste products must be excreted from the body, placing additional strain on the kidneys.

With regards to **vitamins** and **minerals,** a balanced diet typically provides an abundance of these nutrients. Two possible exceptions are calcium and iron. However, like protein, calcium is abundant in low-fat dairy products, and iron is obtained in lean meats, poultry and fish. Although a little extra protein and a daily 100 percent RDA vitamin/mineral pill may be advisable in some situations, a balanced daily diet (12 percent to 15 percent proteins, 20 percent to 30 percent fats, 55 percent to 65 percent carbohydrates) is the best recommendation for meeting normal nutritional needs (see Chapter 4).

Steroids

Anabolic steroids are synthetic derivatives of the male sex hormone testosterone and are taken to increase muscle size and strength. When combined with strength exercise, anabolic steroids may enhance muscle protein synthesis and tissue-building processes. However, the physical and psychological harm that may result from anabolic steroid use far outweighs all possible benefits. The potential consequences of anabolic steroid use include increased blood pressure, decreased levels of **HDL cholesterol,** liver enzyme leakage, liver cancer, testicle **atrophy**, sterility, breast shrinkage, uterus shrinkage and uncontrolled mood swings from depression to aggression. It is strongly recommended that anabolic steroids be avoided for medical and ethical reasons. Sensible strength training and proper nutrition are the keys to muscle development, without the risk of harmful side effects.

Program Discontinuation

If for some reason it is necessary to discontinue strength training, one result is certain. In the absence of a strength stimulus the muscles gradually become smaller and weaker (atrophy). Although the rate of decrease may vary among individuals, strength loss occurs at about one-half the rate of strength gain. For example, during a 12-week training program Natalie gained strength at the rate of 5 percent per week. If Natalie discontinues her training, she will most likely lose strength at the rate of 2.5 percent per week until she is slightly above her pre-training level of strength. Because eating habits tend to remain rather consistent, calories that were previously utilized during strength workouts are stored as fat. Less muscle mass results in a lower metabolic rate, further reducing calorie use and increasing fat stores. Without careful attention to diet, program discontinuation may be followed by simultaneous muscle loss and fat gain for a disappointing change in body composition, **physical capacity** and personal appearance. Fortunately, one or two brief workouts per week are sufficient to maintain strength levels for extended periods of time. It is therefore better to schedule an abbreviated strength-training program than to discontinue strength exercise altogether.

Strength Plateaus

STRENGTH PLATEAUS

After an initial period of strength gain, most clients experience a strength plateau during which their strength level remains essentially the same. Appropriate changes in the training program usually enable the exerciser to make further progress and attain progressively higher levels of strength. The following strategies have proved useful in overcoming strength plateaus.

Training Frequency. As we become stronger, we typically perform more demanding workouts. However, more stressful training sessions may require longer recovery periods for tissue-building processes. Consequently, it is often helpful to reduce the training frequency. For example, a person who normally rests two days between training sessions may obtain better results by taking three days to recover. A person who typically trains all of the major muscle groups three days per week may make further improvement by exercising the lower body muscles on Mondays and Thursdays, and the upper body muscles on Tuesdays and Fridays.

Training Exercises. Because our neuromuscular system adapts to specific movement patterns, it is advisable to change the training exercises occasionally. For example, if progress comes to a halt in the bench press exercise, then the incline press, chest cross or bar dip may serve as excellent substitutes. Although all of these exercises target the pectoralis major muscles, the different movements require different muscle-fiber activation patterns that may stimulate further strength development.

Training Sets. When strength development reaches a plateau, it may be helpful to vary the number of sets performed. People who have been training with multiple sets may benefit from switching to a single-set program. Conversely, single-set trainees may benefit from a multiple-set or a pre-exhaustion protocol. Pre-exhaustion training typically involves two successive exercises for a given muscle group. For example, a set of biceps curls followed immediately by a set of chin-ups may enhance the training stimulus to the biceps muscles.

Resistance/Repetitions Relationships. The neuromuscular system adapts to specific training workloads. Occasional changes in the resistance/repetitions relation- ship may be beneficial. For example, if eight repetitions with 80 pounds becomes a strength plateau, perhaps 12 repetitions with 70 pounds will produce additional strength gains. Some authorities recommend a planned program of **periodization** to enhance the strength-building stimulus. During the first month of training, for example, sets of 12 to 16 repetitions are performed. During the second month, this is reduced to sets of eight to 12 repetitions, and during the third month, it is further reduced to sets of four to eight repetitions. After a week of rest, the three-stage training program is repeated. Although some resistance/repetitions relationships appear to be more effective than others, the main objective is to avoid prolonged periods of training with the same workload.

Breakdown Training. Sometimes the training stimulus must be intensified to maximize muscle development. Breakdown training is one means of recruiting additional muscle fibers during an exercise set. For example, Claudia normally experiences momentary muscle failure after 10 leg extensions with 75 pounds. By immediately reducing the weight load to 65 pounds, Claudia can complete two or three post-fatigue repetitions. Breakdown training, although uncomfortable, enables Claudia to reach two levels of momentary muscle failure, and fatigue more muscle fibers in an extended exercise set.

Assisted Training. Assisted training is similar to breakdown training in that the resistance is reduced in accordance with the muscle's momentary strength capacity.

However, with assisted training a partner actually helps the client perform two or three post-fatigue repetitions. For example, Susan normally encounters momentary muscle failure after 12 leg curls with 70 pounds. By receiving a little partner assistance during the lifting movement, Susan can complete a few more repetitions and fatigue additional muscle fibers. Also, by not receiving assistance during the lowering movement, Susan emphasizes the eccentric muscle contractions.

Negative Training. Because effective muscle force output is greater during eccentric contractions, negative-only training with heavier weightloads may be useful for increasing muscle strength. Lowering weights that are too heavy to lift, however, creates a higher risk of injury for the muscles and connective tissue. It is therefore recommended that negative exercises be carefully controlled and supervised by a competent trainer. As indicated in the previous section, assisted training is an excellent means for emphasizing eccentric muscle contractions.

Another approach to negative training is body-weight exercises such as bar dips and chin-ups. For example, Gayle steps to the top position of a bar dip (elbows extended) and slowly lowers her body to the bottom position (elbows flexed). This exercise, with careful spotting from a trainer, permits controlled eccentric contractions in the pectoralis major and triceps muscles.

Slow Training. Another means for making the muscles work harder is to slow the movement speed. Slower speeds reduce the role of momentum and produce greater muscle tension. A general guideline is to take 10 seconds for each lifting movement, and four seconds for each lowering movement. It should require only four to six slow repetitions to produce temporary muscle fatigue, and the increased muscle effort will be noticeable.

It is not advisable to perform higher-intensity training techniques during every workout. This is because higher-intensity training requires additional recovery and building time. Also, research reveals that higher-intensity strength exercise is much more productive when supervised by an attentive trainer.

TRAINING MOTIVATION

Training Motivation

Though simplistic, exercise recording is an effective means for maintaining a consistent training schedule. By carefully recording each workout, you have a written progress account that provides your clients with added incentive to continue training. Record keeping is even more motivational when the workout charts are routinely reviewed, and appropriate exercise modifications are implemented.

It is hard to overestimate the value of your role as a concerned and communicative personal trainer. One of the best means of motivation is performance feedback, especially when pertinent exercise information is shared in a personal and positive manner. Encouragement and positive reinforcement are highly motivational, particularly for beginners who may be unsure of themselves. To be most meaningful, reinforcing comments should contain specific information emphasizing those things that the client is doing well. Perhaps the most powerful means of motivation is the strength-fitness model. Your physical appearance, training regularity, exercise technique and personal attitude provides an example that can significantly reduce or enhance the client's enthusiasm for strength training. See Chapter 14 for an in-depth discussion of teaching techniques for the personal trainer.

An important aspect of training motivation is maximizing the rate of improvement and minimizing the risk of injury. As a personal trainer, you should monitor each client's exercise intensity and recovery capacity to ensure optimum training results. On the one hand, clients should be encouraged to attain momentary muscle failure during each exercise set. On the other hand, clients should be discouraged from doing too much, and be observed for signs of overtraining. Persistent muscle soreness, prolonged fatigue, performance inconsistency and elevated resting heart rate are indications that the workload should be reduced or the recovery period should be increased. Also, distress symptoms that occur during a workout must be recognized and acted upon immediately. These include chest pain, blurred vision, dizziness, breathing difficulty and nausea. See Chapter 16 for detailed information on emergency procedures.

SUMMARY

Strength training improves **functional capacity** to work and exercise, enhances physical appearance, increases metabolic rate, reduces risk of injury, decreases resting blood pressure, builds bone density and protects against a variety of degenerative problems. To design safe and effective strength-training programs, you must understand the relationship between muscular forces and resistive forces, as well as the factors that affect strength performance. You must also be knowledgeable about the four categories of strength-training equipment: isometric, isokinetic, dynamic constant resistance and dynamic variable resistance.

Almost any form of progressive resistance exercise will stimulate some degree of strength gain. However, many strength-training programs have a high risk of injury and a low rate of muscle development. As a personal trainer, you need to employ guidelines that ensure safe, effective and efficient strength-training experiences for all of your clients.

Finally, you must be prepared to address the problems associated with anabolic steroids and **ergogenic aids**, implement techniques for overcoming strength plateaus, and know how to monitor and motivate clients to achieve optimal training results.

REFERENCES

Campbell, W., Crim, M., Young, V. & Evans, W. (1994). Increased energy requirements and changes in body composition with resistance training in older adults. *American Journal of Clinical Nutrition,* 60, 167-175.

DiNubile, N. A. (1991). Strength training. *Clinics in Sports Medicine,* 10 (1), 33-61.

Evans, W. & Rosenberg, I. (1992). *Biomarkers.* New York: Simon and Schuster.

Faigenbaum, A. D., Westcott, W. L., Micheli, L. J., et al. (1993). The effects of a twice-a-week strength training program on children. *Pediatric Exercise Science,* 5, 339-346.

Fiatarone, M. A., Marks, E. C. & Ryan, N. D. (1990). High-intensity strength training in nonagenarians. *Journal of the American Medical Association,* 263 (22), 3029-3034.

Forbes, G. B. (1976). The adult decline in lean body mass. *Human Biology,* 48, 161-173.

Frontera, W. R., Meredith, C. N., O'Reilly, H. G., et al. (1988). Strength conditioning in older men: Skeletal muscle hypertrophy and improved function. *Journal of Applied Physiology,* 64 (3), 1038-1044.

Harris, K. & Holly, R. (1987). Physiological response to circuit weight training in borderline hypertensive subjects. *Medicine and Science in Sports and Exercise,* 19, 246-252.

Hurley, B. (1994). Does strength training improve health status? *Strength and Conditioning Journal,* 16, 7-13.

Keyes, A., Taylor, H. L. & Grande, F. (1973). Basal metabolism and age of adult man. *Metabolism,* 22, 579-587.

Koffler, K., Enkes, A., Redmond, A., et al. (1992). Strength training accelerates in gastrointestinal transit in middle-aged and older men. *Medicine and Science in Sports and Exercise,* 24, 415-419.

Marino, M., Gleim, G. W. (1984). Muscle strength and fiber type. *Clinics in Sports Medicine,* 3 (1), 85-99.

Menkes, A., Maxel, S., Redmond, A., et al. (1993). Strength training increases regional bone mineral density and bone remodeling in middle-aged and older men. *Journal of Applied Physiology,* 74, 2478-2484.

Messier, S. P. & Dill, M. E. (1985). Alterations in strength and maximal oxygen uptake consequent to Nautilus circuit weight training. *Research Quarterly,* 56 (4), 345-351.

Mochizuki, R. M. & Richter, K. J. (1988). Cardiomyopathy and cerebrovascular accident associated with anabolic androgenic steroid use. *The Physician and Sports Medicine,* 16 (11), 109-112.

Morganti, C. M., Nelson, M. E., Fiatarone, M. A., et al. (1995). Strength improvements with one year of progressive resistance training in older women. *Medicine and Science in Sports and Exercise,* 27, (6), 906-912.

Risch, S., Nowell, N., Pollock, M., et al. (1993). Lumbar strengthening in chronic low back pain patients. *Spine,* 18, 232-238.

Stone, M., Blessing, D., Byrd, R., et al. (1982). Physiological effects of a short term resistive training program on middle-aged untrained men. *National Strength and Conditioning Association Journal,* 4, 116-20.

Tufts University. (1994). Never too late to build up your muscle. *Tufts University Diet and Nutrition Letter,* 12 (Sept.), 6-7.

Westcott, W. L. (1991). Role model instructors. *Fitness Management,* 7 (4), 48-50.

Westcott, W. L. (1993). Strength training for life: How many repetitions? *Nautilus Magazine,* 2 (3), Summer, 6-7.

Westcott, W. L. (1994). Strength training for life: High-intensity training. *Nautilus Magazine,* 4 (1), Winter, 5-8.

Westcott, W. L. (1995). *Strength Fitness: Physiological Principals and Training Techniques,* (4th ed.) Dubuque: Wm. C. Brown Publishers.

Westcott, W. L. (1995). High-intensity strength training. *IDEA Personal Trainer,* 6, 9.

Westcott, W. L. (1995). School-based conditioning programs for physically unfit children. *Strength and Conditioning,* 17 (2), 5-9.

Westcott, W. L. (1995). Twelve reasons every adult should strength train. *Nautilus Magazine,* 4 (3), Summer, 36-37.

Westcott, W. L. (1995). Strength training for life: Women vs. men. *Nautilus Magazine,* 4 (4), Fall, 3-5.

Westcott, W. L. (1995). Strength training for life: The up and down. *Nautilus Magazine,* 5 (1), Winter, 3-5.

Westcott, W. L. (1996). Strength training for life: Make your method count. *Nautilus Magazine,* 5 (2), Spring, 3-5.

SUGGESTED READING

Baechle, T. R. & Groves, B. R. (1992). *Weight Training: Steps to Success.* Champaign: Leisure Press.

Baechle, T. R. & Earle, R. N. (1995). *Fitness Weight Training.* Champaign: Human Kinetics.

Brzycki, M. (1995). *A Practical Approach to Strength Training.* (3rd ed.) Indianapolis: Masters Press.

Brzycki, M. (1995). *Youth Strength and Conditioning.* Indianapolis: Masters Press.

Fleck, S. J. & Kraemer, W. J. (1987). *Designing Resistance Training Programs.* Champaign: Human Kinetics.

Westcott, W. L. (1995). *Strength Fitness.* (4th ed.) Dubuque: Brown & Benchmark.

Westcott, W. L. (1996). *Building Strength and Stamina.* Champaign: Human Kinetics.

CHAPTER 9

Strength Training Program Design

9

IN THIS CHAPTER:

Douglas S. Brooks

Douglas S. Brooks, M.S., holds a master's degree in exercise physiology, and is the author of Going Solo... The Art of Personal Training, *and* Program Design For Personal Trainers: Bridging Theory Into Application, *as well as numerous educational manuals. Mr. Brooks frequently conducts lectures and workshops on exercise physiology, kinesiology, strength training and personal training throughout the world.*

Resistance-training program design is crucial to a well-rounded fitness program and the overall health of your clients. The term resistance training is used to cover all types of "strength" or "weight" training. The best approach to program design is often difficult to identify because there are numerous "training systems" you can choose or create. They can be defined as any combination of sets, repetitions and loads, and every imaginable kind of training system exists, from the light to heavy system, bulks and super-set system to the cheat system. At least 27 different systems are listed by Fleck and Kraemer (1987), and this is not an exhaustive list.

Training systems can be easily understood and categorized by realizing that any system will utilize one or more of the six types of resistance

Table 9.1
Six Types of Resistance Training

1. Isometric force development
2. Concentric contraction
3. Eccentric force development
4. Dynamic constant resistance*
5. Dynamic variable resistance
6. Isokinetics

*Dynamic constant resistance is often labeled as isotonic training, even though this is an imprecise term (see Chapter 1).

training discussed in Chapters 1, 8 and 9 (Table 9.1). Furthermore, all systems fit into the Specificity Chart (Table 9.2) based on the number of repetitions, sets and loads (intensity) that they use. While most scientists agree on some definable parameters for effective program design, the best approach is a combination of science and art.

The defining variables in terms of results may lie in how often a person trains and how they arrange the order and number of sets, repetitions (volume) and loads (intensity), which may be the most important of these factors. Exactly how to vary the frequency, intensity and duration within a periodization plan is the art of resistance-training program design. These factors are of little value, however, until you determine your clients' goals and understand what motivates them.

DESIGNING RESISTANCE-TRAINING PROGRAMS

The real trick in designing your clients' resistance-training programs is determining their unique needs and interests. Develop the goals of the program by first listening to what your clients think they want to accomplish, and second, acting on what you hear. Do not make the mistake of blindly adapting a program simply because it was used, for example, by a successful weight-trained athlete. Researchers have confirmed that there is no one optimal combination of sets and repetitions. Most systems or combinations of repetitions, sets and loads will often produce results in spite of their design, because the body will adapt to any load to which it is not accustomed. However, results in and of themselves do not mean you have the best and safest design. Make sure the training systems you choose, or better yet develop, meet both your client's needs and current situation.

Using and copying one style of training for both athletics and fitness is a common mistake when planning resistance-training programs. The needs of the general fitness enthusiast are different from those of athletes.

Training Smart: Implications for Training Your Clients

Resistance training can be:

- ✔ planned and time efficient
- ✔ results-oriented
- ✔ functional and usable in relation to your clients' personal lifestyles
- ✔ directed toward health and personal wellness

The American College of Sports Medicine (ACSM) recommends resistance training at a moderate-to-high intensity that is sufficient to develop and maintain muscle mass (ACSM, 1990). This should be done at least two days per week for a minimum of one set of eight to 12 repetitions that are executed to fatigue. Complete eight to 10 exercises that challenge the major muscle groups.

These minimal standards influence resistance-training programming in two ways. First, the time it takes to complete a comprehensive, well-rounded program. Those that last more than 60 minutes per session are associated with high dropout rates. Second, although more frequent training and additional sets, or varied combinations of sets and repetitions, elicit greater strength gains, the difference is usually

Table 9.2
Training Specificity and Recovery Time

Relative Loading	Outcome	% 1 RM	Rep Range	# Of Sets	Rest Between Sets
Light	Muscular endurance	< 70	12-20	1-3	20-30 seconds
Moderate	Hypertrophy, strength	70-80	8-12	1-6	30-120 seconds
Heavy	Maximum strength/power	80-100	1-8	1-5+	2-5 minutes

Adapted from Baechle et al., 1992.

small. In fact, strength training two days per week in accordance with these guidelines produces about 80 percent of the strength gains seen when training three days per week. When coupled with significant results, the lower frequency may encourage adherence. Braith et al. (as reported in the ACSM position statement) found that those who performed one set to fatigue showed a greater than 25 percent increase in strength. These results are favorable when compared to other, more time-intensive programs that involve more total repetitions, sets and days of training. By training smart, you can effectively and efficiently utilize your clients' time investment to maximize their health and fitness improvements related to muscular fitness.

When designing programs for your clients, use this simple needs-analysis process. Answers to these questions will largely determine your resistance-training programming approach:

1. What are your clients' goals? Common goals include muscular hypertrophy, increasing maximal lifts, better performance in a particular sport, decreased body fat, feeling stronger, general health enhancement, personal physical independence and increased self-esteem.

2. What are the requirements of the activities or sports your clients participate in? Based on your clients' goals, training scenarios will emerge that may require you to design programs that emphasize general health and fitness, functional strength and balance, and/or training for a competitive sport such as body building, race walking or volleyball. Analyze activities with regard to their requirements for muscular strength and/or endurance, sport specificity with regard to requisite movement patterns, and any special training requirements such as **plyometrics**. It is necessary to weigh these considerations against the current fitness and experience base of your clients.

3. Is training dictated by the needs of the individual or the requirements of a sport? In a competitive coaching situation, athletes continue their participation based on a desire and ability to excel, often at any cost. For example, power lifting requires a full squat; the rules of the sport demand its execution regardless of the risk to the athlete. However, if your clients' needs — such as health, fitness and well-being — are the priority, you have considerable flexibility in the approach you take to program design.

4. How much time will your clients commit? It is impossible to develop an effective resistance-training program without knowing how much available time your clients have. Part of your responsibility, based on the information that you gathered in steps one, two and three, is to let your clients know what kind of time investment they have to make to attain their goals. For example, strength-training goals, unless connected to elite performance, can usually be accomplished as part of a workout that also includes cardiorespiratory and flexibility training components. Work to

accommodate the time offered by your clients, even if it is limited, without creating unrealistic expectations. The key to success with limited client time is to help them plan independent workouts.

Overload

Muscular strength, cardiorespiratory and flexibility training are primary components of a balanced approach to fitness. All three require different overloads to achieve optimum results. Muscular fitness is developed by placing a demand, or overload, on the muscles in a manner to which they are not accustomed. If the overload is applied progressively and sensibly, the neuromuscular system will positively adapt to the demand.

The general guideline for change is a proper and specific overload that uses a progressive increase in resistance over time, causes the targeted muscle(s) to fatigue in about 30 to 90 seconds, and challenges all of the major movements (joint actions) to which the muscle(s) contribute.

A progressive increase in resistance provides continued improvements in muscle strength and endurance. Appropriate **intensity** (attaining momentary muscular fatigue in about 30 to 90 seconds) is necessary to optimize training results. Gradual intensity increases will reduce the likelihood of injury. All of the major movements of the body must be challenged to ensure balanced strength between all of the opposing muscle groups.

FOUR PROGRAM DESIGN SCENARIOS

The following outlines for four program design scenarios, ranging from health and fitness to competitive athletics, present the multitude of approaches available to meet the varied and diverse needs of your clients. These approaches should not be evaluated in terms of absolute correctness, but for their appropriateness to your clients' specific training goals.

Health and Fitness Gains

Significant gains in strength and muscular endurance can be achieved with just two exercise sessions per week. For your clients, this means at least 10 exercises that target all of the major muscle groups. At least one set of eight to 12 repetitions, completed to fatigue, should be performed to gain health benefits.

Most of your clients' health and fitness goals can be optimized by using **active recovery** between sets. For example, performing a stretching exercise or working another body part can facilitate recovery from a previous strength exercise without requiring total inactivity, and allows for more productive use of limited time.

And, because the health benefits associated with resistance training can occur at any age, it's easy to get clients, young and old, excited about resistance training (see Chapter 8).

Functional Training

Functional training requires an integration of balance and intrinsic muscular stability during the exertion of muscular force and often uses closed-chain movement. Exercise can be classified into either closed-or **open-chain** movements. The "chain" refers to the movement chain formed to initiate the activity. In a **closed-chain** activity, the end of the movement chain is fixed against an object such as the floor and supports the weight of the body, whereas in an open-chain activity, the end of the chain remains open, or free. Closed-chain exercises more closely approximate human movement. For example, squats and lunges not only work the glutes, but also important stabilizer muscles, providing for a more functional type of strength. This not only translates into better performance from your body during daily activities, but also helps reduce problems caused by poor body awareness. On the other hand, an open chain exercise such as the leg extension can "isolate" the knee joint in such a way that only the quadricep muscle is used and does not require an integrated response by the body. This does not mean that you should never use this exercise. As a matter of fact, isolation exercises may be used in the beginning of a program where deconditioned or unfit people lack the neuromuscular control and joint stability to safely perform a multi-joint exercise. A stability ball, a large, round air-filled ball, and soft mats, are excellent tools for use in functional training to improve stability and balance.

Bodybuilding

The training goal for bodybuilders centers around balanced muscular size, symmetry and definition. Their training routines encompass a variety of exercises to promote ideal gains in size and symmetry. Generally, a moderate intensity (eight to 12 repetitions to fatigue) is used to allow for the completion of high volume, which is determined by the equation: load x repetitions x sets. A load of eight to 12 repetitions done to fatigue seems logical as the goal of bodybuilding is not superior maximal strength. However, for maximal hypertrophy gains, research suggests training should emphasize increases in resistance, as well as volume. High-intensity volume stress may be the primary stimulus to muscle hypertrophy. The order of exercises within a specific muscle group is more important than the order in which the muscle groups are exercised. Multiple or giant sets are used to accomplish volume overload. These consist of three to six sets and can go as high as 10 to 15 repetitions per exercise. Short rest periods are a distinctive feature of bodybuilding. Thirty- to 90-second rests seem to promote muscular definition, vascularity and a high metabolic intensity that may help lower body fat.

Bodybuilders may work a full-body routine that targets all of the major muscle groups, or split routines, which work different body parts on alternate days. Clients should allow for two workouts per week for most muscle groups. Generally, a split routine schedule requires four to six workouts per week, and some research suggests that three full-body workouts per week may be sufficient to stimulate adaptive responses. This is important to consider since more frequent, all-out training increases the potential for overuse and poor adaptive responses to the workload.

Competitive Athlete

Are sport-specific strength-training movements (i.e., plyometrics and skill practice, which involves trying to preserve movement speed with a load) better than developing base strength traditionally and then "practicing" to see what strength carries over and is applicable to performance? While the question of specificity seems critical in designing a program for the competitive athlete, science has been unable to offer a definitive answer as to whether it is a more effective training method. You should experiment with both approaches or a combination of the two. Individual response and results will dictate the approach you follow.

PROPER INTENSITY

Results depend on proper intensity. If, in the repetition scheme suggested, you can bring the muscle to temporary fatigue (one or two repetitions with good form remain), exceptional results will occur. It is not absolutely necessary for you to force your clients to "true" muscle failure. Most clients will experience significant results if they are close to fatigue. The key is not how much absolute weight or resistance is used, but whether the overload is relative to the individual's current strength level and whether the muscle can fatigue within the goal repetition framework.

Intensity of effort related to strength training and best results can be demonstrated by

Proper Intensity

Table 9.3
Benefits of Controlling the Speed of Movement

1. Consistent application of force
2. More total muscle tension produced
3. More total muscle force produced
4. More muscle fiber activation (both ST and FT)
5. Greater muscle power potential through high intensity force development and, subsequently, through controlled training
6. Less tissue trauma
7. Greater momentum increases injury potential and reduces the training effect on target muscle groups

Exceptions to the above may be appropriate in sport-specific applications and when your client understands the risks.

Source: Westcott, 1991.

a thorough understanding of motor units and their contribution to muscle contraction (see Chapter 1). When the nervous system commands a motor unit to contract, all the muscle fibers of this single motor unit respond together. There is no such thing as a weak or partial contraction from a motor unit — it simply fires "all-or-none." Innervation of a single motor unit does not mean stimulation of the entire muscle. If it did, you could not control movement. The way in which motor units activate fibers is crucial to skilled and/or powerful movement.

Varying the intensity of muscle contraction, or force gradation, occurs in two ways: 1) raising the number of motor units recruited for activity; and 2) increasing their frequency of discharge. By blending these two types of gradation, optimal patterns of neural discharge permit a wide variety of scaled (weak to strong) contractions (McArdle et al., 1991).

Motor units are comprised of two distinct types of fibers: **fast twitch (FT)** and **slow twitch (ST)** (see Chapter 1). During an activity involving muscular contraction, the order in which ST and FT motor units are recruited is relatively constant. It depends upon the type of activity, the force required and the position of the body. This modulatory effect is referred to as a "ramp-like recruitment effect." If a light weight is being lifted slowly, predominantly ST motor units are recruited to perform this movement. If the weight is increased or moved at a faster velocity, FT (Type IIa and IIb) motor units are recruited in addition to the continual contribution of ST units. At maximal force production, all three types of motor units will be required.

The order of recruitment holds the FT motor units, which are highly fatigable, in reserve until the ST motor units can no longer perform the particular muscular contraction. When your clients engage in high-repetition schemes, about 20 repetitions or higher, the intensity is not sufficient enough to significantly call the FT motor units into play. This implies that since the average participant has a ratio of 50 percent FT to ST motor units, 50 percent of the muscle mass in the body, which is especially well-suited for gains in strength and hypertrophy, will not be challenged.

Motor unit recruitment order is important from a practical standpoint for several reasons (Fleck and Kraemer, 1987):

1. As previously discussed, in order to recruit FT fibers and achieve a training effect, the exercise must be higher in intensity.
2. The order of recruitment is fixed for a specific movement (Desmedt & Godaux, 1977; as reported in Fleck & Kraemer, 1987).

If the body position is changed, the order of recruitment can also change (Grimby & Hannerz, 1977; as reported in Fleck & Kraemer, 1987). Furthermore, the order also can change from one movement to another for multifunctional muscles. For example, motor unit recruitment order in the quadriceps is different for the performance of a seated leg extension on a machine than for a knee extension during the performance of a squat (Fleck & Kraemer, 1987). The variation in recruitment order provides some evidence to support the belief that in order to completely develop a particular muscle (all the motor units), it must be exercised through several different movements.

This information suggests that all training done at a slow pace, or with light force, will emphasize the use of mostly the ST fibers, inducing little training effect on the FT IIa or FT IIb fibers. Long, slow training bouts do not prepare the muscle for the demands of competition or higher forces, and do not optimize the stimulation and training effect of your clients' muscle mass.

Movement Speed

For the average client, gains in strength will be best accomplished by moving the weight slowly (about four to five seconds per repetition) through a full range of motion, and accomplishing FT recruitment by using an appropriately intense overload (Table 9.3).

Starting Resistance

A safe starting resistance for most clients is one that allows completion of at least 12 to 20 repetitions. This intensity equates to less than 70 percent of **one repetition maximum (1 RM)** and is generally a safe starting intensity for most people (see Chapter 8). The repetition goal range is determined by a variety of factors that include the client's current fitness level specific to resistance training, current exercise history and their stated resistance training goals, for example, muscle endurance or muscle hypertrophy.

Initially, you may prefer not to test your clients' ability to lift their maximum weight one time (1RM), as this places them in a high-risk, maximal performance situation for which they may not be ready. Instead, start with too little weight and gradually increase resistance when the maximum number of repetitions are performed. The focus of early workouts is not to create muscle failure, but to work on technique and allow the tissues of the body to adapt progressively to new challenges.

Recovery Between Sets

High-intensity resistance training relies primarily on the ATP-CP and lactic acid energy systems, both of which are replenished during the recovery period using the aerobic energy system. Intensity and duration of effort influences the predominance of one energy system over the other (see Chapter 1).

The complete rebuilding of the **ATP-CP energy system**, which is depleted predominantly through short bursts of maximal effort, takes about three to five minutes. That is why, for example, power and Olympic lifters take at least several minutes, usually up to five, to recover from all-out maximal lifts; the ATP-CP energy system must fully recover before these athletes can correctly and safely execute the next lift.

As maximal or strenuous efforts go beyond 10 seconds, the short-term or **lactic acid system** begins to substantially contribute to energy production in an attempt to sustain and assist in the maintenance of a high level, predominantly anaerobic effort (i.e., failure or muscle fatigue in about 30 to 90 seconds).

Half of accumulated lactic acid is metabolized within 25 minutes of recovery and almost all is metabolized within 75 minutes. It would not be practical to rest long enough between sets to completely clear lactate from the body. Fortunately, the body's musculature can sustain quality activity without a complete recovery of lactate levels. Can you imagine your clients waiting 25 minutes to an hour between sets of resistance-training exercise?

Expediting Lactic Acid Clearance

Light activity is encouraged to facilitate lactic acid removal more quickly. Rest periods that use light activity for this purpose must last at least two minutes to be

Proper Intensity

effective if significant lactate has accumulated and recovery is required. The lactic acid system makes a significant energy contribution during hard workouts where sets are performed to failure in one to three minutes. Unless muscular endurance and a high tolerance to high levels of lactate is a goal, fatigue in 30 to 90 seconds is recommended. This is time efficient and will probably enhance most of your clients' health, fitness and muscular strength and endurance goals.

Practical Implications of an Active Recovery

"Active rest" equates to accomplishing more total work in limited amounts of time. An example of active rest would be as follows: have your client perform a chest exercise, then an abdominal exer- cise and then a lower-body exercise. Even though your client is continually active through all three exercises, there is sufficient recovery time for the chest musculature as the body performs the abdominal and lower-body exercises.

Adequate recovery allows your clients to prepare for and perform another quality effort or training set. Shorter recovery times do increase relative intensity. To determine whether adaptations related to shorter recovery times are relevant and useful to your clients, ask yourself:

1. Is the recovery duration appropriate for your client's program goals?
2. Is the recovery duration appropriate for your client's fitness level?
3. What is the client trying to accomplish (i.e., muscular strength, endurance, hypertrophy and/or exercise compliance and health benefits)?

Specificity and Recovery Between Sets

Look at the specificity chart (Table 9.2) and note the recommended amounts of rest between sets for light, moderate and heavy loading by resistance. You will notice that the longest recovery period is five minutes.

Why is it not necessary to recover longer for sets of exhaustive work (i.e., eight to 20 repetitions to fatigue in about 30 to 90 seconds) where major contributions of both the ATP-CP and lactic acid systems are prevalent? First, the question of recovery has been answered regarding the depletion of ATP-CP sources, for example, with 1 RM lifts and heavy relative loading. About two to five minutes are required for complete recovery. During relatively light loading (i.e., 12 to 20 repetitions and less than 70 percent of 1 RM), there are not maximal contributions from either anaerobic energy system (ATP-CP and lactic acid systems). Therefore, complete exhaustion of the ATP-CP system does not occur, nor do significant accumulations of lactate via use of the lactic acid system. Short rests of 20 to 30 seconds, as recommended by the specificity chart, are usually adequate for recovery and allow for another quality set of training. Even moderate loading, which causes muscle fatigue in about eight to 12 repetitions and 30 to 90 seconds, does not require extreme contributions from either the ATP-CP or lactic acid systems. Again, complete recovery of the anaerobic systems is not required. Rests of 30 to 120 seconds between sets is sufficient.

Always let your clients determine if more time is necessary, especially those who are looking for health returns and enjoyment from their exercise routine. In instances where they need a longer period, consider using active recovery and sequence your exercises as suggested above. Include a stretch or two after the set is completed.

In relation to program design, nothing is written in stone. It should be viewed not as an issue of right or wrong, but as a continuum of training possibilities you should operate within to maintain a scientifically valid approach. As a trainer, you have many options for maximizing your clients' training results and individual program needs.

Recovery Between Workouts

Recovery between workouts is based on the intensity of the workout and the individual recovery ability of your clients. Generally, a period of about 48 hours between intense workouts is appropriate for positive adaptations in the neuromuscular system. Adequate recovery is essential to avoid overtraining and strength plateaus, and for progressive improvements in muscular strength and endurance.

Intensity is both relative to, and dependent on, your client's current fitness level. Body-weight exercises serve as a good example. The absolute weight of a person can reflect a light, heavy or even maximal loading. For example, deconditioned clients who perform a traditional pushup may find they can only do four repetitions. This equates to a heavy 4 RM load or greater than 80 percent of 1 RM. These clients need a significant recovery between workouts; in this case, at least 48 hours.

More fit clients may be able to perform 50 to 100 pushups, a relatively light load representing much less than 50 percent of 1 RM. They probably can perform these pushup repetitions every day of the week; recovery is not required because a new workload has not been introduced. It should be noted that by performing 100 pushups, fit clients are not achieving gains in strength. If increased muscular strength is a goal, their time could be used more effectively by progressively overloading the body's musculature in eight to 20 repetitions.

WHEN IS THE RIGHT TIME TO CHANGE A STRENGTH PROGRAM?

When considering a change in a resistance-training program, it is important to consider its motivation. Is it a goal change? Is it the client? Or the trainer? A program that has plateaued in terms of results, resistance or number of repetitions and sets may or may not be a problem. When your clients have reached their goals and are pleased with their body image and level of strength, such a program can be termed "maintenance." Maintenance is a positive state of training, wherein you keep your clients' fitness at their trained level.

Valid reasons for changing a resistance-training program include boredom, lack of motivation, lack of results, desire for change in muscle strength, hypertrophy, muscle endurance or a change in training environment (i.e., equipment availability). Before you consider changing a program, remember that every client should have a muscle strength and endurance base. Establish this strength foundation by training your clients for at least four to six weeks.

When Is the Right Time to Change a Strength Program?

Add Variety by Using Cross Training

If your clients are bored, disinterested or lack motivation, cross train within the muscle strength and endurance components of fitness. This type of training is characterized by variety and the use of different exercises and equipment. Initially, try **cross training** without changing intensity. An often-overlooked variable is to change the movement pattern (Fleck and Kraemer, 1987) of an exercise, or the order of exercise, to stimulate a different pattern of motor unit recruitment. This is in contrast to simply adding or subtracting the amount of resistance your clients work against.

Another first step is simply to change the sequence of exercises the clients are already doing to create variety and a new overload. It is suggested that the fatigue pattern of the involved motor units will be changed, causing your clients to adapt to the new stimulus. The next step might be to replace some or all of the exercises in the foundation routine. For each exercise, look at the joint action(s) and muscle group(s) being utilized and replace it with an exercise that targets the same group(s). For example, the bench press can be replaced by pushups, dumbbell presses or

When Is the Right Time to Change a Strength Program?

incline and decline presses, dumbbell or elastic resistance chest flyes (uses horizontal adduction only) because all these copy elbow extension and horizontal adduction at the shoulder. Machine pullover movements can be replaced by movements that replicate shoulder extension, such as dumbbell or elastic resistance pullovers, one arm or double arm "low" rows, or straight-arm pullbacks with dumbbells or elastic resistance. These exercises help to preserve balance in the foundation routine.

Any change in movement patterns (new exercises or slight body position changes) will require a different motor unit recruitment pattern (Fleck and Kraemer, 1987). This holds true even if you are targeting the same muscle group(s) and utilizing similar joint actions. Cross training can positively affect compliance, motivation and interest, as well as stimulate the body toward additional strength gains. For optimal muscular development, variety is the name of the game.

Exercise Plateau and Overtraining Challenges

Plateaus and overtraining are often the result of continuously using one training program approach. The following approaches can help minimize the possibility of either outcome. Initially, change the exercise sequence, or the exercise, while leaving the relative intensity the same. Next, manipulate frequency, intensity and volume both up and down. Keep the repetitions within the eight- to 20-repetition framework if no sport-specific application is required.

Consider utilizing high-intensity training techniques (see Chapter 8). It seems that the best stimulus for increasing strength gains is to make the muscles work harder, as opposed to longer. High-intensity training may be the edge you need to move your clients who are advanced in their resistance-training gains off strength plateaus. Quality reigns over quantity.

Changing Intensity for the Well-Trained Client

If your clients have been training with you two to three times per week for more than six months, performing 10 to 20 exercises per session, and are looking for additional size and/or strength gains, you should look closely at one factor—intensity.

To increase strength and/or size, intensity with an overload of resistance that keeps your clients training within anaerobic pathways must be maintained. This means that they must fatigue the musculature within a time period of about 30 to 90 seconds. In other words, the body's musculature must be presented with an intensity to which it is unaccustomed on a regular and progressive basis.

If a program remains the same (as within the maintenance phase), muscle endurance and/or the current level of strength will be maintained. This situation should not be evaluated as good or bad, but should be considered within the context of your clients' goals.

High-repetition overloads are usually not sufficient to stimulate significant strength gains (except in deconditioned clients), are rarely useful (except in sport-specific applications) and generally do not engage significant muscle mass to create a cardiorespiratory training effect. This type of training also is usually ineffective in promoting any kind of health and fitness gains and, if the repetitions are redundantly high, could lead to overuse injuries, lack of results and frustration.

For conditioned exercisers, lower the number of repetitions to eight to 12 and/or utilize high-intensity training techniques. This intensity is safe and maximizes adaptations in the neuromuscular systems. How can you apply this information to your client's training programs? Have your clients perform eight to 20 repetitions to the point of temporary fatigue for each exercise set. You will have to communicate to your clients the effort and concentration that is necessary to attain this type of high-intensity training.

PRACTICAL APPLICATION THROUGH A CASE STUDY APPROACH

Do you have clients who focus on elite or advanced strength? Are you dealing with **asymptomatic** average clients or older adults? There is much confusion surrounding the number of repetitions and sets and the amount of resistance you should use with varying populations. The following two case studies, one of an Olympic-style lifter and the other of an older adult (age 63), help clarify some seemingly contradictory recommendations.

Case Study 1: Olympic Lifter

Olympic lifting is a competitive sport that involves two technical and explosive lifting movements known as the "clean and jerk," and the "snatch." John is an Olympic lifter who maintains high levels of muscle strength, joint flexibility and neuromuscular coordination. He has had years of specialized training. His goals are based on the demands of the sport: to accomplish maximal strength development and 1-repetition-maximum (1-RM) lifts. A 1-RM lift is the most amount of weight you can lift once; a 10-RM lift is the most amount of weight you can lift 10 times with good technique. A typical protocol for Olympic lifters is as follows:

Load (resistance)	1-6 RM for max strength development
Sets	Multiple, 3-6 for each exercise
Repetitions	1-10 per set, to fatigue, for strength and power, skill development and periodization effect
Rest/ Recovery	2-5 minutes between each set for full energy system recovery
Frequency	1-3 sessions per day, 4-6 days per week

Case Study 2: Older Adult Exerciser

Janet is 63 years old and participates in a regular walking program. She has just begun a muscular strength and endurance conditioning program. She was motivated by reports that resistance training can positively affect **osteoporosis**, increase metabolism and calorie burning, influence posture and help maintain physical independence. Janet's program resembles the following:

Load (resistance)	12-20 RM during introduction to training; 8-12 RM after 6-8 weeks of training
Sets	1 per exercise, introduction to training; 1-2 after 4-6 weeks of training
Number of Exercises	8-10 challenge all major muscle groups
Repetitions	8-20 range per set (see Load above)
Recovery	1-2 minutes between sets, use active recovery to minimize down time
Frequency	2 times per week, for excellent gains in strength and muscular endurance

Analyzing the Case Studies

Notice that the table does not include how much weight either John or Janet should lift. For both clients, the load is determined by an appropriate resistance that fatigues the muscle within the stated repetition goal range. Remember, the key to strength development is high-effort anaerobic exercise. The resistance should be sufficient to fatigue the target muscle

Practical Application Through a Case Study Approach

group within about 30 to 90 seconds of exercise.

Clearly, John and Janet will be training at different levels of resistance to reach muscle fatigue. But what about Joe, also age 63, who later joins Janet in the same fitness pursuit? Since their goals are similar, their exercise protocols will be the same. But this does not mean they will lift an identical amount of weight. For example, after Joe has trained for eight weeks, both he and Janet may fatigue at 10 RM. However, Janet may use a 12-pound weight for a given lift, while Joe, who has not been training as long, may use an 8-pound weight for the same exercise.

PERIODIZATION

Variety promotes optimal training and helps alleviate **overuse injury**, overtraining and unproductive training. It encourages consistent physical improvements, mental freshness and increased motivation, which leads to a high level of compliance and enjoyment. **Periodization**, or cycling program intensities and exercise variations over specific time periods, should be used to achieve effective program diversity.

Many fitness articles mention that periodization should be incorporated into every program-planning process. However, very few formulas exist that explain how to incorporate a periodized program into the fitness routines of your clients in a time-efficient manner.

There is no consensus in current literature as to the best approach, and more important to the fitness professional, the application link to average participants is difficult to bridge. The encouraging aspect of this seemingly ambiguous and complex training principle is that common characteristics are identifiable when existing models of periodization are carefully studied.

Many trainers think of periodization in terms of planned results. It attempts to provide for adequate recovery, while simultaneously preventing detraining or overtraining. By using known physiological training principles such as progressive overload, progressive adaptation and training effect, as well as your knowledge of maintaining fitness gains, avoiding overuse injuries, peaking for performance and training for health gains, an identifiable formula for periodization emerges for fitness.

To the average participant, periodization means cycling, or varying workouts over set time periods to optimize performance and fitness gains. Ultimately, periodization alternates activities and their intensities to achieve superb results from a progressive, goal-oriented training program.

For your clients, this approach has the potential to:

- ✔ promote optimal response to training stimulus (the work effort)
- ✔ decrease the potential for overuse injuries
- ✔ keep your clients fresh and progressing toward their ultimate training goals
- ✔ enhance your clients' personal efforts
- ✔ enhance client compliance

Timing Fitness: From Athlete to Fitness Client

An important step in creating a periodized program is to develop:

- ✔ short-term micro-cycles, which deal with the daily and weekly variation in volume, intensity, loading and exercise selection
- ✔ mid-term meso-cycles, which usually begin with a high-volume phase and end with a high-intensity peaking phase
- ✔ long-term macro-cycles, each composed of several meso-cycles

A well-planned periodized program considers the short-term, mid-term and long-term needs of the client. Such a planning process, adopted from the training world of the elite athlete, would consider:

1. Daily workouts
2. An agenda that accounts for three to four weeks of training
3. An overall annual scheme, or at least several months of planning

To your average fitness clients, macro-cycle phases translate to 1) preparation or build-up; 2) goal attainment; and 3) restoration/recovery. Within the preparation or goal-attainment phases, specific energy/physiologic system manipulations may be accomplished to attain specific goals that include muscle hypertrophy. To achieve these results, the program should involve changes in frequency, duration and intensity of activity, and should include periods of active recovery.

Periodization Model for Health and Fitness Improvement

Step 1: Set the goal(s).

- ✔ cardiorespiratory
- ✔ muscular strength and endurance
- ✔ flexibility
- ✔ other

Step 2: Determine how to achieve the goal(s).

- ✔ Assess time availability.
- ✔ Identify types (mode) of activity.
- ✔ Match training to goals.
- ✔ Choose activities that the client enjoys.

Step 3: Identify training phases.

1. *Training phases*

- ✔ Develop a three- to 10-day short-term plan (micro-cycle).
- ✔ Develop a three- to four-week training plan (meso-cycle).
- ✔ Develop a yearly organizational training plan (macro-cycle), or at least three to four months of meso-cycles.
- ✔ Plan a general preparation phase of three to four weeks (one meso-cycle), which may repeat several times.

2. *Exercise plan*

- ✔ Manipulate frequency, intensity and duration of each activity for specific results in the body's energy/physiologic systems.
- ✔ Apply frequency, intensity and duration to each fitness component in the general preparation phase and the goal phase.
- ✔ Control results by proper intensity of effort and adequate recovery.

Step 4: Plan volume and intensity.

1. *Vary volume and overload on a cyclical basis.*

- ✔ Change at least every three to four weeks, and possibly within a three- to 10-day micro-cycle.
- ✔ Plan to increase or decrease volume and intensity.
- ✔ Use lower intensities and less duration during active recovery.
- ✔ Start the new meso-cycle after active recovery at a slightly lower intensity than the previous cycle.

2. *Allow for the restoration/recovery process*

- ✔ Never increase progressive overload for more than three continuous weeks.
- ✔ Follow any sustained, progressive overload of about three weeks with at least several days of active recovery activity at a lower intensity. (The effort is less intense when compared to the last overload phase in which your clients participated.)
- ✔ After active recovery, start the new meso-cycle at a slightly lower intensity than the previous cycle.

Step 5: Regularly evaluate the periodization planning process.

- ✔ Monitor results and progress.
- ✔ Conduct a fitness assessment (optional).
- ✔ Recognize goal achievement.

- ✔ Maintain an ongoing dialogue with your clients.
- ✔ Observe client compliance and enthusiasm toward the program.

Case Study: From Periodization Theory to Client Application

Jenna is a beginning exerciser whose goals are weight loss, weight management, increased strength and muscle tone and increased "energy level." Jenna understands that a long-term plan (macro-cycle) that incorporates important fitness components will help her realize her training goals.

1. Set the goals.

An optional first step in creating a periodized program is to assess Jenna's current fitness levels in relation to her goals of weight loss, weight management and increased energy. Fitness testing not only accomplishes this, but establishes a reference point for comparing fitness improvements over time and helps you evaluate the effectiveness of your program.

2. The solution: Determine how to achieve the goals.

Improvements in cardiorespiratory fitness and muscular strength and endurance will be crucial in helping Jenna attain her goals. She understands the important contribution cardiorespiratory fitness makes to calorie burning, and that if she becomes more fit, she will be able to burn more calories and fat, and develop more endurance.

Strength training will enhance Jenna's feeling of power and control. Because gains in muscle strength increase muscle endurance, she will have new energy and strength at the end of the day. Also, increases in lean muscle mass will reshape her body and increase her resting metabolic rate, which will help her lose body fat and maintain her desired weight.

3. Identify training phases.

It is usually unrealistic to plan out an entire year and expect average fitness enthusiasts to stick to this. Instead, stay focused on micro- and meso-cycles.

- ✔ Once the goal(s) and starting fitness level (optional) are determined, plan a menu of workouts (keeping the session length in mind) over a three- to 10-day micro-cycle.
- ✔ Next, extend the micro-cycle to a planned three to four week meso-cycle.
- ✔ A "mini" macro-cycle (long-term planning) of three to four months would be the next step.

This formula will keep you ahead in the planning process and will save valuable time should events in your client's life necessitate a major change in the training program or schedule.

You now start the cycles. Since Jenna is new to fitness and her goals are set, her first three- to 10-day micro-cycle will focus on a preparation phase that reflects the goals of: 1) increased overall endurance, and 2) weight management. Her program looks like this:

- ✔ A series of six or seven micro-cycles (about two months) emphasizing a basic, but progressive resistance and cardiorespiratory program. This series of micro-cycles is equivalent to two meso-cycles.
- ✔ After the first meso-cycle, active recovery should be used for about three to five workouts.
- ✔ A second meso-cycle will emphasize continued, progressive increases in intensity. If Jenna is ready, exercise variety will be introduced within each fitness component.

4. Plan volume and intensity.

After the preparation phase is well established (in about eight weeks), the third meso-cycle begins and progresses to the goal phase of the periodization process. This cycle will emphasize a hypertrophy phase for strength and continued challenges in duration and intensity of effort for cardiorespiratory conditioning. For example, Jenna may have progressed from a 12 to 20 repetition overload to fatigue, to an eight to 12 repetition overload to fatigue. Progressing beyond the base of aerobic endurance built in the first two meso-cycles, the third meso-cycle will manipulate cardiorespiratory intensity, duration and frequency, and utilize interval conditioning.

The goal of these specific time periods is to provide an overload that is challenging, progressive and in sync with Jenna's new fitness gains. Micro- and meso-cycles also create goals that are reasonable, and most important, attainable in short time frames. This keeps the client motivated, compliant and physiologically fresh.

After the completion of this third meso-cycle, active recovery will be used with a variety of cross training activities. Jenna will experience different cardiovascular conditioning activities, will change strength exercises or will switch to an entirely different (non-related) activity during this active recovery.

Active recovery is performed at lower intensities of effort (usually with less quantity or duration) than in the previous micro- or meso-cycle time periods. Active recovery allows for physical recovery and enhancement of the adaptation process. Effort is 50 percent of the training equation, and recovery/restoration is the other important half.

5. Evaluate the program.

Reassessment of goals, results, client interest and enthusiasm can never happen too often. This maintains open and fresh communication with clients, keeps you focused on their current fitness levels and helps you anticipate your next step.

Implementing Periodized Fitness

The key to successful periodization is the ability to challenge the body with new activities and progressive overload (intensity). Three to four weeks of cycling workouts will get results. Just as the body experiences the peak benefits of one meso-cycle of planned workouts and starts to adapt to it, the client moves into a whole new three- to four-week cycle that offers a completely new set of challenges.

There are several ways you can track a periodization program. One idea is to label a manila folder with each meso-cycle and keep each client's workout card in the file. You may have four manila file folders hanging inside one hanging file for each client. You can do the same thing on your computer by creating a file for each meso-cycle and placing the programs you create in the file.

A comprehensive, accurate planning process will draw heavily on your practical experience and knowledge of the scientific theory behind training. It is obvious that periodization, planning and program organization is not an inherently complex task. The main idea of this type of training is to raise the fitness state of an individual to a higher level with a systematic approach. However, implementation does require considerable forethought and time investment. On the other hand, it is well worth it, since periodization makes both the trainer and participant accountable for results.

TRACKING GAINS WITH GOOD RECORDS

Tracking Gains with Good Records

Science has not defined the "best" or "perfect" program, but variation and intensity are two of its most important factors. Make sure that you keep accurate lifting records (repetitions, sets, resistance, order of exercise, name of exercise and periodization planning program) so that you can determine the type of program manipulation that best stimulates your clients' minds and bodies. It is likely that no two people will respond in the same manner to a given training program. Because of this phenomenon, known as individual response, your records, client feedback, strength testing if appropriate, as well as body fat and circumference measurements will help determine the program's effectiveness.

DIRECTING RESULTS

Just how much control do you really have in directing results? Certain genetic factors, such as muscle fiber type, number of fibers and neural and hormonal influences ultimately determine the outer ranges of strength and body shape. However, each person's optimal potential can best be reached by emphasizing the following:

1. Design systems with specific goals in mind.
2. Fit all systems into the specificity chart.
3. Encourage consistent, regular and varied efforts.
4. Teach the use of proper biomechanical techniques.
5. Allow for the recovery/building process.
6. Keep accurate records.

UPPER BODY

Pectoralis Major

Body weight

Push-up (variations: on knees, decline or incline, against a wall or chair)

Performance recommendations

Place hands on the floor with thumbs aligned to nipple-line. Keep elbows straight, but not locked, and maintain a stabilized trunk through the movement. Keep knees hip-width apart and lower the chest to the floor. Push up to starting position.

Spotting

Remind client to avoid hyperextending through the trunk or leading with the hips. Be careful not to place the hands too wide or too narrow.

Pectoralis Major

Free weight

Bench press
(variations: with dumbbells, incline/decline)

Performance recommendations

Lie supine with eyes directly under the bar. Place feet on the bench to maintain neutral spine, if necessary. Retract the scapula, lift the bar off of its supports and lower it to the nipple-line. Pause, and extend the elbows, pressing the bar over the shoulders without locking the elbows. Pause and repeat.

Spotting

Stand behind client, placing hands on bar to assist the lift if needed. Bar should not bounce off the chest, and hips should remain on bench. During the spot, protect yourself by keeping your spine neutral and lifting with your legs.

Pectoralis Major

Machine

Pec deck

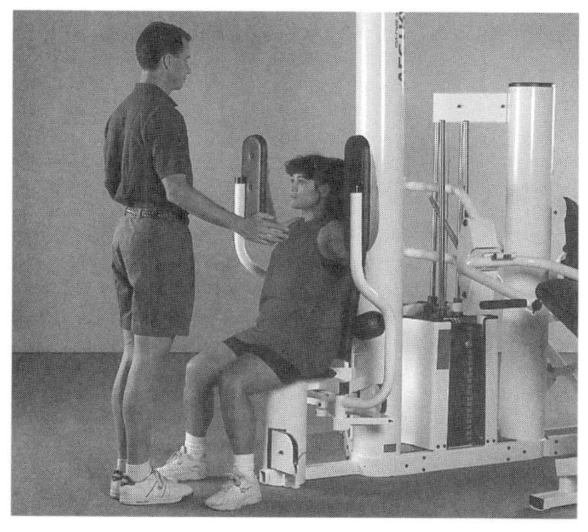

Performance recommendations

Align shoulders with the machine's axis of rotation. Keeping palms open to decrease biceps' contribution, place elbows slightly below the level of shoulders. Contract abdominals to stabilize trunk and retract the scapula while squeezing both pads together. Pause and return to starting position.

Spotting

Stand in front of machine to spot. Provide assistance if needed by squeezing arm pads together. Client may place feet on a stool or bench for better support.

Latissimus Dorsi

Body weight

Pull-up/Chin-up

Performance recommendations

Grasp bar with a pronated or supinated grip, hands shoulder-width apart. Pull body up until chin is over bar, pause briefly and lower body to starting position.

Spotting

Spot from rear; place hands near client's hips to assist with lift, reinforce spinal alignment and prevent rocking; some body weight may be supported by keeping feet in contact with bench for beginners or higher-repetition exercisers.

Latissimus Dorsi

Free weight

One-arm bent-over dumbbell row

Performance recommendations

Hold a dumbbell in left hand while resting right hand, knee and lower leg on bench; keep spine neutral. Flex left leg slightly and the hip 90°. Extend right arm toward the floor and pull the dumbbell straight up toward mid-back, keeping elbow close to side. Pause; return arm to extended position.

Spotting

Make sure the client initiates the movement without using momentum. Watch that they keep shoulder from drooping and the back from swaying or twisting during the lowering phase.

Latissimus Dorsi

Machine

Lat pulldown

(variation: biceps-assisted lat pulldown with a supinated grip)

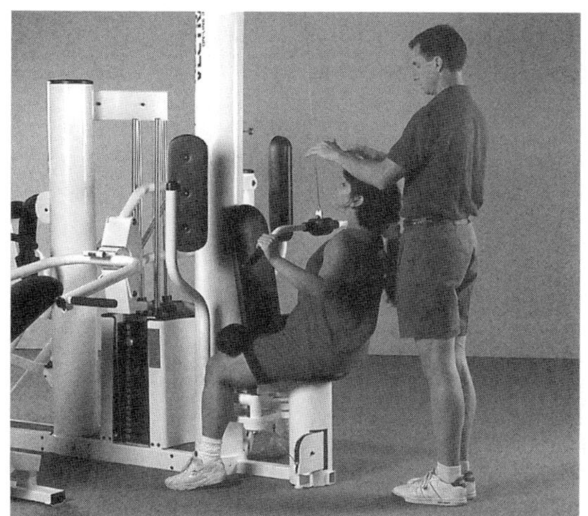

Performance recommendations

Sit facing the weight stack with knees bent under the thigh pad and feet flat on the floor. Grasp the bar slightly wider than shoulder-width apart with a pronated grip. Maintain a neutral spine, keep abs contracted and lean back 30° from hips. Retract the scapula and pull the bar toward the chest. Pause, and return to extended position.

Spotting

Remind client to avoid hyperextension of the lumbar spine, and that wrists should remain neutral throughout the movement. Caution: Behind-the-head lat pulldowns (i.e., external rotation and abduction) increase chances of injury to the shoulder joint. Use only if client is free of any shoulder pain.

Rhomboids

Free weight

Prone scapular retraction

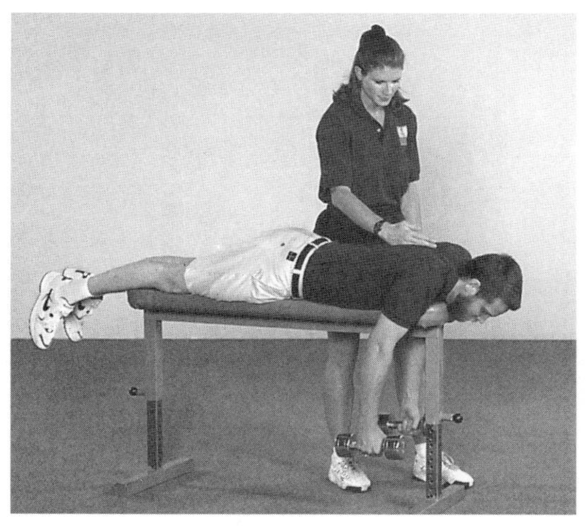

Performance recommendations

Lie prone on a high flat bench, a dumbbell in each hand, arms hanging toward the floor. With the trunk stabilized draw the shoulder blades together and hold for several seconds. Release and repeat.

Spotting

Be sure the client maintains a stable torso. Indicate the rhomboids so they have a clear idea of which muscles they are isolating.

Rhomboids

Machine

Scapular adduction

Performance recommendations

Adjust seat so that the line of pull is even with your shoulders while you are sitting. With both feet flat on the floor, stabilize trunk and grip handles with a pronated grip, keeping arms straight. Retract the scapula and draw the shoulder blades together. Hold for several seconds, release and repeat.

Spotting

Remind the client that this exercise involves a very small range of movement to isolate the rhomboids.

Deltoid (Anterior)

Body weight

Push-up

See Pectoralis Major

Deltoid (Anterior)

Free weight

Bench press

See Pectoralis Major

Deltoid (Middle)

Free weight

Standing lateral raise

Performance recommendations

Stand in a 30° forward-leaning position with cervical and lumbar spine in neutral. Contract the abdominals, retract and slightly elevate the scapula, and bend elbows in a modified short-lever position. Keeping wrists neutral, raise elbows out to sides of the body and then up to shoulder height.

Spotting

Note neutral position in spine and wrists, and watch for excessive internal rotation or shoulder abduction (beyond 90°). In lean position, medial deltoid should be on top.

Deltoid (Middle)

Machine

Lateral raise

Performance recommendations

Align shoulder joints with the machine's axis of rotation and place arms against the movement pads. Retract scapula and raise arms to shoulder height. Pause, slowly return and repeat.

Spotting

Remind client to maintain neutral cervical and lumbar alignment. They shouldn't raise their arms higher than shoulder height.

Deltoid (Posterior)

Body weight

Prone raise (variation: with dumbbells)

Performance recommendations

Lie prone on a high flat bench. Retract scapula and keep neutral alignment from the cervical to the lumbar areas. Palms should face in and arms hang down in line with shoulders. Lift arms to about shoulder height. Pause and repeat.

Spotting

Place hand mid-scapula to reinforce retraction. Be sure client keeps their elbow slightly bent throughout the lift.

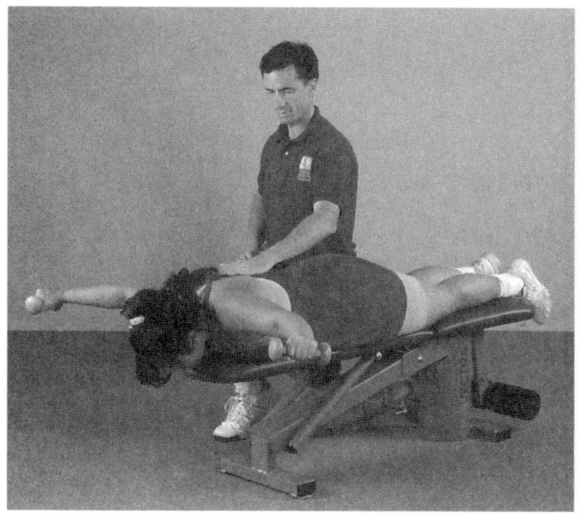

Trapezius

Free weight

Shrug (variation: with dumbbells)

Performance recommendations

Stand erect and hold bar with a pronated grip behind the body. Without rocking body, elevate shoulder girdle toward ears, retract (adduct) scapula, and release to starting position.

Spotting

Be sure the client initiates movement with shoulder girdle, not arms.

Biceps

Body weight

Chin-up

Performance recommendations

See Latissimus Dorsi Chin-up, but use a shoulder-width, supinated grip.

Spotting

Help to maintain a neutral spine and avoid rocking. Be sure a bench or chair is ready if necessary.

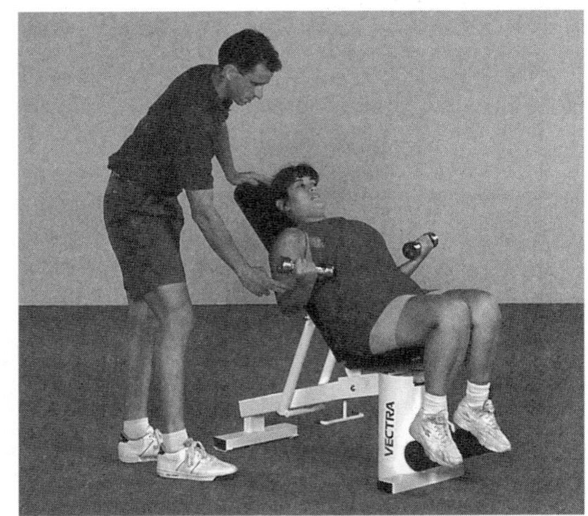

Biceps

Free weight

Seated incline biceps curl
(variations: standing biceps curl, supinated curl, barbell curl, alternate arms)

Performance recommendations

Hold a dumbbell in each hand with an underhand grip. Lie back on an incline bench. Arms should hang straight down with palms forward. Simultaneously curl both dumbbells up to shoulder height. Lower them to full extension, pause and repeat.

Spotting

Assist client in curling in direct alignment with their elbows; all movement should be initiated at the elbow joint. Make sure they do not swing the weight up from the bottom of the lift.

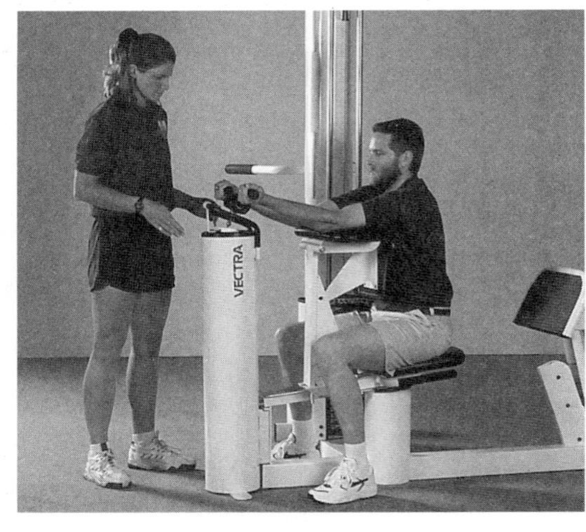

Biceps

Machine

Biceps curl

Performance recommendations

Adjust the seat so the arms rest comfortably over the pad. Arms should rest against the pad at all times. With elbows relaxed and wrists neutral, grasp the bent-angle bar with hands shoulder-width apart (do not hyperextend). Contract the biceps and bring the bar to the top position. Pause and repeat.

Spotting

Small women or men may have difficulty entering some machines. Assist them with proper alignment. Avoid rocking the upper body to lift the weight.

Triceps

Body weight

Dips

Performance recommendations

Sit on a chair or bench with the hands gripping the front edge. Legs may either be straight or the knees bent and feet closer to the chair. With legs together, move forward until the hips are off the seat. Slowly lower the hips toward the floor, and press up to full arm's extension, but do not lock out the arms. Repeat.

Spotting

Advise the client to keep their hips a few inches in front of the chair, and to adjust the distance between their hips and feet according to the degree of difficulty.

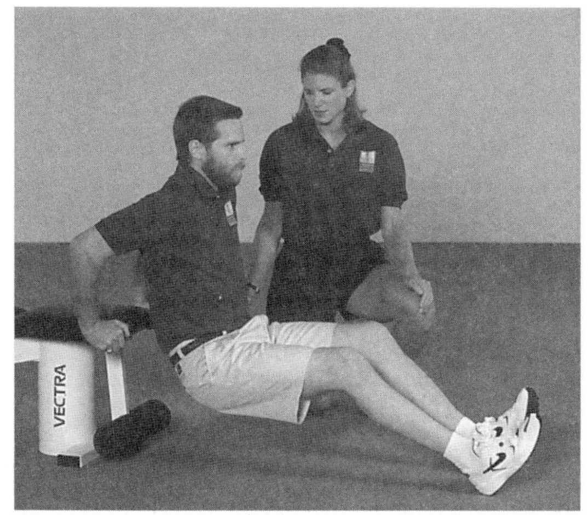

Triceps

Free weight

Triceps kickback

Performance recommendations

Place right knee on one end of a bench. With a dumbbell in left hand, lean forward and place right hand on the other end of the bench. Keep elbows relaxed, spine in neutral position and abdominals contracted. With left foot on the floor, extend left elbow behind until arm is parallel to the floor and palm is facing torso. Contract triceps at the top of the motion. Return to start and repeat.

Spotting

Help client to maintain neutral alignment in the neck, erectors and wrist. To spot, touch the extended elbow and keep it in line with the shoulder. Watch for fatigue in the posterior deltoid, and do not let the upper arm drop.

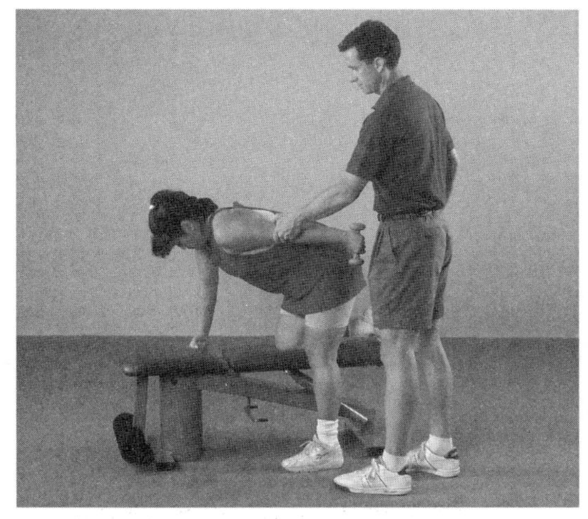

Triceps

Machine

Triceps extension

Performance recommendations

Keeping elbows close to the body, grip handles and pull to slightly above waist level. Push the handle downward until the triceps are fully contracted. Do not permit the elbows to move away from the body. Pause and slowly return to the starting position. Repeat.

Spotting

Do not allow client to lift elbows away from sides and instruct them to keep their body stable.

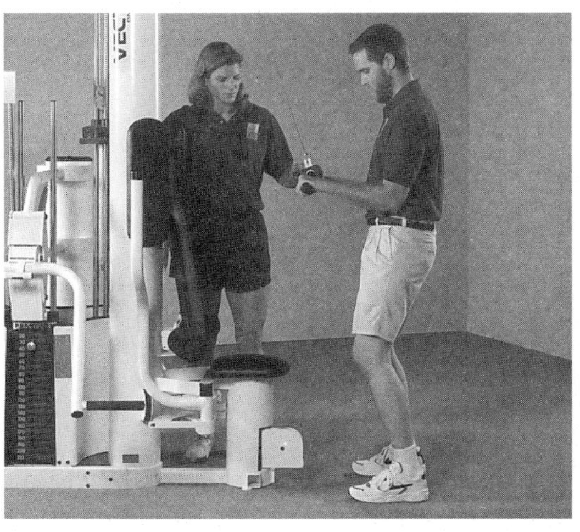

TORSO

Rectus Abdominis

Body weight

Reverse curl

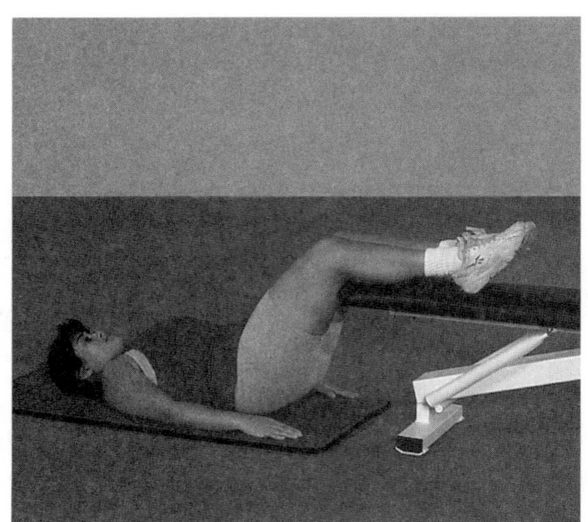

Performance recommendations

Lie supine with lower legs and heels resting on a flat bench. Extend arms flat at sides. Keep spine neutral and contract abdominal area. Without using arms for leverage, bring thighs toward chest slightly and lift hips 1 to 2 inches off the floor. Knees should point to the ceiling throughout this gently rolling movement. Return and repeat.

Spotting

Because the range of motion is very small, remind client not to swing their legs into position. If they experience lower back discomfort, or cannot maintain neutral position, fold a small towel and place it under the lumbar curve.

Rectus Abdominis

Body weight

Crunch (variation: weight plate on chest)

Performance recommendations

Lie supine with knees bent and feet resting on a wall or bench. Cross arms over chest or place them, unclasped, behind head with elbows out. Maintain neutral alignment in the cervical spine and visualize a tennis ball tucked under chin. Tighten the abdominals and exhale as you curl up. Lead with rib cage and raise shoulders and upper back off the floor toward pelvis. Contract at the top of the movement, slowly lower and repeat.

Spotting

Watch for momentum-assisted movements, and remind client to keep elbows back and open. Don't let client pull on their neck.

Rectus Abdominis

Machine

Abdominal curl

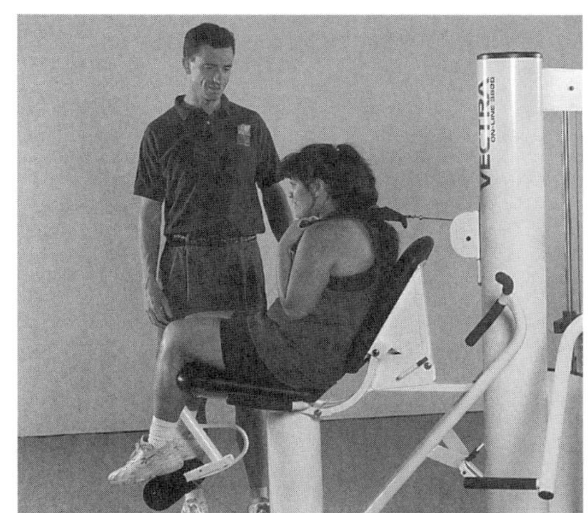

Performance recommendations

Adjust the seat so that the axis point is at the lumbar region. With knees in line with hips, rest chest against the pads, or pull shoulder straps into position, tighten the abdominals and press and contract through the range of motion of the machine. (This will vary with manufacturer.) Pause, slowly return to starting position and repeat.

Spotting

Assist the client in maintaining a neutral cervical spine; 30° to 40° of vertebral flexion is adequate.

External and Internal Obliques

Body weight

Rotation trunk curl

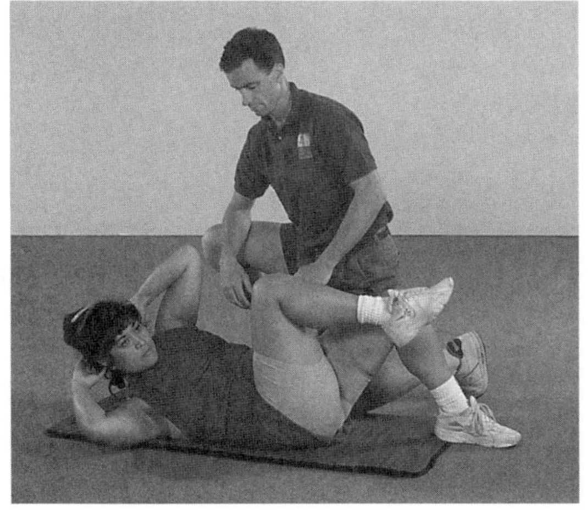

Performance recommendations

Lie supine with knees bent and feet a comfortable distance from buttocks. Cross right ankle over left knee. Place hands at the sides of head (unclasped) with elbows out. Contract the abdominals as you rotate up, keeping head, neck and shoulder blades in alignment. Lead with ribs and cross the left shoulder to the right knee. Contract at the top of the motion, slowly return to the starting position and repeat. Do a complete set of reps on one side before you switch to the other.

Spotting

Remind clients to keep the movement smooth and controlled, concentrating on a shoulder-to-knee movement instead of elbow-to-knee. Watch for momentum-assisted movements.

Erector Spinae

Body weight

Prone back extension (variation: on hands and knees)

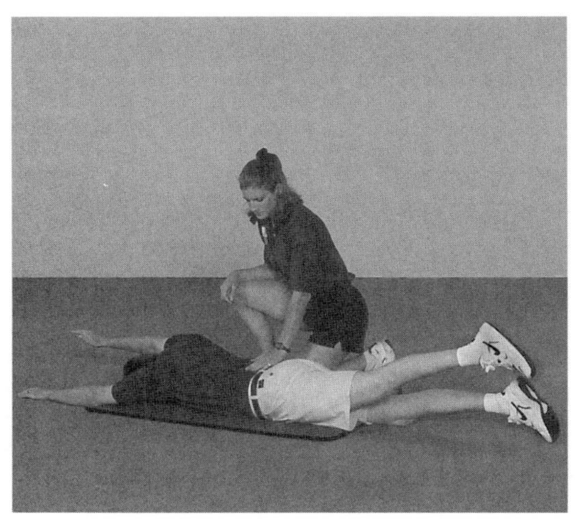

Performance recommendations

Lying prone with hips pressed into the floor and abdominal muscles contracted to stabilize the trunk, lift right arm and left leg. Pause and return to the floor. Repeat on the opposite side. Progress to lifting arms and legs simultaneously.

Spotting

Instruct client to keep head in line with spine and to discontinue exercise if there is discomfort. Watch for hyperextension of the cervical and lumbar spine.

LOWER BODY

Quadriceps

Body weight

Squat

Performance recommendations

Stand with neutral spine and feet shoulder-width apart. Slowly start the descent with hips back, keeping the weight centered over heels or mid-foot. Lower to approximately 90° of knee flexion. Pause and repeat.

Spotting

Assist with balance by placing arms around client's torso, and don't allow bouncing at the bottom of the movement. Remind them to control both the up and down phase of the exercise.

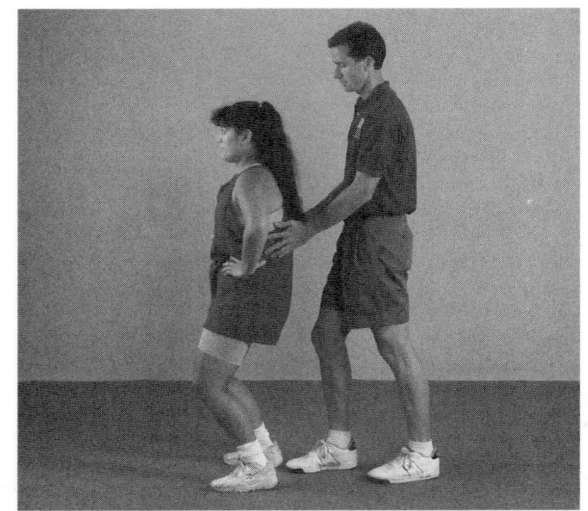

Quadriceps

Body weight

Forward lunge

(variations: with dumbbells, backward lunge)

Performance recommendations

Standing with feet together, take a long step forward with one foot and bend the back knee to a fencer's lunge position; sit straight down. Push back to a standing position. Alternate legs.

Spotting

Have client begin with small steps and progress gradually, keeping the motion controlled. Remind them that the knee of the front leg should not travel forward past the toes during the down phase.

Quadriceps

Free weight

Squat (variation: holding dumbbells instead of using rack)

Performance recommendations

Use a squat rack. The bar should rest on the shoulder blades, off the notch of the neck. Follow movement guidelines for body-weight squat.

Spotting

Don't bounce at the bottom of the movement. Keep the abdominals contracted and the spine neutral. Avoid use of board under heels.

Quadriceps

Machine

Horizontal leg press

Performance recommendations

Sit on a leg-press machine with feet hip-width apart. Hold the handles and contract the abdominals. Bend knees to 90° of flexion, keeping them over the ankles and the entire foot in contact with the foot-plate. Straighten legs until they are fully extended but not locked. Slowly return to starting position. Repeat.

Spotting

Remind client to keep motion smooth and controlled. Avoid hyperextension at the top of the movement. Do not use the lowest foot-pad position.

Hamstrings

Body weight

Squat or Lunge

See Quadriceps

Hamstrings

Free weight

Squat or Lunge

See Quadriceps

Hamstrings

Machine

Standing leg curl

Performance recommendations

Stand with your hips against the pads of a standing leg-curl machine with knees just below the edge of the pad and ankle under the rollers; knees should be slightly bent. Hold on to the handles and press forward with hips while slowly curling the heel toward buttocks. Pause at the top of the lift and repeat.

Spotting

Remind the client to keep their torso stabilized, and not to swing the weight up or lift the hips. Keeping feet relaxed will decrease gastrocnemius involvement.

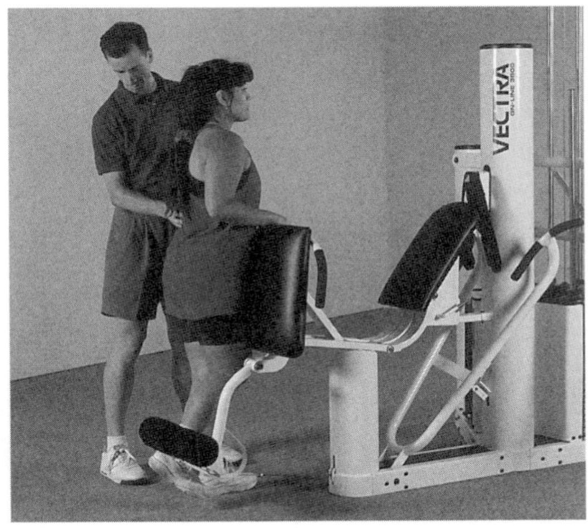

Hamstrings

Machine

Horizontal leg press

See Quadriceps

Gluteus Maximus

Body weight

Prone leg lift

Performance recommendations

Lie prone with legs extended behind and hips against the mat. Rest head in neutral alignment on bent arms. Lift one leg up from the floor and return to start. Repeat, alternating legs.

Spotting

Use caution: this exercise can place stress on the low back. Have client keep chest and hips on the floor, performing the movement in a controlled manner.

Gluteus Maximus

Free weight

Squat

See Quadriceps

Gluteus Maximus

Machine

Horizontal leg press

See Quadriceps

Hip Abductor

Body weight

Side-lying abduction lift (variation: with ankle weight)

Performance recommendations

Lie on side with legs extended, head resting on forearm and hips and shoulders facing forward. While maintaining a neutral spine, bend bottom knee for support, keeping top knee facing forward and relaxed. Lift through the range of motion of the muscle. Pause and return to the starting position.

Spotting

Don't allow client to roll backward on the hip, or let the knee face the ceiling.

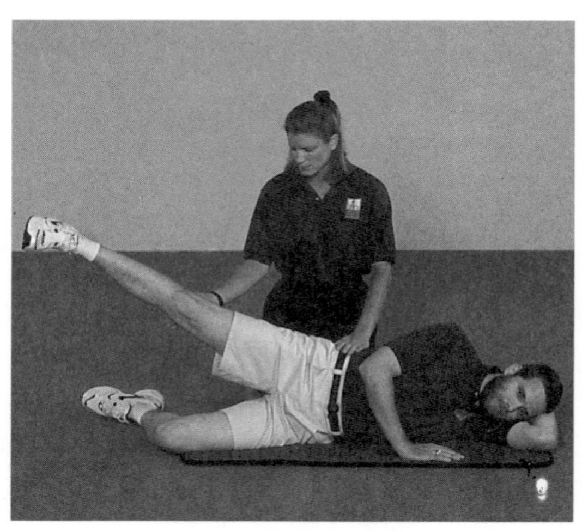

Hip Abductor

Machine

Standing abduction lift with ankle strap

Performance recommendations

Place an ankle strap on outside leg. Balance by holding onto a bar, keeping spine neutral and hips parallel. Relax knees, lift leg to the side and return.

Spotting

Watch for fatigue as client will have difficulty maintaining a neutral spine and may shift hip alignment.

Hip Adductor

Body weight

Side-lying adduction lift (variation: with ankle weight)

Performance recommendations

Lie on side with head resting on the forearm. Hips and shoulders should face forward with spine in neutral position. Straighten bottom leg, then bend and cross top leg over it. Slowly lift the bottom leg as high as possible. Pause, return to starting position and repeat.

Spotting

Keep working knee forward and spine stabilized.

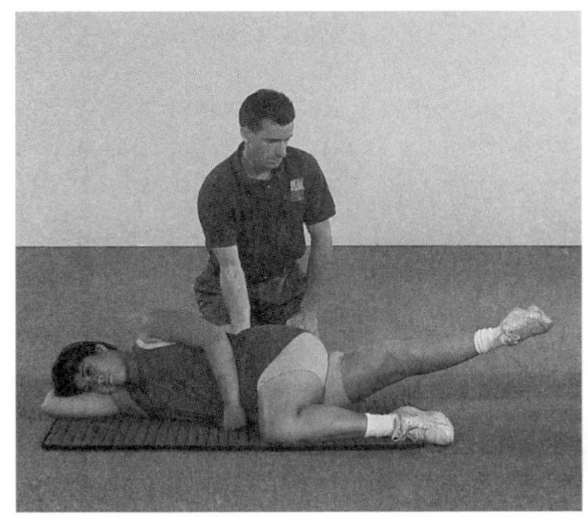

Hip Adductor

Machine

Standing adduction crossover with ankle strap

Performance recommendations

Place an ankle strap on leg, and stand to the side of the cable pulley with feet shoulder-width apart and trunk stabilized. Hold on to the support bar for balance and bring working leg across to the big toe of the supporting leg. Pause, return and repeat.

Spotting

Don't allow client to swing the working leg out too far, and watch for torquing through the knees or spine.

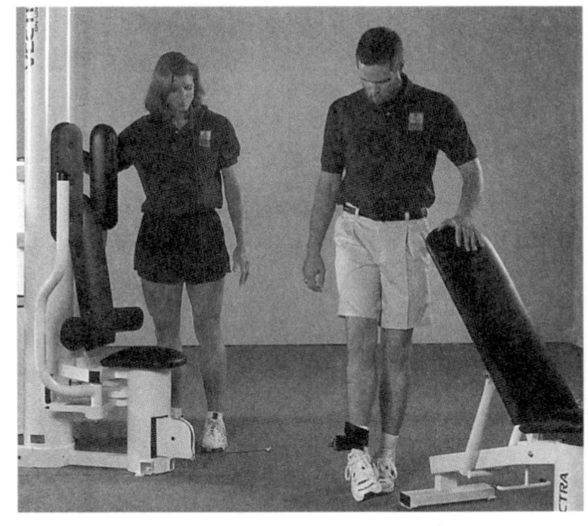

Gastrocnemius

Body weight

Standing heel raise (variation: standing heel raise with weights)

Performance recommendations

Place the ball of one foot on the edge of a block or stair. Wrap the other foot behind the lower leg that is positioned on the block. All weight should be on the standing foot. Use a support for balance and slowly lower the heel of the working leg as low as possible; then rise up on the toe until the calf is fully flexed. Lower and repeat. This exercise may be varied by holding a dumbbell in the hand on the same side of the working leg.

Spotting

Remind the client to emphasize the extension and contraction phase of the range of motion.

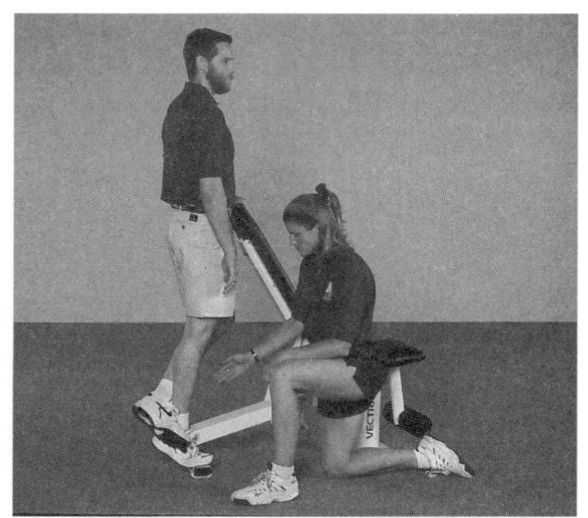

Gastrocnemius

Machine

Standing heel raise (variation: use edge of leg press plate)

Performance recommendations

Stand on the foot plate of the calf machine with centered shoulders. Slowly rise up on toes and contract calves. Pause briefly and lower the heels until they are fully extended. This exercise can be done with one foot crossed over the working leg.

Spotting

Remind client not to slouch, but to maintain proper posture throughout the set.

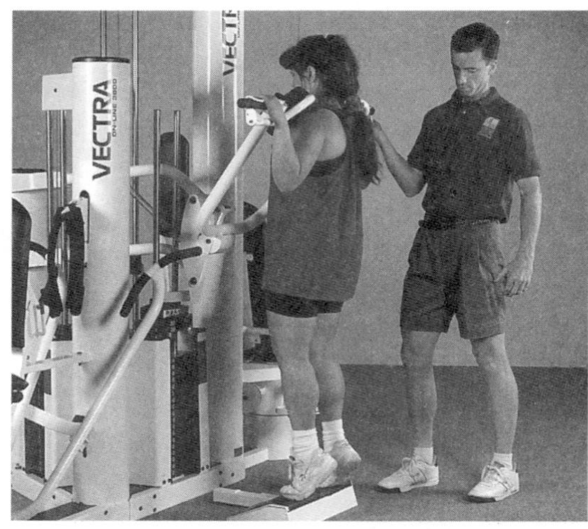

Soleus

Machine

Seated calf raise

Performance recommendations

Sit in a horizontal leg press machine with spine in neutral position. Place the balls of feet on the foot bar with toes pointed forward. Loosely grip the handles or knee pads. Extend heels as low as possible, then raise them, pushing up as high as possible on to the balls of the feet. Slowly lower and repeat.

Tibialis Anterior

Body weight

Toe raise off a block (variation: walk on heels)

Performance recommendations

Stand on a block or stair with feet extended over the edge so that only the heels are supported. Use a bar for balance. Extend toes toward the ground as far as possible. Then bring them to full contraction. Lower them to the starting position and repeat.

Spotting

Emphasize full range of motion.

The editors of this manual would like to thank Diane Buchta, owner of Tri Fitness in San Diego, Calif., for her generous efforts in developing this strength-training exercise section.

SUMMARY

Before you plan resistance-training programs for your clients, remember to look at their current state of psychology, personal needs and level of fitness. When changing programs, be sure to evaluate their physiological needs and their readiness to change.

No program or exercise guideline is written in stone. Err on the side of conservatism. You must know your clients' physical limits and their perception of what is too much; intensity is relative to the individual. Do not join the ranks of trainers who create programs that are too difficult for their clients. Even if you do not injure them, you surely will defeat them. Resistance-training program design is a process that demands constant evaluation, manipulation and change.

REFERENCES/SUGGESTED READING

American Council On Exercise. (1991). *Personal Trainer Manual.* San Diego: American Council on Exercise.

American College of Sports Medicine. (1991). *Guidelines for Exercise Testing and Prescription.* (4th ed.) Philadelphia: Lea & Febiger.

ACSM. (1990). The Recommended Quantity and Quality of Exercise for Developing and Maintaining Cardiorespiratory and Muscular Fitness in Healthy Adults. *Medicine and Science in Sports and Exercise.* 22, 2, 265-274.

Baechle, T. & Groves, B. (1992). *Weight Training - Steps To Success.* Champaign: Human Kinetics.

Basmajian, J. & DeLuca, C. (1979). *Muscles Alive - Their Functions Revealed By Electromyography.* (4th ed.) Baltimore: Williams and Wilkins.

Brooks, D. (1996). *Program Design For Personal Trainers...Bridging Theory Into Application.* Mammoth Lakes: Moves International.

Brooks, D. (1990). *Going Solo - The Art of Personal Training.* (2nd ed.) Mammoth Lakes: Moves International.

Brooks, D. & Copeland-Brooks, C. (1993). Uncovering the Myths of Abdominal Exercise, *IDEA Today,* April, 42-49.

Brooks, D., et al. (1995). *Reebok Interval Program Manual.* Stoughton: Reebok International, Ltd.

Brooks, D., et al. (1995). *Resist-A-Ball: Programming Guide For Fitness Professionals.* Indianapolis: Ground Control Inc.

Evans, W. & Rosenberg, I. (1991). *Biomarkers.* New York: Simon & Schuster.

Fleck, S. & Kraemer, W. (1987). *Designing Resistance Training Programs.* Champaign: Human Kinetics.

Hickson, R.C., et al. (1985). Reduced training intensities and loss of aerobic power, endurance and cardiac growth. *Journal of Applied Physiology.* 58, 492-99.

Kendall, Florence, et al. (1993). *Muscles - Testing and Function.* (4th ed.) Baltimore: Williams and Wilkins.

Komi, P.V., (Ed.) (1992). *Strength and Power in Sport.* Distributed by Human Kinetics Publishers.

Kraemer, W. & Fleck, S. (1993). *Strength Training For Young Athletes.* Champaign: Human Kinetics.

McArdle, W., et al. (1991). *Exercise Physiology - Energy, Nutrition, and Human Performance.* (3rd ed.) Philadelphia: Lea & Febiger.

McDonagh, M.J.N. & Davies, C.T.M. (1984). Adaptive response of mammalian skeletal muscle to exercise with high loads. *European Journal of Applied Physiology.* 52, 139-155.

Pate, R. R., et al. (1995). Physical Activity and Public Health: A Recommendation From the Centers for Disease Control and Prevention and The American College of Sports Medicine. *Journal of the American Medical Association.* 273, 402-407.

Wescott, W. (1991). *Strength Fitness.* (3rd ed.) Dubuque: Wm. C. Brown Publishers.

Wilmore, J. (1991). Resistance Training For Health: A Renewed Interest. *Sports Medicine Digest.* June, 6.

Wilmore, J. & Costill, D. (1994). *Physiology Of Sport And Exercise.* Champaign: Human Kinetics.

Wilmore, J. & Costill, D. (1988). *Training for Sport and Activity: The Physiological Basis of the Conditioning Process.* (3rd ed.) Dubuque: William Brown Publishers.

References Specific to Periodization

Bompa, T. (1983). *Theory and Methodology of Training.* Dubuque: Kendall-Hunt.

Bruner, R. et al. (1992). *Soviet Training and Recovery Methods.* Pleasant Hill: Sport Focus Publishing.

Metveyev, L. (1981). *Fundamentals of Sports Training.* Moscow: Progress Publishers.

Ozolin, N. (1971). *The Athlete's Training System for Competition.* Moscow: Fizkultura Sport Publication.

Siff, Mel, et al. (1993). *Super Training: Special Strength Training For Sporting Excellence.* South Africa: School of Mechanical Engineering, University of the Witwatersrand.

Vorobyev, A. (1978). *A Textbook on Weight Lifting.* Budapest: International Weight Lifting Federation.

Yessis, M. (1987). *The Secret of Soviet Sports Fitness and Training.* Arbor House.

Parts of this chapter are excerpted with permission from *Program Design For Personal Trainers ... Bridging Theory Into Application,* by Douglas S. Brooks. Mammoth Lakes: Moves International, 1996.

CHAPTER 10 Flexibility

10

IN THIS CHAPTER:

Mari Cyphers

Mari Cyphers, P.T., is a physical therapist with an extensive background in orthopedics and sports medicine. She is currently a regional manager for the Physiotherapy Associates clinics in the San Francisco Bay area and frequently lectures for IDEA conventions, ACSM fitness instructor certification workshops, Fitness Associates network and California State University, Hayward.

Few would argue that flexibility is an important component of fitness and a critical factor in achieving peak physical potential. However, flexibility often is overlooked or misused. Some runners and weight lifters, for example, emphasize their cardiovascular or strength training, and pay little attention to their flexibility. Athletes and trainers who do stress flexibility often have different methods of flexibility training, and the scientific data is still not strong enough to support the value of one method over another.

Although controversies remain, and the arguments for flexibility training may not be as strong or well-supported as those for cardiovascular and strength training, it is important for you to include flexibility training in all your fitness programs, especially since recent studies show that injuries do occur as a result of tight or stiff muscles. This chapter presents an overview of the substantial body of knowledge pertaining to flexibility training that can help your clients attain their fitness goals and decrease their risk of injury.

FLEXIBILITY: A DEFINITION

Flexibility is a joint's ability to move freely in every direction or, more specifically, through a full and normal range of motion (ROM). Within each joint and for each activity, there is an optimum ROM essential to peak performance. The optimum range of motion varies depending upon the activity. A number of factors can limit joint mobility: genetic inheritance; the joint structure itself; connective tissue elasticity within muscles, tendons or skin surrounding a joint; strength of the opposing muscle group; and neuromuscular coordination. Flexibility training minimizes the factors that limit flexibility in order to help balance muscle groups that might be overused during physical training sessions or as a result of poor posture.

There are two basic types of flexibility: static flexibility and dynamic flexibility. Static flexibility is the ROM about a joint, with little emphasis on speed of movement. For example, a gymnast holding a split is demonstrating static flexibility. Dynamic flexibility involves speed during physical performance, and strength, power, neuromuscular coordination and tissue resistance or "stiffness" are all factors in one's dynamic or active flexibility. A gymnast performing a split leap must not only possess the static flexibility of a split, but also the power, coordination and minimum tissue resistance to move to that position quickly in mid-air. Both static and dynamic flexibility are important in fitness and sports performance, therefore it is important to become familiar with the different training methods for both static and dynamic flexibility. The benefits derived from each — full, usable and safe ROM at various speeds of movement — include the following:

1. Increased physical efficiency and performance. A flexible joint requires less energy to move through the range of motion.
2. Decreased risk of injury. Although there is insufficient data to support this conclusion, many experts agree that increasing ROM decreases the resistance in various tissues. Your client, therefore, is less likely to incur injury by exceeding tissue extensibility during activity.
3. Increased blood supply and nutrients to joint structures. Flexibility training may also contribute to improved circulation and nutrient transport, allowing greater elasticity of tissues.
4. Range of motion exercises may increase the quantity and decrease the viscosity, or thickness, of synovial fluid enabling better nutrient exchange. Healthy synovial fluid also allows greater freedom of movement and may decelerate joint degenerative processes.
5. Increased neuromuscular coordination. Studies have shown that nerve impulse velocity (the time it takes an impulse to travel to the brain and return) is enhanced with dynamic flexibility training. In attuning the central nervous system (CNS) to the physical demands placed upon it, opposing muscle groups work in a more synergistic or coordinated fashion.
6. Improved muscular balance and postural awareness. Flexibility helps realign soft tissue structures that may have adapted poorly to the effects of gravity and postural habits. Realignment consequently reduces the effort it takes to achieve and maintain good posture in activities of daily living.
7. Decreased risk of low-back pain. Strong clinical evidence indicates that lumbo-pelvic flexibility, which involves

the hamstrings, hip flexors and the muscles attached to the pelvis, is critical in reducing the stress to the lumbar spine.

8. Reduced stress. In general, stretching promotes muscular relaxation. A muscle in a constant state of contraction or tension may require more energy to accomplish activities. Muscular relaxation encourages healthy nutrition directly to the muscle, which decreases the accumulation of toxins, reduces the potential for adaptive shortening and diminishes fatigue.

9. Enhanced enjoyment. A physical training program must be enjoyable if a client is to stick with it. You may find that by relaxing both mind and body, flexibility training increases a client's sense of well-being and personal gratification during exercise.

Although flexibility is a valuable aspect of physical training, it is important for you to be aware of potential disadvantages associated with overtraining for excessive flexibility. How much joint flexibility is necessary varies with the activity and is highly specific to each client. Most experts believe excessive flexibility involves overstretched ligaments, which decreases stability and exposes joint structures to risk of injury. This is sometimes seen in former gymnasts who are hyperflexible, but no longer have the high levels of muscle strength to support it. Instability caused by overstretched ligaments may also lead to decreased joint-protective reflexes and neuromuscular coordination, and ultimately predispose a person to degenerative (arthritic) joint changes. For example, a severe ankle sprain over-stretches the ligaments around the ankle. If the ankle is not properly rehabilitated, the overstretched ligaments can lead to additional injuries.

There may also be muscles that should not be stretched in some clients. Single-joint muscles that are placed in positions of prolonged stretch (usually due to poor postural positions) can develop a stretch weakness (Kendall, et al., 1994). Stretch weakness may increase vulnerability to injury during even mild daily activities. These muscles need to be carefully strengthened and allowed, if possible, to return to normal resting length. These factors emphasize the need for well-balanced programs in muscular strength and flexibility to achieve greater joint stability and thus minimize the incidence of injury.

THE MECHANICS OF STRETCHING

Flexibility is enhanced by using a variety of stretching methods. It is accomplished by applying a force passively or actively to decrease tissue "stiffness" and elongate the musculotendinous unit, thereby increasing the available range of motion. Stretching refers to the process of elongation. It is widely accepted that the most resistance to stretch is not from the more contractile muscle fiber itself, but rather from the connective tissue framework in and around the muscle. Therefore, understanding the mechanical properties of connective tissue under tension is essential in determining the best methods of increasing ROM and flexibility.

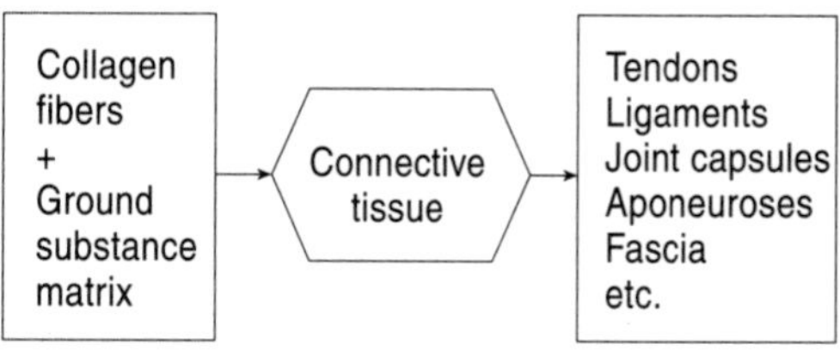

FIGURE 10.1 Organization of connective tissue structures.

Connective tissue is composed of non-elastic collagen fibers and a small number of elastic fibers within a protein matrix that creates various soft tissue structures including tendons, ligaments and fascia (Figure 10.1). Connective tissue has a very high tensile strength, which gives it the ability to support and protect underlying structures from injury. Organized connective tissue is viscoelastic, which means it has a combination of two mechanical

The Mechanics of Stretching

properties relating to obtaining normal flexibility: elasticity and viscosity.

An elastic stretch is an elongation of tissues that recovers when the tension is removed. It is often called temporary or recoverable elongation (deformation), and is frequently compared to a spring-like model (Figure 10.2).

A plastic stretch is an elongation in which the deformation to tissue remains even after the tension is removed. This property is termed permanent or nonrecoverable elongation and is likened to a hydraulic cylinder (Figure 10.3). If a hydraulic cylinder is pulled out, it will usually stay in the end position until another force acts upon it.

To obtain maximum results from flexibility training, you must realize that connective tissue behaves in a viscoelastic manner when stretched. That is, connective tissue exhibits both viscous (plastic) and elastic tendencies during elongation (Figure 10.4). When a soft tissue structure is stretched (in the elastic zone) and the force is removed, the tissue length recovers quickly to resting length. When a soft tissue structure is stretched in the plastic zone, a new resting length is attained, and the results are more permanent. Therefore, to produce more than temporary results, stretching techniques must be designed to increase plastic elongation (deformation).

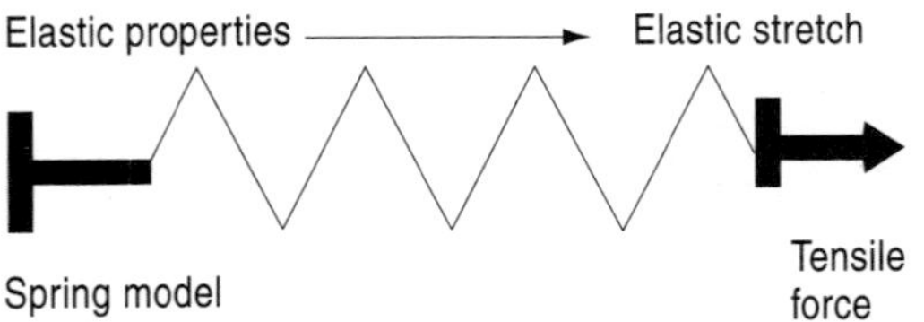

FIGURE 10.2
The "spring" model, representing recoverable (elastic) deformation.

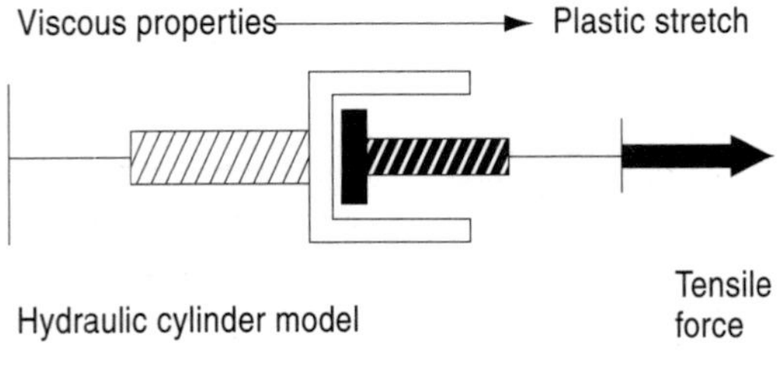

FIGURE 10.3
The "hydraulic cylinder" model, representing permanent (plastic) deformation.

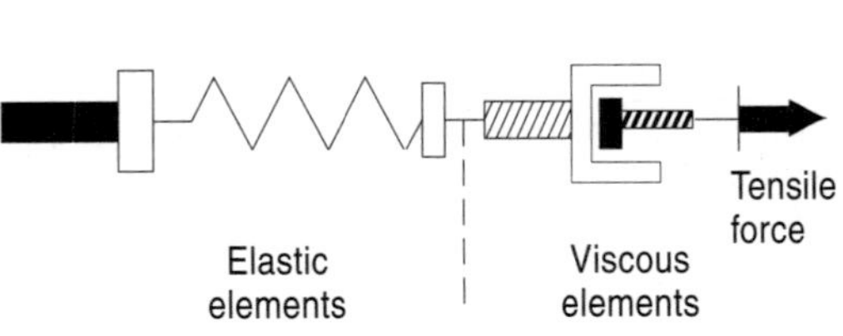

FIGURE 10.4
Viscoelastic connective tissue has both plastic and elastic elements connected in a series.

Whether a stretch effects an elastic (temporary) or plastic (permanent) change in the tissue depends on the methods and condition of the stretch. Two predominant factors in promoting permanent elongation are the force and the duration of the stretch. The degree of tissue lengthening remaining after a force is removed (plastic change) is greatest when a low-force, long-duration stretch (static) is used rather than a high-force, short-duration stretch (ballistic).

Although different stretching methods may be appropriate in different instances, most professionals agree that a static stretch is the safest means to develop passive flexibility. The body, or in this case connective tissue, has the ability to adapt to the stresses placed upon it during physical activity by becoming stronger and better able to sustain increased and progressive levels of exercise intensity. If training conditions exceed the ability to adjust to the current levels of intensity, however, tissues will fail. "Whenever plastic changes are induced in a tissue, this involves a molecular reorganization and weakening of the tissue. However, this stress stimulates the tissue to adapt and the weakening is only short-term, provided training merely involves the stressing of tissue so that it adapts to a new length without any long-term loss of strength" (Enoka, 1994). Connective tissue that is stretched too vigorously and/or for an excessive length of time can fail, leading to serious injury.

Another factor influencing connective tissue extensibility during stretching is an increase in tissue temperature. Exercise physiologists DeVries (1980) and Astrand (1970) concur that an elevation in core body temperature of as little as 1 to 3 degrees produces greater aerobic metabolism on a cellular level and reduced muscle fiber viscosity, increasing muscle elasticity and generally diminishing stiffness. Additional studies have shown that by raising tissue temperature, a thermal transition takes place within collagen microstructures, further augmenting viscous relaxation, and thus permitting enhanced flexibility (Sapega, 1981).

To summarize:

- ✔ A high-force, short-duration stretch performed when the tissue temperature is near or below normal will produce elastic deformation, or temporary, recoverable elongation.
- ✔ A low-force, long-duration stretch at slightly elevated tissue temperature will produce viscous (plastic) deformation, or permanent, non-recoverable elongation.

THE STRETCH REFLEX

A primary component associated with the effects of stretching has a neurophysiologic basis involving reflex activity and is termed the myotatic stretch reflex. The sense organs or neural receptors responsible for the stretch reflex are the muscle spindles lying parallel to the muscle fiber, and the Golgi tendon organs (GTO) found deep within the musculotendinous junctions. Each of these receptors is sensitive to stretch and helps protect a muscle against unnecessary injury.

In general, the muscle spindle passively mimics, or follows, the movements of its adjacent muscle fibers. That is, as the muscle fiber stretches, so does the spindle. The spindle responds to the velocity of the stretch. If the stretch is quick and extreme enough, the muscle spindle responds by sending a signal to the spinal cord, which then returns an order to create a sudden, protective muscular contraction. The spindle ceases to fire when this shortening begins, "unloading" as the muscle fiber contracts and preventing potential tissue damage (Figure 10.5).

The Stretch Reflex

The reflex evoked when the patellar ligament is tapped directly below the kneecap during an examination is a classic example of the stretch reflex. By striking this ligament with a rubber mallet, the physician causes a quick stretch in the quadriceps mechanism. In turn, the muscle spindles react to this unexpected stretch by contracting the quadriceps, resulting in the knee-jerk reflex. Another example is falling asleep in a seated position. As the head relaxes and bends forward, the muscle spindle experiences a sudden stretch, sending a message to the cervical muscle fibers, causing contraction and a sudden jerk to the upright position.

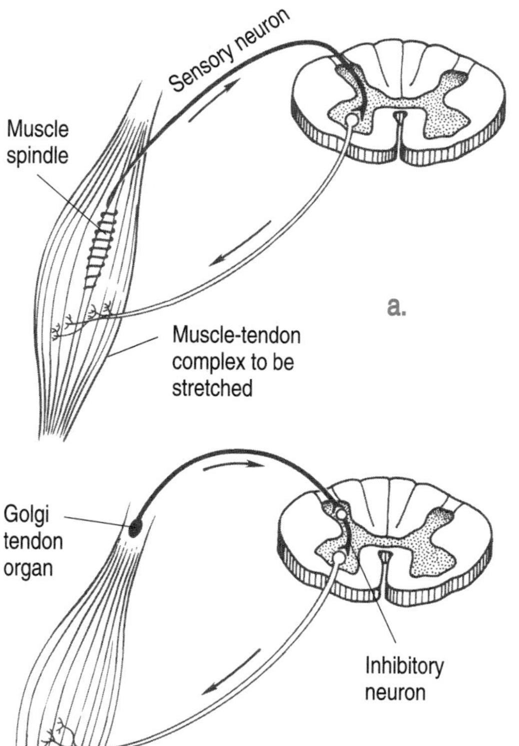

FIGURE 10.5
The stretch reflex and autogenic inhibition.

a. Simple muscle stretch reflex arc: The stretch of the muscle spindle causes reflex contraction.

b. Simple inverse stretch reflex arc: The stretch of Golgi tendon organ causes reflex inhibition (relaxation).

Types of Stretching

It is important to note that as the stretch reflex occurs, antagonist (opposite) muscle action is inhibited. So, when the quadriceps are stimulated with a reflex tap, the hamstrings action is automatically inhibited. This inhibitory response is called reciprocal innervation or reciprocal inhibition.

Up to a point, the harder a muscle is stretched, the stronger the reflex contraction. However, when tension becomes great enough to risk rupture, contraction abruptly stops, and the muscle relaxes. This relaxation response to extreme stretch is called autogenic inhibition and is chiefly dependent on the Golgi tendon organs (GTO). The GTO receptor is actually a weaker and non-dominating system of muscular inhibition. Nevertheless, if all systems are overloaded as a result of excessive stretch or tension, the GTOs transmit impulses to an inhibitory neuron within the spinal cord which finally overrides input from the muscle spindle, causing an immediate relaxation of the entire muscle (Figure 10.5). A greater understanding of the stretch reflex and autogenic and reciprocal inhibition will assist you in determining the effectiveness of various types of stretching techniques used today.

TYPES OF STRETCHING

There are numerous variations in flexibility exercises, but most types can be placed into two main categories: passive stretching and active stretching. During a passive stretch, the contractile components of the muscle are usually relaxed, and the portion of muscle most likely to be loaded is the connective tissue structures mentioned earlier as important in plastic elongation. The static stretch method is an excellent example of passive stretching. On the other hand, active or dynamic stretching has greater effects upon the elastic components — muscles, tendons and musculotendinous junctions (Hubley-Kozen & Stanish, 1984). Because active stretching requires muscle contraction through a range of motion, it has a tendency to load, strengthen and thus prepare these structures for functional activities at hand. As you can see, for maximum benefits in flexibility,

FIGURE 10.6
Static stretching: slow, controlled elongation held for 15 to 30 seconds.

FIGURE 10.7
Ballistic stretching: rapid bouncing or bobbing motions.

Types of Stretching

it is vital to include both active and passive stretching methods in your clients' training programs.

Three popular basic techniques used to increase flexibility are: static stretching, ballistic stretching and proprioceptive neuromuscular facilitation (PNF) stretching. Of these, the static stretching method is advocated by professionals as the least likely to cause injury.

Static Stretching

Static stretching involves a slow, gradual and controlled elongation through a full range of motion. For example, a client stretching the calf (gastrocnemius) would lean (with back straight) over the forward knee until a pull is felt (without pain) in the calf, and hold the position for 15 to 30 seconds (Figure 10.6). This is a low-intensity, long-duration stretch technique. Stretching in this manner physiologically suppresses the stretch reflex. As muscle spindles and the central nervous system (CNS) adapt slowly to a lengthened position, spindle discharge diminishes and muscle relaxation increases.

Ballistic Stretching

Ballistic or dynamic stretching employs rapid, uncontrolled bouncing or bobbing motions (Figure 10.7). This technique incorporates a high-force, short-duration stretch, stimulating muscle spindle activity and, therefore, greater reflex muscular contraction. Uncontrolled or excessive movement also can overload soft tissue structures beyond normal elastic capabilities. Consequently, many trainers, physical therapists and physicians feel ballistic stretching is a higher risk stretching technique, and should be avoided unless specifically needed to prepare for a ballistic sports activity. In this case, there may be a practical advantage to using this stretching method. Ballistic stretching may promote dynamic flexibility and decrease potential injury by preparing tissues for high-speed, volitional-type exercise. Since many movements in sport and exercise are ballistic in nature, a dynamic stretching technique may be appropriate when specifically training for sport competition. Technically, dynamic stretching should consist of rhythmic actions meant to mimic a training

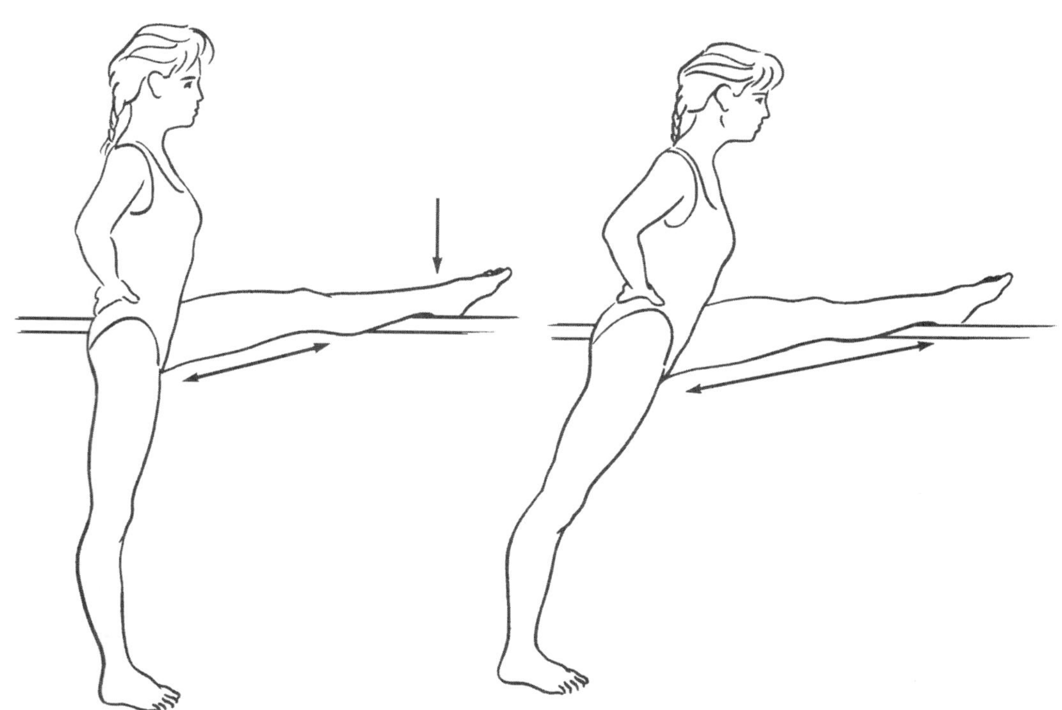

FIGURE 10.8
Proprioceptive neuromuscular facilitation (PNF): contraction followed by relaxation and a slow, passive stretch.

activity, initially small and gradually increasing to larger ranges of motion. However, this method of stretching is not generally recommended for the general population because control may be compromised and the risk of injury increased.

Proprioceptive Neuromuscular Facilitation (PNF)

Proprioceptive Neuromuscular Facilitation (PNF), another common stretching procedure, was first developed by physicians and physical therapists for use in rehabilitation. PNF is a method of hastening neuromuscular responses by stimulating neural proprioceptors (Voss, et al., 1985). Although PNF is extremely complicated and composed of many strategies to promote a variety of results, the aspect most commonly used in training is the contract-relax sequence of PNF. Based on the principle of reciprocal inhibition, this method requires an initial isometric contraction against maximum resistance at the end of the limb's range of motion for approximately six seconds, followed by relaxation and a slow, passive stretch at the point of limitation (Figure 10.8). This sequence is usually repeated several times, and the summation of maximum neural excitations to the muscle being stretched theoretically allows for a greater reflex inhibition and thus a greater stretch. At the end of a contract-relax stretch, it is important to slightly stimulate the antagonist (opposing muscle group) in order to ensure a return to neuromuscular balance. Proponents of this method claim that individuals experience more passive mobility. However, researchers Moore and Hutton (1980) concluded that though the more complicated PNF technique was more effective than conventional stretching techniques, contract-relax was often perceived as more uncomfortable when compared to static stretching. Because PNF exercises were designed to be done with a partner, they should be performed with a knowledgeable and experienced professional.

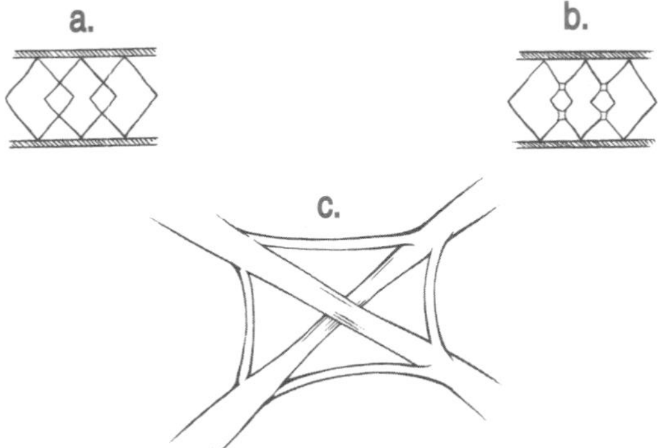

FIGURE 10.9
Age-related changes in collagen fibers.

a. Normal collagen fiber.

b. Age-related collagen fiber crosslinks.

c. Newly synthesized fiber, the result of aging.

FACTORS AFFECTING FLEXIBILITY

Clearly, different stretching techniques produce different results. There also are a number of additional factors specific to each client that contribute to the success or failure of a flexibility program.

Age and Inactivity

Several studies have indicated that there is a distinct relationship between age and degree of flexibility. Developmentally, the greatest increase in flexibility usually occurs up to and between the ages of seven and 12. During early adolescence, flexibility tends to level off and thereafter begins to decline. After age 25, normal aging tends to accelerate, causing significant changes in connective tissue and eventually decreased extensibility. Aging increases both the diameter of collagen fibers and the number of intermolecular cross-links (Alter, 1988) (Figure 10.9). This age-related effect strengthens connective tissue bonds, further increasing the resistance to deformation. A fair amount of dehydration in and around soft tissue structures also occurs as one ages. This lack of water in soft tissue structures diminishes lubrication and the flow of nutrients to the site, ultimately creating a more fragile unit.

Generally speaking, the more active a

person is throughout the aging process, the more flexible they will be. Inactivity, or hypokinesis, as it is often called, permits adaptive shortening within connective tissue structures. When connective tissue is not actively stretched through a full range of motion, it becomes shorter and less resilient, making it difficult to obtain the balance essential for proper alignment during activity. Regular stretching throughout one's life can enhance positive tissue adaptability and reduce natural wear and tear.

Gender

Although conclusive evidence is still lacking, there appears to be a strong gender difference related to flexibility potential. Females are generally much more flexible than males. One hypothesis for this is that, genetically, women are designed for a greater range of flexibility, especially in the pelvic region, in order to accommodate childbearing.

Body Type and Strength Training

Many attempts have been made to relate body type and flexibility. For example, an underweight fragile body type (ectomorph) might be thought to have greater flexibility than a heavier, over-developed or massive body type (endomorph). However, in recent studies, there has been little correlation between weight and body type and the ability to achieve range of motion.

Strength training is an area where misconceptions concerning flexibility continue to exist. Many still believe that weight training causes the body to become muscle-bound and lack overall flexibility. It is true that overdeveloping muscles may encourage muscular imbalances if stretching is not incorporated into the training program, but the perception that strength training independently decreases flexibility is a myth. The 1976 U.S. Olympic weightlifting team ranked second only to gymnasts in joint range of motion testing.

It is important to remember that flexibility has been consistently shown to be highly specific to the individual, to the activity and to each joint. Since each person has different musculature, joint structure and genetic composition, you must create programs that are individual to each of your clients. Flexibility is not necessarily an underlying characteristic of each person, but it is an essential component of physical fitness.

Warm-up

A warm-up is a slow, rhythmic exercise of larger muscle groups performed before an activity, which provides the body with a period of adjustment between rest and performance of that activity. Generally, warm-up prepares the body for what is about to come. Scientists agree that by imitating an exercise activity for a period of five to 15 minutes before high-intensity involvement, overall performance will be heightened. This technique gradually warms tissues, increasing blood flow and nutrients to active structures. Warm-up may also fine-tune CNS receptors to improve kinesthetic awareness during activity. (That is, sensory organs within muscles, tendons and joints facilitate our ability to know where we are in space during an activity.) This kinesthetic awareness helps prepare our bodies for activity, so that we gain a certain amount of protection and psychological readiness necessary for reducing potential injuries. Warm-up can be used to prepare soft tissue structures for the flexibility necessary for any particular activity.

PRINCIPLES OF STRETCHING

Although there is continuing controversy over which flexibility exercises are best, whether to stretch before or after exercise, or just how much to stretch, professionals currently agree on certain guidelines that should be incorporated into your clients' fitness programs.

Principles of Stretching

Most experts recommend stretching both before and after intense activity, but each for different reasons. In preparation for activity, pre-stretch is primarily active and aimed at decreasing tissue stiffness, focusing particularly on the muscles that will be used in the activity to follow. For example, an aerobic dance participant would stretch hamstrings and calves during warm-up, while a tennis player might stretch forearm and shoulder muscles as well.

With intense exercise, body temperature increases and tissues offer less resistance. Therefore, stretching for permanent elongation is emphasized later in the workout rather than at the beginning. Stretching after exercise may also enhance muscle relaxation, facilitating normal resting length, circulation to structures and removal of unwanted waste products. Body core temperature also is found to be highest just after the aerobic or more intense portions of training programs. For these reasons, and in order to achieve maximum gains in range of motion, it is logical and highly recommended to include static stretching exercises at this stage.

How often one should stretch is still not fully understood. Professionals seem to agree, however, that daily stretching is best, or at least before and after activity sessions. In a Swedish study, Wallin et al. (1985) found that once subjects had attained optimal flexibility, stretching just one to two times per week would maintain those ranges. However, when stretching

FIGURE 10.10
Neck/cervical spine stretch. With left arm at side and shoulder down, slowly bend the chin to chest and turn toward right shoulder. Using only the weight of the hand, stretch away from the left shoulder. Repeat on the left side.

FIGURE 10.11
Anterior shoulder stretch (pectoralis stretch). Stand and place your right palm against a wall and rotate the torso away from the hand until a stretch is felt across the chest and shoulder. Repeat on the left side.

FIGURE 10.12
Posterior shoulder stretch. With shoulders down and relaxed, bring right arm across the chest, parallel to the floor. Place the left hand on the upper arm and apply gentle pressure toward the body. Repeat on the left side.

FIGURE 10.13
Triceps stretch. Bend the right elbow and use the left arm to bring the bent elbow up and behind the head until a stretch is felt on the outside of the upper arm. Repeat on the left side.

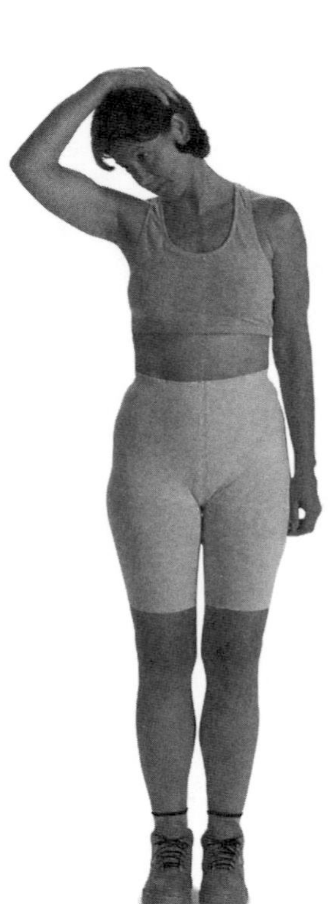

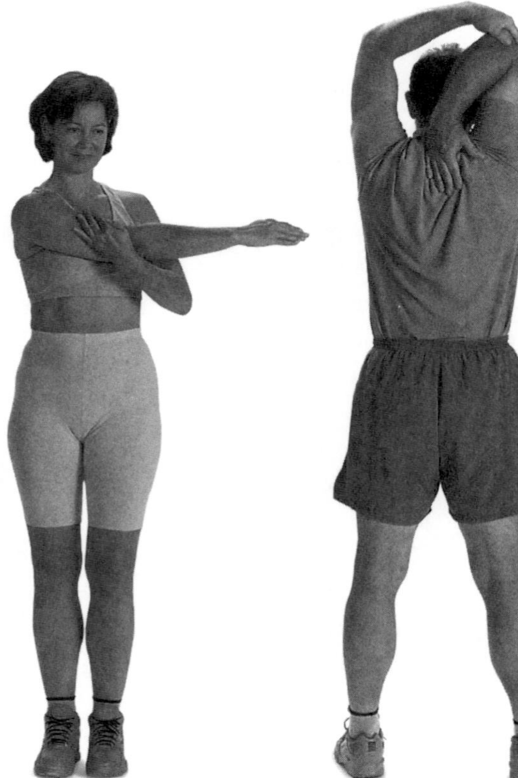

Principles of Stretching

was incorporated three to five times per week after attainment, range of motion was augmented further. Various other studies have demonstrated that increased mobility remains from only 90 minutes to 24 hours after performing stretching exercises. In other words, more frequent stretching would increase and maintain flexibility, while avoiding muscular imbalances created by daily activities or exercise.

When designing a stretching program for a client, you should keep the following in mind:

1. Connective tissue elongation (plastic deformation) is the primary target when stretching.

2. The two most important factors influencing stretching are intensity and duration. A low-intensity, long-duration stretch favors more lasting plastic tissue deformation. A high-intensity, short-duration stretch favors a more temporary elastic tissue deformation.

3. Elevated tissue temperature facilitates range of motion.

4. Flexibility is specific; therefore, exercises must be specific to each joint and/ or group.

5. Proper alignment for each stretch is

FIGURE 10.14
Low back stretch. On back with knees bent, gently pull both knees toward chest, lifting feet off the floor; hold and relax. This exercise may also be done using one leg.

FIGURE 10.15
Outer hip stretch. On back, flex right knee across the body and pull toward left shoulder. Repeat on the left side.

FIGURE 10.16
Cat stretch.
a. On hands and knees, sag back, lifting head up.
b. Arch back, lower head down.

FIGURE 10.17
Torso stretch. On stomach, place hands as if to do a push-up. Lift upper body, keeping hips and lower body on the floor. This stretch may also be performed while keeping the elbows on the ground. Perform this exercise in a pain-free range only.

Flexibility Exercises

critical to achieve maximum effectiveness in any one specific muscle group. By creating a good relationship between one joint and another during exercise, one biomechanically places muscles in positions to achieve maximum effectiveness in stretching, absorb shock and decrease stress to surrounding soft tissue structures.

FLEXIBILITY EXERCISES

Your clients would benefit most by regularly performing the exercises in Figures 10.10 through 10.15, which emphasize major muscle groups important in postural correction, as well as individual sports activities. If there are

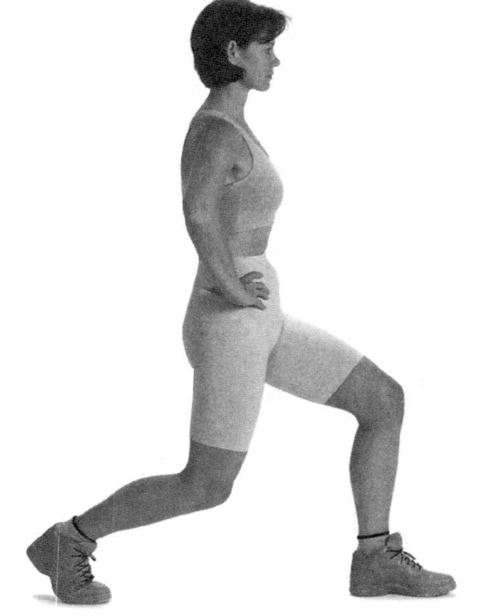

FIGURE 10.18
Hip flexor stretch. Assume lunge position, making sure front knee is directly over the foot and ankle. With weight supported by both hands, press hips toward floor.

FIGURE 10.19
Groin stretch. Sitting erect with soles of feet together, gently pull heels toward groin and press inside of knees toward floor.

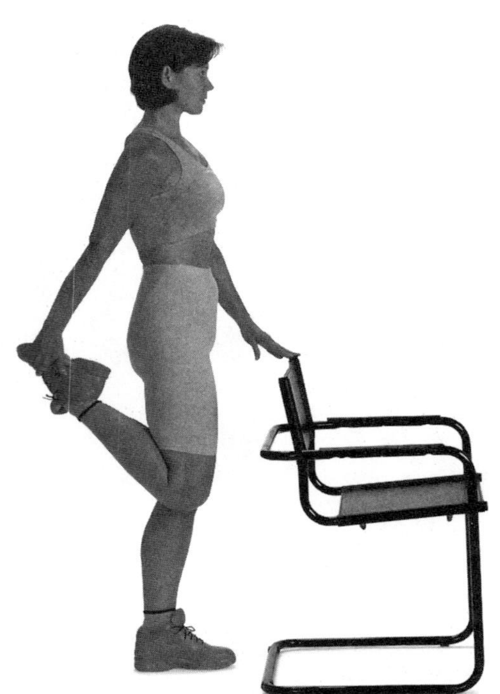

FIGURE 10.20
Quadriceps stretch. Using a wall or chair as support, reach back with right hand and grasp right foot or ankle. Be sure hips are forward and knees are adjacent to each other. Repeat on the left side.

FIGURE 10.21
Hamstring stretch. Stand in front of a low step or bench and place left heel on it. Place hands on right leg for support and lower and lean forward from the hips until a stretch is felt in the back of the leg. Repeat

time constraints, your first priority should be to target your client's individual needs based on flexibility assessments (see Chapter 6). In addition, if your client has overworked a specific muscle group during exercise or daily activities, include a series of stretches addressing that area at the end of the session. Finally, it is important to include exercises addressing your client's chronically tight areas, such as hamstrings, calves, posterior neck, anterior shoulder, hip flexors and low-back musculature.

SUMMARY

Although its role in fitness is not as well-documented scientifically as other components, flexibility is an essential part of a well-balanced exercise program. To understand the effects of various stretching techniques, you need to understand the mechanics and neurophysiology of flexibility. Most professionals agree that of the three major types of stretching — static, ballistic and PNF — static stretching is most beneficial and least likely to cause injury. A static stretch is a low-intensity, long-duration stretch that favors more lasting connective tissue elongation (plastic deformation). Ideally, a client should stretch daily. You also can see that your client stretches both before and after exercise sessions. Because age, gender, level and type of activity play a role in achieving and maintaining full range of motion, it is important that you design a stretching program to meet the assessed needs of each individual client.

Summary

FIGURE 10.22
Stretches for the calf.

a. Gastrocnemius stretch. Using the wall or a chair as support, place one foot behind the other. With front knee slightly bent, back knee straight and heel down, lean hips forward. Repeat on the opposite side.

b. Soleus stretch. Using a wall or chair as support, place one foot behind the other. With both knees bent and heels down, lean forward from the hips. Repeat on the opposite side.

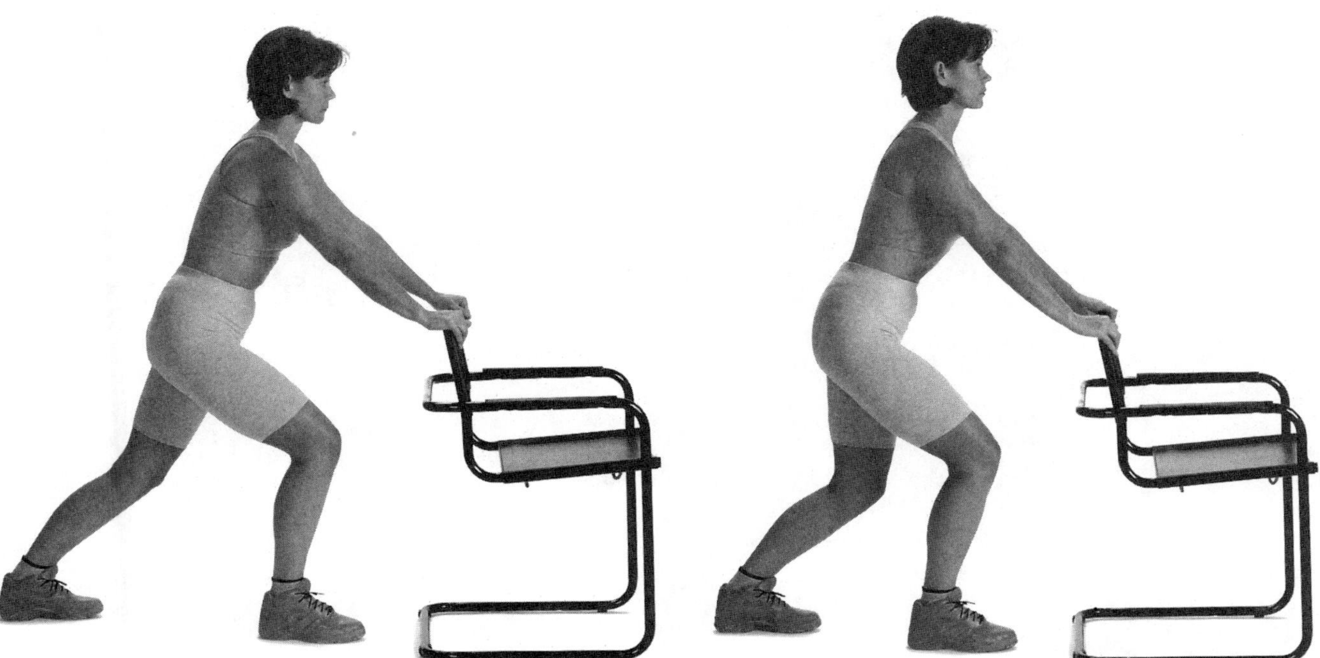

REFERENCES

Alter, M. (1988). *Science of Stretching.* Champaign: Human Kinetics.

Astrand, O. & Rodahl, K. (1970). *Textbook of Work Physiology.* New York: McGraw-Hill.

DeVries, H. (1980). *Physiology of Exercise for Physical Education.* (3rd ed.) Dubuque: William C. Brown.

Ecstrand, J. & Gillquist, J. (1982). The frequency of muscle tightness and injuries in soccer players. *American Journal of Sports Medicine,* 10, 55-58.

Evjenth, O. & Hamberg, J. (1989). *Autostretching: The Complete Manual of Specific Stretching.* Sweden: Alfta Rehab Forlag.

Hubley-Kozey, C. & Stanish, W. (1984). Can stretching prevent athletic injuries? *Journal of Musculoskeletal Medicine,* 9, 25-32.

Kendall, F., McCreary E. & Provance P. (1994). *Muscles: Testing and Function.* (2nd ed.) Baltimore: Williams & Wilkins.

Moller, M. (1984). Athletic training and flexibility. A study on range of motion in the lower extremity. *Linkoping University Medical Dissertations.* No. 182.

Moore, M. & Hutton, R. (1980). Electromyographic investigation of muscle stretching techniques. *Medicine and Science in Sports and Exercise,* 12, 322-329.

Sady, S., Wortman, M. & Blanke, D. (1982). Flexibility training: ballistic, or proprioceptive neuromuscular facilitation? *Archives of Physical Medicine and Rehabilitation.* 63: 261-263.

Sapega, A., Quedenfeld, T., Moyer, R. & Butler, R. (1981). Biophysical factors in range-of-motion exercise. *Physician and Sportsmedicine,* 9, 57-64.

Schultz, P. (1979). Flexibility: Day of the static stretch. *Physician and Sportsmedicine,* 7, 109-117.

Voss, D., Ionta, M. & Myers, B. (1985). *Proprioceptive Neuromuscular Facilitation: Patterns and Techniques,* (3rd ed.) Philadelphia: Harper & Row.

Wallin, D., Ekblom, B., Grahn, R. & Nordenberg, T. (1985). Improvement of muscle flexibility: A comparison between two techniques. *American Journal of Sports Medicine,* 13, 263-268.

SUGGESTED READING

Anderson, B. (1980). *Stretching.* Bolinas, CA: Shelter Publications.

Francis, P. & Francis, L. (1988). *If It Hurts, Don't Do It.* Rocklin, CA: Prima Publishing.

Wirbed, R. (1984). *Athletic Ability and the Anatomy of Motion.* London: Wolfe Medical Publications.

PART IV

IV

Individualized Program Design

CHAPTER 11

Programming for the Healthy Adult

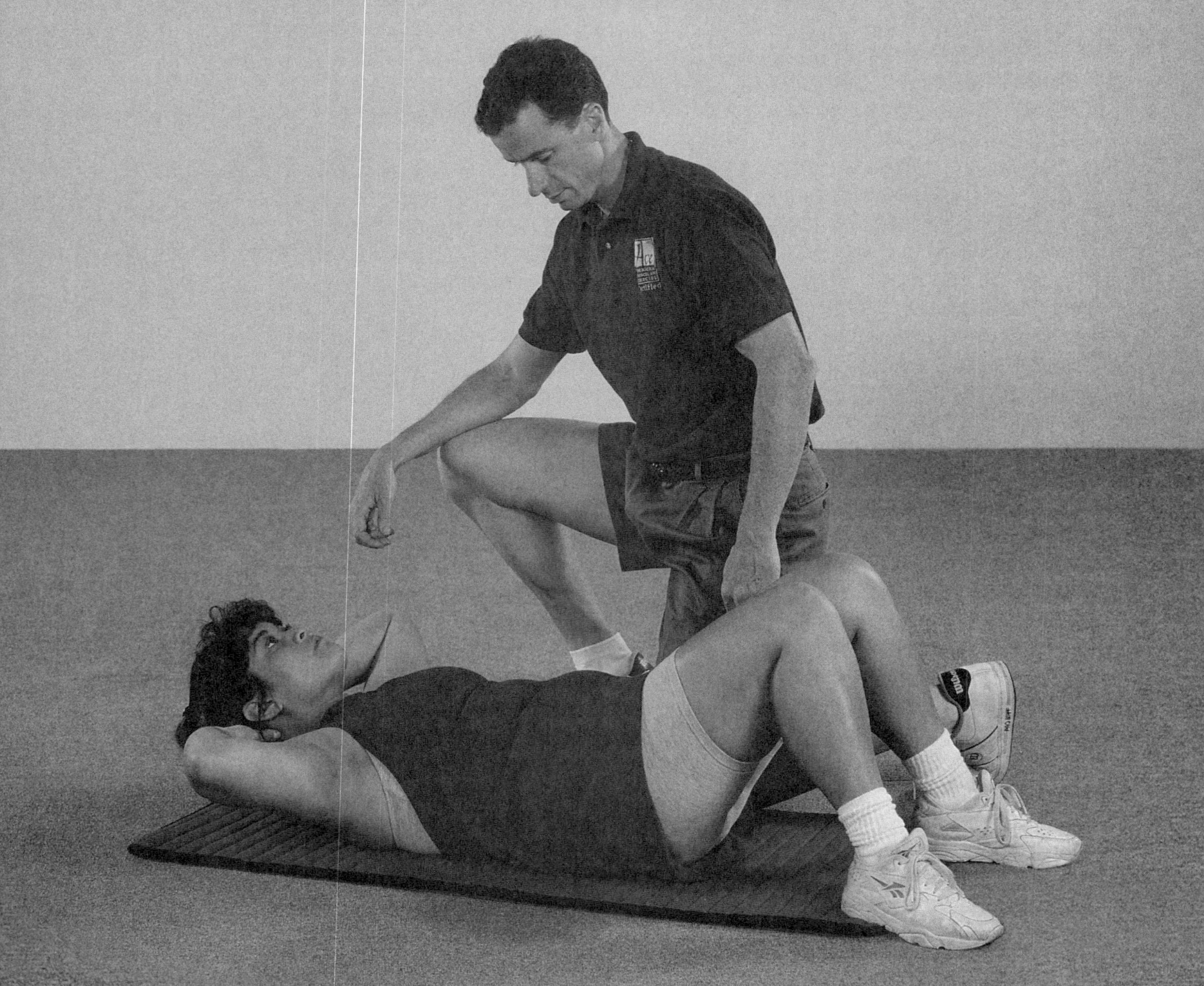

11

IN THIS CHAPTER:

David C. Nieman

David Nieman, Dr. P.H., F.A.C.S.M., is a professor of health and exercise science at Appalachian State University in Boone, NC. He has taught at the college and university level since 1972, and is the author of four textbooks and more than 80 research articles in the areas of sports medicine, exercise and health, exercise immunology, sports nutrition and obesity.

As a personal trainer, you have the unique opportunity to adapt and individualize exercise workouts according to your client's distinctive background and goals. People vary widely in their health and fitness status, motivation, goals, age, needs and desires, education, occupation, health habits and medical background. Developing an exercise program that best meets your client's needs in a safe and effective manner requires a clear understanding of that person.

In previous chapters of this book, information is given on health screening, testing and evaluation, and training regimens for the development of cardiorespiratory and musculoskeletal fitness. In this chapter, emphasis is placed on how these components can be combined to provide comprehensive exercise programs

Exercise for Physical Fitness vs. Health and Disease Prevention

Table 11.1
Physical Activity and Public Health: A Recommendation From the Centers for Disease Control and Prevention and the American College of Sports Medicine: Key Statements

- ✔ The current low-participation rate may be due, in part, to the misperception of many people that to reap health benefits, they must engage in vigorous, continuous exercise. Scientific evidence clearly demonstrates that regular, moderate-intensity physical activity provides substantial health benefits.
- ✔ Every U. S. adult should accumulate 30 minutes or more of moderate-intensity physical activity on most, preferably all, days of the week. One way to meet this standard is to walk two miles briskly.
- ✔ Intermittent activity also confers substantial benefits. Therefore, the recommended 30 minutes of activity can be accumulated in short bouts of activity: walking up the stairs instead of taking the elevator, walking instead of driving short distances, doing calisthenics or pedaling a stationary cycle while watching television.
- ✔ The health benefits gained from increased physical activity depend on the initial physical fitness level. Sedentary individuals are expected to benefit most from increasing their activity to the recommended level.
- ✔ Two other components of fitness — flexibility and muscular strength — should not be overlooked. Clinical experience and limited studies suggest that people who maintain or improve their strength and flexibility may be better able to perform daily activities, may be less likely to develop back pain, and may be better able to avoid disability, especially as they advance in age.
- ✔ If Americans who lead sedentary lives would adopt a more active lifestyle, there would be enormous benefit to the public's health and to individual well-being. An active lifestyle does not require a regimented, vigorous exercise program. Instead, small changes that increase daily physical activity will enable individuals to reduce their risk of chronic disease and may contribute to enhanced quality of life.

Source: Pate, R.R, Pratt, M., Blair, S.N., et al., 1995.

for your clients. The intent of this chapter is best described in the definition of exercise prescription given by the American College of Sports Medicine (ACSM): "the process whereby a person's recommended regimen of physical activity is designed in a systematic and individualized manner."

There are four primary steps in designing a formal, comprehensive exercise program:

1. medical/health screening
2. physical fitness testing
3. selection of exercise mode
4. design of an exercise program for total fitness

This chapter will explain the rationale for each step. You will be referred to previous chapters for specific information on conducting the various screenings and tests.

Before exploring these four steps in designing a formal exercise program, one important point needs to be addressed—the difference between exercise programs designed to develop physical fitness, and those focused on health and the prevention of disease.

EXERCISE FOR PHYSICAL FITNESS vs. HEALTH AND DISEASE PREVENTION

During this century, there have been many opinions about what is the best type of exercise for the American public. During the first half of the century, for example, muscular strength was emphasized by many fitness leaders as the primary goal of an exercise program. During the boom years of the **aerobic** movement in the 1970s and 1980s, development of cardiorespiratory fitness through high-intensity aerobic exercise was emphasized, often to the detriment of musculoskeletal fitness. The focus now is on a comprehensive approach to physical fitness in which three major components—cardiorespiratory fitness,

Exercise for Physical Fitness vs. Health and Disease Prevention

Table 11.2
American College of Sports Medicine Exercise Prescription Recommendations

	Intensity (%VO_2 max)	Duration (minutes)	Frequency (days/week)	Purpose
ACSM, 1990	50-85%	20-60	3-5	Develop, maintain fitness, body composition*
ACSM, 1991	40-85%	15-60	3-5	Designed to encompass activity that may enhance health without having a major impact on fitness**
ACSM, 1993	moderate	30 or more	near daily	Developed to emphasize the important health benefits of moderate physical activity***

* ACSM in 1990 also included recommendations for developing and maintaining muscular strength and endurance for the first time (at least one set of 8 to 12 repetitions of eight to 10 exercises that condition the major muscle groups at least two days a week).

** ACSM also gave general guidelines for developing flexibility and muscular strength and endurance.

*** ACSM also recommended regular participation in physical activities that develop and maintain muscular strength and joint flexibility.

Sources: American College of Sports Medicine, 1995. Pate, R.R, Pratt, M., Blair, S.N., et al., 1995.

"Exercise lite"

musculoskeletal fitness and body composition—are given balanced attention.

In 1993, the ACSM released its "exercise lite" recommendations. With an emphasis on general physical activity and disease prevention, these recommendations caught some people off guard (Table 11.1). The ACSM currently has three different sets of exercise prescription standards, which are compared in Table 11.2. Notice that when the development of **cardiorespiratory endurance** is the objective, the intensity of training should range between 50 percent to 85 percent of **VO_2 max** (or 60 percent to 90 percent of maximum heart rate). When improvement in health is of more concern, the intensity can drop to 40 percent, and people in the general population are simply urged to "accumulate 30 minutes or more of moderate-intensity physical activity over the course of most days of the week."

Because these three sets of standards complement each other, you are urged to adapt these recommendations in accordance with the goals and unique characteristics of your client. The ACSM released its 1993 recommendations in light of concerns that the majority of Americans had not entered the modern-day physical fitness movement because "previous public health efforts to promote physical activity have overemphasized the importance of high-intensity exercise. The current low rate of participation may be explained, in part, by the perception of many people that they must engage in vigorous, continuous exercise to reap health benefits."

For some time now, the ACSM has recognized that most people prefer a less technical, more informal approach to exercise programming, and public health officials will be monitoring the response of Americans to the new guidelines. Year 2000 physical activity and fitness goals for the nation are outlined in Table 11.3. Depending on the survey, only 10 percent to 15 percent of American adults report exercising vigorously (at an intensity of at least 60 percent VO_2 max for 20 or more minutes per session, three or more times per week), the level generally recommended for cardiovascular benefit. Approximately 25 percent of Americans report that they exercise moderately (at an intensity below 60 percent VO_2 max) five or more times per week, while another 25 percent report living essentially **sedentary** lifestyles. The rest of Americans report exercising irregularly, which means that 35 percent to

Exercise for Physical Fitness vs. Health and Disease Prevention

Table 11.3
Healthy People 2000: Year 2000 Objectives to Increase Physical Activity and Fitness

Year 2000 Goals (selected)	Best Estimate of Current Status
Increase to at least 30 percent the proportion of people aged 6 and older who engage regularly, preferably daily, in light-to-moderate physical activity (less than 50 percent VO_2 max) for at least 30 minutes per day.	24% (5 times/wk) 17% (7 times/wk)
Increase to at least 20 percent the proportion of people aged 18 and older, and to at least 75 percent the proportion of children and adolescents aged 6 through 17, who engage in vigorous physical activity (greater than 50 percent VO_2max) that promotes the development and maintenance of cardiorespiratory fitness three or more days per week for 20 or more minutes per occasion.	14% (age 18+ yrs) 66% (ages 10-17)
Reduce to no more than 15 percent the proportion of people aged 6 and older who engage in no leisure-time physical activity.	24% of adults
Increase to at least 40 percent the proportion of people aged 6 and older who regularly perform physical activities that enhance and maintain muscular strength, muscular endurance and flexibility.	16% (adults, weight training)

Source: Public Health Service, U.S. Department of Health and Human Services (1991). Healthy People 2000: National Health Promotion and Disease Prevention Objectives. DHHS Publication No. (PHS) 91-50212. Government Printing Office, Washington, DC 20402-9325.

40 percent of adults exercise fewer than three times per week, 20 minutes per session.

The biggest challenge you face as a personal trainer is motivating clients to adhere to their exercise program. Principles of adherence and motivation are reviewed in Chapter 13. In general, to enhance long-term participation in regular physical activity, several factors should be considered, especially those that pertain to the person (gender, age, occupational status, health status, education, prior exercise experience), the exercise regimen itself (in particular, intensity and mode), and the environment (weather, community facilities, home-based programs, travel distances, time barriers, family and spousal support, employer and co-worker support, government, economic and public-policy support). The personal trainer can do much to control these factors, and reduce the barriers to long-term exercise adherence.

What does all this mean for you, the personal trainer? The exercise program should be designed to meet a client's needs and personal goals, whether they be health-related, fitness-related or both. For the client who merely desires an exercise program to decrease risk of disease and feel better, a walking program with supportive calisthenics may be sufficient. For others who are seeking large increases in physical fitness for improved appearance and performance, a more formal, intensive aerobic and musculoskeletal fitness program should be designed.

Although the natural tendency of most fitness leaders is to urge clients to adopt intensive fitness programs, the ACSM "exercise lite" recommendations will probably better meet the needs of most Americans. During the past decade, there has been a shift from uniform exercise prescription based on intensity, frequency and duration to one that encourages increased levels of general energy expenditure throughout a person's day. Helping clients to increase routine or transportation-related physical activity, and facilitating more convenient forms of leisure-time activity, especially for those who have little interest in formal exercise programs, should now become an accepted part of your counseling skills.

Step 1: Medical/ Health Screening

Step 2: Physical Fitness Testing

Step 3: Selection of the Aerobic Exercise Mode

As mentioned earlier in this chapter, there are four steps in establishing an exercise program for a client. These apply whether the exercise program will follow more traditional guidelines for exercise prescription, or the new, more moderate "exercise lite" guidelines.

STEP 1: MEDICAL/HEALTH SCREENING

As emphasized in Chapter 5, to gain a complete picture of your client's background, current medical and health status, motivation and current goals, a comprehensive questionnaire should be completed and carefully reviewed. There are many good questionnaires available that ask about personal and family history of disease, **risk factors** and symptoms, present medications and treatment, lifestyle habits, social/demographic factors, and exercise history and attitude.

After completing the questionnaire, the client can then be classified as apparently healthy, at higher risk or with disease. Appropriate judgments should then be made for further testing with physician supervision. According to ACSM, this "risk stratification" is important to ensure the safety of exercise testing and participation. It also helps to determine the appropriate type of exercise program, identifies those in need of more extensive medical evaluation and makes appropriate recommendations for an exercise program.

Each year, about 75,000 Americans suffer a heart attack during or after exercise. These victims tend to be individuals who are usually sedentary and at high risk for heart disease. During unaccustomed exercise, a chain of physiological events takes place in the body that lead to a heart attack. With appropriate screening and referral to medical facilities, the incidence of cardiovascular problems during exercise can be greatly reduced.

Information from the questionnaire also can be used to gain a complete background on the client so that you can better meet their needs and goals. As emphasized in the introduction to this chapter, people vary widely. The design of an exercise program for an elderly, obese female will differ greatly from one developed for a young female athlete.

STEP 2: PHYSICAL FITNESS TESTING

In Chapter 6, a complete review of physical fitness testing and evaluation is given. Before the exercise program is designed, you must know how physically fit the client is for at least four reasons:

1. to assess current fitness levels, both strengths and weaknesses
2. to identify special needs for individualized counseling
3. to evaluate progress over time
4. to motivate and educate

The testing process is invaluable, and can be used to help clients learn more about themselves while establishing appropriate health and fitness goals. The very process of administering a fitness test draws attention to what is considered worthy of special attention in the lifestyle. The test results can be used to educate, motivate and stimulate interest in exercise and other health-related topics.

Normative information on each test should be shared with each client. Research results have shown that the testing process, in and of itself, often spurs people to make meaningful and lasting changes in their lifestyles.

STEP 3: SELECTION OF THE AEROBIC EXERCISE MODE

Selection of the aerobic exercise mode by the client is central to the long-term success of the exercise program. Most studies have shown that if frequency, intensity and duration of training are similar, the cardiorespiratory training outcomes are independent of the

Step 3: Selection of the Aerobic Exercise Mode

Table 11.4
Fitness Benefits of Selected Physical Activities

Activities are rated on a 5-point scale in terms of capacity to develop aerobic fitness or muscular strength/ endurance. 1=not at all; 2=somewhat or just a little; 3=moderately; 4=strongly; 5=very strongly. For muscular strength and endurance, the activity is rated high if both upper- and lower-body musculature is improved.

Physical Activity	Aerobic Fitness	Muscular Strength and Endurance
Aerobic dance, moderate-to-hard	4	4
Basketball, game play	4	2
Bicycling, fast pace	5	3
Canoeing, rowing, hard pace	5	4
Circuit weight training	3	5
Handball, game play	4	3
Golf, walking, carrying bag	3	2
Lawn mowing, power push	3	3
Racquetball, squash, game play	4	3
Rope jumping, moderate-to-hard	4	3
Running, brisk pace	5	2
Roller blading/skating	4	3
Shoveling dirt, digging	4	4
Skiing, downhill	2	3
Skiing, cross country	5	4
Soccer	4	3
Splitting wood	4	4
Stair climbing	5	3
Swimming	5	4
Tennis, game play	3	3
Volleyball, game play	3	3
Walking, briskly	3	2
Weight training	1	5

mode of aerobic activity. In other words, if different people cycle, swim or run five days per week, 30 minutes per session at 70 percent **heart rate reserve**, after 10 to 15 weeks, improvement in heart and lung fitness should be comparable. It should be noted, however, that some aerobic activities, like rowing and swimming, also confer considerable musculoskeletal benefits, giving more of a "total fitness" benefit when compared to running or cycling, for example. Table 11.4 summarizes the fitness benefits of selected physical activities.

Aerobic activity mode should be selected on the basis of individual interest, time and facility availability, personal goals and objectives, and fitness level. Present your client with a comprehensive list of suitable aerobic activities and discuss them thoroughly from both a practical and total fitness perspective. Next, have your client choose primary and secondary activities that they can fit into their schedule without creating undue stress and inconvenience.

"Lack of time" is the major obstacle individuals list for not continuing exercise programs, and this potential problem should be discussed from every angle to ensure long-term adherence. To improve compliance, some people like the socialization, competitiveness and pleasure of both dual and team sports. As shown in Table 11.4, many sports can develop aerobic and musculoskeletal fitness, improving compliance for those who enjoy this type of exercise. Others enjoy various work activities such as splitting wood or shoveling dirt, feeling that while overall fitness is being improved, they also are accomplishing a worthwhile task.

National surveys show that the most popular fitness activity continues to be walking, followed by swimming, bicycle riding, exercising with equipment, basketball and aerobic dancing. Moderate-intensity activities of longer duration are being promoted more and more by fitness leaders because these types of activities are more

Step 3: Selection of the Aerobic Exercise Mode

The Exercise Programming Form

Stage One - Cardiorespiratory/Body Composition

1. **Warm-up**
   Purpose: To slowly elevate the pulse to an aerobic level by engaging in 5 minutes of slow aerobic activity.

2. **The Aerobic Session**
   Purpose: To improve the cardiorespiratory system of the body by exercising vigorously for at least 20-30 minutes, 3 times/week, on a regular basis.

	Fitness Status		
F.I.T. Guidelines	**Low**	**Average**	**High**
F Frequency (sessions/week)	3	3-4	≥ 5
I Intensity (% heart rate reserve)	50-60%	60-75%	75-85%
T Time (minutes/session)	10-20	20-30	30-60

Mode Selection (your personal)____________________

Training HR = [(Max HR - RHR) x 50 to 85%] + RHR

__________ = [__________ - __________ x __________] + __________

Days of week and time of exercise sessions

Sun _____ Mon _____ Tue _____ Wed _____ Thu _____ Fri _____ Sat _____

3. **Cool-down**
   Purpose: To slowly decrease the heart rate by engaging in slow aerobic activity for at least 5 minutes.

Stage Two - Musculoskeletal Fitness

1. **Flexibility Exercises** ____________________

   Purpose: To stretch the major muscles and joints, especially those involved in the aerobic session, using static stretching techniques.

2. **Muscular Strength and Endurance Exercises** ____________________

   Purpose: To build muscular endurance and strength, especially in the muscles not developed in aerobic sessions, using appropriate weight training and calisthenic exercises.

FIGURE 11.1
A sample exercise programming form.
Source: Nieman, D.C. *Fitness and Sports Medicine: A Health-Related Approach.* Palo Alto: Bull Publishing, 1995. Used with permission.

Table 11.5
Recommendations for Improving Muscular Strength and Endurance for the General Adult Population*

	Number of Sets	Number of Reps*	Sessions Per Week	Number of Exercises	Overall Purpose
ACSM**	1	8-12	2	8-10	To provide basic development & maintenance of the fat-free mass
CIAR**					
Minimum	1	8-12	2	10	For strength maintenance
Recommended	2	8-12	2	10	For strength improvement
Optimal	3	8-12	2	10	For noticeable strength gains

* In all examples listed, repetitions represent maximal weight lifted to fatigue.
** ACSM = American College of Sports Medicine; CIAR = Cooper Institute for Aerobics Research
Sources: American College of Sports Medicine, 1995. Cooper Institute for Aerobics Research, 1990.

acceptable to the masses, increasing the likelihood of a permanent change in lifestyle. Physical activities such as brisk walking result in low rates of musculoskeletal injury, and have the potential to lower blood pressure, improve the lipid profile, reduce body fat, enhance mental well-being, and reduce the risk of coronary heart disease and cancer. Walking has been found to have a higher compliance rate than other physical activities because it can easily be incorporated into a busy time schedule, does not require any special skills, equipment or facility, is companionable and can be undertaken by individuals of all age groups. Do not be reluctant to prescribe walking for a large proportion of your clients.

Participation in a variety of aerobic activities carries several benefits, including decreased risk of overuse injuries, reduced boredom, increased long-term compliance and increased overall fitness. For these reasons, urge your clients to have at least one secondary activity to supplement their primary mode of exercise. Even for athletes, engaging in two or three different types of exercise modes (i.e., cross training) can help maintain fitness during the off-season, or help maintain fitness during periods of injury or when experiencing burn-out.

STEP 4: DESIGNING AN EXERCISE PROGRAM FOR TOTAL FITNESS

As emphasized in Chapter 6, a comprehensive exercise program considers all components of physical fitness: cardiorespiratory endurance, muscular strength and endurance, **flexibility** and **body composition.** Figure 11.1 is a sample exercise programming form that can be used to ensure all components are given due attention during the training session.

Notice that the exercise programming form is divided into two stages: cardiorespiratory/body composition and musculoskeletal fitness. There are many different combinations that can be used to ensure that both categories of physical fitness are developed. For example, some clients may desire a total physical fitness workout each session, while others may engage in strength training one day and aerobic training the next. Some may prefer a daily walking program supplemented with flexibility and muscular endurance calisthenics.

Once clients have selected a primary and secondary aerobic activity from Table 11.4, have them write these in the "mode selection" blank. Next, go step-by-step through each stage of the exercise programming form, explaining the basic concepts involved (see Chapters 7, 8, 9 and 10).

For the warm-up, emphasize the importance of elevating body temperature through slow aerobic activity, preferably the aerobic activity that will be utilized in the workout session. This will provide a cardiovascular and neuromuscular rehearsal for the aerobic session itself. Explain that flexibility exercises are best conducted after the aerobic session when the body is warm.

Next, circle the appropriate F.I.T. criteria based on the fitness test results. Help clients determine their personal training heart rate using the Karvonen formula, and fill in the appropriate blanks. Explain how to measure the training heart rate, and fill in the blank for the 10-second pulse count. Review the concept of **ratings of perceived exertion** (RPE), explaining that an RPE of "somewhat hard" appears appropriate for most people. For many clients who are more concerned with health-related fitness, using just RPE is sufficient to ensure adequate exercise intensity. Explain the concept of cooling down to help the body through the transition from hard aerobic exercise to rest, especially for those who are engaging in high-intensity exercise.

Review the principles that underlie the development of joint and muscle flexibility, emphasizing the importance of stretching the muscles utilized in the aerobic session (see Chapter 10). Select at least four to six different stretching exercises and have your client complete two to three repetitions of each, sustaining the stretched position for 10 to 30 seconds.

Discuss the principles of resistance training, and develop a program based on your client's personal goals and fitness test results. Remember that a minimum weight-training program, according to the ACSM, involves at least one set of eight to 12 repetitions of eight to 10 different exercises conducted two days per week (see Chapter 8). There are many different weight-training regimens, and this stage of exercise programming should be highly individualized to meet your client's needs (see Table 11.5). Some may prefer a calisthenic program while others may center their entire exercise program around weight training. Weight lifting centers around five different variables (repetitions to fatigue, sets, rest between sets, order of exercises and type of exercise), and these can be manipulated according to specific goals.

TRAITS OF A GOOD EXERCISE CONSULTANT

Traits of a Good Exercise Consultant

Establishing an exercise program for a client, and then supporting the process for the long term, is no simple task. In addition to possessing the knowledge and skills of a personal trainer, it helps to adopt some of the basic traits of a good consultant.

Although no one person can fully motivate another, one can create an environment that will facilitate people to motivate themselves. Motivation comes from within and people tend to become motivated by challenge, growth, achievement, promotion and recognition. Emphasis should be placed on providing a proper environment for self-growth by challenging clients, giving them responsibility, encouraging them and giving full range to individual strength. An effective personal trainer develops warm, personal relationships with each client, and regards each as worthy of genuine concern and attention.

Traits of a good counselor include:

- ✔ Empathy — the ability to climb into the world of the client and communicate feelings of understanding.
- ✔ Respect — a deep and genuine appreciation for the worth of your clients, separate and apart from their behavior. The strength and ability of your clients to overcome and adjust is appreciated.
- ✔ Warmth — the communication of concern and appropriate affection.

Rate of Progression and Retesting

- ✔ Genuineness — being freely one's self. One is congruent and not just playing a role.
- ✔ Concreteness — essential ideas and elements are ferreted out.
- ✔ Self-disclosure — revelations about self are shared at the appropriate time for the benefit of the client.
- ✔ Potency and self-actualization — one is dynamic, in command, conveys feelings of trust and warmth, is competent, inner-directed, creative, sensitive, nonjudgmental, productive, serene and satisfied.

RATE OF PROGRESSION AND RETESTING

The rate of progression in an exercise conditioning program depends on many different factors, including your client's initial fitness and health status, age, needs, motivation and personal goals, family support, and frequency and intensity of training. For example, a middle-aged, overweight, sedentary female will make greater measurable gains during the first three to six months of an exercise program than will a young, normal-weight female.

ACSM defines three progression stages:

Initial conditioning stage. This stage typically lasts four to six weeks. The ACSM recommends that the intensity, frequency and duration of exercise sessions be at the lower end of the training range to help avoid muscle soreness, injury, discomfort and discouragement. Gradual progression is urged so that clients achieve early success in coping with the change in routine and lifestyle.

Improvement conditioning stage. This stage usually lasts 8 to 20 weeks and the rate of progression is more rapid. Frequency, intensity and duration all should be gradually increased to at least the middle of the recommended ranges, with 300 or more calories expended per exercise session. Retesting of all components of physical fitness (cardiorespiratory endurance, muscular strength and endurance, flexibility and body composition) should take place about three months after initiating exercise, and should continue every three months thereafter to help maintain interest and motivation. After each retesting session, physical fitness objectives can be altered to allow the client to aim for a higher standard, or to maintain goals already attained.

Maintenance Conditioning Stage. Once the desired level of fitness is reached, the client enters the maintenance stage of the exercise program. This stage usually begins five to six months after the start of training and, hopefully, extends for a lifetime. To ensure long-term compliance, the exercise program should be enjoyable, fit into the time schedule without undue stress, meet personal needs and goals, and be adaptable to changes in weather and location.

To help maintain client interest, enthusiasm and long-term compliance, there are many strategies you can adopt, including:

- ✔ encourage group participation or exercising with a partner
- ✔ emphasize variety and enjoyment in the exercise program
- ✔ minimize musculoskeletal injuries with a moderate exercise intensity and rate of progression
- ✔ help your client draw up reasonable goals and highlight these in a contract to be signed by the client
- ✔ recruit support from a spouse or significant other
- ✔ provide progress charts to document achievement of goals
- ✔ recognize accomplishments through a system of rewards
- ✔ maximize convenience in terms of time, travel and disruptions in family relationships
- ✔ complement fitness activities with nutrition education, stress management and other health-promotion

activities to improve the overall health of your client

Various studies support the argument that physical activity must be continued on a regular basis if benefits are to be retained. Cessation of exercise training results in a rapid decrease in both aerobic and muscular power. Maintenance of physical fitness, however, is achievable even when training volume (but not intensity) is decreased by half. In other words, it appears to take more energy expenditure to increase aerobic and muscular fitness than to maintain it, as long as training intensity is sustained.

Case History #1: A Middle-aged American Female Location: Client's Home

Data from Medical/Health Questionnaire:

Age: 45 years
Height: 64 inches
Weight: 154 pounds
Desired weight: 130 pounds
Smoking status: quit five years ago
Exercise habits: sedentary both at work and during leisure for all of adult life
Family history of disease: father died of coronary heart disease at age 52
Personal history of disease: negative
Signs or symptoms suggestive of cardiopulmonary or metabolic disease: negative
Dietary habits: fruit/vegetables, two servings/day (low); cereals/grains, five servings/day (low and refined)
Personal goals: lose weight, improve appearance and muscle tone, decrease risk of heart disease
Preferred modes of aerobic exercise: brisk walking, stationary bicycling

Data from Physical Fitness Testing Session (Physician's Office and Fitness Center):

Resting heart rate: 79 bpm (poor)
Resting blood pressure: 142/93 mmHg (mild hypertension) (from two measurements on two days)
Serum cholesterol: 247 mg/dl (high risk)
HDL cholesterol: 33 mg/dl (low)
Cholesterol/HDL-cholesterol ratio: 7.5 (high risk)
Percent body fat: 35 percent (obese)
VO_2 max: estimated from Bruce treadmill test with EKG — 23 ml/kg/min (low); EKG negative
Sit-and-reach flexibility test: -2 inches from footline (fair)
Hand grip dynamometer (sum of right and left hands): 55 kg (below average)

Comments

Using the medical/health questionnaire and laboratory data from recent testing, this client was classified as an "individual at increased risk," according to the ACSM criteria. This classification was given because she has two or more major coronary risk factors (family history, **hypertension, hypercholesterolemia,** sedentary lifestyle). Due to the number of risk factors and family history of coronary heart disease, and the client's desire to engage in moderate-to-vigorous exercise, a medical exam and diagnostic exercise test were recommended. The treadmill EKG test was negative (no evidence of ischemia or arrhythmias), and physician clearance was given for the client to begin a moderate exercise program with gradual progression. Additional physical fitness tests were conducted at a fitness center to determine body composition and musculoskeletal fitness.

Recommended Exercise Program

A home-based program using brisk walking and indoor stationary bicycling, supported with calisthenics for general muscle toning, is recommended. During the first month, have the client warm up with range-of-motion calisthenics and walking for five to 10 minutes, followed by 15 minutes of brisk walking and/or stationary cycling at 50 percent to 60 percent heart rate reserve, three days per week. After cooling down, the client should engage in static stretching activities for five

Rate of Progression and Retesting

Rate of Progression and Retesting

to 10 minutes, followed by toning calisthenics for 10 to 15 minutes.

After the first month has passed, gradually increase the duration of brisk walking and/or cycling to 30 to 45 minutes per session, and the frequency to five to six days per week. The intensity of exercise can also be gradually increased to 70 percent of heart-rate reserve. These increases, along with careful control of dietary habits, will help ensure a steady weight loss of about 1 pound per week. Since the client has 24 pounds of body fat to lose, ideal body weight should be attained after 24 to 30 weeks of training. This degree of weight loss, combined with improvements in physical fitness, should help to bring both hypertension and hypercholesterolemia under control if improvements in dietary quality are made (i.e., less **saturated fat** and **cholesterol**, more fruits, vegetables and whole grains, less sodium and alcohol). The client has a high risk of **coronary heart disease**, and it is imperative that the risk factors be brought under control through weight loss and dietary and exercise lifestyle changes. Enlist the services of a dietitian to ensure adherence to an **anti-atherogenic diet**.

Retest every three months to help ensure motivation and attainment of goals. Long-term compliance can be enhanced by encouraging family support, goal-setting and **contracting,** establishing rewards for attainment of goals, and combating time obstacles.

Case History #2: A 30-Year-Old Male
Location: Fitness Center

Data from Medical/Health Questionnaire:

Age: 30 years
Height: 70 inches
Weight: 160 pounds
Desired weight: 175 pounds
Smoking status: never smoked
Exercise habits: plays golf on the weekends, but no other formal exercise; sedentary at work
Family history of disease: negative
Personal history of disease: negative
Signs or symptoms suggestive of cardiopulmonary or metabolic disease: negative
Dietary habits: has a healthy diet and tries to follow Food Pyramid guidelines
Personal goals: increase muscle weight through weight-training program; improve aerobic fitness moderately
Preferred modes of aerobic exercise: indoor equipment, especially rowing machine and stationary bicycle

Data from Physical Fitness Testing Session (Fitness Center):

Resting heart rate: 67 bpm (average)
Resting blood pressure: 123/82 mmHg (normal) (from two measurements on two days)
Serum cholesterol: 195 mg/dl (within desirable range)
HDL cholesterol: 46 mg/dl (average)
Cholesterol/HDL-cholesterol ratio: 4.2 (average, but above optimal ratio of 3.5)
Percent body fat: 14 percent (desirable)
VO_2 max: estimated from timed Bruce treadmill test — 43 ml/kg/min (average)
Sit-and-reach flexibility test: +2 inches from footline (average)
Hand grip dynamometer (sum of right and left hands): 110 kg (average)
1-RM bench press test: 95 percent of body weight (average)
Pull-ups: 7 (fair)
Push-ups: 25 (above average)
One-minute timed, bent-knee sit-ups: 32 (above average)

Comments

This client has no major risk factors for disease and is, therefore, classified as "apparently healthy" using the ACSM guidelines. According to ACSM, a medical exam or diagnostic exercise test is not needed prior to initiating a vigorous exercise program for this type of client. Although the client has a normal body-fat percentage, his body weight is somewhat low for his height, and he desires to gain

Rate of Progression and Retesting

15 pounds through a weight-training program while moderately improving aerobic fitness. He is especially interested in adding muscle bulk to improve his golf game, which is his weekend passion.

Recommended Exercise Program

The client desires an intensive weight-training program at the fitness center, three days per week, with a moderate aerobic program two days per week. Since the client has never lifted weights seriously, a gradual, progressive-resistance program should be established. During the first month, a one-set, 10-repetition-maximum (RM) program of 10 different exercises will allow the client to adapt to the weight-training program without undue fatigue and soreness (which would interfere with his weekend golf game). Over the next two to three months, gradually increase the sets to three, with the RM lowered to six to eight. On two days of the week, after five minutes of warm-up, the client can use the rowing machine and/or bicycle for 20 to 30 minutes at 60 percent to 75 percent of heart-rate reserve. On weight-lifting days, it is recommended that the client warm up prior to lifting for 10 minutes by rowing and/or cycling. This will allow additional aerobic training and help warm-up the muscles and joints to allow safe and effective weight lifting.

Establish one-RM goal weight lifts for each of the 10 exercises, and retest every three months. Also retest aerobic fitness and body composition every three months. To facilitate a healthy gain in body weight, consult with a dietitian to provide nutrient and energy analysis of the diet every three months. The dietitian also can give recommendations to improve the energy density of the diet.

Case History #3: An Elderly Male Location: Client's Home

Data from Medical/Health Questionnaire

Age: 72 years
Height: 68 inches
Weight: 170 pounds
Desired weight: 150 pounds
Smoking status: quit 20 years ago
Exercise habits: walks 10 minutes after supper with wife, but no other formal exercise
Family history of disease: negative
Personal history of disease: type II diabetic, diagnosed one year ago
Signs or symptoms suggestive of cardiopulmonary or metabolic disease: negative, but has low energy and feels tired much of the day; feels out of breath after climbing stairs; feels weak
Dietary habits: low in fruits and vegetables (2 servings/day); low in whole grains and cereals (3 servings/day); uses whole milk and cheese; likes red meat (2 servings/day)
Personal goals: lose weight to help control diabetes; improve aerobic fitness and increase energy level; increase muscle strength moderately
Preferred modes of aerobic exercise: walking outside on good-weather days; use of a treadmill on bad-weather days

Data from Physical Fitness Testing Session (Physician's Office and Testing at Home):
Resting heart rate: 78 bpm
Resting blood pressure: 135/87 mmHg (high normal) (from two measurements on two days)
Serum cholesterol: 256 mg/dl (high risk)
HDL cholesterol: 30 mg/dl (low, high risk)
Cholesterol/HDL-cholesterol ratio: 8.5 (high risk)
Percent body fat: 27 percent (obese)
VO_2 max: estimated from Bruce treadmill test with EKG test — 20 ml/kg/min (low); EKG negative
Sit-and-reach flexibility test: -3.5 inches from footline (poor)
Hand grip dynamometer (sum of right and left hands): 75 kg (poor)

Comments

Using the medical/health questionnaire

Rate of Progression and Retesting

and laboratory data from recent testing at the doctor's office, this client was classified as an "individual with disease" using ACSM criteria. This is because he is a newly diagnosed type II diabetic, a condition that can often be controlled through weight loss, exercise and improvements in the diet (especially more dietary fiber and carbohydrates). After consulting with the client's physician (who determined that the EKG results were negative), you have been given approval to put the client on a moderate-intensity exercise program. The client is considered to be at high risk for heart disease because of the presence of multiple risk factors (age, diabetes, hypercholesterolemia, sedentary lifestyle). Therefore the physician has cautioned slow progression with retesting conducted every three months to monitor progress. Additionally, the services of a dietitian have been advised to help the client improve dietary intake.

Recommended Exercise Program

A home-based program, using walking supported with calisthenics for general muscle toning, is recommended. During the first month, have the client warm up with range-of-motion calisthenics and walking for five to 10 minutes, followed by 15 minutes of walking at 40 percent to 50 percent of heart rate reserve, three days per week. After warming down, the client should engage in static stretching activities for five to 10 minutes, followed by toning calisthenics for 10 to 15 minutes.

After the first month has passed, gradually increase the duration of walking to 30 minutes per session, and the frequency to five days per week. The intensity of exercise also can be gradually increased to 60 percent of heart rate reserve. These increases, along with careful control of dietary habits, will help ensure a steady weight loss of about 0.5 to 1 pound per week. The client has 20 pounds of body fat to lose, which is considered critical in treating type II diabetes. At the same time, this degree of weight loss, combined with improvements in physical fitness, should help bring the hypercholesterolemia under control if improvements in dietary quality are made. Diabetics tend to be at high risk for coronary heart disease, and attainment of normal serum cholesterol and HDL cholesterol is an important goal.

To ensure long-term success, seek family support of all lifestyle changes. If various goals are met during retesting sessions, organize an incentive system to improve client motivation and interest. During the entire exercise program, close communication and cooperation with the physician and dietitian is crucial.

REFERENCES

American College of Sports Medicine. (1995). *Guidelines for Exercise Testing and Prescription.* (5th ed.) Baltimore: Williams & Wilkins.

American College of Sports Medicine. (1993). *ACSM's Resource Manual for Guidelines for Exercise Testing and Prescription.* (2nd ed.) Baltimore: Williams & Wilkins.

Bouchard, C., Shephard, R.J. & Stephens, T. (1994). *Physical Activity, Fitness, and Health.* Champaign: Human Kinetics.

Cooper Institute for Aerobics Research. (1990). *The Strength Connection.* Philadelphia: Lea & Febiger.

Davison, R.C.R. & Grant, S. (1993). Is walking sufficient exercise for health?. *Sports Medicine,* 16, 369-373.

Haskell, W.L. (1994). Health consequences of physical activity: Understanding and challenges regarding dose-response. *Medicine and Science in Sports and Exercise,* 26, 649-660.

King, A.C. (1994). Community and public health approaches to the promotion of physical activity. *Medicine and Science in Sports and Exercise,* 26, 1405-1412.

Loy, S.F., Hoffman, J.J. & Holland, G.J. (1995). Benefits and practical use of cross-training in sports. *Sports Medicine,* 19, 1-8.

Morrissey, M.C., Harman, E.A. & Johnson, M.J. (1995). Resistance training modes: Specificity and effectiveness. *Medicine and Science in Sports and Exercise,* 27, 648-660.

Nieman, D.C. (1995). *Fitness and Sports Medicine: A Health-Related Approach* (3rd ed). Palo Alto: Bull Publishing Company.

Pate, R.R., Pratt, M., Blair, S.N., et al. (1995). Physical activity and public health: A recommendation from the Center for Disease Control and Prevention and the American College of Sports Medicine. *JAMA*, 273, 402-407.

Robison, J.I. & Rogers, M.A. (1994). Adherence to exercise programs: Recommendations. *Sports Medicine*, 17, 39-52.

U.S. Department of Health and Human Services. (1991). *Healthy People 2000: National Health Promotion and Disease Prevention Objectives.* DHHS Publication Printing Office, Washington, DC 00402-9325.

SUGGESTED READING

American College of Sports Medicine. (1995). *Guidelines for Exercise Testing and Prescription* (5th ed). Philadelphia: Lea & Febiger.

Baechle, T.R. (1994). *Essentials of Strength Training and Conditioning.* Champaign: Human Kinetics.

Nieman, D.C. (1995). *Fitness and Sports Medicine: A Health-Related Approach* (3rd ed). Palo Alto: Bull Publishing Company.

Wilmore, J.H., & Costill, D.L. (1994). *Physiology of Sport and Exercise.* Champaign: Human Kinetics.

CHAPTER 12

Special Populations and Health Concerns

12

IN THIS CHAPTER:

Scott Roberts

Scott Roberts, Ph.D., is an assistant professor at Texas Tech University. He is the author of numerous books, including Strength and Weight Training for Young Athletes, Clinical Exercise Testing and Prescription: Theory and Application *and* Exercise Physiology: Exercise, Performance and Clinical Applications. *Dr. Roberts has also published numerous articles and book chapters on exercise, including the* ACE Aerobics Instructor Manual.

Personal trainers frequently encounter clients with special needs and health concerns. For those who work with clients of middle age or older, this will be a regular event. It is important for a personal trainer to identify health conditions that will influence exercise program development in the initial screening portion of the client-trainer interaction. As a personal trainer you should regularly update your client screening records in order to identify and effectively address changes in health status as they occur.

Once you have identified that a client has a medical and/or health condition, steps should be taken to obtain physician approval before proceeding with exercise program development, testing or training. Along with physician approval you also should request exercise guidelines and limitations from your client's physician. In many cases a physician will appoint another health professional to assist in providing exercise guidelines. This may be, for example, a nurse, physical therapist, clinical exercise physiologist or a diabetes educator, depending on the clinical status of your client. It is important for you to obtain and follow the guidelines given and to maintain close contact with the appropriate health professional to get your questions answered and to provide status reports at predetermined intervals. An ACE-certified Personal Trainer is certified to work with clients with health challenges only after they have been cleared by their personal physician.

This chapter will address basic guidelines for working with clients with the following health conditions and/or special needs:

- Coronary artery disease
- Hypertension
- Stroke
- Peripheral vascular disease
- Diabetes
- Asthma
- Bronchitis
- Emphysema
- Cancer
- Osteoporosis
- Low-back pain
- Arthritis
- Older adults
- Weight management
- Pregnancy
- Children

As a rule of thumb, if a client has been released to take part in independent activities of daily living (including a limited exercise program) they will probably be cleared to work with a personal trainer as well, who can then provide guidance and motivation.

Generally speaking, clients with one or more of these characteristics should follow a low- or non-impact, low-intensity exercise program that progresses gradually. In many cases there are specific exercises or modifications to exercises that will enhance the safety and effectiveness of the exercise program. If you train clients with special needs it is your responsibility to enhance your knowledge and skills in this area through all the varied continuing education opportunities.

CARDIOVASCULAR DISORDERS

Cardiovascular disease is the leading cause of death in the Western world. The majority of these deaths are attributed to coronary artery disease. **Coronary artery disease (CAD)** results from **atherosclerosis**, which is caused by a narrowing of the coronary arteries that supply the heart muscle with blood and oxygen. The narrowing may result from an initial injury to the inner lining of the arteries (due to high blood pressures, high levels of **LDL cholesterol**, elevated blood glucose or other chemical agents, such as those from cigarettes). Once the inner lining has been damaged, the accumulation of plaque (consisting of calcified cholesterol and fat deposits) reduces the diameter of the coronary artery.

Atherosclerosis also is the underlying cause of cerebral and **peripheral vascular diseases**. Manifestations of these diseases include heart attack, **angina**, **stroke** and intermittent **claudication**.

Exercise and Coronary Artery Disease

Regular physical activity reduces the risk of CAD, but how effective is exercise in treating it? In the early '60s, physicians began experimenting with getting patients up and out of bed soon after a cardiac event, and the results were favorable. Unlike those who were advised to stay in bed, cardiac patients who stayed mobile experienced fewer clinical complications, a faster recovery and fewer complications related to bed rest. In almost all cases, individuals recovering from a **myocardial infarction**, cardiac surgery or other cardiac procedure, can benefit from a supervised cardiac rehabilitation program.

Exercise Guidelines for CAD

It is best if clients with coronary artery disease come to you after graduating from a cardiac rehabilitation program. Most clients who have been released to take part in activities of daily living will have been given a home exercise program and some basic activity guidelines. It is appropriate for you to inform prospective clients that cardiac rehabilitation programs are available and that they should ask their physician if participation is recommended. Exercise and activity guidelines are based on the clinical status of the client. A cardiologist or other designated health professional should provide you with an upper-limit heart rate, as well as guidelines and limitations to physical activity.

1. Low-risk cardiac clients should have stable cardiovascular and physiological responses to exercise. The term low risk is generally applied to those clients who have all of the following: a) an uncomplicated clinical course in the hospital; b) no evidence of resting or exercise-induced **ischemia**; c) **functional capacity** greater than 6 to 8 **METS** three weeks following any medical event or treatment that required hospitalization, such as a heart attack, episode of angina or open heart surgery; d) normal ventricular function greater than 50 percent ejection fraction (percent of blood pumped out of the heart with each beat); and e) no significant resting or exercise-induced **arrhythmias** (abnormal heart rhythms identified by an electrocardiogram).

2. Clients or potential clients who have two or more cardiac risk factors or a history of cardiac disease need to have a physician release and referral in order to exercise (see Chapter 5).

3. All clients with documented coronary artery disease should have a **maximal-graded exercise test** to determine their functional capacity and cardiovascular status in order to establish a safe exercise level.

4. Design your clients' exercise programs according to the guidelines given by their personal physicians. These guidelines will usually be based on exercise test results, medical history, clinical status and symptoms. There are published guidelines available to assist you in working with these clients and interacting with their health-care team (ACSM, 1995, AACVPR, 199X).

5. Exercise should not continue if any abnormal signs or symptoms are observed before, during or immediately following exercise. If symptoms persist the emergency medical system should be activated.

Sample Exercise Recommendation

Mode. Low-intensity endurance exercise, such as low-impact aerobics, walking, swimming or stationary cycling, should be the primary exercise mode. Avoid **isometric** exercises because they can dramatically raise blood pressure and the work of the heart. Prescribe a weight-training program that features low resistance and a high number of repetitions.

Note: Any client who has had a cardiovascular event within the last month should, as appropriate, follow the exercise guidelines outlined below. If a low-risk client has been stable for at least six months, follow exercise guidelines for sedentary, healthy adults.

Intensity. **RPE** 9 to 14 (6-20 scale); heart rate can be as low as 20 beats over resting heart rate and up to 40 percent to 75 percent of maximal **heart rate reserve** (Karvonen formula).

Duration. The total duration should be gradually increased to 20 to 30 minutes of continuous or **interval training**, plus additional time for warm-up and cool-down activities.

Frequency. Three to five days per week.

Hypertension

HYPERTENSION

Hypertension is one of the most prevalent **chronic** diseases in the United States. As many as 50 million Americans have chronically elevated blood pressures greater than 140/90 mmHg, or are taking antihypertensive medication. **Hypertension** is related to the development of CAD, increased severity of atherosclerosis, stroke, congestive heart failure, left ventricular hypertrophy, aortic aneurysms and peripheral vascular disease.

Hypertensive individuals are at three to four times the risk of developing coronary artery disease, and up to seven times the risk of having a stroke.

Exercise and Hypertension

Exercise is now recognized as an important part of therapy for controlling hypertension. While we know that regular aerobic exercise reduces both **systolic** and **diastolic** blood pressure by an average of 10 mmHg, how it does this is not completely understood. It appears that regular physical activity reduces both cardiac output and total peripheral resistance when the body is at rest, as well as sympathetic activity.

Exercise Guidelines for Hypertension

Since many hypertensive individuals are obese and have CAD risk factors, non-drug therapy is usually the first line of treatment. This therapy will usually include weight reduction, salt restriction and increased physical activity. Consider these factors when recommending exercise for hypertensives: a) medical/clinical status; b) current medications; c) the frequency, duration, intensity and mode of exercise the individual is currently participating in; and d) how well the individual manages their hypertension.

1. Don't allow your hypertensive clients to hold their breath or strain during exercise **(Valsalva maneuver)**; cue them to exhale on the exertion.

2. Weight training should supplement endurance training. Utilize **circuit training** rather than heavy weight lifting, and keep resistance low and the repetitions high.

3. Use the RPE scale to monitor exercise intensity, since medications can alter the accuracy of the training heart rate during exercise.

4. Be aware of any changes in medications, which should come with written guidelines from your client's physician. Not all medication changes will require a change in an exercise program, but this should be communicated to you by your client's physician.

5. Exercise should not continue if any abnormal signs or symptoms are observed before, during or immediately following exercise. If symptoms persist the emergency medical system should be activated. If symptoms stop, the exercise program should not continue until your client's physician gives clearance.

6. Physicians may instruct their hypertensive patients to record their blood pressures before and after exercise.

7. Instruct your hypertensive clients to move slowly when getting up from the floor because they are more susceptible to **orthostatic hypotension** when taking antihypertensive medication.

8. Both hypertensive and hypotensive responses are possible during and after exercise for individuals with hypertension. Either of these responses should be reported, and additional exercise guidelines given as a result.

9. Carefully monitor your client's blood pressure during exercise initially, and possibly long-term. Blood pressure can be most accurately measured during lower-body aerobic activity (e.g., stationary cycling) and resistance training (e.g., leg extensions). Clients with more severe hypertension will likely be taking one or more hypertensive medications that may affect their response to exercise.

10. Individuals with hypertension may

Stroke

have multiple CAD risk factors, which should be considered when developing their exercise program.

Sample Exercise Recommendation

Mode. The overall exercise training recommendations for mild to moderate hypertensives are basically the same for apparently healthy individuals. Endurance exercise, such as low-impact aerobics, walking and swimming should be the primary exercise mode. Exercises with a significant isometric component should be avoided. Weight training can be prescribed, and should feature low resistance and a high number of repetitions (initially, 12 to 20).

Intensity. The exercise intensity level should be near the lower end of the heart-rate range (40 percent to 65 percent).

Frequency. Encourage your hypertensive clients to exercise at least four times per week. Elderly clients or those with an initially low functional capacity may exercise daily for shorter duration.

Duration. Gradual warm-ups and cool-downs lasting longer than five minutes are recommended. Gradually increase total exercise duration to as much as 30 to 60 minutes per session, depending on the medical history and clinical status of the individual.

STROKE

Stroke-related events were the third leading cause of death in 1990. Strokes also are referred to as **cerebrovascular accidents (CVA)**. Similar to a myocardial infarction, a stroke affects the arteries of the nervous system instead of the heart. When nerve cells are deprived of oxygen because of a blockage or rupture of a blood vessel supplying blood to the brain, those cells die within minutes. The results can be devastating: speech, thought patterns and memory, behavioral patterns and sight all may be affected and the body may become paralyzed. The risk factors for stroke include high blood pressure, heart disease, cigarette smoking, high red blood cell count and **transient ischemic attacks (TIAs)**, which are momentary reductions in oxygen delivery to the brain, possibly resulting in a sudden headache, dizziness or a blackout.

Exercise and Stroke

There is little data on the role of exercise and stroke, as most studies have yielded mixed results. In general, because the risk factors for stroke are the same as those for CAD, exercise may lessen the risk for stroke by reducing overall CAD risk. Hypertension is a primary risk factor for strokes; therefore, exercise, because it reduces hypertension, is a primary lifestyle modification recommended for preventing strokes. It also may be recommended for hypertensive individuals at risk for stroke, or those recovering from a stroke. Seventy percent to 80 percent of strokes are caused by a **thrombosis**, which is the formation of a blood clot within an intact blood vessel. Exercise also may help by enhancing fibrinolytic activity, the system responsible for dissolving blood clots. For clients who are at risk for, or have experienced a stroke, follow the same guidelines and recommendations used for coronary artery disease and hypertension.

Varied degrees of rehabilitation will follow a stroke. A minor stroke could result in very basic home guidelines given as part of the in-patient discharge instructions. Moderate and severe strokes usually require out-patient therapy. These programs are designed to assist a patient's return to an optimal level of functioning. The physical activity portion of stroke rehabilitation will usually be administered by physical, occupational and/or recreational therapists. Ideally, your guidelines should come from this team with approval from your client's personal physician.

Peripheral Vascular Disease

Subjective Grading Scale for PVD

Grade I — Definite discomfort or pain, but only of initial or modest levels.

Grade II — Moderate discomfort or pain from which the client's attention can be diverted, by conversation, for example.

Grade III — Intense pain (short of Grade IV) from which the client's attention cannot be diverted.

Grade IV — Excruciating and unbearable pain.

FIGURE 12.1
Subjective grading scale for peripheral vascular disease.

PERIPHERAL VASCULAR DISEASE

Peripheral vascular disease (PVD) is caused by atherosclerotic lesions in one or more peripheral arterial and/or venous blood vessels (usually in the legs). Common sites for atherosclerotic lesions include the iliac, femoral and popliteal arteries (see Chapter 2). Most people with PVD are older and have long-established CAD **risk factors**; it also is 20 times more common in diabetics than in non-diabetic individuals. The treatment for PVD usually involves a combination of medication (drugs to increase dilation of the arteries and veins), exercise (to improve blood flow and functional capacity), medical procedures (cleaning out the blockages) or surgery (artery by-pass).

PVD is a painful and often debilitating disease, characterized by muscular pain caused by ischemia (reduced blood flow) to the working muscles. This ischemic pain is usually the result of spasms or blockages, referred to as claudication. Some people experience chronic claudication and pain even at rest. For others, activities such as walking, cycling or stair climbing can cause painful, intermittent claudication that is usually relieved by immediate rest. Most people with PVD describe claudication as a dull, aching, cramping pain. The claudication pain scale is a subjective rating of discomfort, which can be used to regulate exercise intensity/duration and frequency (Figure 12.1).

Exercise and Peripheral Vascular Disease

One of the primary benefits of exercise for individuals with PVD is that it helps to lower overall CAD risk (hypertension, hypercholesterolemia, etc.), as well as improve blood flow and overall cardiovascular endurance. Studies have shown that people with PVD can improve their peak work capacity with regular exercise.

Exercise Guidelines for Peripheral Vascular Disease

Individuals with PVD should undergo a complete medical evaluation before embarking on an exercise program. Initially, focus on low-intensity, non-weight-bearing activities. Because of their chronic pain, individuals with PVD often have a high anxiety level when starting out. Gradual progression can build confidence, and additional activities may be added to their program. Individuals with PVD probably don't have ambitions to run a marathon; they simply want to be able to go shopping, climb stairs and go for a walk without a great deal of pain. In addition to exercise, other lifestyle modifications, such as diet modifications and weight management, should be encouraged in an effort to lower overall CAD risk.

1. Encourage daily exercise with frequent rest periods to allow for maximal exercise tolerance.

2. Initially, recommend low-impact, non-weight-bearing activities such as swimming, rowing and cycling. Add weight-bearing activities as exercise tolerance improves.

3. Avoid exercising in cold air or water to reduce the risk of **vasoconstriction**.

4. Interval training, which may involve five- to 10-minute exercise bouts, one to three times per day, may initially be appropriate for some PVD clients.

5. Because many PVD clients also are diabetic, they need to take excellent care

of their feet to avoid blisters and other injuries that could lead to infection.

6. Ideally, individuals with PVD should be closely supervised, such as in a cardiac rehabilitation program.

7. Gradually increase the time, duration and intensity of your PVD clients' programs. The degree of progress (absence or reduction of pain) will dictate how often and how much to increase these variables. As their functional capacity improves, increase these factors accordingly.

8. Encourage your PVD clients to walk as much and as often as they can tolerate.

Sample Exercise Recommendation

Mode. Non-impact endurance exercise, such as swimming and cycling, may allow for longer-duration and higher-intensity exercise. Recommend weight-bearing activities that are shorter in duration and lower in intensity, with more frequent rest periods.

Intensity. Choose low-intensity exercises rather than high-intensity, high-impact exercises. PVD clients should exercise to the point of moderate to intense pain (Grade II to Grade III on the claudication pain scale, Figure 12.1). As functional capacity improves, gradually increase intensity.

Frequency. Daily exercise is recommended initially. As functional capacity improves, frequency can be reduced to four to six days per week.

Duration. A longer and more gradual warm-up and cool-down (longer than 10 minutes) is recommended. Gradually increase total exercise duration to 30 to 40 minutes.

DIABETES

Diabetes mellitus is characterized by reduced insulin secretion by the pancreatic beta cells and/or reduced sensitivity to insulin. **Diabetes** mellitus causes abnormalities in the metabolism of carbohydrates, protein and fat and, if left untreated, can be deadly. This is of particular concern since the symptoms of diabetes mellitus are not always evident in the early stages.

Diabetics are at greater risk for numerous health problems, including kidney failure, nerve disorders, eye problems and heart disease. Prolonged and frequent elevation of blood sugar can damage the capillaries, a condition called microangiopathy, which leads to poor circulation. In addition, diabetics are at greater risk for permanent nerve damage.

Insulin-dependent diabetes mellitus (IDDM) and **non-insulin-dependent diabetes mellitus (NIDDM)** are the two main types of diabetes. IDDM is caused by the destruction of the insulin-producing beta cells in the pancreas, which leads to little or no insulin secretion. IDDM generally occurs in childhood, and regular insulin injections are required to regulate blood glucose levels.

The typical symptoms of IDDM are excessive thirst and hunger, frequent urination, weight loss, blurred vision and recurrent infections. During periods of insulin deficiency, a higher-than-normal level of glucose remains in the blood because of reduced uptake and storage. A portion of the excess glucose is excreted in the urine, which leads to increased thirst and appetite and weight loss. Chronically elevated blood glucose levels is a condition known as **hyperglycemia**.

NIDDM is the most common form of diabetes, affecting 90 percent of all diabetic patients. It typically occurs in adults who are overweight, and is characterized by a reduced sensitivity of insulin target cells to available insulin. Some people with NIDDM never exhibit any of the classic symptoms of diabetes. Treatment for NIDDM usually includes diet modification, medication and exercise therapy.

NIDDM also is characterized by frequent states of hyperglycemia, but without the increased catabolism of fats and protein. Because 75 percent of NIDDM individuals are obese, or have a history of **obesity**, it is important to note that NIDDM is often reversible with permanent weight loss.

Effective Diabetic Control

Long-term regulation of blood glucose levels is necessary to effectively control diabetes. In IDDM, glucose regulation is achieved through regular glucose assessment, proper diet, exercise and appropriate insulin medication. For NIDDM, it is achieved through lifestyle changes centered around proper diet, weight management, exercise, and insulin or oral agents if needed. A combined diet and exercise regime results in weight loss and weight control, improved circulation and cardiorespiratory fitness, a reduced need for insulin, improved self-image and a better ability to deal with stress.

Exercise and IDDM

The role of exercise in controlling glucose levels has not been well demonstrated. Even so, individuals with IDDM can improve their functional capacity, reduce their risk for CAD and improve insulin receptor sensitivity and number with a program of regular physical activity.

Exercise and NIDDM

Exercise plays an important role in controlling NIDDM, because it reduces both cholesterol levels and weight. With excessive blood glucose elevation, blood fats rise to become the primary energy source for the body. Higher-than-normal blood-fat levels put diabetics at greater risk for heart disease.

Exercise Guidelines for Diabetes

Before beginning an exercise program, diabetics should speak with their physician or diabetes educator to develop a program of diet, exercise and medication. The primary goal of exercise for IDDM is better glucose regulation and reduced heart disease risk. The timing of exercise, the amount of insulin injected and the injection site are important to consider before exercising. Exercise should be performed consistently so that a regular pattern of diet and insulin dosage can be maintained. Ideally, the diabetic client should perform a similar exercise routine every day, within 1 hour of consuming a meal or snack.

The primary goal of exercise for the NIDDM diabetic is weight loss and control. Eighty percent of NIDDM diabetics are overweight. By losing weight through diet and exercise, NIDDM diabetics may be able to reduce the amount of oral insulin medication needed. The primary objective during exercise for the NIDDM diabetic is caloric expenditure, which is best achieved by long-duration exercise. Since the duration of exercise is often high for NIDDM diabetics, the intensity of exercise should be kept lower.

1. Do not inject insulin into the primary muscle groups that will be used during exercise because it will be absorbed too quickly, resulting in **hypoglycemia**.
2. Diabetics should check their blood glucose levels frequently and work closely with their physician to determine the right insulin dosage.
3. Diabetics should always carry a rapid-acting carbohydrate (such as juice or candy) in case they develop hypoglycemia.
4. Encourage your diabetic clients to exercise at the same time each day for better control.
5. Avoid exercise during periods of peak insulin activity.
6. A carbohydrate snack should be consumed before and during prolonged exercise.
7. Diabetics need to take very good care of their feet, which should be regularly checked for any cuts, blisters or signs of infection. Good quality exercise shoes also are very important.
8. Physicians will usually instruct their patients to check their blood glucose level before and after exercise. Exercise

should usually not proceed if blood glucose is below 70 mg/dl or greater than 150 mg/dl. Your diabetic client should have specific guidelines to follow in these situations. These guidelines will depend upon a client's clinical status and medical history with respect to blood glucose control.

Sample Exercise Recommendation

Mode. Endurance activities, such as walking, swimming and cycling.

Intensity. Fifty percent to 60 percent of cardiac reserve, gradually progressing to 60 percent to 70 percent.

Frequency. Four to seven days/week. Some clients may need to start out with several shorter daily sessions.

Duration. Individuals with IDDM should gradually work up to 20 to 30 minutes per session. For individuals with NIDDM, 40 to 60 minutes is recommended.

Special Precautions for Exercise and Diabetes

Individuals with IDDM face two potential problems during or following exercise: lack of insulin, which may cause a hyperglycemic effect; and rapid mobilization of insulin, which dangerously lowers blood glucose levels. Low blood glucose is referred to as hypoglycemia. One of the first rules for the insulin-dependent diabetic is to either reduce insulin intake or increase carbohydrate intake before exercise. Individuals with either type of diabetes should exercise one to two hours after a meal, and before peak insulin activity. Because exercise has an insulin-like effect, insulin dosages generally should be lowered prior to exercise. Diabetics should check blood glucose levels frequently when starting an exercise program, and be aware of any unusual symptoms prior to, during or after exercise.

ASTHMA

Asthma

Asthma is a reactive airway disease characterized by shortness of breath, coughing and wheezing. It is due to: a) constriction of the smooth muscle around the airways; b) a swelling of the mucosal cells; and/or c) increased secretion of mucous. Asthma can be caused by an allergic reaction, exercise, infections, stress or other environmental irritants, such as pollens, inhalants, cigarette smoke and air pollution. Asthma is one of the most common respiratory disorders affecting both adults and children.

Approximately 80 percent of asthmatics experience asthma attacks during exercise (referred to as exercise-induced asthma or EIA), that are characterized by moderate obstruction and are not life threatening. The severity of an EIA attack is related to the intensity of exercise and the ventilatory requirement of the task, as well as the environmental conditions. Inhaling cold, dry air, versus warm, moist air seems to cause greater airway obstruction.

The exact cause of EIA is not well understood, but is believed to be caused when the airways become dry as moisture is absorbed from the air as it passes from the nose to the lower part of the lungs. While asthma is not a contraindication to exercise, asthmatics should work with their physicians to develop an appropriate exercise program.

Exercise and Asthma

Most individuals with controlled asthma will benefit from regular exercise, which helps to reduce the ventilatory requirement for various tasks, making it easier for them to participate in normal daily activities with less shortness of breath and fewer asthma attacks. Several studies have shown that regular exercise also can reduce the number and severity of exercise-induced asthma attacks.

Exercise Guidelines for Asthma

1. Before beginning an exercise program, asthmatics must have a medication/treatment plan to prevent EIA attacks.
2. Asthmatics should have a bronchodilating inhaler with them at all times and be instructed to use it at the first sign of wheezing.
3. Keep the exercise intensity low initially and gradually increase it over time since exercise intensity is directly linked to the severity and frequency of EIA.
4. Reduce the intensity if asthma symptoms occur.
5. Using an inhaler several minutes before exercise may reduce the possibility of EIA attacks.
6. Use the results of pulmonary exercise testing to design an appropriate exercise program.
7. Encourage asthmatics to drink plenty of fluids before and during exercise.
8. Asthmatics should extend their warm-up and cool-down periods.
9. Individuals with respiratory disorders will often experience more symptoms of respiratory distress when exercising in extreme environmental conditions (high or low temperature, high pollen count and heavy air pollution).
10. Wearing a face mask during exercise helps keep inhaled air more warm and moist, and may minimize asthmatic responses during exercise.
11. Individuals with respiratory disorders need to be carefully followed by their physician.
12. Only stable asthmatics should exercise.
13. If an asthma attack is not relieved by medication, the emergency medical system should be activated.

Sample Exercise Recommendation

Mode. Dynamic exercise, walking, cycling and swimming are good choices for the asthmatic. Upper-body exercises such as arm cranking, rowing and cross-country skiing may not be appropriate because of the higher ventilation demands. Swimming may be particularly beneficial because it allows asthmatics to inhale moist air above the surface of the water.

Intensity: Recommend low-intensity dynamic exercise based on the client's fitness status and limitations.

Frequency: Encourage your asthmatic clients to exercise at least three to four times per week. Individuals with low functional capacities, or those who experience shortness of breath during prolonged exercise may benefit from intermittent exercise (two 10-minute sessions).

Duration. Encourage a longer, more gradual warm-up and cool-down (longer than 10 minutes). Gradually increase total exercise duration to 20 to 45 minutes.

BRONCHITIS AND EMPHYSEMA

Bronchitis, a form of obstructive pulmonary disease marked by inflammation of the bronchial tubes, is primarily caused by cigarette smoking, though air pollution and occupational exposure may play lesser roles. Acute bronchitis is an inflammation of the mucous membranes as well. However, an acute bout of bronchitis can develop following a cold or exposure to certain dust particles or fumes, and resolve in several days or weeks. Chronic bronchitis persists for a lifetime in most cases.

Emphysema is another form of chronic pulmonary disease caused by over-inflation of the alveoli, resulting from a breakdown of the walls of the alveoli. This causes a significant decrease in respiratory function. The classic signs of emphysema are chronic breathlessness and coughing. Together, emphysema and bronchitis are referred to as **chronic obstructive pulmonary diseases, or COPD**.

Exercise and COPD

Individuals with COPD may or may not benefit from mild exercise training, depending on the severity of their disease. These individuals need to be carefully screened and followed by a physician. While most people with COPD do not improve their pulmonary function, other benefits such as reduced anxiety, body weight and stress, and an improved ability to perform daily activities can be realized through exercise. The primary goals of exercise training for individuals with COPD is to: a) increase functional capacity; b) increase functional status; c) decrease severity of dyspnea; and d) improve their quality of life.

Individuals with COPD who are stable and have obtained all the potential benefits from a medically supervised exercise program, should benefit from participating in a non-medically supervised exercise program. Encourage these individuals to do the best they can, because every little bit of exercise they do can result in potential health benefits.

Exercise Guidelines for COPD

1. Before starting an exercise program, individuals with COPD need to complete extensive pulmonary tests.
2. Individuals with unstable COPD should not participate in a non-medically supervised exercise program.
3. Carefully choose exercise intensity and type to avoid developing shortness of breath. (For a complete review of strategies for setting exercise intensity for pulmonary patients see ACSM's *Guidelines for Exercise Testing and Prescription.*)
4. Apply the exercise guidelines for asthmatics to your clients with COPD.
5. Individuals must be fully recovered from an acute bout of bronchitis before exercising.
6. Individuals with COPD should have a bronchodilating inhaler with them at all times and be instructed to use it at the first sign of wheezing.
7. Individuals with COPD should perform breathing exercises to help strengthen their respiratory muscles.
8. Initially avoid upper-body exercises such as arm cranking or rowing because of the increased strain on the pulmonary system. Upper-body resistance training may be gradually added to a comprehensive exercise program.
9. Some individuals with COPD may require supplemental oxygen during exercise.
10. COPD clients must not smoke.
11. Based on your clients' responses to exercise, review the type and dose of medications with their physicians.
12. If a COPD client's performance in a non-medically supervised program worsens, encourage them to participate in a pulmonary rehabilitation program until their signs and symptoms improve.

Sample Exercise Recommendation

Mode. Dynamic exercise, walking and stationary cycling. Upper-body exercises such as arm cranking, rowing and cross-country skiing may not be appropriate initially because of the higher ventilation demands. Gradually add upper-body resistance exercises.

Intensity. Recommend low-intensity dynamic exercise rather than high-intensity, high-impact exercise. Adjust the intensity according to the client's breathing responses to exercise. Keep the exercise intensity below the point where any difficulty in breathing may occur.

Frequency. Encourage your clients with COPD to exercise at least four to five times per week. They may benefit from shorter, intermittent exercise sessions.

Duration. Encourage a long, gradual warm-up and cool-down (longer than 10 minutes). Gradually increase total exercise duration to 20 to 30 minutes.

CANCER

Cancer affects one out of every four people in the United States, and of those cases, an estimated 80 percent may be prevented through appropriate lifestyle changes. For example, regular exercise, a low-fat, high-fiber diet and not smoking all help reduce the risk of developing cancer. Dietary changes can reduce the risk of developing bowel cancer, the second most common form of cancer diagnosed, while not smoking may prevent the development of lung cancer. Thus, it appears that many types of cancers are highly preventable.

Exercise and Cancer

In general, physically inactive people are more likely to develop cancer, and studies show that cancer **mortality** is higher in those who exercise the least, even after age and cigarette smoking are considered.

Exercise Guidelines for Cancer

There currently are no specific guidelines for exercise and cancer. However, the following five questions should be asked of your client's personal physician before designing an exercise program for clients with cancer:

1. Are there any limitations in activity based on pre-existing conditions or medical procedures?
2. Are there any limitations in activity as a result of nutritional and fluid deficits?
3. Are there any limitations in mobility as a result of disease or treatment?
4. Are there any limitations in oxygen delivery as a result of disease or treatment?
5. Are there any limitations based on risk for anemia, bleeding and infections?

If individuals have any limitations based on the conditions listed above, guidelines should be given by a member of your client's heath-care team, and their exercise program should be adjusted accordingly.

OSTEOPOROSIS

Osteoporosis is characterized by reduced bone mass and an increased susceptibility to fractures, which occur more commonly in men than in women younger than 45 years, and more commonly in women than in men after 45 years of age. **Osteoporosis** affects an estimated 15 to 20 million Americans at a cost of $3.8 billion per year.

After reaching its peak, bone mass declines throughout life because of an imbalance of "remodeling" of the bone. Remodeling refers to the replacement of old bone with new bone, and keeps the skeletal system in peak form and helps maintain calcium **homeostasis**.

Exercise and Osteoporosis

The treatment of osteoporosis is aimed at preventing or retarding bone mineral loss. Estrogen replacement therapy is highly effective in maintaining bone mass and preventing osteoporosis in women by reducing bone reabsorption and retarding or halting **postmenopausal** bone loss. Premenopausal women should consume 1,000 to 1,500 mg of calcium per day, which appears to suppress age-related bone loss. While the role of exercise in the prevention and treatment of osteoporosis is not completely understood, it is known that physical stress determines the strength of bone. Physical inactivity is a known risk factor for osteoporosis, and exercise is recommended for its prevention and treatment because weight-bearing exercise either retards the loss of, or increases bone mass. Even individuals who have led sedentary lives can increase bone mass by becoming more active.

Exercise Guidelines for Osteoporosis

The greater the physical stress and compression on a bone, the greater the rate of bone deposition (this is why weight-bearing exercise is recommended). Since most individuals who suffer from osteoporosis are elderly, refer to the exercise guidelines and recommendations for older adults on page 340. Resistance training also is an important component in the prevention of osteoporosis. Additionally, individuals with osteoporosis may need to avoid:

- jumping, high-impact aerobics, jogging and running
- spinal flexion, crunches and rowing machines
- trampolines and step aerobics
- wood gym floors that may become slippery from sweat drops
- abducting or adducting their legs against resistance (particularly machines)
- moving their legs sideways or across their body
- pulling on their neck with hands behind the head

LOW-BACK PAIN

Back injuries, including sprains and strains, are the number-one disability for people under age 45. It is estimated that 80 percent of the population will experience an episode of low-back pain some time in their lives. Of these, 5 percent will go on to develop chronic low-back pain (LBP), which accounts for 10 percent of all chronic health conditions in the U.S., and 25 percent of days lost from work. LBP has been labeled the most expensive benign health condition in America.

Back injuries translate into millions of lost work days every year and cost billions for medical care, disability payments and legal payments. Reducing back injury rates is a top priority for all employers. In fact, the most common type of workers' compensation claim is a back strain/sprain, which accounts for up to 25 percent of all claims, representing annual payments of $2.5 to $7 billion, including one-half of all disability compensation payments annually.

While the cause of LBP is often elusive, four common causes have been identified: a **herniated disc** (rupture of the outer layers of fibers which surround the gelatinous portion of the disc); **spondylolisthesis** (forward sliding of the body of one vertebra on the vertebra below it); a trauma to the back (accident); and degenerative disc disease (progressive structural degeneration of the intervertebral disc). Lower back problems are often associated with an imbalance of strength and flexibility of the lower back and abdominal muscle groups. Poor flexibility in the hamstrings and hip flexor muscles also have been linked to LBP.

Exercise and LBP

A strong correlation exists between LBP and excess body weight, smoking and decreased physical activity. It makes sense, then, that physical fitness combined with a healthy lifestyle may help prevent LBP. In fact, many physicians feel that the major cause of chronic low-back pain is simply physical deconditioning. More specifically, low endurance in the large muscle groups, particularly the back extensors, seems to put one at a greater risk of developing LBP. Aerobic training and exercises for the low-back should be performed on a regular basis as part of the treatment and prevention of LBP.

Exercise Guidelines for Low-back Pain

Prevention is the key to avoiding LBP, and clients should be screened for low-back pain risk factors. If someone has experienced a recent LBP strain or injury, they should be cleared by a physician before starting an exercise program. In addition to a program of aerobic and resistance training, basic core back exercises should be performed on a regular basis (Table 12.1). Clients with diagnosed low back pain should avoid: unsupported forward flexion; twisting at the waist with turned feet, especially when carrying a load; lifting both legs simultaneously when in a prone or supine position; and rapid movements, such as twisting, forward flexion or hyperextending.

Advise clients with low-back pain to keep

Table 12.1
Exercises for the Low Back

Position	Activity
Supine with knees bent	Slowly, pull one knee to chest and hold for 5 seconds, then do the same with the other knee.
Supine, with knees bent and legs together	Slowly rotate knees from side to side while keeping them together.
Hands and knees	Arch your back up like a cat, hold five seconds and relax.
Hands and knees	Slowly sit back between your knees and then return to hands and knees.
Hands and knees	Slowly bring one knee to the chest then extend the leg straight out behind you. Repeat on the other side.
Standing against the wall. Optional exercise is to place a large rubber ball behind the back.	Squat down so that your lower back is pressed against the wall. Move your feet out from the wall and bend your legs to a "half-squat" and hold. Gradually straighten legs out.
Lie on your stomach, legs and arms straight out.	Lift one arm, hold and relax. Alternate arms. Lift one leg, hold and relax. Alternate legs. Lift one arm and one leg on opposite sides, hold and relax. Alternate sides.
Supine, with knees slightly bent	Flatten your back against the floor by contracting your stomach muscles and rotating your hips backward.
Additional activities	Side stretch, abdominal curls, modified push-ups, lateral leg raises, groin stretch, hamstring stretch, calf stretch, and quadriceps stretch.

in mind the following:

1. Always be aware of proper form and alignment.
2. Always maintain neutral pelvic alignment and an erect torso during any exercise movements (see Chapter 3).
3. Avoid head-forward positions in which the chin is tilted up.
4. When leaning forward, lifting or lowering an object, always bend at the knees.
5. Avoid hyperextending the spine in an unsupported position.
6. Adequately warm up and cool down before and after each workout session.
7. Most low-back pain is caused by muscle weaknesses and imbalances in the hamstrings, hip flexors, lower back muscle groups and abdominals. Exercises should be routinely performed to improve muscle strength and/or flexibility (Table 12.1).
8. Advise your clients with low-back pain, or a history of chronic low-back pain, to consult with a physician and get specific recommendations for exercises.
9. If clients complain of low-back pain following exercise, have them sit or lie down in a comfortable position and apply ice to the affected area. Encourage clients to take a few days off from exercise if they experience a mild back strain.

ARTHRITIS

The most common forms of arthritis are rheumatoid and **osteoarthritis**. Osteoarthritis, also referred to as degenerative joint disease, is a degenerative process in which cartilage wears away, leaving two surfaces of bone in contact with each other. Osteoarthritis is very common in older individuals, affecting 85 percent of all people in the United States over the age of 70. **Rheumatoid arthritis** is caused by an inflammation of the membrane surrounding the joint, and is often associated with pain and swelling in one or more joints. Rheumatoid arthritis affects about 3 percent of all women and 1 percent of all men in the United States.

The treatment of arthritis, which may involve medicine (corticosteroids), physical therapy, physiotherapy (Transcutaneous Electrical Nerve Stimulation [TENS] and hot packs), occupational therapy (to improve activities of daily living [ADLs]) and surgery (joint replacement), depends on the severity and specific form of arthritis.

Arthritis

Individuals with arthritis can be classified into four categories of functional capacity (Table 12.2). Functional Class I and II arthritic individuals are generally able to perform their normal ADLs with little discomfort, while those in Class III and IV typically are seriously limited by their condition.

Individuals with arthritis should not be excluded from participating in a program of regular exercise. Stronger muscles and bones, improved cardiorespiratory fitness and improved psychosocial well-being are some of the benefits arthritis sufferers can gain from appropriate exercise. It is contraindicated, however, during inflammatory periods because exercise can aggravate or worsen the condition.

Exercise and Arthritis

Exercise is recommended for individuals with arthritis to help preserve muscle strength and joint mobility, improve functional capabilities, relieve pain and stiffness, prevent further deformities, improve overall physical conditioning, re-establish neuromuscular coordination and to mobilize stiff or contracted joints.

Fitness programs, which should be carefully designed in conjunction with a physician or physical therapist, must be based on the functional status of the individual. For example, someone in Functional Class I should be able to perform most activities that a typical healthy person can. For those in Class II, non-weight-bearing activities, such as cycling, warm water exercise and walking, are recommended. Individuals in Class III should benefit from a cycling or warm water aquatic program. Exercise should be avoided during acute arthritic flare-ups.

Clients with arthritis may complain of fatigue and some discomfort following exercise. Exercise programs need to achieve the proper balance between rest, immobilization of affected joints, and appropriate exercise to reduce the severity of the inflammatory joint disease.

Table 12.2
Classification of Functional Capacity for Individuals with Arthritis

Class I	Complete ability to carry on all usual duties without handicaps
Class II	Adequate ability for normal activities despite handicap, discomfort or limited motion at one or more joints
Class III	Ability limited to little or none of the usual occupational or self-care duties
Class IV	Incapacitated, largely or wholly; bedridden or confined to a wheelchair; little or no self-care

Source: American Rheumatism Association

Exercise Guidelines for Arthritis

1. Encourage your arthritic clients to participate in low-impact activities such as stationary cycling, rowing and water fitness classes.

2. Begin with low-intensity, frequent sessions.

3. Reduce exercise intensity and duration during periods of inflammation or pain.

4. Extend the warm-up and cool-down periods.

5. Modify the intensity and duration of exercise according to how well the client responds to it, any changes in medication and their level of pain.

6. It is essential to put all joints through their full range of motion at least once a day to maintain mobility.

7. Have the individual take a day or two of rest if they continue to complain about pain during or following an exercise session. Use the two-hour pain rule to adjust exercise levels.

8. Emphasize proper body alignment at all times. Poor posture and decreased joint mobility and strength disrupt the performance of efficient, controlled and integrated movement. Misaligned body positions and awkward movements affect walking gait and increase fatigue. Special

Table 12.3
Exercise Guidelines for Individuals with a Hip Replacement

- ✓ Lift knee no higher than hip level or 90° flexion
- ✓ Toes straight ahead, no "pigeon toes"
- ✓ No adduction past midline
- ✓ Need leg/hip abduction and lateral movements and strengthening

precautions should be taken for clients that have undergone a hip replacement (Table 12.3)

9. While pain is quite normal in people with arthritis, instruct your clients to work just up to the point of pain, but not past it. Movements that are simple for healthy people can be quite painful for individuals with arthritis.

10. Use isometric strengthening exercises, which strengthen the joint structures and surrounding muscles while placing the least amount of stress on the joint itself.

11. If severe pain persists following exercise, clients should consult with their physician.

12. Individuals with rheumatoid arthritis should not exercise during periods of inflammation, and regular rest periods should be stressed during exercise sessions.

13. Keep in mind that arthritic clients may be more limited by joint pain than by cardiovascular function.

Sample Exercise Recommendation

Mode. Non-weight-bearing activities such as cycling, warm-water aquatic programs and swimming are preferred because they reduce joint stress. Recommen- ded water temperature is 83° F (28° C) to 88° F (31° C).

Intensity. Emphasize low-intensity, dynamic exercise rather than high-intensity, high-impact exercise. The exercise intensity should be based on the client's comfort level before, during and after exercise.

Frequency. Arthritic individuals should be encouraged to exercise at least four to five times per week.

Duration. Encourage long, gradual warm-up and cool-down periods (longer than 10 minutes). Initial exercise sessions should last no longer than 10 to 15 minutes.

OLDER ADULT

The United States population is growing older. In fact, by the year 2030, more than 20 percent of our population will be over the age of 65. The most rapid population increase over the next decade will be of those over 85 years of age. This is due, in large part, to modern medicine and health-promotion activities.

But what is the quality of these extended lives? One measure of the quality of life is an individual's ability to perform activities of daily living (ADLs), such as bathing, dressing and eating. While these tasks may become more difficult as an individual grows older, it is possible to stay healthy and lead long, satisfying lives. The things we must do to stay healthy (exercise, eat right, not smoke, etc.), become even more important as we age. Thus, while someone may be 65 years of age (chronological age), they may have a biological age of 45, based on their fitness and health status. The importance of regular exercise and health promotion cannot be emphasized enough when looking at the association of chronological versus biological age.

Physiological Challenges of Aging

Aging is a normal biological process. The signs of progressive aging are familiar to most of us and include loss of height, reduced lean body mass, gray hair, more wrinkles, changes in eyesight and, to some extent, slightly less coordination. There are noticeable changes in the functioning of the cardiovascular, endocrine, respiratory and musculoskeletal systems as well. To what extent these changes may be affected by exercise is not completely understood.

Heart Rate. Maximal heart rate declines with age, diminishing the accuracy of estimating training intensity based on heart rate. Other methods of monitoring exercise intensity, such as the rate of perceived exertion scale (or in conjunction with heart rate), may be more effective. Even though exercise heart rate declines with age, in healthy older subjects who exercise, stroke volume has been shown to increase or be maintained, thus, overcoming the affect of a lowered heart rate.

Blood Pressure. Older individuals generally display higher blood pressure readings during submaximal and maximal exercise. In addition, they may have higher myocardial oxygen consumption requirements, which can result in higher blood pressures. Endurance training can significantly reduce the mean blood pressure and the systemic vascular resistance in older individuals.

Cardiac Output and Stroke Volume. **Cardiac output** (the amount of blood pumped out of the heart per minute) is typically lower in older individuals, and resting cardiac output declines 1 percent per year upon reaching adulthood. Resting stroke volume declines approximately 30 percent from the ages of 25 to 85 and, when combined with the decrease in maximal heart rate, leads to a drop in cardiac output of 30 percent to 60 percent. This effect may be countered, however, by exercise.

Maximal Oxygen Uptake. With normal aging, **maximal oxygen uptake (VO_2 max)** declines approximately 8 percent to 10 percent per decade after age 30. This decline is associated with a decrease in maximal heart rate and stroke volume, and a decrease in oxygen extraction by contracting muscles. It is clear however, that aerobic capacity can be improved at any age.

Bones. With age, bones become more fragile, and serious, often debilitating fractures are common in the elderly. By the age of 90 as many as 32 percent of women and 17 percent of men will have sustained a hip fracture, and many will die of related complications. With age, the loss of calcium results in decreased bone mass, but weight-bearing and resistance-training exercises are known to help maintain bone mass.

Skeletal Muscle. Muscle mass declines with age, resulting in decreased muscular strength and endurance. For each decade after the age of 25, 3 percent to 5 percent of muscle mass is lost. This is primarily attributed to changes in lifestyle and the decreased use of the neuromuscular system. Several recent studies, however, have reported significant strength gains in previously sedentary older adults following a program of regular exercise.

Body Composition. As lean body weight (muscle and bone) declines with age, body fat increases. The changes in body composition resulting from age are primarily due to a decrease in muscle mass, **basal metabolic rate** and lack of physical activity. On average, there is a 10 percent reduction in basal metabolic rate between early adulthood to retirement age, and a further 10 percent decrease after that. Regular physical activity, which preserves lean body mass, decreases fat stores and stimulates protein synthesis, may reverse these adverse changes in body composition that are associated with growing older.

Exercise Guidelines for Older Adults

Before starting an exercise program, older adults should first see their physician. Although the principles of exercise design are similar to those for any group, special care should be given when setting up a fitness program for older participants. A pre-exercise evaluation may need to include a complete medical history, a physical and a treadmill test. The exercise program should combine endurance, flexibility and balance training, as well as muscle strength and joint mobilization. For most elderly patients, low-impact exercise is advisable. Older individuals should be encouraged to become more physically active in all of their daily activities (use the stairs, walk to the store, etc.), and to bend, move and stretch in order to keep joints flexible.

Sample Exercise Recommendation

Mode. Endurance exercise, such as low impact aerobics, walking, cardiovascular equipment and swimming should be the primary exercise mode. Recommend a program of weight training that features low resistance and high repetitions.

Intensity. Keep the exercise intensity level near the lower end of the heart-rate range (40 percent to 65 percent).

Frequency. Encourage your elderly clients to exercise at least four to five times per week. Daily exercise of shorter duration may be appropriate for certain individuals with an initial low functional capacity.

Duration. A longer and more gradual warm-up and cool-down period (greater than 5 minutes) is recommended. Gradually increase total exercise duration to 30 to 60 minutes per session, depending on the medical history and clinical status of the individual.

Special Precautions

Individuals with high blood pressure, heart disease or arthritis should take particular care when performing weight-training exercises. Incorporate an extended warm-up and cool-down period — approximately 10 to 15 minutes. You may find that your older clients have a more difficult time exercising in extreme environmental conditions, and these should be avoided. Some elderly individuals with arthritis or poor joint mobility should participate in non-weight-bearing activities, such as cycling, swimming, and chair and floor exercises.

WEIGHT MANAGEMENT

On any given day, at least one out of every four Americans is on a diet. Americans spend more than $30 billion annually on various weight-loss methods, most of which fail. Excess body weight is associated with numerous health-related problems including increased risk for coronary artery disease, diabetes and **hyperlipidemia**. Unfortunately, 95 percent of people who lose weight are unsuccessful at keeping the weight off. In addition, an obsession with weight and weight loss can lead to practices of self-imposed starvation (anorexia nervosa), which is a serious medical problem. While maintaining a healthy body weight and eating nutritionally is important, it is not an easy task for most people.

The diagnosis and treatment of obesity is difficult and can be frustrating. A detailed medical and dietary history is necessary before a physician can begin to determine the cause(s) of obesity in patients. In many cases, it is caused by complex psychosocial issues, which may require a referral to a psychologist or psychiatrist. Although caloric consumption and physical activity habits are directly related to the increased prevalence of excess weight, they are not the only causes of obesity.

Exercise and Weight Management

Exercise in combination with a sensible eating plan produces the best long-term weight-loss results. Exercise can contribute up to a 300 to 400 kcal deficit per exercise bout. With a constant food intake, an exercise program conducted three times per week (at an intensity and duration eliciting 300 to 400 kcal/session) could result in a 16-pound weight loss in one year. Exercise is important because it helps maintain **resting metabolic rate** and **fat-free mass**. Both strength training and aerobic exercise has been shown to make the greatest contribution to a weight-management program when the caloric intake does not go below 1,200 kilocalories per day. Regular exercise may also help control appetite and improve psychological outlook when trying to lose weight.

Sample Exercise Recommendation

Mode. Walking is a highly effective form of exercise for weight loss and control. Walking, cycling and aerobic dance have been shown to elicit better results than swimming, although the key is to find an activity that is safe, effective and enjoyable enough to become consistent. Variety in aerobic modes has benefits in safety, effectiveness and compliance.

Intensity. The intensity should be low initially (possibly as low as 40 percent to 50 percent of maximal heart rate). As fitness improves, increase the intensity level. The perceived exertion scale can be more useful than monitoring heart rate for determining intensity. Look for signs that a weight management client is working at too high of an exercise intensity level: excessive sweating, higher-than-normal rate of breathing, joint pain, excessive fatigue, inability to complete an exercise session and a flushed color.

Frequency. It is important for overweight clients to make exercise habitual; five to six days of exercise per week is often considered the ideal. Initially, obese clients may need to start out with as few as two to three days per week.

Duration. Since most overweight clients will not be able to exercise at a high intensity level, duration is the essential exercise program variable, especially at the start of an exercise program. Generally, the longer the duration, the greater the caloric expenditure.

Resistance Training. Resistance training can help an overweight client maintain lean body mass when caloric restriction is moderate. Start beginners out with one set of 8 to 12 repetitions of six to 10 exercises. Some clients can progress to higher-intensity programs, while others will benefit more from a consistent and more moderate program. Regardless of intensity, variety in the exercises should be incorporated to optimize compliance and effectiveness (see Chapters 8 and 9).

Keep weight loss goals reasonable. Significant health benefits can be realized by body-weight reductions of only 10 percent. The key to healthy weight management is consistency in both activity and healthy eating. Try not to over-focus on "weight loss;" instead, support your clients in making healthy lifestyle changes.

EXERCISE AND CHILDREN

Within the last decade, a great deal of research has focused on the effects of exercise in children and adolescents. It appears that children respond to exercise in much the same way as adults do. With little encouragement, most children in good health are willing to be physically active. Recent national attention on the health and fitness of American children has sparked a great deal of debate over topics such as: a) how much exercise should children and adolescents be getting, and at what age; b) who is responsible for making sure children get enough exercise; and c) what kind of exercise is important, and at what age. Many of these issues have yet to be resolved.

Over the past two decades, several large-scale youth fitness surveys have been conducted, and the results provide much of the evidence used to judge the past and current health and fitness status of American youth. The only trend in youth fitness that has been analyzed with a high degree of accuracy is skinfold data. There appears to be a systematic increase in skinfold

Table 12.4
General Endurance Training Guidelines for Children

1. Although children are generally quite active, most choose to participate in activities that consist of short-burst, high-energy exercise. Encourage children to participate in sustained activities that use large muscle groups.
2. The type, intensity and duration of exercise activities need to be based on the maturity of the child, medical status and previous experiences with exercise.
3. Regardless of age, the exercise intensity should start out low and progress gradually.
4. Because of the difficulty in monitoring heart rates with children, the use of a perceived exertion scale is a more practical method of monitoring exercise intensity in children.
5. Children are involved in a variety of activities throughout the day. Because of this, a specific time should be dedicated to sustained aerobic activities.
6. The duration of the exercise session will vary depending on the age of the children, their previous exercise experience and the intensity of the exercise session.
7. Because it is often quite difficult to get children to respond to sustained periods of exercise, the session periods need to be creatively designed.

thickness among six- to nine-year-old boys and girls from the '60s and '70s to the '80s — a clear indication of the rise in childhood obesity over the last several decades. Another particularly alarming statistic is the poor levels of strength in American children, particularly upper-body strength.

Exercise Guidelines for Children

Sufficient evidence exists that children can physiologically adapt to endurance training. However, the amount of exercise required for optimal functional capacity and health at various ages has not been precisely defined. Until more definitive evidence is available, current recommendations are that children and youth obtain 20 to 30 minutes of vigorous exercise each day. Physical education classes typically devote instructional time to physical fitness (Table 12.4).

Sample Exercise Recommendation

Mode. Encourage children to participate in sustained activities that use large muscle groups (i.e., swimming, jogging, aerobic dance). Other activities, such as recreational sports and fun activities that develop other components of fitness (speed, power, flexibility, muscular endurance, agility and coordination) should be incorporated into a fitness program.

Intensity. Exercise intensity should start out low and progress gradually. There are currently no universal recommendations available for the use of training heart rate during exercise for children. Using the perceived exertion scale is a more practical method of monitoring exercise intensity with children.

Frequency. Two to three days of endurance training will allow adequate time to participate in other activities, and still be sufficient enough to cause a training effect.

Duration. Since children will be involved in a variety of activities during and after school, a specific amount of time should be dedicated to endurance training. Endurance exercise activities should be gradually increased to 30 to 40 minutes per session. With younger children, it will be necessary to start out with less time.

Although there are fewer resistance-training studies involving children than adults, the evidence that demonstrates increases in strength following structured resistance training in children is mounting. These studies indicate strength increases in children are similar to those observed in older age groups. Furthermore, the safety and efficacy of resistance-training programs for prepubescent children has been well documented.

The risk of injuries to children participating in resistance-training programs is low. However, injuries can occur in any sport or strenuous physical activity. To minimize the risk of injury during resistance training, consider the following:

- ✔ Obtain medical clearance or instructions regarding physical needs.
- ✔ Children should be properly supervised at all times.
- ✔ Do not allow children to exercise unless the weight-training facility is safe for them.
- ✔ Never have children perform single maximal lifts, sudden explosive movements or try to compete with other children.
- ✔ Teach children how to breathe properly during exercise movements.
- ✔ Never allow children to use any equipment that is broken or damaged, or that they don't fit on properly.
- ✔ Children should rest for approximately one to two minutes between each exercise, more if necessary. In addition, they should have scheduled rest days between each training day.
- ✔ Encourage children to drink plenty of fluids before, during and after exercising.
- ✔ Children need to be told that they need to communicate with their coach, parent or teacher when they feel tired, fatigued or when they have been injured.

EXERCISE AND PREGNANCY

Numerous studies of the cardiovascular responses of pregnant women have demonstrated that women can maintain and even improve their cardiovascular, respiratory and aerobic capacities during pregnancy. Since exercise causes a redistribution of the blood flow to the working muscles, it was believed that a reduction of blood flow to the uterus might harm the fetus. However, several recent studies have shown that although there is a slight decrease in overall uterine blood flow during moderate exercise, blood flow to the placenta appears to be adequate.

Cardiac reserve, or the difference between resting and maximum cardiac function, is reduced in pregnant women. As pregnancy progresses, it seems the heart is less able to adapt to the increased demand, especially in the supine position, because they may already be working at a very high level due to the increased demands of pregnancy. This is why pregnant women should be discouraged from exercising at high levels, or participating in activities that require sudden bursts of movement.

Many women are more flexible during pregnancy due to joint laxity. With the release of the hormone relaxin, joints become looser, increasing the risk for injury during exercise.

Women who choose to exercise during pregnancy must be aware of the ambient temperature prior to exercise. Exercise increases body temperature, which can be harmful to the fetus, particularly if the core body temperature exceeds 100° F. Pregnant women should be conservative when exercising in hot, humid environments since body temperature regulation is more difficult for them.

Exercise Guidelines for Pregnant Women

Most women should be able to continue exercising during their first trimester without much difficulty. While morning sickness, mild weight gain and fatigue, might sideline some, most women should be able to continue their normal exercise program. Exercise in the supine position is not recommended after the first trimester, and some forms of exercise, such as running, may be difficult during the second and third trimesters due to increased body weight, edema, varicose veins and increased joint mobility.

A woman should clearly understand the risks and potential benefits associated with exercising during pregnancy, and should make the decision to exercise in conjunction with her physician.

The conclusion of the American College of Obstetricians and Gynecologists that exercise during pregnancy is safe for most women is based on the recommendation that participants be carefully monitored by their physician, and that they understand and adhere to the following guidelines as appropriate:

1. Exercise goals during pregnancy should be discussed with a physician.
2. Do not begin a vigorous exercise program shortly before or during pregnancy.
3. Gradually reduce the intensity, duration and frequency of exercise during the second and third trimesters. For example, a woman who walks or runs an average of 4 miles per day might reduce her mileage to 3 miles per day during the first trimester; to 2 miles per day during the second; and to 1 or 1.5 miles during the final trimester.
4. Avoid exercise when the temperature and/or humidity is high.
5. Try to run or walk on flat, even surfaces.
6. Wear supportive shoes while walking or running during pregnancy.
7. If running becomes uncomfortable during the second and third trimesters, try other forms of aerobic exercise, such as swimming, running in water and bicycling.
8. Extend warm-up and cool-down periods.
9. Body temperature, which should not exceed 100° F (38° C), should be taken immediately after exercise. If body temperature exceeds 100° F (38° C), modifying intensity and duration, as well as exercising during the cooler part of the day, should help.
10. Use the rating of perceived exertion scale rather than heart rate to monitor exercise intensity. Choose an intensity that is comfortable; a pounding heart rate, breathlessness or dizziness are indicators that intensity should be reduced.
11. Eat a small snack before exercise to help avoid hypoglycemia.
12. Drink plenty of water before, during and after exercise.
13. Avoid overstretching or going beyond normal range of motion.
14. Any unusual physical changes, such as vaginal bleeding, severe fatigue, joint pain or irregular heart beats, should immediately be reported to a physician.

SUMMARY

Training clients with health concerns and special needs can be very gratifying. One of the keys to success is to maintain contact with your client's physician and the rest of their healthcare team. Always obtain written guidelines before proceeding with exercise training. Keep programs more conservative than you would for your clients that are without health concerns. This can be an area of tremendous professional growth for you. Investigate continuing education opportunities to maximize the safety and effectiveness of your services.

REFERENCES/SUGGESTED READING

American Association of Cardiovascular and Pulmonary Rehabilitation. (1995). *Guidelines for Cardiac Rehabilitation Programs.* (2nd ed.) Champaign: Human Kinetics.

American College of Obstetricians and Gynecologists. (1994). *ACOG Technical Bulletin #189.* Washington D.C.

American College of Sports Medicine. (1995). *Guidelines for Exercise Testing and Prescription.* (5th ed.) Baltimore: Williams & Wilkins.

American College of Sports Medicine. (1993). Position stand: Physical activity, physical fitness and hypertension. *Medicine and Science in Sports and Exercise.* 25 (10), i-x.

American Diabetes Association. (1993). Standards of Medical Care for Patients with Diabetes Mellitus. *1992-93 Clinical Practice Recommendations.* Alexandria: American Diabetes Association.

Bartram, H.P. & Wynder, E.L. (1989). Physical activity and colon cancer risk? Physiological consideration. *American Journal of Gastroenterology.* 84, 109.

Blair, S.N., Kohl, H.W., Gordon, N.F. & Paffenbarger, R.S. (1992). How much physical activity is good for health? *Annual Review of Public Health.* 13, 99.

Bonnick, S.L. (1994). *The Osteoporosis Handbook: Every Woman's Guide to Prevention and Treatment.* Dallas: Taylor Publishing Company.

Brownell, K.D. & Foreyt, J.P. (Eds.) (1986). *Handbook of Eating Disorders: Physiology, Psychology and Treatment Of Obesity, Anorexia and Bulimia.* New York: Basic Books.

Campaigne, B.N. (1994). *Exercise in the Clinical Management of Diabetes.* Champaign: Human Kinetics.

Cheung, W.Y. & Richmond, J.B. (Eds.) (1995). *Child Health, Nutrition, and Physical Activity.* Champaign: Human Kinetics.

Christianse, C. (1993). Consensus Development Conference on Osteoporosis. *The American Journal of Medicine.* 95 (5a).

Clark, J. (1992). *Full Life Fitness: A Complete Exercise Program for Mature Adults.* Champaign: Human Kinetics.

Danneskiold-Samsoe, B., Lynberg, K., Risum, T. & Telling, M. (1987).The effect of water exercise therapy given to patients with rheumatoid arthritis. *Scandinavian Journal of Rehabilitation Medicine.* 19, 31-35.

Frontera, W.R., Meredith, C.N., O'Reilly, K.P., Knuttgen, H.G. & Evans, W.J. (1988). Strength conditioning in older men: Skeletal muscle hypertrophy and improved function. *Journal of Applied Physiology.* 64, 1038-1044.

Frymoyer, J.W., Pope, M.H., Contanza, M.C., et al. (1980). Epidemiologic studies of low-back pain. *Spine.* 5, 419-423.

Gisolfi, C.V. & Lamb, D.R. (Eds.) (1989). *Perspectives in Exercise Science and Sports Medicine, Volume 2, Youth, Exercise and Sport.* Indianapolis: Benchmark.

Gordon, N.F. (1993). *Arthritis: Your Complete Exercise Guide.* Champaign: Human Kinetics.

Gordon, N.F. (1993). *Chronic Fatigue: Your Complete Exercise Guide.* Champaign: Human Kinetics.

Gordon, N.F. (1993). *Diabetes: Your Complete Exercise Guide.* Champaign: Human Kinetics.

Gordon, N.F. (1993). *Stroke: Your Complete Exercise Guide.* Champaign: Human Kinetics.

Gordon, N.F. & Gibbons, L.W. (1990). *The Cooper Clinic Cardiac Rehabilitation Program: Featuring the Unique Heart Points Recovery System.* New York: Simon and Schuster.

Hanlon, T.W. (1995). *Fit for Two: The Official YMCA Prenatal Exercise Guide.* Champaign: Human Kinetics.

Hiatt, W.R., Regensteiner, J.G., Hargarten, M.E., Wolfel, E.E., Brass, E.E. & Brass, E.P. (1990). Benefit of exercise conditioning for patients with peripheral arterial disease. *Circulation.* 81, 602-609.

Hinson, C. (1995). *Fitness for Children.* Champaign: Human Kinetics.

Holstein, B.B. (1988). *Shaping Up for a Healthy Pregnancy.* Champaign: Life Enhancement Publications.

Institutes of Medicine. (1995). *Weighing the Options: Criteria for Evaluating Weight Management Programs.* Washington: National Academy Press.

Leppo, M. (1993). *Healthy from the Start: New Perspectives on Childhood Fitness.* Washington, DC: ERIC Clearinghouse on Teacher Education.

Miller, P.D. (Ed.) (1995). *Fitness Programming and Physical Disability.* Champaign: Human Kinetics.

Nakamura, E., Moritani, T. & Kanetake, A. (1989). Biological age versus physical fitness age. *European Journal of Applied Physiology.* 58, 778-785.

Osness, W.H. (1990). *Functional Fitness Assessment for Adults Over 60 Years: A Field Based Assessment.* Reston: American Alliance for Health, Physical Education, Recreation, and Dance.

Poehlman, E.T., McAuliffe, L., Van Houten, D.R. & Danforth, E. (1991). Influence of age and endurance training on metabolic rate and hormones in healthy men. *American Journal of Physiology.* 159, 66-72.

Pollock, M.L. & Schmidt, D.H. (Eds.) (1995). *Heart Disease and Rehabilitation.* Champaign: Human Kinetics.

Paciorek, M.J. (1994). *Sports and Recreation for the Disabled.* Carmel, IN: Cooper Publishing Group.

Pangrazi, R.P (1989). *Physical Fitness in the Elementary Schools; A Teacher's Manual.* (2nd ed.) Reston: American Alliance for Health, Physical Education, Recreation and Dance.

Rickers, R. (1986). *Seniors on the Move.* Champaign: Human Kinetics.

Rowland, T.W. (1990). *Exercise and Children's Health.* Champaign: Human Kinetics.

Sammann, P. (1994). *YMCA Healthy Back Book.* Champaign: Human Kinetics.

Shephard, R.J. (1990). *Fitness in Special Populations.* Champaign: Human Kinetics.

Sinaki, M. (1989). Exercise and osteoporosis. *Archives of Physical Medicine and Rehabilitation.* 70 (3), 220-229.

Smith, E.L. (1982). Exercise for prevention of osteoporosis: A review. *The Physician and Sports Medicine.* 10 (3), 72-83.

Tipton, C.M. (1991). Exercise, training and hypertension: An update. In: Hollozy, J.O., (Ed.) *Exercise and Sport Science.* 19, 447-505. Baltimore: Williams & Wilkins.

Van Norman, K.A. (1995). *Exercise Programming for Older Adults.* Champaign: Human Kinetics.

PART V

Chapter 13 Principles of Adherence and Motivation

Chapter 14 Communication and Teaching Techniques

V

Leadership and Implementation

CHAPTER 13

Principles of Adherence and Motivation

13

IN THIS CHAPTER:

Abby C. King and Deborah Rohm Young

Abby C. King, Ph.D., is a licensed clinical psychologist, assistant professor in Health Research & Policy and Medicine, and senior scientist at the Stanford Center for Research in Disease Prevention, Stanford University School of Medicine. She has written numerous articles and papers regarding the behavioral and psychological factors influencing adherence to a variety of health regimens, is a past recipient of a National Institutes of Health research career award to study the effects of physical activity on stress-related response in older adults, and she is federally funded for several research projects examining health benefits of physical activity. Deborah Rohm Young, Ph.D., is an exercise epidemiologist and assistant professor of Medicine at The Johns Hopkins Center for Health Promotion, The Johns Hopkins School of Medicine. She has written articles on exercise adherence and is studying the health benefits of physical activity in community-based samples.

In addition to providing ongoing expert advice and instruction about effective training for a client, a major part of the personal trainer's job is motivating the client to stick with a regular physical activity routine. Motivation, like other aspects of exercise, is a personal issue; what works for one client may not be successful for another. Developing strategies to keep each client interested and motivated will often be as important as designing the exercise program.

The Challenge of Motivating Clients to Adhere to their Physical-Activity Program

THE CHALLENGE OF MOTIVATING CLIENTS TO ADHERE TO THEIR PHYSICAL-ACTIVITY PROGRAM

Those of us working in exercise or physical fitness find physical activity to be an integral part of our lives. Understanding what it can do for us physically and mentally, as well as the sheer enjoyment we get from working out regularly, keeps us with our exercise program regardless of inconveniences or barriers we may encounter from week to week. Indeed, many committed exercisers feel miserable if they can't exercise; the rewards from completing an exercise session, and the negative consequences of not exercising, make the exercise schedule or routine a relatively simple undertaking. For such persons, regular exercise remains a high priority regardless of what life may bring.

Unfortunately, only a relatively small percentage of people in the U.S. and other Western countries share this attitude. While many acknowledge the importance of physical activity to health and well-being, a substantial proportion of the population is underactive. Current estimates suggest that approximately 30 percent of the American population do not engage in any leisure time activity, and only 9 percent are active at an intensity and frequency recommended for enhancing cardiovascular fitness (Caspersen & Merritt, 1995). Citizens of other countries fare no better. The percentage of regularly active persons decreases with age as well as with educational level, and minorities are particularly likely to be inactive. Drop-out rates for those beginning an exercise program are alarming. A number of studies report drop-outs from standard exercise programs to reach 50 percent or more by the end of the first six months (Dishman, 1991).

Why do so many people find sticking with exercise over the long haul such an arduous task? The answer is complex and multifaceted, influenced by factors associated with each client and their environment, the stage a person is in with respect to incorporating regular physical activity into their lifestyle, and characteristics of the exercise program itself.

Definition of Adherence

Adherence has been defined in a variety of ways. For the purpose of this chapter, adherence is defined as the amount of exercise performed compared with the amount of exercise recommended. Exercise refers to the specific program developed by the trainer with input from the client. Depending on the client and trainer's goals or preferences, the amount of exercise can refer to the frequency, duration (including number of repetitions), or intensity of exercise, or some combination of these three dimensions. You must consult with the client to determine adequate markers of adherence or progress toward realistic goals.

Factors Influencing Exercise Adherence

A growing body of scientific research in exercise adherence has identified a number of factors that may influence initial participation in an exercise program as well as how well someone will adhere to the program over the long term. These factors are described below.

Personal Factors. Surveys undertaken in the U.S. and elsewhere show that those most likely to begin an exercise program tend to be younger (especially when the activity is vigorous), more highly educated, white-collar workers as opposed to blue-collar, nonsmokers, whites as compared with minority groups, and not significantly overweight. Some of these factors also are associated with how well someone may maintain an exercise program after the initial adoption period. Persons who are aware of and believe in the positive health benefits of exercise also are more likely to

Exercise Confidence Survey*

How sure are you that you can do these things?

I know I can **Maybe I can** **I know I cannot**

1. Get up early, even on weekends, to exercise.

1 2 3 4 5 6 7 8 9 10

2. Stick to your exercise program after a long, tiring day at work.

1 2 3 4 5 6 7 8 9 10

3. Exercise even though you are feeling depressed.

1 2 3 4 5 6 7 8 9 10

4. Stick to your exercise program when undergoing a stressful life change (e.g., divorce, death in the family, moving).

1 2 3 4 5 6 7 8 9 10

5. Stick to your exercise program when you have household chores to attend to.

1 2 3 4 5 6 7 8 9 10

6. Stick to your exercise program even when you have excessive demands at work.

1 2 3 4 5 6 7 8 9 10

7. Stick to your exercise program when social obligations are very time consuming.

1 2 3 4 5 6 7 8 9 10

8. Read or study less in order to exercise more.

1 2 3 4 5 6 7 8 9 10

To obtain your exercise self-confidence score, simply add together the eight numbers you circled above. The higher your score, the more likely it is that you may eventually discontinue a regular exercise program.

*Adapted from Sallis, J. F., Pinski, R. B., Grossman, R. M., Patterson, T. L., & Nader, P. R. (1988). The development of self-efficacy scales for health-related diet and exercise behaviors. *Health Education Research,*

The Challenge of Motivating Clients to Adhere to their Physical-Activity Program

FIGURE 13.1
Read each of the statements and rate how confident you are that you could really motivate yourself to do these things consistently for at least six months. Be sure to answer every item and try to be as honest and accurate as possible in your responses. No one but you will know your score.

adopt a physically active lifestyle, but these factors are less influential for determining maintenance. Smokers and overweight individuals have poorer adherence rates than their nonsmoking and normal-weight counterparts. Finding ways to make the exercise program less physically demanding, such as promoting lower-intensity exercises or building frequent breaks into the exercise session, as well as using more frequent reminders concerning the physical and mental health benefits of regular exercise, may be particularly important for such clients. For smokers, pointing out how regular exercise may help counteract a number of negative symptoms and side effects associated with quitting (tension, fatigue, depressed mood, weight gain) may be especially helpful.

Other personal factors associated with exercise adherence include health status; past experiences with exercise; the actual skills (both physical and behavioral/psychological) a client has to exercise appropriately and effectively; the client's self-confidence in being able to engage in physical activity or complete an exercise program(self-efficacy); clients ratings, self-motivation or ability to persevere without external rewards; perceptions of program convenience and enjoyability; perceptions that the activity is not overly uncomfortable or difficult; and the client's ability to resolve common barriers to exercise, such as travel, injury, illness, competing demands on time, boredom and high-stress periods.

While some of these factors, such as smoking status or ratings of self-motivation, may be difficult to modify, others, such as self-efficacy and perceptions of enjoyability and convenience, are more amenable to change. These latter factors, discussed in this chapter, should be kept in mind when tackling exercise adherence issues. Assessment tools such as the exercise confidence survey (Figure 13.1) may be helpful in determining early on which clients may benefit from strategies that enhance exercise confidence. McAuley et al. (1994) found that middle-aged adults who were assigned to an exercise intervention designed to increase exercise efficacy (i.e., they provided information on exercise accomplishments over time; showed videos of others with similar characteristics who were exercising and enjoying it; formed buddy groups to provide encouragement; and provided information regarding physiologic changes associated with regular exercise) had greater adherence over a five-month period compared with adults who did not receive this special training.

Program Factors. Factors related to the exercise program or regimen itself may also affect client adherence. Among such factors, convenience is particularly important to most clients in the U. S. and other Western countries. For instance, does the client have choices of time of day for training sessions, and is there some flexibility in scheduling to accommodate changing circumstances? If the client is someone with a typically large number of time constraints, such as a middle-aged working woman who also is a wife and mother, can the personal trainer make arrangements for personal service (e.g., childcare, errand-running) to help ease competing demands? If the exercise program is held away from the client's home, is it reasonably accessible?

Other relevant program-related questions that require consideration include the following:

- ✔ Does the exercise mode itself require special, costly or time-consuming preparation that could reduce participation levels?
- ✔ Is the exercise regimen of a sufficient intensity so that the client finds it challenging but not punishing or aversive?
- ✔ Does the frequency of the exercise program fit the client's expectations, lifestyle and fitness/health goals?
- ✔ Is the program length acceptable to the client? In general, sessions lasting longer than 60 minutes are perceived as overly time consuming.
- ✔ Is the exercise routine varied enough to maintain interest and diminish boredom?

One of the important benefits of the one-to-one relationship between you and your client is the large amount of ongoing individualization of the exercise program that can occur. You should take advantage of every opportunity for enhancing motivation as well as shaping the actual exercise program.

Environmental Factors. For many clients, environmental factors provide some powerful incentives (and disincentives) for continuing exercise. They include the general ambiance of the locale in which the exercise sessions occur, and the time it takes to travel to the locale; token rewards for meeting predetermined goals; regular cues or reminders concerning the exercise training sessions, such as scheduling exercise time on the client's calendar and setting out exercise clothes the night before; weather conditions that may influence either travel to an exercise setting or willingness to exercise outside; limitation of time (either real or perceived); and the amount of support and feedback about exercise.

Ongoing support, in particular, has been found to be extremely important in promoting exercise adherence. This can come, not only from you, but also from the client's spouse, family and friends. Clients can be encouraged to talk with significant others about exercise goals and progression toward them. In addition to face-to-face contact, telephone or mail contacts, as appropriate, can remind clients about upcoming sessions and make them feel part of a larger organization. Encouragement during a time when the exercise workload is increased, or when other demands are competing with exercise time, can provide the client with support to carry on with the program. Lack of a group to which the client can feel they belong may be at least partially offset by using t-shirts, newsletters or other devices to identify the client as a member of your "team."

Social support also includes finding ways to minimize negative comments from others concerning the client's attempts to exercise. For instance, negative attitudes toward a client's exercise program by their spouse, significant other or family have a detrimental effect on attempts to stick with the program. Exploring methods to include members of the family in the exercise enterprise may be quite worthwhile. This may mean finding ways to encourage actual exercise participation on the part of the spouse or significant others, such as undertaking exercise activities at the same time as the client or simply providing that person with information about the exercise program so that they feel included. You should consider all three factors — personal, program and environmental — when developing and carrying out exercise programming.

UNDERSTANDING MOTIVATION

Many of us have the notion that motivation is something that we are born with, or that resides entirely within us. This "trait" notion of motivation suggests that whether a client succeeds in engaging regularly in an activity or not is dependent almost entirely on their personal resources, abilities or strengths, rather than on external factors or circumstances. Faced with a nonadherent client, personal trainers subscribing to a trait notion of motivation will often place either the responsibility or the blame for nonadherence entirely on the client. By assuming that only personal factors influence adherence, they often write the individual off as lazy, incompetent or unmotivated — in essence, engaging in what is known as "blaming the victim."

However, as noted, adherence to health regimens such as exercise is influenced by a host of environmental and situational factors in addition to personal factors. Some of these factors may be out of the client's control. Others may be factors of which the person is completely unaware. Rather than simply placing the blame for nonadherence on the client, you must view motivation as a joint responsibility shared with the client. It also is helpful to view the motivation process as something dynamic; different strategies may be needed for different clients at different stages in the program. For example, the types of strategies used to enhance adherence or attendance during the initial "critical period" of exercise (first three to six months), when many of the difficulties associated with participation typically occur, may well differ from those most useful in helping to maintain exercise over the long haul.

Because motivating the client is one of your most important and most difficult responsibilities, the ability to address the motivational needs of the client in an ongoing, effective fashion may well be the single largest measure of a trainer's success.

Leadership Qualities

Your attitudes, personality and professional conduct are important factors in adherence and motivation. The qualities of an effective exercise leader include the following:

- ✔ Punctuality and dependability in scheduling sessions and communicating with the client. This includes being regularly prepared for training sessions, starting and ending sessions on time, and arranging for substitutes if you cannot attend a planned session.
- ✔ Professionalism in dress, behavior and demeanor. This means treating clients with respect and letting them know (through actions as well as words) that you take the trainer-client relationship seriously. It also means respecting the client's privacy and the confidentiality of what is shared as part of the relationship.
- ✔ Dedication to the exercise training endeavor, demonstrated by putting continual effort into making training sessions fun, rewarding, safe and educational. Attending workshops to keep up on the latest developments regarding exercise training, and finding out answers to questions that the client may have on exercise-related topics indicate dedication.
- ✔ Willingness to plan ahead for things that may interfere with a training session and preparing the client, as much as possible, for any breaks that may occur. In addition, becoming aware of upcoming events or fitness challenges, and making a plan to train for one of them may be appealing to certain clients.
- ✔ Sensitivity to each client's past experiences, current preferences and current and future needs. This includes recognizing that each client is unique, customizing each exercise session to meet their preferences, and working with the client to maximize each exercise session. Providing a regular means for evaluating the client's performance as well as your own, and being open to suggestions and alternatives that may enhance training sessions also are important.
- ✔ Recognizing signs of burnout and taking steps to prevent or ameliorate it by taking time off and enlisting the aid, advice and support of fellow trainers. Apathy toward work and/or irritability with clients that extends beyond a few days is a sign of burnout and needs to be resolved quickly. Overuse musculoskeletal injuries also are a sign that a break is needed.
- ✔ Presenting oneself as a role model for exercise training and other areas of health.
- ✔ Taking responsibility for problems that may arise in the course of helping clients reach their exercise goals. Consider issues of motivation, the training regimen itself, and client safety and well-being. As part of this, the conscientious trainer recognizes when the client may be better served seeking assistance elsewhere, and aids the client in obtaining an appropriate referral.
- ✔ Forming with each client a partnership in the exercise experience, which includes having the client play an active role in developing the training program and any decisions that may be needed to pursue the exercise-training goals.

Methods for Enhancing and Maintaining Motivation to Exercise

The general guidelines listed on the following page for enhancing motivation and promoting exercise adherence should be used to develop a specific plan of action tailored to the motivational needs of each client. They include personal, programmatic and environmental influences on exercise adherence.

1. Structure appropriate expectations at the beginning. As mentioned earlier, a client's personal beliefs about what exercise can and cannot do, as well as past exercise experiences, can influence motivation. Unrealistic expectations ("If I exercise regularly, I should be able to shed all that excess weight within a month or two," or "exercise will completely change my life"), fueled by the media and at times a somewhat overzealous health community, currently run rampant. Such expectations, when unfulfilled, can lead to frustration, disappointment or overexercise that make drop-out more likely.

You can help to structure realistic expectations by exploring what the client expects to achieve early in the program. The client should be informed about the exercise regimens you are best equipped to offer, how the sessions will generally be structured and why. If the client currently is not a regular exerciser, starting a program out at a moderate-intensity level may be preferable while the client is adopting a physically active lifestyle. Explaining to the client the rationale for starting out at a lower level will assist the client-trainer relationship and help to develop trust early on in the program. The use of the Borg Scale (Borg, 1970), which involves the rating of perceived exertion (RPE), can provide an excellent means for evaluating the client's perception of exercise intensity. RPE has been found to provide a useful reflection of intensity and how the client is feeling about the workout. Individuals consistently rating themselves at the upper range of the RPE, particularly early in their exercise program, may be at increased risk for non-adherence, drop-out or potential injury.

Since musculoskeletal injury is the most often cited reason for discontinuing a vigorous exercise program, starting a program out slowly at a moderate intensity will allow the client's muscles, tendons and bones to adapt to the stress of the exercise. Carroll and colleagues (1992) found that the incidence rate of injury was only 14 percent for adults between the ages of 60 and 79 years who engaged in a walking program, which suggests that low-impact activities may be particularly beneficial for older adults. However, most of the injuries occurred in the women, so careful monitoring of older women for proper exercise techniques, as well as adequate warm-up and cool-down periods, is warranted.

The client should be informed about the types of uncomfortable or negative side effects that may accompany increased physical activity, such as stiffness, minor soreness or muscle pain, and some fatigue, particularly early on in the training program. These symptoms usually are transient and will dissipate over time. However, other types of symptoms, such as chest pain and undue fatigue lasting well after the exercise session, require further, and perhaps medical, attention.

2. Find out the client's preferences, needs and exercise history. One of the advantages of being a personal trainer is that usually there is time to assess your client thoroughly. Take advantage of this opportunity to find out not only what level your clients are at physically, but where they are mentally and experientially as well. This is probably best accomplished through a simple questionnaire that all clients should complete at the beginning of their program, either on their own or in an interview format. Questions of interest include the types of exercise programs clients have previously participated in (types of activities; format — with another personal trainer, in a class or on their own; length of time of participation; reasons for drop-out); reasons for seeking a personal trainer at this particular time; what expectations and goals they hope to accomplish

My Responsibilities:

1. To attend all of my scheduled exercise sessions (three times per week) over the next four weeks.
2. For any sessions that I have to miss due to illness or other unavoidable reasons, I will:
   a. Call my trainer to let them know the reason(s) why I had to miss (Trainer's telephone number = ____________________).
   b. Plan to make up the missed session by (specify): ________________.
3. To reward myself at the end of each week that I attend all of my scheduled sessions by engaging in thirty or more minutes of reading for my own enjoyment.

My Helper's Responsibilities:

My designated helper is: ______________________________. They have agreed:

a. To prompt me during work to attend my exercise sessions.
b. In return, I will prompt them concerning a behavior of their choice, as desired.

This contract will be evaluated on ____(date)____.

Signed:

____________________ ____________________
(participant) (date)

____________________ ____________________
(helper) (date)

____________________ ____________________
(trainer) (date)

FIGURE 13.2
Sample four-week contract.

and over what time frame; current preferences concerning specific types of exercise; past and current injuries; potential pitfalls they see ahead based on prior experiences; constraints with respect to time and other issues and questions they would like answered concerning working with you, or concerning your particular style and strengths.

3. Decide on the specific types of activities that will best fit the client's objectives, time, commitments and personal style. Based on the above information, tailor the exercise program to each client. This may mean using indoor exercises for the client embarrassed to be seen in public; water exercises for clients with knee or hip problems; exercise sports for clients motivated by competitive challenges; or relaxed reading time on a reclining cycle for the stressed or exhausted executive. In addition, if a client says that in the past, one of the major reasons why they stopped exercising was boredom, then building in variety within, or across, sessions, as well as varying exercise routes or locations on a regular basis, may be helpful.

4. Set appropriate exercise goals. Once you have both determined the specific activities that will make up the client's exercise routine, the next job is to work with the client to set appropriate, realistic and flexible goals for each portion of it. Realistic goals are important in order to avoid injury and maintain interest. This is particularly true in the beginning, when over-enthusiastic clients may be tempted to set goals that are unachievable, given the common restraints of other commitments for one's time. Short-term goals determined by the personal trainer for each exercise session, in conjunction with longer-term, monthly goals established with the client, allow for flexibility on a daily basis

without jeopardizing the longer-term goals. Goals can be specific to the exercise process, such as training together a predetermined number of times combined with a certain number of individual sessions in the coming weeks, or training for a specific fitness event. Regardless of what type of goal is used, with its achievement, the next one should be discussed. Providing feedback regarding progress towards specific goals and praising and rewarding the client when goals are reached also is a useful strategy.

Goals can be formalized in the form of a **contract** (Figure 13.2). Contracts are written agreements signed by the client and the personal trainer (and additional third parties, such as a spouse or exercise partner, if deemed appropriate) that clearly spell out the exercise goals (such as the duration, type, and/or intensity of exercise engaged in with you), preferably over a short time period (two to four weeks), and the rewards associated with achieving them. Contracts serve to increase the client's personal responsibility and commitment to the exercise program. An exercise contract should contain input from both you and the client, and the responsibilities each has in meeting its terms. The contract should specify goals that are somewhat challenging yet realistically achievable to promote success. You should make certain that the client has the skills necessary to meet the terms of the contract and include precautions to ensure that they do not engage in unhealthy practices to meet contract requirements (such as exercising at a high intensity when ill). Exercise goals should be written in a manner that allows them to be objectively measured, thereby eliminating any questions regarding goal attainment. If you are responsible for delivering a contingent reward, plan ahead so it can be distributed promptly.

To summarize, a series of prudent goals should be negotiated by you and your client that focus on building the exercise habit through gradual increments rather than larger changes that, though more appealing to some clients, can lead to failure, frustration, injury and/or dropout. During the first six to 12 weeks in particular, the goals may need to be focused on simply "showing up," no matter how little the client may feel like, or be able to do. Alternatively, for the zealous overachieving client, goals can aid efforts to diminish overexertion and injury. The important thing is to match the goals to the needs and preferences of each individual.

5. Whenever possible, offer choices. While some structure is typically welcomed by clients attempting to adopt or maintain a behavior such as exercise, many will benefit from being offered some choice of alternatives within the general structure of the program. Doing so helps to stave off boredom that often creeps into an exercise program. Choices may be made available with respect to the exercise regimen itself (types of activity engaged in, frequency, intensity and/or duration factors), or the types of goals, **feedback** and/or incentives used to enhance adherence. An increasingly flexible view is being taken by national organizations regarding types of physical activity and the frequency, intensity and duration suitable for obtaining reasonable health benefits. Current recommendations by the Centers for Disease Control and Prevention and the American College of Sports Medicine (1995) state that moderate-intensity activity (which includes a wide variety of leisure, work and transportation-related activities) carried out for 30 minutes per day on most days of the week is sufficient for a wide variety of health benefits. Personal trainers can now offer clients an increasing number of options for achieving worthwhile health and fitness goals.

6. Remember that exercise, like other behaviors, is strongly influenced by its immediate consequences. Often the immediate feelings and consequences

surrounding actions, rather than more abstract or long-term beliefs or views, have the most powerful effect on daily activities. Despite the best of intentions, if the immediate or short-term benefits of exercise do not outweigh the time and effort required, it is likely that drop-out or relapse to being sedentary will result. You must work with the client to identify short-term benefits (feelings of accomplishment, stress reduction, better sleep, changes in circumference of the legs or arms) rather than focusing only on long-term outcomes (better health, reduction in cardiovascular risk, weight loss). While weight control is certainly an important by-product of regular aerobic exercise, for many clients weight loss through increased exercise alone is a slow process. In addition, in at least some individuals, the loss in fat weight is often compensated for by an increase in lean weight (muscle) resulting in no change on the scale. Periodic measurements of parts of the body might, for some clients, be a better gauge of progress.

7. Increase the immediately rewarding aspects of the behavior and decrease the negative or punishing aspects. Analyze both the positive and negative aspects of the exercise session itself to increase enjoyability and decrease discomfort and boredom. For some, providing a means of distraction from the chore of exercise through social interaction, music or an interesting exercise routine is important. Through regular monitoring of how clients are enjoying the session (using a simple six-point rating scale, with one equaling "extremely unenjoyable," and six equaling "extremely enjoyable"), you can modify the regimen. For instance, if a client dislikes a particular portion of the exercise routine you can substitute a different exercise to achieve the same results. Because what is rewarding or punishing about an exercise program differs from person to person, it is important to individualize strategies for enhancing enjoyment.

For some clients, modifying the exercise session to increase enjoyment will not be enough, especially for those just beginning an exercise program. For them, the uncomfortable aspects of increased exertion (sweating, increased heart rate, sore muscles) may outweigh any positive outcomes. Such clients may need external incentives, such as earning points toward a desirable reward once the goal has been reached. For some clients, an external incentive system can be set up in the form of an achievement club, or related activities, with formal recognition in the form of pins, t-shirts, certificates or other rewards for achieving training goals.

Teaching clients how to successfully monitor their own intensity levels can help them maintain an enjoyable workout. Beginning exercisers should be encouraged to exercise at an intensity that allows them to talk comfortably without undue sweating. Knowing how to accurately monitor their heart rates, through regular pulse taking or the use of a portable heart monitor, is another method of monitoring intensity. The **RPE** scale previously described also provides information regarding the client's perceived intensity of a workout and can be used to gauge how a client is responding to a new routine.

8. Provide feedback whenever possible. Regular feedback that is specific and relevant to the client can be an extremely powerful reinforcer or incentive, particularly early in the exercise program when more intrinsic benefits from exercising, such as an increase in muscle tone or reduction in tension, may not yet be present. Feedback can take many forms. Physiologically based feedback may include changes in resting or exertional heart rate or RPE. Use of a standardized submaximal exercise test, such as the step-test or 12-minute distance test, administered at the beginning of the exercise program and at regular intervals, can provide useful information to both you and the client.

Testing clients every three months or so should provide them with enough feedback to reinforce current activities and motivate future adherence. However, if the client has had to lay off training (due to injury, illness or scheduling problems), it is preferable to allow them to build back up to a reasonable intensity before initiating further testing. Testing during a plateau or down period in the client's training program can lead to discouragement and frustration, which in turn can result in either dropping out or overtraining. It also is important to determine if testing is preferable to an individual client; some may be opposed to regular testing or not find the procedures or results motivating.

Behaviorally based feedback can include regular recordings of the amount of activity (frequency, duration, number of repetitions, distance covered), as well as periodic completion of an exercise balance sheet, in which the client lists both the positive and negative aspects of regular exercise. Through completing such a sheet, clients are often reminded of the reasons they decided to exercise in the first place. For those clients who are amenable to it, regular logging of exercise behavior serves as an immediate, visual record of their session-by-session accomplishments. If the exercise activity is walking, running or hiking, pedometers can be worn to log the distance traveled. Logging of exercise behavior helps to bridge the gap between the exercise sessions and more distant rewards of changes in **body composition**, endurance or strength, and earning something tangible such as a t-shirt. Having clients maintain their own records also helps to drive home the point that they share responsibility with you.

9. Teach the client how to use prompts and reminders to set the stage. Exercise can be one of a long list of activities vying for our time and attention. To keep exercise prominently placed in the client's list of priorities, set up a system of **prompts**, or reminders, about the exercise sessions. This may involve writing the sessions into a daily schedule book or providing the client with a calendar to be prominently displayed on the refrigerator or other suitable place in the home or at work. Encouraging the client to ready their exercise apparel the evening before a scheduled exercise session, and to display it in a prominent place, may help get them to a class or group.

10. Model the appropriate behaviors for the client. Appropriate and consistent **modeling** of exercise-related behaviors can provide motivation in the early as well as later stages of participation. When modeling the actual exercise routines or activities, perform the activity slowly, both as a demonstration as well as along with clients during their execution of the activity. Breaking complicated routines into easily learned segments will help the client increase their self-confidence in performing the routine. Remember that, as a health professional, you are in an excellent position to serve as a role model for other important health behaviors by not smoking or abusing alcohol and by maintaining healthy dietary patterns and prudent weight-control activities.

11. Foster self-management of the exercise regimen. In order to help clients establish exercise as a lifelong habit, foster a sense of personal responsibility and commitment to exercise. It is critical to realize that we must take charge of our exercise as a lifelong goal, rather than as a time-limited commitment that ends when certain goals have been reached or temporary set-backs occur. To do this, train clients in the use of self-management strategies that will help them keep the exercise habit going when circumstances interfere with their usual routine. This may mean equipping clients with strategies to keep them exercising during those periods, such as business travel, vacations or changes in work hours, when they are unable to make

normally scheduled exercise sessions. For a client who will be traveling, this may include packing appropriate exercise attire, being aware of exercises that can be undertaken in a hotel room, and/or making arrangements to stay in a hotel that has in-house exercise facilities. Because anticipated breaks from an exercise schedule can lead to drop-out, planning for them ahead of time can increase the probability of subsequent resumption of the exercise program.

When unplanned breaks in the exercise regime occur, it is important to first let the client know that you care, and then encourage them to get back into the regimen as soon as possible. Expect that many clients will feel at least some level of guilt (that they have let you, as well as themselves, down), in addition to frustration and discouragement. Such feelings breed drop-out. Research shows that even a brief supportive, nonjudgmental telephone call during such a period can help clients maintain their exercise programs.

12. Prepare the client for inevitable **lapses**. Clients should be fully informed about the pitfalls that are often encountered when people attempt to exercise regularly. These may include unplanned breaks in the exercise regimen due to illness, work schedule, unplanned travel, holidays and the like, or failure to observe further gains following a period of significant progress. Preparing clients ahead of time for particularly high-risk situations, when breaks in the exercise regimen are likely, may help prevent the full-blown drop-out often seen following such unplanned breaks. By encouraging the client to also exercise on their own, you will provide them with confidence to exercise without supervision when a scheduled class must be missed. An additional strategy is to promote an abbreviated workout during busy times.

13. Prepare the client for changes in trainers. Perhaps the most disruptive event for many clients is the loss of the regular trainer, even for a brief period. Unfortunately, little, if anything, is typically done to prepare clients for this often unsettling circumstance. Planned transition periods (pregnancy leave, travel, permanent relocation) can be smoothed immensely by preparing clients well ahead of time and, if possible, introducing the instructor who will be stepping in well before the regular instructor takes their leave. Having the regular and new instructor team teach several of the exercise sessions can go a long way to allay fears and prevent clients from dropping out. Even the most healthy trainers will have days when they are unable to work, so all trainers should plan for substitutes and, if possible, introduce them to clients ahead of time. If a substitute is not available, following up with clients by telephone may help to keep them from feeling abandoned, betrayed or discouraged.

14. Utilize as many types of social support as possible. Ongoing social support, in all of its many forms, is invaluable both in the early and more advanced stages of an exercise program. While the face-to-face support provided during the session itself can be invaluable for many clients, don't overlook other potentially important avenues that can complement your personal instruction. These include telephone contacts following missed sessions; regular newsletters or other mailed items that can both educate and motivate continued participation; and the encouragement of support on the part of family members or co-workers through mailed newsletters or other informational pieces.

15. Look for opportunities to promote an overall healthy lifestyle. Exercise does not occur in a vacuum, but rather is only one of a number of activities clients engage in throughout the week. Because for many of us our exercise program has a major impact on the rest of our lives, we often assume that those who exercise regularly will automatically change other

health behaviors, such as smoking and dietary practices. Unfortunately, very little scientific evidence supports this widely held belief. Many people who exercise maintain a regular smoking habit or eat a diet high in saturated fats and sugar. Indeed, some maintain the inaccurate belief that regular exercise will protect them against the other negative health habits. We must help clients recognize that exercise alone is not a panacea for health, but, rather, only one of a number of behaviors that comprise a healthy lifestyle.

As a trained health professional, you are in an excellent position to provide basic, accurate information and encouragement for the development of a healthy lifestyle beyond exercise. Most trainers are deluged by questions on diet, weight control and other health regimens by those concerned about their health and confused by the mixed messages currently being promulgated in the media and by special-interest groups. Regular contact with clients interested in improving their health provides an invaluable opportunity for educating them in a manner not available to many other types of health professionals. The trainer who stays abreast of current scientific information and developments in health promotion can help ensure that health information is responsibly disseminated. Refer to Chapters 4 and 12 for useful information about nutrition and weight control, and consider becoming certified as an American Council on Exercise Lifestyle & Weight Management Consultant.

A healthy lifestyle also involves participating in physical activities beyond the scheduled training session. Encourage clients to look for opportunities to be more active as a way of life (by walking instead of driving, or by using stairs instead of elevators or escalators). Increasing lifestyle-type activities such as these is being promoted by national organizations as a way to accumulate 30 minutes per day of moderate-intensity activity and provide health benefits. Including these types of activities in one's regular routine may also help clients maintain a high energy level when more vigorous activities are not possible. Such activities are particularly important for the older client, as well as other subgroups, such as those who are overweight or those who have been unable to give up the smoking habit. By encouraging physical activity in all of its forms, you can serve as an important teacher and role model for achieving a healthy lifestyle.

SUMMARY

Drop-out rates for those beginning an exercise program can reach 50 percent or more after only six months. Instead of blaming the client, you must view motivation as a shared responsibility. By analyzing each client's preferences, habits and circumstances to anticipate blocks to success, you can design a specific approach to motivate each client to achieve mutually determined goals.

Factors affecting adherence to a health regimen can be complex and interrelated. Motivation is a dynamic process and requires the use of a variety of techniques that will help a client achieve and maintain a healthy lifestyle. These techniques range from structuring appropriate expectations and goals, identifying short-term benefits and providing specific feedback, to serving as a positive role model and training clients in self-management strategies. Understanding and applying the principles of adherence and motivation will make you a more effective teacher and health professional.

REFERENCES

Borg, G. V. (1970). Perceived exertion as an indicator of somatic stress. *Scandinavian Journal of Rehabilitation Medicine,* 2, 92-98.

Carroll, J. F., Pollock, M. L., Graves, J. E., Leggett, S. H., Spitler, D. L. & Lowenthal, D. T. (1992). Incidence of injury during moderate- and high-intensity walking training in the elderly. *Journal of Gerontology: Medical Sciences,* 47, M61-M66.

Caspersen, C.J. & Merritt, R. K. (1995). Physical activity trends among 26 states, 1986-1990. *Medicine and Science in Sports and Exercise,* 27, 713-720.

Dishman, R.K. (1991). Increasing and maintaining exercise and physical activity. *Behavior Therapy,* 22, 345-378.

McAuley, E., Courneya, K. S., Rudolph, D. L. & Lox, C. L. (1994). Enhancing exercise adherence in middle-aged males and females. *Preventive Medicine,* 23, 498-506.

Pate, R. R., Pratt, M., Blair, S. N., Haskell, W. L., Macera, C. A., Bouchard, C., Buchner, D., Ettinger, W., Heath, G. W., King, A.C., Kriska, A., Leon, A. S., Marcus, B. H., Morris, J., Paffenbarger, R. S., Patrick, K., Pollock, M. L., Rippe, J. M., Sallis, J. & Wilmore, J. H. (1995). Physical activity and public health. A recommendation from the Centers for Disease Control and Prevention and the American College of Sports Medicine. *Journal of the American Medical Association,* 273, 402-407.

SUGGESTED READING

American College of Sports Medicine. (1994). *Resource Manual for Guidelines for Exercise Testing and Prescription.* (2nd ed.) Baltimore: Williams and Wilkins.

Dishman, R.K. (ed.) (1994). *Advances in Exercise Adherence.* Champaign: Human Kinetics.

King, A. C., Blair S. N., Bild, D. E., Dishman, R. K., Dubbert, P. M., Marcus, B. H., Oldridge, N. B., Paffenbarger, R. S., Jr., Powell, K. E. & Yeager, K. K. (1992). Determinants of physical activity and interventions in adults. *Medicine and Science in Sports and Exercise,* 24, S221-S226.

CHAPTER 14

Communication and Teaching Techniques

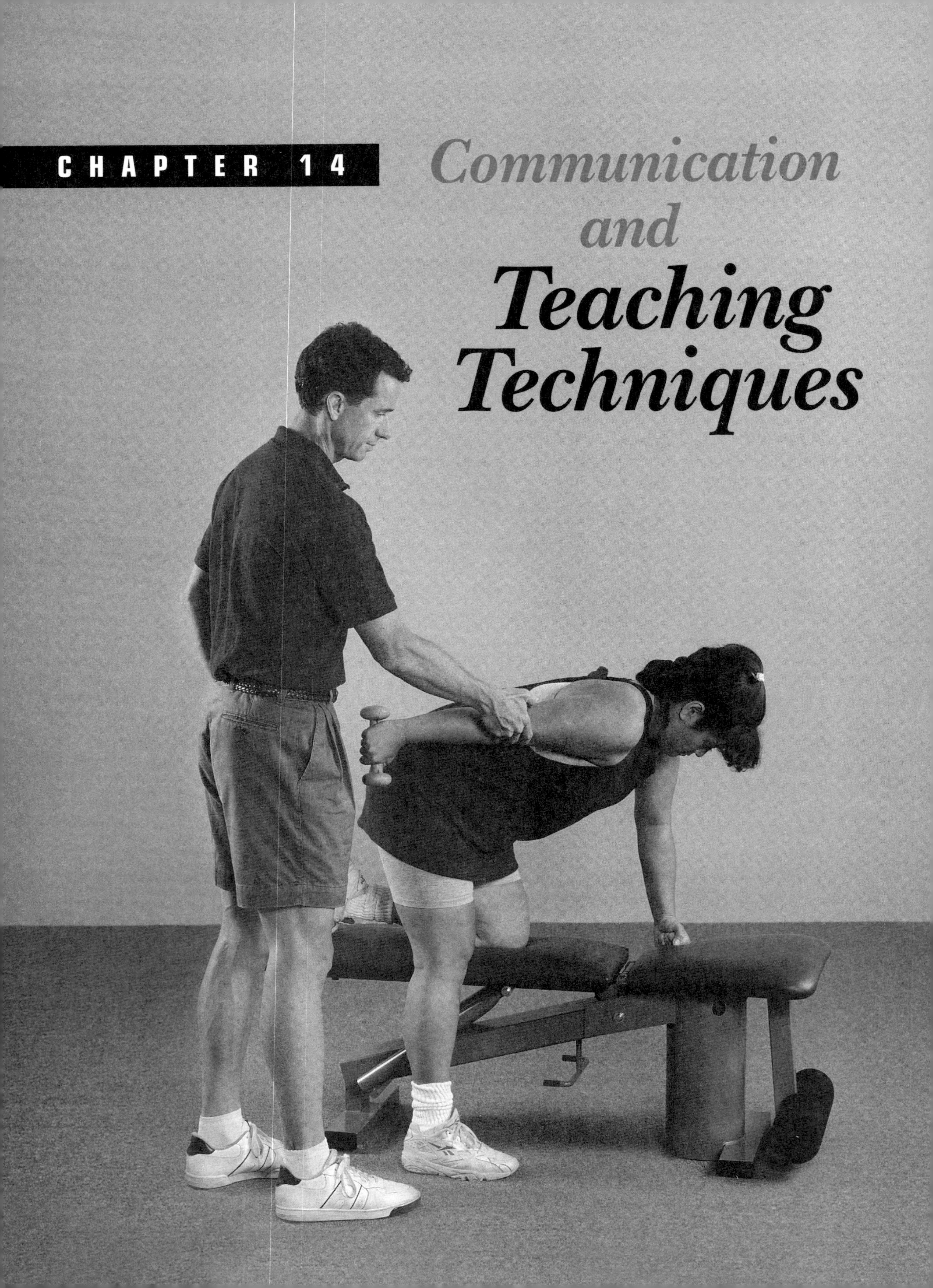

14

IN THIS CHAPTER:

Amy P. Jones

Amy Jones, M.Ed., is a licensed psychotherapist and works with Fortune 500 companies undergoing change or a transition. Much of her time is spent coaching and training executives in communication and organizational effectiveness. She was formerly the director of programs for the Cooper Fitness Center in Dallas for 12 years, and served as a technical advisor to the National Aerobic Championship. She is currently a member of the American Council on Exercise Board of Directors.

A personal trainer's relationship to a client is clearly the helping relationship of educator to student. You are the helper or teacher; the one being helped is referred to as the student or client. Helping relationships differ from most other kinds of relationships encountered in daily routines. Most ordinary experiences are dialogues in which both people seek personal enhancement or the mutual exchange of ideas or information. In the helping relationship, one person temporarily sets aside personal needs to help another person. The focus of the relationship is on the client's needs and on goals that will lead to new behavior. Simply put, helping is enabling another person to change. Instead of encouraging dependence, the purpose of helping is to facilitate the client's taking more

Stages of the Personal Trainer/Client Relationship

control and becoming self-sufficient. Helping is an active process of advising, informing, correcting and directing.

There are many kinds of helping relationships. Because there is usually a fee for service in personal training, you can be classified as a structured, professional helper, like social workers, teachers, school counselors and legal advisors. In contrast to this professional level are unstructured levels of helping such as friendships and family relationships.

Your role is complex as you will function as a teacher, coach, advisor, supervisor, supporter, counselor and negotiator.

Teacher: Explaining to clients what they need to know and must do (e.g., outlining and explaining an aerobic exercise program).

FIGURE 14.1
Stages of the personal trainer/client relationship.

Coach: Training clients in desired skills (e.g., coaching during a free-weight workout).

Advisor: Telling clients the wisest course of action (e.g., warning about dangers of an unsupervised liquid fasting program).

Supporter: Encouraging clients as they work on specific lifestyle changes (e.g., providing emotional support for a client who has stopped smoking).

Counselor: Helping clients sort through personal problems (e.g., listening to a client's frustrations regarding problems at work).

Negotiator: Bargaining with clients to reach an acceptable agreement (e.g., negotiating an exercise contract with a client for a period of travel).

These roles are described only in a general sense. You should be acutely aware of your limitations and must not exceed the professional parameters of offering advice or counseling about personal problems. You can obviously listen and offer support, but you should know when to refer clients to other qualified professionals.

STAGES OF THE PERSONAL TRAINER/CLIENT RELATIONSHIP

There will be distinct stages in your relationships with clients (Figure 14.1), and they form a general model or framework for the divisions and related skills of the helping relationship. They may not always occur in this exact sequence, nor are all stages always present. Their length also may vary from client to client. Generally, the initial contact between the personal trainer and client is made in the rapport stage. The process of gathering information after the relationship has begun forms the investigation stage. This gives way to the planning stage in which the client's goals and steps toward them are mapped out. Finally, the action stage begins when the actual training process starts.

Each stage requires specific skills and techniques. In the beginning, for example, attentive listening skills can build the working relationship; the following stages require more decision-making and behavioral-change skills. Developing these skills can increase your effectiveness as a personal trainer. Because the personal trainer/client relationship is dynamic and ever changing, these stages and skills overlap and may not occur in the exact order given. The specific stages and required skills are outlined as follows:

Stage 1: Rapport — interpersonal communication skills.

Stage 2: Investigation — information gathering skills.

Stage 3: Planning — problem-solving or decision-making skills.

Stage 4: Action — behavioral change skills (feedback, contracting, modeling, etc.).

RAPPORT STAGE

The rapport stage is the foundation for the entire relationship between you and your client. Rapport means a relationship of mutual trust, harmony or emotional affinity. Establishing it entails building a certain level of comfort or shared understanding into a relationship. The rapport stage begins at first contact. Whether in person or on the telephone, the client is "checking out" the personal trainer and answering the question, "Can this person help me?" Confidence or trust in your skills must be established early because only then will the client be willing to receive guidance.

According to Rogers' (1967) research, people in the helping profession need to communicate three basic attributes or qualities in order for the helping relationship to be successful. These three primary qualities are 1) **empathy**, 2) warmth and 3) genuineness. The importance of these qualities has been demonstrated repeatedly in research by Truax and Carkuff (1967) and others. They are the foundation for a successful helping relationship and are key factors during the rapport stage.

Empathy is the ability to experience another person's world as if it were one's own. It is understanding the client's point of view or where the client is "coming from." The empathetic personal trainer will be able to respond appropriately to the client's covert feelings and verbal messages by communicating perceptions to the client. The absence of empathy may lead the client to think the trainer does not understand what they are experiencing and, therefore, will block the entire helping process.

Warmth is an unconditional positive regard or a respect for another person regardless of their individuality and uniqueness. It bridges professional distance through friendliness and consideration regardless of a "liking" for another person. Warmth is about caring and understanding rather than judging and impersonalizing. This quality will convey a climate that communicates safety and acceptance to a client, even when they're making mistakes.

Genuineness can be defined as authenticity or being honest and open without putting up a front. It is a state in which the helper's words and actions are congruent. For example, when you greet a client with "I'm glad to see you're here today," your body language must be consistent with the words of welcome. Genuineness is the ability to relate to people without hiding behind a clipboard or white coat. It is not necessarily being fully self-revealing, but rather being committed to a responsible honesty with others.

Empathy, warmth and genuineness are paramount in establishing trust in a working relationship. At first glance, they may seem simplistic because they are the outgrowth of ordinary effective human qualities. However, relevant research and cumulative experience points out the necessity for continuous monitoring of the timing and amount of conditions that facilitate the development of these qualities.

Interpersonal communication skills are the primary skills needed to establish rapport and thereby build a relationship. They are not only important during the rapport stage, but are necessary throughout the relationship. Interpersonal communication skills can be broadly categorized as nonverbal and verbal. The nonverbal category includes such behaviors as attending, and perceiving nonverbal and verbal messages. The verbal category includes paraphrasing, reflecting and clarifying. Many of these skills are natural for anyone genuinely involved in helping another person, but specific communication skills can be learned, practiced and continuously mastered.

Nonverbal Behaviors

Listening is the primary nonverbal

Rapport Stage

communication skill. It is a complex concept and is not the same as hearing, which is the perception of sound through the ear. Listening obviously involves the physiology of hearing, but also is a more complex psychological procedure of involvement with the other person. In and of itself it involves skills in attending, perceiving verbal and nonverbal messages, and even verbal responding. All of these skills overlap and are difficult to treat separately.

Attending. Attending behaviors are exhibited by the listener to put the speaker at ease and entail being attentive or giving physical attention to them. Instead of interrupting, the listener gives nonverbal acknowledgements during the conversation through posture, eye contact and gestures. Verbal responses also are a form of attending. The listener may say "yes, I see" to encourage the speaker to continue.

Effective attending can build trust and can work wonders in human relationships. Conversely, nonattentive behavior can be devastating. For example, when you are speaking to someone who appears bored, and whose eyes are continually distracted to other things, you may feel ignored and not encouraged to continue the conversation. The trainer interested in developing good attending behaviors or skills needs to be aware of the following:

1. Posture: When you and your client are seated, specific postures can communicate your interest. To show involvement, face the client squarely at eye level and lean toward them in a relaxed manner. Avoid expressing defensiveness by maintaining an open position with arms and legs uncrossed. This posture says, "I am interested in you and am ready to listen." Research has shown that these postural behaviors demonstrate to the client the traits of empathy, warmth and genuineness.

2. Positioning: Position yourself at an appropriate distance from the client to demonstrate a respect for their personal space. Hall (1966) describes an 18-inch or less distance between two people as "intimate space" an 18-inch to 4-foot distance as "personal space" a 4-foot to 12-foot distance as "social distance" and beyond 12 feet as "public distance." Most normal conversation will occur in the personal space (Figure 14.2). However, the very nature of your working relationship demands at times that you enter the client's intimate space. Because of this intimate positioning, be sensitive to the client, particularly when hands-on work is being done. Early in the relationship you may want to ask permission to touch the client and should take care that the client does not misconstrue your touching or presence in their personal space.

3. Mirroring: Another technique you can use to establish rapport is mimicking or mirroring. Mirroring may be either conscious or unconscious, but its purpose is to establish rapport with another person when it previously has not been. The technique of mirroring involves sensitively

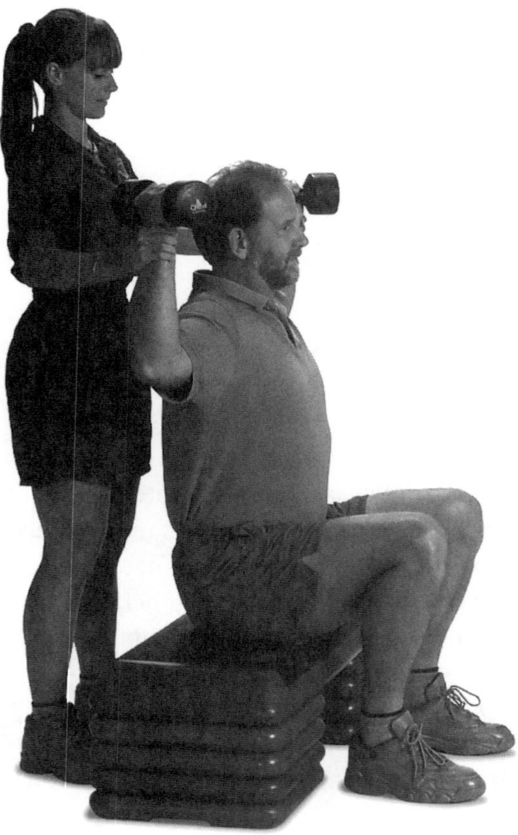

FIGURE 14.2
Trainer working in a client's personal space.

Rapport Stage

matching the posture and gestures of the other person, and may include matching voice tone and tempo, and breathing patterns. These techniques often occur naturally as people interact.

4. Eye Contact: Eye contact is a key vehicle for indicating interest in a person. Good eye contact is not a fixed stare but rather a relaxed focus on the client's eyes, face and body gestures. It enables the client to feel safe and comfortable, and conveys your interest at the same time.

5. Gestures: Appropriate body movement is essential in attending. Try to use relaxed motions instead of appearing rigid and unmoving. Nervous mannerisms such as playing with objects, jingling pocket change, waving to others and drumming fingers should be avoided.

6. Environment: Since much of the personal training process takes place in a gym that is usually full of talking people, blaring music and clanging weights, a quiet place is preferable for effective communication. Pleasant surroundings facilitate conversation, so initial sessions should be conducted in a nondistracting environment. To give someone your undivided attention when distractions are present is difficult. Distractions may consist of a blaring TV or radio, a ringing telephone, people stopping by to talk, uncomfortable room temperature and inappropriate lighting. Another type of distraction is seating arrangement. Sitting behind a desk not only puts up a physical barrier, but can be an interpersonal barrier as well. Attempts should be made to limit environmental distractions so that the client's thoughts are not interrupted and effective communication can take place.

Perceiving Nonverbal Messages. The saying "actions speak louder than words" is especially true in communications. Mehrabian (1972) determined that 93 percent of communication is nonverbal, leaving only 7 percent for actual content of spoken words. A person's expressions, gestures, posture and other actions provide a constant source of information. Therefore, improving your interpretation of body language is a valuable communication skill. Nonverbal messages are usually a means of expressing emotions. We search someone's face to determine feelings of anger, sadness or disgust. Nonverbal messages tend to be more reliable than verbal messages and are essential to understanding many of the most important things others are trying to communicate to us.

The following list of nonverbal cues is not by any means exhaustive.

Feature	Nonverbal Cues
Head	Nodding, cocked to side, thrown back, motioning a direction
Facial expression	Frowning, grimacing, animated, distracted
Eyes	Squinting, wide open, closed, winking, blinking, rolling, teary
Mouth	Smiling, pursed lips, lip licking, lip biting, open, closed
Skin	Blushing, paleness, perspiration, rashes
Body posture	Relaxed, rigid, stooped shoulders, leaning forward, leaning backward, chest extended out
Hands/arms	Fidgeting, tapping, laced fingers, fisted, pointing, touching, crossed arms
Feet/legs	Foot tapping, legs crossed, legs open, knee knocking

Although voice intonation is verbal and explained in more detail later, it is appropriate to mention it as a nonverbal behavior. The sound of the voice communicates beyond the specific words. The words spoken may be fast, slow, high-pitched, loud or whispered. The voice tells much about the mood of the speaker. For example, some people may speak very rapidly or at a high pitch when they are nervous or fearful.

General appearance also is a nonverbal

cue. The way in which a person grooms and dresses is a statement to others.

One aspect of interpreting body language is noting discrepancies between verbal and nonverbal messages. It is easy to note incongruence in a person who says he is not angry while slamming his fist on the table. When you note a difference between words and nonverbal behavior, it may be helpful to search for the meaning of both. Body language can have multitudes of meanings and should be interpreted in context. A single gesture does not stand alone, but should be seen in relationship to other body movements and related to a person's words.

Misunderstandings often occur when listening only to words or observing only body language. Clarify the accuracy of your interpretation with the client.

Perceiving Verbal Messages. To understand verbal messages, you must be able to recognize both the apparent and the underlying content. The apparent or cognitive content is comprised of the actual words and facts of the message. Cognitive messages are more easily recognized because they are stated and usually involve talking about things, people or events and may include one or more themes or topics. The underlying or affective content is comprised of emotions, attitudes and behaviors. Affective messages are communicated both verbally and nonverbally and are more difficult to perceive and interpret. The client may not even be aware of their own feelings and might be surprised when you reveal your perceptions of what they are saying. Generally, emotions can be grouped into four major categories—sadness, anger, fear and happiness—and a feeling from one category may often cover up a feeling from another.

Discriminating between cognitive and affective messages will allow you to respond appropriately to the client. Many cognitive themes may be communicated at once, but hearing the emotional message will help you to establish priorities for cognitive topics. It seems listeners will often respond to the most recent verbal theme instead of the most important one. To illustrate, a client says to a personal trainer in their first meeting, "There is so much going on right now. I have gained 25 pounds since starting school. I'm about to flunk chemistry and if I do, my dad said he would take me out of school. I can't concentrate and I'm not sleeping at night. It seems I just keep gaining weight." In this situation, it is necessary for the personal trainer to listen to the whole message and prioritize the cognitive themes. It may be helpful for this client to learn some stress-reduction techniques from a qualified professional even before being put on a weight control and exercise program.

Verbal Behaviors

Verbal responses are a form of listening and they demonstrate to the client an understanding of what they are saying and feeling. Appropriate responses will encourage the client to continue talking and will allow for more exploration. The following are commonly used verbal responses:

- ✔ Minimal encouragers — brief words or phrases that allow the client to continue speaking. These verbal prods let them know that you are following what is being said. Example of minimal encouragers are "Mmm-hmmm," "I see," "Yes" and "Go on."

- ✔ Paraphrasing — a response that concisely restates the essence of the speaker's content. For example:
  Client: I didn't sleep well and don't feel like working out.
  Personal Trainer: You're tired today.

- ✔ Probing — an attempt to gain more information. Statements such as "I'm wondering about ..." and "Let's talk about that" will help reveal more information.

✔ Reflecting — restating feelings and/or content in a way that demonstrates understanding. You can reflect stated or implied feelings, non-verbal observation, specific content and even what has been omitted. Examples of reflecting are "You're feeling uncomfortable about starting an exercise program," and "Sounds like you are angry at your husband for insisting that you come today."

✔ Clarifying — an attempt to understand what the client is saying, "I'm confused about ..." and "Could you please explain that again?" are examples of clarifying statements.

✔ Informing — sharing factual information, as when you explain the pros and cons of a liquid diet.

✔ Confronting — providing the client with mild or strong feedback about what is really going on. Confrontations are more easily heard when communicated with "I" messages such as "I feel you really don't want to be here today." Another example of confronting is "It seems to me you say ... and yet you do ... "

✔ Questioning — asking for a response. Questions may be closed or open. Closed questions direct the client to give a short response such as "yes" or "no." Open questions provide space for them to explore their own thoughts without being hemmed in. "What's on your mind today?" is an example of an open question.

✔ Summarizing — recapping what has been communicated and highlighting major themes. Effective summarizing can tie loose strands of a conversation together at its conclusion. A summary might begin with "Let's recap what we've discussed so far."

As mentioned earlier, the way in which we speak is often more important than what we actually say. An effective communicator is aware of the quality of delivery of their message. The elements of voice in delivery are intensity, pitch and pace. The intensity, or force, is an important factor in delivery. Some trainers speak so softly that they cannot be heard, while others speak with such volume that they are annoying. Delivery should be loud enough to be heard, while reserving a range to emphasize important points. Working in the weight room, you may find an unusual amount of interference from others talking, background music and weights clanging. This situation provides you with a challenge to determine an effective intensity for your voice. Decreasing voice volume in a noisy situation can actually increase the attentiveness of the other person. For example, instead of shouting to a client in a noisy gym, you can experiment with lowering your voice volume to encourage them to listen more intently. This technique also will reduce vocal stress.

Pitch is the general level of the voice on the musical scale. Everyone has a characteristic pitch. Some speak in a singsong fashion while others speak in a monotone. Some people may end their sentences with an upward inflection while others end with a downward inflection. A noticeable rise in pitch level may decrease effective delivery because it usually denotes incompleteness of thought or indecisiveness. Experienced trainers cultivate a wide range of pitch, which they use effectively during delivery.

Rate means the speed of the utterance, or the number of words spoken per minute. Most people speak at the rate of 115 to 150 words per minute. Variations in rate depend upon such factors as the importance of the material, the desire for emphasis and the mood of the content. Speaking too quickly reduces clarity and can be confusing for those listening. Even though speaking at a slower rate allows others time to absorb what is being said, speaking too slowly may bore the listener. Pausing gives people time to think about what is being said and can accentuate important information.

The rapport stage, which begins at first contact, is critical to establishing a good working relationship between the trainer and client. Sometimes a level of comfort may be quickly established, while at other times more time and energy may have to be expended to win a client's trust. Interpersonal communication skills can be learned and mastered. Merely reading about these skills does not necessarily improve application to everyday situations; they must be continuously practiced. Even though the rapport stage is presented as the first stage, there is really no end to it. The primary qualities (empathy, warmth and genuineness) and the interpersonal communication skills are important and valuable throughout the entire trainer/client relationship.

INVESTIGATION STAGE

The goal of the investigation stage is to gather information about your client's present fitness level, personal goals and physical and psychological limitations. This may begin in the initial interview, when the client is encouraged to talk about desires and expectations for training. The health history and lifestyle questionnaires discussed in Chapter 5 will yield a wealth of information. Additional data can be gathered from fitness assessments (Chapter 6). Historically, health history and lifestyle questionnaire forms are filled out by the individual client. However, you are encouraged to ask these questions orally. This method requires more time, but it can be valuable in establishing rapport. In addition, clients will probably reveal more about themselves when they observe your interest. The least interaction that should occur is that you and your client discuss their written responses to the questionnaire. During the discussion you can probe, question and clarify in order to gain more information. After all the information is gathered, you and your client can begin planning by setting goals and making decisions about how to achieve them.

PLANNING STAGE

Up to this point, most of your time with your client has been spent building rapport and gathering appropriate information regarding their lifestyle behaviors and current fitness levels. In the planning stage, the trainer and client begin setting goals according to the client's needs and desires. Because there are usually several ways to reach any goal, you must make use of decision-making skills to determine the best course of action. The outcome will be more effective if the process is done together than if you dictate to the client what to do each step of the way.

Decision-making occurs frequently as we go about our daily activities; we must constantly decide how we'll spend our time, money and energy during any given day. Many of these decisions are second nature for us, so we do not consider the process we go through in determining what is best in a particular situation. Even though there are many decision-making models, the basic process for the personal trainer/client relationship consists of the following steps:

1. Setting goals
2. Generating alternatives
3. Exploring the alternatives
4. Making the decision
5. Formulating a plan
6. Evaluating the implementation

Setting Goals. Clients will seldom approach you with neatly stated goals. They are usually expressed in vague statements, such as "I want to be in better shape" or "I want to lose some weight." It is your

Planning Stage

responsibility to translate these general aims into precise goals.

Effective goals must be SMART, which means they are:

Specific — The goals must specifically tell what is to be accomplished. They must be easily understood and unambiguous.

Measurable — The goals must be measurable so there is no question of attainment. Examples of measurement would be percent body fat, number of pounds or a specific fun run.

Attainable — The goals must be attainable, not too difficult or too easy. Easy goals don't motivate and overly difficult ones may frustrate.

Relevant — The goals must be relevant or pertinent to the particular interest, needs and abilities of your client.

Time-bound — The goals must be time-bound with specific deadlines for completion.

It is difficult to know when a client has obtained a goal that is expressed in terms such as "I want to get in better shape." However, both parties would know when the goal is attained if it is stated as, "I want to be able to walk three miles in 45 minutes by March 31st," or "I'd like to drop 20 pounds by the end of the year." According to Dick and Carey (1990), one method of clarifying a broad goal is to follow these steps:

1. Write the goal down.

2. Write down things the client can do to demonstrate they have achieved the goal (i.e., lose 20 pounds, drop to 12 percent body fat, fit into a size 10 dress they haven't worn in three years).

3. Sort through the statements and pick out the ones that best represent the original goal.

4. Rewrite the original goal to include your new statements or make smaller goals.

Express the goals in terms of client actions rather than trainer actions. A goal stated as "the trainer will get me in shape" does not give the client ownership of or responsibility for the goal. The goals must also be attainable. It would not be attainable for a non-runner client to say, "I want to run a 10K next week." Attainable goals will help ensure the client's success. Finally, setting both short- and long-range goals will be helpful. For example, a female client who is 30 percent body fat may have a long-range goal of obtaining 20 percent body fat in six months. The short-range goal might be to reach 27 percent in the next four weeks. Setting a time line, or date of completion, often creates a sense of urgency for both the client and the trainer and can be effective in overcoming client procrastination. You also can help the beginner client create behavioral goals that will remove intimidating evaluation procedures like body-fat tests, tape measures and weight scales. An example behavioral goal can be stated as "I want to exercise three times per week, for 30 minutes of aerobic training, 20 minutes of strength training and 10 minutes of stretching, for 12 consecutive weeks starting January 1st." In this example, the trainer and client are establishing positive lifestyle changes rather than strictly emphasizing physiological changes.

Generating Alternatives. This step in the decision-making process involves proposing all possible alternatives for reaching the goal. This brainstorming process gives the client more choices. For example, a client might define their goal as "I want to get my thighs stronger for the upcoming ski season." In exploring alternatives to reach this goal, you and your client might generate the following:

a. I could increase my thigh strength by riding the stationary cycle.

b. I could increase my thigh strength by performing squats with free weights.

c. I could increase my thigh strength by climbing stairs.

d. I could increase my thigh strength by

Table 14.1
Learning Pathways

	Visual	Auditory	Kinesthetic
Client actions	Watches intently Prefers reading	Listens carefully Prefers hearing	Touches or holds Prefers to be spotted
Client statement	"Oh, I see" "Let me see that again."	"Yeah, I hear you" "Say that one more time."	"I feel that" "This does not feel right."
Strategy	Demonstrations	Question and answer	Hands on supervision

stepping up and down on a bench.

The client now has several viable options for obtaining their goal.

Exploring Alternatives. After brainstorming the list of options, the next step is to weigh or rank them. Evaluate the alternatives for implementation realities and hypothesized consequences. Some options may immediately be thrown out because they are impractical, making it easier for the client to prioritize the remaining alternatives. From the previous example, a client may discard option b because of its impracticality. With your help, they may then rank the rest of the alternatives according to interest, availability and time.

Making the Decision. You and the client now decide on one or more of the alternatives. Choose the most effective strategy or a combination of the options for this person at this time. For example, our skier may choose to train for skiing by doing squats with free-weights at the gym at least two days a week. In addition, they can climb stairs at home when they do not have time to get to the gym.

Formulating a Plan. At this point you and the client determine a specific sequence of action that likely will result in the accomplishment of the goals. Formulating an action plan includes who needs to do what, when, where, what materials are required and so forth. This step is further developed as exercise programming, which is covered in Chapter 11.

Evaluating the Implementation. This step measures accomplishment in relation to the predetermined goals and may occur in a formal setting where the client's fitness level is reassessed. The appropriate fitness assessments are described in Chapter 6. The evaluation process may also occur informally during the training sessions as both client and trainer report progress. Either way, together you determine the accomplishment and, if necessary, a new set of action steps.

ACTION STAGE

Once rapport has been established, information has been gathered and goals have been set, the action stage, or actual training, begins. You coach the client toward their goals. As a teacher or tutor, you may use many methods of education. In a broad sense, personal training is similar to an individual approach to direct instruction, which is essentially active learning. It consists of the trainer's explaining a new concept or skill to the client. Afterwards, the client demonstrates understanding by practicing under the trainer's direction, while the trainer encourages them to continue to practice until the skills become natural. The climate of direct instruction is task-oriented and is high in expectations. The client will be more motivated to learn in areas they find interesting and may actively resist learning in areas they don't. You can increase motivation by teaching information that meets the needs and desires of the client. Once an area of interest is discovered, you can use a variety of teaching techniques to help the client feel successful with learning. According to Wlodkowski (1984), an initial small success can lead to greater confidence in the learning process, improved self-esteem and increased motivation to learn new things. Your selection of techniques will depend upon your style and that of the client. What works well for one client may not work for another. Having a variety of teaching techniques is essential to the success of the trainer/ client relationship.

Action Stage

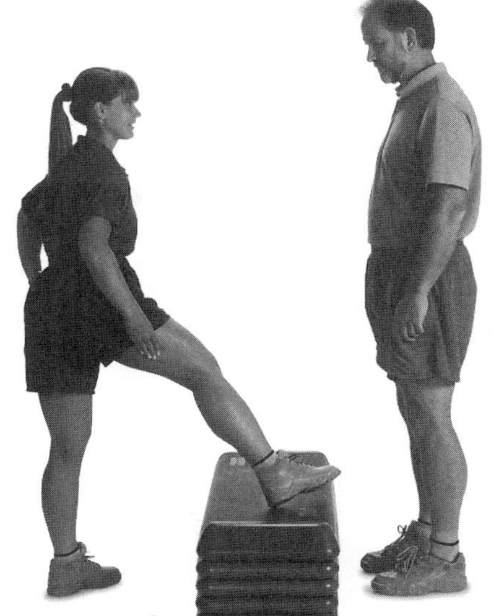

a.

b.

c.

FIGURE 14.3
"Tell, Show, Do."
a. Trainer explaining hamstring stretch.

b. Trainer demonstrating hamstring stretch.

c. Trainer watching client perform hamstring stretch.

Multisensory Input

Clients gather information through their senses (visual, auditory, kinesthetic, smell, taste) and this creates a pathway for information to be received and processed by them. Pathways often overlap with clients showing a "preference" for gathering information in one pathway over others. Approximately 60 percent of the population prefer a primary visual pathway, while 20 percent access information auditorily and another 20 percent prefer to kinesthetically receive data. Even though a client may enjoy charts and pictures because they prefer to gather information visually, the client is still able to gather information verbally although it is not their dominant pathway.

You can identify which pathway the client prefers to gather information through by observing their actions during learning situations and by listening for clues in their language (Table 14.1). For example, a trainer is discussing basic anatomy with a client using an anatomy chart on the wall. The visual learner may focus directly on the chart, and may walk right up to it while the trainer is talking. The auditory learner may ignore the chart and focus directly on the trainer's words. The kinesthetic learner may touch the chart, or touch and move

Action Stage

their corresponding muscles as the trainer describes them.

If you can identify the learning pathway that the client prefers, you can match your words and behaviors to their preference (Table 14.1). This not only enhances learning, but it also allows you to maintain rapport with your client.

"Tell, Show, Do"

I hear and I forget
I see and I remember
I do and I understand
-Anonymous

This proverb is at the heart of day-to-day personal training. As early as the 1930s, John Dewey advocated "learning by doing." Probably the most effective systematic method of teaching a skill is by explanation, demonstration and execution, also known as "tell, show, do." It involves observing how something is done correctly and then performing it under the supervision of an instructor (Figure 14.3). The instructor provides the student with an auditory, visual and kinesthetic learning experience, thus stimulating all learning pathways.

Explanation. The explanation should be a concise verbal description of the skill that gives a clear understanding of what is to be accomplished. A simple skill may only require one sentence while a more complex skill may require more detail. During this time, the client should be told what to watch for during the demonstration. For example, the trainer might say, "I'm now going to show you how to perform a biceps curl. Watch how I control the movement and do not use momentum to help lift the weight."

Demonstration. The demonstration is the visual presentation of the skill. It is critical that it be an accurate representation of the desired action. Therefore, you must be keenly aware kinesthetically so that proper form is communicated to the client. If you have just explained that there should be no use of momentum or swinging during the biceps curl, then you must perform the curl with complete control without using momentum for the lift.

Demonstrating the movement slowly will help the client see what is happening. Repeating the demonstration at normal speed while reiterating the main points also will aid learning. The explanation and demonstration steps can be effectively combined in order to save time.

Performance. The performance is the client's opportunity to practice the skill. You should carefully monitor and supervise the client's performance to correct errors and encourage proper form. Constructive feedback and more practice time complete the learning loop. The problem in many teaching programs is that all the above steps are not followed. Often the explanation or "tell" step is not followed by the "show" and "do" steps. Telling a person exactly how to perform a skill does not ensure that they will be able to do it correctly. Simply telling a client to "stretch the hamstrings after you jog" does not ensure that they will perform the stretch effectively. To complete the process, the client should be shown how to perform a hamstring stretch properly, and then given an opportunity to practice it while you coach proper form and execution.

You must decide if a skill should be taught as a whole or if it should be broken into parts. These methods of teaching are often referred to as the whole approach and the parts approach, respectively. Less complex skills are usually taught as a whole to establish a general idea and feel for the movement. Practicing the biceps curl from start to finish is an appropriate application of the whole approach. More complex exercises that require much attention may be demonstrated by you as a whole movement, and then broken down into lower-torso and upper-torso movements so that the student may master each part of the skill. Breaking down race walking into individual parts makes it easier to perform the activity in its entirety.

Association. You can also help the client learn by creating links or bridges between old and new information. By discovering what the client already knows, beginning in the rapport stage, you can build on their pre-existing knowledge. Each client will have their own unique experiences to draw from. For example, when working with a client who skis, you can redirect their feet during a standing calf stretch by telling them to "point both skis downhill." By using an association, you allow the client to place meaning to the instruction, and, ultimately, they learn more deeply and are more likely to make a lasting improvement on performance.

Modeling

Humans want to identify with other humans. We look at others and imitate traits we would like to have. The concept of emulating another's behavior or attitudes is called modeling and the individual demonstrating the behavior is known as the model. We see many examples of modeling in our daily lives. Children adopt parent's language patterns and nonverbal cues, and they can learn aggressive behavior from watching television. Prestigious models have a profound impact on clothing and dress, hair styles, music and food. Consider the widespread use of leg warmers in exercise classes after Jane Fonda's "Workout" videotape came on the market. According to Bandura (1977), modeling is probably the most efficient and effective form of learning a new behavior. This places both enormous opportunity and responsibility on the teacher.

Two forms of modeling are identified by Good and Brophy (1987). The first is simply imitation or "monkey see, monkey do." The observer adopts the behavior of the model, as in the leg warmer example. The second is more complex because the observer must infer attitudes, values, beliefs or personality characteristics as a result of watching the model. The observer draws their own conclusions and, over time, may change their behavior. This is a common occurrence in the trainer/client relationship. As a result of observing your dedication to a healthy and fit lifestyle, the client may choose a healthier alternative to their regular Friday afternoon happy hour. In this form of modeling, people often communicate attitudes unconsciously and are unaware of the effects. Students constantly observe a teacher's approach to a subject, studying the teacher's attitudes and beliefs. They watch the way the teacher interacts with students and other colleagues, and the student may then make inferences regarding the learning process. The way in which a teacher responds to a student's question can affect the learning climate. The response, "I don't know ... let's find out," models enthusiasm for learning and makes not knowing the answer acceptable. This form of modeling is both subtle and powerful.

There are several factors that influence modeling. The first is the state of the learner. The more uncertain a learner is, the more significant the effects of the model will be. Therefore, a client is more susceptible to the effects of your modeling at the beginning of the relationship. A second factor that influences modeling is the status of the model in the eyes of the learner. Students are more likely to adopt the behaviors of a teacher they like and respect than of one they do not.

You cannot escape being a model. However, you can decide what kind of model you will be. Who a personal trainer is and what they do sends loud and clear messages to the client about what is important and how the program is really supposed to work. In other words, the way you behave is just as important as what you say. The trainer who advocates doing what they are unwilling to do will more than likely be

Action Stage

unconvincing. For example, it is fruitless for a trainer to tell clients that steroids are bad for their health when it is known that the trainer uses steroids. "Do as I say, not as I do" has no place in the trainer/client relationship. The client views you as an expert and will generally believe everything that you say and do with regard to fitness. Therefore, it is critical that you be aware of your influence. Be competent and wise in fitness matters and obtain at least a level of fitness that corresponds to the level of teaching. Going beyond mere competence is even more desirable.

Contracting

Contracting finds its roots in the behavioral theory of reinforcement that says rewarded behavior tends to be repeated. Contracting systematically arranges the rewards so that the probability of the desired response is increased. Most behavioral **contracts** are verbal or written agreements between two or more people and consist of two primary parts (Figure 14.4). The first part is specifying the behavior to be achieved. The second part is stating specific reinforcements that will reward the desired behavior. It may take the form of, "If you will do _________, I will do ________." A contract does not necessarily require involving other people. It is possible for a person to make an agreement with himself by preparing a self-contract (Figure 14.5).

All helping relationships have implied contracts or understandings that both people will have responsibilities to carry out. Verbal or informal contracts are used when there is little chance of a misunderstanding of the conditions. The written contract is used to prevent those misunderstandings and to add impact by having the client sign their name to indicate a commitment.

Several features are necessary for an effective contract. The terms should be explicitly stated so that the expectations are clearly understood by all parties. An example of an unclear contract statement is "I agree to lose some weight so I may do something I enjoy." A more clearly stated contract term might be "I will lose 5 pounds and then I'll be permitted to buy that new dress." Many contracts fail because of impossible terms, so they should be feasible and reasonable. "I will lose 50 pounds this month so I can buy that new dress," is an unreasonable goal. "I will lose 1 to 2 pounds a week for the next two months," is a more reasonable goal. Composing the contract in positive rather than negative terms will encourage a more favorable attitude toward the contract. "If you do not quit smoking, I will not work with you," is a negative approach. A more positive approach would be to determine a reward given upon smoking cessation.

To ensure satisfactory results, contracts need to be evaluated frequently and perhaps renegotiated. This renegotiation can occur any time or during the formal evaluation process. What appeared to be fair and reasonable initially may not be so later. If a client discovers they cannot meet a specified commitment you should discuss the difficulty, and a new contract can be negotiated, drafted and signed. This evaluation process will help ensure that the contract remains effective.

The following questions will help you trouble-shoot while writing contracts:

1. Are the terms of the contract clear?
2. Is the contract fair?
3. Is the contract positive?
4. Is the target behavior clearly specified?
5. Does the contract provide for immediate reinforcement?
6. Is the reinforcement frequent and in small amounts?
7. Does the client understand the contract?
8. Is there a time specified for evaluation?

Feedback

Feedback is a powerful contributor to

Action Stage

I, the undersigned, agree to the following conditions, which I will follow to the best of my ability.

From __________ to __________, for a period of one week, I will choose to eat at meal time only.

From __________ to __________, for a period of one week, I will eat foods recommended by the American Heart Association and the American Dietetic Association.

At the end of the week, as a reward for fulfilling the above conditions, I will attend a movie or other social function with my husband.

Date __________________

Signature of wife ____

I, the undersigned, agree to take my wife to a movie when the above conditions are met.

Date __________________

Signature of husband ____

FIGURE 14.4 Example of an exercise contract between two people.

I will walk in my target zone a minimum of ______ minutes ______ times per week.
I will record my progress in my personal log.
The following people will help me reach my goal:

____

Person	Method
1. ______________________	1. ______________________
2. ______________________	2. ______________________
3. ______________________	3. ______________________
4. ______________________	4. ______________________

I will reward myself for adhering to the above for ______ weeks with the following:

____

____

____

I will begin the program __(date)__ and will reevaluate it on __(date)__.

FIGURE 14.5 Example of a personal exercise contract.

effective learning and client performance. It is any information about current or past behavior that can be used to improve performance and can be given verbally or nonverbally. It usually occurs after a client has asked a question or done something related to the exercise session. Feedback informs the client of the correctness of their performance and recognizes their effort. You will naturally respond and react to clients' behavior, and they are greatly influenced by the way you behave toward them. They monitor their trainers' reactions and adjust their performance in accordance with what they interpret.

In order for feedback to be effective, a clearly defined standard of performance must be given. For example, a trainer defines the standard of performance for proper placement and movement of the arms in race walking during their explanation and demonstration of the skill. The client's performance is then measured and corrected according to the demonstrated criteria. The performance standard may need to be set at frequent intervals during instruction by continuing to explain and demonstrate. In order for the feedback to be effective and learning to occur, there must be a practice session that gives the client an opportunity to correct their performance and reach the preset standard.

Research indicates that effective feedback has three characteristics: 1) it is specific; 2) it is contingent on performance; and 3) it provides corrective information for the learner. Specific feedback is clear about what was right and/or wrong. You may watch a client incorrectly perform a lat pulldown on the weight equipment and then exclaim, "That's not right, Susie!" Your response does not aid Susie's understanding of the performance, it only lets her know that it was wrong. By contrast, you might respond, "Not quite Susie, let's reverse the position of your hands." Corrective feedback helps the client know what was wrong with the performance and what to do to get back on track. The number of different cues is infinite, and striving for unique ones will require your creativity and committed practice.

Feedback should not be given for every single move because too much of a good thing can have a negative effect; people tend to disregard excessive compliments. The feedback should match the achievement and specifically relate the response to the performance. For example, a personal trainer observing a client performing a biceps curl might respond with "That's good," which is only a statement of general praise. However, an even more effective response would be "That's it John, you're really isolating the biceps muscle now." This response gives the client specific information as to why the performance is correct. To maximize the effect, cues can be personalized by using a client's name, for instance, "That's the right idea, Jennie." Typical verbal cues are:

Good	Excellent
Right	Correct
All right	OK
Very good	Fine

These words are less effective because they have been overused. Examples of other, more effective cues that you might use are:

That's an effective thought.
You've got it.
You're on the money.
You are really with it today.
I'd give that move a 10.

Nonverbal feedback is far more effective than verbal feedback. Clients tune into facial expressions and gestures. When used properly, nonverbal cues are the epitome of personalization. How else can a "thumbs up" signal and a generous smile be interpreted? Nonverbal positive feedback interactions include:

Smiling	Making an "Okay" sign
Nodding	Patting on the back
Shaking hands	Touching
Clapping	Winking
Thumbs up	Applauding

Nonverbal negative feedback interactions include:

Frowning	Thumbs down
Shaking head	Drumming fingers
Looking away	Rolling eyes
Grimacing	

A final and important point needs to be made regarding verbal and nonverbal feedback. As in all interpersonal communication, when both verbal and nonverbal cues are given, they must be congruent. For example, if you frown while telling a client that they are doing a great job, the two behaviors are incongruent and the conflicting messages are confusing. The client will receive a mixed message and will probably believe the frown rather than the words. On the other hand, when verbal and nonverbal cuing are congruently combined, you can have a powerful influence on the client.

SUMMARY

Summary

Your relationships with clients are helping relationships throughout the stages of establishing and building rapport with them, gathering vital information, developing fitness goals and implementing a plan to accomplish them. As a helper, you create conditions and use techniques that will help bring about the desired outcomes for the client. Merely possessing a fit body, technical skills and a wide-based knowledge of health and fitness does not ensure your success. Probably the most crucial factor for determining a positive climate for the working relationship is the trainer's repertoire of communication skills. These skills include both verbal and nonverbal behaviors, such as attending, perceiving nonverbal messages, perceiving verbal messages and verbal responding. These interpersonal communication skills can be learned, practiced and mastered, and are important not only in the first stage of establishing rapport, but throughout the entire process.

Personal training is about behavioral change, which is the true measure of a successful trainer/client relationship. Every personal trainer is unique and brings into the relationship their own personal experience and opinions about what brings about lifestyle changes in people. Each client also is uniquely different. Therefore, you must be flexible in matching teaching techniques and changing strategies to meet the goals, needs and personality of the client. A technique that is successful for one client does not ensure the same achievement or change for another. A skilled personal trainer will get to know the client and apply various techniques with wisdom, while another may resist to the point of discontinuing the relationship.

The flexibility required to do your job sometimes demands that you be deeply personal and at other times remain an objective observer. Being able to move freely along the full range of interpersonal skills and teaching techniques will permit you to respond appropriately at various stages of the relationship. On one hand, the process of sizing up and assisting a client toward a healthy lifestyle is naturally intuitive, but, on the other hand, it needs to be a deliberate, rational process.

REFERENCES

Bandura, A. (1977). *Social Learning Theory.* Englewood Cliffs: Prentice Hall.

Dick, W. & Carey, L. (1990). *The Sytematic Design of Instruction* (3rd ed.). Harper Collins.

Good, F. & Brophy, J. (1987). *Looking in classrooms.* New York: Harper & Row.

Hall, E.T. (1966). *The Hidden Dimensions.* Garden City: Doubleday.

Krumboltz, J. (1966). *Stating the Goals of Counseling* (Monograph No. 1). Fullerton: California Personnel and Guidance Association.

Mehrabian, A. (1972). *Nonverbal Communication.* Chicago: Aldine-Atherton.

Rogers, C.R., Gendlin, E.T., Keisler, D.J. & Truax, C.D. (1967). *The Therapeutic Relationship and Its Impact.* Madison: University of Wisconsin Press.

Truax, C.B. & Carkuff, R.F. (1967). *Toward Effective Counseling and Psychotherapy.* Chicago: Aldine.

Wlodkowski, R. (1984). *Enhancing Adult Motivation to Learn.* San Francisco: Jossey-Bass.

SUGGESTED READING

Bolton, R. (1979). *People Skills.* New York: Simon & Schuster.

Carkhuff, R.R. & Anthony, W.A. (1979). *The Skills of Helping.* Amherst: Human Resource Development Press.

Jacobson, D., Eggen, P.D. & Kauchak, D. (1989). *Methods for Teaching: A Skills Approach.* Columbus: Merrill.

Kauchak, D.P. & Eggen, P.E. (1989). *Learning and Teaching: Research-based Methods.* Needham Heights, MA: Allyn & Bacon.

Knowles, M. (1989). *The Making of an Adult Educator.* San Francisco: Jossey-Bass.

Mitchell, G. (1987). *The Trainer's Handbook.* New York: AMACOM.

Mosston, M. (1966). *Teaching Physical Education: From Command to Discovery.* Columbus: Merrill.

Okun, B.F. (1987). *Effective Helping Interviewing and Counseling Techniques.* Monterey: Brooks/Cole.

Rogers, C. (1961). *On Becoming A Person.* Boston: Houghton Mifflin.

Wheels, A. (1973). *How People Change.* New York: Harper & Row.

PART VI

Injury Prevention and First Aid

CHAPTER 15

Musculoskeletal *Injuries*

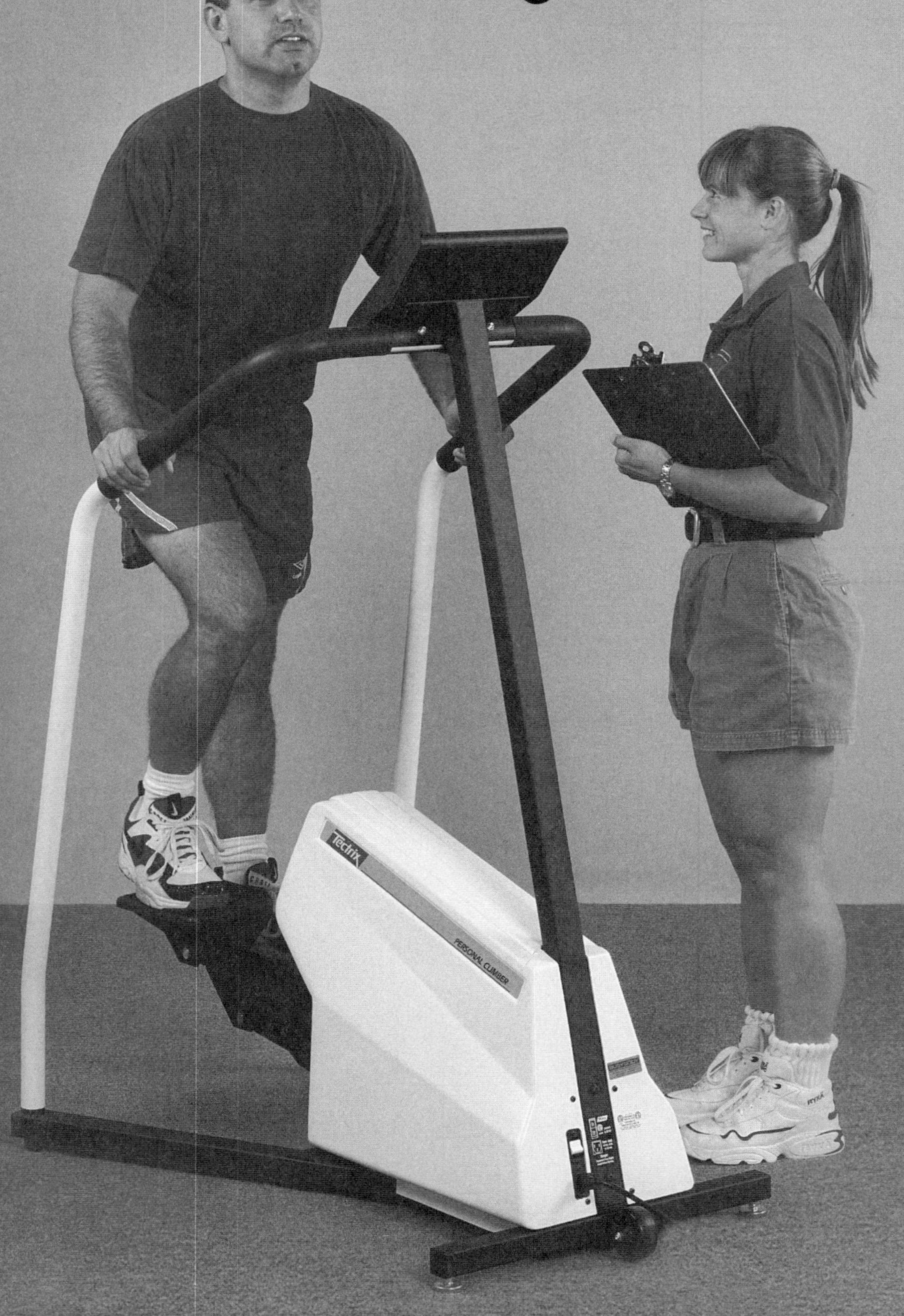

15

IN THIS CHAPTER:

Denise M. Fandel

Denise Fandel is the head athletic trainer at the University of Nebraska, Omaha where she oversees the entire athletic facility, and is an instructor in UNO's School of HPER. She is director of the athletic training program within HPER, and president of the National Athletic Trainer's Association (NATA) Board of Certification. Ms. Fandel has been a contributing author to numerous texts on sports medicine and athletic injuries.

Musculoskeletal injuries are probably the most common injuries that occur in active individuals. They also are one of the most common reasons people stop being active. To help prevent musculoskeletal injuries, you must focus on the following areas when developing a total fitness program for your clients: strength, flexibility, muscular endurance and proprioception. Even when programs are designed properly, injuries can happen. However, a properly conditioned client can rehabilitate an injured area quickly and more completely.

Types of Tissues

TYPES OF TISSUES

Four tissues of the body are of concern when discussing musculoskeletal injuries: muscle, **tendon, ligament** and bone. Each has individual characteristics that, when understood, can help you prevent musculoskeletal injuries.

Muscle Tissue

Muscle tissue is elastic and able to withstand an enormous amount of stress. Muscle tissues act as springs for the body by absorbing a tremendous amount of shock. They also facilitate movement. Preventing injuries to the muscles and the joints is dependent upon a muscle being strong and flexible. Flexibility in any exercise program is important for preventing injuries.

An injury to muscle tissue is called a **strain** or a rupture. Strains are classified as mild, moderate or severe. A severe strain may be called a rupture or complete tear. These injuries heal with scar tissue, known as **collagen** tissue, that is not elastic. The collagen tissue goes to the injury site and is laid down in an unorganized pattern. If left in this unorganized state, the tissue will be very weak. Therefore, it is important that some stretching be initiated, gradually adding weight to the injury to help the collagen tissue organize. Stretching and added weight will cause the tissue to "line up" in the direction of the surrounding muscle fibers. This organization increases the strength of the collagen tissue. However, even in an organized state, this tissue will not be as strong or flexible as the surrounding tissue.

Tendon Tissue

Another part of a muscle group that can be injured is the tendon. Tendons connect muscle to bone. The tendon area of muscle is supplied with less blood than is the belly of the muscle. Because of this anatomical difference, injuries to tendons heal more slowly.

Ligament Tissue

Ligaments are nonelastic tissue designed to connect bone to bone. They are found around joints, and when injured, they do not contract as muscle tissues do to protect the area. Once stretched, the ligaments allow greater joint motion, thereby necessitating increased strengthening of surrounding muscle tissues.

Joint capsules, larger versions of ligaments that surround joints, provide stability. They may be injured in more severe **sprains** and can result in serious dislocations and subluxations.

Bone Tissue

Bone is the only tissue in the body that, when injured, repairs itself with exactly the same type of tissue. Bone can develop cracks from abnormal types and amounts of stress, resulting in stress fractures. Complete breaks in the bone also are called fractures. They result from excessive stresses, and usually involve a large amount of trauma. When a client complains of pinpoint pain over a bone, or of hearing or feeling a "snap," you should consider the possibility of a fracture. It is not true that, "if you can move it, it isn't broken."

TISSUE REACTION TO INJURY — INFLAMMATION AND THE HEALING PROCESS

When tissue is injured or damaged, the body immediately begins the repair process. This creates inflammation, which acts as a protective, as well as a healing, mechanism. Some relate the process to an army fixing a weak spot in a line that has been penetrated by the enemy. The body's main transportation system is the circulatory system. It transports the foot soldiers, the white blood cells, to the area of injury. Here, the white blood cells encircle the injury, containing it and thereby preventing damage to other tissues.

Injuries can often be recognized by the swelling, black and blue color (ecchymosis), pain and decreased range of motion that accompanies them. These are just a few of the signals that the body is defending itself from the injury and is repairing the damage. You must recognize these signs and symptoms, and provide proper referral to a medical professional. In addition, if appropriate, you must provide the proper instruction for participation in exercise that will not make the injury worse.

Signs and Symptoms of Inflammation

The body is a predictable machine when handling injuries. Tissue that is injured relies on the inflammatory reaction for its early defense and to begin the healing process. It is important for you to be able to recognize the following signs and symptoms of inflammation:

Increased temperature — is the result of an increase in blood flow to the injured area due to damaged blood vessels and the need to supply the area with increased numbers of white blood cells. Much as the body develops a generalized fever when ill, an injury to a soft tissue of the body causes a "local fever." This is why heat, hot packs or hot soaks are not used on a new injury. Why turn up the heat under a boiling kettle?

Redness — is due to the increase in blood flow to the area.

Swelling — also is due to the increase in blood flow to the area. Additionally, damage to the cells, small capillaries and lymphatic vessels in the area may allow the leaking of some fluid.

Pain — is often due to pressure on nerve endings from increased swelling.

Loss of function — is caused by swelling in the area and "guarding" of the muscles surrounding the injury. This also produces an increase in pain.

ACUTE TREATMENT OF MUSCULOSKELETAL INJURIES

Acute Treatment of Musculoskeletal Injuries

The acronym RICE is the most common method of describing the **acute** treatment for musculoskeletal injuries. This acronym stands for Rest, Ice, Compression and Elevation, the four steps of the accepted first aid standard for the treatment of these types of injuries.

Though swelling is a key protective mechanism and a part of the healing process, it is still important to reduce swelling. Little can be done to stop initial swelling, but the RICE principle can be applied to reduce secondary swelling, which occurs when injuries are not properly treated. Secondary swelling slows the healing process and decreases one's ability to safely participate in activity.

Remember that it may not always be prudent to actually apply treatment. Check with local governing associations for the most current standards for providing emergency treatment. Of course, the more education you have in first aid and injury management, the more comfortable you will feel if an injury situation develops. Therefore, the guidelines for RICE are included below:

Rest	Avoid continuing the activity that has caused injury or will make the injury worse.
Ice	Ice should be applied for 20 to 30 minutes. There should be some sort of insulating layer between the skin and the ice to prevent frostbite. Never apply ice to an already numb area.
Compression	Elastic bandages can help prevent or reduce excessive swelling. The elastic bandage

should always reach from the largest muscle area below the injury, to the largest muscle group above the injury.

Elevation	The force of gravity can reduce swelling. After applying the first three steps, the injured area should be raised as high as possible while still being comfortable. The injured areas should be raised at least level with, or slightly above, the heart.

Flexibility and Musculoskeletal Injuries

Flexibility is described by some as the key to longevity. A flexible muscle is better able to absorb shock and periodic overstretching than an inflexible muscle. Unfortunately some believe that if a little **flexibility** is good then more must be better. When it comes to injury prevention, however, this is not always the case.

A client's flexibility should be compared to that of the average population. If their measurements fall below what is considered normal for flexibility (hypoflexibile), they should be instructed in a solid, well-designed flexibility program. These clients are more prone to muscle injuries, strains and ruptures. Conversely, if their measurements are above normal (hyperflexibile), their program should place more emphasis on strength development. These clients are at increased risk of joint dislocations and **subluxations**. Guidelines for the development of the flexibility program are discussed in Chapter 10.

EXERCISE TECHNIQUE AND PREEXISTING JOINT INJURIES

Working with clients who have preexisting joint injuries is often a challenge. Postural conditions such as "knock-knee" and "sway back" often make certain activities difficult. Clients who are loose-jointed or have joint injuries may not be able to perform all exercises using traditional methods and body positions. It is critical that you strictly reinforce the importance of proper technique for these clients. Correct exercise technique is essential to a safe, effective and enjoyable exercise experience.

PREEXISTING CONDITIONS AND EXERCISE SELECTION

You may have a client who has had previous injuries, which makes it a bit more difficult to design safe and effective personalized programs. The medical history form each client completes should list any previous injuries, surgeries or conditions that have made exercise difficult in the past. The medical staff working with the client will dictate

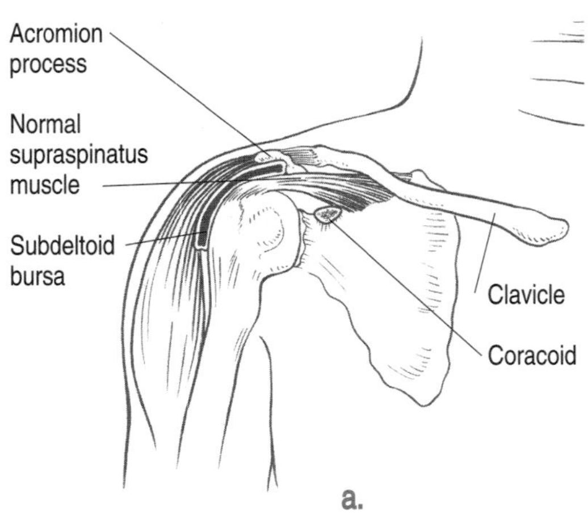

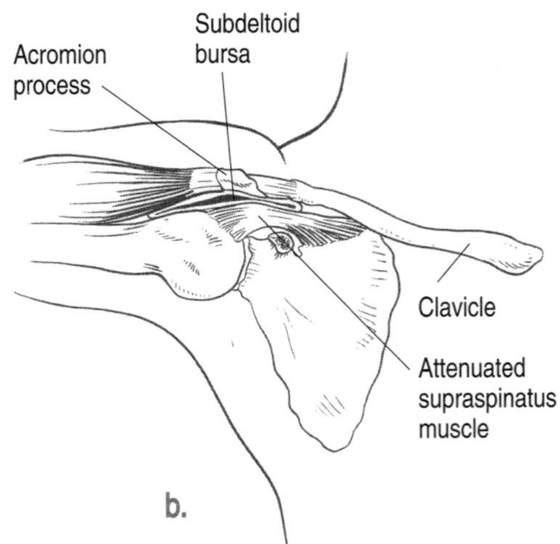

FIGURE 15.1
Impingement of bursa and supraspinatus under the coracoacromial arch with abduction movement:

a. with arm adducted.

b. with arm abducted.

Preexisting Conditions and Exercise Selection

when it is safe to begin exercising again. They may provide additional information or suggestions for the exercise program. With this information and guidance, you can design a safe, effective and personalized program for your clients.

Upper Extremity Conditions

Impingement syndrome makes it difficult to perform exercises that require the arms to be above the head for extended periods of time (Figure 15.1). Exercises such as overhead presses, military presses, lat pulldowns and incline presses may aggravate this condition. It is up to you to substitute non-aggravating exercises for these.

Dislocating shoulders are usually more susceptible to injury when they are in an abducted and externally rotated position, such as the starting position of a lat pulldown or bench press. Most commonly, the front or anterior ligaments of the shoulder have been stretched. When the client places their shoulder in this position, the shoulder is more likely to "slip" forward and recreate the dislocation.

Avoiding these positions is critical. You may want to "block" the full range of motion for these individuals. For example, a client can perform the bench press on a machine where the trainer can place a pin in the weight stack after the handle has been lifted up to a safe position. A second pin can then be used to set the desired weight. This will protect the shoulder from excessive abduction and external rotation.

Lateral epicondylitis and medial epicondylitis are similar conditions (Figure 15.2). They most commonly result from a lack of flexibility and overuse of the flexor and extensor groups of the forearm, especially when beginning a new exercise. "Tennis elbow" is a common name for lateral epicondylitis. The pain is located at the elbow on the radial or thumb side. "Little League Elbow" is the common name for medial epicondylitis and describes the inflammation on the opposite side of the elbow.

Both conditions respond well to conservative treatment by medical professionals. You should understand these conditions and implement appropriate flexibility exercises for these muscle groups. In addition, refrain from any activities that may aggravate the condition.

Carpal tunnel syndrome is most commonly seen as an occupational illness (Figure 15.3). It is usually seen in persons who do repetitive tasks, such as typing or working on a cash register. It also can result from weight training and other athletic activities. Individuals with carpal tunnel syndrome may complain of numbness in the middle fingers of their hands, usually after doing some kind of repetitive work using the wrist and finger flexor muscles. Once again, flexibility plays a key role in preventing and treating the symptoms of carpal tunnel. The flexor group should receive extra flexibility attention to prevent this injury. Physician referral may be necessary if symptoms persist.

Lower Extremity Conditions

Ankle sprains, one of the most common athletic-related injuries, may be prevented through the proper use of proprioceptive training, proper footwear and ankle bracing.

The most common ankle injury is a sprain of the ligaments on the **lateral** or outside of the ankle (Figure 15.4). Sprains to the **medial** or inside of the ankle are relatively rare. Because the lateral aspect of the ankle is more frequently injured, you should focus on strengthening the peroneal muscles to prevent, or make an injury less severe.

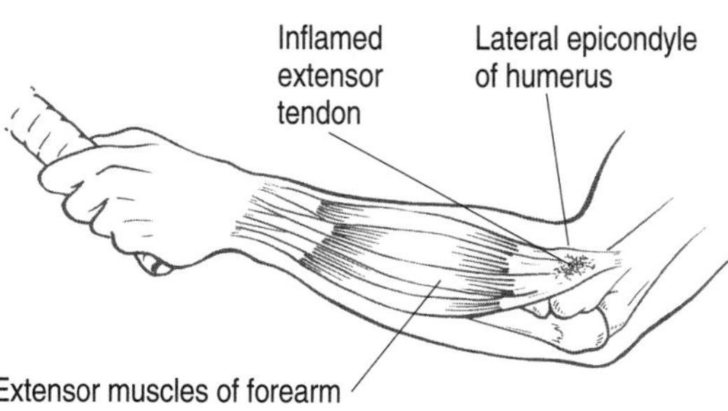

FIGURE 15.2 "Tennis elbow."

Preexisting Conditions and Exercise Selection

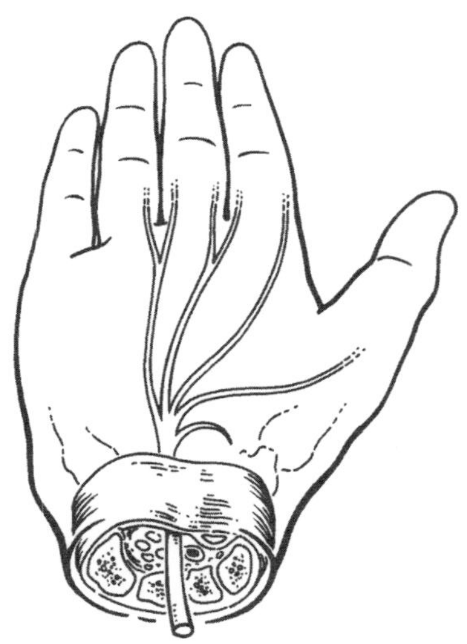

FIGURE 15.3
Carpal tunnel syndrome.

Proprioceptive training can be as simple as rope skipping. Many footwork drills also can increase ankle **proprioception**. If an ankle has been recently sprained, basic proprioceptive training may be as simple as having the client stand on the injured ankle and try to maintain their balance.

Recent research has confirmed that the use of ankle braces will decrease the incidence of ankle sprains without sacrificing speed or agility. However, convincing clients of this may prove difficult if they have had a negative experience with athletic taping.

Knee ligament injuries are often the most feared among active individuals. The knee is an inherently unstable joint and depends heavily on muscular strength for its dynamic support. Muscle strength should be balanced, so the hamstrings have 60 percent to 70 percent of the strength of the quadriceps.

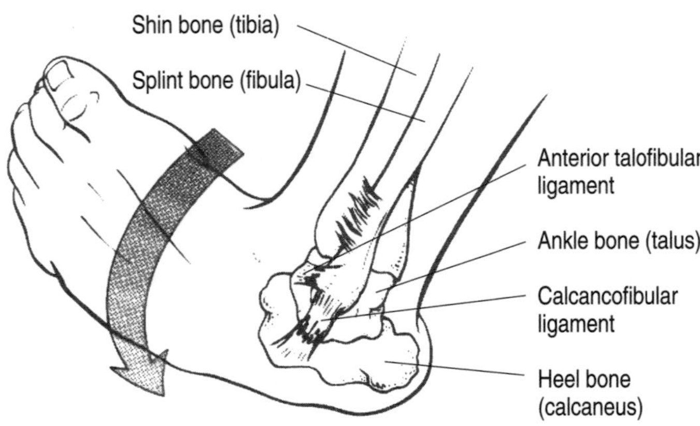

FIGURE 15.4
Lateral ankle sprain.

The medial collateral ligament (MCL) is located on the inside or medial aspect of the knee (Figure 15.5). The medial side is the major weight-bearing side of the knee. A sprain of the MCL can lead to varying degrees of disability, so you must take care not to stress it when prescribing activities such as squats, lunges, slide board and lower-extremity flexibility exercises.

Anterior cruciate ligament (ACL) injuries are the most dreaded of the knee injuries (Figure 15.5). The importance of a healthy ACL in an active individual has been demonstrated by the large number of athletes who have been able to rehabilitate an injury to it completely and return to pre-injury form. You must have solid communication with the client's orthopedic surgeon and physical therapist to determine the limitations of activity for the client. No two surgeries are exactly alike. Also, no two surgeons or therapists will use the same rehabilitation protocol. You will most likely be supervising upper-body strengthening and cardiovascular training early in the rehabilitation process, and lower-extremity and functional activities as the process moves into the later months.

The knee cap joint, also called the patellofemoral joint, is a common site of pain (Figure 15.6), which has been referred to by different terms, such as runner's knee, jumper's knee, etc. It is generally caused by two things: decreased hamstring and calf flexibility, or improper tracking of the patella (kneecap) in the femoral groove. You can work with the client on hamstring and calf flexibility exercises to reduce the stress on the quadriceps. If there is a tracking problem, this will be diagnosed by a medical professional. Physical therapists or athletic trainers will work with the client on the specifics of this problem. Generally, there will be a substitution for knee extension exercises.

Eccentric strength training should be

stressed for clients who seem predisposed to injuries in this area. The patellofemoral joint is under constant **eccentric** stress during **ballistic** activities such as running and jumping. This stress is similar to that placed on a car's brakes. The quadriceps muscles are constantly absorbing shock and decelerating the leg. If the muscles are not trained eccentrically, they will fatigue earlier. This fatigue can lead to changes in the client's movements and sometimes a substitution of other muscles to absorb the shock to the lower extremity. Unfortunately, it is not a common practice in most conditioning programs to do eccentric training of the quadriceps group. A complete conditioning program should emphasize some of this type of training.

Shin splint syndrome is a term often used to describe any pain in the lower leg (Figure 15.7). Shin splint syndrome may be the result of decreased flexibility of the Achilles tendon and posterior muscles of the calf, decreased strength of the anterior muscles of the lower leg, fallen arches or flat feet. Once again, the lower leg is the initial shock absorber during activities. If the shock-absorbing system begins to fail, the client may begin to experience pain. Shin splint syndrome pain will decrease when the aggravating activity is stopped. It is important that the client be referred to a medical professional to rule out the possibility of a stress fracture. The medical professional will often prescribe flexibility and strengthening exercises for the lower leg and/or shoe orthotics for corrective support.

Stress fractures are commonly seen in the lower extremities (Figure 15.8). The most common sites are the lower one-third of the medial tibia and the third, fourth and fifth metatarsals of the foot.

Stress fractures are the result of excessive stress on the bone that causes the outer lining of the bone, the periosteum, to crack. The periosteum is one of the most sensitive structures in the body, and cracking is the initial cause of pain. Small cracks will initially produce pain only with activity, but as the stress fracture progresses, the pain will occur outside the activity.

Some biomechanical and postural considerations can contribute to the healing of stress fractures. Clients with "knock knee" or flat foot have decreased shock absorption ability. These conditions must be evaluated by a medical professional.

The spine is another common site of injury. The lower back is often injured due to excessive stress, such as using improper techniques when lifting objects. Poor posture also can contribute to low back pain.

You may have a client who has a predisposing condition such as **scoliosis** (Figure 15.9). This is an abnormal lateral curva-

Preexisting Conditions and Exercise Selection

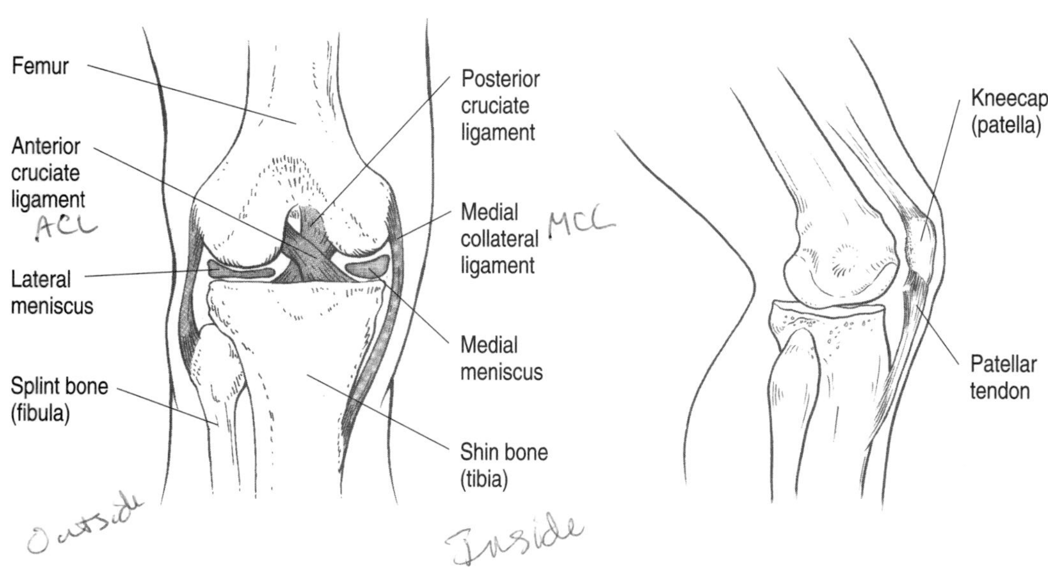

FIGURE 15.5 Knee joint anatomy depicting the anterior cruciate ligament (ACL) and medial and lateral menisci.

FIGURE 15.6 Injuries of the patella. The roughened area on the undersurface marks the region of chondromalacia and patellofemoral pain syndrome. The frayed area is the region of patellar tendinitis.

ture of the thoracic spine that places abnormal stress on the muscles of the upper back. The muscles on the side, away from the curvature, are stretched while the muscles on the opposite side are pinched. You may have to work with the client to balance strength and flexibility. If the client has problems with their upper spine, they should be evaluated by a medical professional before significantly modifying their strength program.

Another spine condition that you may see, especially in older clients, is **kyphosis** (see Chapter 3). This is often called a "hunchback" or a dowager's hump. It is an excessive posterior curvature of the upper thoracic spine. This condition places increased stress on the upper trapezius, cervical spine and rhomboids. You should work in close communication with the client's physicians to determine the best exercises for their condition.

The final, and probably most common, spinal condition is excessive **lordosis**. This is an abnormal or excessive curvature of the lower back, sometimes called "swayback." Weak abdominal muscles and poor posture contribute to pain in this area, so emphasizing abdominal strengthening and hamstring flexibility is important.

If a client complains of low back pain, encourage them to be evaluated by a physician. A condition that can mimic some of the common muscular pain patterns of the lower back is **spondylolysis**. This is a stress fracture of the vertebrae of the spine. Those who do heavy lifting as a part of their jobs, and athletes and active people who perform squats or Olympic-style lifts can also develop a spondylolysis. Strengthening for these clients may demand a creative approach to protect the lower back during exercise.

ENVIRONMENTAL IMPACT ON INJURIES

One of the caveats of human physiology is that the body is constantly in search of balance or **homeostasis**. Environmental conditions can wreak havoc on the body. Clients should be encouraged to maintain a proper water or hydration level to prevent adverse reactions to the environment.

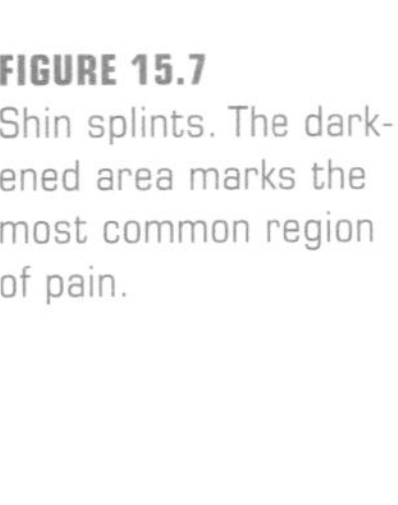

FIGURE 15.7
Shin splints. The darkened area marks the most common region of pain.

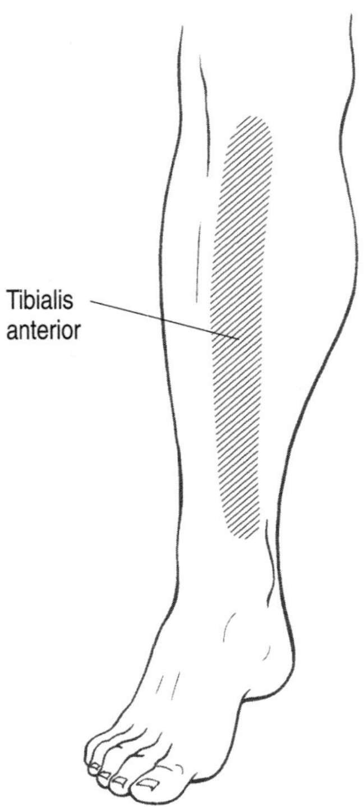

FIGURE 15.8
Types of stress fractures.

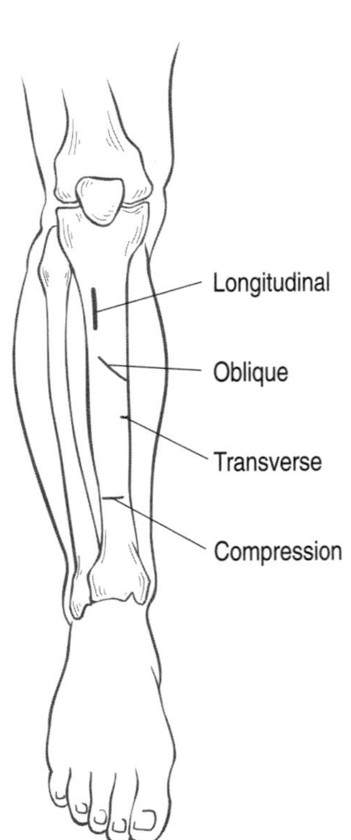

Record Keeping for the Personal Trainer

To ensure that there is an adequate amount of water in the body, an active individual should consume a minimum of eight to 10 eight-ounce glasses of water each day. If this is done, the color of the urine in an active person who is not taking any supplements will be clear. Supplements and some medicines will make the urine appear a dark yellow to orange, no matter how much water is consumed.

When an active individual loses too much water, one of three conditions related to heat illness or **hyperthermia** are likely to occur: heat cramps, heat exhaustion or heat stroke. Heat stroke is the most serious of the three and is considered a true medical emergency.

Recognizing the signs and symptoms of heat illness is important. **Heat cramps** are usually seen in the dominant, active muscles such as the gastrocnemius and abdominals. A person who is suffering from **heat exhaustion** may look pale, have cool, clammy skin and a rapid, weak pulse. They may sweat profusely yet exhibit a normal body temperature for an active individual. The person suffering from **heat stroke** will most likely have hot, red and dry skin. Their core body temperature will be elevated, sometimes as high as 105° Fahrenheit. They are usually not sweating because the body is trying to conserve body fluids.

Immediate care for the victim of a heat-related condition is simple. Stop exercising, remove the client from the hot environmental conditions and, if conscious, give fluids. For the client with heat cramps, stretching can be helpful.

If a client is exercising in a cold environment, be mindful of the possibility of hypothermia (low core body temperature) and/or frostbite. Attention to proper clothing can prevent many cold-related injuries. Layering clothes and using hats, mittens, ear protection and nose covering will prevent the majority of injuries related to cold.

A person who is the victim of a cold injury or **hypothermia** will display many of the signs of a person who is diabetic or one who is intoxicated. First aid for those suffering from cold injuries is to remove them from the cold environment, warm them as quickly and gently as possible and, if conscious, give warm fluids. Those with frostbite should not rub or massage the frozen tissue. This will only cause more significant tissue damage.

RECORD KEEPING FOR THE PERSONAL TRAINER

Prevention of injuries comes from expecting the unexpected. If you have some knowledge of the medical history of a client you will be, at

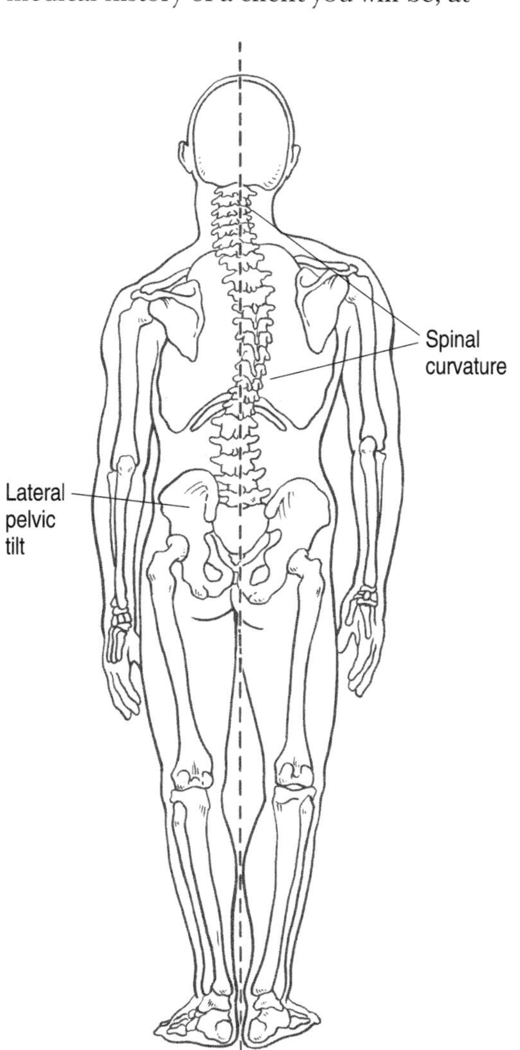

FIGURE 15.9 Scoliosis.

Summary

the minimum, more prepared. The use of medical history forms and emergency information forms is essential in case of an emergency or injury. For any conditions noted on the medical history form, ask the client for additional information. When possible, note any musculoskeletal injuries and ask for information from the client's medical professionals.

These documents are, of course, confidential, and should be kept in a secure location and never released without the permission of the client.

It also is pertinent that you keep detailed records of your conversations with, and observations of, those clients who have known injuries or illness while under your supervision. These notes should be completed daily and include the client's level of activity and progress toward recovery. Keep these records in a secure location.

SUMMARY

You will most likely deal with clients who have sustained, or will sustain, musculoskeletal injuries in the course of their activities, supervised or unsupervised.

Avoid those exercises that aggravate pre-existing conditions. An understanding of how the body reacts to injury and the resulting repair will help you plan an appropriate program. Recognizing the signs and symptoms of inflammation and knowing the proper steps in acute injury care can help the injured client recover more quickly.

It also is important for you to know the common injuries associated with activity. The ability to design a program for a client that will avoid injury is critical to the success of the program.

Receive as much training as is available in first aid and injury recognition. This will increase your confidence in dealing with your clients in these types of situations.

REFERENCES AND SUGGESTED READING

Arnheim, D. & Prentice, W. (1990). *Principles of Athletic Training.* (8th ed.) St. Louis: Mosby.

Booher, J. & Thibodeau, G. (1991). *Athletic Injury Assessment.* (3rd ed.) St. Louis: Mosby.

Galaspy, J. & May, J. (1996). *Signs and Symptoms of Athletic Injuries.* St. Louis: Mosby.

Starkey, C. & Ryan, J. (1995). *Orthopedic Athletic Injury Evaluation.* Philadelphia: F. A. Davis.

Taber's Cyclopedic Medical Dictionary. (1989). (16th ed.) Philadelphia: F. A. Davis.

CHAPTER 16

Emergency Procedures

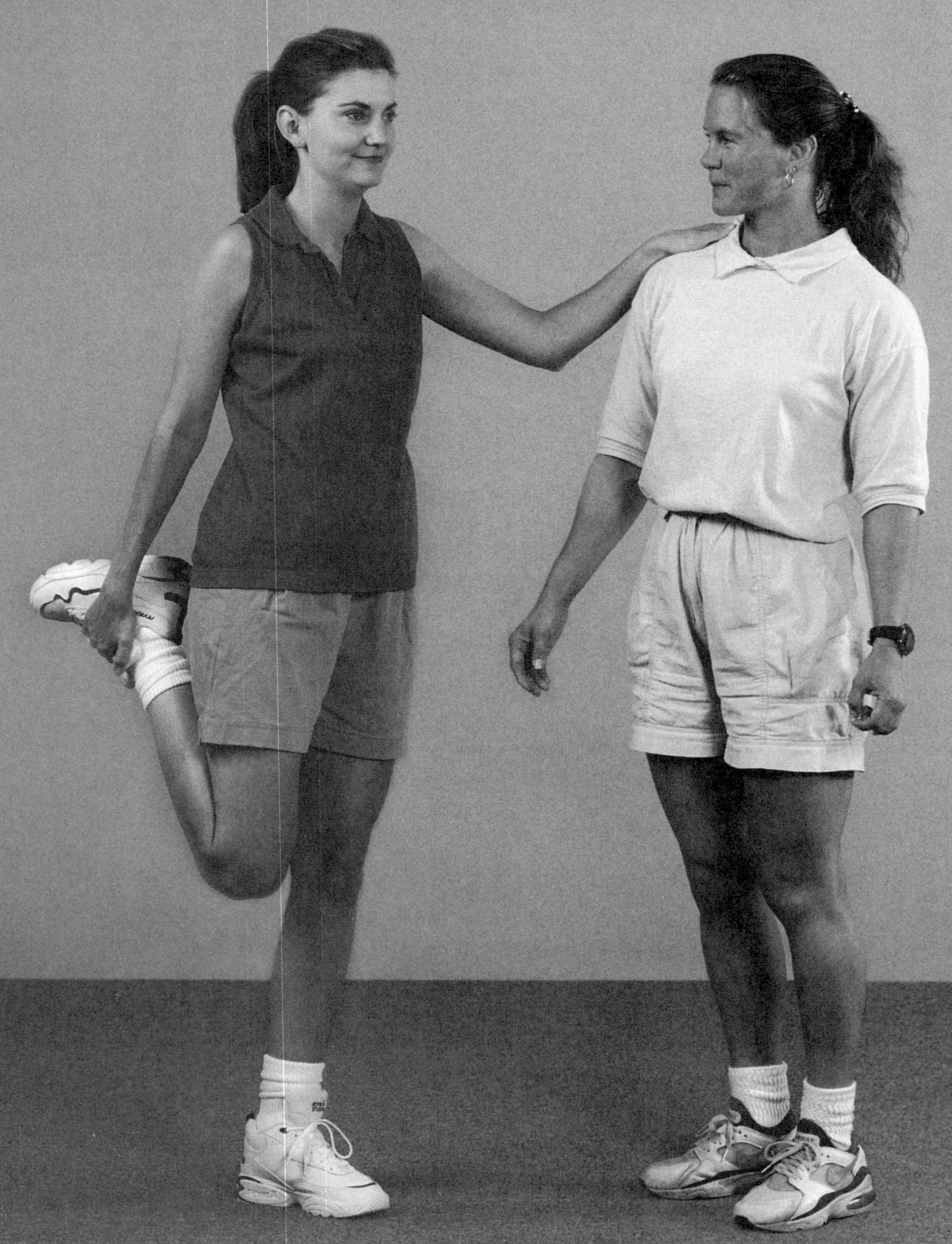

16

IN THIS CHAPTER:

Kathleen M. Hargarten

Kathleen Hargarten, M.D., F.A.C.E.P., is a clinical assistant professor at the Medical College of Wisconsin and medical director for several Emergency Medical Services Systems in Wisconsin. She is board certified in emergency medicine and is a fellow of the American College of Emergency Physicians. She currently serves on the American Council on Exercise's aerobic instructor examination committee and is a former member of the personal trainer examination committee.

As a personal trainer, you encourage your clients to realize a healthier lifestyle through exercise and improved nutrition, minimizing the risk of injury. However, no matter how knowledgeable you are or how well-designed your program, a medical crisis or acute injury may occur. Although most people who actively engage in regular physical activity are healthy adults with no serious medical problems, some may have an underlying disease that has not yet manifested itself. Appropriate health screening and fitness testing, before an exercise program begins, will help identify these persons. You can then simply refer them to their physicians for medical clearance, thereby forestalling emergency conditions. But what if the unforeseen happens? Knowing what to do during those first critical

Emergency Equipment and Emergency Medical Services

moments, or how to access the emergency medical system, can make the difference between life and death, between temporary and permanent disability, between rapid recovery and a long hospital stay.

This chapter will familiarize you with several procedures for preventing and coping with emergencies. Although the following information is a good overview of first-aid procedures, it is not comprehensive nor is it a substitute for formal training in first aid. As a personal trainer, you should take the American Red Cross Standard First Aid and Personal Safety Course. You also are required to take a course and become certified in airway management and cardiopulmonary resuscitation (CPR). Should injury or medical conditions arise, clients should be referred to their physicians for diagnosis and medical advice.

EMERGENCY EQUIPMENT AND EMERGENCY MEDICAL SERVICES

Whether you work in a health club, out of a home or in clients' homes, you need a telephone and first-aid kit nearby. Rapid access to a telephone is vital for contact with emergency medical personnel if they are needed. The first-aid kit should be completely stocked and systematically maintained. It should contain the following supplies:

For airway management:
- ✔ CPR microshield or pocket mask with one-way valve for protected mouth-to-mouth ventilations (Figure 16.1)

For assessing circulation:
- ✔ sphygmomanometer (blood pressure cuff)
- ✔ stethoscope
- ✔ penlight or flashlight

For general wound management:
- ✔ personal protective equipment, including latex gloves, mask and eye protection
- ✔ sterile gauze dressings (medium and larger sizes)
- ✔ adhesive tape (1-inch and 2-inch sizes)
- ✔ bandage scissors
- ✔ liquid soap (if soap is unavailable in the workplace)

For suspected sprains or fractures:
- ✔ splinting material (see the section on fractures, page 419)
- ✔ chemical cold pack, or ice and plastic bag

You should check the first-aid kit at least every three months to replace outdated items and become familiar with the contents. Any items used from the kit should be immediately replaced. Tape a list of contents to the inside cover so that nothing will be inadvertently omitted during restocking.

FIGURE 16.1
Mouth-to-mask ventilations: A small pocket mask with a one-way valve prevents contact with a victim's face during mouth-to-mouth resuscitation.

Accessing the Emergency Medical Services System

Every personal trainer needs a well-thought-out plan of action, for any emergency, that takes into account services available in the community. When an emergency occurs, you must know how to activate the **emergency medical services (EMS) system**, and who to call for immediate stabilization of a person in critical condition. Most large cities have a 911 telephone number that will automatically set the EMS system in motion. When someone dials 911, a dispatcher trained in recognizing emergencies will answer the telephone and ask questions that help determine which medical unit is needed. In communities without centralized dispatch, you must choose the police, sheriff, fire department or ambulance emergency number. For either system, you must be prepared to provide the name, address and telephone number at that location. The dispatcher will ask questions about the sex and approximate age of the victim, the nature of the illness or injury (for example, level of consciousness, respiratory difficulty, location of pain, presence of trauma or bleeding), and past medical history that may affect the victim's condition.

When a centralized dispatch number is not available, it is important for you to know the difference between emergency medical technicians (EMTs) and paramedics. EMTs are trained to recognize the nature and seriousness of a patient's illness or injury, and to provide basic care to sustain life and prevent further injury. This basic care includes splinting fractures, handling simple wounds, controlling bleeding, maintaining open airways and administering CPR. Some EMTs also are trained in **defibrillation**, which involves delivering an electric shock to a victim in cardiac arrest in an attempt to restart the heart beat. Some may be trained in inserting an advanced airway and administering epinephrine (EpiPen) for serious allergic reactions. Paramedics, on the other hand, are specially trained to administer advanced care and work under direct physician supervision, usually by radio. With approximately 1,000 hours of training, they are qualified to perform many lifesaving procedures, such as interpreting heart rhythm, managing advanced airways, starting intravenous fluids for shock, administering multiple medications and performing simple lifesaving surgical procedures. Clearly, any victim of a potentially life-threatening emergency needs a paramedic's services immediately. When in doubt about which help is needed, call the paramedics to be safe.

EMERGENCY ASSESSMENT

Most injuries or illnesses allow enough time for you to obtain a history, perform a brief examination, obtain assistance from emergency systems and provide reassurance to the victim. Unfortunately, a few situations require prompt action to save a life. Any condition that prevents the victim from breathing adequately or getting enough oxygen could cause death. A few basic principles will help you to identify these situations and act appropriately.

Oxygen, the basic fuel for sustaining life, is required by the cells of all the body's organs to carry out their functions. The three vital organs that must function to sustain life are the heart, lungs and brain. The heart is a pump that supplies oxygen-rich blood to the cells through the arteries, and then returns oxygen-depleted blood back to the lungs through the veins. The brain coordinates most of our functions, including movement, sensation, emotion, speech, wakefulness, sleep and thought. The lower brain level coordinates body functioning, as well as life-support systems, such as respiration and arterial blood pressure. Important for sustaining life, these brain cells are so sensitive to oxygen depletion that they will die within minutes after circulation to the brain stops.

Although many types of injuries and medical emergencies may occur, anything affecting your client's airway (A), breathing (B), or circulation (C) must be promptly acted on. The most obvious

Emergency Assessment

example is a person who suffers a cardiopulmonary arrest. An asthma attack, airway obstruction, injury to the trachea, heart attack or heavy hemorrhage from a wound has the potential to be just as serious a threat to life. When assessing an injury or illness, ask the ABC questions:

A. Does this person have a compromised airway?
B. Is this person breathing adequately?
C. Is blood circulation interrupted to prevent oxygen getting to their heart, lungs or brain?

Once you have identified a true emergency, you must respond rapidly and appropriately.

You need two skills to determine the nature of an emergency: 1) the ability to extract key information from the victim and other people around; and 2) the ability to assess the condition of the victim. If the victim is awake and responding, you may ask what problems they are experiencing and whether these problems have occurred before. Usually, the victim can talk about what is wrong: "My asthma is acting up again," "I'm having chest pain that feels the same as my last heart attack," "I think I broke my ankle" or "I'm having an insulin reaction." The victim may even give information about the help needed: "My inhaler is in the locker room," "If you could get my nitroglycerine pills from my purse, I think I'll be fine" or "I need some sugar to reverse my insulin reaction."

Unfortunately, it is not always this easy. If the victim is unconscious, cannot breathe easily or has never experienced these symptoms before, you must rely on physical assessment of the victim for answers. The **primary assessment** includes rapid examination to identify life-threatening or disabling circumstances. When help is on the way and the victim is out of immediate danger — breathing without assistance, bleeding controlled, pulses present — you can proceed to a more complete **secondary assessment**.

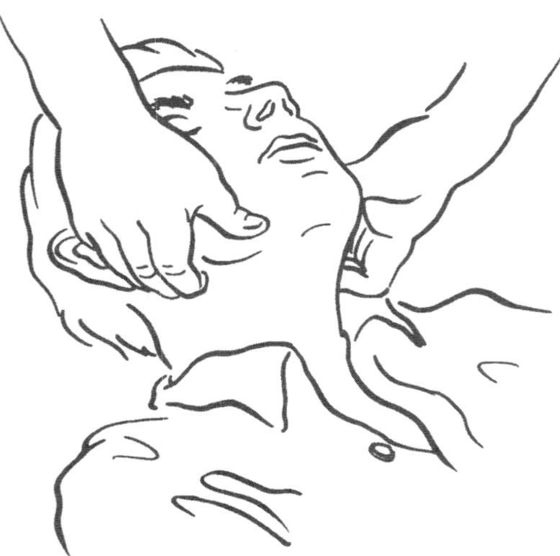

FIGURE 16.2
The jaw-thrust maneuver: The victim's head is carefully supported, without tilting or turning it in any direction. While kneeling at the head, push the lower jaw forward by exerting pressure with four fingers behind the angles of the jaw.

Primary Assessment

The purpose of the primary assessment, which may take only one or two minutes, is to identify any threats to life or limb that need immediate attention. This examination provides not only enough information to start first aid, but also valuable information for the EMS dispatcher, the paramedics or a physician.

The first moments after an emergency occurs can be so frightening that logic and experience are insufficient; to be able to respond appropriately and rapidly enough, you need to follow a systematic approach to assessing the victim. You may recruit other people on the scene to summon the EMS once an emergency has been identified, freeing yourself to continue assessment and apply first aid.

Begin with the ABCs of basic life support. Although the canned question from the Basic Life Support (BLS) course, "Are you OK?" may seem trite, asking the victim a simple question can give an assessment of the ABCs in less than five seconds. If the victim can answer, the airway is open, breathing is sufficient to sustain life for the moment and circulation is adequate to supply the brain with oxygen. If the victim is unable to answer a simple question, you

Emergency Assessment

must individually assess airway, breathing and circulation by physical examination.

1. Assess the airway. If the victim is not breathing or is making "snoring" respirations, the airway may be obstructed. You should establish an open airway by using the chin-lift or jaw-thrust maneuver (Figure 16.2). A simple sweep of the fingers clears foreign debris from the airway. With anyone who has sustained an injury above the clavicle (collar bone), you should suspect cervical spine injury and use the jaw-thrust maneuver to avoid extension of the neck. Excessive movement of the neck could convert a cervical spine fracture without neurological damage into a fracture dislocation with paralysis.

2. Look to see whether the victim's chest rises and falls. If the chest does not move, and if exhaled air cannot be felt coming from the mouth or nose, begin mouth-to-mouth or mouth-to-mask ventilations at 12 breaths per minute (Figure 16.1).

3. After two breaths, check the victim's circulation by feeling the carotid pulse. If pulses are absent and the victim is not breathing spontaneously, begin CPR.

4. Look quickly for signs of bleeding, and control hemorrhage with direct pressure over the wound. Victims who are bleeding profusely will not get enough oxygen-rich blood to vital organs. Even when they are alert at first, they will go into shock and quickly lose consciousness if appropriate measures are not taken.

5. Perform a rapid neurological examination. It is important to ascertain the victim's level of consciousness, pupil size and pupillary reaction. You can perform this exam by asking the victim to state their name, where they are and what day it is. You also should check whether the victim's pupils are equal, as well as whether the pupils constrict when a light shines on them. Although this brief exam is somewhat crude, it provides useful information to medical personnel should the victim's condition deteriorate later.

Secondary Assessment

Once the life-threatening needs of the victim have been addressed (airway, breathing and circulation) and help is on the way, you can conduct a more thorough evaluation. Again, a systematic approach will prevent you from missing a subtle but important injury. The simplest method is to survey the victim from head to toe.

1. Look at the victim's general appearance. Do they look sick or seriously injured? Are they having obvious respiratory difficulty?

2. Look at the skin. Skin color and condition can give clues about amount of pain, amount of bleeding and underlying injuries. A victim who is sweating excessively may be in severe pain. Pale, cool, clammy skin may indicate significant blood loss. Any break in the skin (lacerations, bruises, swelling or deformity) may reveal an underlying injury.

3. Check the head and face. Look for lacerations (cuts), hematomas (bumps) or bruises, and then ask whether the victim is having pain in the neck. If any evidence of head or neck injury appears, you should immediately immobilize the victim's neck to prevent spinal-cord damage and permanent disability.

4. Observe the chest for injury. The chest should rise and fall evenly with each respiration, and both sides of the chest should be symmetrical. Look for lacerations or bruising.

5. Ask whether the victim has abdominal pain. Look for signs of obvious trauma, such as bleeding or breaks in the skin.

6. Protect the spine if a fall has occurred. You can assess spinal injury by simply asking if the victim is in pain. If the person cannot answer or is unconscious, you must assume a spinal injury until proven otherwise. The victim should not be turned over for examination but should be kept on their back and prevented from moving until a physician can perform an examination and order X-rays. Do not move a

victim who falls in a side-lying position and is having back pain. Wait for help to arrive so the victim can be properly positioned on a backboard to immobilize the spine. Your actions may prevent permanent paralysis.

7. Check for injury to arms and legs. If swelling, discoloration or deformity are present, prevent the victim from moving until help arrives. If the victim must be moved because of a long delay in getting help or a dangerous situation, you should immobilize the limb with a simple splint.

8. Perform a more thorough neurological examination. Now that the more urgent problems have been addressed, you can take a moment to ask whether the victim is noticing any weakness, numbness or "pins-and-needles" feeling in their extremities. If the victim complains of these symptoms, you should prevent unnecessary movement and then report the symptoms to the emergency medical personnel so that they can take precautions against spinal injury. You may also reevaluate the victim's level of consciousness by repeating the same simple question asked during the primary assessment: "Are you OK?"

9. Check vital signs. You should note blood pressure, pulse rate and respiratory rate. These vital signs provide valuable information about the cardiovascular system, the amount of bleeding and the severity of respiratory problems.

COMMON MEDICAL EMERGENCIES AND INJURIES

You may encounter a variety of injuries and medical emergencies over the course of your career as a personal trainer. Here are some of the most common, along with guidelines for treatment.

Dyspnea (Difficult Breathing)

Labored breathing that persists after an exercise session may have several causes. The sudden feeling of **dyspnea** may result from emotional excitement, airway obstruction, emphysema, **asthma** attack or acute metabolic abnormalities. Victims may feel they cannot get enough air (air hunger) and may display an anxious expression. Their breathing may be audibly labored and their nostrils flared, or their neck and chest muscles may retract with each breath, indicating their distress. **Cyanosis**, a bluish discoloration, may appear around the lips and fingertips. Breathing may be rapid and shallow. If left untreated, the condition may progress to respiratory arrest. Following are basic first-aid procedures you should use with someone who is having respiratory difficulty:

1. Stop all activity immediately. Have the victim sit down in a comfortable position. Never urge a victim to lie down if they are resisting; the supine position may make the symptoms worse.

2. Question the victim about any history of medical problems. However, a victim in severe respiratory distress needs energy for the work of breathing and may not be able to respond to extended questioning.

3. Administer oxygen if it is available. Allow the victim to take their inhaled medication.

4. Administer mouth-to-mouth or mouth-to-mask ventilations if the victim is unconscious and has no spontaneous respirations.

Asthma. Many asthmatics are active people who do not need to restrict their activities, but some may need occasional modifications to their exercise schedule. During an asthma attack, the smooth muscles surrounding the airway goes into spasm. Mucous plugs or excessive secretions in the airway also contribute to respiratory difficulties. Most attacks result from allergic reactions to things in the environment, such as mold, pollen, dust, trees, grass, animals and certain foods. Some people suffer asthma attacks that are influenced by the type, intensity and duration of exercise. Some also suffer asthma attacks or more intense symptoms if they inhale cold air. During a typical asthma attack, the victim wheezes, breathing with a musical or "whistling" quality. Severe breathing difficulties will produce retracted neck and chest muscles, flared nostrils, cyanosis and the inability to speak. A victim who cannot speak in complete sentences because of the struggle to breathe needs immediate treatment and rapid transport by paramedics. Advanced airway maneuvers may be necessary and delay could mean the difference between life and death.

The asthmatic client can easily manage mild symptoms by decreasing the intensity of the workout. Other asthmatics may need to use their inhalers to reverse the symptoms quickly. If the symptoms resolve, the client can continue exercising as before. Here are some steps to prevent an asthma attack:

1. Use a prolonged warm-up to prevent or reduce the symptoms of **exercise-induced asthma**.
2. Decrease the intensity and increase the duration of the aerobic phase to avoid asthma symptoms while maintaining the cardiovascular benefits of the exercise.
3. Using a medicated asthma inhaler before beginning exercise may prevent an asthma attack. The client should consult with a physician before using this strategy.
4. Urge clients to comply with prescribed medication and follow up with a physician to maintain an active lifestyle while controlling asthma symptoms.

Chest Pain

Chest pain can originate from any structure in or near the chest, such as the esophagus, aorta or other large blood vessels, muscles, cartilage, lungs or heart. The most alarming cause of chest pain is **coronary artery disease**, which is still the number-one killer of adults in the United States. Every year more than 2 million people sustain a heart attack — approximately 700,000 of these result in death. With the population of physically active older adults growing, more personal trainers may find themselves providing first aid to clients complaining of chest pain or other signs and symptoms of a heart attack.

Coronary Artery Disease. The coronary arteries supply blood rich in oxygen to the myocardium (heart muscle). When plaque build-up or a spasm of the artery wall impedes blood from flowing through the arteries, the victim will feel chest pain. This pain originating from the heart is called **angina**. Someone who has coronary artery disease may experience angina during or immediately following physical exertion. The pain generally goes away when the victim dissolves a nitroglycerine pill under the tongue. However, if the myocardium continues without enough oxygen for a prolonged period, or if complete blockage of the artery stops flow to the heart, the muscle will die. This permanent damage to the myocardium is called a heart attack or myocardial infarction.

Victims of a **myocardial infarction** will complain of pain in the middle or on the left side of their chests. Frequently, they describe this pain as a pressure sensation over the anterior chest. Others have described this pain as "vise-like," "heavy" or "squeezing." The pain may radiate to the left shoulder and arm, up the neck or around the back. In addition, victims commonly have shortness of breath, nausea and vomiting, palpitations (heart pounding) and lightheadedness. You may observe excessive sweating, difficult breathing and an anxious expression in the victim.

About half of all cardiac deaths occur within two hours after the onset of symptoms, often before the victim reaches the hospital. Immediate recognition of symptoms and effective treatment within the first few moments are crucial to the victim's survival. Upon observing cardiac symptoms, you should immediately activate the EMS system or recruit a bystander to assist with this task. Paramedics are needed because they are trained in advanced life-support and can begin treatment immediately. If the victim has a cardiac arrest, paramedics or EMTs trained in defibrillation (EMT-Ds) can use electric stimulation to convert an erratic heartbeat into a functional rhythm. Paramedics also have been trained to perform advanced airway procedures and administer intravenous medications to resuscitate the victim. Before paramedics arrive, these first-aid measures should be followed:

1. Have the victim stop all activity immediately.
2. Place the victim in a comfortable position. Victims frequently ask to sit up, especially if dyspnea (breathing difficulties) accompany the chest pain.
3. Allow the victim to take prescribed medication (nitroglycerine) if they request it.
4. Administer oxygen if available. The myocardium is not getting enough oxygen for the demands made on it.
5. Keep the victim still until help arrives, thereby avoiding excessive exertion and increased demands on the heart. Reassurance that help is on the way will reduce stress and anxiety.
6. If the victim is unconscious, check their airway, breathing and circulation. Begin CPR as needed.

Syncope (Fainting)

Fainting, or **syncope**, is a transient state of unconsciousness during which the person collapses from lack of oxygen to the brain. Some common causes of syncope include rapid or irregular heartbeat, vasovagal reaction, heat illness and insulin reaction (hypoglycemia). Anything that causes a relative decrease in blood volume, such as excessive blood loss or severe dehydration from vomiting or diarrhea, also can cause fainting.

Angina or a heart attack may disrupt the normal electrical activity coordinating the heartbeat. The resulting rapid or erratic heart rhythm can cause the victim to collapse. If the heart loses its ability to pump, quivering instead, the brain may incur irreversible damage within four minutes, and death may occur.

The most common and least serious form of fainting results from an increase in vagal nerve tone combined with dilation of the arteries, a vasovagal reaction. Such an attack typically occurs with the victim in a standing position, and follows an unpleasant or anxiety-provoking event, such as pain, fright or the sight of blood. The victim typically experiences profuse sweating, loss of skin color, nausea and restlessness. Heart rate and blood pressure drop dramatically, decreasing flow to the brain so that the victim loses consciousness. These symptoms resolve rapidly when the victim lies down.

Insulin Reaction (Insulin-induced Hypoglycemia)

Hypoglycemia occurs when there is a deficiency of sugar in the blood. The most common cause of hypoglycemia is an insulin reaction in a person with **diabetes mellitus**. Insulin, the antidiabetic hormone secreted by the pancreas, is necessary for the utilization of glucose (blood sugar) by the cells and for maintenance of proper blood-sugar levels. Inadequate production or utilization of insulin leads to improper metabolism of glucose and fats for energy production and brings on diabetes. Diabetes mellitus, a chronic and incurable disease resulting from poor insulin production or utilization, is characterized by high blood sugars and excretion of glucose in the urine. A diabetic can control their symptoms and prolong life by using insulin injections and by closely monitoring blood sugars.

A diabetic may experience a hypoglycemic episode from too much insulin, too much exercise or insufficient food. The episode produces fatigue, excessive sweating, headache, trembling, slurred speech and poor coordination. The diabetic may feel faint, lose consciousness or have a seizure. Other physical symptoms, such as pale moist skin, full rapid pulse, tremors and elevated blood pressure, may also appear. Many diabetics are aware of early symptoms and can quickly reverse the process by simply consuming candy, fruit juice or some other food rich in simple sugars. Other people may have no warning and go into insulin shock suddenly. Your prompt response may prevent hospitalization or serious complications. Basic first aid for a diabetic with a hypoglycemic reaction includes the following steps:

1. If the victim is conscious, prevent injury by having them lie down or sit while someone gets help.
2. Give the victim sugar in the form of fruit juice, soft drinks sweetened with sugar, candy and so on.
3. Prevent the diabetic client from resuming activity after the insulin reaction.
4. Encourage the victim to eat a meal and consult a physician to prevent further reactions.

If the victim loses consciousness, first-aid treatment changes. Following is a list of procedures in order of priority:

1. If the victim is unconscious, check the airway, breathing and circulation. Artificial ventilations may be started as needed. Protect the victim's cervical spine if a fall has occurred.
2. Activate the EMS system. Paramedics or EMTs certified to start IVs can administer intravenous glucose that will quickly reverse a potentially life-threatening insulin reaction.
3. Protect the victim and prevent injury if they have a seizure. During a seizure, avoid restraining the victim. Place a soft object (towel, jacket, blanket) under the head to keep it from banging on the floor during violent muscular contractions.
4. Do not give anything by mouth. An attempt to give sugar by mouth to an unconscious person could cause aspiration of the substance and airway or respiratory compromise. If the victim vomits, turn the victim on their side to prevent aspiration (Figure 16.3).

Adapting a Training Regimen for Diabetics. Most physicians today encourage their diabetic patients to exercise because of the many physical and psycho- logical benefits. In consultation with their physicians, experienced and knowledgeable diabetics can safely embark on a training program, maintain good diabetic con- trol and avoid hypoglycemic reactions. The following methods will help the diabetic athlete:

- ✔ Athletes on insulin may need to reduce their doses by 20 percent to 40 percent when beginning an exercise program. Diabetics need to work closely with their physicians during this process to ensure the appropriate dosage of insulin.
- ✔ Diabetics respond best to exercises that have a predictable duration, intensity and frequency. Some examples of exercise that allow consistent and

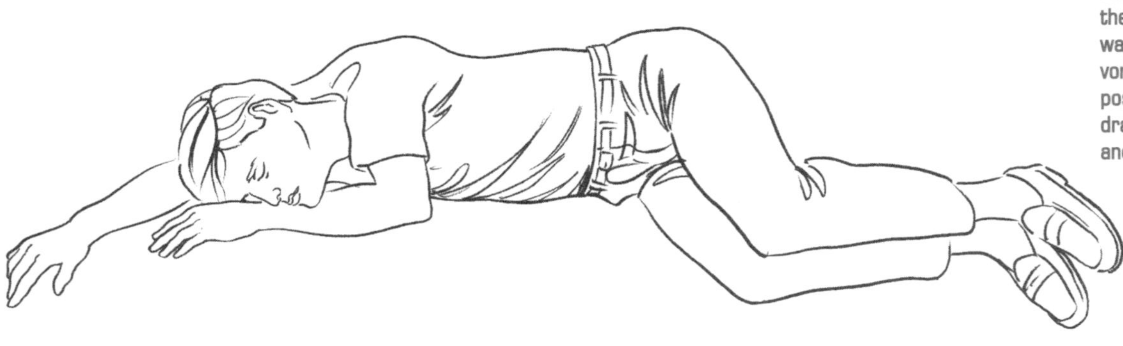

FIGURE 16.3
Side position for unconscious victim: Placing the victim on their side prevents airway blockage in case vomiting occurs. This position allows fluids to drain from the nose and mouth.

predictable energy expenditure include aerobic activities: walking, running, cycling, dance exercise, step training and cross-country skiing.

✔ Diabetics should avoid injecting insulin into exercised extremities. The increased circulation in the exercised limb may allow the insulin to be absorbed too rapidly, causing hypoglycemia. Abdominal sites may be safer for insulin administration.

✔ During sustained exercise, a quick source of energy containing 10 grams of **carbohydrates** should be taken every 15 to 20 minutes. This could include one-half cup of a soft drink with sugar, six to eight hard candies p of gelatin dessert (Sperling, 1988).

✔ Several hours before competing in an athletic event, diabetics should eat a meal high in carbohydrates and relatively low in **fats** and **protein**. Within one hour before prolonged strenuous exercise, a mixed snack containing 15 to 20 grams of carbohydrates should be consumed. This could consist of one-half cup of milk and two or three crackers (Sperling, 1988).

✔ Diabetics must take responsibility for their own care by closely monitoring blood sugars, taking insulin as recommended, eating properly, exercising regularly and keeping all medical appointments.

Heat Illnesses

Hot climates present serious health hazards to athletes. Runners, especially enthusiastic novices, are particularly vulnerable to heat illness. Runners may attempt to finish a race by exceeding their training levels or running too fast for their level of fitness. The normal metabolic processes of the body continuously produce heat that is dissipated to a cooler air temperature.

Normal body temperature is about 98.6° F (37° C). When the body gains excess heat — from increased metabolism during exercise, a hot environment, impaired dissipation of heat to the environment, or a combination of these — the brain's temperature regulatory center, the hypothalamus, activates several cooling mechanisms. Sweating, the most important method the body has to release excess heat during exercise, produces heat loss through evaporation. Also, the superficial veins in the skin dilate, losing heat through convection (transfer of heat to air currents) and radiation. The amount of evaporation and heat loss depends on the air temperature, humidity and wind speed. When humidity is high and the air is still, evaporation will diminish or cease completely. Convection of heat will cease when the air temperature approaches 100° F (38° C).

Anyone who exercises in a hot, humid environment, indoors or outdoors, runs a risk for heat illness. Injuries from heat occur in three forms: **heat cramps**, **heat exhaustion** and **heat stroke**. Although the following description separates them, they overlap a great deal. A person with heat illness may display a combination of these symptoms.

Heat Cramps. The mildest heat illness, heat cramps typically occur during or after strenuous physical activity. This disorder is characterized by painful muscle spasms affecting those muscles worked the hardest. For example, runners most often feel heat cramps in their calf muscles, while racquetball players are more likely to have them in their arms. It is not clear what causes heat cramps, although they appear to be related to profuse sweating accompanied by loss of body salt (sodium). Hyperventilation and accumulation of lactic acid in the muscles also may contribute to the condition. The heat-cramp victim exhibits painful muscle cramps, sweating and a normal body temperature. Treatment consists of drinking a commercially available electrolyte solution and massaging the affected muscle. If the cramps do not respond to these simple measures, the victim should be transported to a hospital for intravenous fluids and, possibly, muscle-relaxing medication.

Heat Exhaustion. The most common heat illness that occurs in athletes, heat exhaustion typically follows intense exercise in a hot, humid environment. Profuse sweating with resultant fluid and electrolyte loss and inadequate fluid replacement may produce a dramatic drop in blood pressure. The victim's temperature may be normal or slightly elevated, and they will be sweating profusely. Other signs and symptoms may include early fatigue, lightheadedness, nausea, vomiting, severe headache, decreased coordination and staggering, hypotension (blood pressure lower than 90 systolic), tachycardia (heart rate higher than 100 beats per minute) and syncope (fainting).

A victim of heat exhaustion needs rest and fluid replacement. Follow these simple first-aid measures:

1. Move the victim to a cool place to reduce further sweating and fluid loss.
2. If the victim is profoundly hypotensive (blood pressure lower than 90 systolic), call paramedics to transport the victim to the hospital.
3. If the victim is alert and mildly hypotensive (blood pressure 90 to 100 systolic), offer an oral electrolyte solution until help arrives. The victim can be more effectively rehydrated in the hospital with intravenous saline.
4. Victims of heat exhaustion should avoid activity for at least 24 hours following the condition and be sure to drink adequate amounts of fluids during that time. Furthermore, they should refrain from exercising in the heat for at least one week because they are especially susceptible to repeat episodes within that period.

Heat Stroke. The least common but most serious heat illness, heat stroke results from heat overload and impairment of the body's ability to dissipate heat. A true medical emergency, it may result in significant complications or death. The three classic symptoms of heat stroke are high body temperature (106° F or higher), altered consciousness and lack of sweating. However, in heat stroke induced by exertion, dry skin is not a reliable sign because the victim may be sweating from exercise. People affected by heat strokes have commonly been exercising in hot, humid weather. The conditions that predispose someone to heat stroke include:

- ✔ older age
- ✔ exercise and exertion
- ✔ hot, humid weather
- ✔ dehydration
- ✔ obesity
- ✔ heavy clothing
- ✔ infection and fever
- ✔ certain drugs: alcohol, amphetamines, diuretics, beta blockers and anticholinergics
- ✔ cardiovascular disease
- ✔ poor acclimatization
- ✔ hyperthyroidism

Older people and those who have been using drugs (including alcohol) may not be able to protect themselves from a high environmental temperature, leaving them susceptible to heat stroke. Alcohol dilates the blood vessels, making it easy for the body's temperature to increase if the air temperature is higher than the body's. Any condition that increases metabolism can increase heat production and susceptibility to heat stroke. The excess thyroid production seen in people with hyperthyroidism, any exercise or exertion, infections and stimulants such as amphetamines all increase metabolism.

Acclimatization refers to the body's ability

to adapt to heat stress over time, resulting in an increased capacity to work in hot, humid conditions. On the first day of rigorous exercise in a hot environment, a person may experience severe fatigue, elevated body temperature and a heart rate near maximum. Over the next four to eight days of similar exposure, the body will compensate by improving blood distribution and increasing blood volume, sweating at a lower temperature to improve heat loss, reducing urination to preserve body fluids and reducing salt concentration in the sweat glands. People with inadequate acclimatization tolerate heat poorly and are more susceptible to heat stroke.

Anyone who is dehydrated, has cardiovascular disease, or takes diuretics or beta blockers may have reduced skin circulation. Adequate skin circulation is needed to dissipate heat. Anticholinergic drugs, such as certain medications prescribed for depression, can impair the body's ability to sweat and thus impair cooling from evaporation. Many other drugs that affect mood and thinking can also impair the brain's temperature-regulatory center.

Once heat stroke is suspected, the victim needs rapid treatment aimed at lowering the body temperature by whatever means are available. For immediate first aid you should:

1. Activate the EMS system. At the same time, move the victim to a cool area and remove excess clothing to expose the skin to air.
2. Immediately apply ice packs to areas of increased blood flow — the groin, underarms and neck.
3. Apply cool water to the skin surface and then fan the victim by hand or machine to increase evaporation.
4. If the victim begins shivering, remove ice packs and use only cool sponging. Intense shivering increases metabolism and promotes heat production.

After transportation to an emergency room, the victim will receive care to minimize the damage from prolonged and intense heat to various organ systems.

Prevention of Heat Illness. All heat illnesses may be prevented with proper planning and common sense. To minimize risk of problems with heat, you should:

- ✔ Avoid exercising in extreme heat and humidity.
- ✔ Urge clients to wear sensible, porous, light-colored, loose-fitting clothing while exercising in the heat.
- ✔ Train clients for competition in heat by acclimating them slowly, increasing the intensity and duration of exercise over eight days.
- ✔ Help your client avoid **dehydration** by urging them to drink adequate amounts of water before, during and for 24 hours after vigorous exercise. Commercially prepared **electrolyte** and glucose solutions are unnecessary except for long periods of exertion in the heat, as in running a marathon. In fact, excessive salt intake can cause stomach cramps, weakness and high blood pressure. Use of solutions containing too much glucose can retard absorption from the gastrointestinal tract by keeping the solution in the stomach longer.
- ✔ Encourage clients to use table salt more liberally the day before prolonged exercise (eight hours or more) in heat. Plenty of fluids should be consumed before the event (8 ounces, 20 to 30 minutes ahead), in anticipation of fluid loss through sweating and breathing. A **hypotonic** electrolyte solution containing less than 0.9 percent concentration of sodium chloride (salt) should be consumed every 10 to 15 minutes during

a long event. A commercially made or homemade solution consisting of one-quarter teaspoon of salt dissolved in a quart of water, can be used. Salt tablets should be avoided.

- ✔ Recognize the early symptoms of heat stress–dizziness, cramps, clammy skin and extreme weakness.
- ✔ Have your client take more frequent rest periods and find a cool shaded area for these breaks.
- ✔ Encourage clients to avoid drugs (including alcohol) that may predispose them to heat injury.

Seizures

A **seizure**, or convulsion, originates from the brain and causes disturbances in movement, behavior, sensation or consciousness. Symptomatic of another condition, a seizure can result from an irritation in the brain from trauma, infection, blood clot or hemorrhage. Other causes include decreased blood supply to the brain from cardiac or respiratory disturbance; metabolic abnormalities in sodium, calcium, magnesium or glucose (hypoglycemia); poisons; alcohol withdrawal; high fever (especially in children); and complicated pregnancy. Epilepsy is a seizure disorder without an underlying cause. Epileptic seizures usually appear during childhood and recur spontaneously throughout life. With the use of an anticonvulsant medication, epileptics can lead normal lives and control their symptoms.

A major motor seizure, called a **grand mal seizure**, causes violent and uncontrollable muscular contractions. It can be frightening to see for the first time. It has four phases:

- ✔ The aura, when an unusual sensation of smell, taste or sound warns a person that a seizure is imminent.
- ✔ The tonic phase, in which the victim loses consciousness, becomes rigid with all extremities extended, and holds their breath. As a result of not breathing, they appear cyanotic.
- ✔ The clonic phase, in which the muscles alternate between contraction and relaxation, making the victim appear to jerk.
- ✔ The postictal phase, in which the victim is comatose and their muscles become flaccid (limp). Consciousness returns slowly, with some initial confusion, headache and extreme fatigue.

First Aid For Seizures. Your first task is to protect the victim from injury that might result from the flailing head and extremities. The simplest method is to put something soft under the victim's head and move all objects out of the way. Never attempt to hold the victim's arms or legs down, because this restraint may inadvertently cause a fracture or dislocation. Facial muscle spasms may cause the victim to bite their tongue. If a padded tongue blade or bite block is readily available, it may be gently placed between the victim's teeth to prevent tongue biting. You should avoid placing fingers or a pencil into the victim's mouth for fear of damage. The jaw muscles are creating an enormous force that has the potential for serious injury.

It is important not to panic or attempt to force open the jaw during the tonic phase, when the victim may stop breathing and look cyanotic. This phase will pass and the clonic phase will bring renewed breathing and improved skin color.

During the postictal phase, the victim's muscles will become flaccid. A snoring sound during respiration usually indicates an airway obstruction. If the victim has fallen to the floor and has noisy respirations, you can make a big difference by protecting their neck from further movement and controlling the airway with the jaw-thrust maneuver (Figure 16.2). You also should call an ambulance to immediately transport the victim to a hospital emergency room.

Soft-tissue Injuries

Tissues, such as skin, muscles and nerves, are composed of groups of cells that act together for a specific function. Bone, the hardest connective tissue in the body, is discussed later. This section will present identification and first aid for common wounds, sprains and acute strains.

Wounds. A break in continuity of the soft tissue, a wound can be open or closed. An open wound is manifested by broken skin, while a closed wound involves injury to underlying tissues without a break in the skin. Types of open wounds are:

- ✔ **Abrasion** — a scraping away of the skin or mucous membrane. Bleeding from an abrasion may be minimal, perhaps just a little oozing. However, abrasions still have potential for contamination and infection.

- ✔ **Incision** — a cut in the skin, typically from contact with a sharp object. The amount of bleeding depends on the size, depth and location of the incision.

- ✔ **Laceration** — a jagged, irregular cut or tear in the soft tissues, usually caused by a blow. Bleeding may be brisk in a laceration and tissue destruction is greater than with an incision. A laceration has great potential for contamination and resulting infection.

- ✔ **Puncture** — a piercing wound from a sharp object, such as a nail, pin or wood splinter, that makes a small hole in the skin. If external bleeding is minimal, the risk of infection is high. Bleeding flushes the area and assists in removing dirt and bacteria. A puncture wound over the trunk (chest, back, abdomen) can damage the underlying organs, causing internal bleeding.

- ✔ **Avulsion** — a forcible tearing away of tissue from the body. Damage may be small, as when a minor accident tears away a little skin, or extensive, as when a crushing injury tears a limb from the body. In more serious avulsion injuries, significant bleeding may occur and infection may develop if precautions are not taken.

FIGURE 16.4
Direct pressure for hemorrhage control.

Hemorrhage Control. Wounds usually result from external physical forces, such as falls or mishandling of equipment. First aid for open wounds emphasizes controlling bleeding and reducing the risk of infection. If an open wound is bleeding profusely, bleeding control takes precedence over infection control. Once the dressing has been applied and the bleeding is under control, the dressing should not be removed until the victim reaches the hospital. You should attend to the most life-threatening condition first. Following are some simple techniques you can take to control bleeding.

1. Elevate above the heart any briskly bleeding wound of the head, neck, arm or leg. This elevation reduces arterial bleeding from the force of gravity, and also encourages venous blood to return to the heart by draining excess blood from the elevated body part.

2. Apply direct pressure over the bleeding point, using a gloved hand over a gauze dressing (Figure 16.4). If bleeding is brisk and gauze dressings are not readily available, firm pressure with a small towel over the wound may be used.

3. Place a victim who has lost a significant amount of blood, looks pale and sweaty, and has a weak pulse in the shock position. Elevating the legs above the level of the heart assists venous return of blood to the heart.

Caution: a tourniquet can be dangerous and should only be used by medical personnel. Direct pressure and the measures discussed above will control nearly all bleeding wounds. A tourniquet shuts off the down-stream blood supply to the extremity. All viable tissue will die. Medical personnel may consider using a tourniquet only under life-threatening conditions, bearing in mind that its use means saving a life at the cost of losing a limb.

Preventing Infection. Contamination of a wound leads to infection, and open wounds are vulnerable to contamination from several sources, including the object that inflicted the injury, air-borne bacteria and particles and normal skin bacteria. To minimize the risk of infection, you may take several measures:

1. Remove all debris, such as wood splinters, pieces of glass, clothing particles or dirt by gently flushing the wound with warm water. For a superficial wound, you may remove embedded particles by gently brushing them off with a cotton swab or pulling them out with tweezers. Particles embedded deep in a wound should be left for a physician to remove, because pulling them out could disrupt an artery or sever a tendon or nerve.

2. Encourage the victim to wash a superficial wound with mild soap and warm water, rinsing thoroughly with warm, running tap water. The wound may be blotted gently with a clean towel or sterile piece of gauze and covered with a dry sterile bandage. If signs of infection develop – redness, warmth, swelling, tenderness – the victim should seek medical attention.

3. Obtain immediate medical attention for any wound that may need stitches. Delay in closure of the wound increases infection risk.

4. Place a dressing over any open wound to protect it from additional contamination. The dressing may be secured with tape or a gauze strip.

First Aid for Closed Wounds. Closed wounds typically result from external forces, such as a fall, or blow from a blunt object (a racquetball hitting the body or a free-weight falling onto it, for example). Even when the skin has no visible break, injury may still occur to underlying skin and other organs, muscles, tendons, ligaments and bones. Internal bleeding may produce a contusion (bruise), hematoma (collection of blood) or bleeding within the body cavity. Closed wounds are much less susceptible to infection than open wounds because the skin keeps out environmental bacteria. Although most closed wounds heal by themselves, some may involve deep structures with significant internal bleeding. Here are some tips for managing a closed wound:

1. If the wound is minor, apply ice to the area to reduce swelling and slow bleeding within the tissues.

2. If the victim has no outward signs of injury but complains of pain and tenderness, suspect an internal injury. **Call paramedics immediately if the following signs and symptoms appear:**

- ✔ Pale, cool and clammy skin; rapid and weak pulse; complaints of lightheadedness.

These may be signs of shock from internal bleeding.

- ✔ Extreme pain and tenderness over the injured area.
- ✔ Vomiting or coughing up blood, or blood in the urine or feces. These may be signs of significant injury to the chest or gastrointestinal tract.
- ✔ Rapid, painful or difficult breathing (dyspnea). Breathing difficulty may result from injury to the chest wall (ribs, cartilage, muscles) or to the respiratory system.

3. Examine the victim's extremities for swelling, discoloration or deformity that might indicate a fracture or dislocation. If these indications are present, avoid moving that body part. Keep the victim quiet and wait for help to arrive. The limb may be immobilized using simple splinting techniques if the victim must be moved before EMTs or paramedics arrive (see the section on Fractures, page 461).

Sprains. When the ligaments that normally stabilize a joint tear, the resulting **sprain** can range from a simple twist that causes minimal symptoms, to a complete tearing of the ligaments that produces an unstable joint, severe pain and swelling. The ankle is the most commonly sprained joint, typically from an inversion injury (turning in of the foot) caused by landing off balance or exercising on an irregular floor surface. When a joint is sprained, the victim may hear a popping sound if a significant tear has occurred. Pain, swelling, discoloration or the inability to bear weight also may be present. It is often difficult to distinguish between a sprain and a fracture without X-rays. Treatment of a sprain consists of RICE (rest, ice, compression, elevation). If a sprain is suspected, you should:

1. Stop all activity immediately and have the victim rest the injured extremity.

2. Apply an elastic bandage and ice to the injury. Elevate it to minimize swelling.

3. If pain or swelling is severe, do not allow the victim to walk. Immobilize the extremity with simple splinting maneuvers, and arrange for transportation to a hospital where the limb can be examined for fracture or other disabling injury.

Muscle Strains. A tear in a muscle or its tendon, a muscle strain is often called a "pulled muscle." This injury can be minor, involving less than 5 percent of the muscle fibers, or it can be severe, with complete disruption of the muscle or its tendon. There are several causes. The muscle may have been warmed up insufficiently before vigorous use, or it may have been overtrained and fatigued. It also could have been weakened by a previous injury. A tense muscle or tendon may be injured in movements that demand flexibility. And muscles exposed to cold weather have less capability of contracting than normal. The following are symptoms of a muscle strain:

- ✔ At the moment of injury, a sharp pain is felt; contracting the injured muscle reproduces this pain.
- ✔ Localized tenderness and swelling may occur over the damaged muscle or tendon.
- ✔ Pain may inhibit the muscle from contracting if it is partially torn; the muscle will not be able to contract at all if completely torn.
- ✔ Bruising and discoloration may appear 12 to 24 hours after the injury.

Treatment of minor muscle strain consists of RICE (rest, ice, compression, elevation). If the injury affects the leg and walking causes discomfort, the victim should use crutches until a medical evaluation can be obtained.

Fractures

A fracture, or break in a bone, may be closed or open. A closed (simple) fracture has no opening from outside the skin to the broken bone. An open (compound) fracture, which is more serious, results when the broken ends of the bone pierce the skin, or when a sharp object penetrates the skin and fractures the underlying bone. In either case, the opening between the skin and the injured bone brings a high risk of infection. A fracture is a serious injury not only because the bone is broken, but because of the potential injury in the surrounding soft tissue. Tendons, ligaments, muscles, nerves and blood vessels may be damaged, with a threat of permanent disability. Fractures may result from a direct blow or a more indirect cause, such as a fall. Following are signs of possible bone fracture:

- ✔ audible snap at the time of injury
- ✔ abnormal motion or position of the injured limb
- ✔ inability to bear weight on the limb (stand or walk)
- ✔ swelling
- ✔ deformity
- ✔ discoloration
- ✔ pain or tenderness to the touch

First Aid For Suspected Fracture. Immediate care for a victim with a suspected fracture involves controlling hemorrhage, preventing further injury to the bone and soft tissue, and providing first aid for shock, if necessary. If you suspect a fracture, take the following steps:

1. Keep the victim quiet; do not allow them to move the injured part or attempt to put weight on it.

2. Remove or cut away clothing that covers the injury. This step allows more thorough assessment and prevents contamination of an open fracture.

3. Cover an open fracture with a sterile gauze dressing or clean cloth to prevent further contamination. Activate the EMS system immediately and keep the victim lying down if there is significant bleeding to improve circulation to the heart and brain until help arrives. Apply gentle pressure to slow or stop the bleeding, using care not to disturb the fractured site.

4. Leave the protruding ends of bone where they are. Attempting to push them back in place will increase risk of infection and further injury to soft tissues.

5. If the injury is not too serious, splint the limb to immobilize it. However, if the extremity is grossly deformed and splinting may be difficult, merely prevent the injured limb from moving until medical help arrives. An untrained person's attempts to move a fractured limb can convert a closed fracture into an open one, or cause nerve and vascular injury in an uncomplicated fracture.

Splinting Techniques. Splinting or immobilizing a fractured limb protects it against further injury during transportation, reduces pain and prevents bone fragments from injuring arteries or other tissues. Many household objects or pieces of equipment in a health club may be converted to emergency splints — any object that provides support and prevents movement. Some examples include heavy cardboard, newspapers, rolled blankets or towels, exercise mats and straight sticks. The splint should simply be long enough to extend past the joints above and below the suspected fracture and should be padded to prevent pressure injuries from hard surfaces or sharp edges. A first-aid course will teach you the how to splint an extremity.

Figures 16.5 and 16.6 illustrate properly applied splints of the forearm and ankle, using materials commonly found in the home or health club.

Head Injuries

Typically the result of a blow or a fall, head injuries are less common than extremity injuries, but their complications can produce long-term disability. Thus, it is important for you to be able to identify a potential head injury and take appropriate precautions. When the skull accelerates or decelerates suddenly, the brain can move within the skull, and its impact on the skull may injure the brain. Bleeding may occur within the brain tissue, as in cerebral contusions (bruising of the brain) and hematomas (collection of blood). Bleeding also may occur from vessels between the membranes covering the brain. Because the skull is a rigid bony structure filled with brain tissue, it contains little room for expansion. Any bleeding or tissue swelling exerts compression force against the brain cells, and can result in serious neurological damage.

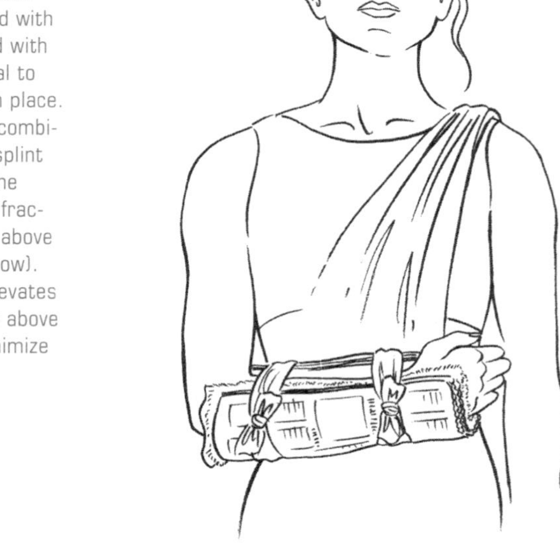

FIGURE 16.5
Splinting the forearm: The bone has been immobilized by newspaper that has been rolled up, padded with a towel, and tied with strips of material to hold the splint in place. Using a sling in combination with the splint will immobilize the joints below the fracture (wrist) and above the fracture (elbow). The sling also elevates the hand slightly above the elbow to minimize swelling.

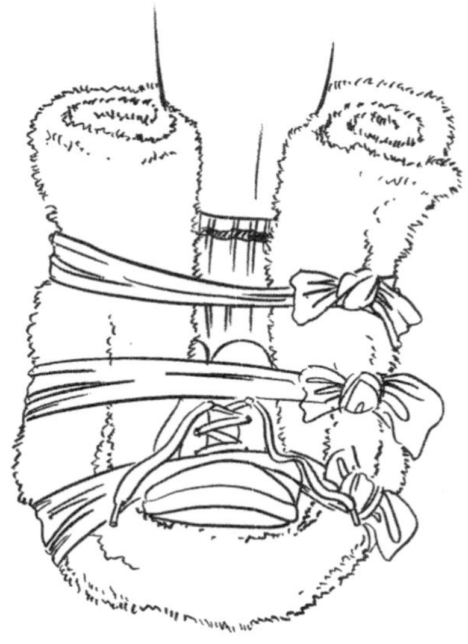

FIGURE 16.6
Splinting the ankle: Remove the victim's shoe and check circulation and sensation. If the shoe cannot be removed without moving the leg, just loosen the laces. Splint the ankle using a rolled blanket (or exercise mat), applying it around the ankle and sole of the foot and tying it into place with cloth strips.

Symptoms of head injury may be fairly minor, such as headache, dizziness, nausea and vomiting. They may be severe, including speech disturbance, partial or complete paralysis, seizures and coma. A force strong enough to cause a temporary loss of consciousness is strong enough to cause serious complications or death. **Any victim of head injury who loses consciousness, however briefly, needs immediate transportation to a hospital emergency department for neurological evaluation.**

Visible signs of trauma to the head or face are further clues that hidden injury to the brain may have occurred. A laceration or large hematoma of the scalp (collection of blood under the scalp that feels like a large bump) needs a physician's attention. Signs of a possible skull fracture include discoloration and swelling around the eyes (raccoon sign), visible blood in the ear canals and clear fluid draining from the nose or ears. This seepage may be cerebrospinal fluid, the fluid that surrounds the brain and spinal cord. A fractured skull needs further evaluation that may include a radiological scan or observation in the hospital. The excessive force required to fracture the skull may also have produced injury to the underlying brain.

Head injuries seldom occur in isolation. Damage to the cervical spine (neck) accompanies 15 percent to 20 percent of head injuries, so it should always be considered when caring for the victim, especially someone with altered mental status, unconsciousness, or any of the visible signs listed previously. You must take precautions to immobilize the neck, thereby preventing disabling injury. When in doubt, always protect the cervical spine until the victim is thoroughly examined

Common Medical Emergencies and Injuries

by a physician and X-rays are taken. The jaw-thrust maneuver will assist the airflow, without moving the neck of a comatose victim whose airway is compromised. Paramedics are needed immediately to open the airway and transport the victim to the hospital.

Neck and Back Injuries

Airway Compromise. Blunt force against the front of the neck, the face or the jaw can produce airway compromise. For example, a client may bench press too much weight, become fatigued and drop the barbell on the front of their neck. Extensive swelling may occur around the trachea, or the larynx may fracture, either of which may result in airway obstruction. Time is critical and paramedics should be summoned immediately for rapid transport to a hospital, where a surgically made airway (tracheotomy) may be necessary. If the victim sustains a respiratory arrest, you should begin mouth-to-mouth or mouth-to-mask ventilation while waiting for help to arrive.

Spinal Cord Injury. Injuries to the vertebral column occur most frequently when excessive force is applied from the top or bottom, as in a fall or a dive into a shallow pool. The resulting fractures or dislocation of the vertebrae disrupt the ligaments that hold the bones in place. The spinal cord, normally protected within the vertebral canal, may be injured, the blood supply to the cord interrupted, and neurological dysfunction with paralysis may result.

It is extremely important to keep in mind the possibility of vertebral injury for any victim of head trauma, or for someone with several areas of trauma. It is easy to overlook the neck during the initial assessment when, for example, a large laceration or bone deformity may distract one's attention. However, many victims of multiple trauma also have spinal cord injuries. For the purpose of first aid, anyone with one or more of the following signs should be considered to have an injured spinal cord:

- ✔ altered level of consciousness
- ✔ obvious numbness, tingling, weakness or paralysis
- ✔ a fall or injury that might have injured the spinal cord
- ✔ head or facial injury
- ✔ pain or tenderness over the spine
- ✔ swelling or deformity over the spine

Emergency Response to Neck and Back Injury. Initial management of a neck or back injury is extremely important to the long-term outcome. Improper management may turn a simple bone injury into permanent neurological disability and paralysis. Following are techniques you can use to protect the spinal cord while help is on the way:

1. Handle the victim carefully, avoiding movement of the head and neck or bending of the neck. Simply hold the head and neck stationary to prevent the victim from moving until help arrives (Figure 16.7).
2. Do not attempt to reposition or move the victim until an ambulance arrives with trained EMTs equipped with spinal immobilization devices.
3. If the victim's airway is compromised, or they require artificial respirations, you may need to roll the victim onto their back, keeping the entire spine straight as a board to protect the neck and back ("log roll"). The victim will then be in a position

FIGURE 16.7
Immobilization of the head and neck: Kneel at the victim's head, place your hands on either side of the head and neck, and hold them firmly in place. Keep the victim quiet and prevent movement of the head. Do not try to reposition the victim.

conducive to establishing an airway. The most effective and appropriate airway maneuver to avoid hyperextension of the neck is the jaw-thrust.

PROTECTION AGAINST BLOODBORNE PATHOGENS

There are many bloodborne diseases that you could be exposed to while caring for an injured client. These include non-A hepatitis, non-B hepatitis, hepatitis B and delta hepatitis. Other diseases transmitted though blood include syphilis, malaria and human immunodeficiency virus (HIV). Of these, the most common and serious diseases are hepatitis B (HBV) and human immunodeficiency virus (HIV).

Hepatitis B

Hepatitis B virus (HBV) is one of the most common bloodborne hazards you may face on the job. Hepatitis is defined as an inflammation of the liver ("hepatic" = liver, "itis" = inflammation). Among healthcare workers alone (nurses, doctors, laboratory technicians, etc.) more than 8,000 persons become infected with hepatitis annually, resulting in approximately 200 deaths.

Some of the signs and symptoms of HBV are similar to the flu, and may include abdominal pain and vomiting severe enough to necessitate hospitalization. Some persons have no symptoms at all, but their blood, saliva and other body fluids may be infected.

Acquired Immune Deficiency Syndrome (AIDS)

The first reported case of AIDS in the United States occurred in 1981. Initially, it was considered a "gay" disease because most individuals who contracted AIDS were homosexual. As more cases were discovered in the population at large, it became clear that AIDS did not discriminate against certain populations. AIDS has now gained recognition as being an epidemic due to the alarming number of new cases discovered each year.

The human immunodeficiency virus (HIV) attacks the body's immune system causing the AIDS disease. This weakens the body's ability to fight off infections from bacteria, viruses and parasites. The HIV may remain inactive for years in some individuals, and the person infected may be completely asymptomatic.

When the virus becomes active, the person infected may begin to experience headaches, fatigue, swollen lymph glands, night sweats and fever, nausea, diarrhea, loss of appetite, skin rashes and sores in the mouth, nose or anus. AIDS is the last stage of HIV infection and causes such diseases as pneumonia, infections of the brain, Kaposi's sarcoma (a rare skin cancer), severe weight loss and eventual death.

Universal Precautions

An individual may be infected with HIV or HBV and not show visible signs or symptoms. Some clients may be carriers without knowing it and a careful history or examination may not pick up those who are infected. You cannot afford to risk exposing yourself to these communicable diseases. All human blood and certain body fluids should be handled utilizing universal precautions. It is possible to reduce your risks from bloodborne pathogens by understanding the facts and taking the following precautions:

- ✔ Contaminated razors, broken glass or other sharp objects should be carefully placed in a disposal container that is puncture-resistant and leak-proof.

- ✔ If infected material gets on your hands, wash them immediately with soap and running water

Summary

✔ Personal protective equipment such as gloves, masks, gowns, faceshields, protective eyewear and CPR protective mouthpieces should be used when appropriate. The type of protective equipment you use will depend on the type of exposure that is anticipated when assisting a client or responding to an emergency.

✔ If personal protective equipment or street clothes become contaminated, remove them as soon as possible and place them in the designated area for disposal or washing.

✔ If you are at risk of exposure to HBV on the job, your employer will make the hepatitis B vaccination available to you at no cost. Currently, there is no vaccine to prevent AIDS.

SUMMARY

As a personal trainer, you may work closely with clients of various ages and fitness levels. This requires you to have 1) a basic knowledge of common injuries and medical emergencies, and 2) a well thought-out plan of action for all emergencies. This chapter is not comprehensive, but it has presented most of the common medical emergencies you might encounter, and first-aid procedures for responding to them. You should be competent in CPR and take additional training in first aid. A well-stocked and systematically maintained first-aid kit should always be near at hand, whether you work in a health club or in a client's home. Your ability to recognize a true emergency, as well as your ability to respond correctly, can play a critical role in the ultimate outcome of an illness or injury. Immediate treatment for such common injuries as sprains and strains can reduce pain and swelling and shorten a client's recovery time. By familiarizing yourself with the signs of a heart attack, insulin shock or seizure, you may be able to save a life. Finally, it is important to remember that you should never attempt to provide medical advice. Instead, your responsibility is to provide immediate first aid, refer injured clients to their physicians and, when necessary, call for emergency aid.

REFERENCES AND SUGGESTED READING

American Diabetes Association. (1995). Reiderman, N., Phil, D. & Devil, J.T. (Eds.) *The Health Professional's Guide to Diabetes and Exercise.*

American Red Cross. (1993). *Community First Aid & Safety.* St. Louis: Mosby Publishers.

Kulund, D. (1988). *The Injured Athlete.* (2nd ed.) Philadelphia: Lippincott.

Peterson, L. & Renstrom, P. (1994). *Sports Injuries: Their Prevention and Treatment.* St. Louis: Mosby Publishers.

PART VII

Chapter 17 Legal Guidelines and Professional Responsibilities

VIII

Legal Issues

CHAPTER 17

Legal Guidelines and Professional Responsibilities

17

IN THIS CHAPTER:

Independent Contractors vs. Employees
- Legal Tests

Contracts

Business Structure
- Sole Proprietorship
- Partnership
- Corporations

Scope of Practice
- Health Assessment
- Nutritional Counseling

Legal Responsibilities
- Facilities
- Equipment
- Supervision
- Instruction
- Safety Guidelines
- Exercise Recommendations and Testing

Legal Concepts and Defenses
- Standard of Care
- Assumption of Risk
- Negligence

Liability Insurance
- Protection for You
- Independent Contractors
- Locating Coverage
- Riders
- Words to Choose Your Policy By
- Coverage Where You Need It
- Make Sure Legal Fees Are Covered
- Find Out What Is Not Covered
- Past, Present and Future Claims

Other Business Concerns with Legal Implications
- Music
- Certification
- Bloodborne Pathogens
- Risk Management

David K. Stotlar

David K. Stotlar, Ed.D., teaches sport management and sport law and is the director of the School of Kinesiology and Physical Education at the University of Northern Colorado. He is a consultant, author and lecturer, has contributed to numerous publications and conducts management seminars throughout the world.

Although the majority of personal trainers may be well trained and comfortable with their responsibilities for designing exercise programs and working with clients, they may be far less comfortable with legal concepts important to running a fitness business. This chapter is intended to increase your comfort level, and to address some of the legal and business concerns you may have as a personal trainer. It also will describe the scope of practice in personal training, and summarize your legal responsibility as a personal trainer. The guidelines offered here, while based on sport law and the experience of fitness professionals, are not intended as legal advice, but

Independent Contractors vs. Employees

rather as guidance. You should always consult lawyers in your own state for specific legal questions and problems.

INDEPENDENT CONTRACTORS vs. EMPLOYEES

Personal trainers who work in clubs are either independent contractors or employees, while self-employed personal trainers are usually independent contractors. This term evolved from the concept of a leased employee. For example, a homeowner might hire a bulldozer and an operator to move some dirt in their backyard. The bulldozer operator would not legally be considered the homeowner's employee, but rather an employee of the bulldozer company. The driver merely came along with the equipment, making the bulldozer company responsible for any **negligent** actions of the driver. Similarly, clients who hire personal trainers do not usually intend to hire them as employees, but prefer to lease their services for a brief period of time.

Some owners of fitness clubs use independent contractors, thereby avoiding the expense of training, medical benefits, social security withholding, worker's compensation or unemployment coverage for these workers. However, most clubs still require independent contractors to follow club rules. Clubs also may prefer to deal with **independent contractors** because it is legally more difficult to fire an **employee** than it is to simply not renew a contract.

As a personal trainer with independent contractor status, you would enjoy the following benefits:

- ✔ choosing when and where to work
- ✔ charging variable fees for different situations
- ✔ having professional freedom in conducting work

These freedoms must be weighed against the disadvantages of not having training, benefits or equipment provided for you.

Legal Tests

Both independent contractors and club employees must be certain that all details of their agreements are clear from the beginning of their professional relationship with a club or fitness center. Often the legal nature of the relationship is ambiguous, and people have filed lawsuits attempting to collect worker's compensation or unemployment insurance from clubs that consider them independent contractors. Personal trainers, whether as employees or as independent contractors, are often left without health benefits or insurance coverage. In addition, trainers quickly discover the penalties of neglecting payments to tax and social security accounts if they assume that the clubs they worked for were paying into the accounts for them. Clubs only do this for people they consider employees, not for independent contractors.

Court cases have established 10 legal tests for determining whether someone is an employee or an independent contractor. These tests include the following:

1. How much control can the employer exercise over the details of the work? The right to control indicates an employer-employee relationship.

2. Are people paid by the hour or by the job? People paid regularly by the hour or by the week are generally considered employees. On the other hand, people who receive a single payment for services rendered more easily qualify as independent contractors.

3. How long has the person been working in this establishment? People hired for short periods (a few days or weeks) are more easily defined as independent contractors than people employed over several months or years.

4. How much training does the person

require? If the worker brings specialized or technical skills to the employer, the worker typically may be considered an independent contractor. On the other hand, if the employer provides training to a recently hired person, the court usually considers that person an employee.

5. Does the person provide service to more than one client or business? If so, this person may be seen more easily as an independent contractor. If the person provides services for only one business or client, they would probably be considered an employee.

6. Who provides the equipment? In general, independent contractors provide their own equipment. However, using the club's or client's equipment, in itself, would not disqualify a trainer from independent contractor status.

7. Is the work integral to the business? If so, the worker will more likely be considered an employee. Supplemental services are more likely to support the status of independent contractorship.

8. In other clubs, is the work traditionally performed by an independent contractor or an employee? Current practices in the field may help determine if a trainer is an employee or an independent contractor.

9. What did the club and the trainer intend when they made their agreement? If the trainer believed they were hired as an independent contractor, as did the club, the court would attempt to enforce their original intent.

10. Is the employer engaged in business? If a client hires a trainer to perform personal training, the court will probably consider the trainer an independent contractor. The intent is to protect clients from being misconstrued as employers.

All of these questions have arisen in court cases over employment status, each with varying degrees of authority. Both you as a personal trainer and the clubs you work with must understand these issues when you initiate an agreement.

CONTRACTS

Contracts

To perform your work, get paid for it, and avoid costly legal battles with clients and employers, you need to understand legal **contracts**. Whether you work as an independent contractor or as an employee of a club or fitness center, you must be aware of basic contract law. The following elements are necessary for a binding contract:

- an offer and acceptance with a mutual agreement on terms
- consideration — an exchange of valuable items, such as money, for services
- legality — acceptable form under the law
- ability of the parties to enter into a contract with respect to legal age and mental capacity

For example, you may talk to a prospective client and mention the services you can provide, such as designing individualized exercise sessions to meet their goals. You and your client also may agree on dates and times for exercise sessions. This negotiation constitutes an offer and an acceptance. Stating a fee of $50 per hour for services sets up an exchange of consideration, i.e., training services for money. Once these negotiations are settled, you should prepare a written contract by filling out a basic contract form or by having one specifically written for each agreement. In either case, you should consult legal counsel to ensure that the written form is valid under contract law. This document becomes a valid contract when signed by both you and the client, if both of you are of legal age to enter into contracts.

Some personal trainers beginning in business may feel that written contracts are unnecessary, that a brief chat and a handshake are enough. However, in case of a misunderstanding or injury, legal complications can arise from such a simple oral contract, which can be enforceable under law. Business matters are less likely to lead to problems when the parties put the contract in writing, spelling out details to avoid potentially expensive misunderstandings. It is useful to pay for the services of a lawyer to develop the basic agreement. You can then personalize this agreement for each client and avoid additional legal fees. Whether the contract is to be used with clients or with a fitness club, you and your attorney should address the following considerations in developing it:

- ✔ identification of the parties to the contract, such as you and the client or club
- ✔ description of services (fitness training and consultation)
- ✔ specification of compensation, payment method, or rate of compensation per hour, day or month
- ✔ confidential relationship — an agreement by each party not to divulge personal or business information acquired through the relationship
- ✔ business or employment status
- ✔ term and termination — defining the length of the contract and the conditions under which termination will be allowed by either party

BUSINESS STRUCTURE

Early in your professional life, you must decide whether you are acting as an individual, as a corporation or as an employee of fitness centers. If you conduct business independently from a fitness center or club, you have three types of business structures available: **sole proprietorship, partnership** and **corporation.**

Sole Proprietorship

As the name implies, a sole proprietorship is a business owned and operated by one person. This person owns all assets and is responsible for all income, losses and liabilities. Forming a sole proprietorship establishes a legal right to conduct a business and gives the owner legal title to it. The owner — the personal trainer, in most cases — has sole control over decisions and profits. This business structure offers the advantages of ease and low cost when the business is started. Furthermore, profits are taxed at the owner's individual rate, which is typically lower than a corporation rate. The owner reports income and taxes on a schedule that is attached to the personal income tax form instead of a separate business tax return. Government regulation is minimal compared to other business structures.

The risk of **liability**, however, is a drawback that often convinces people to choose other business structures. In sole proprietorships, the owner is completely responsible for all liabilities, court awards or damages incurred by the business. An injured person who sues the owner and wins a sizable judgment can be awarded, if necessary, the proceeds from seizure of the owner's personal savings and property, such as house and auto. If the owner's business liabilities exceed their personal assets, the owner could be paying for today's problems years into the future.

Another disadvantage of sole proprietorships is the difficulty of getting away for vacations, illness or emergencies. It may be impossible to find someone to watch the shop with the same care and interest as the owner. Often, the owner does not recognize these pressures in the early days of establishing the business, but later, the stress and pressure of successful operation may suggest a break from daily routine.

Partnership

Two or more people who agree to operate a business and share profits and losses may form a partnership. Two personal trainers, for example, could form a company, or a trainer could become part owner of a club. Although partnerships may be

Business Structure

loosely created without legal documents, serious business relationships benefit from a partnership agreement that establishes rules of operation. This agreement should lay out the structure for authority, the partners' rights, expected performance and contributions from each partner, buy-out clauses, income distribution and responsibility for debts. The agreement also should stipulate whether the business is a general or limited partnership.

General Partnership. In a general partnership, all partners are fully liable for the actions of the business. For example, suppose you and a friend go into business together. You will be the personal trainer and your friend will run the office as well as do the marketing and promotion. Because the business was your idea, you will put up $50,000 to get started; your friend agrees to work at minimum wage until things get rolling. Early on, a video company approaches your friend to produce and sell videotapes to your clients as part of the fitness package. Your friend agrees to a deal for $25,000, payable in 90 days. Shortly thereafter, your friend suffers a breakdown, gets a divorce, squanders all personal assets and stops managing the business. After 90 days, the video company can legally collect from you all the money owed. It makes no difference that you owned only 50 percent of the business, or that you had an agreement that each partner would be responsible for only 50 percent of all debts. You also are liable for all debts if a court judgment is entered against your partner for activities of the business. You could sue your partner to try to recover your losses, but you might never benefit from your suit.

Limited Partnership. To avoid such devastating personal liability, limited partnerships allow certain partners, usually those who have invested in the business, to limit their liability to the amount of money they have contributed. The law usually prevents limited partners from taking an active role in managing the business. Although it might seem intriguing to limit financial liability by organizing a business with only limited partners, the law also requires that at least one person be designated as a general partner. The general partner may be anyone in the business, typically the person who runs the day-to-day operations. General partners are personally liable, while limited partners risk only their original investment.

All partnerships have the same tax advantage as sole proprietorships: profits are taxed at personal rates. This advantage makes partnerships attractive to investors because the partnership passes on to them the tax losses, credits and deductions, while providing the limited partners with many of the legal protections they would only find in corporate structures.

Corporations

Regulated by state laws, corporations exist as legal entities and are independent of their owners. They are taxed separately from their owners, and corporate assets may be easily sold or transferred. In most cases, any number of people may own the corporation through shares issued by the business. Typically, the shareholders elect a board of directors to represent their interests. If you intend to form a corporation, you must first choose a company name that has not been previously registered. Then you should file a notice of incorporation with your state, paying the appropriate fees and designating a registered agent as a contact for the state. You may want to retain an attorney to guide you through this process, or simply call your secretary of state directly. Often a friendly and knowledgeable state clerk can talk applicants through the incorporation procedures, saving them hundreds of dollars in legal fees.

Many businesses form corporations to limit the financial liability of their shareholders. Creditors can attach the assets of a corporation if it owes money or has a judgment against it, but the personal assets of the corporate officers, board and shareholders are typically not at risk for liabilities of the corporation. Taxes, however, can be more burdensome in a corporate structure. As an independent legal entity, a corporation must pay taxes, usually at a rate higher than for individuals. In addition, all corporate profits after taxes are paid as dividends to the shareholders, who in turn must declare them as income and pay taxes on them. This double taxation may be avoided if shareholders play an active part in the corporation management and draw salaries as managers. These salaries may offset the corporate profits, eliminating a tax on corporate earnings. The Internal Revenue Service requires that the salaries be reasonable for the work performed. The salaries, of course, are subject to individual tax as earned income.

A second method of avoiding double taxation, known as the S corporation, may be a better choice for personal trainers just starting out. This structure passes its profits through to shareholders, where the income is taxed at the individual rate. S corporations have certain restrictions, such as limiting the number of shareholders to 35.

Table 17.1 offers a brief summary of the advantages and disadvantages of each of these business structures just discussed. Few personal trainers will choose to take on the complicated tax structure, government regulations and legal procedures necessary to begin and maintain a corporation. Most will simply register at their county courthouses as sole proprietors. In most cases, it is helpful to consult a lawyer when making this choice.

SCOPE OF PRACTICE

Whether you work as an employee in a fitness club or as an independent business person, you will find that clients ask for your advice on a variety of problems. Not only is it important for you to be well-educated and familiar with your own discipline, but it also is important for you to understand the limitations of your practice. Personal trainers are not usually licensed or qualified physicians, physical therapists, dietitians, marriage counselors or social workers. You should avoid practicing these disciplines without appropriate training.

Personal trainers should note, however, that many of these allied health professionals can provide meaningful information and services to their clients. Establishing a network of counselors, dietitians, physicians and physical therapists can be valuable. Clients who need the specialized services of these healthcare professionals should be referred for treatment and counseling. In turn, your network of professionals may refer clients to you who need or desire personal training.

Health Assessment

According to fitness law expert David Herbert (September 1989), "wellness-assessment documents should be utilized for ... [the] determination of an individual's level of fitness ... never for the purpose of providing or recommending treatment of any condition."

As a personal trainer, you should use the health history form to screen the client for appropriate placement in a fitness program. In cases where any significant risk factors are indicated, you should refer the client to a physician for clearance before the program begins. If you were to use this form to recommend treatment, you could be accused of practicing medicine without a license. It is far better to have a physician sign the form, indicating the types of training suitable for this client, or clear the client for exercise by writing a letter on their letterhead. Some trainers prefer a physician's letter to avoid the possibility of a client forging the doctor's signature on a

Table 17.1
Advantages and Disadvantages of Sole Proprietorships, Partnerships and Corporations

Sole Proprietorships and Partnerships	Corporations
✔ Easily formed under the law	✔ Complicated legal requirements
✔ Low costs of formation	✔ High costs of formation
✔ Unlimited liability (except limited partners)	✔ Limited liability for corporate acts
✔ Typically can operate in different states without registration	✔ Must be registered in each state where business is conducted
✔ Owners pay taxes, but business does not	✔ Both corporation and owners are taxed, except for S corporation
✔ Minimal government regulation	✔ Extensive government regulation

fitness form. However, if a client fakes a physician's signature in order to obtain acceptance to a fitness program, the trainer probably would not be held liable.

You must understand how to use the information collected on the health history form, asking only those questions you know how to interpret and apply. If you request information about the types of medications your client is taking, you may be held responsible for knowing the biochemical and physical reactions to these drugs. You must read and fully understand the answers to other questions as well. One sports administrator required all participants to complete health and physical appraisal forms, and then filed them without reading them. When a participant who had noted his heart defect on his form died, the sports administrator had little legal defense in the ensuing lawsuit.

Nutritional Counseling

According to the American Dietetic Association, more than one-half of the 50 states regulate or license dietitians or nutritionists. In a recent Ohio case, a personal trainer was prohibited from providing nutritional counseling without a license. The plaintiff centered his case around the titles he was using: nutritionist or registered nutritionist. The court determined that, regardless of his title, he was not a registered dietitian and was in violation of Ohio law by practicing dietetics without a license. This included advising his client to use nutritional supplements. You should check the laws in your own state to ensure that you are not violating any of them by advising your clients about food, vitamins or calorie consumption. You should avoid giving advice on any subject in which you have not received training. Clients with complex dietary concerns should be referred to a registered dietitian (RD).

LEGAL RESPONSIBILITIES

Liability simply means responsibility. Certain obligations and responsibilities arise from the legal relationships between you and your clients, specifically those responsibilities that a court would recognize as part of your employment as a fitness professional. These responsibilities may include facilities, equipment, supervision, instruction and exercise recommendations and testing.

Facilities

As a personal trainer, you have an obligation to make sure that the facilities you use are free from unreasonable hazards. This may pose a problem if you conduct exercise sessions in your clients' homes or in places of business where you have little control over the setting. You must select the workout area carefully, giving special attention to the following:

- ✔ Floor surface. Many exercises require floor surfaces that will cushion the feet, knees and legs from excessive stress.
- ✔ Adequate free space around workout stations.
- ✔ Appropriate use of public spaces. Use of public beaches, parks or public trails for business is illegal in some areas. Check with a local attorney.
- ✔ Ethical use of other business establishments. Accompanying a client into a fitness center may violate laws as well as ethical business practice. A local attorney can advise you.

Because your primary responsibility is your client's safety, inspect facilities regularly using a safety checklist. If you notice an unsafe facility, you must notify the club management or client. If a club owner does not repair the problem and your client is injured, you are technically responsible. However, juries have often looked favorably on employees who have tried unsuccessfully to persuade management to correct dangerous conditions.

Often, the client may not wish to follow your suggestions for making a safer environment because it does not fit their home's decor. In this case, the client is assuming responsibility for these conditions. Whether a dangerous situation occurs in a club or at a client's home, you must make a professional assessment and decide whether or not to continue.

Equipment

Fitness programs may utilize a variety of equipment, and injuries from the use of exercise equipment give rise to a majority of the litigation in the fitness industry. To protect both you and your clients, all of your equipment should meet the highest safety and design standards. Avoid using homemade equipment because your liability is greater if it causes injury to your client. You must be concerned about the selection, maintenance and repair of the equipment you use with your clients, and inspect it on a regular basis. Here's why: An injured woman claimed that she had not been properly warned of the risks involved in the use of a given piece of equipment. She further claimed that the equipment had not been properly maintained and that she had not been thoroughly instructed on how to safely use it. The court agreed and she was awarded $20,000.

You may find a conflict between professional practice and legal protection when it comes to equipment owned by a client. A conservative legal stance would be to avoid any contact and adjustment to the client's equipment, but most personal trainers accept some liability by using their expertise to adjust a client's equipment or to recommend maintenance. Here's an example: A personal trainer arrives at a client's home for an initial fitness session and finds a leg extension machine with a frayed cable. The trainer should inform the client that the equipment needs repairs, suggest that they call the company to order a replacement part, and then conduct sessions without using this equipment until it has been repaired.

Recommendations. If a client asks for recommendations about exercise equipment, clothing or shoes, you should be cautious in giving advice, particularly if you receive payment for endorsing a product or retail store. Before giving advice, you should become completely knowledgeable about the products and equipment available, as well as their advantages and disadvantages. Your other option would be to protect yourself by referring clients to their choice of retail sporting goods stores. Advice based solely on personal experience should be given with that express qualification.

Supervision

Although an instructor conducting a large aerobic class may have difficulty ensuring each client's safety, as a personal trainer, you should always be in direct control and in close contact with each client to ensure their safety. You should never leave the client during an exercise session in which direct supervision is needed. If you are working with a couple, position yourself where you can observe both persons during an activity without turning your back on one or the other. If you ask one client to perform an exercise that requires direct supervision, don't ask the other client to perform the same exercise. Instead, engage them in an activity requiring only general observation to ensure safety. For example, you wouldn't ask one client to do squats with a heavy weight while the other is doing a one-rep max in the bench press. You can't spot both clients at the same time. A safer option would be to have one client stretching or working out on a stationary bike while the other is lifting and being spotted. Proper supervision requires planning to ensure that each client can be monitored at all times.

You also must adequately plan for any emergencies that may arise (see Chapter 16). When training a client, you should always have their emergency medical information with you. This eliminates the need to call back to your office for critical information about your client in the event of an emergency. Determine the availability and location of your client's telephone, as well as the address of your training location. Whether in independent practice or in a club, you should know how to activate the emergency medical system (this is done by calling 911 in most areas).

Instruction

To avoid potential litigation, your instructional techniques should be consistent with current professional practices. If you fail to demonstrate a movement or give proper instructions on how to use a piece of equipment, and your client is injured, you may be found negligent. Legal standards require that you give a client "adequate and proper" instruction before and during an activity. In a courtroom, an expert witness could be asked to assess "proper" or factually correct instruction. Adequate and proper instruction also means avoiding contraindicated exercises, or those not recommended by professional peers. Advocating dangerous or controversial exercises puts you at risk for a lawsuit if a client is injured.

A relatively new aspect of instructional liability concerns touching clients. You should avoid touching a client unless it is essential in instruction. Furthermore, you should inform your clients about the purpose of touching; if the client objects, find an alternative. Charges of sexual assault, even if groundless, can have disastrous consequences on your personal training career.

Safety Guidelines

In reference to the above mentioned areas of responsibility, personal trainers should adhere to the following safety guidelines in the conduct of their activities.

- ✔ Be sure that all sessions are well-planned, sequential and documented.
- ✔ Communicate and enforce all safety rules for equipment use.
- ✔ Be sure that equipment meets or exceeds all industry standards.
- ✔ Inspect all equipment prior to use and document maintenance.
- ✔ Never allow unsupervised activity by the client.
- ✔ Limit participation to those under contract (i.e., no friends).
- ✔ Clearly warn clients about the specific risks of planned activities.

- ✔ Be sure that all activities selected are within the areas of your training.
- ✔ Be sure that clients are wearing any necessary protective equipment (i.e., weight lifting belts, athletic supporter or sports bra.)
- ✔ Review your emergency plan (access to a phone and 911 for EMS).
- ✔ Stay up-to-date with certifications and education in the field.

Exercise Recommendations and Testing

Many states allow exercise prescriptions to be developed only by licensed doctors. It is important for you to be sure that you are providing exercise programs, not exercise prescriptions. Although the difference between these terms may sound like a technicality, it could become an important issue in a courtroom. To protect yourself, be sure you are following exercise program guidelines recommended by professional organizations such as the American Council on Exercise (ACE), the National Strength and Conditioning Association (NSCA), the American College of Sports Medicine (ACSM) and the American Heart Association (AHA). According to fitness and legal expert David Herbert (1992), guidelines such as these, while not bearing the same legal impact as a specific law, may well establish an acceptable **standard of care**. Of course, the age, medical history and previous activity patterns of each client must be taken into consideration. An excellent resource for applicable standards of practice for personal trainers is *The Standards Book for Exercise Programs,* (Professional Reports Corporation).

Trainers also should be familiar with the position statements (papers) for specific populations developed by these organizations. The NSCA has produced a position paper on weight training for prepubescent youth; the American College of Obstetricians and Gynecologists has produced resource material on women and exercise; and an extensive article in *The Physician and Sportsmedicine* details the exercise precautions for pregnant women.

You may administer fitness assessments if the tests are recognized by a professional organization as appropriate for the intended use and are within the scope of your qualifications and training. For example, the ACSM has established protocols for fitness assessments as well as training and **certification** in several areas of testing. You should carefully follow ACSM procedures when conducting these tests; never attempt to administer a test that you have not been trained to perform. You can legally administer tests that do not require maximum effort, therefore, you should not hook up electrodes and administer a maximum capacity test, such as a treadmill stress test, unless a qualified physician is present and oversees the test. Any highly specialized testing should be conducted by physicians or exercise physiologists. Some states regulate the administration of tests such as **Graded Exercise Tests (GXTs)**. In addition, some professional associations, such as the ACSM, the American Heart Association and the American College of Cardiology, provide certification for testing as well as guidelines for the role of physicians in GXTs. Even physicians can be sued in the area of testing. In one recent case, a physician examined a man who wanted to begin an exercise program and gave the man a resting electrocardiogram (ECG), not a GXT. A few days later the man died while jogging, and the courts found in favor of the plaintiff, awarding $500,000 to his estate.

The development of exercise technology has offered several dilemmas for personal trainers, among them the legal concern over monitoring clients who can attach electrodes to their chests and continuously monitor their heart rates while exercising. You must make every effort to monitor your clients during exercise, with or without the fancy technology currently available. Failure to do so may constitute a breach of legal duty.

Legal Responsibilities

"I, ________________, have enrolled in a program of strenuous physical activity including, but not limited to, aerobic dance, weight training, stationary bicycling and the use of various aerobic-conditioning machinery offered by ____[name of business]____. I hereby affirm that I am in good physical condition and do not suffer from any disability that would prevent or limit my participation in this exercise program."

"In consideration of my participation in ____[name of business]____ exercise program, I, ________________, for myself, my heirs and assigns, hereby release [name of business]____ (its employees and owners), from any claims, demands and causes of action arising from my participation in the exercise program."

"I fully understand that I may injure myself as a result of my participation in [name of business]____ exercise program and I, ________________, hereby release [name of business] from any liability now or in the future including, but not limited to, heart attacks, muscle strains, pulls or tears, broken bones, shin splints, heat prostration, knee/lower back/foot injuries, and any other illness, soreness, or injury, however caused, occurring during or after my participation in the exercise program."

____

Signature

____

Date

I hereby affirm that I have read and fully understand the above.

____

Signature

FIGURE 17.1 Sample waiver of liability/informed consent.

This form should not be adopted for use without individual legal review and consultation.

Please note that this waiver is only a guideline, compiled from the forms upheld in Illinois, Minnesota and Tennessee. The rules vary from state to state, so do not expect this particular waiver to hold up in your state court. See your attorney for advice.

If your attorney discovers that waivers of liability are not upheld in your state, redraft your waiver to comply with these recommendations anyway. You never know when the law may change.

Legal Responsibilities

FIGURE 17.2
Sample informed consent form reprinted with permission from Herbert, D.L. and Herbert, W.G., *Legal Aspects of Preventive and Rehabilitative Exercise Programs,* Professional Reports Corporation. All rights reserved.

This form should not be adopted for use without individual legal review and consultation.

Informed Consent for Exercise Testing Procedures of Apparently Healthy Adults

Name ______________________________________

1. Purpose and Explanation of Test

It is my understanding that I will undergo a test to be performed on a motor driven treadmill or bicycle ergometer with the amount of effort gradually increasing. As I understand it, this increase in effort will continue until I feel and verbally report to the operator any symptoms such as fatigue, shortness of breath, or chest discomfort which may appear. It is my understanding, and I have been clearly advised, that it is my right to request that a test be stopped at any point if I feel unusual discomfort or fatigue. I have been advised that I should immediately upon experiencing any such symptoms, or if I so choose, inform the operator that I wish to stop the test at that or any other point. My stated wishes in this regard shall be carried out. **IF CORRECT, AND YOU AGREE AND UNDERSTAND, INITIAL HERE ______.**

It is further my understanding that prior to beginning the test, I will be connected by electrodes and cables to an electrocardiographic recorder which will enable the program personnel to monitor my cardiac (heart) activity. During the test itself, it is my understanding that a trained observer will monitor my responses continuously and take frequent readings of blood pressure, the electrocardiogram and my expressed feelings of effort. I realize that a true determination of my exercise capacity depends on progressing the test to the point of my fatigue. Once the test has been completed; but before I am released from the test area, I will be given special instructions about showering and recognition of certain symptoms which may appear within the first 24 hours after the test. I agree to follow these instructions and promptly contact the program personnel or medical providers if such symptoms develop. **IF CORRECT, AND YOU AGREE AND UNDERSTAND, INITIAL HERE ______.**

Before I undergo the test, I certify to the program that I am in good health and have had a physical examination conducted by a licensed medical physician within the last ______ months. Further, I hereby represent and inform the program that I have accurately completed the pre-test history interview presented to me by the program staff and have provided correct responses to the questions as indicated on the history form or as supplied to the interviewer. It is my understanding that I will be interviewed by a physician or other person prior to my under- going the test who will, in the course of interviewing me, determine if there are any reasons which would make it undesirable or unsafe for me to take the test. Consequently, I understand that it is important that I provide complete and accurate responses to the interviewer and recognize that my failure to do so could lead to

Legal Responsibilities

FIGURE 17.2 continued

possible unnecessary injury to myself during the test. **IF CORRECT, AND YOU AGREE, INITIAL HERE ______.**

2. Risks

It is my understanding that there exists the possibility of adverse changes during the actual test. I have been informed that these changes could include abnormal blood pressure, fainting, disorders of heart rhythm and very rare instances of heart attack or even death. These risks include, but are not necessarily limited to, the possibility of stroke or other cerebrovascular incident or occurrence; mental, physiological, motor, visual or hearing injuries, deficiencies, difficulties or disturbances; partial or total paralysis; slips, falls, or other unintended loss of balance or bodily movement related to the exercise treadmill (or bicycle ergometer) which may cause muscular, neurological, orthopedic, or other bodily injury; as well as a variety of other possible occurrences, any one of which could conceivably, however remotely, cause bodily injury, impairment, disability or death. Any procedure such as this one carries with it some risk however unlikely or remote. THERE ARE ALSO OTHER RISKS OF INJURY, IMPAIRMENT, DISABILITY, DISFIGUREMENT, AND EVEN DEATH. **I ACKNOWLEDGE AND AGREE TO ASSUME ALL RISK. IF YOU UNDERSTAND AND AGREE, INITIAL HERE _____.**

I have been told every effort will be made to minimize these occurrences by preliminary examination and by precautions and observations taken during the test. I have also been informed that emergency equipment and personnel are readily available to deal with these unusual situations should they occur.

Knowing and understanding all risks, it is my desire to proceed to take the test as herein described. **IF CORRECT, AND YOU AGREE AND UNDERSTAND, INITIAL HERE ______.**

3. Benefits to be Expected and Alternatives Available to the Exercise Testing Procedure

I understand and have been told that the results of this test may or may not benefit me. Potential benefits relate mainly to my personal motives for taking the test, i.e., knowing my exercise capacity in relation to the general population, understanding my fitness for certain sports and recreational activities. Although my fitness might also be evaluated by alternative means, e.g., a bench step test or an outdoor running test, such tests do not provide as accurate a fitness assessment as the treadmill or bike test, nor do those options allow equally effective monitoring of my responses. **IF YOU UNDERSTAND, INITIAL HERE ______.**

4. Consent

I hereby consent to voluntarily engage in an exercise test to determine my circulatory and respiratory fitness. I also consent to the taking of samples of my exhaled air during exercise to properly measure my oxygen consumption. I also

Legal Responsibilities

FIGURE 17.2 continued

consent, if necessary, to have a small blood sample drawn by needle from my arm for blood chemistry analysis, and to the performance of lung function and body-fat (skinfold pinch) tests. It is my understanding that the information obtained will help me evaluate future physical fitness and sports activities in which I may engage. **IF CORRECT, AND YOU AGREE, INITIAL HERE ______.**

5. Confidentiality and Use of Information

I have been informed that the information which is obtained in this exercise test will be treated as privileged and confidential and will consequently not be released or revealed to any person without my express written consent. I do, however, agree to the use of any information for research or statistical purposes, so long as same does not provide facts which could lead to the identification of my person. Any other information obtained, however, will be used only by the program staff to evaluate my exercise status or needs. **IF YOU AGREE, INITIAL HERE ______.**

6. Inquiries and Freedom of Consent

I have been given an opportunity to ask questions as to the procedures. Generally these requests, which have been noted by the testing staff, and their responses are as follows:

____

____

____

____

IF THIS NOTATION IS COMPLETE AND CORRECT, INITIAL HERE ______.

I acknowledge that I have read this document in its entirety or that it has been read to me if I have been unable to read the same.

I consent to the rendition of all services and procedures as explained herein by all program personnel. Date ________

________________ Witness' Signature	________________ Participant's Signature
________________ Witness' Signature	________________ Spouse's Consent
	________________ Test Supervisor's Signature

Legal Responsibilities

AGREEMENT AND RELEASE OF LIABILITY

1. In consideration of being allowed to participate in the activities and programs of ____________________ and to use its facilities, equipment and machinery in addition to the payment of any fee or charge, I do hereby waive, release and forever discharge ____________________ and its officers, agents, employees, representatives, executors, and all others from any and all responsibilities or liability from injuries or damages resulting from my participation in any activities, or my use of equipment or machinery in the above mentioned activities. I do also hereby release all of those mentioned, and any others acting upon their behalf, from any responsibility or liability for any injury or damage to myself, including those caused by the negligent act or omission of any of those mentioned or others acting on their behalf, or in any way arising out of or connected with my participation in any activities of __________________ or the use of any equipment at ____.
(*Please initial* ______)

2. I understand and am aware that strength, flexibility, and aerobic exercise, including the use of equipment, is a potentially hazardous activity. I also understand that fitness activities involve a risk of injury and even death, and that I am voluntarily participating in these activities and using equipment and machinery with knowledge of the dangers involved. I hereby agree to expressly assume and accept any and all risks of injury or death.
(*Please initial* ______)

3. I do hereby further declare myself to be physically sound and suffering from no condition, impairment, disease, infirmity or other illness that would prevent my participation or use of equipment or machinery except as hereinafter stated. I do hereby acknowledge that I have been informed of the need for a physician's approval for my participation in an exercise/fitness activity or in the use of exercise equipment and machinery. I also acknowledge that it has been recommended that I have a yearly or more frequent physical examination and consultation with my physician as to physical activity, exercise and use of exercise and training equipment so that I might have his/her recommendations concerning these fitness activities and equipment use. I acknowledge that I have either had a physical examination and been given my physicians permission to participate, or that I have decided to participate in activity and use of equipment and machinery without the approval of my physician and do hereby assume all responsibility for my participation and activities, and utilization of equipment and machinery in my activities.

Date ____________________ Signature ____

FIGURE 17.3
Sample waiver of liability reprinted with permission from Koeberle, B. E., *Legal Aspects of Personal Fitness Training*, Professional Reports Corporation.

This form should not be adopted for use without individual legal review and consultation.

Legal Concepts and Defenses

LEGAL CONCEPTS AND DEFENSES

It is essential that, as a personal trainer, you conduct your professional activities with the highest standards, not only for your professional competence and training, but also for your ethical and legal position. In court, certain concepts have special meanings that you should be familiar with in order to protect both yourself and your clients. Some of these concepts have already been discussed. The remainder of this chapter will present several other legal concepts that are important to you.

Standard of Care

Your actions as a personal trainer must be appropriate for the age, condition and knowledge of the client, as well as for the program selected. To evaluate the standard of care, a court would typically ask an expert witness to describe the current professional standards — what other fitness professionals of similar training would do (or should have done) in the same situation. This manual, for example, constitutes a standard for personal training. With ACE certification in personal training, your competence could be verified. In addition, your conduct would be compared to the standards presented in the manual and your ethics would be equated to the ACE **Code of Ethics** located in Appendix A. In a legal dispute, a court would almost certainly look to the practices described in this manual to evaluate the appropriateness of a trainer's actions.

Assumption of Risk

If a client voluntarily accepts the dangers known to be part of an activity, the trainer can use the **assumption of risk defense.** However, the two most important issues here are "voluntarily" and "known danger." If a client's participation was involuntary, this defense cannot be used. Furthermore, if the client was not informed about the specific risks of the program or test, the client cannot be held to have assumed them. Does this defense imply that a trainer must describe every injury that might occur? Yes, in general, but the best way to take care of this issue is to use standard forms for **informed consent** (express assumption of risk) or **waiver** forms.

Known technically as exculpatory agreements, waivers, informed consents and warnings fall under contract law, and are often used by exercise leaders and fitness centers to absolve themselves of liability. Although many fitness professionals have little faith in the value of these documents, the courts have been increasingly willing to uphold them.

Informed Consent. When a client signs an **informed consent** form, they are acknowledging that they have been specifically informed about the risk associated with the activity they are about to engage in (Figure 17.1). Some personal trainers use an informed consent form in a similar manner to a waiver (Figure 17.2), but it is primarily intended to communicate the dangers of the program or test procedures to the client. You should obtain signed informed consent forms from every person who enters your programs and before every test you administer. Nygaard and Boone (1989) recommend that you let your clients know that questions about the program or testing are welcome, and that they are free to withdraw consent and discontinue participation at any time. You should inform your clients about:

- ✔ The exercise program or test, providing a thorough and unbiased explanation of the purpose of each.
- ✔ The risks and possible discomforts involved.
- ✔ The benefits they might expect.
- ✔ Alternatives that may be advantageous to them.

Warnings. In one Colorado case, a health club's failure to warn a client about the dangers of an activity and piece of equipment was judged "willful and wanton" misconduct. You should obtain signed proof that you have warned your clients about any foreseeable hazards and risks.

Waivers. A voluntary abandonment of the right to file suit, waivers are used to release you from liability for injuries resulting from an exercise program. Waivers must be clearly written and indicate that the client waives all claims for damages, even those caused by the trainer's negligence (Figures 17.1 and 17.3). Occasionally, these documents are so poorly worded that they hold little value in court.

Case law regarding the validity of waivers, warnings and informed consent documents is complicated. One such case, Brown vs. Racquetball Centers, Inc. (1987), shows that the specific wording of the form is critical in the eyes of the court. In this particular case, the form did not contain language clearly stating the risks of participating in the program (Herbert, July 1989). Other cases demonstrate support for well-written waivers (Gimpel vs. Host Enterprises, Inc. (1986); Schlobohm vs. Spa Petite (1982); Larsen vs. Vic Tanny International (1984). Courts prefer to deal with these issues on a case-by-case basis. You should consult with attorneys in your own state, providing them with examples to use as a model.

Negligence

Someone who fails to perform as a reasonable and prudent person would under similar circumstances is considered negligent. This definition has two important components: failure to act and appropriateness of the action. A person can be sued both for neglecting something that should have been done, such as not spotting a client in a free-weight bench press, and for doing something that should not have been done, such as prescribing straight-leg sit-ups for a client with low-back problems. This action may be found inappropriate as compared with what a reasonable and prudent professional would do.

To substantiate a charge of negligence in court, the plaintiff must establish four elements:

- ✔ The defendant had a duty to protect the plaintiff from injury.
- ✔ The defendant failed to exercise the standard of care necessary to perform that duty.
- ✔ Damage or injury to the plaintiff occurred.
- ✔ This damage or injury was caused by the defendant's breach of duty (proximate causation).

Negligence in personal training could occur, for example, if you agreed to provide instruction and supervision (duties) in weight lifting, and during the first session told the client you would spot them during a lift but failed to do so (breach of duty). Perhaps the client suffered broken ribs and was unable to work for three months, incurring both medical bills and lost wages (damages). The damages would not have occurred if you had not failed to spot for the client during the lift (proximal causation).

Contributory Negligence. If the client played some role in getting injured, a few states prohibit the recovery of damages (check your local state laws). For example, a client might exceed their recommended heart rate. It would be important to determine whether the trainer was present when the client was hurt, or whether the client was exercising alone and following the trainer's guidelines. If present, the trainer might have noticed the client's over-taxation and warned them about exceeding the recommendations.

Comparative Negligence. A court may apportion guilt and any subsequent award for damages, measuring the relative fault of both the plaintiff and the defendant.

Table 17.2
Make Sure You're Covered

General Liability	Disability
There are several types of coverage available to health and fitness professionals. General liability insurance covers basic trip and fall injuries that occur in a nonbusiness environment. These policies will not provide coverage for accidents that occur at work.	Disability insurance, which provides income protection should you become injured, may or may not be supplied by your employer. If it is not provided, you may want to consider purchasing this type of insurance for yourself. While worker's compensation covers you when you are injured on or by the job, disability insurance will provide income even if your injury occurs outside of work.
Professional Liability	**Medical Insurance**
Professional liability insurance is designed to protect you against a broad spectrum of claims. This includes allegations claiming injury to students or clients as a result of improper supervision of fitness activities, failure to adequately instruct, improper use or recommendation of equipment and exposure to injury from substandard facilities. This coverage should extend to acts of omission (things you didn't do) as well as acts of commission (actual conduct). Most policies also extend coverage for violations of a client's civil rights, such as sexual harassment, an important element to consider in today's sensitive environment. Defense coverage should be extended even if the charges are groundless.	Individual medical insurance, which provides hospitalization and major medical coverage, is another type of coverage that may be supplied by your employer. These plans vary widely and, because of increasing costs, many clubs have reduced or eliminated these benefits as a cost-saving measure. Rarely are independent contractors granted benefits.

The court or jury then determines the percentage of responsibility of each party to prorate the award. This defense can be useful if a client is somewhat to blame in injuring themself.

LIABILITY INSURANCE

Whether you are a seasoned veteran or a newcomer to the fitness profession, a complete understanding of insurance is essential to your success. Because of the rise in litigation throughout the healthcare industry, purchasing insurance has become one of the best risk-management strategies available to health and fitness professionals. Judgments for millions of dollars are not uncommon, and few could weather such a substantial financial blow. Insurance protection also provides peace of mind; you can be secure in the knowledge that if someone were to be injured as a result of your actions, insurance coverage would be adequate to recompense that individual for their losses.

Protection for You

Generally, an insurance policy is a contract designed to protect you and your assets from litigation. There is, however, a sarcastic yet often accurate saying that insurance companies are in the business of collecting premiums and denying claims. Table 17.2 provides a breakdown of the types of coverage available and the provisions of specific policies. It is important to familiarize yourself with these terms before you rush out to purchase an insurance policy.

Independent Contractors

If you are an independent contractor working for clubs or other facilities, you should pay special attention to your coverage. It is imperative that all aspects of any coverage that may be provided for you are understood and included in the written agreements for services. If insurance coverage is not provided by the club, it is in your own best interest, as well as that of your clients, to provide yourself with adequate coverage.

Locating Coverage

Insurance is predicated on a system whereby the risks of financial loss are distributed over policy holders. Therefore, policies available through various professional associations often provide the best value because the risks are spread over a large number of policy holders. Membership in these organizations does not automatically provide this coverage, but these organizations have arrangements that give members the right to purchase policies at a reduced rate. Individual policies are available in the marketplace but are considerably more expensive.

Riders

Some companies offer "business pursuits riders" or "umbrella coverage" that extend current coverage on your residential property or apply a blanket amount to both personal and professional activities. These policies are often less expensive than the policies available through professional associations, but may exclude certain professions. A check with your insurance carrier is certainly warranted.

Words to Choose Your Policy By

The basic tenet of insurance is to obligate the company to defend you as well as to pay for any damages adjudged against you. The following statement, or some version of it, should be included in any basic agreement:

We agree to pay those sums that the insured becomes legally obligated to pay as damages because of bodily injury or property damage to which this insurance applies, and will include damages arising out of any negligent act, error or omission in rendering or failing to render professional services described in this policy.

A key provision here indicates that the company will pay even if you fail to provide a service. For example, if an injured person needed first-aid attention and you did not provide it, the policy would still protect you. If "failure to render" or "omission" were not specified, the policy would cover you only if the services you provided were inadequate or improper.

Coverage Where You Need It

When choosing an insurance policy, be sure to describe in detail all of the types of professional services for which you are seeking coverage. If a claim is made, the company will look very closely at the nature of the activity in which the injury occurred. If it was not specified in the policy, the company might deny the claim. Carefully examine the types of services covered to be sure that the ones you provide your clients are included.

Make Sure Legal Fees are Covered

Another important element of an insurance policy is related to coverage of legal fees, settlements and defense charges. Look for the following clause before signing on the dotted line:

We will have the right and duty to defend any suit seeking damages under this policy, even if the allegations are groundless, false or fraudulent and may, at our discretion, make such investigation and settlement of any claim or suit deemed expedient.

The best policies cover the cost of a legal defense and any claims awarded. Policies that only cover an amount equal to awarded damages are not recommended. If you go to court, all of the trial expenses incurred will be your responsibility. A good policy should cover the cost of a legal defense as well as the amount of damages awarded.

Find Out What Is Not Covered

While it is important to identify and understand what is covered, it is also critical to know what is not covered. Most policies delineate specific exclusions. The following liabilities are often excluded in fitness professional policies: abuse, molestation, cancer (resulting from tanning), libel and slander.

You should also inquire whether your bodily insurance coverage will protect you if a suit is filed alleging mental stress. Most policies differentiate between the two, and a standard bodily injury clause does not include mental injuries. A client filing a suit might claim that you were overly critical and, as a result, they suffered mental injuries. The courts are split on the issue of inclusion. Recent litigation in New York found that bodily injury included mental distress, while a California court said it did not.

Past, Present and Future Claims

Finally, most policies exclude coverage for acts committed before the policy was purchased. Coverage also might be excluded for claims that occurred during the policy period, but are filed after the coverage has been terminated. These issues are related to the "claims-made basis" of a policy. You can purchase "prior acts coverage" from most insurance carriers for an additional cost. An analysis of your past actions should guide your decision in this area. An "extended reporting endorsement" will insure that claims made in the future for injuries during the policy period will be covered even if you decide to cancel your policy.

As with all business endeavors, you should closely evaluate an insurance company before purchasing a policy. The most reputable insurance carriers have a national affiliation, are licensed, have strong financial backing and have a reinsurer (corporate policy to insure that policy holders' claims will be met even if their business collapses). You may also want to check whether or not the company has had complaints filed with state insurance commissions or the Better Business Bureau.

While understanding the language and details of insurance policies can be difficult, keep in mind that your insurance agent works for you. It is their responsibility to give you a complete explanation and answer any questions you may have. By understanding the basic principles outlined here, you will have a head start on finding the insurance coverage to meet your professional needs.

OTHER BUSINESS CONCERNS WITH LEGAL IMPLICATIONS

In addition to your legal responsibilities in the areas of **scope of practice**, facilities, equipment, testing, instruction and supervision, you must be aware of the legal implications of such business concerns as use of musical recordings and certification.

Music

All the popular recordings on radio and television have been protected by artists and studios with copyrights. Any use of this material for profit is a violation of federal law, even if you have purchased the recording. Recordings sold commercially are intended strictly for the private, noncommercial use of the purchaser. Although two groups, ASCAP and BMI, will issue licenses for the commercial use of recordings, their fees are probably prohibitive for most personal trainers. You might find it more economical to use recordings designed and sold for fitness and aerobic programs. Another option is for your clients to purchase their own recordings for use during workouts. In effect, the clients are then using these recordings for their own private, non-commercial enjoyment during exercise.

Certification

Although there are currently no federal laws requiring licensure or certification for personal trainers (Herbert, 1992), certification from a professional organization can assist a defendant by providing evidence of **competency**. It also is important to note that certification does not protect against findings of negligence. In fact, some trainers believe that juries will hold certified personal trainers to a higher standard of care than noncertified trainers. In reality, however, negligence is negligence, and a competent attorney can expose a substandard performance in either case. Most legal experts acknowledge that certification demonstrates minimal competency in the fitness profession. It also will help you assure clients that they are receiving instruction from a knowledgeable and recognized professional.

Bloodborne Pathogens

In special circumstances, you may be involved in situations where a client bleeds. For instance, you may be working with a client who is a boxer or is engaged in other contact sports. In situations where you are exposed to a client's blood, special precautions must be followed. The Occupational Safety and Health Administration (OSHA) has issued guidelines for handling exposure to blood. Because a variety of maladies can be transmitted through contact with human blood (human immunodeficiency virus, hepatitis, etc.), trainers should have access to protective gloves and exercise caution when exposed to and disposing of any blood-contaminated materials. Trainers involved in contact sports should contact OSHA for more complete details.

Risk Management

Periodically reviewing programs, facilities and equipment to evaluate potential dangers to clients allows you to decide the best way to reduce costly injuries in each situation. This is called **risk management**.

Most authorities recommend a risk management protocol that consists of the ensuing five steps:

1. Identification of risks — the specification of all risks that may be encountered by the personal trainer in the areas of instruction, supervision, facilities, equipment, contracts and business structure.

Table 17.3
Risk Probability

	Frequent	Likely	Occasional	Seldom
Catastrophic	Extreme	Extreme	High	High
Critical	Extreme	Extreme	High	Medium
Moderate	Extreme	High	Medium	Low
Negligible	High	Medium	Low	Low

2. Evaluation of each risk — the personal trainer must review each risk with consideration given to the probability that the risk could occur and if so, what would be the conceivable severity. Table 17.3 can be used to assess the identified risks.

3. Selection of an approach for managing each risk — several approaches are available to the personal trainer for managing and reducing the identified risks.

Following are the most common methods of reducing risk:

- ✔ transfer of risk, as with insurance policies
- ✔ reduction (through continuing education)
- ✔ retention (budgeting for minor emergencies)
- ✔ avoidance of certain activities or equipment

The recommended approach for risks that are extreme is to avoid the activity completely or transfer the risk through appropriate insurance. Risks that fall into one of the high categories can be managed either through insurance or viable actions to reduce the likelihood of occurrence or severity of outcome. Reduction is also the preferred method for addressing risks in the medium category while risks with low impact can be handled through retention.

4. Implementation — putting your plans into practice.

Summary

5. Evaluation — assessing the outcome of your risk management endeavors.

You also can manage risk by examining procedures and policies and developing conduct and safety guidelines for your clients' use of equipment. Strict safety guidelines for each activity, accompanied by procedures for emergencies, are particularly important. You must not only develop these policies but become thoroughly familiar with them, mentally practicing your emergency plans. Several lawsuits have resulted in substantial judgments against fitness professionals who failed to respond to the emergency medical needs of clients. Once risks are identified, you should carry out the actions needed to reduce them.

SUMMARY

Although often overlooked when considering the technical aspects of providing quality personalized fitness instruction, the legal, ethical and business concerns are of paramount importance. You accept a tremendous amount of responsibility when you assume the role of personal trainer. You must always be aware of your scope of practice and, because of the rise in litigation across all aspects of the profession, it is absolutely essential to maintain adequate insurance coverage. This chapter touched on the legal, ethical and business issues that must be considered. The guidelines offered are not legal advice. Rather, they are a condensed presentation of the technicalities that you, as a responsible trainer, must understand.

REFERENCES

Herbert, D.L. (1989). Appropriate use of wellness appraisals. *Fitness Management,* September, 23.

Herbert, D.L. (1989). Prospective releases must conform to law. *Fitness Management,* July, 24.

Herbert, D.L. (1992). *The Standards Book for Exercise Programs.* Canton: Professional Reports Corporation.

Nygaard, G. & Boone, T.H. (1989). *Law for Physical Educators and Coaches.* Columbus: Publishing Horizons.

SUGGESTED READINGS

Brooks, D. (1990). Going Solo: *The Art of Personal Training.* (2nd ed.) Los Angeles: Moves International.

Herbert, D.L. & Herbert, W. G. (1989). *Legal Aspects of Preventive and Rehabilitative Exercise Programs.* Canton: Professional Reports Corporation.

Koeberle, B.E. (1990). *Legal Aspects of Personal Training.* Canton: Professional Reports Corporation.

Koeberle, B.E. (1989). Personal fitness liability: A trainer's guide to legal fitness. *The Exercise Standards and Malpractice Reporter,* October, 74-79.

Kooperman, S. (1989). Liability waivers: Can they really work? *IDEA Business Today*, May, 2-3.

Kooperman, S. (1989). Should you sign a waiver? *Shape,* August, 99.

Kooperman, S. (1986). In defense of health clubs. *Dance Exercise Today,* September, 29-30.

Stotlar, D.K. (1988). The liability crises. *Dance Exercise Today*, March, 26-31.

Stotlar, D.K. (1987). The dance-exercise industry and independent contractors: The legal issues. *Dance Exercise Today*, May, 45-46.

APPENDIX A Code of Ethics

ACE-certified Professionals are guided by the following principles of conduct as they interact with clients, the public and other health and fitness professionals.

ACE-certified Professionals will endeavor to:

- ✔ Provide safe and effective instruction.
- ✔ Provide equal and fair treatment to all clients.
- ✔ Maintain an understanding of the latest health and physical activity research and its applications.
- ✔ Maintain current CPR certification and knowledge of first-aid services.
- ✔ Comply with all applicable business, employment and copyright laws.
- ✔ Uphold and enhance public appreciation and trust for the health and fitness industry.
- ✔ Maintain the confidentiality of all client information.
- ✔ Refer clients to more qualified fitness, medical or health professionals when appropriate.

APPENDIX B

ACE Personal Trainer Certification Examination Content Outline

PURPOSE

In October 1994, the American Council on Exercise® (ACE®) and Columbia Assessment Services, Inc. conducted a role delineation study to identify the primary tasks performed by personal trainers. The fundamental purpose of this study was to establish and validate appropriate content areas for the ACE Personal Trainer Certification Examination. The result of this process includes this exam content outline which sets forth the tasks, knowledge and skills necessary for a personal trainer to perform job responsibilities at a minimum professional level. It is the position of ACE that the recommendations outlined here are not exhaustive to the qualifications of a personal trainer but represent a minimum level of proficiency and theoretical knowledge.

Please note that not all knowledge and skill statements listed in the exam content outline will be addressed on each exam administration.

DESCRIPTION

An ACE-certified Personal Trainer works in a health/fitness facility or in another appropriate setting administering individualized physical activity programs to asymptomatic individuals, or individuals who have been cleared by a physician.

ACE-certified Personal Trainers will be competent to assess a client's health/medical/ fitness status effectively, design safe and effective physical activity programs utilizing goal setting, exercise science principles and safety guidelines, implement the exercise program safely and effectively, modifying the program as necessary in order to achieve reasonable goals, and adhere to all codes, laws and procedures applicable within the recognized scope of practice for personal trainers.

The ACE Personal Trainer Certification will be given to those who meet the following prerequisites: maintaining current adult CPR certification, being at least 18 years of age, and passing an entry-level examination measuring ACE-identified competencies. This certification is appropriate for individuals working one-on-one, with small groups or as floor staff, etc. The certification will be valid for a two-year period at which time it may be renewed. Requirement for renewal will be 1.5 continuing education credits (CECs) and applicable fee.

Attention Exam Candidates!

When preparing for an ACE certification exam, be aware that the material presented in this manual, or any text, may become outdated due to the evolving nature of the fitness industry, as well as new developments in current and ongoing research. These exams are based on an in-depth job analysis and an industry-wide validation survey. By design, these exams assess a candidate's knowledge and application of the most current scientifically-based professional standards and guidelines. The dynamic nature of this field requires that ACE certification exams be regularly updated in order to ensure that they reflect the latest industry findings and research. Therefore, the knowledge and skills required to pass these exams are not solely represented in this or any industry text.

In addition to learning the material presented in this manual, ACE strongly encourages all exam candidates and fitness professionals to keep abreast of new developments, guidelines and standards from a variety of valid industry resources.

Percentages indicate how much of the examination is devoted to each area. The number of questions on the exam is shown in parentheses. Please note that a basic knowledge of anatomy, exercise physiology, kinesiology and nutrition is assumed for this examination.

I. Client Assessment

24% (43 questions)

A. Establish rapport to collect accurate, comprehensive information

B. Obtain health/medical and lifestyle information to aid in client evaluation, program design and referral

C. Identify client expectations and preferences

D. Perform fitness evaluations and periodic re-evaluations

II. Program Design

22% (38 questions)

A. Establish realistic and measurable short- and long-term goals

B. Integrate goals, assessment data and principles of exercise science to design program

III. Program Implementation

37% (65 questions)

A. Teach safe, effective exercise technique

B. Monitor, record and evaluate progress to make appropriate program modifications

C. Facilitate adherence to exercise

D. Maintain a supportive relationship to facilitate goal achievement

E. Consult with medical/health professionals, as necessary

IV. Professional Responsibility

17% (29 questions)

A. Adhere to ACE code of ethics, laws, regulations and procedures within recognized scope of practice

B. Use informed consents and waivers appropriately

C. Develop and follow safety and emergency procedures

D. Ensure competence through ongoing education

E. Obtain adequate insurance

F. Evaluate safety of equipment, facilities and locations

G. Ensure client confidentiality

PERFORMANCE DOMAIN I: CLIENT ASSESSMENT

A. Establish rapport through effective communication in order to obtain accurate and comprehensive information.

Knowledge of:

1. Communication techniques (e.g., active listening, appropriate eye contact, reflecting, other attending behaviors).
2. Techniques that build and enhance rapport.
3. Individual differences that may influence behavior (e.g., gender, age, culture, ethnicity).
4. Environmental factors that affect communication (e.g., location, noise, privacy).
5. Body language and nonverbal behavior.
6. Influence of learning style (e.g., comprehension rate, visual, auditory, kinesthetic) on communication.

Skill in:

1. Applying interview and communication techniques.
2. Selecting an appropriate environment for client consultation.
3. Using interview techniques (e.g., open-ended questioning, active listening, responding nonjudgmentally).
4. Modifying interaction style based on client's individual differences (e.g., gender, age, culture, ethnicity).

B. Obtain health/medical information in order to determine appropriateness for exercise, aid program design, and identify the need for medical referral using questionnaires, interviews and other available records.

Knowledge of:

1. Health conditions and risk factors that may interfere with the ability to exercise safely (e.g., diabetes, high cardiovascular risk, cardiovascular disease, hypercholesterolemia, orthopedic considerations, pregnancy).
2. Qualified local health/medical professionals to use as referral sources (e.g., physicians, psychotherapists, registered dietitians, physical therapists, athletic trainers, clinical exercise physiologists).
3. Criteria for referral to appropriate health/medical professionals.
4. Accepted exercise guidelines and their applications for test administration and participation in physical activity (e.g., American College of Sports Medicine [ACSM], American College of Obstetricians and Gynecologists [ACOG], American Heart Association [AHA]).
5. Components of a health history form that adequately document the client's health status (e.g., demographic information, health risk factors, medications, illness, surgery and injury history, family history).
6. Cardiovascular risk factors and their significance relative to referral, appropriate application of assessment tools, and physical activity.
7. Physiological effects of and appropriate precautions to take with a client taking medications and other substances (e.g., beta blockers, diuretics, antihistamines, tranquilizers, alcohol, diet pills, cold medications, caffeine, nicotine, antihypertensives).

Skill in:

1. Selecting, administering and interpreting health/medical information forms in order to make referrals as necessary.
2. Investigating client health conditions based on information obtained.
3. Applying industry guidelines (e.g., ACSM, ACOG, AHA) to referral, exercise test administration and physical activity programming.

C. Obtain lifestyle information as needed

in order to aid program design and optimize program adherence using interviews and/or questionnaires.

Knowledge of:

1. Components of a lifestyle information form (e.g., family support, career, physical activity habits, dietary patterns, social habits, stressors).
2. The relationship of lifestyle to health.

Skill in:

1. Developing and/or selecting and interpreting lifestyle information forms.

D. Identify the client's expectations and personal preferences to aid program design using interviews and/or questionnaires.

Knowledge of:

1. Techniques for obtaining client's preferences and expectations.
2. Techniques to determine the client's desire to maintain a program of regular physical activity.

Skill in:

1. Obtaining and assessing client's preferences, expectations and desire to maintain a program of regular physical activity.

E. Perform baseline evaluation and periodic re-evaluations of fitness levels and physical limitations using established protocols in order to aid program design and ensure safety and effectiveness.

Knowledge of:

1. Factors that determine appropriate intervals for re-evaluation (e.g., program goals and progress, client motivation, injury).
2. Factors that affect test results (e.g., test error, test conditions, client-related factors).
3. Procedures for converting raw data into a meaningful assessment of fitness (e.g., estimated oxygen consumption, muscular strength and endurance, flexibility, body composition).
4. Currently accepted fitness test norms.
5. Test selection criteria (e.g., client's age, gender, health, fitness, goals, test advantages and disadvantages, duration, safety, expense, facilities).
6. Techniques for obtaining heart rate and blood pressure.
7. Warning signs that require intervention (e.g., shortness of breath, dizziness, chest pain).
8. Techniques for assessing cardiorespiratory endurance (e.g., step test, field tests, cycle ergometer) and advantages and disadvantages as assessment tools.
9. Techniques for assessing body composition (e.g., hydrostatic weighing, skinfold calipers, bioimpedance, girth measurement, infrared refraction) and their advantages and disadvantages as assessment tools.
10. Techniques for assessing flexibility (e.g., sit and reach, shoulder ROM, hip flexion) and associated advantages and disadvantages of assessment tools.
11. Techniques for assessing muscular strength and endurance (e.g., push ups, sit ups, hand grip dynamometer, repetition-maximum tests) and advantages and disadvantages as assessment tools.
12. Physiological effects of, and appropriate precautions to take with a client taking medications and other substances (e.g., beta blockers, diuretics, antihistamines, tranquilizers, alcohol, diet pills, cold medications, caffeine, nicotine, antihypertensives).

Skill in:

1. Performing fitness tests, including cardiorespiratory endurance, muscular strength and endurance,

flexibility and body composition.
2. Applying test selection criteria and modifying test protocols based on health and medical information.
3. Obtaining heart rate and blood pressure.
4. Recognizing warning signs that require intervention (e.g., shortness of breath, dizziness, chest pain) and taking appropriate action.
5. Converting raw data into a meaningful assessment of fitness.
6. Recognizing inconsistencies between data and observations.
7. Communicating evaluation and re-evaluation results to client in a meaningful manner.

PERFORMANCE DOMAIN II: PROGRAM DESIGN

A. Establish realistic, measurable short- and long-term goals by acknowledging the client's expectations and reviewing assessment and re-assessment data in order to design and/or modify a safe and effective program.

Knowledge of:

1. Methods used to identify client goals (e.g., communication, questioning).
2. Qualities of a well-stated goal (i.e., specific, measurable, action-oriented, realistic and time-bound).
3. Safe and effective rates of change in physical fitness and body weight with respect to the development of exercise program recommendations.
4. Motivation, exercise adherence and behavior modification with respect to goal setting.
5. Fitness, health and lifestyle assessments and utilization of this data in goal setting.

Skill in:

1. Utilizing assessment and evaluation results for goal setting, adjustment and reinforcement.
2. Goal setting.

B. Apply the principles of exercise science in designing and modifying an individualized physical activity program by integrating the specific, measurable goals and interpreting assessment and re-assessment data in order to develop safe and effective programming.

Knowledge of:

1. Cardiorespiratory, musculoskeletal and basic neuromuscular anatomy.
2. Basic exercise science (e.g., cardiorespiratory, metabolic and neuromuscular exercise physiology, applied kinesiology and biomechanics).
3. Basic exercise psychology with respect to motivation, adherence and behavior modification.
4. Comprehensive physical activity program design and modification based on individual goals, evaluation and re-evaluation results, program progress and motivation.
5. Energy systems (e.g., aerobic, anaerobic, nonaerobic) and the relationship of these to training techniques.
6. The integration of the four components of fitness (cardiorespiratory endurance, muscular strength and endurance, flexibility and body composition) into a comprehensive physical activity program.
7. Principles and techniques of cardiorespiratory, muscular strength and endurance and flexibility conditioning.
8. Motor learning as it applies to skill acquisition (e.g., developmental stage, coordination considerations, neuromuscular patterning, visualization).
9. Biomechanical principles as they apply to exercise technique.
10. Exercise programming utilizing mode, intensity, frequency, duration and progression.
11. Exercise programming with respect to physical fitness, performance and health.

12. Physical activity programming for populations with special needs (e.g., conditions relating to aging, obesity, cardiovascular disease, arthritis, orthopedic disorders, pregnancy, youth, athletes, diabetes, osteoporosis) that have been cleared by their physician to take part in a program of regular physical activity.
13. Environmental conditions (e.g., heat, cold, altitude, smog) and their impact on physical activity.
14. The characteristics and application of exercise equipment (e.g., resistive, cardiorespiratory endurance).
15. The characteristics and application of isometric, isotonic and isokinetic exercise.
16. Modification of an exercise program with respect to a client's injury history and injury risk.
17. Benefits of participation in regular physical activity.
18. Applicable standards, guidelines and position statements published by accepted organizations (e.g., ACSM, YMCA, ACOG, ADA, AHA) to use in the formulation of recommendations.

19. Ergogenic aids (e.g., sports drinks, anabolic steroids, ginseng, amino acid supply) and their effectiveness and impact on performance.
20. Macronutrient (e.g., protein, fat, carbohydrates, water) sources and function as they apply to physical activity and weight management.
21. Micronutrient (e.g., vitamins, minerals) sources and function as they apply to physical activity and weight management.
22. Current nutrition guidelines and concepts (e.g., food pyramid, yo-yo dieting, U.S. Department of Agriculture recommendations).
23. Factors affecting metabolic rate (e.g., level of activity, muscle mass, genetic, hormonal, thermic effect of food, exercise intensity and duration).
24. Storage and release of fat as they apply to physical activity and weight management.
25. Effectiveness and integration of complementary physical activity (e.g., yoga-based exercise, tai-chi, mind-body exercise programs, pilates, Feldenkrais).
26. Safety guidelines as they apply to program design.
27. Appropriate educational resources (e.g., electronic, print, audiovisual) for use in client instruction.
28. Physiological effects of and appropriate precautions to take with a client taking medications and other substances (e.g., beta blockers, diuretics, antihistamines, tranquilizers, alcohol, diet pills, cold medications, caffeine, nicotine, antihypertensives).

Skill in:

1. Designing a safe, well-balanced, comprehensive physical activity program specific to the client's health status, special needs, desires and goals.
2. Selecting, integrating and modifying methods for cardiorespiratory endurance, muscular strength and endurance, and flexibility conditioning based on client needs.
3. Selecting and integrating appropriate educational resources for use in client instruction.

PERFORMANCE DOMAIN III: PROGRAM IMPLEMENTATION

A. Teach safe and effective exercise technique by using a variety of methods and resources in order to attain desired results.

Knowledge of:

1. Cardiorespiratory, musculoskeletal and basic neuromuscular anatomy.

2. Basic exercise science (e.g., cardiorespiratory, respiratory, metabolic and neuromuscular exercise physiology, applied kinesiology, biomechanics).
3. Communication techniques (e.g., active listening, appropriate eye contact, reflecting, other attending behaviors).
4. Teaching techniques (e.g., demonstrating, rehearsal, verbal cueing, modeling, correction).
5. Concepts, principles and techniques related to muscular strength and endurance training, cardiorespiratory training and flexibility training (e.g., overload, specificity, reversibility, progression, frequency, training effect).
6. Proper spotting techniques for various activities and equipment (e.g., free weights, variable resistance machines, calisthenics).
7. Exercise equipment set up, use, maintenance and safety.
8. Normal joint range of motion as it applies to conditioning and physical activity.
9. Methods to determine appropriate conditioning intensities and workloads.
10. Effects of various environmental conditions on exercise performance.
11. Modification necessary for various situations as they occur (e.g., progress plateau, increase in intensity, decrease in intensity, compensation for injury, newly diagnosed condition with physician approval).
12. Proper form and techniques for a variety of activities (e.g., walking, running, intervals, circuit training).
13. Warning signs/symptoms that may occur while working with a client and how to react safely and effectively to them.

Skill in:

1. Applying basic biomechanics and kinesiology to movement analysis and correction.
2. The use of a variety of exercise equipment.
3. Teaching safe and effective exercise techniques.
4. The application of teaching and communication techniques.
5. Identifying improper exercise techniques and facilitating a change in the client's form or technique.
6. Utilizing and demonstrating proper spotting techniques.
7. Determining appropriate intensity for cardiorespiratory conditioning and appropriate workload for resistive exercise.
8. Choosing appropriate equipment and activities with respect to the client's level of fitness.

B. Make appropriate modifications by monitoring the client's progress, systematically recording all relevant data, and evaluating program effectiveness in order to support the client's progress toward program goals.

Knowledge of:

1. The importance and application of subjective record keeping (e.g., observation, client self-report, moods) to progress monitoring and program modification.
2. The importance and application of objective record keeping (e.g., frequency, intensity, duration) to progress monitoring and program modification.
3. Appropriate exercise program modification as a result of change in client status (e.g., progress, pregnancy, new health conditions).

Skill in:

1. Using client feedback to modify a physical activity program.
2 Keeping records of subjective and objective data.
3. Modifying physical activity program

based on available data.

C. Facilitate exercise adherence by understanding the dynamics of exercise compliance in order to maintain progress toward program goals.

Knowledge of:

1. The principles and techniques of exercise adherence and compliance.
2. Lifestyle characteristics that influence adherence to a program (e.g., affordability, convenience, time management).
3. Relationship of program variability, enjoyment, social interaction, and goal attainment to exercise adherence.

Skill in:

1. Facilitating exercise adherence.

D. Maintain rapport through a constructive and supportive relationship in order to facilitate efforts toward achieving program goals.

Knowledge of:

1. Communication techniques (e.g., active listening, appropriate eye contact, reflecting, other attending behaviors).
2. Factors that build and enhance rapport (e.g., empathy, genuineness, nonjudgmental responses).
3. Age, gender, cultural, ethnic and personal differences as they affect communications, lifestyle, physical activity habits, and personal and interpersonal behavior.
4. Body language, other nonverbal behaviors, and the incongruities between verbal and nonverbal behaviors.

Skill in:

1. Building and maintaining rapport through a constructive and supportive relationship.
2. Active listening.
3. Modifying interaction style based on client age, gender, cultural, ethnic and personal differences.
4. Recognizing and interpreting nonverbal cues.

E. Attend to the client's needs by referring to, or consulting with, other medical/health professionals, as necessary, in order to progress safely and effectively.

Knowledge of:

1. Factors and conditions that may necessitate referral to, or consultation with, a medical/health professional (e.g., injuries, changes in health status, health risk factors, pregnancy, medication changes, psychological challenges).
2. Qualified local health/medical professionals to use as referral sources (e.g., physicians, psychotherapists, registered dietitians, physical therapists, athletic trainers, clinical exercise physiologists).
3. Physiological effects of, and appropriate precautions to take with a client taking medications and other substances (e.g., beta blockers, diuretics, antihistamines, tranquilizers, alcohol, diet pills, cold medications, caffeine, nicotine, antihypertensives).

Skill in:

1. Recognizing factors and conditions that may necessitate referral to, or consultation with, a medical/health professional (e.g., injuries, changes in health status, pregnancy, medication changes).

PERFORMANCE DOMAIN IV: PROFESSIONAL RESPONSIBILITY

A. Conduct oneself in a professional manner by adhering to the ACE Code of Ethics, ACE Application and Certification Standards, all applicable laws, regulations and procedures, and by operating within the recognized scope

of practice for personal trainers and within personal bounds of competence in order to protect the client and contribute to the integrity of the profession.

Knowledge of:

1. ACE Code of Ethics.
2. ACE Application and Certification Standards.
3. Negligence laws, both comparative and contributory, as they pertain to personal training.
4. Applicable business laws (e.g., truth in advertising, full disclosure, taxation, billing/refund policies, employment law).
5. Copyright laws as they apply to music, video, written text and trademark usage.
6. The recognized scope of practice of personal training and personal bounds of competence.
7. Currently accepted standards of care for personal training.
8. Contributions of other allied health/fitness professions (e.g., athletic training, physical therapy, chiropractic) to the personal training client.
9. Personal limits of knowledge and skill.
10. Signs, symptoms and strategies to recognize and address instructor burnout (e.g., forgetfulness, irritability, apathy, insomnia, lethargy, tendency toward injury to self and others).

B. Inform the client of the risks and benefits of physical activity through the use of informed consents and waivers in order to protect the client and minimize liability.

Knowledge of:

1. Selection and use of informed consents, waivers and other such documents.
2. Limitations of waivers and informed consent.
3. Risks of exercise (e.g., muscle strains/sprains, morbidity/mortality, dizziness, nausea, abnormal heart rate/rhythm, shortness of breath, heart attack, stroke).
4. Benefits of exercise (e.g., increased HDL cholesterol, decreased LDL cholesterol, improved blood pressure, improved cardiorespiratory function, weight management, increased lean muscles mass, flexibility enhancement).

Skill in:

1. Explaining a waiver and an informed consent.

C. Implement a risk-management protocol by developing and following safety and emergency procedures in order to protect the client and reduce liability.

Knowledge of:

1. Accepted CPR and first-aid procedures as established by the American Heart Association, American Red Cross and other appropriate organizations.
2. Emergency medical system activation.
3. Principles of Rest, Ice, Compression and Elevation.
4. Components of a risk management protocol and its application.
5. Components of an emergency action plan as it pertains to the training environment.
6. Warning signs that require intervention (e.g., shortness of breath, dizziness, chest pain).
7. Scope of practice with respect to advice given to injured client.

Skill in:

1. Identifying potential risks and taking appropriate action.
2. Performing CPR.
3. Filling out a complete accident/incident form.
4. Managing a crisis situation.
5. Recognizing warning signs that

require intervention (e.g., shortness of breath, dizziness, chest pain).

D. Ensure continuing competence and professional growth through ongoing education in order to provide quality service.

Knowledge of:

1. Requirements for maintaining personal training and CPR certification.
2. Sources for acquiring continuing education offered by individuals, conferences, colleges, universities, seminars, workshops, etc.
3. Accepted professional resources and publications (e.g., texts, journals, audio and video tapes).

E. Obtain adequate insurance in order to protect the client and minimize financial risk.

Knowledge of:

1. Characteristics, types of coverage and appropriate limits for professional liability insurance.
2. Characteristics, types of coverage and appropriate limits for general liability insurance.
3. Sources of applicable insurance.

F. Provide a safe environment by evaluating all equipment, facilities and locations in order to ensure safe and effective physical activity.

Knowledge of:

1. Equipment maintenance and signs that indicate potential equipment hazards and/or equipment malfunction (e.g., frayed cables, worn electrical wires, loose or missing parts, abnormal noise or operation).
2. Environmental factors and their impact on physical activity (e.g., terrain, surface instability, space, temperature, humidity, pollution, altitude, wind chill).

Skill in:

1. Recognizing, identifying and modifying potential hazards.
2. Modifying established exercise programs/activities, modalities and/or environments to avoid unnecessary risks.

G. Ensure client confidentiality by following governmental regulations pertaining to client information, as applicable, and securing all data in order to protect the client and minimize liability.

Knowledge of:

1. Laws and governmental regulations regarding reporting and confidentiality.
2. Acceptable practices and procedures for acquiring, recording and securing all client information to ensure confidentiality.

APPENDIX C

Performance Guidelines
One-rescuer CPR: Adult

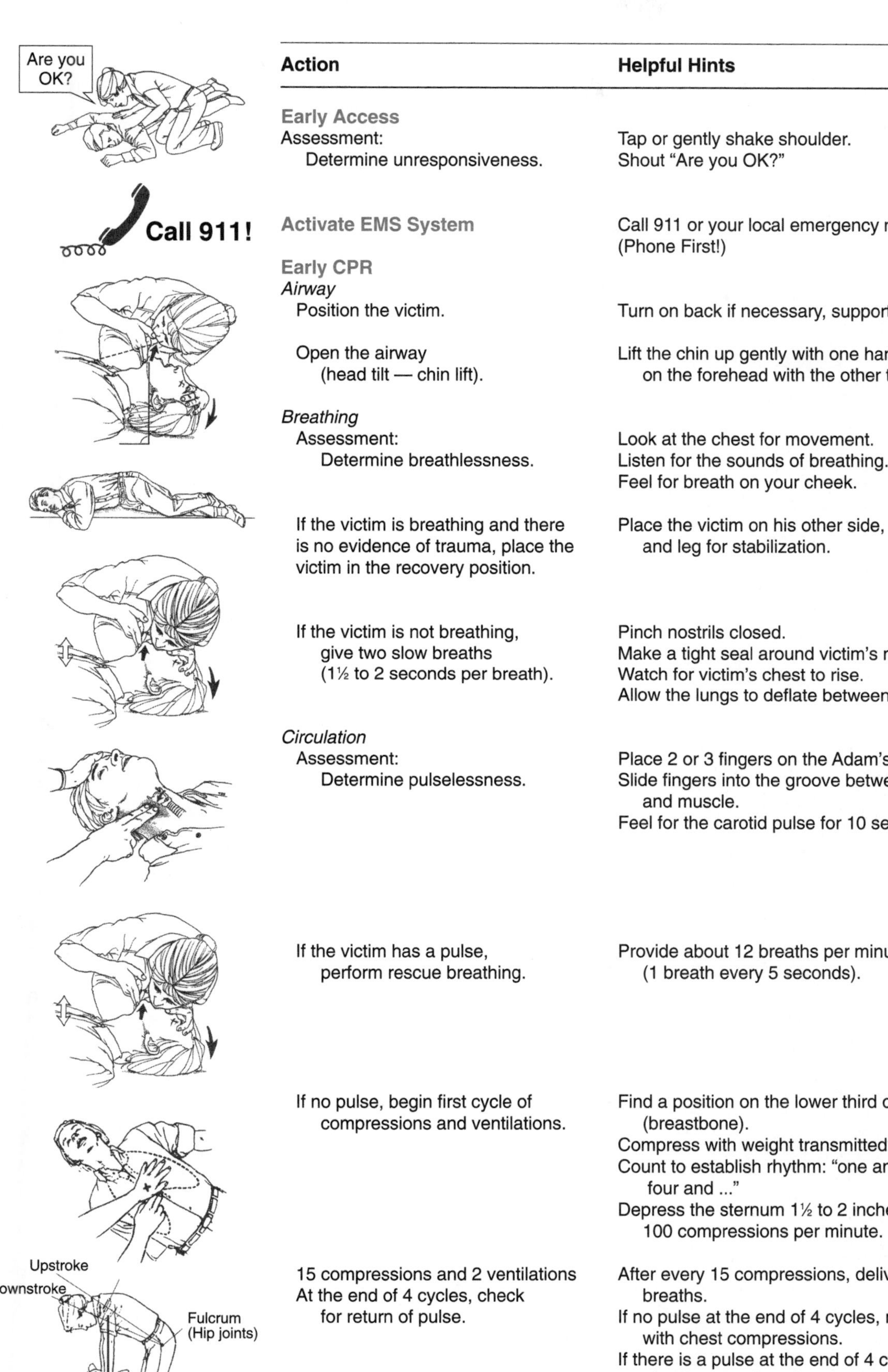

Action	Helpful Hints
Early Access	
Assessment: Determine unresponsiveness.	Tap or gently shake shoulder. Shout "Are you OK?"
Activate EMS System	Call 911 or your local emergency number. (Phone First!)
Early CPR	
Airway	
Position the victim.	Turn on back if necessary, supporting head and neck.
Open the airway (head tilt — chin lift).	Lift the chin up gently with one hand while pushing down on the forehead with the other to tilt the head back.
Breathing	
Assessment: Determine breathlessness.	Look at the chest for movement. Listen for the sounds of breathing. Feel for breath on your cheek.
If the victim is breathing and there is no evidence of trauma, place the victim in the recovery position.	Place the victim on his other side, using the victim's arm and leg for stabilization.
If the victim is not breathing, give two slow breaths (1½ to 2 seconds per breath).	Pinch nostrils closed. Make a tight seal around victim's mouth. Watch for victim's chest to rise. Allow the lungs to deflate between breaths.
Circulation	
Assessment: Determine pulselessness.	Place 2 or 3 fingers on the Adam's apple (voice box). Slide fingers into the groove between Adam's apple and muscle. Feel for the carotid pulse for 10 seconds.
If the victim has a pulse, perform rescue breathing.	Provide about 12 breaths per minute (1 breath every 5 seconds).
If no pulse, begin first cycle of compressions and ventilations.	Find a position on the lower third of the sternum (breastbone). Compress with weight transmitted downward. Count to establish rhythm: "one and, two and, three and, four and ..." Depress the sternum 1½ to 2 inches, at a rate of 80 to 100 compressions per minute.
15 compressions and 2 ventilations At the end of 4 cycles, check for return of pulse.	After every 15 compressions, deliver 2 slow rescue breaths. If no pulse at the end of 4 cycles, resume CPR, starting with chest compressions. If there is a pulse at the end of 4 cycles, but no breathing, give 1 rescue breath every 5 seconds.

Source: *Basic Life Support Heartsaver Guide*, American Heart Association, 1993.

GLOSSARY

Abduction Movement of a body part away from the midline of the body; opposite of adduction.
Abrasion A scraping away of a portion of the skin or mucous membrane.
Acclimatization The process whereby the body physiologically adapts to an unfamiliar environment, and achieves a new steady state. For example, the body can adjust to a high altitude or a hot climate and gain an increased capacity to work in those conditions.
Actin Contractile protein in a myofibril.
Active (dynamic) stretching A stretching of muscle and tissue that requires muscle contraction through a range of motion. No outside force is involved.
Active recovery Performing stretching exercises or working other body parts to facilitate recovery after intense exercise to allow for more productive use of exercise time.
Acute Descriptive of a condition that usually has a rapid onset and a relatively short and severe course; opposite of chronic.
Adduction Movement of a body part toward the midline of the body; opposite of abduction.
Adenosine triphosphate (ATP) A high-energy phosphate molecule required to provide energy for cellular function. Produced both aerobically and anaerobically, and stored in the body.
Adherence The amount of programmed exercise a client engages in during a specified time period compared to the amount of exercise recommended for that time period.
Adipose tissue Fatty tissue; connective tissue made up of fat cells.
Aerobic With, or in the presence of, oxygen.
Aerobic composite training An individualized combination of numerous training methods characterized by a variety of intensities and modes, primarily for those in the maintenance phase of conditioning. Example: jog 15 minutes to a pool, swim for 20 minutes and jog home (see also Cross training).
Aerobic system The metabolic pathway that, in the presence of oxygen, uses glucose for energy production; also known as aerobic glycolysis.
Agonist muscle A muscle that is directly engaged in contraction; opposes the action of an antagonist muscle.
All-or-none principle The principle of muscle contraction that states that when a motor unit is activated, all of the muscle fibers will maximally contract.
Amenorrhea The absence of menstruation.
Amino acids Nitrogen-containing compounds that are the building blocks of proteins.
Anabolic androgenic steroids Synthetic derivatives of the male sex hormone testosterone. Used for their muscle-building characteristics.
Anaerobic Without the presence of oxygen; not requiring oxygen.
Anaerobic glycolysis The metabolic pathway that uses glucose for energy production without requiring oxygen. Sometimes referred to as the lactic acid system or anaerobic glucose system, it produces lactic acid as a by-product.
Anaerobic threshold The point during high-intensity activity when the body can no longer meet its demand for oxygen and anaerobic metabolism predominates. Also called lactate threshold.
Anatomical position Standing erect with the feet and palms facing forward.
Anemic Characterized by a reduction below normal of the number of red blood cells or hemoglobin in the blood.
Angina Pain originating from the heart that is characterized by a substantial "pressure" sensation within the chest, commonly radiating down the arm, up into the jaw, or to another site. Generally caused by decreased blood flow through the coronary arteries supplying oxygen to the myocardium (heart muscle) due to partial occlusion from plaque or clot formation or spasm of the artery itself. Also called angina pectoris.

Anorexia nervosa An eating disorder characterized by an intense fear of becoming obese, a distorted body image, extreme weight loss and self-starvation. Metabolic abnormalities are commonly associated with this disorder and can sometimes be fatal.

Antagonist muscle The muscle that acts in opposition to the action produced by an agonist muscle.

Antecubital space The space just in front of the cubitus (elbow).

Anterior Anatomical term meaning toward the front. Same as ventral; opposite of posterior.

Anthropometric assessments Measurement and analysis of parts of the human body. Examples include skinfold, girth and body weight.

Anti-atherogenic diet A diet designed to minimize atherosclerosis, usually one that is low in cholesterol and saturated fat.

Antioxidants Substances that boost the body's defense against excessive numbers of unstable oxygen molecules (free radicals) to prevent them from causing damage. Five nutrients have been identified as having antioxidant properties: beta carotene, vitamin C, vitamin E, sulfur and selenium.

Aponeurosis A white, flattened, tendinous expansion that mainly serves to connect a muscle to the parts that it moves.

Arrhythmia Abnormal heart rhythm or beat.

Arteries Vessels that carry oxygenated blood from the heart to the tissues.

Arterioles Smaller divisions of the arteries.

Arthritis Inflammatory condition involving a joint. See Osteoarthritis and Rheumatoid arthritis.

Articulation Place of union or junction between two or more bones.

Assumption of risk A legal defense used to show that a person understood the possible occurrence of known dangers of a specific activity and chose to participate anyway.

Asthma A disease of the pulmonary system characterized by episodes of dyspnea (difficult breathing) due to narrowing of the airways from constriction of bronchial smooth muscle and overproduction of mucous. See Chronic obstructive pulmonary disease.

Atherosclerosis A specific form of arteriosclerosis characterized by the accumulation of fatty material on the inner walls of the arteries, causing them to harden, thicken and lose elasticity.

ATP See Adenosine triphosphate.

ATP-CP system See Creatine phosphate system.

Atrium One of the two (left and right) upper chambers of the heart (pl.: atria).

Atrophy A decrease in the cross-sectional size of a muscle resulting from inactivity or immobilization following injury.

Attending (behavior) Nonverbal acknowledgments during conversation to encourage the speaker to continue.

Auscultation The act of listening to sounds (through a stethoscope) arising within bodily organs (e.g., the heartbeat).

Autogenic inhibition An automatic reflex relaxation caused by excessive stimulation of Golgi tendon organs (GTOs).

Avascular Not vascular; without blood supply.

Avulsion A wound involving forcible separation or tearing of tissue from the body.

Axis of rotation The imaginary line or point about which an object, such as a body or a lever, rotates.

Ballistic High-impact, rapid, jerking movements.

Ballistic stretch A high-force, short-duration stretch using rapid bouncing movements.

Baroreceptors A sensory nerve ending that is stimulated by changes in pressure, as those in the walls of blood vessels.

Basal metabolic rate (BMR) The energy expended by the body while at rest to maintain normal body functions.

Beta-blockers (beta-adrenergic blocking agents) Medications that "block" or limit sympathetic nervous system stimulation. They act to slow the heart rate and decrease maximum heart rate, and are used for cardiovascular and other medical conditions.

Bioelectrical impedance (BIA) A method of determining body composition by measuring the body's resistance to electrical flow.

Blood pressure The pressure exerted by the blood on the walls of the arteries; measured in millimeters of mercury with a sphygmomanometer.

Body composition The makeup of the body in terms of the relative percentage of fat-free mass and body-fat.

Body mass index (BMI) A relative measure of body height to body weight for determining degree of obesity.

Bradycardia Slowness of the heartbeat, as evidenced by a pulse rate of less than 60 bpm.

Bronchioles The smallest tubes that supply air to the alveoli (air sacs) of the lungs.

Bronchitis Acute or chronic inflammation of the bronchial tubes. See Chronic obstructive pulmonary disease.

Bronchodilators Medications inhaled to dilate (enlarge) and relax the constricted bronchial smooth muscle. Example: Proventil.

Bursitis Painful inflammation of a bursa, occurring most often in the knees, hips, shoulders and elbows.

Bulimia nervosa An eating disorder characterized by episodes of binge eating, followed by self-induced vomiting or the use of diuretics or laxatives.

Calorie The amount of heat required to raise the temperature of one kilogram of water one degree Celsius. Also called kilocalorie.

Capillaries The smallest blood vessels that supply blood to the tissues, and the site of all gas and nutrient exchange in the cardiovascular system. They connect the arterial and venous systems.

Carbohydrate (CHO) An essential nutrient that provides energy to the body. Dietary sources include sugars (simple) and grains, rice and beans (complex). 1 gm CHO = 4 kcals.

Carbohydrate loading Sequence of up to a week-long regimen of manipulating intensity of training and carbohydrate intake to achieve maximum glycogen storage for an endurance event.

Cardiac cycle The period from the beginning of one heart beat to the beginning of the next; the systolic and diastolic movement, and the interval in between.

Cardiac output The amount of blood pumped by the heart per minute; usually expressed in liters of blood per minute.

Cardiorespiratory endurance The ability to perform large muscle movement over a sustained period; the capacity of the heart-lung system to deliver oxygen for sustained energy production. Also called cardiovascular endurance.

Cardiovascular disease (CVD) General term for any disease of the heart and blood vessels. Includes coronary artery disease, hypertension, stroke, congestive heart failure, peripheral vascular disease and valvular heart disease.

Cardiovascular endurance See Cardiorespiratory endurance.

Cartilage A smooth, semi-opaque material providing a "frictionless" surface of a joint.

Cell membrane The enveloping capsule of a cell composed of proteins, lipids and carbohydrates.

Cerebrovascular accident (CVA) Damage to the brain, often resulting in a loss of function, from impaired blood supply to part of the brain. More commonly known as a stroke.

Certification The act of attesting that an individual or organization has met a specific set of standards.

Cholesterol A fat-like substance found in the blood and body tissues and in animal products. Essential for body production of hormones, steroids and so on. Its accumulation in the arteries leads to narrowing of the arteries (atherosclerosis).

Chronic Descriptive of a condition that persists over a long period of time; opposite of acute.

Chronic disease Any disease state that

persists over a long period of time.

Chronic obstructive pulmonary disease (COPD) A condition, such as asthma, bronchitis or emphysema, in which there is chronic obstruction of air flow. See Asthma, Bronchitis and Emphysema.

Circuit training A form of training that takes the participant through a series of exercise stations, sometimes with brief rest intervals in between. Can emphasize muscular endurance, aerobic conditioning, muscular strength or a combination of all three.

Circumduction The active or passive circular movement of a joint. A combination of flexion, abduction, extension and adduction movements.

Closed chain exercise (CCE) Exercises that use the body muscles in a weight-bearing position. Co-contractors, postural stabilizers and the neuromuscular system are all trained at the same time. Examples: squats and lunges.

Co-contraction The mutual coordination of antagonist muscles (such as flexors and extensors) to maintain a position.

Code of ethics Code, supplementary to other professional standards of practice or legal requirements, developed by professional organizations to govern professional conduct. Adherence to these codes is necessary to maintain professional standing or certification with such organizations.

Collagen The main constituent of connective tissue, such as ligaments, tendons and muscles.

Competencies Specific skills or knowledge that one must possess in order to have the capacity to function in a particular way (provide appropriate standard of care) for a specific job.

Complete proteins Foods that contain all 10 essential amino acids. Most meats and dairy products are considered complete protein foods.

Concentric contraction (action) A contraction in which a muscle exerts force, shortens and overcomes a resistance.

Connective tissue The tissue that binds together and supports various structures of the body. Examples: ligaments and tendons.

Continuous training Conditioning exercise, such as walking, jogging, cycling or aerobic dancing, in which the prescribed intensity is maintained continuously between 50 percent and 85 percent of maximal oxygen consumption (functional capacity).

Contract A written agreement signed by the participant and the trainer (and additional third parties as appropriate) that clearly states the exercise goals to be achieved over a given time period. Also, a legally binding agreement stating services, fees and other pertinent information regarding the trainer/client relationship.

Contracting Systematically providing rewards for positive behavior; stems from the behavioral theory of reinforcement.

Coronary artery disease (CAD) The major form of cardiovascular disease; almost always the result of atherosclerosis. Also called coronary heart disease (CHD).

Coronary heart disease (CHD) See Coronary artery disease (CAD).

Corporation A legal entity, independent of its owners and regulated by state laws. Any number of people may own a corporation through shares issued by the business.

Creatine phosphate (CP) A high-energy phosphate molecule that is stored in cells and can be used to immediately resynthesize ATP. One of the phosphagens.

Creatine phosphate system System of transfer of chemical energy for resynthesis of ATP supplied rapidly and without oxygen from the breakdown of creatine phosphate (CP). Also called ATP-CP system.

Cross training A method of physical training in which a variety of exercises and changes in body positions or modes of exercise are utilized to positively affect compliance and motivation, and also stimulate additional strength gains or reduce injury risk.

Cyanosis A bluish discoloration, especially of the skin and mucous membranes, due to reduced hemoglobin in the blood.

Deep Anatomical term meaning internal; that is, located further beneath the body surface than the superficial structures.
Defibrillation Termination of atrial or ventricular fibrillation (rapid, randomized contractions of the myocardium), usually by electroshock.
Dehydration A condition of having a less than optimal level of body water.
Delayed onset muscle soreness (DOMS) Muscle soreness that occurs 24 to 48 hours after intense exercise. Typically associated with eccentric muscle contractions, and thought to be the result of microscopic tears in muscle or connective tissue.
Diabetes mellitus A disease of carbohydrate metabolism in which an absolute or relative deficiency of insulin results in an inability to metabolize carbohydrates normally.
Diastole The relaxation phase of the cardiac cycle during which blood fills the ventricles.
Diastolic blood pressure The pressure exerted by the blood on the blood vessel walls when the heart relaxes between contractions.
Distal Anatomical term meaning away from the attached end of the limb, origin of the structure or midline of the body; opposite of proximal.
Diuretic Medication that produces an increase in the volume of urine and sodium (salt) that is excreted.
Dorsiflexion Movement of the dorsum (top) of the foot up toward the shin (proximally); opposite of plantarflexion.
Dynamic flexibility The range of motion about a joint when speed is involved during physical performance. Strength, power, neuromuscular coordination and tissue resistance are all factors.
Dynamic (isotonic) constant-resistance Strength-training exercises and/or equipment that provide a constant resistance throughout the movement range.
Dynamic (isotonic) variable-resistance Strength-training exercises and/or equipment that automatically vary the resistance throughout the movement range.
Dyspnea Shortness of breath, resulting in difficult or labored breathing.
Eccentric contraction (action) A contraction in which a muscle exerts force, lengthens and is overcome by a resistance.
Ejection fraction The percentage of the total volume of blood that is pumped out of the left ventricle during the systolic contraction of heart.
Elasticity Temporary or recoverable elongation of connective tissue.
Electrolytes The minerals sodium, potassium and chlorine, which are present in the body as electrically charged particles called ions.
Emergency medical services (EMS) system A local system for obtaining emergency assistance from the police, fire department or ambulance. In the United States, most cities have a 911 telephone number that will automatically set the EMS system in motion.
Empathy The ability to experience another person's world as if it were one's own. Understanding another's point of view.
Emphysema A chronic lung disease characterized by loss of air sacs resulting in a decreased ability to exchange gases. Carbon dioxide levels are increased and oxygen levels are decreased, causing rapid breathing and dyspnea.
Energy balance The principle that body weight will stay the same when caloric intake equals caloric expenditure, and that a positive or negative energy balance will cause weight gain or weight loss, respectively.
Energy balance theory The principle that body weight will stay the same when caloric intake equals caloric expenditure, and that a positive or negative energy balance will cause weight gain or weight loss.
Enzymes Proteins necessary to bring about biochemical reactions.
Ergogenic aids Substances thought to enhance energy availability or utilization to improve endurance or strength.
Essential amino acids Eight to 10 of the 20 different amino acids needed to make

proteins. Called essential because they must be obtained from the diet, since they cannot be manufactured by the body.

Essential fat Fat that cannot be produced by the body and must be supplied by the diet. Linoleic acid is the only essential fat.

Essential fatty acids See Essential fat.

Essential nutrient A nutrient that must be supplied by the diet because it cannot be produced by the body.

Eumenorrheic Having normal menstruation.

Eversion Movement of the sole of the foot outward; opposite of inversion.

Excess post-exercise oxygen consumption (EPOC) Increased oxygen requirement above RMR following a bout of exercise. Historically referred to as oxygen debt.

Exercise-induced asthma Intermittent labored breathing precipitated by exertion during exercise. See Asthma.

Extension Movement at a joint that brings two parts into or toward a straight line, thereby increasing the angle of the joint, such as straightening the elbow; opposite of flexion.

Fartlek training A form of training similar to interval training, except the work-rest intervals are not systematically measured, but instead are determined by how the participant feels.

Fascia A sheet or band of fibrous tissue that lies deep to the skin or forms an attachment for muscles and organs.

Fast-twitch (Type II) fiber Large muscle fiber characterized by its fast speed of contraction and a high capacity for anaerobic glycolysis.

Fat An essential nutrient that provides energy, energy storage, and insulation and contour to the body. 1 gram fat = 9 kcals.

Fat-free mass That part of the body composition that represents everything but fat — blood, bones, connective tissue, organs and muscle; is the same as lean body mass.

Fat-free weight See Fat-free mass.

Fat soluble Able to be dissolved in fat. Relating to vitamins, those that are stored in the body fat, principally in the liver.

Fatty acid The building block of fats. An important nutrient for the production of energy during prolonged, low-intensity exercise.

Feedback Verbal or nonverbal information about current behavior that can be used to improve future performance.

Flexibility The range of motion possible about a joint.

Flexion Movement about a joint in which the bones on either side of the joint are brought closer to each other; opposite of extension.

Food Guide Pyramid A guide to assist the public with daily food choices that will accomplish dietary goals. Published in 1992 by the U.S. Dept. of Agriculture and the U.S. Dept. of Health & Human Services.

Frontal plane An imaginary longitudinal section that divides the body into anterior and posterior halves; lies at a right angle to the sagittal plane.

Fulcrum The support on which a lever rotates when moving or lifting something.

Functional capacity The maximum physical performance represented by maximal oxygen consumption.

Gait The manner or style of walking.

General liability insurance Insurance for bodily injury or property damage resulting from general negligence.

Glucose A simple sugar; the form in which all carbohydrates are used as the body's principal energy source.

Glycogen The storage form of glucose found in the liver and muscles.

Golgi tendon organ (GTO) A sensory organ within a tendon that, when stimulated, causes an inhibition of the entire muscle group to protect against too much force.

Graded exercise test (GXT) A treadmill or cycle-ergometer test that measures or estimates maximum aerobic capacity by gradually increasing the intensity until a person has reached a maximal level or voluntary exhaustion.

Grand mal seizure A major motor seizure characterized by violent and uncontrollable muscle contractions.

HDL High-density lipoprotein; a lipoprotein that contains more protein than cholesterol. Labeled "good" cholesterol because it removes excess cholesterol from the body.

Heart rate (maximum) reserve The result of subtracting the resting heart rate from the maximal heart rate; represents the working heart-rate range between rest and maximal heart rate within which all activity occurs.

Heat cramps A mild form of heat-related illness that generally occurs during or after strenuous physical activity and is characterized by painful muscle spasms.

Heat exhaustion The most common heat-related illness; usually the result of intense exercise in a hot, humid environment and characterized by profuse sweating, which results in fluid and electrolyte loss, a drop in blood pressure, light-headedness, nausea, vomiting, decreased coordination and often syncope (fainting).

Heat stroke A medical emergency that is the most serious form of heat illness due to heat overload and/or impairment of the body's ability to dissipate heat. Characterized by high body temperature (>105°F), dry, red skin, altered level of consciousness, seizures, coma and possibly death.

Hernia A protrusion of the abdominal contents into the groin (inguinal hernia) or through the abdominal wall (abdominal hernia).

Herniated disc A condition in which the disc between two vertebrae of the spine bulges backward, often compressing a nerve root and compromising its function.

High-density lipoproteins (HDLs) A plasma complex of lipids and proteins that contain relatively more protein and less cholesterol and triglycerides. High HDL levels are associated with a low risk of coronary heart disease.

Homeostasis The tendency toward stability and balance in normal body states.

Hydrostatic weighing An underwater test used to measure body fat and lean body mass percentages, based on the relative density of fat and lean tissue.

Hypercalciuric effect The tendency to excrete excessive calcium in the urine. Usually caused by leaching of calcium from the bones.

Hypercholesterolemia An excess of cholesterol in the blood.

Hyperextension Extreme or excessive extension of a joint.

Hyperglycemia An abnormally high content of glucose in the blood.

Hyperlipidemia An excess of lipids in the blood.

Hypertension High blood pressure, or the elevation of blood pressure above 140/90 mmHg.

Hyperthermia Abnormally high body temperature.

Hypertrophy An increase in the cross-sectional size of a muscle in response to progressive resistance (strength) training.

Hyperventilation A greater-than-normal rate of breathing that results in an abnormal loss of carbon dioxide from the blood; dizziness may occur.

Hypoglycemia A deficiency of sugar in the blood commonly caused by too much insulin, too little glucose, or too much exercise in the insulin-dependent diabetic.

Hypokalemia A deficiency of potassium in the blood.

Hypokinesis Lack of activity or energy.

Hypothermia Abnormally low body temperature.

Hypotonic A solution having less tonicity (effective osmotic pressure equivalent) than bodily fluids.

Impingement syndrome Reduction of space for the supraspinatus muscle, and/or the long head of the biceps tendon, to pass under the anterior edge of the acromion and coracoacromial ligament. Attributed to muscle hypertrophy and inflammation caused by microtraumas.

Incision A cut in the skin, frequently from

a sharp object.

Incomplete proteins Foods that contain less than the nine to 10 essential amino acids.

Independent contractors People who conduct business independently on a contract basis and are not employees of an organization or business.

Inferior Anatomical term meaning situated below or nearer the soles of the feet in relation to a specific reference point; opposite of superior.

Informed consent Voluntary acknowledgement of the purpose, procedures and specific risks of an activity in which one intends to engage.

Insulin-dependent diabetes mellitus (IDDM) Form of diabetes caused by the destruction of the insulin-producing beta cells in the pancreas, which leads to little or no insulin secretion. Generally develops in childhood and requires regular insulin injections.

Intensity The physiological stress on the body during exercise; indicates how hard the body should be working to achieve a training effect.

Interval training Short, high-intensity exercise periods alternated with periods of rest. Example: 100-yard run, one-minute rest, repeated eight times.

Inversion Moving the sole of the foot inward; opposite of eversion.

Ischemia A local deficiency of blood supply caused by the constriction or obstruction of the arteries, which results in a decreased supply of oxygen to the tissues.

Isokinetic Exercises or equipment that provide a fixed speed of movement and vary the resistive force according to the muscle force.

Isometric contraction A contraction in which a muscle exerts force but does not change in length.

Isometric equipment Equipment that does not permit joint movement, resulting in static (isometric) muscle contractions.

Isotonic See Dynamic constant-resistance; Dynamic variable-resistance.

Karvonen formula The mathematical formula that uses maximum heart-rate reserve to determine target heart rate.

Ketone An organic compound (e.g., acetone) with a carbonyl group attached to two carbon atoms. See Ketosis.

Ketosis An abnormal increase of ketone bodies in the body; usually the result of a low-carbohydrate diet, fasting or starvation. See Ketone.

Kinesiology The study of the principles of mechanics and anatomy in relation to human movement.

Kinesthetic awareness One's sense of one's position and movement in space during various activities.

Korotkoff sounds Five different sounds created by the pulsing of the blood through the brachial artery. Proper distinction of the sounds is necessary to determine blood pressure.

Kyphosis Exaggerated sagittal curvature of the thoracic spine; often accompanied by a forward-head position.

Kyphosis-lordosis An increase in the normal inward curve of the low back, and increased outward curve of the thoracic spine.

Lactic acid (Lactate) A waste product of anaerobic energy production known to cause localized muscle fatigue.

Lactic acid system See anaerobic glycolysis.

Lacto-ovo vegetarian A person who consumes milk and eggs, but not meat, poultry or fish.

Lapses The expected slips or mistakes that are usually discreet events and are a normal part of the behavior change process.

Lateral Anatomical term meaning away from the midline of the body. Pertaining to the side; opposite of medial.

Law of acceleration The force (F) acting on a body in a given direction is equal to the body's mass (m) multiplied by the body's acceleration (a) in that direction: $F = ma$, or $a = F/m$.

Law of impact and reaction forces The earth exerts a force against the body that is equal to the force applied to the earth as one moves.

Law of inertia The tendency of all objects

and matter to remain at rest, or, if moving, to continue moving in the same straight line unless acted on by an outside force. Proportional to body mass.

LDL Low-density lipoprotein; a lipoprotein that contains more cholesterol than protein. Labeled "bad" cholesterol because it deposits cholesterol on the artery walls.

Lever A rigid bar that rotates around a fixed support (fulcrum) in response to an applied force.

Liability Legal responsibility.

Ligament A connective tissue that functions to connect two bones.

Lipoprotein The vehicle that transports fat throughout the body; made up of protein, fat and cholesterol.

Lordosis An exaggerated forward curvature of the lumbar spine, often resulting in a protruding abdomen and buttocks. Sometimes referred to as a swayback.

Low-density lipoproteins (LDLs) A plasma complex of lipids and proteins that contains relatively more cholesterol and triglycerides and less protein. High LDL levels are associated with an increased risk of coronary heart disease.

Maximal graded exercise test See Graded exercise test (GXT).

Maximal heart rate (MHR) The highest heart rate a person can attain.

Maximal oxygen consumption (VO_2 max) The highest volume of oxygen a person can consume during exercise; maximum aerobic capacity.

Maximal oxygen uptake See Maximal oxygen consumption (VO_2 max).

Medial Anatomical term meaning toward the midline of the body. Pertaining to the center; opposite of lateral.

Megadose A dose of a substance that is extremely high compared to the needs of the body.

Menopause Cessation of menstruation in the human female, usually occurring between the ages of 48 and 50.

Metabolic equivalents (METs) A simplified system for classifying physical activities where one MET is equal to the resting oxygen consumption, which is approximately 3.5 milliliters of oxygen per kilogram of body weight per minute (3.5 ml/kg/min).

MET See Metabolic equivalents (METs).

Minerals Organic substances needed in the diet in small amounts to help regulate bodily functions.

Mirroring Imitating another's behavior or attitudes.

Mitochondria Specialized subcellular structures located within body cells that contain oxidative enzymes needed by the cell to metabolize foodstuffs into energy sources.

Modeling The process of learning by observing and imitating others' behavior.

Monounsaturated fats A type of unsaturated fat (liquid at room temperature) that has one spot available on the fatty acid for the addition of a hydrogen atom. Moderate intake is associated with a lower risk for cardiovascular disease. Example: oleic acid in olive oil. Generally considered to be a "healthy" fat.

Morbidity The disease rate; the ratio of sick to well persons in a community.

Mortality The death rate; or ratio of deaths that take place to expected deaths.

Motive force The force that starts or causes a movement.

Motor learning effect Improvement in performance during the initial weeks of strength training due to more efficient motor unit utilization.

Motor unit A motor nerve and all the muscle fibers it stimulates.

Muscle fiber A muscle cell.

Muscle spindle The sensory organ within a muscle that is sensitive to stretch and thus protects the muscle from being stretched too far.

Muscular endurance The capacity of a muscle to exert force repeatedly against a resistance, or to hold a fixed or static contraction over time.

Muscular strength The maximum force that a muscle can produce against resistance in a single, maximal effort.

Myocardial infarction (MI) Death of a portion of the heart muscle from an interruption of the blood supply. Commonly called a heart attack.

Myofibril Contractile protein in a muscle fiber.

Myosin Contractile protein in a myofibril.

Myotatic stretch reflex Muscular reflex created by excessive muscle spindle stimulation to prevent potential tissue damage.

Negligence Failure of a person to perform as a reasonable and prudent professional would perform under similar circumstances.

Net caloric cost Exercise energy expenditure minus resting energy expenditure during the same period of time.

Non-insulin-dependent diabetes mellitus (NIDDM) Most common form of diabetes; typically develops in adulthood, is characterized by a reduced sensitivity of the insulin target cells to available insulin and is usually associated with obesity.

Nutrient density Quantitative analysis of the amount of nutrients versus the amount of calories in a given food. Nutrient-dense foods provide more nutrients than calories.

Obesity An excessive accumulation of body fat. Usually defined as more than 20 percent above ideal weight, or over 25 percent body fat for men and over 30 percent body fat for women.

One repetition maximum (1RM) The amount of resistance that can be moved through the range of motion one time before the muscle is temporarily fatigued.

Open chain exercise (OCE) Exercises in which a muscle or muscle group is isolated to function alone. Example: seated leg extension.

Opposing muscle group See Antagonist muscle.

Orthostatic hypotension A drop in blood pressure associated with rising to an erect position.

Osteoarthritis Degenerative joint disease occurring chiefly in older persons; characterized by degeneration of the articular cartilage, hypertrophy of the bones and changes in the synovial membrane.

Osteoporosis A disorder, primarily affecting women past menopause, in which bone density decreases and susceptibility to fracture increases.

Overload principle One of the principles of human performance that states that beneficial adaptations occur in response to demands applied to the body at levels beyond a certain threshold (overload), but within the limits of tolerance and safety.

Overuse injury An injury caused by activity that places too much stress on one area of the body over an extended period.

Oxygen debt See Excess post-exercise oxygen consumption (EPOC).

Oxygen extraction The amount of oxygen taken from the hemoglobin and used in exercising muscle cells. Often referred to as the arterio-venous oxygen difference or A-VO_2 diff.

Palpation The use of hands and/or fingers to detect anatomical structures or an arterial pulse (e.g., carotid pulse).

Partnership A relationship where two or more people agree to operate a business and share in the profits and losses.

Passive stretch A stretch in which the elastic components of the muscle are relaxed and the portion of muscle most likely to be loaded is the connective tissue. Example: a static stretch.

Peripheral vascular resistance Impedance of blood flow in the peripheral (farthest from the center) blood vessels.

Phosphagens Adenosine triphosphate (ATP) and creatine phosphate (CP), two high-energy phosphate molecules that can be broken down for immediate use by the cells.

Physical working capacity The maximal amount of physical work (cardiorespiratory activity) that can be attained by an individual. Also referred to as aerobic capacity or functional capacity. See Maximal oxygen consumption (VO_2max).

Plantarflexion Distal movement of the planter surface of the foot; opposite of dorsiflexion.

Plastic or viscous property Permanent or

nonrecoverable elongation of connective tissue.

Plyometrics Exercises that maximize the myotatic or stretch reflex to teach muscles to produce maximum force faster. Plyometrics are usually sport-specific and utilize exercises such as hops, bounds and depth jumps; may cause overuse tendon injuries in some athletes.

Polyunsaturated fats A type of unsaturated fat (liquid at room temperature) that has two or more spots on the fatty acid available for hydrogen. Examples: corn, safflower, soybean oils.

PNF See Proprioceptive neuromuscular facilitation.

Posterior Anatomical term meaning toward the back; opposite of anterior.

Post-menopausal The period of time after menopause.

Premenopausal Pertaining to the time before menopause.

Primary assessment A rapid examination to identify life- or limb-threatening injuries or illnesses that need immediate attention.

Prime-mover muscle The muscle that contracts concentrically to accomplish the movement in any given joint action.

Principle of Specificity Training One of the principles of human performance that states that a specific demand (e.g., exercise) made on the body will result in a specific response by the body.

Professional liability insurance Insurance to protect against professional negligence or the failure of a trainer to perform as a competent and prudent professional would under similar circumstances.

Pronation A triplanar motion at the subtalar joint consisting of abduction, dorsiflexion and eversion; closely resembles eversion. Position of the forearm with the palm facing backward or down.

Proprioceptive neuromuscular facilitation (PNF) A method of promoting the response of neuromuscular mechanisms through the stimulation of proprioceptors in an attempt to gain more stretch in a muscle. Often referred to as a contract/relax method of stretching.

Proprioception The reception of stimuli produced within the body.

Proprioceptors Specialized nerve endings in muscles, tendons and joints that are sensitive to changes in tension during activity; gives a body part a sense of where it is in space.

Protein An essential nutrient made up of 22 amino acids that builds and repairs body tissues. 1 gm = 4 kcals.

Protraction Scapular abduction.

Proximal Anatomical term meaning toward the attached end of the limb. Origin of the structure, or midline of the body; opposite of distal.

Range of motion (ROM) The number of degrees that an articulation (joint) will allow one of its segments to move.

Rapport A relationship of mutual trust, harmony or emotional affinity.

Rating of perceived exertion (RPE) Developed by Borg, this scale provides a standard means for evaluating a participant's perception of their physical exertion. This original scale was 6-20; the revised scale is 0-10.

Reciprocal innervation (inhibition) Reflex coacting with stretch reflex to inhibit activity of an opposing muscle group.

Recommended Dietary Allowances (RDA) Recommended vitamin and mineral intake for most people to obtain optimum health.

Residual volume Usually refers to the volume of air left in the lungs after complete expiration.

Resistive force A force that resists the motion of another external force.

Resorption The act of dissolving and assimilating.

Resting heart rate (RHR) The number of heart beats per minute when the body is completely at rest; usually counted first thing in the morning before any activity.

Resting metabolic rate (RMR) The number of calories expended per unit time at rest. It is measured early in the morning after an overnight fast and at least 8 hours of sleep.

The sleep is at home and the measurement is in the lab.

Retraction Scapular adduction.

Rheumatoid arthritis An autoimmune disease that causes inflammation of connective tissues and joints.

Risk factor A condition, behavior (such as smoking), inherited trait or a disease that increases one's risk for a given disease.

Risk management Minimizing the risks of potential legal liability.

ROM See Range of motion.

RPE See Rating of perceived exertion.

Sagittal plane Anatomical term referring to the imaginary longitudinal line that divides the body or any of its parts into right and left sections.

Sarcomere Repeating unit of a muscle fiber.

Saturated fats Fatty acids carrying the maximum number of hydrogen atoms. These fats are solid at room temperature and are usually of animal origin.

Scoliosis A lateral curvature of the vertebral column, usually in the thoracic area.

Scope of practice The range and limit of responsibilities normally associated with a specific job or profession.

Secondary assessment After immediate life- or limb-threatening injuries/illnesses have been identified, this more thorough evaluation is performed to identify more subtle, yet still important, injuries.

Sedentary Doing or requiring much sitting; not active.

Seizure A disorder originating from the brain in which there is a disturbance of movement, behavior, sensation or consciousness.

Set-point theory The weight control theory that states that each person has an established normal body weight. Any deviation from this set point will lead to changes in body metabolism to return to the normal weight.

Sliding filament theory A generally accepted theory explaining the interaction between actin and myosin proteins and ATP to cause muscle contraction.

Slow-twitch (Type I) fiber A muscle fiber characterized by its slow speed of contraction and a high capacity for aerobic glycolysis.

Sole proprietorship A business owned and operated by one person.

Sphygmomanometer An instrument for measuring blood pressure in the arteries.

Spondylolisthesis Forward displacement of one vertebra over another. Usually occurs at the 4th or 5th lumbar vertebrae.

Spondylolysis Dissolution (dissolving into another) of a vertebra; usually begins with a stress fracture.

Sprain A traumatic joint twist that results in stretching or tearing of the stabilizing connective tissues. Mainly involves ligaments or joint capsule, and causes discoloration, swelling and pain.

Stabilizer muscles Muscles that stabilize one joint so a desired movement can be performed in another joint.

Standard of care Appropriateness of an exercise professional's actions in light of current professional standards and based on the age, condition and knowledge of the participant.

Static flexibility Range of motion (ROM) about a joint with little emphasis on speed of movement.

Static (passive) stretch A low-force, long-duration stretch that holds the desired muscles at their greatest possible length for 15 to 30 seconds.

Steroids See Anabolic androgenic steroids.

Strain A stretch, tear or rip in the muscle or adjacent tissue such as the fascia or tendon.

Stretch weakness The weakening effect on muscles remaining in the elongated position for an extended period of time.

Stroke A sudden and often severe attack due to blockage of an artery into the brain.

Stroke volume The amount of blood pumped from the left ventricle during one heartbeat.

Subluxation A partial dislocation of a joint that usually reduces itself.

Submaximal aerobic exercise test A cardiorespiratory fitness test designed so that the intensity does not exceed 85 percent of heart-rate reserve or maximal oxygen uptake. This provides an estimation of maximal oxygen uptake without the risks associated with maximal exercise testing.

Superficial External; located close to or on the body surface.

Superior Anatomical term meaning higher or toward the head; opposite of inferior.

Supination A triplanar motion at the subtalar joint consisting of dorsiflexion, adduction and inversion. Looks like inversion. Position of the forearm with the palm facing forward or upward.

Supine The position of the body when lying face upward.

Sympathetic nervous system A division of the autonomic nervous system that activates the body to cope with some stressor (i.e., fight or flight response).

Syncope A transient state of unconsciousness during which a person collapses to the floor as a result of lack of oxygen to the brain. Commonly known as fainting.

Synergist A muscle that assists another muscle in its function.

Synergistic Working together in a coordinated fashion.

Synovial fluid Transparent, viscous lubricating fluid found in joint cavities, bursae and tendon sheaths.

Systole The contraction phase of the cardiac cycle during which blood leaves the ventricles.

Systolic blood pressure The pressure exerted by the blood on the blood vessel walls during ventricular contractions.

Talk test A subjective method for measuring exercise intensity using observation of respiration effort and the ability to talk while exercising.

Target heart rate (THR) The number of heartbeats per minute that indicate appropriate exercise intensity levels for an individual. Also called training heart rate.

Tendinitis Inflammation of a tendon.

Tendon Strong, fibrous connective tissue that attaches a muscle to a bone.

Thrombosis The formation, development or presence of a blood clot (thrombus).

Torque A force causing rotation about a fixed axis of rotation; the act or process of turning around on an axis.

Training heart rate range Target heart rate represented as a range of numbers. See Target heart rate (THR).

Transient ischemic attack (TIA) Momentary dizziness, loss of consciousness or forgetfulness caused by a short-lived lack of oxygen (blood) to the brain. Usually due to a partial blockage of an artery, it is a warning sign for a stroke.

Transverse plane Anatomical term for the imaginary line that divides the body, or any of its parts, into superior and inferior parts. Also known as the horizontal plane.

Triglyceride The storage form of fat consisting of three free fatty acids and glycerol.

Valsalva maneuver Increased pressure in the thoracic cavity caused by forced exhalation with the breath held.

Vasoconstriction Narrowing of the opening of blood vessels caused by contraction of the smooth muscle cells in the walls of the vessel.

Vasodilation Increase in diameter of the blood vessels, especially dilation of arterioles leading to increased blood flow to a part of the body.

Vasodilator An agent (motor nerve or drug) that acts to relax (dilate) a blood vessel.

Vegan A pure vegetarian who excludes all animal-derived foods from the diet.

Veins Blood vessels that carry blood, usually deoxygenated, to the heart.

Venous return Return to the heart of the circulatory fluids by way of the veins.

Ventricle One of the two (left and right) lower chambers of the heart. The muscular left ventricle pumps blood to the body; the smaller right ventricle pumps blood to the lungs.

Viscoelastic A combination of elastic and

plastic properties found in all connective tissue.

Vitamins Organic compounds that function as metabolic regulators in the body. Classified as water soluble or fat soluble.

VO_2 max See Maximal oxygen consumption.

Waist-to-hip circumference ratio (WTH) A measure for determining health risk due to the site of fat storage; taken by dividing the abdominal girth (waist measurement) by the hip measurement to form a ratio.

Waiver Voluntary abandonment of a right to file suit; not always legally binding.

Water soluble Dissolvable in water. Relating to vitamins, those that require adequate daily intake since the body excretes excesses in the urine.

INDEX

A

C

D

G

H

I

J

K

N

O

P

Q

R

S

T

U

V

W

Y